# CRITICAL
# MASS

## THE **D**ANGEROUS **R**ACE FOR
## **S**UPERWEAPONS
## IN A **F**RAGMENTING **W**ORLD

—

### William E. Burrows
### & Robert Windrem

**SIMON & SCHUSTER**
New York   Toronto   London   Sydney   Tokyo   Singapore

SIMON & SCHUSTER
Rockefeller Center
1230 Avenue of the Americas
New York, New York 10020

Copyright © 1994 by William E. Burrows and Robert
Windrem

DESIGNED BY BARBARA MARKS
Manufactured in the United States of America

10   9   8   7   6   5   4   3   2   1

Library of Congress Cataloging-in-Publication Data
Burrows, William E., date.
   Critical mass : the dangerous race for superweapons in
a fragmenting world / William E. Burrows & Robert
Windrem.
      p.      cm.
   Includes index.
   1. Arms race.   2. World politics—1989–
3. Developing countries—Armed Forces—Weapons
systems.   4. Nuclear weapons—Developing countries.
5. Biological weapons—Developing countries.
6. Chemical weapons—Developing countries.   I. Windrem,
Robert.   II. Title.
UA10.B87   1994
327.1'17—dc20                    93-36604   CIP
ISBN 0-671-74895-5

# ACKNOWLEDGMENTS

**A**uthors like to call their books their own. But that is seldom the case in nonfiction, and certainly not with a work as heavily investigative as this one. There are necessarily a lot of bad characters in this book, but it required a great deal of help from some very good characters to find them and give them the exposure they deserve.

First, we would like to thank everyone who facilitated the reportage. In particular, we are indebted to NBC News and in particular its former veteran Pentagon correspondent Fred Francis with whom Windrem has shared many long days in faraway places with strange-sounding names (from Rawalpindi to Zug).

Others at NBC who merit special thanks include Bill Wheatley and Steve Friedman, who served as executive producers of "NBC Nightly News" over the past five years. It was Wheatley who first assigned Windrem to the proliferation beat and Friedman who continually found space in his program for ever-lengthening reports. Foreign news directors David Miller and John Stack provided more than ample support, as did Nightly News producers Jack Chesnutt, Cheryl Gould, and Michael Bass. Other correspondents who have worked on the proliferation beat with Windrem include Jim Maceda, Arthur Kent, Brad Willis, and Ed Rabel. There was also much help from producers and researchers Rich Gardella, Jerry Bornstein, Scott Lewis, Liora Ben-Haim, Michelle Neubert, Sue Burt, Sofia Perez, Kristin Matthews, Peter Meryash, Steffi Fields, Shane Keats, and Tammy Kupperman. Rollo Pereyra, who works for NBC News out of Buenos Aires, lent his knowledge of both Spanish and South America to Windrem's efforts, particularly in the search for Carlos Cardoen and Condor.

The list of reporters and television producers whose work we have respected and used is long. In particular, we have deep respect for Alan George, a British freelancer who first broke the stories of Gerald Bull's supergun, the Iraqi and Iranian procurement networks, and the Condor program (all from his tiny but tidy office in Southfields, London), and Mark Hibbs, European editor for McGraw-Hill's nuclear trade journals, who is simply the best in the business of covering nuclear proliferation. We appreciate their friendship as well as their considerable help.

Others whose work has been invaluable include Jane Hunter of *Israeli Foreign Affairs*, who has long tracked Israel's dealings with South Africa and other weapons-hungry states and who provided a stream of invaluable FBIS reports; Hans Leyendecker of *Der Spiegel*, who has exposed German industrialists' transgressions from Libya to North Korea; Alejandra Rey of *Somos* in Buenos Aires, who provided excellent directions to the Condor's nest; Herbert Langsner of *Focus* in Vienna, who was kind enough to arrange interviews with sources who worked in Iraq's missile program; Claudio Gatti of *Europeo* in Milan and Alan Friedman of London's *Financial Times*, who have closely followed the trail of Banca Nazionale del Lavoro; John Fialka of *The Wall Street Journal* and Ruth Sinai of the Associated Press, whose work on any number of subjects in this area we have long admired; Doug Frantz, Jim Mann, and Murray Waas of the *Los Angeles Times*, who did the best job of exposing Iraqgate; Steve Coll and Jeff Smith of *The Washington Post*; Michael Gordon, Elaine Sciolino, Dean Baquet, and columnist William Safire of *The New York Times* for their fine coverage of defense and intelligence and, in Safire's case, for pointing the way; Rich Greenberg of ABC News; and Dick Meserve of Covington & Burling.

Special thanks, too, go to Ken Timmerman for *The Death Lobby* and to Sy Hersh for *The Samson Option* and "On the Nuclear Edge," which appeared in *The New Yorker*. All three are goldmines of information that reflect countless hours of research and interviews. Indian author Sreedhar is in their category as well.

In Congress, three staffers stand out: William C. Triplett II of the Senate Commerce Committee; Randy Rydell of the Senate Government Affairs Committee; and Dennis Keane of the House Banking Committee. All three have shown a remarkable commitment to the ideals of public service, attempting to ferret out the causes of proliferation and correct them through the legislative process. Triplett has been particularly resolute on the issue of procurement; Rydell on the issue of technology transfer; and Keane on the issue of financing weapons deals. They have generously shared their time and the product of their research with us. Deserving our appreciation, too, are those diplomats from Israel, India, Pakistan, Argentina, Russia, and Australia who have provided us with their special knowledge of the issue.

In addition, three public policy researchers deserve great credit for bringing the issue of proliferation to public attention. Gary Milhollin of the Wisconsin Project for Nuclear Arms Control, Leonard Spector of the Carnegie Endowment for International Peace, and William C. Potter of the Monterey Institute for International Studies are men of profound integrity and commitment whose long labors are only now being appreciated. Others who provided us with advice and help include Frank von Hippel of Princeton University; Peter Hayes of Northwestern University; John Ellicott of Covington & Burling; and Mac Bundy, now of the Carnegie Corporation of New York, who generously shared his own proliferation research and considerable experience in international relations.

Bill Arkin of Greenpeace and Jeff Richelson, a widely respected expert on intelligence, provided first-rate advice on nuclear weapons technology and intelligence, respectively. We owe special thanks to Jeff, who not only ran what amounted to a clipping service for us, but even provided Knicks tickets when deadline pressure was crushing.

We also appreciate the help we received from a number of U.S. specialists at the Departments of Commerce, Defense, Energy, and State; at the CIA and DIA; at the Customs Service; at the Office of Foreign Assets Control; and at the three national weapons laboratories: Los Alamos, Sandia, and Lawrence Livermore. The Freedom of Information Act Office at Energy was especially adept at cutting through the blizzard of requests and returning answers.

In Bob Bender, too, we are lucky to have an editor whose well-known professional skill is matched by his serious interest in the subject and the great stock he puts in projects like this one. It was he, as well as we, who turned an idea floating in the ether into what we hope and

7

believe to be useful reportage. We are also indebted to Esther Newberg of International Creative Management for believing in this project from its inception and for using her renowned skill to get its message told.

Finally, our profound appreciation goes to our wives, Joelle and Patti, who bore the brunt of what was in effect a two-year lost weekend with patience, encouragement, and considerable support. Their "widow's benefits" are less tangible than most. But we hope they are infinitely more profound.

STAMFORD, CT
*May 9, 1993*

*To Joelle and Lara
and Patti and Gregory*

# CONTENTS

This development [of a key uranium refining component for nuclear weapons] could only be accomplished by industrialized countries with an established scientific and engineering infrastructure.

—Office of Technology Assessment report, 1977

Revenge takes forty years; if not my son, then the son of my son will kill you. Someday we will have missiles that can reach New York.

—*Abu Abbas, leader of the Palestine Liberation Front, reacting to the U.S. attack on Iraq in 1990*

# PREFACE

$A$ writer with an imagination to match even Tolstoy's would be challenged to invent what follows. Here are the ingredients of the epic novel: treachery, greed, murder, dreams of conquest,
intrigue, heroism, corruption, duplicity, deception, genius, pervasive self-
delusion, and multiple ironies. But the setting for all of this is not Moscow's drawing rooms or Borodino's bloody redoubts. It is the real world.

This is the story of the men and machines that threaten that world,
the story of the cold war's most lasting and dangerous legacy: a new arms
race driven, not so much by competing political philosophies or socioeconomic differences, but by pervasive ethnic and religious hatred. The
passing of the old order in Eurasia—the disintegration of the Soviet Union,
liberation of eastern Europe, realignment of western Europe, and quickening withdrawal of the United States from Asia and elsewhere—is leaving
a chaotic vacuum that is being filled by ambitious new antagonists. Old
hatreds, no longer subverted, repressed, or bribed into temporary remission by the superpowers and their proxies, are surfacing around most of
the world.

Far from being an aberration, Saddam Hussein is in the avant-garde
of international politics, a specter of the future. His war against his own

Kurds and Shiites, against Jews, and against the revivalist mullahs in Iran is mirrored in varying degrees by relations between India and Pakistan; Japan, China, and the Koreas; Israel and the Arab states; Iran and Sudan versus secular neighbors like Libya, Algeria, and Egypt; and all of the factional wars that have exploded from Bosnia and Herzegovina to Armenia, Afghanistan, Tajikistan, and beyond.

The kaleidoscope of convulsions that are occurring throughout the world is in most cases centuries old and is the geopolitical equivalent of plate tectonics: old and implacable ethnic and religious entities, stubbornly irreducible masses that seethe with unyielding hatred, are moving against each other with tremendous force. This is creating friction, heat, fire, tremors, fissures, and an occasional explosion. The eight-year war between Iraq and Iran was one such eruption. India's wars and close calls with China and Pakistan are others. So are Israel's mortal conflicts with its Arab enemies.

There are two basic differences, however, between the old eruptions and the new. The moderating influence of the two old superpowers is diminishing as both turn their attention to internal affairs. With the age of the superpowers over, the world arena is open to new contenders for regional domination.

The end of the old age and start of the new was marked by events that took place during one forty-eight-hour period: May 18–19, 1990.

It began with a handshake in the Kremlin on May 18. Forty-five years of staggeringly expensive and dangerous competition between the two superpowers—a competition that defined an epoch—came to an end when Soviet President Mikhail Gorbachev and U.S. Secretary of State James Baker agreed to the START-1 nuclear arms reduction treaty. With the U.S.S.R. imploding like one of its own nuclear weapons because of seven decades of fundamentally flawed economic and social policies, and its old rival exhausted, heavily debt-ridden, and in a tenacious recession, both sides concluded that trust in each other provided more national security than all of their strategic forces combined. The cold war was over.

The new era began the next day when Baker and his boss, President George Bush, hurriedly dispatched then Deputy National Security Adviser Robert M. Gates to Islamabad and New Delhi. The future Director of Central Intelligence had instructions to keep two nations that were as poor as they were hate-filled from starting the first nuclear war. While Baker held the limelight in Moscow, Gates quietly defused a situation on the subcontinent that was threatening to go out of control with horrendous consequences.

The peace terms upon which Baker and Gorbachev agreed were as complicated as the weapons that haunted them. Each side bristled with the most sophisticated engines of death. More than 100,000 nuclear weapons had been built since the start of the cold war, most of them secreted in blast-proof silos, in bomb bays, or in the bowels of fat black submarines that silently prowled the world's oceans. For four decades the atomic and thermonuclear bombs and warheads, plus a vast array of other ferocious devices that included chemical and biological agents, were kept ready at the ends of short electronic leashes. They were kept ready but they were not used. Meanwhile arms control—the complicated and frustrating path that promised to lead to relative safety in incremental stages—progressed to that May Friday in Moscow.

No knotty technical issues bedeviled Indian and Pakistani strategic forces the next morning, however. Neither side had a nuclear weapon as advanced as the one that had cored Hiroshima or a missile more advanced than those that battered London in World War II. Hate, not capabilities, was the issue. India's and Pakistan's differences went back, not to a political event like the storming of the Winter Palace, but to at least 1526, when hated Muslims invaded India and established a Mogul empire out of Delhi that repressed Hindus for more than three centuries. The Hindus found ample ways to gain revenge and they still do. For both sides, rivalry between economic systems—capitalism and communism—is a relative trifle compared with cultural and religious passions that run like blood itself through the two societies. That was the ominous world into which Gates stepped on May 20, when he landed in Islamabad.

More ominously, the weapons used in the conflicts are becoming ever more powerful. Superweapons are replacing superpowers as the arbiters of the world order.

At the same time, every nation in the Third World with geopolitical ambitions knows that First World governments and arms salesmen are as fundamentally undependable as they are venal. Iraq and Iran, Israel, India, Pakistan, North Korea, and others have long understood that dependence on their sponsors for advanced weapons made them subject to their sponsors' whimsy and that, in turn, was inimical to sovereignty. Marionettes must forever dance to the tune of the fingers that control their strings. True independence, they believe, rests on military self-sufficiency.

Several Third World countries have therefore provided themselves with superweapons: the so-called unconventional weapons or weapons of mass destruction, which include chemical and biological agents, ballistic missiles, and above all nuclear weapons. Others are trying to do so with quiet tenacity. They have been helped by greedy, shortsighted, and manipulative governments, companies, and individuals, all trying to make large profits and exert influence.

This is therefore primarily a story about people, not merely atomic bombs, poison gas, missiles, and other weapons. The characters who populate these pages—who build, buy, sell, finance, or steal superweapons—include a right-wing German arms dealer who sent a photograph of himself in military uniform on Christmas cards; an Israeli movie mogul in Hollywood whose own life would compete with any film he has produced; a disgruntled Canadian-born ballistics genius who went into the business of designing killer cannons and missiles because he couldn't stand the sight of blood; a remorselessly amoral death merchant who attacked journalists in his Mercedes and threw a party the night hundreds of Iranians were slaughtered by his weapons; an ultrasuave South American financier who had a taste for champagne and piloted his own helicopter; an avaricious and self-deluded Atlanta banker who endangered the world monetary market by funding Iraq's superweapon program; a British-educated organizational genius who, working for a murderous thug, came within months of giving Iraq the atomic bomb; a former high-ranking U.S. Air Force scientist who was presented with an award for helping his country right before he fled it to avoid prosecution for smuggling nuclear triggers; Israel's first family of mass destruction, which treated U.S. weapons laboratories like a nuclear Kmart; and a self-effacing Pakistani scientist who plied Dutch secretaries with bon-bons while stealing their government's nuclear technology.

The supporting cast includes a legion of greedy and corrupt businessmen and government officials, and many equally conscientious and even heroic investigators, agents, analysts, aides, and news reporters. There are also a number of scientists, engineers, journalists, and at least one prostitute who have been bludgeoned, pushed out of windows, hanged (with ropes and shirts), and run down. Beneath these storied individuals, the pyramid widens to procurement networks operating out of front companies and then to a legion of otherwise anonymous corporate executives and engineers quietly doing business in a Hansel and Gretel Swiss town

18

and in modern offices from Minneapolis to Miami, Monte Carlo, Munich, Moscow, and Mosul.

All of them have succeeded in spreading superweapon technology beyond its traditional domain and, finally, out of their control. Nuclear, chemical, and biological weapons, together with such delivery systems as ballistic and cruise missiles, aircraft, and submarines, are pervasive and expanding.

In January 1992, then Director of Central Intelligence Robert M. Gates told the Senate Governmental Affairs Committee that more than twenty countries had, were suspected of having, or were developing nuclear, biological, or chemical weapons and the means to deliver them over long distances. A year later, outgoing Vice-President Dan Quayle estimated that sixteen nations had some indigenous capability to use space to control their military operations and the number may double by the end of the decade.

The CIA took Saddam's Iraq to be the harbinger of a perilous future. It was so concerned about the threat of unpredictable, radical regimes acquiring and using superweapons that it established its own Non-Proliferation Center before the fires in Kuwait had been put out. President Clinton followed suit by placing superweapons proliferation at the top of his foreign policy agenda and succinctly describing the fear of "old animosities and new dangers" in his Inaugural Address.

There are now several crucial aspects of the problem. First, the weapons themselves are more genocidal than political. They are taking hold in cultures where fierce emotions—long-held ethnic and religious hatreds coupled with what are taken to be the spiritually purifying effects of martyrdom—often dominate the cooler logic of secular politics. The restraints of Mutual Assured Destruction—the doctrine that shaped U.S.-Soviet nuclear strategy—are less important to religious fanatics and ethnic militants than the appeal of Mutual Assured Annihilation. Increasing competition for scarce renewable resources like water and fertile land, as well as nonrenewable ones like oil and minerals, on a dangerously overpopulated planet is also likely to make superweapons attractive as instruments of intimidation or the ultimate arbiters of territorial disputes.

Furthermore, while greed, nationalism, ethnoreligious rivalries, and resource scarcity fuel the proliferation process, the rails upon which it moves are greased by the intercontinental jet, instantaneous satellite telephone and computer links, the fax machine, and, above all, the increase in world trade. Hardware needed to build nuclear weapons can cross frontiers looking like furnaces that mold artificial limbs or like small capacitors that store electricity for hundreds of purposes. A huge gun barrel designed to hurl a conventional or chemical warhead hundreds or even thousands of miles can pass for oil pipe. Ingredients for nerve gas agents intended for homicide are similar to those used for pesticide, while the 400 pounds of nitric and sulfuric acid and urea used in the World Trade Center bombing in February 1993 are common ingredients in fertilizers. The same engine that propels a scientific sounding rocket beyond the atmosphere can be used to fire a ballistic missile to a foreign capital.

But more ominously, the new danger is not so much the flow of components but of ideas. Weapons technology is now moving across borders, not only on compact discs and through modems, but in the heads of engineers and scientists who roam the world looking for fat profits or simply for employment. Ideas are infinitely harder to stop than finished missiles or supercomputers.

Then, too, the notion that proliferation can be capped by technical means alone, let alone reversed, is misguided. The most shocking part about Iraq's nuclear weapons program was that it was derived from open sources, from techniques so antiquated that the United States government had long since abandoned and declassified them. There are now many thousands of scientists and high-level technicians worldwide who are intimately acquainted with nuclear weapons design and production— 7,000 in Iraq alone and many times that number in the former Soviet Union—plus the large quantities of fissile material and the easily obtainable means of manufacturing much of the necessary equipment.

It is therefore our belief that while the best export control possible can slow the superweapon proliferation process, technical fixes alone cannot by themselves stop this most dangerous situation. The history of weapons technology is one of constant improvement in destructive capacity and range. While it is tempting to think of superweapons as being confined to far-off lands, it is only a matter of time before their reach and lethality extend everywhere. Nor do the deadly weapons need to fly on pillars of fire to reach their targets. More insidiously, they can be packaged for use by terrorists and carried anywhere.

The answer, we believe, is worldwide political resolve. As Canada, Sweden, Switzerland, Italy, and several South American countries demonstrate, would-be superweapon states need to be persuaded that, far from guaranteeing sovereignty, superweapons erode it because of their enormous expense and tendency to be matched in kind. While treaties and agreements like the Non-Proliferation Treaty and the Missile Technology Control Regime are undeniably useful for slowing proliferation, they are also dangerously porous. Iraq's being a party to the NPT did not prevent it from trying to obtain nuclear arms, nor did Russia's adherence to, if not membership in, the MTCR prevent it from trying to sell advanced rocket engines to India, to take only two examples.

Finally, the range of the devices described on these pages has increased steadily over the years, and there is no evidence that the trend will reverse itself. The push for miniaturized nuclear weapons, ballistic missiles with increased range, cruise missiles that can be carried offshore by submarine or freighter, air-to-air refueling, and a great deal more is substantially shrinking the safety zone between the traditional powers and their restive, ambitious, and increasingly well-armed neighbors. Having already come to that conclusion, several European nations are planning a defense system to protect them against missile attacks from North Africa and the Middle East. It is supremely ironic that the weapons and technology that threaten them are the very ones that they themselves spread because of greed and political expedience. And it is doubly ironic that, by the end of 1993, they were negotiating with their old antagonist—Russia—for the possible means of their salvation: SA-12 defensive missiles. The proliferators were prepared to pay their former adversary to rescue them from a potentially catastrophic threat caused by their own avarice and stupidity. But no place will be safe until every place is safe.

W.E.B. AND R.W.

# THE

# **E**QUALIZERS

—

# 1

## IRAQ:
## LAWRENCE OF ARABIA
## MEETS DR. STRANGELOVE

**I**t was the most dramatic, expensive, and violent product recall in history.

The streams of warplanes that thundered through the predawn darkness over Iraq early on the morning of Thursday, January 17, 1991, hit their targets with unrestrained ferocity. The coalition's attackers—American, British, French, Italian, Saudi Arabian, and Kuwaiti fighter-bombers—streaked over eastern Iraq, over Baghdad, and over scores of other sites along a wide corridor that went roughly from the Euphrates east to near the Iranian border. The planes, heavily laden with bombs, missiles, and fuel tanks to extend their range, came from several directions at once and headed unerringly through the night until they reached the highest priority targets. "There was a great deal of high-prestige bombing that went into that high-prestige target," one observer would later recall. The prelude to the liberation of Kuwait from Iraqi occupation had begun.

Most of the targets were in Baghdad and its suburbs, but some were strung out on both sides of the Tigris, from just south of the capital to the far north. Even before the invasion, intelligence analysts and strategists in the United States had begun sifting through growing evidence that certain places in Iraq were carrying out advanced weapons research.

The pace had abruptly quickened after Iraqi forces rumbled into Kuwait on August 2, 1990, however, as military and civilian intelligence analysts tried to divine, for the most part unsuccessfully, what was happening in the scattered, often sprawling, facilities.

Since security was exceptionally tight in Iraq, most of the intelligence came from so-called techint systems: technical intelligence operations that included electronic eavesdropping and reconnaissance satellites which sent down imagery of the suspect facilities. Not only had the analysts tried to figure out what was happening inside individual sites, but what was even more difficult, they tried to learn how, if at all, the separate work was interrelated. It was an exasperatingly difficult, immensely complicated business that was reminiscent of the game in which children connect dots on a piece of paper. The dots had names like Samarra, Sa'ad-16, Al Fallujah, Salman Pak, Taji, Tarmiyah, Ash Sharqat, Al Atheer, Qabaysah, Al Anbar, Tuwaitha, Al Qaim, Baiji, Al Iskandriyah, and Mussayib. When they and more than a score of other sites were connected, which did not happen until many months after the fighting ended, it would be seen that they formed a vast, heavily redundant superweapon network for the development and production of chemical and biological agents, ballistic missiles, and atomic bombs. No one in the West had any idea on war day how extensive Iraq's superweapon program was. One reason: no one had looked. In June 1990, there were only two analysts assigned by the Defense Intelligence Agency to Iraq. By comparison, forty-two were working on POW/MIA issues left over from the Vietnam War.

Daily briefings from the start of the heavily censored Desert Shield operation, including those conducted by General Norman Schwarzkopf, were largely designed to impress the Americans and Europeans back home with the technical proficiency of U.S. weapons as well as with the bravery and dedication of the men and women who used them. The idea was to demonstrate that countless American and other coalition combatants' lives, as well as those of the Iraqis themselves, were being saved by so-called smart weapons that could smash enemy targets with unprecedented accuracy. Videotapes showed the four walls of a building being blown out after one of the weapons apparently went down a chimney. Another showed "the luckiest man in Iraq" racing off a bridge just as the part of the span immediately behind him was destroyed by another "smart" bomb. Still another showed a Navy cruise missile slicing a radio antenna in half.

Those who watched the evening news as it was systematically distorted through the Pentagon's looking glass were left with the impression that the United States was spearheading a juggernaut whose relentless destructive capability came from the unmatched technical superiority of its weapons.* The colossal amount of money that had been pumped into the military during the preceding decade, much of it to develop high-tech weapons, seemed to be paying off. But whatever short-run benefit this had in saving the lives of coalition ground personnel and buoying morale at home—and it was considerable—it would also have the highly negative long-term effect of proving to those in the Third World who watched from the sidelines that advanced military technology could more than offset traditionally armed opponents. In depicting Iraq as being at the mercy of an opponent using the most modern weapons, and then being made humiliatingly impotent by them, the United States was fostering a problem that would prove to be even more pernicious than Iraq itself: quality beat quantity. Nor would it escape many Third World leaders that Baghdad would never have been attacked in the first place if it had actually managed to acquire its own atomic bombs.

That last possibility was precisely what Saddam Hussein had in mind all along. He did not have to watch coalition F-16 and Tornado fighter-bombers dropping "smart" bombs on his munitions plants, bridges, and generating stations to appreciate high-tech weapons. Superweapons—not mere "smart" bombs, but true weapons of mass destruction and the means of delivering them—were the linchpin for both his own power and for Iraq's concomitant role as the major Arab force in the Middle East and beyond. But the relentless drive for long-range missiles, nuclear arms, and the other accoutrements of big-power war machines had cost big-power money. They had cost so much, in fact, that Saddam brazenly tried to annex Kuwait and its petroleum to pay for them.

The United States and its allies responded, not to instill democracy in the sheikdom (which would be anathema), but for three less altruistic reasons: to protect the oil on which their economies functioned; to defang an unpredictable sociopath who was suddenly seen as being dangerously

---

*The bombs were guided by the pilots flying the aircraft that released them. The videos at the news briefings showed what the pilots had seen in their cockpits. While many structures were seen to have been knocked out, Pentagon public relations people were careful to omit scenes showing dead Iraqis. This lent an almost unreal quality to the scenes, as if the attacks had taken place on a practice bombing range. While the repeated carpet bombing of the "elite" Republican Guard by B-52s was frequently mentioned, no aerial reconnaissance photos were released showing what were unquestionably grisly scenes of thousands of soldiers who had been blown up in the open desert.

out of control; and to show other Third World countries what to expect if they, too, seriously threatened the establishment. There had never been any illusions about Saddam Hussein. He had always been taken to be a jackal. But he spent eight years and rivers of Iraqi blood fighting anti-Western and anticommunist Islamic revivalists in Iran—doing Washington's, Moscow's, and Riyadh's dirty work—and he had therefore been *their* jackal. Now, with the Iran-Iraq war over, he was too much his own jackal, and so he had to be stopped before it was too late. This was to be done chiefly from the sky.

Whatever the camouflaged briefing officers in Dhahran told the reporters, however, the air war did not get off to an auspicious start. On January 18, the day after the initial attacks, senior Iraqi nuclear scientists who were waiting to hear which of their secret sites had been detected and destroyed were pleasantly surprised. The nuclear research center at Tuwaitha, the only well-known facility in the vast nuclear program, had survived the night with little damage. The installation, just southeast of the capital, was where uranium enrichment and weaponization experiments had been carried out and where Iraq had small research reactors. When the attackers reached Tuwaitha, though, they found it all but obscured by thick smoke pouring out of cleverly positioned smoke pots.

As the F-16 pilots—part of a seventy-two-plane assault force—worked to get a clear shot at the reactor, strange things were going on deep inside. Iraqi weapons scientists were conducting experiments whose purpose remains a mystery.

"On the night the air war started, the Iraqis were running their research reactor at full power with two fuel elements being explicitly irradiated for plutonium separation," said David Kay, who headed the International Atomic Energy Agency inspection team that searched Iraq after the war in an effort to unlock the secrets of its nuclear weapons program. "One of the hallmarks of research reactors in developing countries is they virtually never run at night." The small reactor could never produce enough plutonium for a bomb. And all the evidence gathered before and after the war seemed to indicate that Iraq was not pursuing the plutonium route to the bomb, but rather the highly enriched uranium route. Why, then, was Iraq frantically trying to separate plutonium on the night of the attack?

"The Iraqis admitted they were prototyping a fuel assembly," Kay explained. This indicated that Iraq either was planning to build a plutonium production reactor or had one ready for operation and thus was working to develop the fuel rods to run it. Kay, among others, found the prospect of Iraq's being able to produce plutonium deeply frightening. It was a mystery that would remain unsolved.

Ordinarily, the fighter-bombers would have lingered, waiting for some of the smoke to dissipate, or tried to punch through it. But they also ran into such thick antiaircraft fire that swarming around Tuwaitha for a clear shot would probably have caused unacceptably high casualties. So they left after inflicting only slight damage.

Better yet, Tarmiyah, Iraq's first operational uranium enrichment facility, thirty miles on the other side of Baghdad, had not been touched. Neither had its twin at Ash Sharqat, which was then 85 percent complete. Al Atheer, the nation's equivalent of Los Alamos, had also escaped untouched, as had the four plants where components for Iraq's enrichment facilities were to be made.

Seeing that damage assessments showed Tuwaitha to be virtually intact, and knowing that the place was protected by a heavy concentration of antiaircraft guns, the coalition command sent out eight F-117A stealth fighters and a pair of tankers a few nights later to finish the job. Unseen by Iraqi radar, the black planes penetrated the air defense network and wiped out the facility's key laboratories and three of its four reactors. A couple of weeks after that, Tarmiyah and Ash Sharqat were discovered only by accident by Air Force targeteers and were also damaged but not destroyed.

Coalition planes, 288 cruise missiles, "smart" bombs, and armor made short work of Saddam's military. The air attacks were particularly effective. The sky over Iraq was first cleared of enemy fighters and was then used to carpet-bomb the "elite" Republican Guard and systematically break communication links, disrupt transportation, and blast known military and war manufacturing facilities. For the most part, the high-tech weapons worked as they were supposed to. Intelligence, on the other hand, was another matter.

The most sophisticated aerial and space reconnaissance apparatus on and over Earth—a $100 billion-plus system of satellites that could see (but not read) license plates from 100 miles and eavesdrop on telephone conversations from 22,300 miles, as well as thousands of analysts and buildingsful of the most modern computers and other support equipment—had decidedly mixed results. Pentagon claims during the war that mobile Scud batteries were being obliterated in large numbers were simply not true. While fixed sites were hit with devastating results, mobile launchers escaped destruction by being moved repeatedly, whatever the claims of the attacking pilots. What the pilots actually destroyed were ordinary flatbed tractor-trailer trucks.

Far more important was the fact that an extraordinary number of superweapon facilities, especially those relating to Iraq's nuclear weapons program, remained concealed until U.N. inspectors were able to prowl through the country long after the last "smart" bomb had fallen.* Even they, a normally taciturn bunch of scientists and engineers, expressed amazement at the true breadth of the nuclear weapons enterprise and the cleverness with which it was kept hidden from prying eyes both on the ground and above it. While much of the success was no doubt due to the Iraqis' inherent talent—they are at least as good at camouflage and deception as anyone else in the region—they also received generous amounts of help from their chief antagonists, the Americans themselves. During the Iran-Iraq War, while the United States was providing arms to Iran in the hope of getting hostages in Lebanon freed, it was also rushing highly classified satellite intelligence to Iraq as soon as it came in from space. The richly detailed data showed military equipment, the size and location of Iranian troop concentrations, and fixed targets, at least some of which were presumably concealed. While the imagery itself may not have been sent to Baghdad, the information it yielded provided the Iraqis with an excellent idea of what U.S. spy satellites could see and, by inference, how they could be foiled. This, combined with the Iraqis' own guile, resulted in decidedly mixed results where vital strategic intelligence was concerned.

In July 1991—five months after the end of Operation Desert Storm— the commander of the U.S. Central Command Air Forces told aerospace industry executives back home that the forty-three-day air campaign was a resounding success. Allied air forces had destroyed "100 percent of the nuclear facilities in Iraq that we knew about," Lieutenant General Charles A. Horner said, adding that "possibly 80 percent of all Iraqi

*The inspectors, themselves, became unintentional target-finders for the U.S. Navy. George Bush's parting gift to Saddam Hussein was delivered on January 17, 1993—three days before Bush left office—when forty-five Tomahawk cruise missiles were fired at the Zaafaraniya industrial complex in the southeast Baghdad suburbs. The facility, discovered by the inspectors, had been used to make computer-generated hardware for the calutrons that enriched uranium to bomb-grade and probably ballistic missile components as well. It should be noted, however, that the inspectors were also directed to many Iraqi facilities by U.S. space reconnaissance assets. Ground-to-air missile sites along the northern and southern "no-fly" zones were also hit during the days immediately before and after the attack on Zaafaraniya.

nuclear facilities were hit." While Horner, an unusually outspoken and forthright officer, had his aircrews strike whatever the intelligence analysts said bore striking, an incredible number of targets were missed because they were not known to exist.*

Whatever the effectiveness of the intelligence and bombing, Horner admitted, they had not been good enough to annihilate Iraq's nuclear weapons potential. Not by a long shot. The Iraqis suffered through the most sophisticated aerial bombardment in history—the first war of the space age, as Air Force Chief of Staff General Merrill A. McPeak quickly dubbed it because of the heavy use of reconnaissance, ballistic missile warning, communication, and other satellites—only to emerge, in Horner's words, with enough nascent nuclear capability to be able to produce weapons by the year 2000.

He was echoed more than a year later by the Director of Central Intelligence. "Baghdad probably still has more than 7,000 nuclear scientists and technicians—more than enough to reconstitute a weapons program—and may have enough equipment and material to make enough fissile material for a nuclear weapon in five to seven years if U.N. inspections and sanctions were to cease," Robert M. Gates warned an audience in California.

David Kay, the U.N.'s chief inspector of Iraqi nuclear efforts, contends that even Gates's figure is woefully conservative, that as many as 20,000 employees worked in the nuclear weapons and related programs. In emphasizing the size, stealth, and resilience of Iraq's nuclear program, all three men—the air force general, the spymaster, and the U.N. inspector—were unintentionally paying tribute to a fourth. His name is Jafar Jafar and he remains a formidable adversary.

Jafar Jafar and his brethren in other places are part of an atomic priesthood that is dedicated to harnessing the power of nuclear energy for devastation. The high priesthood's secret is to be able to take natural uranium, a common metal, and turn it into an explosive. They must learn to isolate enough of two fissile elements—uranium-235 or plutonium-239—so their natural instability can be used to release energy in the form of heat, light, and radiation: an explosive force that has been likened to 1,000 suns. But this trick is not easy.

---

*Contrary to reports and supposition during the war, Iraqi communication links remained operational until the end of hostilities. Horner said later that they were largely unscathed. (Burrows interview with Horner on April 28, 1993.)

Uranium ore—U-238—contains less than one percent of uranium-235 and has no plutonium-239, which is not found in nature. The U-235 must therefore be separated—enriched—from the rest of the ore through several processes until it is pure enough to be bomb grade. This is done by using electromagnets, ultra-high-speed spinning centrifuges, lasers, or chemical reaction.

Cyclotrons, for example, use electromagnets to separate lighter U-235 atoms from the much more numerous U-238. Since an electrically magnetized atom travels in a circle whose radius is determined by its mass, lighter U-235 atoms fly in tighter circles than their heavier counterparts. The U-235 ion flux—a beam of vapor—can then be skimmed in a collecting pocket like cream from milk. Plutonium-239, the deadliest of substances, can be found and chemically reprocessed from fuel rods used in either research or civilian power reactors.

The priests—nuclear physicists—understand these processes and use them to examine the ways in which the refined elements can be focused with deadly effect. For Jafar Jafar and others, that work entailed the mastery of every successive stage of the process, from finding the uranium to refining it to the immensely complicated business of designing and constructing bombs. His work was carried out on behalf of a ruthless tyrant who felt no qualms about plunging the world into a calamitous war in order to fulfill what he believed to be his destiny.

Jafar Dhia Jafar, the J. Robert Oppenheimer of the Iraqi nuclear weapons program, is the scion of one of his country's most powerful—and durable—families. In some ways, he is a cinematic figure: a combination of Lawrence of Arabia and Dr. Strangelove who mixes Muslim fatalism, Arab nationalism, and modern technocracy. The grandson of one of T. E. Lawrence's comrades-in-arms and the founder of the modern Iraqi Army, the son of a man who held seven different cabinet positions in Baghdad, Jafar was officially Deputy Minister of Industry and Military Industrialization (MIMI), Vice Chairman of the Iraq Atomic Energy Commission, and Director of Reactor Physics at the Tuwaitha Nuclear Research Center when the war erupted. What is certain is his position as the father of the aborted Iraqi atomic bomb. By the time the coalition's planes arrived, Jafar's empire included a complex of more than two dozen weapons plants, most of them clustered around Baghdad, the legion of employees, and

remarkable research and development laboratories that concentrated exclusively on fissile materials and their weaponization. The whole enterprise
had one specific long-range goal, according to Kay: the production of
fifteen to twenty nuclear weapons a year. Production of the first, he and
others believed, was as little as six months away when coalition bombers
struck, and not more than eighteen months. And all of that was undertaken
without once raising the suspicions of the International Atomic Energy
Agency, which was charged with making certain that Iraq lived up to its
obligations as a signatory to the nuclear Non-Proliferation Treaty.

"They certainly couldn't have got as far as fast as they did without
him," said Kay. "He was and is a very bright scientist as well as an
inspirational leader of his team. It's quite clear from talking to people
there [that] they respected him. They worked very hard because they, in
part, believed in him. And he actually participated very actively in the
program." Kay ought to know. He had an opportunity to talk with Jafar
and his subordinates several times, including on four blistering days in
the late summer of 1991 when he and his own colleagues were trapped
in a Baghdad parking lot. Jafar refused to let them collect and confiscate
weaponization, procurement, and personnel records from the nuclear program.

In common with countless Iraqi officers and bureaucrats, Jafar wears
a thick, neatly trimmed moustache in the manner of his leader. But that
is where the affectation ends. Unlike the soldiers, he does not wear
fatigues, nor even the shirt sleeves and open collar favored by scientists
and engineers who must work in a climate renowned for its scorching
heat. Unlike the others, Jafar's taste runs to Italian-style haircuts and silk
suits.

The Western demeanor is deceiving, though. In spite of his European
education, Jafar is a patriot who shares Saddam's dream to make Iraq a
world power. He, like his Iraqi colleagues, used his knowledge of Western
science and commerce in an effort to develop the ultimate superweapon
for a ferocious despot who was unafraid to use it. In that regard, Jafar
combines science and strident nationalism the way other nuclear patriots
do. He has much in common with Iran's Reza Amrollahi, India's P. K.
Iyengar, Pakistan's A. Q. Khan, Israel's Yuval Ne'eman, South Africa's
Jacobus W. DeVilliers, and Brazil's Brigadier General Hugo Oliviera Piva.
All share a Western education and total dedication to securing for their
countries what they see as the ultimate equalizer: nuclear weapons. Jafar

and Ne'eman, whose atomic missiles would have been aimed at each other had the Iraqi war program succeeded, both studied at the University of London's Imperial College, though not together.

And Jafar, like the others, startled the West and exposed its profound cultural arrogance toward the Third World by dint of the magnitude of what he accomplished on his own. "Ragheads *can* make bombs," one surprised Pentagon official exclaimed after hearing about Iraq's success in the chase for nuclear weapons.

After Desert Storm ended, journalists and intelligence analysts looked for Western companies and even technicians who had sold out to Iraq and other Third World nations. To be sure, the duplicity was staggering, particularly where so-called dual-use products and nuclear materials were concerned. Private or state companies in Brazil, France, Germany, Great Britain, the United States, and Yugoslavia, among others, thought of the Iraqis the way city slickers think of country bumpkins whose pockets are stuffed with money and who are out for a good time. Yet the reporters and analysts missed the most startling, and in the long-run most ominous, aspect of the Iraqi nuclear program: how much the Arabs—and others—had managed to accomplish on their own. Jafar, together with his counterparts in Teheran, Tel Aviv, and Islamabad, had shown that increasingly free trade had opened the way, not only for more equipment and material to cross borders, but for ideas to cross them as well. Iraq in fact had a library of 60,000 nuclear weapons–related documents, including many Manhattan Project designs that carried U.S. patents. One, 2,709,222, was Ernest Lawrence's design for the electromagnetic separation of uranium isotopes. The patent and other documents laid out designs for calutrons—which Jafar patriotically renamed "baghdatrons"—the very means by which the U.S. had separated the lighter (and more valuable) U-235 from the far more abundant U-238 for its Hiroshima bomb. Brainpower and open knowledge counted now, and no nation could claim a lock on them.

And there was something else Jafar and his Third World counterparts had in common. The bombs upon which they labored so furiously were to be aimed, not at political adversaries as was the case with the United States and the Soviet Union, but at enemies who were distinguished by their cultural, religious, or ethnic "otherness." The Third World's nuclear weapons programs existed to provide the means for settling ancient scores, some of them centuries or even millennia old. The Iraqi bomb was being built specifically to kill masses of Jews and Persians; the Israeli bomb was perfected to kill Arabs and Persians; the Iranian bomb to kill Arabs and Jews; the South African bomb to kill blacks; the Pakistani bomb to kill Hindus and other "infidels"; the Indian bomb to kill Muslims and Chinese. Unlike Western and Soviet bombs that were produced to end the political scourges of communism, capitalism, and fascism, Third World nuclear weapons are genocidal. The bomb is a weapon for ethnic "cleansing" or "purification" on an awesome scale.

Jafar Jafar is so important to Iraq's nuclear weapons program that he is a prisoner in his own country. He is no longer permitted to leave, as he once did, for fear that enemy assassins will execute him.* Jafar is so close to Saddam that he lived in the presidential compound near his (Jafar's) younger brother, Yahia, an electrical engineer who was an Iraqi government computer expert.

The Jafar family, which is part of a network of cosmopolitan Shiite families in Baghdad, has links with Iraq's and other countries' ruling elites that go back to the turn of the century. Jafar Jafar's father, Dhia Jafar, was a favorite of Iraq's King Faisal II, taking on a long series of trusted ministerial assignments for him. The elder Jafar was in London on an official visit on July 14, 1958, when he learned that Faisal, his son the crown prince, and the prime minister were murdered in yet another coup. The family patriarch used connections to remain in England with his two sons, Jafar and Hamid, and later to send for his wife and young Yahia. He never returned home, electing instead to educate his sons in the best British schools.

Jafar went to the University of Birmingham for his baccalaureate and master's degree in physics and then completed a doctorate at Manchester before marrying a British woman and starting a family. His first job was as an associate researcher at the prestigious Institute for Nuclear Physics in London University's Imperial College.

In a pattern that was familiar elsewhere, Jafar began to absorb the knowledge that would later be applied to his country's most advanced weapons program. During a visit to CERN, the European nuclear research center in Geneva, from May through December 1971, he became increasingly familiar with cyclotron technology. What he learned about the "atom smashers" became the basis for the "baghdatrons," the electromagnetic

---

*It can be assumed that, where Baghdad is concerned, the Mossad leads the list.

isotope separators that he would develop years later to enrich uranium until it was bomb-grade. A stint at Harwell, the British nuclear research center, provided a firsthand look at the type of military cyclotron technology that had been used to make the highly enriched uranium for the Manhattan Project. Two decades later, few knowledgeable outsiders would guess that it was primarily calutrons, the dinosaurs of the enrichment world, that were Jafar's machines of choice to produce the highly fissile material for his country's first atom bomb. Nor did the similarity end there. The American bomb was called "The Gadget" by those who worked on it; its Iraqi counterpart was referred to as "The Mechanism."

Jafar applied for a professorship at Imperial College early in 1975. He had by then evolved into that most contradictory creature, an urbane Shiite bon vivant who loved "starred" restaurants, excellent whiskey, bridge, squash, and tailor-made suits from Milan, his favorite city. Yet the young physicist remained an abidingly serious fellow. He drove a Volkswagen Beetle, not an MG, and never succumbed to the gaudy temptations and arrogant decadence that were the hallmarks of many well-off Arab expatriates living in Europe and "the States."

"Even though Jafar displayed a certain elegance when dressing, he wasn't the type to boast his wealth," said D. S. Websdale, a British colleague who had accompanied Jafar to Geneva. Whatever his scientific virtues, however, he did not land the professorship. It was a fateful decision. Rebuffed by academe, Jafar decided to return with his family to the land of his birth.

His arrival in Baghdad in April 1975 coincided with the start of a government drive to recruit nuclear scientists. It was an open secret that both Israel and Iran, Iraq's sworn enemies, were after nuclear weapons (the Israelis not only had them, but had considered using them against overwhelming Egyptian forces in the Yom Kippur War two years earlier). Some 4,000 scientists were attracted between 1974 and 1977, with Jafar being the biggest catch. For whatever reason—patriotism, wealth, power, nostalgia—the thirty-three-year-old physicist became the willing instrument of the man behind the recruiting effort, Vice-President Saddam Hussein. His new job was with the Iraq Atomic Energy Commission, whose operations were about to expand with the construction of a French-supplied reactor called Osirak.

Saddam believed that the embryonic nuclear weapons program had within it the key to his nation's lasting greatness and, by inference, his own. He therefore took a special interest in its health. He went to France in 1976 to close the deal for Osirak, the forty-megawatt research—not power—reactor that was to be the nucleus of the most ambitious atomic weapons program in the Arab world. Osirak was well named. It stood for Osiris, the Egyptian god of the underworld, who myth had it was slain by his evil brother Set. In keeping with such treachery, Jafar recommended that Iraq agree to a French demand that it sign the nuclear Non-Proliferation Treaty as a condition of the reactor sale and then, if need be, renounce it after the facility was completed. To figure out what France's client had in mind for Osirak, all anyone needed to do was read an interview Saddam had given to a Beirut magazine in 1975 in which he stated explicitly that his country was engaged in "the first Arab attempt at nuclear arming." But dwelling on their clients' motives could have had the effect of inhibiting commerce, and it was therefore not encouraged. A favorable balance of trade helped win elections, after all, not an over-fastidiousness about customers' intentions. The West Germans, who were also ringing up huge sales in Iraq, couldn't have agreed more. So everyone tried to think good thoughts.

Jafar's only equal in Iraq was another foreign-educated Shiite, Hussain al Sharistani, with whom he had worked at the Imperial College. While both men had much in common, including excellent educations, foreign-born wives, and an intense loyalty to Iraq, they differed profoundly in one major respect: religion. Jafar was secular. Sharistani, the nephew of a Shiite ayatollah and the friend of Iraq's leading ayatollah, was intensely religious—so religious, in fact, that when the two men dined out in Paris or Rome while on nuclear equipment shopping expeditions in the late 1970s, Sharistani would pepper the waiters with questions about how the food was prepared to ensure that neither lard nor wine had been used.

By 1979, Jafar became Vice Chairman of the Iraq Atomic Energy Commission and was responsible for dealing with the French on Osirak. Sharistani was the commission's Chief of Research and the scientific adviser to Iraq's new president, Saddam Hussein. With oil revenues projected to be $60 billion over the next five years, and Osirak coming together, Jafar predicted to friends in Geneva that a "great day" was about to dawn.

But it did not come. Personal problems got in the way when his wife became ill and retreated to Europe with their two young sons. Then the Mossad got in the way. First the Israelis infiltrated Osirak's training program and then they sabotaged it. On April 7, 1979, only two days before a pair of reactor cores were to be shipped to Iraq, seven Israeli agents stole into a warehouse in the port of La Seyne-sur-Mer, near Toulon, and blew them up.

Next, Saddam himself got in the way. The toppling of the Shah of Iran in February of that year, followed by the seizure of the government by the Ayatollah Khomeini and the other revivalist zealots who were intent on exporting their religion, made Saddam, a Sunni, deeply suspicious of the Shiite sect. Shiite demonstrations did nothing to ease his fears. He therefore ordered increasingly brutal reprisals against the demonstrators. Overcome by persistent paranoia, he had Sharistani arrested in his office at the Atomic Energy Commission on September 18. His wife, two daughters, and year-old son were initially taken in. The scientist was known to have deep ties to the Shiite clergy. More important, he was rumored to have helped the Israelis destroy the reactor cores in France and even to have planned the destruction of the Osirak reactor itself. It was all absurd, of course, except in Saddam's always leery mind. Sharistani was therefore tortured into paralysis for twenty-two consecutive days at the Abu Gharib military barracks and, after a brief appearance at a military hospital in January 1980, was not seen again for eleven years.

The following month, Jafar's attempt to get his friend released landed him in prison, too. According to the ample lore of the era, Barzan al-Tikriti, Saddam's brutal stepbrother and then chief of the secret police, separately offered the two men a choice: continued imprisonment or a return to the country's nuclear weapons program, complete with perks as extravagant as a suite in the presidential palace. Following a rejection of the offer by Sharistani (the story goes), he was sentenced to twenty years in prison and was so completely shut away that even human rights groups gave him up for dead. "They offered me great privileges, but also revealed that the program's main objective was the bomb. Because of ethical and religious considerations, I refused three times," Sharistani would later maintain. Al-Takriti was eventually rewarded by being sent to Iraq's U.N. Mission in Geneva, where he traded his military beret for a diplomat's top hat.

Jafar Dhia Jafar capitulated, however, and in doing so became the chief of his nation's nuclear weapons program. Jafar may not have been good enough to teach nuclear physics at the Imperial College, he undoubtedly reflected, ruefully, but he would be good enough to make his country a power that would eclipse the United Kingdom itself. In the process, Jafar would also became a born-again Saddam loyalist. And throughout the rest of the decade, few outside the Iraqi inner circle knew that he had even been released from jail, let alone was directing his country's ambitious nuclear weapons program.*

Jafar brought a degree of energy to the task that amounted to fanaticism. When the Iran-Iraq War began a few months later—and the weapons programs were first speeded up—he went on a recruiting drive, enticing gifted high school and university students with a compelling inducement: deferments from the war with Iran and large salaries after graduation. He sent thousands of the young military scientists to school abroad, mainly in England, and made it clear that they would apply themselves to their studies or suffer the consequences on the front lines. "The Kuwaitis would party all night," an Egyptian student who was in a British university in the mid-1980s recalled. "The Iraqis, on the other hand, had to file monthly progress reports. These were always very serious." Sami Arajj, the director of the Tuwaitha Nuclear Research Center, received both his bachelor's degree and doctorate in nuclear physics from Michigan State University and worked at the Commonwealth Edison nuclear reactor outside Chicago before going home.

France took some of the recruits for training at Saclay, its own nuclear training facility, so they could operate the Osirak reactor to its fullest advantage. Since the French believed that a robust economy was its own reward, they had performed the same service for the Israelis who operated the secret French research reactor at Dimona, deep in the Negev. Since the nuances of nuclear science and engineering vary slightly from country to country, Jafar sent his young charges to the United States and the Soviet Union as well as to Britain and France, thereby adding depth to the program. He quickly became the young Iraqis' father figure—the disciplinarian who was totally dedicated to their nation's taking its rightful place among the real powers of the world, one way or another.

Whatever his charges believed, however, their education was not free. The debt run up by their government-sponsored studies was paid back by absolute loyalty or certain liquidation. Every scientist and engineer who studied in the West or participated in a conference there understood that defection or passing information to a hostile intelligence

---

*One was Simon Henderson, a skilled and knowledgeable reporter for *The Financial Times*'s "Mideast Markets." In December 1989, Henderson quoted "Western officials" as saying that Jafar Jafar might have overall responsibility for a nuclear weapons program and that the bomb itself was a complicated implosion device, not a relatively simple gun-barrel type. ("Iraq and the Bomb," *The Financial Times*, December 11, 1989.)

service would bring swift and deadly reprisal not only to the transgressor but to his family. "The first Iraqi defector after the war came out and gave us some of the basic information about the calutron process," David Kay recalled. "He had staged his own death on the highway to Mosul, and he thought they would not find out that he was still alive and had defected. He had been out for less than two months when a journalist printed the story. His entire family down to a second cousin were killed."

The search for scientific talent extended to rival Egypt as well. According to Kenneth R. Timmerman, author of *The Death Lobby*, Saddam himself ordered Jafar to hire Dr. Yahia al-Meshed, one of Egypt's top nuclear physicists, and send him to Saclay as well. Meshed's specialty was the chemical reprocessing of bomb-grade plutonium from spent reactor fuel. His flirtation with the Iraqis was a short one, however. On June 13, 1980, at the end of his first week of training at Saclay, al-Meshed returned to Paris and was beaten to death that night by Israeli agents in his room at the Hotel Meridien. Far from wanting to keep the nature of the murder a secret, Israel used it as an open warning to others who might be tempted to enlist in the Iraqi cause. Israeli radio announced the killing that very night, claiming that the "Iraqi project to acquire an atomic bomb has been set back by two years." A month later, a prostitute who had been with al-Meshed the night he was killed was herself struck and killed by a hit-and-run driver. And a month after that, on August 7, 1980, the Rome office of Techint, the Italian firm that supplied plutonium reprocessing technology to the Iraqis, was bombed. To make sure that Techint got the message, a bomb went off that same night outside its director's home.

On June 7, 1981, the Israelis delivered the most crippling blow of all. Late that afternoon, F-16s protected by F-15s streaked out of a setting sun to drop a succession of 2,000-pound bombs on Osirak, scoring enough direct hits to knock out the reactor permanently. The surprise attack left the smashed core entombed in a mound of concrete rubble and Saddam Hussein's dream temporarily entombed with it. One American official quoted a dejected and embittered Jafar as saying that his countrymen had "found themselves paying billions of dollars and ended up with nothing." Jafar exaggerated. The whole complex—the reactor and its labs—actually cost $750 million.

Two weeks later, Saddam wrathfully told his cabinet that the pursuit of nuclear weapons had not ended with the destruction of Osirak. "No power can stop Iraq acquiring technological and scientific know-how to serve its national objectives," he said: not the war with Iran; not the relentless Israelis; not the Non-Proliferation Treaty.

By 1982, with Jafar still in charge, a special committee developed a master plan to realize that end. It was a far-reaching, comprehensive program, political as well as technical. And it was to be fed with the nation's oil. The key decision was to take the enriched uranium route to the bomb. Without a reactor like Osirak, Iraq could not obtain plutonium in large enough quantities to fuel a bomb. That meant Iraq would have to build large and secret facilities where natural uranium would be enriched to bomb grade—a major violation of the NPT.

Iraq would not only not renounce the NPT, Jafar decided, but would seem to embrace it. Inspectors from the International Atomic Energy Agency would be welcomed twice a year for tours of Tuwaitha. Iraq would look like a good citizen to the IAEA and get the bomb at the same time. Ripping up the NPT, he said, would be counterproductive. It would scare off European suppliers whose equipment was essential, especially in the program's early stages. Instead, the inspectors would be shown records proving that Iraq could account for the eighty pounds of highly enriched uranium that it had long ago bought from France and the Soviet Union.

The statements Jafar's commission prepared for Saddam reflected the deceit. "Today, late in the twentieth century, we appear, through the feverish nuclear arms race, to be set upon committing mass suicide," the Iraqi dictator said in a message to the World Conference Against Atomic and Hydrogen Bombs in 1982. "The proliferation of weapons of mass destruction has surpassed the limit of all anticipation." The words might have come from an acceptance speech for the Nobel Peace Prize. For his part, Jafar was so proud of the massive deception that he would one day joke to a United Nations inspector that he should have given an address before the U.N. itself on how to beat the Non-Proliferation Treaty.

While the IAEA was complimenting Iraq for its forthright position on nuclear proliferation, the quest for reactors continued. The French, now sensitive to international publicity, turned down an offer to rebuild Osirak. Saddam and Jafar then began looking for someone to build a top-secret underground reactor near the Al Multhanna chemical weapons facility, just north of Samarra. There were negotiations with a French-Belgian consortium, with other foreign firms, and with the Soviet and Chinese governments themselves to build the reactor. There is also evidence that the parent organization of Brazil's nuclear program was approached to construct an underground uranium dioxide facility to provide fuel for the reactor. At the same time, huge amounts of graphite, as well as a graphite mill, were purchased by Iraq. Graphite, nuclear weapons scientists point out, is used to construct plutonium production reactors. This lends more credence to David Kay's theory that Jafar was trying to become self-sufficient in plutonium production. Although evidence that a reactor had been built was never found, the fact that Saddam wanted to site it underground reflected not only an attempt to protect it from being spotted and attacked, but the high degree of secrecy with which the new nuclear program in general would be run. This time, it was decided, there would be no speeches, no magazine articles, no bluster to rouse the ire of the West.

The core of the Iraqi plan was to set up an Iraqi Manhattan Project whose goal was nothing short of establishing an *indigenous* capability to build not only nuclear weapons but the entire research and development support structure that went with them. Between 1982 and 1987, Jafar's scientists set up at least six disguised weapons labs at Tuwaitha, in the shadow of the bombed Osirak reactor. The Nuclear Physics Building contained laboratories for the research and testing of baghdatrons. Another, faster method of enrichment, using spinning centrifuges to separate U-235 from U-238, took place in the Chemical Research Building. The centrifuges were to succeed and complement the baghdatrons, which ultimately cost between $4 billion and $8 billion.

Scientists in the Polymer Chemistry Research Laboratory worked on enriching uranium through a tedious and expensive chemical process developed by the French and Japanese. The Iraqis had legally obtained detailed data from the French owners of the process and then, U.N. inspectors later learned, tried to duplicate the process without French help. Others, in the Chemical and Radiochemical Analysis Laboratory, worked at reprocessing gram quantities of plutonium from depleted uranium that had been obtained for use in artillery shells. More important by far, it was in the chemical analysis lab that uranium metal was to be melted and cast for bomb cores.

Although Jafar ran the entire program, he brought knowledge of calutrons from Harwell, CERN, and elsewhere to the baghdatron operation and was unquestionably its guiding light. "In the uranium enrichment area, he was the scientific, really the guiding scientific investigator, in one of their major enrichment methods; that is, the calutron . . . ," said David Kay, Jafar's eventual nemesis. "That was very close to his own scientific field and he actively participated as a member of the design and production group." The operation remained so secret that even the Israelis, who prided themselves on the quality of the intelligence they got from Iraq, were surprised to discover its depth and breadth after the war. "In general we knew what was going on and we tried to tell the Americans about it," a senior Israeli official remarked, "but we were surprised as well when we learned the extent of what there was in Iraq."

Later, Saddam and his advisers decided to develop a long-range ballistic missile in conjunction with the nuclear weapons. It was to be called Condor-2, or Badr-2000, and was designed to reach targets 600 miles from Iraq's frontiers. The Iraqi atomic bomb program would be run by the Atomic Energy Commission's Department of Studies and Development. The entire integrated nuclear and missile programs and everything that went into them were collectively called Project 395.

The nuclear weapons program required a clandestine logistical effort of immense proportion. Highly specialized equipment, from computers to nuclear triggers, high-temperature furnaces, and electron-beam welders, had to be imported overtly or otherwise—sometimes in pieces. This was handled in Baghdad by two "private" firms set up by Iraqi intelligence to do the high-priority shopping: the Al Araby Trading Company and Industrial Projects Company. There was also a shadowy network of dummy trading companies established in England and elsewhere to quietly buy and send home whatever equipment was needed. Whole companies, like Britain's Matrix-Churchill, a precision tool maker with a sister company in Ohio, were quietly taken over to assure that specialized hardware for precise machining could be imported without interruption.

Architects and construction firms were hired to design and build, not dozens, but hundreds of specialized buildings at secret locations throughout the country. Ever mindful of what had happened to Osirak in 1981, Jafar and his colleagues in intelligence came up with a specialized security plan that included building a twin of every critical facility and separating the two by as many miles as possible. Facilities for the fabrication of small parts were kept separate. Buildings were cleverly designed so their purpose would not be detected. They were constructed so that radioactive and other telltale emissions did not leak out, for example. Many were also dual-use plants, one of which produced both baghdatrons and window frames. Buildings that performed the same function were sometimes shaped differently. All of it was done to fool the spy satellites, which, they knew from firsthand experience, were very good.

43

Tarmiyah, which was largely designed and completely built and equipped by Yugoslavia's Federal Directorate of Supply and Procurement and EMO Electrical Engineering Corporation/Ohrid, a private Yugoslav company, was not easy to hide. The complex, which cost between $2 billion and $3 billion, comprised nearly 400 buildings spread over more than two square miles of desert a half hour's drive north of Baghdad. The entire facility was surrounded by a light fence to give photointerpreters the impression that little of importance was happening inside.

Building 33, its centerpiece, measured 250 feet by 370 feet and contained the first operational baghdatrons. The uranium would be enriched until it was bomb-grade by using the same technology that U.S. weapons scientists used in the Manhattan Project, declassified in 1949, and finally abandoned in the 1950s. The first step in the two-step baghdatron, or electromagnetic isotope separation (EMIS), process for enriching uranium took place inside Building 33. A second, nearby building could complete the process until the uranium was 93 percent pure U-235, or bomb-grade. Two satellite structures containing 132 one-megawatt transformers flanked Building 33 and fed electricity into the power-hungry baghdatrons. Knowing that large power cables leading to the transformer buildings would arouse the suspicion of U.S. and Soviet photointerpreters who knew that nuclear enrichment facilities use great quantities of electricity, the 100-megawatt-plus plant that fed the transformers was built ten miles away and was connected to Tarmiyah by underground cables. And what, officially, did the sprawling facility make? Transformers. Tarmiyah was so sophisticated that bar codes and computer inventories were used to keep track of and order spare parts from the Ministry of Industry and Military Industrialization (MIMI).

Ash Sharqat, Tarmiyah's twin (in cost as well as structure), was being built near the Badush Dam (another huge Yugoslavian project) when the Persian Gulf War broke out. Iraq bought heavy construction equipment from companies like Caterpillar, Mack Trucks, Rotec, and Dresser Industries, claiming it was going to be used for the dam when, in fact, it was being diverted to the new enrichment facility. The manual labor was done by 12,000 Vietnamese, each of whom was paid premium wages (for Vietnamese): $3 a day.

Jafar and the intelligence chiefs needn't have lost sleep worrying about Tarmiyah and Ash Sharqat's being discovered. Analysts in the Lawrence Livermore National Laboratory's classified Z Division, who were responsible for spotting nuclear proliferation worldwide, were derisively dismissing a suggestion from another national laboratory that the Iraqis could be studying EMIS. The other lab, Oak Ridge, pointed to a classified study done in 1984 that showed twenty nations having research programs in EMIS technology. But the Livermore group, whose facility was named after Edward Lawrence, the inventor of the calutron, just wouldn't buy the idea that Iraq could even contemplate using Stone Age technology. They would have been even more surprised to learn that much of the calutron and centrifuge technology came from open literature and that the machines themselves were homemade.

The facility most critical to the nuclear weapons program was at Al Furat, south of Baghdad. There, Iraqi scientists had built, with the help of Interatom, a Siemens subsidiary, a workshop for the design and fabrication of centrifuges, which offer the most efficient, least expensive way to enrich uranium until it is bomb-grade. The baghdatrons developed by Jafar were indeed ingenious. But they would limit Iraq to a paltry three bombs a year. Thousands of centrifuges operated in tandem arrangements called cascades would lead to an atomic bomb assembly line just like Israel's, which can produce twenty bombs or warheads a year. More important, the calutrons and centrifuges would work, not in parallel, but in sequence. The calutrons would do the hard work enriching natural uranium from 0.7 percent to 20 percent, a process requiring brute force. The centrifuges would then take it the rest of the way to 90 percent, a relatively easy task.

The centrifuge design data were Germany's great gift to the Iraqi superweapon program. The data had been provided in 1987 by an ingenious route. German scientists simply let their Iraqi customers download the data over international telephone lines. That way, no blueprints were smuggled out of Frankfurt, no floppy discs were air-expressed to Baghdad. The key technology was transferred over modems by a special team of Iraqi computer hackers.

Al Atheer, code-named Petrochemical Complex-3 and comprising nearly 100 buildings disguised as a materials processing facility south of Baghdad, was Jafar's crown jewel. Al Atheer was a "gold-plated" mini-Los Alamos where the final step—bomb assembly—was to take place. There were buildings containing computer-controlled drills and lathes and the presses, induction furnaces, and plasma coating machines that were necessary to shape and mold the uranium bomb cores. There was a weapon design complex that used standard personal computers (IBM PS/2s, the same model that was used to write this book) to test possible weapon configurations and a larger NEC-750 as a backup. Al Atheer even had a firing bunker to test the conventional explosives that would be needed to implode the bomb core.

Leaving no possibility untried, the Iraqis even used the Internet electronic bulletin board, a vast international computer network that was originally set up by the Pentagon, to get answers to their most vexing problems. According to Kay, Jafar Jafar's minions would couch their nuclear weapons problems in innocuous terms and simply send them out and wait for some unsuspecting expert to answer. Kay said that in a number of instances, the baffled Iraqis actually got back useful answers.

Despite everyone's surprise, Iraq had followed the same path in its pursuit of nuclear weapons as in its chemical and biological programs and its missile development program. The Geneva Protocol of 1925 forbids the use of chemical agents except in retaliation against another nation that uses them. The Biological and Toxin Weapons convention of 1972 prohibits the possession or use of such biological weapons as cholera, anthrax, tularemia, and equine encephalitis. Baghdad signed both agreements, though it never ratified the BW convention. Yet Saddam Hussein hadn't been in command when the accords were reached. He evidently saw both, as he saw the NPT, as being irrelevant and obstructive but excellent cover. In fact, Iraq's Revolutionary Command Council decided not only to stock chemical weapons but to build indigenous manufacturing facilities as early as 1974, even before Hussein officially came to power. In this area, no less than with nuclear weapons and ballistic missiles, self-sufficiency was the thing.

Accordingly, a front organization, the Iraqi State Enterprise for Pesticide Production, was set up to search for European or American companies that would build a pilot "pesticide" plant in Iraq. Karl Kolb, a small West German company, got the contract and was soon joined by other similarly sized firms. Since development of the new Al Multhanna chemical complex near Samarra was heavily fragmented among the firms, some did not know what they were helping to create.

Management was the Iraqi genius, as it would be in the nuclear effort a decade later. Al Multhanna was shortly to move from a pilot plant to a full-scale chemical weapons production facility, turning out an estimated 3,000 tons a year of mustard gas and sarin and tabun, as well as trying to develop a gas called VX, a persistent nerve gas, and BZ, a hallucinogen. Suffice it to say that Al Multhanna was not run by a pesticide enterprise. Just as the Iraqi Atomic Energy Commission was a peaceful-sounding front for a deadly program, so too was the State Enterprise for Pesticide Production merely a cover. Both operations would eventually come under the control of MIMI.

If anyone doubted that Saddam would use nuclear weapons if he got his hands on them, a look at his record with poison gas would dispel the notion. By 1985, Iraq had realized a goal it never reached with nuclear weapons. It was manufacturing its own mustard gas and both nerve agents in locally operated, if foreign-built, plants. Iraq used the "poor man's atom bomb" against Iranian troops between 1983 and 1988 and against Kurdish civilians in 1987 and 1988. Teheran claims that 50,000 Iranian soldiers were killed, wounded, or disfigured by Iraqi chemical agents. And Massoud Barzani, a Kurdish leader, complained to the United Nations in September 1988 that Iraqi forces bombed Kurdish villages with chemical weapons twenty-four times during the preceding eighteen months. Barzani's message was brought forcefully home after grotesque scenes showing gassed women and small children lying in the streets of the Kurdish town of Halabja were broadcast on television around the world and appeared in color in news magazines in March 1988.* Since several Western nations, including the United States, were supplying Saddam Hussein with arms to fight the Iranians, they mostly kept silent about the atrocities at Halabja and elsewhere.

And a little-known incident occurred during the second week of the Gulf War that could have added an especially nasty new dimension to the combat. At one point, F-117As blasted Soviet-made TU-16 and Chinese Xian B-6D Badger bombers at Al Taqqadum. According to General Horner, the Iraqi aircraft were being loaded with chemical weapons when the attack took place. Had the Iraqis used poison gas against coalition forces, a reprisal in kind almost certainly would have been launched. The reaction of Americans at home to their sons and daughters being gassed by Arabs, as well as immediate and extreme pressure on

---

*Although U.S. officials and the Kurds themselves have maintained that Iraq gassed Halabja, some experts said after the war with Iraq in 1991 that both Iran and Iraq used chemical weapons against that town and others in the area. "The fact is that both sides used chemical weapons," one intelligence analyst said. "There probably wasn't an attempt on either side to kill the villagers, but instead, they were fighting over the territory." ("Years Later, No Clear Culprit in Gassing of Kurds," *The New York Times*, April 28, 1991.) Any lingering doubts about the use of gas against the Kurds were put to rest by soil tests conducted five years after the attack. ("Tests Indicating Iraq Gas Warfare," *The New York Times*, April 30, 1993.)

the White House to retaliate massively, would undoubtedly have escalated the war. U.N. inspectors later found the chemical weapons—specifically mustard gas—where Horner said they were.

The freedom with which Saddam operated in the chemical area expanded steadily. Iraq had built a pilot plant for the production of the precursor chemicals used in mustard gas in the 1970s. In 1988, as the war with Iran drew to a close, a larger facility for the precursors was begun near Mussayib, and a brand-new installation for nerve gas precursors was started near Fallujah. These were the chemical weapons analogues to the uranium enrichment plants. Once again, German companies—Preussag and a Karl Kolb subsidiary—sold the equipment and provided the training, just as they were to do in the nuclear program. German authorities believed that as many as five companies were involved.

With such facilities, Saddam Hussein had every reason to believe by the summer of 1990 that at least his chemical arsenal was formidable. Not only had the chemical weapons taken a heavy toll in dead and wounded, but they proved to have considerable political value in terrorizing adversaries, particularly civilians. By April 1990, even as he was preparing to move on Kuwait, Saddam Hussein's stockpile of chemical weapons emboldened him enough to issue this warning to Israel: ". . . by God, we will make the fire eat half of Israel if it tries to do anything against Iraq. We don't need an atomic bomb because we have the dual [binary] chemical," he said, referring to chemical weapons that become deadly when two otherwise nonlethal precursor chemicals are mixed. "Whoever threatens us with the atomic bomb," he added, "we will annihilate him with the dual chemical."

Similarly, Iraq violated the Biological Weapons Convention, the single most prohibitive of the superweapons treaties. It categorically bans all biological weapons and permits only defense research. Saddam's scientists, nonetheless, set up research labs and at least one production facility at Salman Pak, not far down the Tigris from the nuclear research facility at Tuwaitha. Again, Iraq had a foreign company, this time Germany's Thyssen, build the basic facility. Baghdad then developed the foundation stones for a weapons program. In this case, they were bacteria that would be used to fill weapons canisters: anthrax, botulism, and tularemia. Thousands of bottles of the agents were carefully filled and stored at Salman Pak. If the coalition bombers hadn't been careful about the kinds of munitions they used against these targets and the way they attacked them, it was estimated that as many as six million Iraqis would have perished because of their own country's deadly arsenal.

To the scientists and technicians in Iraq's biological weapons program who mixed the witch's brew, the ingredients carried suitably sterile-sounding names: *Clostridium botulinum, Clostridium perfringens, Bacillus anthracis, Brucella abortus, Brucella melitensis, Francisella tularensis, Bacillus subtilis, Bacillus cereus,* and *Bacillus mageterium.* The scientists' victims, however, would know them with terrible intimacy: botulism, gas gangrene, anthrax, very high fever, rabbit fever, and bloody diarrhea. Gas gangrene, the worst of the lot, literally causes skin tissue to first discolor and then explode. One plan, U.N. inspectors later learned, called for the biological agents to be used in "terrorist activities."

Iraq steadfastly maintained, both before and after its war with the coalition, that it had never used biologicals against either the Iranians or the Kurds. A 1987 Iraqi Army document seized by Kurdish guerrillas in northwest Iraq in the aftermath of the Gulf War tells a far different story, however. The top-secret order, issued "in the name of God, the merciful, the compassionate," instructed the recipients to take an annual inventory of all "biological and chemical materials." Another document relating to chemical weapons derogatorily referred to the Kurds as "sons of treachery" and "saboteurs." Kurdish physicians and the Iranian government cited the orders as proof of what they had believed for years: that Saddam Hussein had, indeed, resorted to using biological weapons against his foes.

The Iraqi strongman was in fact so confident about the effects of his superweapons that, in the spring of 1990, he began to boast about them, much the way he had boasted about the possibility of using nuclear weapons fifteen years earlier. And why not? Saddam's stockpile of chemical weapons, then in excess of 150,000 bombs, rockets, missile warheads, artillery rounds, and even landmines, emboldened him to the point at which he had issued his annihilation warning to Israel. Tel Aviv responded the next day with the launch of a rocket that could have easily laid an atomic bomb on Baghdad with less than ten minutes' warning. The Israelis thought they knew Saddam well enough to call his bluff in a way that could not be misinterpreted. (Over the next three weeks, however, Saddam responded by firing five Scuds.)

Israel and the coalition nonetheless took the threat with utmost seriousness. When the first eight Scud missiles were fired at Israel during the second day of the war, for example, it was widely assumed that they carried chemical warheads. Initial reports on television quoted sources at the Tel Aviv hospital where the wounded were taken as saying that they showed signs of having been exposed to chemical agents. Yitzhak Malkian, a resident of the city, had his gas mask blown off his face by the force of one of the Scuds exploding nearby. "I was sure it was chemical weapons," he said afterward, "and that I was dead."

If Jafar Jafar was the atomic bomb program's Oppenheimer, its General Leslie Groves—the managerial genius who ran the organization that supported the Manhattan Project scientists—was General Amir Hammoudi al-Saadi. The title of general was strictly honorific. Like Jafar, al-Saadi was a foreign-educated scientist, with a doctorate in chemistry from the University of Munich and practical experience working in the arms industries of East Germany, Czechoslovakia, and Yugoslavia. He endeared himself to Saddam by developing the Al Abbas missile, the extended-range Scud that was used against Israel and Saudi Arabia in the Persian Gulf War. Not the least of al-Saadi's attributes was a good working knowledge of both German and English and an understanding of West German export laws. As MIMI's Senior Deputy Minister, al-Saadi was responsible for integrating all the superweapons programs—nuclear, chemical, biological, and missile—plus building engineering facilities for those programs, procuring equipment, negotiating with foreign suppliers, securing financing, and keeping his immediate boss, General Hussein Kamel, and Saddam happy. Pleasing Kamel was important because he was Saddam's nephew, son-in-law, and deadly protégé. As head of the Republican Guard, Kamel had been responsible for gassing the Kurds. As Saddam's chief bodyguard, he was a remorseless assassin who would kill unhesitatingly for his master.

Working with Iraqi intelligence, al-Saadi built a vast suppliers' network that sold Iraq the components, technology, and training necessary to develop its own nuclear and chemical weapons and long-range missiles. For their part, Jafar and his opposite numbers in the other superweapons programs drew up highly detailed shopping lists of what they needed to keep the various programs moving. Al-Saadi also established the far-flung network to fill those lists. The tentacles stretched to Paris, Milan, Los Angeles, Cleveland, Sao Paolo, Santiago, and Krefeld, Germany. All of the little firms in those places had the freight-forwarding contracts for

Iraqi Air, which facilitated the movement of equipment back home. The network was only one manifestation of Baghdad's massive effort to build an indigenous superweapon program, as the United Nations Special Commission's teams were to discover after Desert Storm. The colossal amount of money required to pay the superweapons bill was as carefully and clandestinely collected as the components and technology themselves. It required an elaborate subterfuge involving the Atlanta branch of the Italian government's Banca Nazionale del Lavoro, or BNL. In one of the most bizarre aspects of one of the most bizarre weapons procurement efforts in history, al-Saadi befriended the branch's manager—an otherwise unexceptional American named Christopher P. Drogoul—who became the superweapon program's chief fund raiser. The funds he raised exceeded $5 billion.

While many companies that did business in the Iraqi netherworld knew what they were doing, others insisted that their sales were negotiated in total ignorance of their products' end-use. They insisted both before and after the war in the Gulf that their merchandise was so-called dual-use or multipurpose, meaning it could be used for either civilian or military purposes. They maintained that they had dealt with the Iraqis in good faith on the assumption that their products would be used only for peaceful ends. This was disputed by the U.N. teams that inspected the weapons research and development sites after the war. "While much of the equipment is multipurpose in the sense of being used in a number of manufacturing processes," the inspectors concluded in a December 1991 report, "the presence of application-specific fixtures removes most doubt as to the intended use."

In other words, the IAEA maintained, there could have been little doubt on the part of Leybold Heraeus, a German firm, that its electron-beam welder was being purchased for nuclear weapons work, despite its claim that the welder was for rockets. Nor could H & H Metallform, Neue Magdeburger Werkzeugmaschinenfabrik, Degussa, Acomel, NUPRO, VAT, and Balzer have believed that their oxidation furnaces, high-frequency converters for operating centrifuges, electrically controlled bellows valves, and other equipment were destined for anything other than a superbomb program. The large cold isostatic press made by the Swiss firm Asea Brown Boveri could be used only for shaping explosive charges, the inspectors reported. Two streak cameras made by Hamamatsu in Japan, which were found at Baghdad's Technical University, were suspected of having as their primary purpose the taking of ultrahigh-speed photographs of simulated nuclear weapon detonations. Arthur Pfeiffer Vakuum Technik GmbH, the inspectors found, should have had no doubt that its very high temperature vacuum induction furnaces were to be used in the development of an atomic bomb. One U.S. firm, Du Pont, made the list by selling the Iraqis Krytox, a lubricant used to keep centrifuges running. Nonetheless, most of these companies, including Du Pont, dispute the report's charges.

Another report, prepared by the Thirteenth On-Site Inspection Team, which visited Iraq in mid-July 1992, specifically listed three German suppliers—Degussa, Leybold, and Siemens—and a large French firm, Thomson CSF, as selling Iraq research and production-size nuclear equipment. This included oxidation furnaces, annealing and brazing furnaces, roughing vacuum pumps, diffusion and control systems for the centrifuges, and switching gear for the baghdatrons.

While Germany would become notorious for playing a major role in helping Iraq in its relentless quest for superweapons—and rightly so— it shared that dubious distinction with another country, one that shared Iraq's dream: Brazil. United Nations investigators subsequently found mounds of evidence showing that Brazil's military, which ran the government from 1975 to 1990, worked very closely with Saddam on both the nuclear weapons and ballistic missile programs, as well as a spy satellite for target selection. Brazilian scientists worked in parts of Osirak that even its builders were forbidden to see. When the Israelis bombed the reactor, in fact, Brazilian scientists were completing their fourth secret mission to the facility.

"Brazil sold uranium under the table; trained Iraqi nuclear scientists; shared knowledge of uranium enrichment; and Brazilian scientists and technicians helped Iraq develop long-range rocket technology and improve the range of Scud missiles," Gary Milhollin and Diana Edensword of the Wisconsin Project on Nuclear Arms Control have reported. In fact, twenty-seven tons of uranium oxide was sold to Iraq in a secret deal in 1981. U.N. inspectors believe that the key engineers who helped the Iraqi centrifuge program were Germans who had delivered their data to Brazil before it somehow was passed on to Iraq. One of the most important of the group, Karl-Heinz Shaab, fled to Brazil ahead of German authorities, who wanted to arrest him. He was eventually arrested and sent home for prosecution.

General Piva, a retired Brazilian Air Force officer who was also an affable, swashbuckling, wine-loving entrepreneur and weapons scientist, was his country's pointman in Baghdad. He personified the nightmarish figure that haunted U.S. proliferation specialists: the man who brought nascent nuclear nations together in deadly consortiums that were difficult to track and stop. Piva talks freely of his work for Iraq and for Libya before Iraq. He is careful to say that he did not transfer "sensitive [nuclear] technology" to Baghdad, though he does not define that term. "There were times when tension with Argentina was rather unpleasant," he told a Brazilian journalist in March 1993, "and we sort of blew the dust off the files that contained the technology for possible military use." The fact that Brazil itself possessed such technology was bad enough. But the possibility that some or all of it was sold to Saddam Hussein was doubly confounding.

The number and lethality of the Iraqi-manufactured "products" made from the imported equipment and then discovered and destroyed by members of the United Nations Special Commission were extraordinary. In the area of chemical and biological weapons alone, inspectors at various sites turned up 30 chemical-filled ballistic missile warheads; 160 bombs filled with mustard gas; 6,000 empty containers intended for filling with nerve gas and then inserting into tactical rocket warheads; 6,394 mustard gas–filled 155-millimeter artillery shells; and 6,120 sarin-filled 122-millimeter rocket warheads. Though no ready biological weapons were found, earlier denials of involvement in that area disintegrated when the inspection teams uncovered laboratories dedicated to such research.* In some instances, the Iraqis volunteered information about their chemical, biological, and even missile programs, perhaps to distract their visitors from concentrating on the nuclear weapons program. The technique of letting out pieces of information about CBW activities to lead enemies off the nuclear trail had been used against the Israelis for years. Understandably, U.N. inspectors received no such cooperation when they tried to uncover Iraq's atomic bomb program, which was considered infinitely more important.

*The Iraqis told the inspectors that the biological warfare program had begun in 1986 and ended in 1990. While the inspectors found no weapons, they unanimously agreed that the program as it existed would logically have included a serious development and production component. (United Nations, Office of the Special Commission, "Report by the Executive Chairman of the Special Commission Established by the Secretary-General Pursuant to Paragraph 9 (b) (i) of Security Council Resolution 687 (1991)," pp. 28–30.)

• • •

One day in mid-May 1991, three months after Desert Storm had ended and one month after Iraq had flatly denied that it had any undeclared nuclear weapons material, four Iraqis drove up to the U.S. Marine checkpoint at Dahuk, a hamlet on the road to the nearby Turkish border that had been set up to protect the Kurds. "I am Saddam Hussein's top nuclear scientist," one of the automobile's occupants told a skeptical marine. "I want to defect now." If there was any doubt in the marines' minds that the man was someone important, a glance at what appeared to be a distant Iraqi secret policeman turning a sniper rifle in their direction settled it. The defector, his wife, brother, and a friend were spirited away for interrogations, first in Turkey and then, a week later, in a safehouse in Munich that had been routinely used for those who fled eastern Europe. His was the family whose other members were put to death because he fled.

The "walk-in," as a seeker of asylum is called in the argot of counterespionage, was not Jafar Jafar, of course, but a high-ranking physicist who had worked at Ash Sharqat's baghdatron separation facility, which had been close to completion when the war broke out. He revealed for the first time that Iraq had refined EMIS technology and added that he knew of several sites where the separation facilities existed. Furthermore, the U.S. bombing raids had missed key nuclear targets, many of which were expertly camouflaged or so well fortified that they were only partially damaged. On the top of his list: Tarmiyah. Only the week before, U.N. inspectors had combed through the huge complex but had found nothing incriminating. The defector's most amazing revelation, however, was that he had been assured by a colleague that "Petrochemical Complex-3" had a secret cache of eighty-eight pounds of bomb-grade uranium that had already been enriched by Jafar Jafar's baghdatrons, or enough for two bombs. Although that part of the scientist's story never checked out, it sent the U.S. intelligence community into a panic.

In one respect, it was fortunate that the baghdatron technology was American. Surviving alumni who had worked on the Manhattan Project were pressed into service to ferret out critical facilities and components. They were amazed at what they saw in highly detailed satellite imagery and other data supplied by the CIA. The Iraqis had used the Freedom of Information Act and piles of other material to copy whole facilities. They had erected an enrichment building at Tarmiyah, for example, that was a duplicate of one at Oak Ridge. "My God," one of the American scientists exclaimed on seeing satellite imagery of the place, "I've worked in that building all my life."

The week the defector was moved to Munich, KH-11 and radar reconnaissance satellites (originally called Lacrosse) were put on "constant watch" over Iraq. Photointerpreters who studied the pictures saw that after the U.N. inspectors left Tuwaitha on May 21, the Iraqis uncovered and removed disc-shaped objects that were buried outside the nuclear research center. It didn't take the Oak Ridge irregulars long to conclude that the objects were almost certainly magnets for the baghdatron program. Other reconnaissance imagery was used to send the inspectors to the Abu Gharib military barracks, where Sharistani had been imprisoned and from which he had escaped during an air raid in the Gulf War. The pictures showed more disc-shaped objects, the same ones that had been dug up at Tuwaitha and removed. Three days after being denied access to the prison, the inspectors were finally admitted, only to find that the magnets had disappeared. A fast-paced shell game was developing, with the Iraqis managing to stay one step ahead of the IAEA.

New intelligence sent the inspectors to Fallujah, thirty miles west of the capital. On June 28 they arrived for the first in a series of "zero-notice" inspections and were again refused entry. What happened next could have been produced in Hollywood. David Kay, the inspection team's diminutive, but doughty leader, confronted impassive, beret-clad military men. He told the stone-faced officers that either equipment that had been taken out of the place be returned or else he would inform an already angry Security Council in New York.

Then, Kay was to recall later, "one guard made a terrible mistake; terrible for him, very lucky for us." After being harangued by the IAEA inspectors, Kay said, one exasperated guard told them that nothing was being hidden and that they would be able to see as much for themselves if they climbed a nearby water tower and simply looked around. Three inspectors carrying binoculars, video cameras and walkie-talkies did just that. Ninety seconds later, they were excitedly telling their colleagues on the ground that a convoy of large trucks loaded with heavy equipment was speeding out of the facility's rear entrance and raising clouds of dust as it went.

Two other inspectors jumped into one of the white U.N. vehicles and raced after the trucks, in the process taking a twenty-mile, tire-screeching shortcut through village bazaars to head off the flatbeds on the main road. The sight that greeted the inspectors when they made their successful interception, driving parallel to the convoy on an adjacent road, was astonishing: a line of ninety-four trucks speeding away from Abu Gharib with the nuclear equipment tied down under flapping tarpaulins that in many cases revealed what was under them. The inspectors shot pictures of the trucks while the guards who accompanied the trucks shot bullets at them. The two men were finally stopped by Iraqi security agents and searched, but they adamantly refused to give up the film they had risked their lives to get.

The great escape had been directed by Jafar Jafar himself, who finally appeared in mid-July after persistent stonewalling threatened to bring renewed coalition air attacks. It happened at the Al Mansour Hotel in Baghdad, where thirty-seven IAEA inspectors were questioning Iraqi nuclear experts. The Iraqis seemed unsure of what to say. "As we asked more and more questions, they kept looking around to see if it was okay to give answers," Cal Wood, a Lawrence Livermore physicist later recalled. "This went on for a time, and then suddenly this well-dressed man in the back, in impeccable English with a British accent, said, 'I will answer all your questions.'" It was Jafar himself. But he never answered all the questions. In the days that followed, Jafar seemed alternately detached and cold and then effusive, sometimes agreeing to arrange visits to baghdatron facilities and storage locations, and at other times evading questions and feigning ignorance. During the coming months, he would first raise the stakes by denying the team access to facilities and documents and then, after talking to "the highest authorities," back down. And each time, the damning evidence accumulated.

It was "like peeling skins off the side of an onion, and one gets the impression that Saddam Hussein is keen to retain as much in the center of that onion as he possibly can," observed Derek Boothby, a member of the U.N. Special Commission, which ran the teams conducting the missile, toxic agent, and atomic inspections. "When he's forced to shed another skin, he'll shed one. Now, the work of the Special Commission is to try to make sure that we get all the skins off we can."

The last, and most famous, of the confrontations happened during the third week in September. Although the IAEA inspectors had by then uncovered a great deal of atomic hardware, they still lacked solid documentary evidence that Saddam was after nuclear weapons. The big break came in the Nuclear Design Center in Baghdad on September 23, however. Once again the news was carried by walkie-talkie. "We've found it," team members on the building's eighth floor suddenly heard from their colleagues in the basement. "You won't believe this!" What they found was a large cache of documents—thousands of them, including a highly detailed progress report from Al Atheer—describing the bomb program in copious detail. Elsewhere, records turned up listing the 20,000 people who had worked in the program, together with their facilities. Each installation carried as many as three code names.

The evidence was so incriminating that the IAEA inspectors soon found themselves trapped in the Iraq Atomic Energy Commission's sweltering parking lot. Having loaded four trunk-size metal boxes of data onto their vehicles, the inspectors were prohibited from leaving the lot by security men, who then forcibly unloaded them (but not before one batch had been evacuated). The IAEA team, now convinced that the most incriminating material would disappear overnight if they retreated, decided to camp in the parking lot rather than hand over their own records, including photographs, film, videotapes, and copies of documents they had already made. With the temperature raising both sweat and flies, the U.N. scientists dug in again.* This time, though, they kept in constant telephone contact with IAEA headquarters in Geneva as well as with the world press. Kay was making direct phone calls to America's leading television anchormen to discuss what they had found and their precarious situation. The reporters understood the standoff's dramatic possibilities and stayed on it to the end. It would last four days.

Now, the natty Jafar reappeared, still guarding his nest and demanding all of the records and film. "These documents, for us, have an historic value," he told the inspectors with characteristic calm and not the slightest trace of deceit. "We want to keep the historic value of the documents," he said again, "and this is our right. This is our main documentation center. If you take these without our having a copy of them, we prefer them to be destroyed." He also insisted on keeping the personnel records. "We feel such information will be used by hostile security organizations to hunt our personnel, and we are very anxious for their safety," he said, evidently thinking about Gerald Bull and

---

*The inspection teams suffered more than flies and heat, even long after the cease-fire. They were repeatedly threatened, harassed, intimidated, and abused in orchestrated efforts to discourage them. This included being pelted with garbage and menaced by large crowds, receiving threatening telephone calls through the night in their hotel rooms, and being physically attacked. (Robert M. Gates, "Weapons Proliferation: The Most Dangerous Challenge for U.S. Intelligence," an address made by the CIA Director at the Comstock Club, Sacramento, California, on December 15, 1992.)

the Arab scientists who had been killed by the Mossad. It was his last card.

Jafar's composure masked deep anxiety because he knew that the inspectors had hit the mother lode. The documents provided detailed descriptions of the nuclear weapons program's procurement network and the training its engineers received by the European suppliers. They linked the nuclear weapons and Condor-2/Badr-2000 programs, with one Ministry of Defense document even instructing the Iraq Atomic Energy Commission to postpone an experiment until after the missile had been tested. They showed that, contrary to earlier speculation that Iraq's nuclear weapons program had been directed by some mysterious foreign genius, Jafar was himself its senior administrator. Most important, they showed conclusively that, irrespective of what Iraq told the IAEA, it had a highly advanced program for developing "an implosion-type nuclear weapon": an atomic bomb.

The most damning document was a top-secret progress report from Al Atheer which covered the period between January 1 and May 31, 1990. It stated that Al Atheer's goal was to design and manufacture "The Mechanism," which would comprise a nuclear initiator, an enriched uranium core, a reflector made of natural uranium, a tamper, explosive lenses, and electronic trigger, control, and guidance systems for missile delivery. All but the enriched-uranium core had been produced indigenously, the amazed U.N. inspectors discovered. The report stated that a small amount of plutonium had already been produced, that natural uranium had been shaped into cylinders for eventual casting into discs, and that the discs would be used to model the manufacture of part of the core of the implosion mechanism. It went on to say that Iraq had gone through five designs, that twenty detonation tests had been carried out using explosive lenses, and that experiments were done to test "the internal initiator."

A later analysis of the whole cache by U.S. intelligence revealed that "The Mechanism's" design had an ominous genealogy. It was ominous because the Iraqis were working mostly from publicly available documents, including some detonation codes that were sold as software packages. At least one helpful code may have been obtained from the U.S. Department of Energy's National Energy Software Center at Argonne National Laboratory near Chicago. The Iraqis had simply subscribed to a code catalogue offered by the National Technical Information Service. What was not directly known was deduced. The Iraqis were developing increasingly sophisticated designs with increasingly unsophisticated computers. Jafar had proven that computers were no longer a strategic chokepoint for stalling nuclear weapons programs. If a nation wanted to mimic the United States and the Soviet Union and develop an advanced thermonuclear weapon—an H-bomb—a Cray was helpful. But if that nation wanted to settle for an A-bomb like the one that vaporized much of Hiroshima, a PC would do just fine.

The United Nations had made an open-and-shut case against the first country ever caught abrogating the IAEA's safeguards agreement. The IAEA concluded that Iraq had enough material and equipment to eventually make more than 20,000 centrifuges. Together with the baghdatrons, they would have yielded enough fissile material to produce twenty "Nagasaki-Hiroshima" bombs a year. The Gulf War was indeed propitious. Operation of the huge baghdatron facilities had just begun and no bomb-grade uranium had been produced. But no one was deluded into believing that Iraq's quest for the bomb was over. All 20,000 of the skilled workers and scientists remained in place and on the payroll. So did the records, irrespective of the number of boxes full of them that were taken out of the country by the U.N. Jafar had seen to it that all of the reports and other documents were put on microfilm and hidden. The Iraqis had lost a great deal. All their uranium had been seized and much of their nuclear infrastructure blown up, either during the war, by U.N. inspectors, or in George Bush's final riposte the week before he left office.

So, far from sounding triumphant, the IAEA report raised a disquieting specter. "Although there might be other explanations, in the light of the continued attempts to conceal the true extent of Iraq's nuclear weapons program and some very recent correspondence relevant to the program found at one site, the question remains open whether Iraq has given up its nuclear weapon aspirations."

There was no such question in Jafar Dhia Jafar's mind. "You can bomb our buildings. You can destroy our technology," he told the U.N. inspectors one day while sharing a meal with them. "But you cannot take it out of our heads. We now have the capability."

# 2

# PAKISTAN:
# A HORRIBLE
# EXAMPLE

**T**he incongruity of it all had to have been obvious to the three people who gathered outdoors in Islamabad that lovely morning in late June 1990. The two Americans had insisted on speaking with their hostess in her garden since they believed—erroneously—there were no listening devices there.

The beautiful and charismatic Benazir Bhutto, Prime Minister of Pakistan, listened intently to her old and trusted friends as they told her that, whatever she believed, she was in control of neither her government nor her country. One of the men was Peter Galbraith, son of John Kenneth Galbraith, the Harvard economist and ambassador to India during the Kennedy presidency. Young Galbraith was the south Asia specialist on the Senate Foreign Relations Committee. More to the point, Bhutto had been one of Galbraith's closest friends since their days at Harvard, and he had revered her ever since. He had affectionately called her "Pinky" back then; now, appropriately, he referred to her as "the Islamic Bombshell." She was the Ivy League- and Oxford-educated female leader of a populist party in a staunchly Muslim country where most women's rights were strictly confined to the home. She had already done time in jail for practicing her politics (and credited Peter with engineering her release in 1983). In 1988, with the death of the increasingly devout Islamic dictator, General Zia ul-Haq, she had become chief of government in the ensuing election. The Prime Minister of Pakistan was also the de facto defense minister and commander-in-chief of the armed forces. But even in those exalted positions one might not be privy to certain state secrets.

Mark Siegel, the other American, was Bhutto's Washington lobbyist. Even more than Galbraith, he idealized her and constantly worried about her fate in the violent and potentially deadly cauldron of Pakistani politics. His going-away present to her before she left for a series of huge rallies in Pakistan in 1986 had been a bulletproof vest.

Siegel had worked as a domestic policy adviser in the Carter White House and was responsible for liaison with the Jewish community. His previous work as an Israeli lobbyist had earned him the epithet of "Benazir's Jew" from Bhutto's many enemies. Yet his considerable effort for Pakistan had paid off. It had become the third largest recipient of U.S. foreign aid, after Israel and Egypt, and only fifteen months before had been promised forty more F-16s. Siegel's task had been made considerably easier by Pakistan's being a Mujahedeen staging and supply area during the war between the Soviets and the American-backed rebels in Afghanistan. But it had been made more difficult by recurring reports that the Pakistanis were trying, with quiet desperation, to get an atomic bomb. And that was precisely why Galbraith, Siegel, and Benazir Bhutto were walking in her garden that June morning, thinking they were out of earshot of her own military intelligence people.

U.S. intelligence had determined that her country finally had an atomic weapon capability, Galbraith and Siegel told her; Pakistan had "crossed the line," as it was euphemistically called in Washington's nuclear precincts. The CIA had learned that the previous month Pakistani scientists had succeeded in converting highly enriched uranium from a gas into 275 pounds of bomb-grade heavy metal. The uranium had undergone successive changes, going from gas to pellets to the molded and machined spheres—perfect spheres—that constituted the cores of atomic bombs. The CIA knew that the cores were then stored near the other components needed to make a complete weapon so the Pakistani bomb— the long-feared "Islamic bomb"—could be assembled in as little as three hours at Chagai, an air base in the Baluchistan desert well out of reach of Indian jets. There was enough metal to make between six and eight nuclear weapons, Galbraith and Siegel told their stunned friend, each with an explosive capability equivalent to the bombs that devastated

Hiroshima and Nagasaki.* Although that was tiny by superpower standards, it was enough to obliterate the Bhabha Atomic Energy Research Center in the Bombay suburbs or, for that matter, to reduce the heart of New Delhi to rubble. The consequences would be particularly horrific for those who lived in south Asian cities, where population density reached 900,000 a square mile.

The prospect of a Holocaust-like conflagration between India and Pakistan kept U.S. intelligence busy for weeks, since a series of events signaling preparation had been picked up by eavesdropping stations and spy satellites. The Pakistanis, the U.S. believed, not only had gone over the line, but had actually prepared some bombs for delivery. Now that the analysis was complete and tempers in India and Pakistan had cooled, it was time to make the adjustments required by U.S. law.

The news Galbraith and Siegel delivered took Benazir Bhutto by surprise. She had been well aware of her country's nuclear weapons program, particularly since her own father, Zulfikar Ali Bhutto, had initiated it in 1972—two years before India's "peaceful bomb," the "smiling Buddha," had gone off. It was her father who, in his last political testament before being executed by Zia ul-Haq, revealed his long-held belief that it was imperative for Islam to have the bomb. She knew, too, that Zia himself had pushed the program along, using mostly Chinese, German, and American technology.

Zia ul-Haq may have been a scoundrel, but he also had been an astute enough politician to see that the West cared more about using Pakistan to defeat the Soviets in Afghanistan than it did about heading off his country's nuclear weapons program. When presidential candidate Ronald Reagan was asked on January 31, 1980, how he felt about nuclear proliferation in Pakistan and elsewhere—five weeks after the Red Army invaded Afghanistan, killed its president, and seized the nation—he provided an answer that resonated in Islamabad, where Zia was searching for ways to ingratiate his country to Washington while pursuing the bomb. "I just don't think it's any of our business," Reagan said. That was splendid news, not only for Pakistan and every other nation that wanted super-

*The final number was seven. Two cores had been machined during the previous month, during the most recent flare-up with India over Kashmir, and five more would be turned out by the end of July, the CIA had since learned. The first two cores used about forty pounds of uranium each, while the last used about twenty-six pounds each, proving that experience was very important.

weapons, but for those who wanted the business that spreading super-weapons would bring.

For Zia ul-Haq, every Soviet tank that rumbled into Kabul, every land mine buried in the countryside, every Hind helicopter gunship that sent rockets slamming into Mujahedeen strongholds, was a gift from God. Ostracized for killing Ali Bhutto only eight months earlier, he now presided over a nation seen by Washington as an indispensable bulwark against communist expansion. That meant almost boundless American largesse. It would come through vast increases in foreign aid, in advanced weapons like F-16s, and in an unprecedented, if blatantly expedient, political flirtation. Best of all, Pakistan's powerful new suitor would occasionally grumble in public about its nuclear weapons program while, as Reagan had promised, not seriously interfering. The United States would spend the next decade using Pakistan to turn Afghanistan into Moscow's Vietnam. And if that meant looking the other way while work on the bomb continued at what was obviously a feverish pace, so it had to be.

It was a policy that was as cynical and shortsighted as it was arrogant. But it was not unique. The United States was doing precisely the same thing at the same time in Iraq, where Saddam Hussein, the Zia ul-Haq of Baghdad, was fighting Washington's other enemies, the militant mullahs of Iran.

Benazir Bhutto knew that her army chief of staff, Mirza Aslam Beg, was not only an ardent supporter of Pakistan's nuclear program, but had actually offered nuclear weapons technology to the mullahs in Teheran in return for a strategic alliance that would use Iranian money to pay off his country's worsening national debt. She knew the mullahs' desires only too well. A month before, in mid-May, President Hashemi Rafsanjani himself had made a similar proposal to her in his office. When she rejected it, she did not know that she could have delivered the Islamic bomb immediately.

Bhutto hated Beg. She also hated her other nemesis, President Ghulam Ishaq Khan, who for thirteen years had run the bomb program in one position or another. Ishaq Khan not only had been instrumental in funding the program when he was finance minister under Zia, but was one of the few whom Zia consulted before ordering the execution of her father. The world beyond the garden was alive with enemies.

However shocked she was to learn that her country was a nuclear power, she at least understood why it had happened: Kashmir. Pakistan and India had gone to war four times over the Islamic enclave between 1948 and 1972. As India vowed to get the bomb after its devastating defeat by the Chinese Army at Ladakh in 1962, Pakistan did the same a decade later when the victorious Indians brazenly turned East Pakistan into Bangladesh. Another defeat at the hands of India could mean that what remained of Pakistan would be further divided into rump states carved out of the always warring provinces. In the months before the June meeting, the two bitter rivals had nearly fought again; even Bhutto had been so engaged by the passion of the moment that she swore a 1,000-year war to free Kashmir and appropriated $5 million for pro-Pakistani rebels in the Indian-held region. Yet the astounding thing was that even with a possible war imminent, she had been deliberately kept ignorant about the ultimate weapon that might have been used in that war.

"I think it's criminal that the Prime Minister, who is ultimately responsible in the eyes of the people and in the eyes of history, should not be taken into confidence on such a major issue," she would say later with abiding anger. "I did not know."

There is in the affairs of nations, no less than in those of individuals, a presumption that, within reasonably broad parameters, events can be controlled. Control—not letting situations get out of hand—becomes increasingly important as the affairs of both nations and individuals coincide. This is especially true where nuclear weapons are concerned because of the catastrophic consequences that would come from a loss of control. The need for control increases in proportion to the killing capacity of the weapons. It was the imperative to keep maximum control over their nuclear war-fighting systems—to insulate them as much as possible against chaos—that forced both the United States and the Soviet Union to adopt stringent fail-safe mechanisms.

Wise leaders know that it is prudent to factor bad luck into their political and military plans as a kind of buffer against catastrophe. But they also know that bad luck can end control and bring dire consequences no matter what they do. A panic-stricken Soviet brigade commander's firing a tactical nuclear missile at a Marine battalion invading Cuba in 1962 would have been bad luck with dire consequences. Disgruntled French generals in Algeria or a Chinese warlord in Xingjiang seizing and using atomic bombs also would have been bad luck that brought dire consequences. Disgruntled Russian generals appropriating the suitcase that contained their country's nuclear war codes on August 18, 1991, the day before the coup against Mikhail Gorbachev, could also have created havoc. And so, too, would the dropping of an atomic bomb on India by a deliriously vengeful Pakistani chief of staff who had deliberately kept his own commander-in-chief ignorant of its existence.

It was bad luck that Benazir Bhutto was not told about her country's Islamic bomb. But there was even more bad luck in store. During the first week in July, a few days after the meeting with Galbraith and Siegel, U.S. Ambassador Robert Oakley informed her that, as she well knew, U.S. law required a cutoff in aid to Pakistan if it possessed a "nuclear explosive device." In May, he had told her that the United States had indications that her own military was getting dangerously close to crossing the line. But he had added that Washington lacked specifics and that he was therefore trying to head off a serious confrontation. The generals steadfastly denied to her that they were anywhere near the forbidden line. Now, in July, Oakley told Bhutto that the intelligence was unassailable: the generals and their scientists had crossed the line.

During the years of war in Afghanistan, Pakistan had been lavished with billions in military aid and $800 million worth of dual-use equipment. And none of it, including $250 million worth of advanced computers, had so much as been reviewed by the Pentagon's Defense Trade Security Administration to see whether it was too sensitive to export. The particularly sensitive equipment included high-capacity computers, some of which could have been used for refining a bomb design, plus millions more in oscilloscopes, zirconium, pressure-measuring equipment, laser systems, neutron generator systems, and telemetry systems for missiles.

Congressional investigators came to believe that tens of millions of dollars' worth of the equipment was diverted to the nuclear program, a figure higher than similar exports to Iraq. All the military sales and other aid would end with the new fiscal year beginning October 1, Oakley now warned Bhutto, unless the genie was stuffed back into the bottle; unless the metal was turned back to gas.

A 1984 amendment to the Foreign Aid Act, sponsored by Senator Larry Pressler of South Dakota (and, ironically, written by Peter Galbraith), required the President to make an annual assurance to Congress before aid was approved that Pakistan did not have a finished nuclear bomb. While the war was under way in Afghanistan, Reagan and Bush had gotten around the so-called Pressler Amendment because of the stipulation that Pakistan had to possess a "nuclear explosive device," though that definition was not further defined in the amendment. It was only after Bhutto was elected in late 1988, four and a half years after the amendment was passed, that the gas-to-metal definition was put in writing and given to her.

But it was 1990, the Afghan war was over, and Pakistan no longer figured importantly in Washington's plans. If anything, the collapse of the Soviet Union opened new possibilities for better relations with bigger, stronger India. So Pakistan had to get rid of its "explosive nuclear device," or face the consequences, and that was that.

Bhutto contacted Ghulam Ishaq Khan, relayed Oakley's warning, and called for a meeting with Ishaq Khan. The President replied that Oakley had raised the matter of aid with him, too, and that he had had a meeting with the American ambassador "to satisfy him." Three times over the next month she asked Ishaq Khan to convene the top-secret committee that ran the nuclear weapons program. Three times he said he would get back to her on the request. But he never did. The Prime Minister also asked Beg for an explanation and was assured one would be forthcoming. It never was. What was forthcoming, however, was Benazir Bhutto's ouster. On August 6, 1990, with the world's attention focused on Saddam Hussein's brazen drive into Kuwait, Ghulam Ishaq Khan went on television to denounce Bhutto's government as being corrupt and incompetent and to dismiss her. The generals made their position on the matter absolutely clear by sending tanks to surround Bhutto's house. Whatever Ishaq Khan said, Bhutto and her supporters considered the action to be a "nuclear coup."

While the attention of the United States, its European allies, and the Persian Gulf sheikdoms was focused on Saddam's invasion of Kuwait and growing evidence that he was working hard to get an atomic bomb, they ignored the fact that Ishaq Khan in fact already had seven of them.

"I have no proof for this, but I feel that someone may have turned on the switch in the spring of 1990 to justify the dismissal of my government," Benazir Bhutto told NBC News two years later. "And now, having done that, [he] does not know how to turn that switch off and explain to the people who turned it on that she was right and they were wrong."

The October 1 deadline came and went. With the installation of a new government stalled in a partisan political snarl, and not an ounce of bomb-grade uranium having been turned back into gas, American aid to Pakistan was abruptly stopped. Meanwhile, Islamabad had its seven atomic bombs. The story of how they came to exist illustrates why the West has lost the battle against superweapon proliferation in the Third

World through a series of arrogant, Faustian bargains. Some of the bargains were wise. Many more were foolish. But in the end, no matter what they were, everyone lost.

In order to understand how this happened, it is necessary to go back to the beginning and look at events as they unfolded, and particularly as they were shaped by the United States. It is a cautionary tale.

**W**here the development of nuclear weapons is concerned, no nation has done more with less than Pakistan. By any measure, Pakistan is one of the poorest nations on Earth. Its statistics are appalling. In 1992, Pakistan ranked 120th out of 160 nations in terms of overall human development. Its per capita gross domestic product (GDP) was $370. Thirty-six million Pakistanis, or 30 percent of the population, live below the poverty line by the U.N.'s calculation. Life expectancy is only 57.7 years. Of every 1,000 children, 158 live in squalor and die before their fifth birthday. Nearly a million children under the age of five die each year from malnutrition or disease, while nine and a half million others are so badly malnourished that their growth is stunted. Fifty-five million Pakistanis have no access to health services or safe drinking water, and a million have no access to sanitation. Forty-three million are illiterate, including almost 80 percent of the women (the average woman receives only eight months of formal education in her entire life). The country spends 2.6 percent of its GDP on education and 6.7 percent on the military. There are 50 percent more Pakistani soldiers, in fact, than teachers.

"Pakistan displays all the negative characteristics of an underdeveloped economy," *The New Book of World Rankings* reported in 1991. "[It has] a rigid, highly stratified, and largely illiterate society; overdependence on agriculture; and limited infrastructure and natural resources."

But Pakistan does excel. While it ranks 144th on *The New Book*'s Physical Quality of Life Index—behind even Haiti and Bangladesh—it ranks 11th on the CIA's Nuclear Weapons List, after the United States, Russia, Kazakhstan, Ukraine, Belarus, China, France, Great Britain, Israel, and India. Furthermore, Pakistan's arsenal was built without the advantages that other members of the nuclear club have. It lacks the oil wealth of Iran, Iraq, and the peninsula sheikdoms. It does not have the vast industrial base of its adversary, India. It has neither Israel's abundance of trained scientific and technical talent nor North Korea's obsessive secrecy. Pakistan is therefore the exception that makes the rule. It is a model of how far a down-and-out nation can go in acquiring nuclear arms when its leaders combine unwavering resolve with flexibility and imagination. Pakistan is the Horatio Alger nation of the atomic age.

Wherever it was actually constructed, the Islamic bomb was conceived as a result of a kind of political version of Newton's Third Law: for every action, there is an equal and opposite reaction. The action was the establishment of close ties between the Soviet Union and India in the 1960s. The intimate relationship between the two giants made Pakistan strategically important to both of the Soviet Union's major opponents: the United States and China. They therefore reacted by courting Pakistan. And given the depth of Pakistan's fear and loathing of India, it courted them in return.

To be sure, Pakistan served the United States and its allies well during the war in Afghanistan. But even before that, it served both Washington and Beijing by acting as a bridge between them after the Nixon administration decided to improve relations in the early 1970s. Close ties with Pakistan had the double advantage for China of opening diplomatic avenues to the West while gaining a military counterweight on India's left flank. For their part, the Pakistanis had found two big, powerful brothers who they determined would be used to full advantage.

China was the chief instrument by which Pakistan got its bomb. The Chinese did for the Pakistanis in the 1980s exactly what the Russians had done for the Chinese three decades earlier: they provided critical technology, design data, training, and even nuclear materials. In fact, as U.S. and Soviet intelligence would later learn, China actually supplied Pakistan with essentially the same design and trigger mechanism that it had perfected in 1966, when it tested its fourth nuclear weapon (and the first to be mounted on a missile). Chinese scientists visited the Pakistani weapons design facility in the town of Wah in late 1982 or early 1983 to help determine whether the slightly modified design would work. They supplied Pakistan with enough uranium hexafluoride to get its centrifuge program started, a particularly valuable service since the Pakistanis, themselves, were unable to get the equipment needed to make their own feedstock. Chinese scientific and technical delegations also spent a "substantial amount of time" at the Pakistanis' secret centrifuge plant near Kahuta, according to one expert. China, in turn, invited hundreds of

Pakistani scientists and technicians to witness and evaluate its own nuclear weapons tests throughout the 1980s. They had a very symbiotic relationship.

By 1993, in fact, the aggressive Chinese had sold Pakistan a 300-megawatt power reactor that was being built at Chashma on the Indus River. What doubly vexed proliferation experts was the fact that the Pakistanis planned to expand the already controversial centrifuge plant so it could produce still more enriched uranium, saying it was needed to power the new reactor.

But delivery systems were not ignored. In return for $300 million in seed money—a substantial amount of which was no doubt freed up because of help from the U.S. Treasury—China agreed to codevelop and build twenty-five M-11s for Pakistan. In addition, the two nations jointly developed the K-8 fighter-bomber, which has the potential to drop Pakistan's chemical and biological weapons.

If Beijing's role in providing Pakistan with the atomic bomb was active, Washington's was passive and ambivalent. Unlike in Iraq, which was an intelligence failure of major proportions, the CIA had enough assets and analysts in Pakistan to closely follow both its research and its ties to the Chinese program. Yet throughout the 1980s, the imperatives of the war in Afghanistan dictated giving Islamabad's nuclear program a wide berth. That policy, too, had amounted to a sharp change in direction.

The United States had expressed fear in forthright, even excessively blunt and threatening, language during the 1970s. Armed with detailed intelligence reports about the Pakistani program, including projected purchases of foreign equipment that left no doubt where the Pakistanis were headed, Secretary of State Henry Kissinger stopped in Islamabad in 1976. He warned the Pakistani Prime Minister that unless he reneged on an agreement to buy a plutonium reprocessing plant from France, the United States was prepared to make "a horrible example" of both him and his country.

In an interview with NBC News several years later, Benazir Bhutto said that she remembered the heated exchange between her father and Kissinger quite vividly. "I was in the hall at the time Henry Kissinger came in and said, 'We will make a horrible example out of you.' . . . He said that you should either delay this program or you should scrap this program, and if you don't delay this program and you don't scrap this program, we will make a horrible example out of you. And my father said, 'That's no way to talk to the head of an elected government in a country. We are developing this for peaceful purposes. If you have any fears, let's talk about those. If you have any apprehensions, let's talk about them. But it is not fair to just come and say that . . . do this or that or we will make a horrible example out of you.' " Although the French deal never went through, Ali Bhutto's daughter and political heir would come to suspect that her father's intransigence on the issue led to his downfall and ultimate death at the hands of Zia. The crafty general had no quarrel with Bhutto's nuclear weapons ambitions. It's just that he wanted power for himself.

In the summer of 1977, with Kissinger's warning of a year earlier still in mind, Ali Bhutto nevertheless toured the Middle East trying to cadge enough Muslim money to prop up his country's sagging financial structure. U.S. intelligence learned that during at least two meetings, one with Saudi Arabia's King Khalid and the other with Qaddafi, Bhutto offered his own country's embryonic nuclear weapons technology in return for cash. Neither of the men took him up on the offer, perhaps because Pakistan's weapons research was then so anemic that it wasn't worth any significant amount of money.

Anemic but growing healthier every day. Early research and development on uranium enrichment was taking place in something called the Engineering and Research Labs at Islamabad Airport, where Pakistani airliners and Air Force C-130s flew in a stream of equipment, most of it from Germany. In the meantime, work was also progressing on reprocessing plutonium, a much faster route to the bomb.

The pace quickened following the Soviet invasion of Afghanistan. Kissinger's warning evaporated three years after it was given when the Soviet tanks rolled over the Afghanistan border. Washington's sudden embracing of Islamabad emboldened Pakistani nuclear procurement operatives to press their search. In 1980 and 1981, two key illegal exports were uncovered in the United States, one involving uranium enrichment technology and the other plutonium. It was the same in Europe. The Department of State's Bureau of Intelligence and Research, among other U.S. agencies, was aware of what was happening. "We have strong reason to believe that Pakistan is seeking to develop a nuclear explosives capability," one State cable reported. "Pakistan is conducting a program for the development of a triggering package for nuclear explosive devices."

One element in the analysis was clear evidence that the Kahuta enrichment plant had begun operations in 1980. Another was that the

A. Q. Khan Research Laboratories at Kahuta were named after the man whom the BBC had recently identified as the "father of the Islamic bomb." The analysts were also aware that, deprived of plutonium reprocessing capability they might have gotten from France, Pakistan was using centrifuge technology Khan had stolen in the Netherlands during the mid-1970s. When questioned about their program, the Pakistanis borrowed a page from their Indian enemies and said it was strictly peaceful. But secret internal deliberations suggested otherwise.

A Pentagon assessment written in 1983 was explicit in regard to Islamabad's motives: "There is unambiguous evidence that Pakistan is actively pursuing a nuclear weapons development program." It went on to identify the centrifuge facility at Kahuta as the program's centerpiece, noting that its "ultimate application . . . is clearly nuclear weapons."

Still more evidence came from a high-level spy inside China's nuclear weapons program who, at great personal risk, first described the assistance his country was providing Pakistan and later even helped the CIA to obtain the actual design of Pakistan's first weapon, whose fundamental attributes were decidedly Chinese. CIA and other U.S. intelligence analysts turned up unambiguous data on Pakistan's atomic bomb program throughout the 1980s. Yet like some viscous substance, the thicker the evidence became, the more difficulty it had rising to the top of the structure that contained it.

One CIA analyst who studied the Pakistani nuclear weapons program said that the rules of evidence laid down by the National Security Council and the Department of State were stricter than those laid out by the judicial system. "We joked that the standard was beyond beyond reasonable doubt. It is difficult to get a smoking gun in this business. Without one, we have to prove the best analysis. They wouldn't want to hear it, so they raised the standards to an unattainable level."

On June 24, 1981, Undersecretary of State James Buckley told the Senate Government Affairs Committee that he had been "assured by Pakistani ministers and by the President himself that it was not the intention of the Pakistani government to develop nuclear weapons." Three months later, he declared: "I fully accept the statement of President Zia that Pakistan has no intention of manufacturing nuclear weapons or acquiring nuclear weapons." In December 1982, Zia himself assured the Foreign Policy Association of New York that his country's nuclear program was benign. "I would like to state once again, and with the emphasis at my command, that our ongoing nuclear program has an exclusively peaceful dimension and that Pakistan has neither the means nor, indeed, any desire to manufacture a nuclear device."

Meanwhile, duplicity reigned in the White House. By early 1983, the Chinese-Pakistani bomb design had been analyzed by U.S. weapons experts and certified to be workable. A mock-up was then made and sent to the Foreign Ministry in Islamabad by the Reagan administration to show its allies that it was aware of what they were doing.

The Pakistanis knew they were developing the bomb. The United States knew they were developing the bomb. Now the Pakistanis knew the United States knew they were developing the bomb. But Washington decided that the short-term goal of ejecting the "Evil Empire" from Afghanistan took precedence over the creation of the Islamic bomb. Lies therefore continued to flow to Congress and the public even as massive amounts of aid continued to flow to Pakistan. Washington also refused to mount a serious diplomatic effort to get West Germany and other European nations to stop selling high-tech equipment to Pakistan. It limited its effort to sending Bonn more than 100 notoriously weak, pro forma demarches: the same ones Richard Perle, an assistant secretary of defense, contemptuously dismissed as "demarche-mallows."*

The American look-the-other-way policy toward Pakistan's furious chase after the bomb was in sharp contrast to the campaign it waged against the German-built poison gas works at Rabta in Libya and at Qaddafi himself. If the lenient American attitude toward Islamabad resembled anything, in fact, it was the blind-eyed reaction to the equivalent program in Iraq. There was a very good reason for the difference, however. The only real danger Washington perceived in North Africa was Libya itself. There were no other immediate threats. Since the other nations of the Maghreb were not in immediate danger, and since Qaddafi himself showed little sign of changing his belligerent attitude toward the United States, he was a safe target and, in Washington's view, one uncomplicated by nuance.

Not long after he became president, Reagan directed that a five-year, $3.2 billion aid program be targeted for Pakistan. During the same 1982 visit in which Zia assured his New York audience of his country's benevolent intentions, he received a twenty-one-gun salute at the White

*Richard N. Perle's use of the term "demarche-mallows" was reported in "Germans Accused of Exporting Arms," *The New York Times*, May 3, 1989.

House and the blessings of Ronald Reagan, who promoted him as an anticommunist freedom fighter: the beleaguered leader of a bastion of American democracy.

In addition to the foreign aid package sent to Congress, other billions began to quietly move out of the government's secret accounts and into Pakistan's war chest. This was done through William J. Casey. The Director of Central Intelligence was an ardent believer in exacting revenge or, as it was often put in the circle in which he moved, of paybacks. As the United States had been bled and humiliated by Soviet-backed Vietcong in the seemingly endless quagmire in Vietnam, so would the Soviets be bled and humiliated by American-backed Mujahedeen. Afghanistan became Casey's personal crusade.

In 1984, Casey and his Pakistani counterpart, General Akhtar Abdul Rahman Khan, concocted a plan to step up the then five-year-old war in Afghanistan. Not satisfied with helping the Mujahedeen expel the Soviets from Afghanistan itself, Casey advocated sending the guerrillas to strike inside the Soviet Union. The Soviets, William Casey ruefully decided, had to feel the sting of Mujahedeen forays and rocket and artillery strikes on their own land. Even the United States had not been subjected to that kind of punishment in Indochina.

ISI, the Pakistani intelligence service, would be the one to get its hands dirty in Afghanistan. The CIA would, for the most part, provide funds for the operations. "The foremost function of the CIA was to spend money," one of Akhtar's protégés said later. "The CIA supported the Mujahedeen by spending the American taxpayers' money, billions of dollars of it over the years, on buying arms, ammunition, and equipment. It was their secret arms procurement branch that was kept busy. It was, however, a cardinal rule of Pakistan's policy that no Americans ever became involved with the distribution of funds or arms once they arrived in the country. No Americans ever trained or had direct contact with the Mujahedeen."

That year alone, 1984, overt and covert aid to Pakistan totaled $1 billion. But the Americans were not the only ones footing the bill for Islamabad's arms buildup and the secret war in Afghanistan. The CIA's hefty contribution was matched by King Fahd, who succeeded to the Saudi throne in 1982, and who was persuaded to help his fellow Muslims wage their holy war against the communist oppressors. The other backer was the Bank of Credit & Commerce International (BCCI), which not only set up accounts for the American and Saudi arms donations, but simultaneously acted as the chief financial agent for Pakistan's nuclear weapons program.

Meanwhile, the United States Senate was growing increasingly restive about Pakistan's nuclear program. In early 1984, Senators John Glenn and Alan Cranston backed a strong amendment to the Foreign Assistance Act that would have closed a loophole in the existing law: namely, that a nation had to actually explode a nuclear weapon in order to become ineligible for continued aid. (The Chinese had obligingly helped Pakistan skirt that problem by providing them with the tested design.) The two legislators wrote a law stipulating that aid would be stopped unless the President confirmed in writing that Pakistan neither had a "nuclear explosive device" nor, more important, was acquiring material to manufacture or detonate one. The Senate Foreign Relation Committee unanimously adopted the amendment on March 28, 1984.

The White House reacted to Glenn and Cranston's amendment, particularly to the part about acquiring material, with panic. It was totally unacceptable, the senators were told, because it would ruin delicate relations with Islamabad and subvert the Mujahedeen at the same time. And by arming the Pakistanis to the teeth with conventional weapons, the administration added with brazenly transparent disingenuity, it would make them so strong relative to the Indians that they wouldn't even feel the need to acquire nuclear weapons for protection.

A compromise was needed, and the task of putting it together fell to Peter Galbraith and Benazir Bhutto, then only a political dissident. At the time the compromise was being worked out, Bhutto herself was in Washington, lobbying for human rights in her own country after seven years' house arrest and imprisonment. Asked by Senate Foreign Relations Committee Chairman Charles Percy if she favored a cutoff of assistance, Bhutto answered very carefully, with characteristic diplomacy. "Both our countries would be better served if aid were linked to the restoration of human rights and democracy in Pakistan," she said.

The more conciliatory amendment, which passed on April 3, held that aid could continue so long as the President certified annually that the aid recipient did not have a nuclear explosive device. All reference to the acquisition of material disappeared. From 1984 to 1989, Presidents Reagan and Bush would repeatedly assure Congress that Pakistan did not have the device, despite incontrovertible evidence to the contrary.

Eleven weeks after the amendment passed, with the debate over, Cranston took to the floor of the Senate to deliver a stinging reproach to the executive branch. He spoke passionately, delineating the enrichment plant at Kahuta, a new plutonium reprocessing facility in Islamabad, the secret weapons design team at Wah, and the extraordinary help the Pakistanis received from China. The California Democrat ended his impassioned speech with a call for the Reagan administration to end the politicization of intelligence to meet its own ends, stop subsidizing Pakistan's nuclear weapons program, and halt all sales of F-16s—the "world's best penetrating fighter-bomber for delivering nuclear weapons"—until Pakistan agreed to place its nuclear facilities under IAEA inspection and end its drive for an atomic bomb. "To continue foreign aid without such assurances," he concluded, "is like paying ransom money after the kidnap victim is found dead."

Not only was Alan Cranston ignored, but during the foreign aid debate itself Casey made the first of four clandestine annual trips to Islamabad under a guise bestowed by the Pakistanis themselves: "Mr. Black." The appellation was appropriate. "It was always during darkness that the aircraft arrived," General Mohammed Yousaf, who was in charge of operations supporting the Mujahedeen, would recall. "Usually at around 9 P.M., or just before dawn, General Akhtar and I, along with the local CIA staff, would be waiting at Chaklala [Air Base] for the huge black C-141 Starlifter to taxi up to a secluded part of the terminal. No U.S. Embassy personnel were ever present, at either the plane's arrival or departure.

"The aircraft had flown nonstop from Washington, some 10,000 miles, with KC-10 tanker aircraft based in Europe or the Middle East intercepting it for midair refueling. The crew were always in civilian clothes, as were all the passengers," Mohammed Yousaf continued. "Apart from the U.S. markings on the outside, there was no way of identifying the plane. Inside, the enormous transporter had been transformed into a flying hotel and communications center. Up front, the VIP area was luxuriously appointed with couches, easy chairs, bed and washing facilities: super first-class. The rear portion contained the ultrasophisticated communications [equipment] that allowed the occupants to speak securely to Washington or anywhere else in the world. The aircraft was protected with the latest electronic jamming devices and radar to counter incoming missiles."

The Central Intelligence Agency was by no means the only U.S.

government organization helping Pakistan. The Department of Energy invited more than a score of Pakistanis to visit the national weapons laboratories. Some of the DOE's own security people thought that some of the Pakistanis were spies. In fact, after returning home, one of the Pakistani scientists who had put in a brief stint working at Los Alamos requested a publication—by title and number—on the fabrication of thin shells of plutonium. It was a process that was applicable only for nuclear weapons development work. Having worked at Los Alamos, the Pakistani knew that the paper he wanted had once been classified but was then downgraded. Although the heart of their bomb was a direct transfer from China, the Pakistanis, like their Iraqi counterparts, looked for and found fertile fields of information in the open literature.

The Department of Defense, always worried about transferring high technology that could be used for nuclear and other superweapons against U.S. servicemen and women, was pressured not to oppose such exports, and the export review process was deliberately undermined. Steve Bryen, who was Deputy Undersecretary of Defense for Technology Security from 1981 to 1987, has asserted that his office was simply cut out of the review process early on, despite DIA reports that Pakistan was developing both nuclear weapons and the means to deliver them.

"Originally, we asked for access in 1985, and we got some access for a short time," Bryen recalled. "Then, the administration signed an agreement with Pakistan, and part of the arrangement was that the Defense Department would no longer review export licenses for Pakistan. And so we were dropped and that was it. . . . We were cut off; out of business. They were in a very big hurry to sign the agreement," Bryen said of the Pakistanis. "They hurried to the door and signed it and it was a very general agreement, quickly done. But there was an equal enthusiasm on the U.S. side to make them happy."

What Islamabad could not pick up legally in Washington's $800 million aid package, it tried to acquire by other means. The year Bryen and his office were cut out of the review process, the U.S. Customs Service uncovered two export control violations. One, involving krytrons, went through; the triggers found their way to the nuclear export program. The other, for a flash x-ray camera needed to test the reliability of weapon designs, was stopped in time.

The lack of tight export controls by the United States and its freewheeling ways of dispensing military and scientific aid also signaled other Western nations that Pakistan was a preferred customer for all manner of dubious equipment. One German exporter, NTG, even shipped an entire $8 million plant to manufacture tritium, which is well known for its use in boosting atomic bombs to 100 or more kilotons.

"We not only turned a blind eye," said a disgruntled John Glenn. "In some cases, we even abetted what they were doing by following up with additional sales and not cutting off shipments of things—of equipment—and not stopping the flow of technology, which American law says we have to do. How could it be in our best interest, no matter what our requirements were for shipping through Pakistan into Afghanistan during that war, or whatever? There certainly was a far, far greater danger here in Pakistan's efforts to get nuclear weapons than there was in what we were opposing in Afghanistan."

By 1986, the Pakistani program had reached critical mass. It was widely reported that Islamabad had enough highly enriched uranium and other components to make at least one bomb. One report even quoted a classified National Intelligence Estimate to that effect. *The Washington Post* reported the DIA had concluded that Pakistan "detonated a high explosive test device between September 18 and 21 as part of its continuing effort to build an implosion-type nuclear weapon."

The Pakistanis, now emboldened by the support they were receiving from their American friends, began to brag about their nuclear capability. Late that year, Zia and Khan could no longer contain their pride in their country's accomplishment. "It is our right to obtain the technology, and when we acquire this technology, the Islamic world will possess it with us."

Khan was explicit in a January 1987 interview with an Indian reporter. "What the CIA has been saying about our possessing the bomb is correct. They told us Pakistan could never produce the bomb and they doubted my capabilities, but they now know we have it." Of course Pakistan did not want to use the bomb, Khan continued, but "if driven to the wall there will be no option left." The "drive" he had in mind may have had something to do with Operation Brass Tacks, an Indian exercise then taking place which involved moving 400,000 troops within 100 miles of Pakistan's border. In July 1993, Beg himself was quoted as admitting that Pakistan had actually cold-tested a bomb in 1987. "Pakistan carried out the test in cold laboratory conditions, and it was very successful," he was quoted as telling *Awaz International*, a London-based Urdu language newspaper. Cold testing involves bringing two small quantities of fissionable material together to create an instant critical mass, which is needed to produce a chain reaction, without causing an explosion. Beg subsequently denied that he made the statement.

Still, no action was taken to brake the program. What Glenn, Percy, Pressler, Bryen, and others did not know was that throughout 1986 and into 1987 the Mujahedeen was striking inside the Soviet republics of Turkmenistan, Uzbekistan, and Tajikistan, just as Casey wanted. The forays began with deliveries of written propaganda and progressed to hit-and-run guerrilla attacks and fusillades of rockets. The CIA provided maps and lists of targets that were within the range of the rockets it supplied to the Mujahedeen. The attacks drew a sharp protest by the Soviet ambassador to the Pakistani foreign minister. More important, they provoked ferocious Soviet reprisals: massive bombing and helicopter gunship attacks on Afghan villages. The riposte was so furious and threatening, according to Yousaf, that even the CIA station chief in Islamabad begged the foreign minister not to "start a third world war by conducting these operations inside Soviet territory." The incursions were stopped on April 25, 1987. Casey died eleven days later.

In August of the following year, General Zia and General Akhtar, his intended successor, perished when their C-130 crashed under mysterious circumstances. That November, Benazir Bhutto's Pakistan Peoples' Party took control of parliament, making her prime minister. Lacking enough votes for a clear majority, however, she had to negotiate a series of compromises with Ghulam Ishaq Khan and Mirza Aslam Beg. The secret negotiations had an even more secret interlocutor: the United States. Not only was Ambassador Oakley called on for help, a Bhutto aide recalled, but National Security Adviser Brent Scowcroft even made a surprise appearance at one critical juncture. Scowcroft's chief concern was Afghanistan. On Oakley's advice, she agreed to continue backing the Mujahedeen and use her influence to get Ishaq Khan appointed as permanent president. The position's power had increased significantly under Zia, and Khan's occupying it filled her with dismay, but she yielded to her country's benefactor after she became prime minister in December.

By February, the law of unexpected consequences had begun to affect the entire region. On February 11, General Beg announced that the Haft-2 short-range missile, which many believed was helped along by China, was a success. Four days later, General Boris Gromov, commander of Soviet forces in Afghanistan, strode out of that country hand in hand with his teenage son and behind his demoralized army. The Afghans were now free to turn their wrath on each other in a series of political and ethnic feuds that would ultimately end with the nation's fragmenting into at least three hostile subentities over which Iran, Saudi Arabia, and Pakistan itself vied for influence.

The fight for Afghanistan had turned both superpowers into losers. Growing chaos at home and a decade of hemorrhaging in combat had soured Moscow's adventure. Ten years of unremitting combat had cost thousands of lives, dispirited Soviet society, and depleted funds that were desperately needed at home. For the United States, the disintegration of the country it wanted to save from communism led to a worse evil: the resurgence in the west of Hazaras who were loyal to the revivalist Muslims in Teheran. At war's end, many of them departed from Afghanistan with Korans and Kalasnikovs to carry the *jihad*, the holy war, westward to Bosnia, northeast Africa, and even New York. But that setback paled in comparison with a far more serious one: Pakistan had the atomic bomb. And if it got the weapon through conspiracy, which was the case, then the United States had been a willing coconspirator. At war's end, Earth had a new nuclear power.

That month, February 1989, Mark Siegel flew to Islamabad carrying information from both official and unofficial sources that he used to brief both Bhutto and Yacub Khan, the foreign secretary. The news was that her military had the wherewithal to turn the uranium gas that had been produced for several years into bomb-grade metal, and thus into atomic bombs. Six months after Zia's death and three after her own election, she learned a secret from an American that her own scientists and soldiers had studiously kept from her: Pakistan was a nuclear power. The two Pakistanis expressed surprise at the size, scope, and progress of the clandestine program. Privately, Bhutto assured her lobbyist that she had no intention of actually assembling a bomb and urged him to relay that message to Washington.

But it was too late. During the decade since the Soviet invasion of Afghanistan, Pakistan had developed an extensive and far-flung nuclear infrastructure that Generals Zia and Beg, the redoubtable Ishaq Khan, and others were not about to dismantle because U.S. foreign policy had taken yet another turn. The nuclear weapons program represented billions of rupees, uncounted millions of man-hours, and an unparalleled degree of ingenuity, persistence, and sheer guile.

The network to which Mark Siegel referred astounded Bhutto. Kahuta, the most important of the many facilities in the foothills of the Himalayas, could churn out enough bomb-grade uranium in gas form to make a dozen bombs a year. PINSTECH, the site of a reactor that had been provided by Eisenhower in the Atoms for Peace program, was at that moment being upgraded and modernized by Chinese technicians. Spent fuel rods from the U.S. reactor and the KANUPP power reactor in Karachi could be reprocessed into bomb-grade plutonium at the nearby and, aptly named, New Labs. There were two research and development facilities for centrifuges, a tritium production plant capable of making tritium gas for boosted weapons, heavy water plants, fuel fabrication plants, a weapons design facility, and more, all dispersed within a 100–mile radius of Islamabad.

And more important than these facilities was a top-secret plutonium production reactor that Pakistan began building in the mid-1980s at a secret location along the Indus. By 1992, half of the construction and assembly work had been completed on the 70-megawatt reactor which, had it ever been started up, could have produced enough plutonium for another five bombs a year.

In the military's view, the program could yield a weapon that counterbalanced India's vastly superior conventional force, and which was therefore the nation's ultimate means of salvation. The generals were damned if they were going to relinquish it, particularly because of pressure from an entity as fickle and mercurial as the United States of America. The line *they* were not going to cross separated pride, strength, and sovereignty from intimidation, unending fear, and inevitably doom. Relations between the two countries would soon begin to deteriorate.

Siegel flew home carrying Bhutto's dovish message and a pertinent request. She asked for a clear definition of what the term "nuclear explosive device" meant relative to the Pressler Amendment. The only definition Pakistan had at that point had come in a sharply worded message that Reagan sent to Zia in September 1984. It specified that Pakistan should not enrich uranium beyond the 5 percent needed to run commercial reactors and threatened "grave consequences" if Islamabad surpassed that level. The Department of State set about shaping an answer for the Pakistani prime minister.

When Bhutto arrived in the United States in late June 1989, marking the first state visit in George Bush's presidency, her first stop was not 1600 Pennsylvania Avenue but Blair House, across the street. There, William Webster, the Director of Central Intelligence, picked up where

Siegel left off. He arranged for her to be shown a mock-up of the Pakistani bomb. "The briefing was more detailed" than anything she had ever seen, Siegel would recall. Bhutto had gotten her first indication that the military and Ishaq Khan had been hiding a great deal from her. More important, the CIA director drew the line that defined the possession of a "nuclear explosive device." If Pakistan turned highly enriched uranium gas to metal, he warned, it would cross the line.

The next day, Bhutto addressed Congress, assuring it that her country neither possessed a nuclear "device" nor intended to possess one. She then met with Bush in the Oval Office, where they discussed mutual problems. Although nuclear weapons were high on the list, the President, unaccountably, placed a higher priority on resolving the deteriorating situation in Afghanistan. Specifically, Bush pointed out that his country and hers were backing opposing factions. The problem was left unresolved. Also left unresolved was the question of whether Washington would deal directly with Bhutto, as the civilian head of government, or with Ishaq Khan, the hawkish pronuclear chief of state, and the military cadre backing him. The reconciliation of that question would itself play a decisive role in U.S.-Pakistan relations.

Events on the subcontinent the following year conspired to undermine Bhutto's peaceful pledge. Following the forced resignation of the intensely unpopular Hindu government of Kashmir during Muslim rioting in January 1990, New Delhi flew in additional troops to restore order. As tensions mounted in both capitals, Bhutto went to Kashmir to make her $5 million pledge and warned of the 1,000-year war to free the Muslim state. Meanwhile, her Indian counterpart, V. P. Singh, responded by telling his own countrymen to prepare psychologically for war. Tensions continued to rise through May, when the Indian Army sent an elite strike force on maneuvers near the Pakistani border. More ominously, Pakistani intelligence got wind of the movement of short-range missiles which General Beg's staff believed—wrongly—could be armed with atomic warheads.

India outnumbered Pakistan in virtually every military category, both quantitatively and qualitatively. Its army was two and a half times the size of Pakistan's and it had 220 military aircraft that were nuclear-capable. The great Pakistani fear was an Indian thrust across the Rajasthan desert to the Indus River valley, a move that would cut Pakistan in two from north to south, effectively ending its nationhood.

Worse, as a result of the obsessive secrecy surrounding the Indian nuclear weapons program, outsiders, including the Pakistanis, had been forced to guess how many of the weapons New Delhi actually had. The high figure, calculated by private analysts, was 100. The low figure, the CIA's, was fewer than a dozen. The Pakistanis themselves figured that the Indians had between thirty-six and forty-eight of the weapons.

As winter turned to spring, Pakistan had enough bomb-grade uranium in gas form to begin the process of putting together a nuclear weapon, but it had not yet put one on the shelf. Yet India not only believed otherwise, but had decided that the weapons could be delivered by M-11 missiles and F-16s. In fact, Pakistan's F-16s had deliberately not been configured to drop nuclear weapons when they were shipped by General Dynamics.

Whether Pakistan had been able to steal or reverse-engineer the electromechanical devices needed to arm the bombs in flight was the subject of a debate in the U.S. defense and intelligence communities. There was evidence that the F-16s had flown training missions that mimicked the delivery of nuclear weapons. Although the arming system needed by the fighters was classified, it wasn't that difficult to replicate, certainly not as difficult as making an atomic bomb. Yet Reagan and Bush administration officials continued to testify that the F-16s were not nuclear-capable. To state otherwise would almost certainly have led to an aid cutoff or, at minimum, to some very embarrassing questions. When Pentagon analyst Richard Barlow wrote to his boss to suggest that testimony on the F-16s be changed to reflect their nuclear capability, he was fired for being a national security risk.

There was solid evidence, however, that another aircraft had been reconfigured to drop an atomic bomb on New Delhi. It was the turboprop C-130 Hercules, which would drop a bomb out of its back like any other cargo, allowing it to descend slowly enough under a parachute so the transport plane had time to escape before the shock wave from the blast caught up with it. There was every reason to believe that dropping an atomic bomb from a four-engine propeller-driven aircraft would work, just as it had over Japan.

Seeing the threat increasing, General Beg and Ishaq Khan ordered the country's uranium gas to be turned into metal so the bombs would be ready to use. Although U.S. intelligence did not then know precisely what was happening, it was able to piece together enough to alert the National Security Council. The first intelligence probably came from a National Security Agency intercept. U.S. intelligence monitored the subcontinent from Diego Garcia, the site of a large U.S. naval base and listening post due south of the India-Pakistan border. As alarm spread, lights burned into the night in the White House and across the Potomac in the Pentagon and the CIA.

The orbital flight paths of reconnaissance satellites were moved to get better views, and therefore better imagery, of key nuclear facilities in both countries. White House officials who were assigned to south Asia were soon shocked by what CIA analysts showed them on the digital imagery. Kahuta had been evacuated out of apparent fear of attack. This caused a division among the area experts. Some thought the evacuation showed that Pakistan assumed the nuclear facility would be attacked in response to a Pakistani first strike. Others believed that the exodus only reflected a simple precaution: an assumption that Kahuta would be the first target in any Indo-Pakistani war.

A second indicator was more ominous. At Chagai, near the mountains where Pakistan had tested its weapons design in September 1986, imagery analysts believed that they had spotted a nuclear storage facility. A review of other data increased their confidence in that conclusion. A source inside Pakistan, for example, had revealed that A. Q. Khan had recently visited Chagai. Furthermore, another reconnaissance satellite— probably one of the newer radar-imaging types that could peer through the night—had picked up a convoy of trucks that moved exactly the way their U.S. counterparts did when they delivered nuclear weapons to U.S. bases. Sure enough, the Pakistani convoy was headed to a nearby air base. Finally, at that base, there appeared to be the smoking gun: F-16s were on full runway alert, with pilots sitting in cockpits ready to light their engines and ordnance hanging from the fighters' wings.

One analyst remembered his reaction quite vividly. "I believed that they were ready to launch on command and that that message had been clearly conveyed to the Indians. We're saying, 'Oh, shit.' We've been watching the revolution in Kashmir, the internal problems in India, and we look at the Pakistani pre-positioning. These guys have done everything that will lead you to believe they are locked and loaded."

Secretary of State Baker, who was then meeting with Soviet Foreign Secretary Eduard Shevardnadze in Moscow, was also alerted that his and his host's south Asian proxies were on the brink of nuclear war. Ironically, both men were discussing the reduction of their own country's nuclear weapons stockpiles when the call came. Still, cold war thinking prevailed in some quarters, with one senior military aide in the White House

Situation Room suggesting that the United States should try to convince the Pakistanis to aim their bombs, not at New Delhi, but at Tarapur, the Indian reactor complex north of Bombay. It was right out of a superpower war-gaming scenario. Except this time it was for real.

Deputy National Security Adviser Robert M. Gates was therefore dispatched on a White House aircraft from Moscow to the subcontinent to meet with Ishaq Khan, Bhutto, and Singh in an effort to reduce the tension. His attempt to meet with Ms. Bhutto failed because she was traveling around the Persian Gulf trying to rally Muslim support for her country's position on Kashmir.

Over lunch, Ishaq Khan hinted darkly to Gates that should Pakistan's fate be threatened by India, he would use atomic bombs early in the conflict. But the meeting with Ishaq Khan and Beg did not go the way Ishaq Khan had planned. Gates was less than tactful. "General," he told Beg, "our military has war-gamed every scenario between you and the Indians and there isn't a single way you can win." The message was really directed, not at Beg, but at Ishaq Khan, who the United States believed had not been fully briefed by his excitable chief of staff. "Don't expect any help from us," Gates added for emphasis.

This turn of events embittered Ishaq Khan. After years of helping the United States in its relations with China and in its covert war in Afghanistan, his country was being double-crossed. It had been seduced. Now it was being abandoned. He and Beg therefore offered Gates a deal. They wanted President Bush, at the very least, to reward Pakistan for not going nuclear in an all-out war with India. An appropriate reward, they explained, would be a massive airlift of conventional arms to Pakistan: exactly as President Nixon had done for Israel under similar circumstances in the 1973 war with the Arabs. Nixon may have agreed to such a deal, but Bush would not.

Bhutto would very likely not have pushed Gates the way her vitriolic countryman did. But Gates never spoke with Bhutto. Whose fault that was remains unclear. He saw her as an incompetent and her failure to meet with him on his terms confirmed that opinion. On the other hand, she and her friends in the U.S. Congress viewed Robert Gates as arrogant and wanting to deal exclusively with the man who had been so helpful during the cold war.

The decision to meet with Ishaq Khan while she was out of the country had consequences that were wasted neither on her supporters nor on Ishaq Khan's. The United States had chosen to talk with the hawks, not the doves, about the nuclear weapons program. This had the effect of emboldening Ishaq Khan at Benazir Bhutto's expense. Neither did it go unnoticed in India. At the moment of the great crisis, Pakistan's superpower sponsor decided to meet with Ishaq Khan and Beg, not with Ms. Bhutto. The message, at least where Indian Premier V. P. Singh was concerned, was clear: Bhutto was a mere figurehead. Gates underscored that point when he met with Singh by noting that it was Ishaq Khan, not Bhutto, who had threatened to go nuclear if threatened. The finger on the button was obviously not Bhutto's.

Six weeks later, after confidence-building measures undertaken by both Gates and young Galbraith finally succeeded, Pakistan and India pulled back from the brink of what would have been the first nuclear war.

Richard Kerr, who was deputy director of the CIA during the crisis, later told investigative reporter Seymour M. Hersh that "It was the most dangerous nuclear situation we have faced since I have been in the U.S. government. It may be as close as we have come to a nuclear exchange. It was far more frightening than the Cuban missile crisis."

Yet when "NBC Nightly News" and *The New Yorker* reported on the impending war in the winter of 1992–93, Pakistan insisted that the stories were sensationalist and that the two nations were never close to nuclear war. But how could that square with the preparations for war that were seen throughout Pakistan?

One answer that was later given credence in some intelligence circles was that the Pakistanis were engaged in a colossal bluff of the sort Israel concocted in 1973 and would try to do again in 1991. Pakistan may have had only one option to save its soul—the nuclear one—but its credibility was minimal. The leaders in Islamabad knew full well that a nuclear attack on India would work only as a last resort because India could respond on the order of ten megatons to one. They therefore decided to use a dramatic hoax to get conventional arms instead. Those who believe that scenario note that the data collected by U.S. intelligence systems, far from being ambiguous, were almost unbelievably explicit.

Yet the threat remained as irreversible as the law of unexpected consequences. Two and a half years later, the two relentless antagonists were once against poised for war, as reports of Pakistan's seven nuclear bombs and the delivery of twenty-five M-11 missiles to Karachi were aired on television. The situation was made even more dangerous when, in December 1992, a revered Muslim temple in the northern Indian town of Ayodhya was demolished by crazed Hindu fanatics. Thousands of Muslims died in communal violence then, and hundreds of Hindus perished a few months later when Muslims planted dozens of bombs in Bombay's financial district out of revenge. Once again, both sides edged toward a final confrontation, and then drew back.

Meanwhile, where Washington was concerned, Pakistan had turned from being an asset to being a liability, from a valuable and well-cared-for ally into an ignominiously abandoned embarrassment. It was denied $1.1 billion in humanitarian and military aid during fiscal years 1990–1992. The effect was dramatic. "Tell me," Abida Hussain, the Minister of Population Control and later ambassador to the United States would ask, bitterly, "what does the enrichment of uranium have to do with condoms?" Pakistan, trying to get Washington to reverse its decision, first denied that anything in the nuclear weapons program had changed since Bush last certified it as being clean. Then Foreign Secretary Shahryar Khan, becoming desperate, blamed the weapon's creation on Bhutto. That, too, was ineffective.

Now desperate, Pakistan successively stopped producing highly enriched uranium at Kahuta and plutonium at the New Labs and even promised to sign the NPT and open its facilities to inspection if India would do the same. It also proposed a regional nuclear arms control agreement that would include China, Russia, and the United States, as well as India. But the Indians, seeing that their smaller opponent, now thrown on the defensive and being denied desperately needed funds and military equipment, knew they had an advantage they could press. They also realized what had become obvious: there was only one superpower left in the world, and it was not its old patron, the Soviet Union. If it was to modernize both its economy and military and take what it believed was its rightful place among nations, it would have to deal with the United States.

India therefore rejected Pakistan's regional proposal. The world had changed, it replied. Pakistan's notion of the region was too limited. It should include the five new central Asian states, including the nuclear-armed Kazakhstan, and other nations, as well. Saudi Arabia's Chinese-supplied missiles could easily strike India. So too could the North Korean missiles being ordered by Iran. Everyone knew that the mullahs craved their own atomic bombs.

So Pakistan was trapped. It still would not do what it knew it had to do to restore U.S. aid: it would not relinquish its nuclear weapons because it could not trust India. New Delhi began accelerating not only its nuclear weapons programs, but those devoted to chemical weapons as well. U.S. intelligence had determined that India was designing new and better atomic bombs, machining plutonium bomb cores, and even pursuing a hydrogen bomb.

By the end of 1992, India had also placed its first indigenously produced "Earth resources" satellite in orbit. The spacecraft was capable of providing both intelligence and targeting data. And the Indians also successfully launched an Agni missile while seeking nuclear and chemical weapons capability for the fighter-bombers it assigned to its aircraft carriers.

Worse, from Islamabad's perspective, its former benefactor was now wooing India. Joint U.S.-Indian naval and ground exercises were held in May 1992 and March 1993, respectively. At the same time, the Indian military was preparing an extensive shopping list for American arms makers who were looking for new clients in the wake of the end of the cold war.

Pakistan was now thrown on the defensive in the corridors of Congress and at the Department of State. Indian diplomats lobbied to have Pakistan declared a terrorist state because of its support for Islamic rebels in Indian-occupied Kashmir. State let Pakistan off with a warning. A few years earlier, India wouldn't have even received a hearing on such a request, yet now it was being listened to attentively. Perhaps most ignominiously, Islamabad was even reduced to answering charges about its allegedly ineffective antidrug policy, its support for certain Afghan rebel groups, its new friendship with Iran.

Even Japan took a swipe. In December 1992, after terrible floods killed thousands and left much of the Indus valley devastated, Bhutto's successor, Muhammad Nawaz Sharif, planned for a trip to Tokyo to seal an agreement in which Japan agreed to give Pakistan $400 million in humanitarian assistance. But in early December, Japanese television reran NBC News reports on how Pakistan had prepared for nuclear war against India. The Japanese Foreign Ministry reacted by calling its Pakistani counterpart to say the aid money would not be provided after all. Japan, ever mindful of its history, would not provide succor, even for flood relief, to any nation possessing nuclear weapons.

Pakistan had become the first nuclear pariah. It had the good luck to be pursuing nuclear weapons when its help was needed by the United

States. But it had the bad luck to possess them when they had become politically awkward for Washington. The Pakistanis argued, justifiably, that they had been singled out for retribution while Israel and India not only went unpunished but remained on cordial relations with the United States. But like disciplinarians in some reform school, Senators Larry Pressler, John Glenn, and others determined that Pakistan could be made to serve as an example—a horrible example—of what would happen to other Third World nations that either developed nuclear weapons or refused to abandon those they had. If the aid cutoff was unfair, Glenn fumed, so be it: "They lied to us!"

At best, America's harsh policy might have the effect of limiting, if not reversing, Pakistan's capacity to engage in nuclear catastrophe. If, on the other hand, abandoning Pakistan leaves it so destitute that it is forced to sell what it has created to the likes of Iran in return for basic sustenance, the policy will have failed. The second possibility seems the more likely. Bhutto's supporters claim that in late 1990, not long after aid was cut off, Ghulam Ishaq Khan secretly flew to Teheran for a fifteen-minute meeting with Rafsanjani to conclude an agreement under which Iran would make up the shortfall in aid in return for nuclear weapons assistance. The claim was rejected by both Ishaq Khan and the CIA. But similar rumors continued to circulate. Two years later, Rafsanjani reportedly went so far as to offer to pay Pakistan's entire defense bill—$3.5 billion—in return for its nuclear know-how. The following year, 1993, both Muhammad Nawaz Sharif and Ghulam Ishaq Khan were forced to resign because of their incessant feuding. By late October, Benazir Bhutto would return to power. Whatever the case, the ever-nervous military remained the custodian of the nation's nuclear weapons.

During a debate for the presidency of the United States in October 1980 the incumbent, Jimmy Carter, made a short but prophetic remark about the future. Carter was a graduate of the U.S. Naval Academy, was trained in nuclear submarine engineering, and was the second most scientifically and technologically literate president after Thomas Jefferson. He therefore found more credence in his typically homespun observation than he indicated. Carter said that his daughter, Amy Lynn, then a thirteen-year-old high school student, had told him that her and her friends' deepest worry about the future was the spread of nuclear weapons. As Ronald

Reagan looked on with apparent pleasure, the audience broke into laughter and a chorus of derisive hisses.

It was a telling moment. It is unlikely that Reagan's stance on superweapon proliferation was born that evening. Rather, the crowd's reaction would have reinforced his notion, later demonstrated, that the spread of nuclear weapons, deadly toxins, and the means of propelling them over great distances was of no serious concern compared with waging war against godless communism and other tyrannies that threatened the United States and the rest of the white, industrialized, democratic world. An insular, sinister brand of patriotism soon took hold in Washington that lasted through the Bush administration. Charles Wilson's notoriously ecocentric tenet that what was good for General Motors was good for the country was dusted off and retrofitted to serve an equally cynical agenda: classical capitalism, unfettered by ethical standards that were considered subversive, had to be invigorated and turned loose under the protection of overwhelming military force and through any alliance necessary. Intelligence was bent to fit that requirement. Soviet arms control transgressions, no matter how insignificant, were leaked to the media at every opportunity while data about the Iraqi and Pakistani nuclear programs were routinely ignored. Relatively unimportant Argentina was bludgeoned into abandoning work on the Condor-2 missile. In the meantime China, representing a colossal market for U.S. manufacturers, committed murder and spread nuclear and missile technology far afield while George Bush evangelized about the need to bring Beijing into the fold with patience and understanding (read investment).

This double standard, epitomized in relations with Iraq and Pakistan, had at its heart a policy of forging temporary marriages of convenience by favoring one side over another with little or no regard for long-term consequences. There was, of course, no deliberate attempt to provide superweapons to those countries. Yet America's eagerness to see Iraq and Pakistan succeed in battling its own foes in Teheran and Kabul was interpreted as allowing them a free hand to collect or pilfer whatever it took to achieve superpower weapons status.

But the policy was as shortsighted as it was dangerous. It sent an unmistakable message to industrialized and Third World nations alike that under the right circumstances the proliferation of superweapon technology is permissible. It showed that the United States can be highly selective in adherence to export control regimes, allowing relatively short-term political and economic considerations to take precedence over long-term arms control requirements. It proved that whatever help the United States did provide in the way of weapons and weapon technology could be arbitrarily cut off for political reasons while a vilification campaign was launched against the old ally. That kind of policy reversal, with which many Third World nations are only too well acquainted, is yet another reason for becoming self-sufficient in superweapons. A loaded arsenal seems to be the best insurance against a fickle benefactor. Finally, it helped to spread a fearsome technology from which the United States itself is by no means safe.

# 3

# A BEWILDERING
# VARIETY OF
# POISONOUS SNAKES

**E**arly on the morning of May 22, 1989, a rocket named Agni roared off a launch pad at India's Chandipur test facility, about 150 miles southwest of Calcutta at Balasore. As some 300 scientists and engineers watched on television monitors, murmuring appreciatively and heartily patting each other on the back, the pencil-shaped missile rose straight up on a stream of fire and then gently arced eastward, high over the Bay of Bengal. Agni's solid-fuel first stage separated and fell into the sea minutes after the launch, followed by the jettisoning of its second stage, which ran on liquid propellant. Then, with Indian electronic monitoring ships and hovering helicopters stationed 650 miles downrange to record Agni's telemetry—the missile's vital signs—its dummy warhead plunged into the sea due east of the Andaman Islands and disappeared. Fifteen years after the successful testing of its first nuclear bomb, New Delhi finally possessed a ballistic missile that could carry it. All of Pakistan, as well as large parts of central Asia, the Arabian Peninsula, and China, suddenly lay within striking distance of India. A nuclear warhead miniaturized to 1,000 pounds could be hurled all the way to Beijing.

In an interview shortly after the test, the father of India's space program declared that Agni could carry either conventional or nuclear warheads. But, Avul Pakir Jainulabuddin Abdul Kalam added, "It can also carry flowers to offer as a symbol of peace." The remark was reminiscent of Mahatma Gandhi, the great pacifist himself, and brought to mind the fact that India had even called its first nuclear weapon a "peaceful bomb." No one, however—certainly no one who spoke Hindi—would have been taken in by Kalam's allusion to flowers. Agni does not mean chrysanthemum. It means fire.

And fire was precisely what Agni's designers had in mind. "Agni, deployed operationally and with a conventional warhead, could destroy a major military installation anywhere in Pakistan, in fact, in most of south Asia including Afghanistan," one influential Indian news magazine crowed. "For India, the greater strategic importance is that it can reach major targets in southern and central China. But of more vital import is its deterrent factor. Armed with a nuclear warhead, Agni offers the potential to put India on a par with China as far as military deterrence is concerned."

Should deterrence fail, however, the uses of nuclear-tipped ballistic missiles seemed readily apparent. Here is one Indian journalist's appallingly simplistic dream account of a popular war scenario in which the means of national salvation is the nation's ultimate silver bullet. It is used against Pakistanis in a decisive patriotic catharsis.

"India is reeling under a surprise attack along its western borders. After a short desperate battle, enemy armoured columns smash through Indian front lines and wheel toward New Delhi. Division after division of Indian troops are knocked aside as they rush to stanch the gap in their forward defences. The Indian Prime Minister summons an emergency meeting of senior Cabinet colleagues and military chiefs. According to the prognosis, the way the enemy army is crunching ahead, it is a matter of days before the first enemy columns reach the outskirts of New Delhi. A decision is taken and within a couple of hours an Indian medium-range missile streaks into the atmosphere. A few minutes later, the grim mushroom of a nuclear explosion reddens the sky near the border and a brilliant radioactive flash incinerates the head of the advancing enemy army. A few hours later, the war is over."

The enemy in this fantasy has been set up. The smaller Pakistani force, ignoring the fact that India is known to have a huge army equipped with high-tech conventional weapons, chemical and biological toxins, and atomic bombs, not only invades its Brobdingnagian neighbor, but thrusts so deep into its territory that it menaces the capital (dangerously extending its own supply lines in the process). It nevertheless routs its hapless opponents until its own otherwise indomitable spearhead is annihilated by the wonder weapon. The Pakistanis, awed by Indian invincibility, retreat in terror and do not retaliate in kind. India is saved.

The scenario has sold well in India and in any number of other countries, including Pakistan. It is easy to say that hack journalists and fiction writers can indulge in flights of fancy that statesmen and stateswomen must eschew. No responsible head of state, diplomat, or soldier would for a moment lend credence to the invasion and redemption fantasy spun by the Indian. It fails on strategic and political grounds because it is so simplistic as to be wholly unrealistic. Yet on some primal level, the apparent benefit of possessing the ultimate zap, the master weapon, is at least as old as the Arthurian legend's Excalibur. Revolvers were called "equalizers" in the old West not only because they offset the advantage gunslingers had in being armed, but because they compensated for being outnumbered; they made the prey equal to the predator. If Japan had possessed an atomic equalizer, there would have been no Hiroshima and Nagasaki. That much has not changed.

The possession of nuclear weapons and quick, far-reaching delivery systems by both the United States and the Soviet Union caused a profound change in the strategic equation. All of the generals' and other strategists' elaborately concocted war plans—all of the intricately designed first- and second-strike scenarios, three-dimensional war games, triads, flying command posts, cleverly dispersed bomber bases, ballistic missile early warning systems, multiple silo-busting warheads, and the like—masked one new, irreducible fact. The true and only real purpose of nuclear weapons is political: to hold civilian populations hostage.

The reality behind the fantasy is that the Soviet Union developed nuclear weapons to hold American civilians hostage; China developed them to hold Russian and American civilians hostage; India then developed them to hold Chinese civilians hostage; and finally Pakistan developed them to hold Indian civilians hostage. A Chinese army that first announced its unalterable intention to invade India and then encamped on its own side of the border for a couple of weeks without dispersing might indeed offer India's atomic missileers an inviting target. But no Indian strategist has ever believed that his Chinese counterparts would be so stupid as to do such a thing. Rather, India developed an atomic bomb so that any army sent to invade it would understand that much of the country it left behind would be turned into radioactive rubble before it returned. The Indians' decision was therefore not military, but political, and had as its basis the same strategic doctrine that was used by the superpowers themselves: Mutual Assured Destruction, or MAD.

MAD depends on intimidating large numbers of people, civilian and military, with the expectation that they will convey their fear to their national command authorities and that a permanent standoff will result. The standoff, in turn, depends on rational leaders at every level understanding the doctrine—that there is a tacit agreement not to commit mutual suicide. It also depends on reason and on there not being an accident. A miscalculation or other fracture anywhere in the chain could have apocalyptic consequences.

Such a fracture nearly occurred during the Cuban missile crisis in October 1962 despite the fact that neither President Kennedy nor Premier Khrushchev was willing to start a nuclear war over medium- and inter-mediate-range ballistic missiles on the island. Thirty years after the crisis, a former Soviet general revealed that his country had more than MRBMs in Cuba during those dangerous days. Soviet field commanders, he told an international conference, also had six mobile launchers and nine Luna tactical missiles with nuclear warheads. The officers were instructed to use the missiles at their discretion to repel a U.S. invasion, which the Soviets came to believe was imminent.

Kennedy, who knew nothing about the presence of the small missiles, was in the meantime assuring an angry and frustrated Joint Chiefs of Staff that he would order the invasion of Cuba within forty-eight hours unless Khrushchev pulled the big ones out. Had the invasion taken place, it is likely that at least one of the tactical nuclear missiles would have been used to save the large Soviet garrison from what its commanders probably thought would be a battle with a far stronger force and an ensuing defeat. Robert McNamara, who was secretary of defense at the time, said at the conference that had the Soviets used one of the nukes against U.S. forces, the pressure for the United States to launch a nuclear counterstrike either at Cuba or at the Soviet Union would have been irresistible. The apoc-alypse would have been started, not by a head of state in consultation with his best informed and thoughtful aides, but by some panicked colonel in fatigues on a beleaguered island far from home who was just trying to do the best he could to save his men and himself.

The possibility of nuclear war, however, is not restricted to aber-rational acts by individuals. Nuclear war has nearly erupted at least twice between India and Pakistan, as we have seen, not because a deranged chief of state had his or her finger on the button, but because of appalling miscalculations made in secret by otherwise competent people. And in the heat of the 1973 Yom Kippur War, Israel, still haunted by the ghosts of the Holocaust and suddenly faced with the specter of annihilation, readied its own nuclear missiles for use against Egyptian and Syrian military headquarters.

The theory that superweapons, particularly nuclear ones, are useless because they are unusable rests on a presumed degree of reason, restraint, tolerance, and compassion that is not borne out by history. Every class of superweapon has already been used. Hiroshima and Nagasaki are graphic examples of what can happen when cities are transformed from hostages to actual targets for nuclear weapons. Ballistic missiles have been used by Nazi Germany against England, Belgium, and France, by Iran and Iraq against each other, by the Afghan and Soviet armies against the Mujahedeen guerrillas, and by Iraq against Israel and Saudi Arabia.

Cruise missiles like the French Exocet, Chinese Silkworm, and American Tomahawk, which are more insidious than their big brothers because they are smaller, more difficult to detect, and easier to make, have been used by Germany and Argentina in wars with England and by the United States against Iraq. A report circulating in the Department of Defense in January 1992 indicated that low-flying, stealthy cruise missiles were becoming the number-one proliferation threat. That is understandable. A cruise missile with a 300-mile range carrying a chemical, biological, or atomic warhead can be made with a standard jet engine and commercially available gyroscope and autopilot. It could be launched from a "fishing boat" or "freighter" undetected and strike anything from the White House to the Super Bowl. A conventionally armed cruise missile would become atomic if targeted to strike one of the more than 100 nuclear power reactors in the United States. And as Kosta Tsipis, MIT's arms expert, has noted, not only are cruise missiles more accurate than ballistic missiles—currently to within 30 feet compared with 1,000 feet for ballistic missiles—but they are impervious to defense systems like the abortive Strategic Defense Initiative.

Poison gas has been used repeatedly, from Ypres in 1915 to Halabja in 1988. Eventually, what can be used will be used, whether accidentally or on purpose, whether to win a war or to keep from losing one. The more weapons there are, the greater the chances that they will be used.

Nor are most of the new weapons indigenous, in the strict sense of the word, whatever their owners claim. India's Integrated Guided Missile Development Program, which masterminds the development of New Delhi's ballistic missiles, insists that its products are home-grown. Indian journalists have repeated that assertion, calling Agni "the most spectacular of a series of success stories in indigenous missile development." Agni was indeed spectacular. But although its development was indigenous, its technology was definitely imported.

If the so-called world car is designed in one country, put together in another, and uses parts from still others, Agni is a world ballistic missile. Its heritage traces back to 1963, when the United States started New Delhi's space program by launching a small scientific sounding rocket in India.* It also helped design the Thumba test range, where more than 350 U.S., Soviet, British, and French sounding rockets were fired in the ensuing years. During that time, Abdul Kalam himself studied rocketry at NASA's Langley Research Center in Virginia, where the advanced Scout rocket was developed, and at the Wallops Island Test Center, off the Virginia coast, where Scouts were used to launch small payloads into orbit. NASA was even willing to sell a Scout to India with the blessings of the Commerce Department, according to one missile expert, and was only prevented from doing so by the Department of State. No matter. Kalam was able to collect so much material on the unclassified rocket that it eventually metamorphosed as Space Launch Vehicle No. 3. The indigenously developed element is Kalam's organizational genius.

SLV-3 not only was India's first satellite launcher, but became the scientific prototype and political cover for Agni. That is how the line between civilian and military programs can be blurred to the point of being meaningless. The technology required to orbit a satellite or drop a warhead onto an enemy target is similar; it's basically only a matter of how high the sights are set and what the rocket carries.

Even before Agni's successful test, the missile was decried in Washington as "a highly destabilizing development in the region." Twenty-two senators sent a letter to President Bush denouncing the weapon as being "in direct contradiction of U.S. and Soviet efforts to lessen global tensions by reducing ballistic missiles." The sentiment was commendable. It was

---

*Programs started by the United States for legitimately peaceful purposes have been subverted in a number of countries because of the commonality of the basic technology. This was the case, for example, with Dwight Eisenhower's Atoms for Peace program, which started a number of nations, including Israel, on the path to nuclear weapons.

also hypocritical. U.S. aid to India's missile program was extensive and did not end in the space age's formative years.

Historically, Agni was the true son of Scout, which was first used in 1960. Yet, incredibly, only a week before Agni's successful test, meetings were scheduled between American and Indian officials to discuss new ways in which Washington could expedite the sale of advanced space technology to India—technology, for example, that would help Kalam and his colleagues simultaneously test how a missile performed when it was vibrating and accelerating during launch. The Department of Commerce, which is supposed to foster exports, again approved the sale. But the Pentagon and the CIA, which worry about superweapon proliferation, blocked it.

Ironically, even as intelligence reports on the Agni launch were coming into Washington that May 22, two special agents of the Department of State's Office of Munitions Control were busily pounding out a telling memorandum to the U.S. Attorney in Newark. It reported on the progress of their investigation into how radiation-hardened General Electric computers and microchips used to guide and control U.S. nuclear missiles had found their way into the Indian Space Research Organization's inventory. What it all boiled down to, the agents explained, was that their investigation was dead. The computers and chips were ambiguous, so-called dual-use items, which meant that they could have as easily gone into a civilian rocket as a military one. Since U.S. policy encouraged the peaceful uses of space by other countries, particularly with products made in America, export law would no doubt allow the transaction. That being the case, as it often was, the U.S. Attorney decided that pursuing the matter further was futile.

The U.S. contribution to India's missile program pales, however, in comparison to France's and is nearly eclipsed by Germany's and the Soviet Union's. France not only launched sounding rockets from India, but licensed Indian production of one of them, Centaure, in the late 1960s. More important, it licensed India to build its own version of the same Viking high-thrust liquid rocket motor that is used to propel the European Space Agency's heavy-duty Ariane satellite launch vehicle.*

The indefatigably aggressive Germans contributed by selling India

---

*Salesmen from the Société Européene de Propulsion, which manufactures Viking, performed the same service in Brazil.

three technologies that are crucial for guided missile development: the guidance system that was to become Agni's brain, test facilities, and the use of composite materials. The last are used to make ballistic missile engine nozzles and ablative nose cones, which protect warheads from the intense heat generated during reentry into the atmosphere.

The Soviets sold the Indians SA-2 Guideline surface-to-air missiles—the same weapon that brought down the U-2 spy plane piloted by Francis Gary Powers in 1960—which had a surface-to-surface range of up to twenty-seven miles when paired and specially configured. The Agni rocket's upper stage is identical with India's Prithvi, a Scud-like short-range tactical missile, which is in turn powered by a pair of SA-2 engines mounted side by side.

The lineage of India's first long-range ballistic missile is, therefore, as complex as the television monitors that were used to follow its launch. It is the result of Indian technical and managerial skill and a great deal of help by Western corporations and Soviet ministries, all out to make a profit with the encouragement of governments that wanted to extend their economic and political spheres of influence. India, in common with several other nations, was and remains determined to use superweapons to lay to rest the ghost of a colonial past, assure its survival in a precarious and heavily armed world, and project military power within its region and commensurate political power in it and beyond.

Any lingering doubts on that score should be dispelled by the Polar Satellite Launch Vehicle and ABR 200 (I). The former, a fourteen-story-high, 275-ton brute of a rocket, was designed to place a satellite weighing as much as an automobile in a 500-mile-high polar orbit. It will therefore also be adaptable to the intercontinental ballistic missile role. The ABR 200 (I), which has been successfully tested, is a top-secret airbreathing rocket engine that uses oxygen from the atmosphere instead of carrying a tankful of it from the ground. The highly advanced concept is also under investigation by U.S., Russian, German, and French scientists for possible use as a hypersonic space plane capable of orbiting Earth with reconnaissance cameras, bombs and missiles, or other military equipment. The test model has already reached twenty-three times the speed of sound.

Alarmed because of the deal India made with Russia in 1992 to buy advanced rocket engines (and which ultimately collapsed because of U.S. pressure on Moscow), the United States slapped an embargo on the export of its own rocket technology to India. But it was too late. The years of deals had made India virtually independent. U. R. Rao, head of the Indian Space Research Organization, reacted to the U.S. freeze by saying that it would have "only nuisance value." Referring to the PSLV's powerful satellite launch capability, he quipped proudly, "We would then be among the big boys in space."

This has led to an irony that Sophocles would have savored. Having been tightly bound to Mutual Assured Destruction for more than four decades, the United States and the Soviet Union finally managed to end the dangerous tension with a monumental series of actions that followed Mikhail Gorbachev's perestroika. Beginning in 1987, both countries agreed to a succession of arms control treaties,* for example, that broke new ground in reducing conventional, intermediate- and long-range nuclear forces. But even as the old adversaries emerged from all the years of unrelenting danger to what they hoped would be an era of reduced tension, they remained mindful that the means of causing an international catastrophe was hardly theirs alone. It exists, as it has since the first Chinese nuclear test in 1964, within the Third World. The difference, however, is that the threat is spreading, thanks in large measure to their own shortsighted policies.

The new danger comes from a proliferation of superweapons for which they, themselves, were in large part responsible. During the cold war, the two superpowers as well as France and the United Kingdom sold advanced weapons, technology, and information to their puppets and proxies while showing by example that nuclear weapons seemed to guarantee sovereignty, power, and a healthy economy. Charles de Gaulle took French forces out of the NATO military command in 1967 and created an independent strike command, the *Force de frappe*. This seemed to imbue France with a dignity and independence that was not lost on the Third World. With the exception of an occasional war in Asia and the Middle East, the Northern Hemisphere remained reasonably stable, as NATO

---

*They were the Intermediate Range Nuclear Forces Treaty of 1987, which called for the dismantling of medium- and short-range land-based missiles; the Conventional Forces in Europe Treaty of 1990, which greatly limited the number of tanks, artillery, combat aircraft and helicopters and other weapons each side could have in Europe; the first Strategic Arms Reduction Treaty of 1991, which called for the reduction of Soviet long-range warheads from 11,012 to 6,163 and their American counterparts from 12,646 to 8,556; and the second START agreement of 1993, which further slashed the weapons to 3,000 and 3,500, respectively.

and the Warsaw Pact armed and rearmed their Third World clients at considerable profit. All of this took place under their respective nuclear umbrellas.

Meanwhile, it became clear to the "developing nations," as they were called in the 1960s, that "have" and "have-not" had to do with more than economics. It also had to do with nuclear weapons and the means to deliver them. All the rhetoric about a brave new world and equality among the family of nations notwithstanding, starting in 1964 all five permanent members of the Security Council were nuclear powers. The underlying reality of the "family" metaphor was therefore that the adults had the wherewithal to administer the ultimate punishment and the children did not have it.

As the following pages show, superweapon proliferation was and remains a right of passage from national political adolescence to adulthood for an alarming number of Third World nations. Although circumstances vary, all superweapon aspirants equate nuclear arms, missiles, long-range aircraft, and deep-water naval capability, and to a lesser extent chemical and biological weapons, with enhanced sovereignty and regional power. "We have learned that preserving our independence and survival in this unsuitable international climate is not possible without science, technology, and the necessary tools," Iran's President Hashemi Rafsanjani has maintained, echoing any number of his predecessors both in Iran and elsewhere. Not only is his country in a region also occupied by two enemies—a nuclear-armed Israel and a nuclear-aspiring Iraq—but the revivalist cleric has his own plans to make Iran a major power in the area and beyond. He believes that the necessary tools include atomic and chemical and biological weapons, as well as the aircraft, missiles, and submarines to deliver them. To provide his country with anything less, he and other Third World leaders believe, would amount to treason.

And they want not only the weapons but, like their role models, the capability to produce and maintain them independently. No atomic bomb bestows sovereignty if someone else can take it away. Technological and manufacturing independence is therefore the bedrock of superweapon proliferation.

The drive for independence has had two direct consequences. First, it has spawned weapons that are indigenously developed and produced. The basic technology and some essential hardware may have come from the superpowers, their industrialized allies in eastern and western Europe, and China. The baghdatron and ultracentrifuge technology used by Iraq was, indeed, developed in the United States and Germany, respectively. But there was never a doubt in Jafar Jafar's mind that he would have to make his own calutrons and centrifuges or forever forgo nuclear weapons. Neither was there any doubt that Iraq would have to have an indigenously developed ballistic missile to carry them. This scenario has played out elsewhere, from North Korea to Pakistan, Iran, and Brazil.

The second consequence of independence is that because the weapons are indigenous, they are also freely marketable. Proliferation's new dimension is transnational and almost completely free of the strictures of the First and Second Worlds. By the start of 1993, for example, twenty-two nations had agreed to adhere to the Missile Technology Control Regime, which was set up in April 1987 to limit the spread of ballistic missiles by curtailing the export of key technologies. The MTCR is undoubtedly helpful in restricting some technology transfer. Ominously, however, not one country that agreed to observe MTCR guidelines was from the Third World.* This is because they want to be assured the freedom to not only develop their own long-range missiles but to transfer—sell—the technology to offset their own considerable design and development costs. Eager buyers of superweapon technology within the Third World are not a new phenomenon; eager sellers are.

The Agni missile wears a thousand faces. It is an Egyptian submarine that was designed in the Soviet Union, made in China, and modernized by an American electronics company. It is an intermediate-range ballistic missile that was based on U.S. and German technology, funded by Saudi Arabia, managed by a Swiss company, engineered by Austrians, and put together in a hollowed-out mountain in Argentina and at a Nile delta factory for use by Iraq. It is a Libyan poison gas factory that was developed, built, and stocked by Germans with construction help from Thais and with a neighboring bomb factory supplied by Japan. It is an Iranian poison gas factory patterned by Thai engineers after a prototype in Libya. It is an Indian observation satellite that is launched and controlled by Russians

---

*The nations are Australia, Austria, Belgium, Britain, Canada, Denmark, Finland, France, Germany, Greece, Ireland, Italy, Japan, Luxembourg, the Netherlands, New Zealand, Norway, Portugal, Spain, Sweden, Switzerland, and the United States. Russia, Ukraine, Khazakhstan, and other members of the former Soviet Union that have advanced ballistic missile technology were also conspicuous by their absence. ("U.S. and 21 Others Expand Pact on Spread of Weapons," *The New York Times*, January 8, 1993.)

and whose pictures are enhanced to intelligence quality by an American supercomputer. It is a world main battle tank that is made in South Korea and incorporates an American fire control system, a French gun barrel, and a German engine. It is an Iraqi poison gas factory that was built by Germans and that used American and Japanese chemicals engineered for Yugoslavian rockets. It is an Iranian biological agent, genetically engineered by Cuban scientists. It is a South African ballistic missile whose technology was perfected in France and the United States and whose design came from Israel. It is an Israeli nuclear reactor whose blueprints and major components came from France and whose fuel was supplied by South Africa. It is an Iraqi missile that was conceived and built in the Soviet Union and modified with German help so it could hit Israel and other distant targets. It is Algerian nuclear reactors that come from Argentina and China; Argentine, Turkish, Indian, South Korean, and Brazilian cruise missile–capable U-boats built under license from Germany; Iranian missiles that were made by North Koreans using Soviet plans and Chinese parts; and Libyan air-to-air refueling capability that used American, French, and Soviet aircraft and German technical expertise. It is the Paris Gun and Big Bertha's great granddaughter: an Iraqi monster cannon that was designed by British engineers in Belgium for a Swiss company headed by a Canadian-born American, and which was built with British, Spanish, and Italian components and financed by the Atlanta branch of an Italian bank through an account in a Luxembourg bank.

This is the face of superweapons proliferation at the end of the twentieth century. Military technology, both conventional and unconventional, has become a commodity whose elements can be combined and reverse-engineered in ways that even its creators and sellers often cannot, or do not want to, imagine.

Twenty nations now have sizable stockpiles of chemical weapons, which are attractive because they are relatively cheap—"the poor man's atomic bomb"—and literally use garden-variety chemicals (some of which are used to make pesticides). At least eighteen governments have biological warfare stockpiles or are scrambling to get them.

More than twenty countries possess ballistic missiles or are in the advanced stages of acquiring them. Israel has the Jericho-2, Saudi Arabia the Chinese CSS-2, and India its Agni. Each has a range of well over 1,000 miles and a nose cone big enough to accommodate a nuclear warhead. And since civilian and military rocketry are governed by exactly the same basic principles of physics, today's space launch vehicle carries within it the fully formed embryo of tomorrow's long-range ballistic missile. Japan's massive H-2 superbooster, for example, has been heralded as the linchpin for that country's ambitious space program. The H-2 was conceived to carry very heavy satellites to low Earth orbit and to send lighter ones to the Moon and Mars. Its lifting capacity is comparable with that of the Titan 34D launch vehicle that was used until recently by the U.S. Air Force to loft 30,000-pound reconnaissance satellites and other heavy loads into low orbit. Titans were designed as ICBMs and were then converted to launch vehicles. Reverse engineering, however, could as easily turn the H-2 launch vehicle into an ICBM with a range far in excess of 5,000 miles. The wherewithal to do so is now in place. Meanwhile, roughly 100 less ambitious countries are trying to develop relatively cheap but lethal cruise missiles and other kinds of flying bombs.

Three Third World nations—India, Israel, and Pakistan—have inventories of nuclear weapons (Israel's numbers more than 200 A-bombs). Five others are in various stages of acquiring them: North Korea, Iran, Iraq, Libya, and Algeria. Others can be described as quiescent possibilities: South Korea, South Africa, Taiwan, Argentina, and Brazil. It is also possible—some would say inevitable—that a unified Germany leading a unified Europe will have access to British and French hydrogen bombs and warheads.

In addition, four former Soviet republics—Russia, Ukraine, Belarus, and Kazakhstan—have their own cold-war-surplus nuclear stockpiles. All four were left not only with more than 40,000 nuclear warheads of all sizes and 1,200 ICBMs among them, but with conventional weapons from MIG-29s to KGB patrol boats to T-72 tanks that have been hastily dumped into the largest liquidation sale in history. Worse, tens of thousands of restive nuclear weapons and missile designers and technicians in the former Soviet Union, many of them either unemployed or toiling for $5 a month or less in make-work positions, are looking for employment while the West belatedly tries to come up with ways of keeping them out of the clutches of nations that would pay substantial sums for their services.

Although Japan has no nuclear weapons or known plans to produce them, it could do so very quickly if it felt sufficiently threatened by a neighbor such as North Korea, the vociferously insecure "hermit kingdom." The Japanese are aware that their years of occupation on the Korean peninsula and elsewhere, much of it brutal, left wounds that still fester. Certainly Japan has the necessary scientists and engineers, fiscal resources, computer technology, precision machinery, a growing glut of plutonium, and a suitably competitive spirit to attain superweapons if it feels sufficiently threatened to do so.

Meanwhile, 400 or so large diesel-powered submarines, owned by forty-one nations (not counting the United States and some of the nations of the former Soviet Union), prowl the world's oceans. Nineteen countries are either building them or have recently done so, while three or four others are preparing to turn them out. Seven nations—China, France, Germany, Great Britain, the Netherlands, Russia, and Sweden—have exported most of the new ones. Germany led with the worldwide sale of fifty of its U-209 diesel subs, which are popular because they can stay underwater for up to three weeks by using an air-independent propulsion system and can fire cruise missiles while submerged.

Aside from the United States and Russia, five countries—France, India, Israel, China, and Japan—now have space reconnaissance capabilities; and six others—Germany, Italy, Spain, Pakistan, South Korea, and Taiwan—are not far behind. The Western European Union itself is planning an integrated reconnaissance satellite program, largely to monitor arms control and to keep an increasingly nervous eye on missile proliferators in North Africa and the Middle East. (Further down the line, the Europeans are also planning to install their own ballistic missile defense system.) "Spy" satellites that take pictures from space for intelligence purposes are not generally considered to be weapons. But they are. They are routinely used to locate and pinpoint targets as well as to collect intelligence. Since bombers and missiles are useless unless they can hit their targets, strategic nuclear forces and space reconnaissance go hand in hand. Civilian imaging satellites like the American Landsat and the French SPOT, together with dedicated military spacecraft, have made every place on Earth precisely targetable.

Tactical ballistic missiles, such as India's Prithvi, China's M-series, and the ubiquitous Scud (in all of its guises), are also on the move. Twenty-one countries had them at the beginning of the 1990s, including India, Iran, Iraq, Israel, Libya, North Korea, Pakistan, and Yemen.* All

*Three others—Germany, Bulgaria, and the Czech Republic—are still holding SS-23s, which have a range of 300 miles. Seventy-two of the solid-fuel missiles were transferred to Soviet allies in 1985 and 1986, the year before the superpowers concluded the Intermediate Nuclear Forces treaty that called for the United States and the Soviet Union to scrap such weapons. While the Germans and the Czechs have agreed to destroy their missiles, in keeping with the spirit of the agreement, the Bulgarians refuse to do so because of continuing warfare in their region.

but Yemen can make their own. Antiship cruise missiles, which are also nuclear-capable, have spread in the wake of the loss of HMS *Sheffield* to a single Exocet missile fired from an Argentine fighter during the Falklands war in 1982. Thirteen nations, including the United States, are aggressively marketing the ship killers and 121 nations already have them.

Land-based delivery systems are also spreading. Fighter-bombers like the American A-4, F-4, and F-16, Russia's SU-24 and SU-25, and France's stable of Mirages, all capable of carrying chemical, biological, and nuclear weapons, have proliferated around the world. F-16s now wear the insignias of Israel, Egypt, Bahrain, Belgium, Greece, the Netherlands, Denmark, Norway, Turkey, Portugal, Finland, Indonesia, Singapore, Thailand, South Korea, Pakistan, and Venezuela besides, of course, the United States. And some Egyptian F-16s are being manufactured in Turkey, making it the first all-Islamic fighter. The venerable F-4 Phantom II, designed by McDonnell Aircraft in the 1950s for fleet defense and dogfighting, was turned by Israel into a top-secret bomber that could carry nuclear bombs all the way to Moscow and then refuel in the air to make it home. A squadron of F-16s, piloted by elite air crews, has replaced the Phantoms on twenty-four-hour alert in underground revetments at Tel Nof air base near Rehovot. There are seventy atom bombs in nearby bunkers.

During the five years between 1986 and 1990 the ten biggest exporters of conventional weapons and the value of their wares (in constant 1985 dollars) were the Soviet Union ($61 billion), the United States ($54 billion), France ($14 billion), the United Kingdom ($8 billion), China ($8 billion), West Germany ($5 billion), Czechoslovakia ($2 billion), the Netherlands ($2 billion), Sweden ($2 billion), and Italy ($1.5 billion). Soviet arms exports accounted for an estimated 11.9 percent of its gross national product.

The biggest importers during the same period were India ($17 billion), Japan ($11 billion), Saudi Arabia ($11 billion), Iraq ($10 billion), Afghanistan ($6 billion), Spain ($6 billion), North Korea ($5 billion), Poland ($5 billion), Egypt ($5 billion), and Czechoslovakia ($4.5 billion). North Korea's arms imports cost 20 percent of its gross national product and accounted for an estimated 32.3 percent of all its imports.

Unconventional weapons technology is itself phenomenally expensive and profits to proliferators can therefore be enormous. Libya's poison gas factory at Rabta cost $175 million. Algeria paid about $65 million for its weapons-capable research reactor. Iraq spent $750 million on Osirak and its labs and as much as $8 billion for the baghdatrons. Indonesia's research reactor cost $54 million. Argentina's uranium enrichment facility and related installations cost $200 million, and so did the facilities for its ill-fated Condor-2 missile. Equipment for the missile cost $500 million more. Not to be outspent by its rival, Brazil had pumped $330 million into its nuclear submarine program through 1990 and planned to spend up to a billion more before the boats became operational.

The postwar proliferation of unconventional weapons—the supers— has gone through a series of overlapping and increasingly dangerous phases. But there have been two constants through it all. The deadly technology has steadily improved, raising its cost and increasing the political consequences of both selling and buying it. At the same time, globalization of science and communication on every level have enhanced the flow of even the most complicated data about superweapon technology and related matters. Put another way, the handful of scientists—Oppenheimer, Ulam, Bethe, Feynman, Teller, and the others—who worked on the Manhattan Project in utmost secrecy and with relatively primitive equipment have given way to a transnational network of Ph.D.s in physics who share a common knowledge of atomic energy in its various civilian and military manifestations, read the same journals, and attend many of the same meetings. This is not to say that making atomic and hydrogen bombs is child's play. But the process, particularly for a government that will settle for what is euphemistically called a "primitive" bomb, is more dependent on logistics and getting the right equipment than on scientific breakthroughs. The important nuclear breakthroughs occurred in the 1940s and need only to be copied, as Jafar Jafar has demonstrated.

Similarly, a new generation of engineers around the world has learned from and surpassed its predecessors in the design of rockets and missiles. The equations and other design criteria are now widely known by scientists and engineers like India's Abdul Kalam who have studied throughout the East and West. It's just a matter of buying or making the right components.

No wonder the relief many thought would come if the cold war ever ended—an age of peace and tranquility—has not materialized. "Yes, we have slain a large dragon," Clinton administration CIA Director R. James Woolsey said in reference to the former Soviet Union during his congressional confirmation hearings. "But we live now in a jungle filled with a bewildering variety of poisonous snakes."

. . .

**D**uring the 1970s and 1980s the exporting of weapons and even super-weapon technology was transformed from a disjointed and somewhat malodorous enterprise to a normal business activity. Increasing numbers of arms manufacturers in Asia, South Africa, and South America stepped out of the shadows and into the light of respectability. They bought space at trade fairs to show off their wares, started to market and advertise aggressively, arranged attractive financing for customers, developed arms exclusively for export (Northrop's F-5 Freedom Fighter being a notable example), relaxed some arms import restrictions while often violating export guidelines, sold some weapons that were so new even the military in the producer's country hadn't gotten them yet,* and went into licensing agreements and joint ventures with buyers.

The pace of arms transfers not only quickened but became firmly institutionalized in the mid-1970s and throughout the 1980s as sellers began to fully grasp their benefits, which were considerable. Selling high-tech weaponry and the machines to make it brought in hard currency, reduced unit cost to producers, spread out research and development costs, paid for oil imports (in the case of France), improved the balance of payments, maintained a healthy defense industry, reduced marginal costs by spreading them among a greater number of buyers, bolstered defense industry employment, and advanced defense industry policy goals.

There were Frenchmen, for example—from heads of state to lowly salesmen—plying their wares almost everywhere in the Middle East and Asia during the late 1970s and throughout the 1980s. Their motives were particularly interesting because they had to do, not only with profits in the many billions of francs, but with a streak of nationalism laced with a subliminal inferiority complex. To some degree, French weapons and weapons technology transfers seem to have been driven by a subtle current of wounded Gallic pride that needed mending. With the exception of the conquest of Algeria in 1830, France has suffered an unbroken string of military defeats going back to Napoleon's rout in Russia in 1812 and the Battle of Waterloo three years later. France successively lost the Franco-Prussian War, required foreign help to eject occupying Germans in two

---

*Aerospatiale's AS-30L laser-guided air-to-ground missile was used by Iraq against Iran before it entered the French Air Force's own inventory.

world wars, was publicly reined in by Dwight Eisenhower after the invasion of Suez, and was forcibly thrown out of colonies in both Asia (Vietnam) and the Maghreb (Algeria). To invent and manufacture war-fighting machines of the highest technology was proof of the Fifth Republic's scientific and military prowess. But to provide those weapons and advanced superweapon technology to appreciative customers around the world—to send them out like warrior-emissaries—seemed to make France something its army had not been able to make it for almost two centuries: *formidable.*

It appeared that the pair of research reactors that France sold to Iraq, and from which plutonium could be harvested, was the ultimate in weapons transfers—a great prize that was the reward for persistent and aggressive salesmanship. But the reverse was actually true, and is still not widely understood, even by arms experts. The reactors, one of which was the doomed Osirak, were only sweeteners offered to promote the much more lucrative sale of off-the-shelf weapons and large civilian projects. This was standard French operating procedure. In the 1960s, France had sold Israel its reactor at Dimona and missile technology in order to get the door open so Marcel Dassault, the aircraft manufacturer, could sell Tel Aviv its Mirage III fighters (which arrived in time for the 1967 war). In the 1970s, it sold Iraq the reactors partly to get Saddam to order Mirage F-1s (it was a particularly frustrating business; he haggled over the avionics like a car buyer trying to get free air-conditioning and a stereo). In the 1980s, France sold India some of the technology for Agni so that Dassault could peddle its Mirage 2000 (which can go from 0 to over Mach 2—twice the speed of sound—in about four minutes and which is referred to as "the height of perfection" in trade ads).

The reactor sale to Iraq paved the way for weapons sales that included 143 Mirage fighter-interceptors; Alouette, Gazelle, and Super-Puma helicopters; several thousand Exocet, Milan, Magic, Martel, HOT, Roland, AS-30L, R-530, and Armat missiles; AMX 30–GCT howitzers, and the Tiger-G radar system for the Iraqi AWACS.

The French made similar deals with South Africa and Pakistan. They built the Koeberg reactors for the South Africans as a sweetener for the 1978 sale of Mirage IIIs. They sold Pakistan sounding rockets called Dauphin and Dragon, both of which were refined to become the nuclear-capable Hatf missiles, also as part of a deal for another batch of Mirages.

As is often the case, some of the weapons were eventually used against nationals or allies of the country that supplied them. Aerospatiale, the French rocket and missile maker, boasted in an advertisement after Operation Desert Storm that its tactical missiles had been used by the winning side with great effect. "Defense is our obligation because war can be hell," the ad proclaimed, sanctimoniously. The ad failed to say that the war was particularly hellish for the losing side, which had also used Aerospatiale weapons: Milan and HOT antitank missiles. Another French company, Thomson CSF, also tried to cash in on the role its equipment played in the victory. ". . . we're at the forefront of many of the advanced technologies—like optronics—that stormed to supremacy in the Gulf in 1991," its two-page spread in a trade publication boasted. Omitted, however, was the fact that Thomson CSF had also been heavily involved in arming the losers. It provided an electronic countermeasure (ECM) system that was specifically designed to help Iraqi Mirages elude U.S. fighters, a laser guidance system for the Iraqi "smart bombs" that were used against Iranian positions on Kharg Island,* and whole semi-conductor factories that supplied most of the electronics for Iraq's nuclear weapons program as well as a Soviet Il-76 transport that was modified for AWACS duty. As valuable as those weapons contracts were to France, however, even they earned a relative pittance compared with an immense array of planned construction projects. These included petrochemical, automobile, desalinization, fertilizer, and gas liquefaction plants, tele-communications systems and broadcasting networks, housing projects, defense electronics factories, a subway, a navy yard, and even a new airport.

This was market penetration on a scale that would make any government, let alone the corporate sector, salivate. While the reactors figured prominently in Saddam Hussein's plans, they were relatively inconsequential to France, which used them mainly to establish a symbiotic relationship. *Le Monde* described the nature of the relationship perfectly. Baghdad saw France "as the most natural ally on the geopolitical scene today to help it escape the hegemony of the superpowers. . . . If Paris is seeking to convert its political capital into economic gains, Baghdad hopes to turn its economic strength into political gains."

Baghdad also wanted to turn its economic strength into weapons self-sufficiency. The importance of escaping not only the superpowers'

---

*The laser system was designed by Martin Marietta in the United States for Thomson CSF in a $37 million contract signed in 1975. (Timmerman, *The Death Lobby*, pp. 212–13.)

hegemony but that of all other First and Second World suppliers, including France, had begun to spread throughout the Third World by the end of the 1970s. But the lesson was brought home to Saddam in a particularly dramatic way during Iraq's latest war with Iran.*

In 1979, the United States abruptly cut off military aid to the mullahs after they overthrew the Shah; and the following year, the Soviet Union did the same to Iraq following the attack on Iran that began the two countries' eight-year war of attrition. The Pentagon cut off military aid for the very good reason that the Islamic militants who ran Iran openly despised "the Great Satan," as they called the United States, and took actions that reflected their attitude.† A year later, the Soviet Union stopped selling arms to Saddam because it had no wish to alienate the mullahs on the other side of its border by continuing to supply weapons to their ancient enemies. The men in the Kremlin knew that drawing the wrath of revivalist Shiites, particularly the vengeful, draconian Ayatollah Ruhollah Khomeini and his disciples, was definitely unwise. But greed eventually got the better of them and they lifted the embargo two years later.

The abrupt termination of U.S. arms sales to Iran and of Soviet sales to Iraq convinced the leaders of both nations that the superpowers and their European allies were ultimately undependable as sources of both conventional and superweapon technology and that they had to become self-sufficient or suffer the consequences. This was a historic development in the proliferation process.

At the time of the cutoff, neither Iran nor Iraq had an arms industry in almost any sense of the term. Teheran had nothing whatever. Baghdad's total arms manufacturing capability consisted of two factories, one making sniper rifles under a Yugoslav license, the other, gunpowder under a Soviet license. A decade later, Saddam's vast weapons complex was the largest in the Middle East; it was even preparing for serial production of

---

*The inaugural war was begun by Mebaragesi, the first king of Sumer, who attacked the Elamites in 2700 B.C. in the area that is now Basra. Unlike Saddam at the outset of the war with Iran, the Sumerians made their own high-tech weapons, including well-crafted metal helmets, axes, and wheels, which were used for the first time in combat. Like Saddam, however, they also relied on imports; the helmets were made of bronze smelted with tin that came all the way from the British Isles via the Phoenicians. The point is that some of the scores that belligerents in the area and elsewhere want to settle with weapons of mass destruction—with genocidal bombs—go back millennia. (Richard A. Gabriel and Karwen S. Metz, *From Sumer to Rome: The Military Capabilities of Ancient Armies*, Westport, Conn.: Greenwood Press, 1991, pp. 4–5.)

†The secret arms-for-hostages deal was an exception.

atomic bombs and doing research on hydrogen bombs. Oil money and insecurity had been used to assemble American and European super-weapons technology, send scientists and engineers abroad for training, set up a vast procurement network that included foreign companies and, perhaps most important, develop a large and largely anonymous technological, commercial, and financial elite that could integrate many diverse elements into cohesive weapons programs.

The Kremlin's action and the Iraqi dictator's reaction were the most important developments in the modern history of both conventional and unconventional weapons proliferation. In showing Iraq that they were as undependable as they were avaricious, the Soviets—and by extension their counterparts in western Europe and North America—left many of their customers convinced that they had to institutionalize the production of their own arms or forever remain bound to the political whims and machinations of their benefactors.

India was one of those customers. Following that first successful test of Agni, Dr. Kalam was asked by a reporter what would happen if the West slapped a technology embargo on India. "If there are restrictions," the rocket scientist explained, "we must beat the system. At that time," he added in reference to Agni's formative years in the early 1980s, "we had anticipated this problem and taken a consortium approach toward critical components. An industry, a lab, and an academic institution were identified for a particular problem, and we generated indigenous bases in various critical areas. If embargoes come in a particular area, we will activate the relevant groups. They cannot throttle us."

And the Soviet and American embargoes had another pernicious effect: they left a $100 billion vacuum that accelerated the trade of superweapon technology and components within the Third World itself. China, in particular, embarked on a large-scale effort to sell its exotic but relatively cheap technology to a host of willing buyers. It contracted to transfer missiles and nuclear know-how not only to Iran and Iraq but to Pakistan as well. It also transferred missile technology to Syria and missiles to Saudi Arabia, a research reactor to Algeria, and poison gas chemicals to Libya, among others. The Saudi missile deal, the biggest bonanza of all, came to $3.2 billion for an estimated thirty of the huge weapons.

Iran and Iraq were even able to steal a page from their mercurial benefactors. By turning to other Third World countries to supply them with weapons—Brazil, Chile, South Africa, North Korea, Argentina, and

China—the two Islamic nations made those suppliers increasingly dependent on *them*. In the process they and other Third World countries practically built entire arms industries. Brazil pumped enormous resources into its military industries, largely to arm both combatants during the Iraq-Iran war. Brazil not only never made large profits from the enterprise, however, but invested so much capital in it that it couldn't get out once the war had ended. That and sheer greed were two major reasons for frequent visits by Hugo Piva to Iraq during the frenzied buildup between 1988 and August 1990. The other reason was that Piva, the Caltech graduate, was trying to keep the Brazilian superweapon program alive. He was one of two men identified as masters of both the nuclear weapon and missile programs of Brazil and was desperate for enough cash to keep programs alive that Brazil's political leadership abandoned. Iraq had cash.

Some of the seller nations, in turn, developed niche markets, which were exploited in order to jump-start their own superweapons programs. One Brazilian firm, which started with twenty employees making oil field equipment, branched into low-cost armored personnel carriers, soon becoming the world leader in that specialized enterprise. Saddam bought enough of the vehicles so that the company could branch out yet again. It went into ballistic missiles, first selling short-range versions to Iraq and then forming a joint venture that became the core of Brazil's ambitious intermediate ballistic missile program. Another, Brazil's Avibras, went from being primarily involved in space and communication projects to exporting large quantities of tactical missiles, particularly to its biggest customer, Iraq. Once again expertise in the civilian sector led to important military programs. Basic work on the Sonda series of scientific sounding rockets evolved into the Astros (Artillery Saturation Rocket Bombardment System), which can carry poison gas up to forty miles. During the early 1980s, Avibras became one of Brazil's leading export companies. By 1990, Iraq was preparing a site south of Baghdad to manufacture its own Astros under license.

Saddam's voracious procurement of weapons turned Armscor, the South African weapons producer, from an obscure outfit to the world's eighth largest arms exporter. He accomplished that by ordering $1 billion worth of Gerald Bull–designed howitzers and the ammunition to go with them. In another of the many ironies that haunt the international arms trade, though, Armscor may have used Iraq's howitzer money to finance its part of joint arms manufacturing deals with Israel, Iraq's most implacable enemy. Armscor funds almost certainly went into the missile project that led to the development and production of Israel's Jericho-2 and South Africa's Arniston, an intermediate-range missile derived from Jericho-1. North Korea's Super-Scud program was bankrolled by Iranian oil money. Teheran bought relatively primitive Scud Bs from Pyongyang during the early 1980s. Revenues from the sale were in turn used to develop the Scud Cs that were sent to Syria in February 1992, Scud Ds with a reported range of 650 miles, and no doubt even North Korea's nuclear weapons program.

Throughout the 1980s, the United States watched with growing apprehension as the widespread scramble for superweapons accelerated. Accordingly, it began to urge its allies to curtail the export of superweapon technology. The pressure to do so was mostly ignored by France and totally ignored by Germany. At the same time China, India, North Korea, and the others were admonished to abandon their own thriving arms businesses in favor of such international arms limitation agreements as the nuclear Non-Proliferation Treaty (NPT),* which had gone into effect in March 1970 and the MTCR.

Western Europe reacted to America's stern admonitions by quietly ignoring them. But Asia paid close attention. It listened and then it snarled with unconcealed contempt. China and the others saw the Western arms control treaties as being hypocritical, exclusionary, and racist. Where China and India were concerned, this was not new. Sanctimonious attempts to get them to renounce superweapons dated at least from the testing of the first Chinese atomic bomb in 1964 and the Indian test ten years later. At that time, both nations steadfastly maintained that they were no less entitled to the protective benefits of atomic and thermonuclear weapons than were the members of NATO and the Warsaw Pact.

This attitude hardened during the ensuing years, developing into a cohesive, blatantly negativistic rationale for creating all sorts of weapons of mass destruction. First, and most obviously (the argument went), it was the superpowers, not the Third World, that introduced intercontinental ballistic missiles and nuclear weapons in the first place. And the United States remained the only nation on Earth that had ever used atomic bombs in war. Furthermore, the United States, the Soviet Union, and their proxies remained in possession of the most sophisticated weaponry on the planet,

---

*It is technically the Treaty on the Non-Proliferation of Nuclear Weapons.

all of which could and had been used to subjugate Third World peoples everywhere. Subtle but real political and economic domination by the superpowers would go on forever, the Asians believed, unless the atomic monopoly was broken once and for all.

Treaties that inhibited the spread of superweapons were therefore taken to be doubly insidious. They were concocted by the superpowers and their lackeys to institutionalize the geopolitical imbalance of power while simultaneously inhibiting Third World economic growth by restricting trade. Beijing branded the Non-Proliferation Treaty and the Missile Technology Control Regime as racist ploys concocted by Europeans to impede China's legitimate growth. But because of Western pressure, it decided to pay lip service to them anyway.

Dr. A. Q. Khan, the father of Pakistan's atomic bomb program, had this to say about U.S. pressure to stop France from helping his country. "Behind the non-implementation of the agreement on supplying the reprocessing planet to Pakistan is the same attitude of anti-Islam of the Western countries which they have toward the developing countries generally, and toward Islam countries particularly: that no advanced technology should come into the possession of these countries and they should always remain at their mercy. In pursuance of this policy, they (Western countries) are all as one."

Ironically, this was one key area in which the Pakistanis and Indians shared common ground. "If England and France can have it, why not we?" Kavel Ratna Malkani, the vice-president of India's militantly Hindu Bharatiya Janata Party, asked in January 1993. "We don't want to be blackmailed and treated as Oriental blackies. Nuclear weapons will give us prestige, power, standing. An Indian will talk straight and walk straight when we have the bomb." Accordingly, the BJP went on record as saying that the day it ousted the Congress Party from power, it would deploy nuclear weapons.

The NPT was designed to stop the spread of nuclear weapons through a system of safeguards that required knowledgeable scientists from the International Atomic Energy Agency (IAEA) to inspect reactors and other facilities to make certain that fissile material was not being diverted from them to make bombs and warheads. The reactors were said to be "safeguarded" through supposedly strict bookkeeping and inventory procedures. The NPT was signed by the United States, the United Kingdom, the Soviet Union, and fifty-nine other countries. A number of developing nations sought guarantees during the NPT negotiations that renouncing nuclear arms would not put them at a permanent military disadvantage and make them vulnerable to nuclear intimidation by countries that already had nuclear weapons. What they got was a U.N. resolution declaring that nuclear aggression or the threat of it against any signatory would set off immediate action by the Security Council. This mollified many nations, but not China, India, Pakistan, North Korea, Israel, Algeria, and some others, which refused to sign the document.

The MTCR is a consensual agreement, not a formal treaty, that was initially adopted by the United States, Canada, France, West Germany, Italy, the United Kingdom, and Japan and had twenty-two signatories by 1993. It sets guidelines for use in national export codes to stem the spread of ballistic and cruise missiles with payloads over 1,100 pounds and ranges roughly exceeding 200 miles. The numbers are not arbitrary; they are specifically geared toward halting the spread of long-range nuclear-capable missiles. It encompasses a long list of missile components, many of them dual use, and chemicals that are not supposed to be sent beyond the producing nation's borders.

The Chinese, Indians, and the others didn't need lawyers and Ph.D.s in international relations, however, to tell them that the MTCR was as full of holes as a downrange test site. All they had to do was read American newspapers. In May 1989 *The New York Times* reported that government witnesses told a congressional committee that some of the parties to the MTCR, notably West Germany, were continuing to sell missile technology to the Third World in flagrant disregard of both the agreement's guidelines and Washington's incessant grumbling.

Two months later *The Washington Times* carried an article quoting unnamed senior U.S. defense and arms control officials as voicing concern about an impending deal in which France was going to transfer "sensitive" missile technology to Brazil. It was the Ariane space launcher's Viking engine. Brazil was then allegedly going to pass it on to Colonel Muammar el-Qaddafi, who at the time was fantasizing about showering ballistic missiles on two U.S. bases in the central Mediterranean in retaliation for the American air raid on Libya in 1986. "To have France exporting technology to Brazil knowing of Libya's intense interest in acquiring long-range missiles is outrageous," one frustrated U.S. official said.

The implications of this were not lost on the Chinese, Indians, Pakistanis, Israelis, Argentines, and others who steadfastly ignored both the NPT and the MTCR. Both, it was charged with some justification, had the effect of allowing Western nuclear and missile technology (and sales) to continue while stopping everyone else's. Article VI of the NPT was particularly infuriating. It avowed that the superpowers would shed their nuclear weapons. But to the contrary, they had no intention of disarming and were then actually stockpiling more thermonuclear arms than they would ever need.

And to the extent that the MTCR worked at all, it had the unwanted effect of stimulating missile transfers within the Third World itself. Starting in the late 1980s buyers like Iran, Syria, and Saudi Arabia, which suddenly found it difficult or impossible to acquire missile and related technology from their traditional suppliers, were forced to look to China and North Korea for the weapons. It also had the effect of making Third World missile producers determined to stand their ground in the face of what they interpreted as the West's persistent double standard. This ultimately led several buyers, including Iran, Iraq, Egypt, and Saudi Arabia, to look even beyond China and North Korea as suppliers. It led them to look to themselves.

"Unless they see the inequity and the futility of such nonproliferation efforts that seek to preserve the monopoly over missile technology," one Indian editorial writer warned after the Agni test, "other forms of pressure are bound to mount on the nations at the missile threshold in a bid to prevent entry. . . . Even while facing up to such pressures, India would have to push towards capability to launch geo-stationary satellites and intercontinental ballistic missiles so that self-reliance can be achieved in all spheres."

The Third World emerged from the ninth decade of the century convinced that ultimately only high-tech weapons could ensure survival in a world that seemed to be shrinking dangerously. Indigenous super-weapons production capability seemed to guarantee independence from the atomic chauvinists on both sides of the Iron Curtain. Furthermore, spreading that capability within the Third World itself appeared to have two positive consequences: it was both ennobling and lucrative.

The current phase in strategic weapons proliferation began during three tumultuous years, 1989–91, with the end of the cold war and the coming to light of the Iraqi phenomenon.

The disintegration of the Soviet Union and the consequent breakup of the Warsaw Pact loosed unprecedented forces on the world. First, and most obviously, thousands of advanced tanks, planes, submarines, and other military equipment went on sale at rock-bottom prices, attracting eager buyers from Iran to China. More ominously, the collapse created an economic wasteland and near-anarchy within the old empire. This quickly led to the development of a kind of rogues' market of financially strapped weapons scientists and engineers, the machines they worked with, a vast store of nuclear arms and marketable plutonium and highly enriched uranium (HEU), and impoverished, insecure, and alienated former republics, some of them possessing nuclear weapons and the bombers to carry them and all possessing the know-how to produce them.

By 1992 the former Soviet Union had already begun to leak both brains and hardware, and it seemed to be only a matter of time before the fissile material began spilling out as well. A handful of scientists had been put to work in Algeria, Libya, China, and North Korea, according to U.S. intelligence officials and a highly knowledgeable Russian source. Meanwhile, David Kay was warning that it was only a matter of time before part of the old Soviet Union's immense horde of uranium and plutonium was smuggled out and found its way into the clutches of terrorists. As Kay had every reason to know from his experience in Iraq, creating weapons-grade bomb fuel is the hardest part of making a nuclear weapon. That is why a ready-made stock of fissile material is so potentially dangerous. Spending even $1 billion for 120 pounds of the material, which would be highly transportable and would make at least three atomic bombs, is far cheaper than starting from scratch.

However salubrious the end of the cold war was in easing the threat of a nuclear holocaust, it had the immediate effect of putting people in the arms industries on both sides of the old Iron Curtain out of work. It was particularly hard on eastern European nations, which had fickle economies in the best of times. Like their Western counterparts, eastern European and Soviet weapons makers thrived for almost a half century on wars, real and imagined. It brought to mind the sober observation by Dr. Harvey R. Colten, a member of the National Academy of Sciences, that "more people live off cancer than die from it." Those who had run Czechoslovakia's renowned armaments industry were therefore stunned when their resolutely ethical President, Vaclav Havel, set them to making things like tractors instead of tanks. "We have to divide personal feelings from business," Jan Segla, manager of the ZTS Martin plant, explained in a television interview. The firm, which had manufactured Soviet-designed T-72 tanks, was suffering 30 percent unemployment. "As a human being, I am essentially against the export of arms. But it's not just a question of morality; it's a question of economics," Segla said before adding an afterthought. "I think you journalists should stop writing about the export of arms. This is not something that concerns the rest of the world."

It certainly concerned the United States and, for a change, France, Germany, and other west European weapons and weapons technology exporters. No sooner had the Eastern bloc begun to crumble than Iraq invaded Kuwait. The United States, now the only remaining superpower, felt compelled to lead the coalition against Iraq.

But nothing had prepared either the coalition or onlookers in the Third World for just how formidable Saddam's arsenal really was. His brazen attack on Kuwait, followed by the surprising discoveries that were made afterward about the advanced state of Iraq's weapons production complexes, particularly its nuclear facilities, had a clarifying effect on the West's attitude toward superweapon proliferation.

It took the revelations in Iraq, coupled with the madcap weapons spread that was going on elsewhere, to awaken the United States and its western European trading rivals to the fact that the situation had fundamentally slipped out of their control. Early in 1992, in the wake of revelations about its companies helping Qaddafi acquire the poison gas plant and Saddam his missile and nuclear technology, even Germany decided that braking proliferation was imperative. Its parliament finally enacted long-stalled legislation to seriously tighten controls of weapons and technology exports and created a new agency to monitor such exports.

George Bush's New World Order had foreseen the U.N. Security Council, run by a superpower coalition, keeping the lid on the upstarts indefinitely. But suddenly, incredibly, one of the two superpowers had begun to stagger and then collapse from political malnutrition and economic hemorrhaging. China, another member of the council, was not inclined to help, since it derived a substantial portion of its foreign exchange by exporting precisely the stuff that frightened the United States.

This left the United States in the ethically untenable position of selling more conventional arms around the world than any other nation while making strenuous efforts to plug the superweapon hole almost singlehandedly. It remonstrated against China, for example, trying vainly to pressure Beijing to increase human rights and end the export of missile and nuclear weapon technology in return for most favored nation trading status. But at the same time it agreed to sell F-16s to Taiwan, deeply angering China and raising embarrassing questions about what the Chinese and others saw as a double standard. When Washington complained about Russia's selling reactors and submarines to Iran, Moscow noted that concerns about proliferation in the Middle East had not stopped the United States from selling seventy-two F-15s to Saudi Arabia.

In fact, during the year and a half after the 1990 Iraqi invasion of Kuwait, the United States sold an average of $1 billion in arms a month around the world. By late May 1991, even as President Bush was unveiling a proposal to ban weapons of mass destruction from the Middle East, the United States was becoming the biggest provider of weapons of limited destruction to the area. Several Arab nations were trying to restock inventories that had been depleted by the war or make substantial additions to them. The Saudi F-15 order alone was worth $9 billion and 7,000 jobs. The order, along with Taiwan's F-16s, was approved during Bush's unsuccessful reelection campaign.*

By the end of February 1992, the Bush administration lifted the trade sanctions against China, clearing the way for that nation to buy U.S. satellite parts, supercomputers, and jet engines despite intelligence reports that Beijing was still selling missile technology to Syria and Pakistan and both missile and nuclear technology to Iran. The Pentagon also pointed out, to no apparent avail, that the jet engines were better than any engine China had in its cruise missiles and would very likely be copied and used in those weapons. China, in the words of one knowledgeable observer, was by then making the transition from "a regional power to a regional superpower."

The Chinese insisted that a return to most favored nation status would go far toward convincing them to finally abide by the terms of the Missile Technology Control Regime and possibly even the Non-Proliferation Treaty. But by then it mattered little whether they formally ascribed to the arms control treaties or not. Signing the documents could provide no guarantee that Beijing would honor their provisions. Saddam Hussein's lasting contribution to arms control will have been to demonstrate that the NPT as originally drawn was no match for a determined and clever cheater, that documents in and of themselves are all but meaningless in

---

*France's share would not be inconsiderable, either, and neither would Britain's. More than half of the $5.4 billion in total arms sales France would register after Desert Storm came from the Middle East and North Africa, up from only a third in 1989. In January 1993, the British also struck a bonanza in Saudi Arabia: $15 billion for seventy-two Tornado strike fighters, thirty Hawk jet trainers, and three minesweepers. They also landed a $227 million contract to sell thirty-six Challenger tanks and four armored personnel carriers to Oman. (The French deals are from "Talks Begin on Arms Sales to Third World," *The New York Times*, July 9, 1991; Britain's are from "British to Sell Saudis Warplanes and Supplies Worth $7.5 billion," *The New York Times*, January 30, 1993.)

the absence of real political and economic disincentives to acquire superweapons.

As the century draws to an end, the world realignment caused by the collapse of the Soviet empire and the wrenching economic shifts in Latin America, the Middle East, and the Pacific rim will profoundly affect the spread of unconventional arms. The death of communism where it began showed that ideological lip service is no longer enough to keep nations together. Some countries in the Southern Hemisphere that are threatened or are actually in serious decline will very likely want to adopt superweapons—certainly chemical and biological arms and appropriate delivery systems—as the cheapest long-term defense against the specter of extinction. *The New York Times* observed, "For some messianic fundamentalists in the Middle East, Mutual Assured Destruction is not a deterrent but a temptation."

At the same time, other Southern nations—the exporters—will be under equally heavy pressure to sell what they can to assure their own survival. It will be a buyer's market in which apparently nothing can be gained by holding back.

Superweapon technology has a way of outlasting motives, regimes, and alliances. The North will have to come to terms with the deadly flowers that are sprouting, out of control, in the garden it took such pains to cultivate.

# TOOLS OF THE TRADE

—

# 4

# "SHOP
# TILL YOU DROP"

**I**t was the sort of unremarkable snapshot that tourists take all over the world every day and that is given a perfunctory glance at journey's end before being entombed in a shoebox. Family members and friends would glance at such a picture, mumble something to feign appreciation, and quickly move on. An intelligence analyst who studied the same picture, however, would have made more out of the three men in it and the huge hole behind them than any casual observer could.

The man on the left, a portly individual in his forties whose white shirtsleeves were partly rolled up and whose hands were placed on his waist, was Zuhair Abbas, an engineer. The one in the middle, Fadel Kadhum, was a lawyer. Kadhum, who wore a thick mustache in the style of the president of his country, peered without expression at the photographer from behind brown-tinted glasses. The third man, taller and leaner than the other two, wore a blue and white polo shirt. Less accustomed to the dazzling sun than they were, he squinted and wrinkled his nose. He was an American banker named Christopher P. Drogoul and he was in his late thirties. His two companions were Iraqis.

The photographer, fiftyish and a partner of Drogoul's, was named

Paul von Wedel. Even as he squinted through the lens to capture his three companions, he heard an argument break out between a military officer and a construction chief who stood nearby. The soldier was insisting that taking the picture violated security regulations. He was referring, not to the individuals, but to the very large excavation behind them.

The intelligence analyst would have known that the hole was part of the Badush Dam, a huge engineering project on the Tigris, just north of Mosul, that was designed to generate 400 megawatts of electricity. By itself, that information would not have been very meaningful. But the analyst who combined it with an understanding of what the men in the picture were doing there would have made a very valuable discovery indeed.

Zuhair Abbas was actually the manager of Project 395, the umbrella organization for Iraq's combined nuclear weapon and Condor-2 missile programs. As the project manager, he was in charge of all its civil engineering works, including the dam. Kadhum was the general counsel for the Ministry of Industry and Military Industrialization (MIMI), the superweapon program's overall procurement organization. More important, he was an officer in Al Amn Al Khas, the special security organization established by MIMI to "aid procurement and to report on other Iraqi intelligence organizations." Drogoul and von Wedel were in Iraq that April 1989 to chart the dam's progress. They had already financed it to the tune of $200 million in construction equipment and would, within a matter of days, sign an agreement to provide $1.15 billion more for other, bigger projects as part of Baghdad's single largest external military funding effort.

What neither banker had any way of knowing, however, was that when completed the dam at Badush would feed power to a hungry nuclear uranium enrichment facility at Ash Sharqat, twelve miles away. Still more electricity would be sent to Sa'ad-16, the ballistic missile research and development center, also near Mosul. Drogoul and von Wedel, his Sancho Panza, also did not know that the cranes, trucks, bulldozers, and other heavy earthmoving equipment they financed for the building of the dam were also being used to construct Ash Sharqat itself.

Meanwhile, even as their Arab guides explained how the project was being handled, another Iraqi named Safa al-Habobi was waiting anxiously in Baghdad for Drogoul and von Wedel to return to the capital. Al-Habobi ought to have been in the picture because he was the spider at the center of Iraq's entire procurement web. A forty-three-year-old Ph.D. in engineering, he was also a member of the Iraqi intelligence apparatus and had made a number of trips to the United States for equipment to form the superweapon program's infrastructure. He had tried to buy American steel mills; an oil refinery; an aluminum mill; a helicopter factory; car and truck assembly plants; a brass foundry; and factories for making tungsten carbide tool bits to machine uranium metal, semiconductors, circuit boards, and high-tech composites.* He was also trying to buy into companies in England and elsewhere that had expertise in making the components that were to be used in the superweapons.

Drogoul had a very special place in the master procurement plan. His job was to bankroll a very large part of it: a supremely devious effort that would become the biggest bank fraud in American history, risk more than 65 percent of BNL's net worth, and besmear George Bush in the so-called Iraqgate escapade. Banca Nazionale del Lavoro (BNL), founded in 1913, had 424 branches worldwide and was Italy's largest bank. It was 96.5 percent owned by the Italian government.

It had all begun on February 4, 1985, when Drogoul applied for and received permission from BNL's home office in Rome to grant the Iraqis a line of credit that was not to exceed $150 million at any one time. The alleged purpose of the loan was to buy grain under the Department of Agriculture's Commodity Credit Corporation loan program. The CCC was set up to help American farmers by guaranteeing that loans taken by foreign governments to buy their crops would be underwritten by the U.S. government. Some of the money that was channeled from BNL-Atlanta to Baghdad did, indeed, buy grain. But starting in February 1988, when he made the first in a series of unauthorized and unsecured loans to Iraq—

---

*In some cases, Habobi wanted to buy old factories, dismantle them, ship them to Iraq. In other cases, he wanted major U.S. companies to build brand new factories over there. Among the steel mills Habobi had targeted were U.S. Steel's Baytown works in Texas, two LTV mills, and one Bethlehem mill in Pennsylvania. He also went after the Indyll aluminum mill in Louisiana, the Powerine oil refinery in California, the G.M.-Volvo truck assembly plant in Utah, and the American-built Learfan composites plant in Belfast, Northern Ireland. He also negotiated with Bell-Textron for a new helicopter factory; with Kennametal for the tungsten carbide factory; with Glass International for a circuit board factory; with Semetex for a semiconductor manufacturing facility; and with SerVaas for the brass foundry. (Correspondence related to all of these except Powerine are part of documents used by the House Banking Committee investigation into the Iraqi procurement network. Powerine is from Windrem's interviews with Hamid Jafar and a Powerine official.)

$200 million for Badush and therefore for Project 395—Drogoul was directly financing the superweapon program. By the time the end came, in 1989, he contributed more than $5.1 billion in other peoples' money to Saddam Hussein. All but a tiny percentage of the money was transferred without the apparent knowledge of the bank's officers in the home office, according to federal prosecutors.

According to what he subsequently told federal investigators, he extended credit to Iraq at interest rates that were so low—as little as three-sixteenths of a percentage point above borrowing costs—that other banks could not match them. Drogoul seems to have never doubted that his scheme would cut out the competition and allow BNL—him—to corner the Iraqi business. Doing so not only would impress his superiors, leading to recognition, promotion, and a place in the pantheon of great bankers but, more important, would also line his pockets with considerable kickbacks. And that suited his Iraqi clients perfectly, since it meant that the United States Department of Agriculture and Italian bankers were underwriting a sizable chunk of their weapons development program.

If the United States government knew about the scheme, it never let on. Beginning in November 1984, when the Reagan administration resumed diplomatic relations with Saddam Hussein, Iraq had been the steady beneficiary of American largesse. Drogoul may have operated his electronic ledgers—routing the secret loans to Iraq through a so-called gray book—illegally, but he did so within an exceptionally friendly political environment. On December 12, 1985—five months after Assistant Secretary of Defense Richard Perle warned his boss, Caspar W. Weinberger, that there was evidence Iraq was actively pursuing nuclear weapons—Drogoul and von Wedel had signed an unauthorized agreement to provide $556 million so Baghdad could buy grain under the CCC program. In October 1987, as Baghdad and Teheran again began exchanging Scuds in a flare-up of the war of the cities, the Atlantans had approved an additional $665 million in secret funding for the purchase of "grain." Then, four months later, that first loan went out to Project 395 and there was no going back. It was followed by a second medium-term loan for $300 million that was quietly approved on October 6, 1988, followed by a third that December for an additional $500 million. In April 1989— at the time Drogoul and von Wedel made their pilgrimage to Baghdad— the fourth and last of the major medium-term, unsecured loans was made for a whopping $1.15 billion.

By then, all pretense about the money's going for grain had been dropped. The third and fourth installments went directly to MIMI. As a result, there was a blizzard of contracts for construction and weapons manufacturing equipment, starting in 1988 and continuing until Kuwait was overrun.* Whole factories were being constructed, and negotiations were even under way to buy a mobile satellite tracking system.†

Meanwhile, warnings such as Perle's went unheeded, as did graphic evidence in news magazines and on television that the Iraqis were committing atrocities. Following the use of poison gas to kill 200 Kurds and injure 1,000 more in Halabja in 1988, both houses of Congress passed legislation that imposed widespread sanctions against Iraq. But neither bill became law because of Reagan's opposition. Bush followed suit right up until the day before Saddam Hussein made his move to turn Kuwait into his country's nineteenth province.

They were wonderful, exciting years for Christopher Drogoul, international banker extraordinaire. During the time he manipulated his electronic ledgers in Atlanta using the "gray book"—secret computer codes and hidden discs—for the surreptitious loan transfers to Iraq, Safa al-Habobi hopped around the United States on his shopping spree for the steel mills, refineries, and other major assets. At one point, according to a government source, Drogoul even conducted business through a fax machine plugged into the cigarette lighter of his car, which was parked across the street from the bank.

Whatever Drogoul and von Wedel knew about their role in the arming of Iraq, they could have no idea just how big the procurement program really was. It was an undertaking that, in its breadth, depth, and managerial brilliance, matched the weapons program it served. Drogoul was a vital component, but only a component, in a meticulously conceived plan that entailed nothing less than the domination of the Arab world.

---

*Suppliers were in the United States, Canada, India, West Germany, Czechoslovakia, Belgium, Italy, Switzerland, Sweden, Turkey, the Netherlands, Great Britain, Bulgaria, Austria, Japan, and France. Equipment included arc furnaces, a rotary forging plant, armored steel, telecommunications equipment, a water purification plant, dies, milling and boring machines, heavy engineering equipment, and various electronic components. (United States District Court for the Northern District of Georgia, Atlanta Division, *United States of America v. Christopher P. Drogoul et al.*, February 28, 1991, pp. 72–75.)

†In March 1989, Drogoul was asked to provide a $36 million letter of credit for the purchase of such a system from Comtech Systems, Inc. Since the satellite intelligence the U.S. shared with Iraq during its war with Iran showed the Iraqis how adept the Keyhole satellite was, it can be surmised that Baghdad wanted the tracking system so it could follow the whereabouts of the American spacecraft. That would provide a large measure of protection for projects it did not want spotted from the sky.

Iraqi financing and procurement efforts during those years were persistently dismissed by an arrogant West as fragmented, essentially unrelated events. "Ragheads" (Arabs) were taken to be a disorganized, hopelessly backward, even comical bunch who were as inept at modern managerial skills as they were at fighting Israelis. But the opposite was the case. Mesopotamia—the land between the rivers—has contained advanced civilizations at least since 4000 B.C. Complex Babylonian and Assyrian empires thrived in the area two thousands years before Christ. The forebears of today's Iraqis, many of whom became practiced smugglers by necessity, were then successively dominated by Persians, Macedonians, Arabs, Mongols, Ottomans, and the British. As a consequence, whatever the West has to teach Iraq about high-tech weaponry, it has little to offer in the way of cunning, tenacity, organization, and a sure instinct for survival and resurrection. Far from being backward, Baghdad's pursuit of superweapons showed managerial genius on every level, from dealing with greedy bankers like Drogoul, to suckering the Reagan, Bush, Thatcher, and Mitterand governments into supporting it, buying and infiltrating companies, establishing front organizations, and persuading German and other technology exporters to bend or break their own countries' laws for the sake of fat profits.

Nor were the Iraqis alone in trying to start the financial and technological equivalent of a self-sustaining chain reaction. Similar enterprises were by then also under way in Israel, Pakistan, India, Brazil, North Korea, Iran, and South Africa, as the impetus for atomic and other superweapon independence spread and took hold.

With the exception of a single, terrible mistake, in fact, the Iraqi program could have been a model of indigenous development and almost undoubtedly would have succeeded. But the mistake was decisive. Saddam's rush for superweapons was undertaken so quickly and massively that he overextended his financial resources to the point of collapse. Badush and Ash Sharqat, the two facilities Drogoul and von Wedel were leaving behind, would cost almost $4 billion between them. While Jafar Jafar was all too mindful of the fact that he was copying the Manhattan Project, he may not have known that Oak Ridge, the model for his operation, used more electricity than Canada. And he almost certainly did not know that the organization that developed the first atomic bomb, and employed a small army of physicists, was as large as the entire U.S. automobile industry at the time. Saddam Hussein's total debt the night Drogoul and von Wedel arrived in Baghdad amounted to the staggering sum of nearly $80 billion. The invasion of Kuwait was a last-ditch, desperate attempt by Iraq to stave off national bankruptcy while still keeping the superweapons programs going.

Part of the problem stemmed from the fact that the all-out effort to develop superweapons was matched by a corresponding drive to expand the civilian sphere within Iraq itself: to build factories, refineries, and other industrial facilities. They, too, were stupendously expensive. There were plans for a $1 billion iron works; a $2 billion petrochemical complex (a *real* petrochemical complex); and a new $500 million refinery. The facilities would make Iraq strong, and its strength would make it prestigious. Prestige was so important to Saddam Hussein that, in imitation of Hitler's having brought the 1936 Olympics to Berlin, he was prepared to spend $1.3 billion to bring the Olympics to Baghdad. The Fuhrer was one of Saddam's idols.

In 1986, Hussein Kamel and Amir Hammoudi al-Saadi, MIMI's Senior Deputy Minister, sent a secret invasion force across the English Channel to London. It consisted of a small group of businessmen, lawyers, accountants, and others whose mission it was to plant the seeds for what was to grow into the Iraqi superweapon foreign procurement network. They were led by al-Habobi, who was under specific orders to set up a weapons purchasing system, mainly for the nuclear program, by making contact with Westerners whose resources and expertise were needed. The Iraqis began by quietly establishing front companies and simultaneously buying the names of small to mid-size defunct firms and then reopening them as import-export or "trading" firms. The front companies immediately established overt, but low-keyed, ties with the state-owned import firms in Baghdad.

The tenants of 2 Stratford Place, a nineteenth-century West London office building, for example, soon included TDG (Technology Development Group); TMG (Technology Management Group); and TEG (Technology Engineering Group). Together, they constituted the heart of MIMI's worldwide operation. Among them, they were supposed to contract for whatever technology and equipment was needed for the nuclear weapons program and see to it that the stuff made it safely back to Baghdad. Fundamental to the subterfuge was that all commercial transactions be done by civilians, not military officers, to further reduce the operation's profile.

Purchases and even smuggling operations during the following five years went from the mundane to the almost unbelievable. It was the London group, for example, that arranged for the sections of "petroleum pipe" that, when welded together, were supposed to turn into five supercannons with ranges well over 500 miles. The monster guns were planned for use against the hated Khomeini and his followers. They were designed by Dr. Gerald V. Bull, a disgruntled ballistics genius, who would be murdered in Brussels before the project could be completed.

The Iraqis also quietly bought into healthy firms. The idea was to become self-sufficient in stages, just the way crime bosses did when they first infiltrated a company and then squeezed out its owners. Al-Habobi's irregulars acquired 18 percent of Schmiedemechannica and half of H & H Metalform, Swiss and West German outfits that built the machines needed to manufacture key components for the gas centrifuges Jafar needed to enrich uranium until it was usable in bombs. They also bought 92.5 percent of Matrix-Churchill, a British precision tool manufacturer, for $9 million and made Habobi its chairman. He tried to buy half of Industrias Cardoen, a large international arms firm that was headed by an effervescent and suave Chilean entrepreneur named Carlos Cardoen. Although the Cardoen deal fell through, the Iraqis worked closely with both him and Gerald Bull on a variety of projects, from the superguns to missiles and fusing technology. The Iraqis even set aside more than $125 million in low-interest loans from the Banca Nazionale del Lavoro's Atlanta branch to buy their own bank in either London or New York. The Iraqis had targeted the London operation of First National City Bank of Texas, suggesting that Drogoul might be an ideal choice to run it.

By 1988, a clear procurement pattern had formed. Some standard items, such as machine tools, special presses, and computers, would be purchased directly by state enterprises or ministry offices. More sensitive equipment would pass through the front companies. When there was no other way, material was smuggled back to al-Saadi's Technical Corps for Special Projects (TECO), the ambiguously named umbrella organization for superweapon development. Several key sections of Bull's "pipes" were eventually intercepted in Greece and elsewhere as they were smuggled across Europe, headed for Iraq. At one point, the London group even tried to smuggle nuclear triggers from the United States through Euromac, a tiny "food exporter" that allegedly specialized in frozen French-fried potatoes and was situated in the hamlet of Thames-Ditton, outside of London. That ended in a famous sting by U.S. and British Customs and several arrests.

In common with most other dictatorships, particularly in the Middle East and the Orient, the men who formed Iraq's extended junta were kept loyal and hard-working by allowing them to skim some of the cream off the deals they made. All foreign contracts with MIMI had to be approved by TDG, which also raked off a 10 to 15 percent "consulting fee," von Wedel asserted. Al-Habobi channeled most of that money to Kamel, von Wedel claimed, but also kept a percentage for himself. Letters and other documents relating to MIMI's European and American operations show that "commissions" were routinely built into the contracts and agreements that were made between the Iraqis and their suppliers.

The Iraqis appreciated the Americans so much they even sent them Easter cards—by telex. But the cards were the least of what Drogoul, von Wedel, and a few others in BNL-Atlanta received from their grateful clients. According to the government's indictment, Drogoul himself skimmed $2.5 million in bribes from exporters whose goods were paid for by the loans. Von Wedel got a new house. Following Drogoul's agreement four months earlier to extend an additional $1.15 billion in unsecured credit to Iraq, Raja Hassan Ali, the director of MIMI's Economic Department, gave a third member of BNL's Atlanta office a $12,000 diamond necklace as a "gift from the President." The recipient, a woman named Leigh Ann New, was Drogoul's ambitious secretary. Besides the house and a $6,000 piece of jewelry, von Wedel at one point had been given a wristwatch with a familiar countenance on its face. "This is great," he had exclaimed, enthusiastically, after two Scotches. "My kids will love it: a GI Joe watch!" The image, a red-faced Drogoul had then quietly explained, was in fact that of Saddam Hussein in his fatigues.

If von Wedel was as disgusted by the corruption as he claimed, the former Brooklyn used-car salesman was doubly upset to learn that his business partner's father also played a role in the scheme. Pierre Georges Drogoul was employed by Babil International, another "import-export" company that Habobi had set up in Paris the previous year, in September 1988. It was suspected that Babil's purpose was to launder and funnel the kickbacks paid to Matrix-Churchill into Ba'ath Party accounts in French banks. According to Justice Department documents, the elder Drogoul channeled a minimum of $424,000 in Iraqi bribes and kickbacks to his son for Christopher's invaluable work on behalf of Iraq. The transactions and other activities were in the meantime closely followed by both French and West German intelligence.

• • •

**F**adel Kadhum and the two Americans returned to the capital from their "tourist" excursion to Badush on the night of April 25, 1989, on a government-owned Falcon business jet. On the flight back, the Arab confided that he would soon be negotiating with General Motors to build an assembly plant in Baghdad for Oldsmobile Cutlass Cieras and 4-Wheel Blazers. The latter would have made very good military vehicles. One of the conditions GM imposed for building the plant, von Wedel would later claim Kadhum told them, was "that Iraq had to buy 10,000 1990 Cutlass Cieras."

The following day, Drogoul and von Wedel saw and heard things that should have left little doubt about the enterprise in which they were engaged. The day began with a visit to MIMI, a round of briefings, and then a meeting with Raja Hassan Ali.

The scene inside the ministry was reminiscent of Berlin in 1938. The Americans were first thoroughly frisked and ordered to leave all their possessions, including a gift for Hussein Kamel, outside his office. Then Ali introduced them to the killer himself: to Saddam's guard dog, the man who had personally supervised the gassing of Halabja. Kamel's fatigues, red Republican Guard beret, and automatic, holstered at the waist, were unmistakable evidence of the paranoia and ruthlessness upon which his master's regime was built. Whatever the government had to do to court foreigners, it suffered no trouble from its own people, as Drogoul and von Wedel had learned even before they stepped off their commercial flight two days earlier. The thugs who had come aboard to greet them treated them like celebrities. But the Iraqi passengers were a different matter. "All of a sudden," von Wedel would recall, "bodyguards push people aside and take us off the plane."

With Ali interpreting from the Arabic, Hussein Kamel briefly sketched his country's economic plans and assured Drogoul and von Wedel that he was grateful to them for helping Iraq to industrialize during its "time of need." The visitors could not have had a more informed briefer. His paramilitary getup notwithstanding, Hussein Kamel was the guiding force behind his country's drive for economic self-sufficiency.

The Atlanta bankers' next stop was the Nasser industrial complex and a meeting with al-Habobi himself. The Nasser State Enterprise for Mechanical Industries at Taji, thirty miles outside Baghdad, was a government-run armaments firm. There, al-Habobi's plant manager showed them research and development areas where they saw, among other things, computerized tooling machines that came from the Soviet Union and East Germany, other machines that had been made by Matrix-Churchill, and bomb casings.

Much of what Nasser was making was displayed two days later at Hussein Kamel's coming-out party: the first Baghdad International Exhibition of Military Production. With one exception, the show was the kind of military carnival that takes place around the world every year as weapons manufacturers try to peddle their wares. The exception, however, was a dramatic counterpoint to the festive atmosphere. It underscored the true nature, not only of the wares on display but of Saddam Hussein's always jittery regime. The night before the opening, an Egyptian Alphajet—one of thirty close-support aircraft bought from the French-German Dassault-Breguet-Dornier consortium—ventured too close to Saddam Hussein's presidential palace. It was immediately blown out of the sky in a hail of antiaircraft fire coming from the building's roof. The pilot and another crewman parachuted to safety in the darkness, but the stricken aircraft kept flying until it crashed in a suburb, killing twenty people. Von Wedel, who with Drogoul was staying at the Al Rashid, was awakened by the explosion. (The hotel itself would be hit by a Tomahawk cruise missile three years later when the U.S. Navy went after a nearby nuclear component facility.)

The next morning he and Drogoul arrived at the exposition in a limousine at the head of a motorcade of diplomats, generals, and other dignitaries. Peering out of the window, they could see Kamel, al-Saadi, and Ali hurrying up to the car to greet them. Seeing the three Iraqi notables eagerly extending their hands to the Americans, the press also descended on the limo. But the paparazzi, undoubtedly expecting a defense minister or even a prime minister, were disappointed. "The press was there in droves and their [sic] were hundreds of flash bulbs going off," von Wedel later recalled. ". . . and then the door to our car was opened and out climbed Chris and me. Suddenly, their chins hit the ground in disappointment when they saw who was getting out of the car." But the reporters and photographers had gotten it right the first time, despite appearances. However unlikely it may have seemed, they were looking at the two most important visitors at the show.

As they walked around the exhibition areas, Christopher Drogoul and Paul von Wedel looked into Iraq's future as it was seen by Hussein Kamel and his father-in-law. There was an IL-76 AWACS, renamed the

Baghdad-1, complete with French electronic gear in its large radome. Nearby stood a MIG-23 modified to refuel other fighters in the air, thereby giving them the capacity to strike deep within Israel or Iran. The Russian aircraft were among a fleet of others sent by twenty-eight nations eager to do business with a country they had every reason to believe—however erroneously—was well-off. The single fuel-air explosive on display represented two others that were also under development, thanks to a $100,000 contract with Honeywell. There were prototypes of 155-millimeter and 210-millimeter self-propelled howitzers designed by Gerald Bull and a gatling for air defense. Elsewhere, Al Hussein and Al Abbas—the super-Scuds that were to be used against Israel and Saudi Arabia, and which already had been used against Iran—were displayed on their mobile launchers.

Unlike other Third World arms shows, this one amounted to a demonstration of how a single developing nation could mix, match, and manufacture hybrid weapons systems to suit its own, specialized needs. Not much off-the-shelf stuff here. If no one would provide the Iraqis with an air-to-air refueling capability, they would draw on a variety of otherwise unrelated outside technologies to create their own. If no one would sell them a ready-to-fly AWACS so they could control air battles, they would buy a suitable plane from the Soviets, the right kind of electronic package from the French, and marry them. That, laid bare, was the daring philosophy Iraq's rulers believed would lead to its greatness. But instead, it would lead to disaster. Custom-made weapons, like custom-made clothes, can be ruinously expensive.

The most bizarre weapon was not only hidden from public view, but was in fact still only in model form. On a table at Astra Holdings, a British financial group that was backing Bull in hopes of landing a $1 billion contract, was a 1/35th scale model of Bull's monster cannon. When completed, the 1,000-millimeter supergun would be able to barrage Iran from deep inside Iraq. Or so it was hoped.


When he invited the Americans to the exhibition, Hussein Kamel had more in mind than merely showing off his weapons. He needed to secure the $1.15 billion loan from them. But even that wasn't enough. Starved for hard currency, he was frantically chasing any possibility that promised to keep his war machine on track.

Among other things, he had decided the year before to pursue a bold new course: freeing up his country's industry, especially its oil industry, to raise the needed cash. The key was to find an oil company chief executive who would serve as a willing partner and then use him to make a profitable alliance overseas. That man was to be Hamid Jafar, the owner of the Crescent International Petroleum Company and the younger brother of the director of Iraq's nuclear weapons program.

The idea was to use Crescent to buy into an established Western oil company's "downstream" operation: its refineries, pipelines, transportation fleet, and gas stations. This would mean profits, not just at the wellhead, but at the refinery and the gas pump. Venezuela owned Citgo. Kuwait had the Q-8 chain in Europe. Why should Iraq not enter that business, too, Hussein Kamel had reflected.

Hamid Jafar, Kamel's intended partner, thought highly of him, particularly since Kamel was Hamid's brother's boss. "You know," Hamid would say later of Kamel, "he was a very powerful figure. On the one hand, he is a capable person, young and dynamic; and on the other hand, he had a strong family link with the President." Indeed.

Hamid Jafar, working with Kamel and al-Saadi, the superweapon czar, made a deal within two weeks of the close of the arms show. The arrangement promised profits for Crescent and therefore a steady flow of oil income for MIMI and its superweapon programs, including Jafar Jafar's atomic bomb.

Under the terms of a deal that would be signed on May 14 between Hamid Jafar and al-Saadi, the Ministry of Industry and Military Industrialization would sell 200,000 barrels a day of Iraqi crude to a joint venture put together by Crescent and a foreign oil company. At the going rate of $18 a barrel, that meant MIMI would collect $3.6 million a day, plus a share of the downstream profits. Such an arrangement would be a breakthrough for Kamel, since his ministry no longer would have to depend on the Ministry of Oil for the crude it used to pay its bills. It would sell oil directly to Crescent and its foreign partner, and they would provide money for all the weapons.

Hamid Jafar was quick to distance himself from the reasonable suspicion that his brother, who worked for Hussein Kamel and who had promised to make a present of an atomic bomb to his superior, had a hand in the scheme. "Absolutely none whatsoever," he protested when asked about Jafar Jafar's influence. "In fact, it was somewhat negative. Involvement of any official in business transactions actually carries a death penalty," Hamid Jafar added so matter-of-factly that he might almost have believed it himself.

After negotiating with five American companies, Crescent eventually settled on Fina, the nation's fourteenth largest. Fina owned two refineries, had contracts with 3,100 gas stations, and did $500 million in credit card business annually. At one point, Hamid was so convinced that the deal was going to go through that he had Asprey's, jewelry purveyor by appointment to the Queen of England, send a $5,000 gold-plated commemorative pistol to Hussein Kamel as a memento of the occasion. But the deal, like so many others, came apart under the treads of the tanks that rumbled over the Kuwaiti border on August 2, 1990. Had it gone through, American motorists would have supported the Iraqi superweapons program with every gallon of gas they bought at a Fina station. A congressional staffer who investigated the deal dreamed up a snappy slogan for the abortive enterprise: "Put a tyrant in your tank."

Drogoul, meanwhile, was churning out letters of credit for MIMI. One was for a $3 million water purification plant, to be built by Rossmark van Wijk of the Netherlands, and which U.S. intelligence believed was needed for the enrichment of uranium. Another was for a $100 million steel pipe plant to be constructed by Endeco-Barazuol of Italy. Still another was for Thomson CSF electronic components valued at $7 million. Thomson CSF was already deeply involved in MIMI's operation, having built a giant electronics plant that U.N. inspectors later found was involved in nuclear weapons development. In all, Drogoul would issue an astonishing 2,500 letters for the Iraqis before he was arrested.

At the end of July 1989, three months after the Baghdad arms show, a lawyer representing two employees of BNL-Atlanta told the U.S. Attorney in Atlanta that illegal activities at the bank were a potential threat to the world monetary market. The employees, Mela Maggi and Jean Ivey, later turned state's evidence in return for immunity from prosecution.

At 4:50 on the afternoon of August 4, the receptionist at BNL-Atlanta's small, tastefully appointed Peachtree Street office heard the buzzer and, assuming a business deal was in the offing, opened the branch's door. Instead, she confronted several FBI and Federal Reserve agents, who pushed their way into the suite, herded employees into a conference room for four hours of grilling, and began collecting records. Less than an hour later, other agents were knocking at von Wedel's door. They got right to the point: "Do you know anything about a 'gray book'?"

Drogoul, who was vacationing in Paris with his father, got the news that night from von Wedel. Panicked, he immediately called his Iraqi cohorts, including al-Habobi and Ali, who told him to meet them in London. After conferring with Baghdad, the Arabs spent several hours with Drogoul, and finally told him to return to the United States. BNL-Atlanta's vice president and manager returned to New York on August 7 and then proceeded to Atlanta, where Umberto D'Addosio, BNL-Rome's general vice-president, fired him on the spot. After his arrest, he told federal investigators that neither BNL's New York office nor headquarters in Rome knew about his massive deception. Following an exhaustive investigation, he and nine accomplices (including al-Habobi, but not von Wedel, who also turned state's evidence) were slapped with a 347-count indictment that variously charged them with mail and wire fraud, making false statements, fraud against the Commodity Credit Corporation, interstate transportation of stolen money, forgery, and, in Drogoul's case alone, tax evasion.

By the fall of 1993, the BNL case was coming to a conclusion that left many unsatisfied. In late August, the judge in the case sentenced five of Drogoul's underlings to probation, after they had pleaded guilty to charges that they had defrauded BNL. Only Von Wedel received an additional sentence, being ordered to serve six months in home detention. Drogoul, who had pleaded guilty in 1992, had succeeded in having the plea rescinded, claiming that he had been a scapegoat for a broader conspiracy that included the Bush administration and the bank's Rome office. In September 1993, Drogoul again pleaded guilty to three indictments—one for wire fraud and two for making false statements.

**V**irtually every Western nation that sold weapons and weapon technology to Iraq in return for BNL-initiated and other money knew early-on that work was proceeding on nuclear weapons. Documents declassified after the war in the Gulf show that by 1989 American, British, German, and Italian intelligence organizations were well aware of what Jafar Jafar and his colleagues were doing.* But for a variety of reasons, the heart of

---

*SISMI, the Italian intelligence service, possessed a lengthy list of firms doing business with Iraq which were connected to the BNL operation. They included Consen, Matrix-Churchill, Gildemeister, Al Arabi, FIAT, SNIA Techint, APV Chemical, Euromac, XYZ Option, TDG and TEG, Thyssen, and Kintex. ("BNL Affair: Atlanta Branch," an undated confidential memorandum generated by SISMI.)

which was monetary, their governments chose not to enforce their own laws.

MI 6 (British intelligence) had excellent reason to know what the Iraqis were up to for the very good reason that for several years it had a spy in Matrix-Churchill: Paul Henderson, its chief executive. Henderson enjoyed the best of two worlds. He simultaneously acted the patriot by giving MI 6 information about his Iraqi masters' plans while making a good living sending them millions of dollars worth of machine tools, much of it going to the very nuclear weapons program upon which he spied.

When U.N. inspectors visited Taji in April and May 1992, they found thirty-nine Matrix-Churchill machine tools. Almost all of them were suspected of having had uses related to the nuclear program. At least six were essential to it. The British decided not to interfere in the operation, however, for at least two reasons: they didn't want their country to lose the Iraqi money, and they wanted to keep their spy in place. William Waldegrave, the Minister of State, dismissed Matrix-Churchill's procurement effort as strictly benign and showed contempt for what he considered to be unnecessary meddling. "Screwdrivers are also required to make hydrogen bombs," he told J. R. Young, a Foreign Office analyst. Young had few doubts about Matrix-Churchill's role in the Iraqi superweapon program, but he nevertheless wanted to keep the firm in business to protect the British "intelligence access to Habobi's network. We have a clear interest in maintaining the source in the hope of obtaining incriminating evidence that we can use to persuade our partners to act collectively to counter Iraqi nuclear procurement efforts."

In other words, continuing to collect intelligence on Iraq's atomic bomb had an even higher priority than preventing it from being built. That being the case—in the surreal world on the other side of Young's looking glass—there was a positive side to Saddam Hussein's possession of nuclear weapons: it would just go to show how good MI 6's intelligence was.

The Americans were as confused and naive about the Iraqi procurement system as the British were avaricious and myopic. In October 1989, Bush signed National Security Directive 26, which maintained that he would cooperate with Saddam in an effort to coax him back into the community of nations. Within a month, the kid gloves approach was already causing trouble for export officials, particularly for the Subgroup on Nuclear Export Controls. SNEC is supposed to coordinate nuclear export policy between the Departments of State, Defense, and Energy and the CIA. Without a recommendation from SNEC, Commerce was unlikely to approve any nuclear export. On November 8, nine such applications came in, all of them having to do with sensitive material to be sold to Iraq. Twelve days later, a CIA briefer described Iraq's nuclear weapons program, including activities at Taji, in some detail for SNEC.

The group had to weigh its President's proexport policy against the intelligence agency's explicit warning about those exports' end use. SNEC's members were so upset about the situation that on November 21, they expressed the misgivings in a secret memorandum to their superiors. "SNEC policy for some years has been not to approve exports for Iraq's nuclear program, except for very insignificant items for clearly benign purposes, such as nuclear medicine," the memo said. "However, at the same time, U.S. policy as confirmed in NSD 26 has been to improve relations with Iraq, including trade, which means that exports of non-sensitive commodities to 'clean' end-users in Iraq should be encouraged," the memo said. The officials pointed out that among the factors "complicating" their job was "a presumption by the intelligence community and others that the Iraqi government is interested in acquiring a nuclear explosive capability."

The members of SNEC, mindful that they served at the pleasure of the President within the Executive Branch, ended up approving eight of the licenses. The VAX and other computers, machine tools, and workstations later found by IAEA inspectors to be part of the dedicated nuclear weapons effort were among the items SNEC approved under pressure from the White House.

And there was more. The same month that Bush signed NSD 26—two months after the BNL scandal broke and even as Italians were ridiculing his administration and calling the episode "Iraqgate"—Secretary of State James A. Baker telephoned the Secretary of Agriculture to push for increased agricultural credits for Iraq. "We want to get this important program back on track," Baker told Clayton Yeutter. In November, while SNEC was wrestling with the nine license applications, Agriculture was persuaded by the White House to raise CCC-guaranteed loans to Iraq from $400 million to $1 billion. "Our ability to influence Iraqi behavior in areas from Lebanon to the Middle East peace process to missile proliferation is enhanced by expanded trade," State's dour Lawrence S. Eagleburger wrote to Treasury in defense of the go-easy plan. It was precisely the same policy that Bush had crafted for China despite that nation's record on human rights abuse and flagrant weapons proliferation.

Meanwhile, nagging questions lingered over possible White House meddling in the U.S. Attorney's investigation of Drogoul and getting the CIA to withhold relevant intelligence on the matter. The motive, according to conspiracy theorists, was that the Bush administration and BNL-Rome had known what Drogoul was up to and had quietly sanctioned it as yet another way of helping Saddam Hussein to reform.

"It defied logic to believe that one man down here in a little branch bank in Atlanta could orchestrate $5 billion in loans," said Judge Marvin H. Shoob of the U.S. District Court in Atlanta. Shoob, who believed that the U.S. Attorney had not conducted a thorough investigation, made the remark after spending a year and a half presiding over the BNL case.

But Frederick B. Lacey, a special prosecutor appointed by Attorney General William P. Barr, disagreed. After an intense six-week investigation of his own, he came away convinced that BNL-Rome had no knowledge of Drogoul's crime. This was based in part on Drogoul's own frequent assertions that he acted without his superiors' approval. In addition, Lacey concluded, "The sheer magnitude of the fraud is consistent with the USAO's [U.S. Attorney's Office] theory that Drogoul lacked authority for the loans. The sums were so enormous (and the terms to BNL so unfavorable)," Lacey reasoned, "that it is doubtful that any prudent bank would have willingly and deliberately exposed itself to so much risk." Finally, Lacey cited evidence that Rome lacked adequate capability to monitor its own worldwide loan transactions while Drogoul was engaging in "undeniable acts of concealment."

Judge Shoob never changed his mind on whether there was a larger conspiracy. When the Clinton administration Justice Department told him at the sentencing of certain defendants that Judge Lacey had also concluded the bank was victimized by Drogoul and the other employees, Shoob interrupted: "If Judge Lacey had investigated the Teapot Dome scandal, he would have awarded medals rather than jail terms."

Whatever the truth, the undeniable U.S. fawning over Iraq had so emboldened Saddam Hussein that by the following April he threatened to burn half of Israel if it attacked him. Only then did Bush begin to put the brakes on U.S. aid. Worse, he had come to believe by then that the West would go on humoring him, or at least look the other way, if he annexed Kuwait.

•  •  •

On August 22, 1991, A. Q. Khan, the father of Pakistan's nuclear weapons program, addressed a reception given in his honor by the Karachi Chamber of Commerce and Industry. Dr. Khan was a metallurgist by training. But it had taken a great deal more than a doctorate in metallurgy to provide Pakistan with the atomic bomb. It had taken a sound knowledge of atomic physics, engineering, and management. It had taken a long stint in the Netherlands, where he had filched the secret formula for reprocessing uranium until it was bomb-grade from right under the noses of his trusting Dutch hosts. It had taken a degree of patriotism that only one adjective could adequately describe: fanatical. It had taken monumental self-absorption and egotism. And it had taken money—real money.

Khan assured his audience that the work he had begun for his beloved country would continue because he had groomed a team of scientists at Kahuta, where the uranium was enriched to bomb-grade. Kahuta was also Dr. Khan's roost—a laboratory that specialized in nuclear weapons research and bred the scientists and technicians to whom the master referred.

The speech was vintage Khan. Kahuta, as everyone in the audience knew, was much more than a nuclear facility to the Edward Teller of Pakistan. Like Teller's Lawrence Livermore Laboratory, Kahuta was the womb in which the means of national deliverance—the fearsome weapons that assured Pakistan's survival in a threatening world—would grow. Accordingly, A. Q. Khan assured the businessmen before him that day that nothing would stop what went on at Kahuta: not his own death by natural causes or otherwise, and not what he called "conspiracies against Pakistan."

He ended his presentation by announcing that an institute for science and technology was being established at Swabi to provide advanced training for Pakistanis specializing in metallurgy, mechanical engineering, physics, mathematics, electronics, and computer sciences. That news was interesting in itself. But there were two details about the proposed facility that were at least as interesting. First, the institute was not going to be named after A. Q. Khan, but after another Khan: Ghulam Ishaq Khan. Second, half of the institution's $50 million cost was going to be donated by a bank.

Ghulam Ishaq Khan had been finance minister during the most critical phase of Pakistan's nuclear weapons development program and had therefore kept the nation's purse strings wide open for the top-secret project. That post had led him to the presidency. Naming the institute after Ishaq Khan was like naming the Los Alamos National Laboratory

after Henry Morgenthau, who was Franklin D. Roosevelt's Secretary of
the Treasury while the atomic bomb was being developed there. The bank
was BCCI: Pakistan's own, eventually scandalized Bank of Credit &
Commerce International.

Pakistan's atomic bomb and missile programs and BCCI were like
a philharmonic and its patrons. In this case, a single patron was providing
half of the orchestra's financing. In a newspaper interview as far back as
1984, A. Q. Khan went out of his way to show particular appreciation to
then President Zia ul-Haq and Ishaq Khan for the crucial role they played
at Kahuta. "I would say that this work would never have been done without
the patronage and encouragement" of the two men, Khan told a journalist.
"They encouraged us at every step and gave us all facilities."

And they did even more than that. They gave the nuclear researchers
a free hand to experiment as they wished and to procure as much of the
fabulously expensive equipment as they needed, from computers to special
steel. So whatever success he and his apprentices and colleagues had,
Khan added, "we owe to the President and Finance Minister. Without
their help, guidance and sympathy, the completion of this difficult and
important task would have been altogether impossible."

BCCI was started in 1972 by a Pakistani named Agha Hasan Abedi. Its
ostensible purpose was to be Islam's first world-class bank: a challenger
to Citibank, the Bank of America, Lloyds, Barclays, Crédit Lyonnais,
Deutsche Bundesbank, and other international heavyweights. But BCCI
was an institution apart: a full-service bank in the darkest sense of the
term. Whatever side Abedi and his managers showed the West—it appeared to be eminently respectable and as conservative as its counterparts
elsewhere—BCCI had two distinctions that were unique in its business:
it was avowedly Islamic and it had no scruples whatsoever. There would,
in fact, be no Islamic bomb had it not been for the Islamic bank.

From its inception, BCCI unabashedly acted as a secret worldwide
cash transmission network for thousands of dirty deals involving arms and
arms technology transfers, drug trafficking, and influence peddling of
every kind. Some of the deals were legal—the brokering of Italian and
North Korean battle tanks and artillery pieces for Abu Dhabi, for example—but very many were not. BCCI helped Manuel Noriega, Ferdinand
Marcos, and Saddam Hussein loot their own treasuries and launder what
was stolen. It financed the Colombian drug lords and engaged in other

shady enterprises with Daniel Ortega, Peruvian President Alan Garcia, Nicaraguan Contra leader Adolfo Calero, and Adnan Khashoggi, the millionaire Arab arms dealer. BCCI officers acted as the middlemen who channeled funds from Saudi Arabia to the Nicaraguan Contras during the Reagan administration's Irangate years and as bagmen for both the CIA and British intelligence.

"Bank" is a misnomer. BCCI was a murky multinational empire with more than 400 tentacles—branches and subsidiaries—in 70 countries. It was spawned in Karachi, had its major office in Luxembourg, where it was incorporated, and had important branches in England, Switzerland, Canada, Hong Kong, the United States, Brazil, Abu Dhabi, and Grand Cayman, the largest of the Cayman Islands. Not coincidentally, Luxembourg, Switzerland, and Grand Cayman are notoriously lax in monitoring banking transactions. And Pakistan, being the country that gave BCCI to the world, benefitted from its gratitude and was therefore unswervingly supportive of all of its dark undertakings.

The bank's fingerprints were all over Pakistan's bomb, as well as others', since its modus operandi made it ideal for such undertakings. In fact, BCCI was more reminiscent of Ian Fleming's SPECTRE, the Special Executive Committee for Terror, Revenge, and Extortion, than Chase Manhattan.* The idea was to create a financial institution so vast, intricate, and camouflaged that its labyrinthine transactions could not be tracked. BCCI's structure was therefore made into a maze of shell companies, offshore banks, and obscure subsidiaries. Its unique accounting system used longhand notations written in Urdu on old-fashioned ledgers. This, in addition to the extensive use of unsupervised accounts in Luxembourg, Grand Cayman, and elsewhere, as well as scores of other devious procedures, made BCCI impossible to regulate. That being the case, the bank was free to loot its worldwide deposits, making certain that there was always enough money on hand to pay some customers on demand.

BCCI was therefore a $20 billion multinational cartel, complete with a diplomatic corps and a 1,500-member clandestine secret service. It was, in effect, a financial suzerainty. The secret service, known as the

---

*At least once, however, BCCI acted more like Fleming's Q Branch, the part of the British secret service that invented James Bond's portable helicopter, trick attache case, and other high-tech hardware. One customer, the terrorist Abu Nidal, ordered six armor-plated Mercedes sedans complete with concealed grenade and rocket launchers. The order was canceled when the prospective buyer decided that the rocket launchers were too obvious, even from a distance. ("BCCI's Arms Transactions for Arab Terrorist Revealed," *The Los Angeles Times*, September 30, 1991.)

"Black Network," was part global intelligence operation and part enforcement squad. It contained the elite of the organization's dirty dealers. It was headquartered in Karachi and named by those who worked for it. The network originally specialized in paying bribes, heading off investigations, intimidating authorities and employees, enforcing particularly sleazy deals, and collecting intelligence. Given the amount of money it had to work with to seduce heads of state and lesser politicians and soldiers, the last chore was relatively easy. BCCI's relationship with several presidents, premiers, and potentates, as well as with the CIA and the National Security Council (it maintained accounts for the former and channeled money to the Nicaraguan rebels for the latter), made it particularly well positioned to collect useful information and ward off political probing.

Sometime in the early 1980s, when Iraq and Iran were slugging it out with vast arsenals that were in constant need of replenishment, the Black Network branched out into weapons transfers. According to some accounts, it also regularly resorted to physical intimidation and even to murder.

"Look," said one arms dealer, "these people work hand in hand with the drug cartels; they can have anybody killed. I personally know one fellow who got crossed up with BCCI, and he is a cripple now. A bunch of thugs beat him nearly to death, and he knows who ordered it and why. He's not about to talk." Neither is at least one former BCCI employee who was suspected of being unreliable. After the bank learned that he was trying to quietly liquidate his assets and sell his house, his brother was murdered and his wife was gang-raped. The man finally fled to the United States and has been in hiding ever since.

The arms connection permeated the bank. Several of its major stockholders were men whose fortunes had been built by arms deals. Shayk Kamal Adham, a wheeler-dealer and former head of Saudi intelligence, owned 2.94 percent of the bank's stock. Abdul Rauf Khalil, another Saudi, who was a major supplier of computers and illegal technology transfers to the Iraqi military, owned 3.08 percent. Ali Muhammad Shorafa of Abu Dhabi, who made fat commissions from supplying U.S. military equipment to Egypt, also had a cut. These men and others not only controlled the bank, but were beneficiaries of nearly $500 million in loans that were never paid back.

But because Abedi and most of the bank's middle managers were Pakistani, it had a special relationship with Islamabad. Not surprisingly,

Abedi was a friend of Gen. Zia ul-Haq, one of A. Q. Khan's two patron saints. Told that Abedi had a heart attack and was rushed to the hospital, Zia left a dinner table and guests to be with him. The other saint—the finance minister whose name went on the institute to which BCCI donated $25 million—was unquestionably also a friend and no doubt a close ally as well.

By the early 1980s, BCCI was therefore the obvious choice to help acquire nuclear weapons for a consortium of three nations that badly wanted them: Argentina, Libya, and Pakistan. Many of the "black holes" in BCCI's accounts—credit lines involving billions of dollars that couldn't be accounted for and probably never will be—went to finance a series of attempts to buy nuclear components for Colonel Qaddafi, the three successive iron-fisted juntas led by Generals Viola, Galtieri, and Bignone in Argentina, and Zia ul-Haq at home. An investigative report by *The Guardian* in England during the summer of 1991 alleged that for more than a decade before it was shut down, BCCI moved money and gold around the world to bankroll the atomic sweepstakes.

Besides paying for nuclear-related hardware, BCCI arranged air freight, shipping, and insurance for the equipment and provided operating funds for the consortium's spies and agents. It even paid for top legal counsel when the spies and agents were caught. In 1983, Dr. A. Q. Khan was convicted in absentia in the Netherlands for stealing plans for a uranium enrichment factory (which became Kahuta). He was defended by S. M. Zhfar, a former Pakistani justice minister, who was paid by BCCI. The following year, three Pakistani nationals were indicted in Houston for trying to illegally buy and export the kind of high-speed switches that are used to implode nuclear bombs. The source of their funding was, again, BCCI. The bank also underwrote the $1 million purchase of high-speed computers for Khan's institute in 1982 and 1983.

Two BCCI branches played a key role in financing a plot to smuggle 50,000 pounds of maraging steel C-350, a very high strength metal used in centrifuges, and bomb-enhancing beryllium out of the United States in 1987. The operation was run by a retired Pakistani brigadier general named Inam ul-Haq, who was identified by U.S. and German intelligence organizations as a key buyer for the Pakistan Atomic Energy Commission. Ul-Haq's relationship with BCCI seems to have been intimate, although he denies any connection with it. Ul-Haq's Lahore-based company, Multinational, was literally next door to the International Travel Corporation, a BCCI affiliate. The corporation's specialty, according to Western intelligence officials, was to make elaborate and clandestine "travel arrangements" for the material needed by A. Q. Khan for his big bomb.

Ul-Haq in turn contracted with a Canadian businessman, Arshad Z. Pervez, to buy the steel for $333,450 and then secretly ship it from the United States to Karachi by steamer. Canadian police who searched Pervez's home found documents that showed involvement by BCCI's London and Toronto branches. One document was an irrevocable letter of credit made out specifically for the transaction and issued by the Habib European Bank, Ltd., to BCCI's Toronto branch. Habib, which was located on the Isle of Man between Ireland and England, was tightly held by Pakistanis with close ties to their government and access to the ruling families of the oil sheikdoms, particularly in Abu Dhabi. It was also directly linked to the BCCI branches in London and Toronto. Furthermore, its senior vice-president was A. Q. Khan's brother.

Ul-Haq was arrested on July 11, 1991, at the Frankfurt International Airport during a passport check. The United States immediately filed for his extradition. Asked about reports linking ul-Haq with BCCI, the Pakistani general's German lawyer professed astonishment. "That's the first time I heard something like that about my client," said Hans-Wolfgang Euler. Pervez was convicted of trying to bribe an undercover U.S. Customs agent posing as a Department of Commerce licensing officer.*

Agha Hasan Abedi and his associates understood from the outset that arms transfers and superweapon technology could be immensely profitable for at least two reasons. First, conventional weapons—tanks, fighter planes, howitzers, and so forth—are made in serial production and are therefore extremely profitable. Second, unconventional arms technology— for atomic bombs, chemical and biological weapons, and long-range missiles—is at the same time technically forbidden and politically taboo. This makes it inherently scarce and therefore colossally expensive and profitable. And, as is usual in the arms business, greed chases profit unabashedly. With reputable banks for the most part unwilling to get

---

*Carpenter Technology, a Reading, Pennsylvania, import-export firm, notified U.S. Customs that Pervez's AP Enterprises wanted to buy the steel. Frank Rovello, an undercover agent, played the part of the corrupt Commerce Department official in the sting operation. (NBC News interview with Rovello on March 3, 1992, and letter from Pervez to Carpenter dated February 20, 1987.)

involved in such deals, BCCI became a natural funding source. It was willing to make deals that few, if any, others would touch.

The moral standard by which BCCI peddled weapons and weapons technology was to treat them as though they were party favors or bon-bons placed on hotel room pillows.

"BCCI is functioning as the owners' representative for Pakistan's nuclear bomb project," Senator John Glenn said at one point in a letter to the Justice Department. But while the Pakistan superweapon procurement system was the beneficiary of much of BCCI's largesse, it was by no means alone. The shadowy bank was an equal opportunity lender in a growing market.

The war between Iran and Iraq offered a particularly good investment opportunity. BCCI was the middleman in the sale of South African G-5 artillery pieces and Brazilian Astros-2 rocket launchers to Iraq, both of which could be used for long-range chemical attacks. It also was involved in the sale to Saddam Hussein of French Roland antiaircraft missiles. But BCCI's evenhandedness was evidenced by the fact that the Kuwaitis who rolled back into their country behind the fleeing Iraqis on February 28, 1991, did so on BCCI-financed M-84 tanks, which were Yugoslav knockoffs of Soviet models.

But BCCI also provided a more personal service to the Iraqi dictator. He used secret accounts in BCCI branches in Luxembourg, Switzerland, and Grand Cayman to stash away money for himself and his Tikriti relatives against the day when he, like so many of his kind, would be forced to flee Iraq for his life. U.S. and U.N. investigators are still searching for that "bunker" fund.

BCCI's impartiality even extended to India, provided Pakistan— through the bank—could make some money. During the 1980s, for example, a Pakistani multimillionaire weapons purveyor named Asaf Ali enjoyed a substantial business relationship with Marcel Dassault, the French fighter and missile maker. He was therefore able to broker forty-nine top-of-the-line Mirage-2000 fighter-bombers, which would make excellent nuclear bombers, to India in 1991.

He then supplied his own country by arranging to divert twenty-four of the aircraft from delivery to Peru, which had not yet paid for them. And why did Peru want new Mirages? To replace those it had sold to Iraq, also with BCCI funding, during the war with Iran. A Peruvian legislator was to tell a congressional committee in August 1991 that the deal was greased in typical BCCI fashion. He suggested that his nation's then president, Alan Garcia, and some officials of the Peruvian government had a cozy relationship with BCCI. It was so cozy that someone in the Peruvian bank placed $250 million in government reserves into numbered accounts at the BCCI branch in Panama.

It is therefore no coincidence that, with a single exception, Mexico, the Third World's leading debtors are all nations that are now pursuing, or have pursued, nuclear weapons and ballistic missiles. Brazil, to take one example, led the dubious achievement list in 1990 with a total foreign debt of $111.3 billion (in 1990 dollars). More than $550 million will have been spent on the nuclear submarines that are supposed to project Brazilian power "at distant waters of the South Atlantic," according to the head of the Brazilian Navy, while $2 billion more is going into diesel subs. Another chunk—more than $300 million—has been spent on the VLS satellite launcher, a rocket that could double as a long-range ballistic missile. Hundreds of millions more went into a furtive fifteen-year attempt to produce an atomic bomb: $300 million for an enrichment pilot plant, for example, and another $150 million for mineral exploration. The bomb project drew a great deal of technology from the country's civilian nuclear program and was to use homemade enriched uranium, which is produced in prodigious quantity at Ipero, the site of the Navy Technological Center's 1,000 centrifuges. Meanwhile, Argentina's debt load was $64.7 billion; India's $62.5 billion; Iraq's an estimated $65 billion; Indonesia's $53.1 billion; Egypt's $48.8 billion; Israel's $32 billion; and Pakistan's $18.5 billion.

The real price of procuring superweapons is incalculable. But it is written in wretchedly poor, disease-filled ghettos the world over. In 1981, while Ishaq Khan was bestowing tax-free status on the "BCCI Foundation" and its rapacious officials were returning the favor by financing his bomb, their country staggered under a debt that reduced the life of most of its citizens to bare subsistence. Uncounted millions of the citizens the weapons were allegedly being developed to protect were dying of undiagnosed and untreated diseases. They were dying or were condemned to exist in misery, not by the hated Indians, but by their own would-be protectors. That is the final irony of the coming of superweapons to the Third World. The means of salvation and of destruction are the same.

# 5

# DOCTORS
# OF DEATH

The new arms merchants, an abidingly cynical lot, believe that warfare is as much a part of human nature as love and the maternal instinct. Thinking creatures inevitably have differences of opinion, the reasoning goes, and that usually leads to conflict. Warfare is large-scale conflict in its ultimate form: violence and mass killing. So it has always been, the purveyor of superweapon technology sighs with resignation, and so it will always be. War is a fact of society as death is a fact of life. And besides, it's profitable.

Three tenets follow from the belief in the inevitability of war. First, the moral responsibility for war rests with those who conduct it, not with their suppliers, any more than those who manufacture chemicals are responsible for dumping them in the ocean. Carlos Cardoen, the Chilean arms dealer who eschews that job description in favor of "manufacturer," has said, "I think that the moral issue of the use of armaments is within the people that use them, and not within the people that manufacture them. I feel very comfortable doing what I am doing."

Second, the immutable law of the marketplace dictates that those who want to buy superweapon technology will inevitably find those who want to sell it irrespective of the scruples of any one person. This not only shifts the moral responsibility for dangerous technology transfers from the individual to society as a whole, but implies that winning such contracts in the face of certain competition is laudable.

Third, since national independence ultimately rests on military strength, and since losing wars can be catastrophic, customers will spend lavishly to buy the most ferocious new machines and will use them unhesitatingly if necessary. Indeed, the record of despotic regimes in Africa, the Middle East, and elsewhere proves that weapons purchases can have a higher priority than importing food, even for a starving citizenry. This means there are colossal profits to be made by supplying weapons or the wherewithal to make them.

In addition, the rationale for selling weapons and weapons technology—particularly plans and components for superweapons—is usually cloaked by deliberate self-delusion. Purveyors of such dual-use items as high-speed computers, machine tools, rocket engines, and chemicals that can be combined to constitute pesticides, for example, usually have a very good idea of how their products are going to be used. They, therefore, salve their consciences by looking away rather than forcing themselves to come to grips with the likely results of their dealings. Looking away attained the level of an art in West Germany during the 1980s, but the Germans were far from alone.

Ready-to-use dreadnoughts and Big Berthas, the superweapons of Sir Basil Zaharoff's time, have given way to some-assembly-required poison gas factories and the intricate and diverse components of intercontinental ballistic missiles and nuclear weapons.* Sir Basil's successors, therefore, sell a vast array of wares that are often unrecognizable for what they are: maraging steel for centrifuge cylinders; heavy water to moderate fission in "research" reactors; machine tools to fabricate precision nuclear warhead parts; vats for mixing poison gas or rocket fuel (or rubber for ordinary tires); krytrons that start the conventional explosive process in nuclear weapons; HMX and RDX, the conventional explosives themselves; rocket engines suitable for ballistic missiles; and plans and

---

*Zaharoff, the notorious "Merchant of Death," was an international financier and munitions maker. He was chairman and director of the Vickers-Armstrong munitions firm in England and was reputed to have holdings in the Krupp and Skoda companies as well. Sir Basil, who was decorated by the French and knighted by George V for providing weapons to the Allies in World War I, was a man of intrigue. Rumor had it that he used his political connections with European statesmen to foment wars because they were good for business.

machinery for thousands of otherwise innocuous items which, when fitted together, become superweapons.

Not only is most superweapon technology dual-use, so are many finished weapons themselves. A little imagination can turn a conventional weapon into a great deal more than that; into more than even its manufacturer intended. A military helicopter that can be converted from a gunship to a pesticide sprayer can become a poison gas–carrying superweapon in the hands of a Saddam Hussein. HMX and RDX, the conventional explosives used in many kinds of bombs, are also the preferred detonators for nuclear warheads. A conventional 2,000-pound bomb can be turned into a pseudosuperweapon by replacing its standard explosive with the fuel-air variety. This is not new. Reconnaissance planes in World War I were made lethal by adding machine guns and those carrying machine guns were made still more lethal by hanging bombs on them. What has changed, however, is the killing capacity of the modified weapons.

While some of the men who deal in superweapon technology are driven by patriotism, most are studiously apolitical. They readily sell anything to the highest bidder, regardless of the cause. What makes most of them different from run-of-the-mill arms merchants is the diversity of their wares, the scope of their operations, the breadth of their vision, and the fact that they carry their assets in their head, not in inventories that can be scrapped or blown up. They roam the globe in a relentless drive to create, build, and ship weapons and superweapons outside the control of the superpowers.

The two characters who inhabit this chapter were far removed from the squalid offices, back rooms, and dreary life-styles of many of their lackluster counterparts. Their expertise was rooted in Ph.D.s in science and engineering from excellent universities. Carlos Cardoen's sumptuous skyscraper office in Santiago, Chile, was conspicuously decorated with plaques from Saddam Hussein, each thanking him for helping Iraq defeat Iran in a particular battle. There was a photograph of him shaking hands with the uniformed sociopath (the suave Chilean in a silk suit; the beret-topped Iraqi sporting a holstered automatic). There were expensive rugs of Middle Eastern origin, tasteful art, and Tiffany-class baubles. Cardoen's vision was to be the complete, upscale arms supplier, providing a weapons supermarket in which his customers could shop for everything from standard cluster bombs to killer helicopters, superweapon components, and their own turnkey armament factories.

Gerald Vincent Bull, the prodigy of ballistics, worked out of a small office in Brussels to provide standard artillery weapons of splendid quality to a number of nations, and one supergun—the intended forerunner of others having intercontinental range—to Iraq. Bull was made a U.S. citizen by act of Congress and had security clearances most generals would envy. He evolved into an international management and engineering consultant who sold several countries, most notably Iraq, a wide array of weapons and related services.

Like Cardoen, Bull also dabbled in superweapon technology, the "line" of the future. These were not men secreted behind some nation's inner curtain, the hidden masterminds conjuring a Third World nation's superweapon program. Most such nations have their own J. Robert Oppenheimers and, in any case, would never dare trust their ultimate means of survival to a foreigner. Rather, Cardoen and Bull were to advanced weaponry what "Dr." Henry Hill was to band instruments in *The Music Man*. They were full-service salesmen and consultants who were called in to fill the often large gaps in Third World nations' scientific or technical bases: to provide designs, equipment, new technology, and training for a cadre of local specialists. Both were paid well and worked for a variety of customers. Cardoen's claim two weeks before Iraqi armor rolled into Kuwait that he "never, ever, ever worked for an enemy of the United States" was ludicrous on the face of it. And while Bull maintained that he never trafficked in weapons with the Soviet Union, he did deal with those who did. "They were willing to supply Iraq with everything it needed," one knowledgeable congressional investigator said of the pair.

Nor were they alone. Hugo Piva, another technomercenary (and graduate of the California Institute of Technology), was in Baghdad with several engineers on the day Iraq rolled into Kuwait. They were working on Iraqi missile programs and on a projected Brazilian-Iraqi spy satellite. And behind Cardoen, Bull, and Piva there is a small but dedicated legion of lesser freelance scientists, engineers, and computer specialists who are training Third World nations in the new black arts.

Carlos Cardoen reached his zenith on March 28, 1990, when Industrias Cardoen showed its deadliest wares in a small rented hangar on the west side of El Bosque air base's main runway, outside Santiago. The occasion was the opening of Fidae 90, the biannual weapons exposition that Chile hosts for the world, and Cardoen was in top form as generals, journalists, and war buffs from Europe, Asia, and North America strolled through, perusing the merchandise. He enthusiastically glad-handed anyone who wanted to make serious inquiries about his product line, as well as an occasional priest and the newly elected President of Chile.

At that moment Carlos Cardoen was worth $400 million and feeling very expansive about it. He was dressed in a conservative black-and-white herringbone sports jacket, a white shirt, black pants, and a subdued tie with a dark floral pattern. (Two years earlier, in a scene straight out of a James Bond film, the effervescent entrepreneur, then forty-six, swooped out of the sky over El Bosque in a Learjet from Miami, emerging in a white suit, holding a bottle of champagne in one hand and a glass in the other.) But that very day in the spring of 1990, unknown to Cardoen, British and American customs agents were conducting the nuclear trigger sting operation at London's Heathrow Airport that would sound the first public alarm about Iraq's relentless search for nuclear weapons. It would also set in motion a chain of events that wrecked most of Carlos Cardoen's meticulously constructed empire.

Carlos Cardoen Cornejo, the son of a well-off Chilean family of Belgian descent and holder of a Ph.D. in metallurgy from the University of Utah, had a grand design that was shaped by true panache. He loathed the idea of selling arms the way street vendors peddle dirty postcards. His military wares—the 206 L-111 "Cardoen Bell" attack helicopter, small commando hovercraft, cluster and high-explosive bombs, and a variety of armored personnel carriers and self-propelled artillery pieces— were featured in a professional eighteen-minute sales film, for example, that was photographed in color and set to a modern jazz score. It drove home the company's motto—"imagination and talent in ideas"—with carefully timed shots of designers and draftsmen working at advanced computers within state-of-the-art facilities. Cardoen's flair and his ultra-modern business practices led some Chilean associates to call him "more American than Chilean." Uniquely, for Latin America, the observation was meant as an accolade.

But Cardoen's carpeted hangar held more than a continuously running videotape and signs advertising his products. Several samples were on display. There was a Mowag-Cardoen "Piranha" multipurpose land-water armored vehicle designed in Switzerland and built by Cardoen under license to perform antitank, antiaircraft, or antipersonnel functions, as well as to serve as a troop carrier, communications and command head-quarters, or ambulance (this particular model sported a rotating cannon, not stretchers). Piranhas proved to be extremely effective against the students who occasionally rioted against Chile's brutal dictatorship.

There was a 155-millimeter self-propelled howitzer called the G-6. It was largely designed by Gerald Bull, licensed by Armscor, South Africa's national weapons company, and assembled by Cardoen. Bull, in fact, had been assassinated only six days earlier, leaving Cardoen to wonder aloud that day whether he would meet the same fate. The G-6 was nicknamed the "Kalahari Ferrari" because it could travel at fifty miles an hour on flat terrain, stop in a short distance, be quickly set up, and fire a round up to twenty-five miles. The impressive range (a sure sign of Bull's involvement) was especially important for buyers who wanted to fire poison gas at an enemy while keeping their own troops safely away from the deadly cloud. This was an advantage with which Iraq, Cardoen's chief customer, was very well acquainted.

Following an agreement with Magnus Malan, the South African defense minister who spent two weeks in Chile in March 1989, Cardoen began assembling G-6s and an unpropelled relative called the G-5 in northern Chile. They went for about $1 million each. "Assembling" was the key word, however. Although both partners claimed that Cardoen was merely using South African technology to build the guns from scratch, parts for them were actually made for Armscor in South Africa, Canada, Germany, and elsewhere and then shipped to Chile for assembly. Pretoria had roughly similar agreements with Israel and Taiwan for other weapons systems. In this way, the South Africans were able to circumvent the United Nations arms embargo placed on them because of their policy of apartheid.

A bloated Honduran colonel looked hungrily at the G-6, but he was helped by a lowly technician. Cardoen's salesmen paid no attention to him. The Honduran had no money and everybody knew it. Iraq and the United Arab Emirates had the money and they were the ones being courted for the sale of the G-6. Iraq had, in fact, already bought sizable quantities of the G-5 from South Africa and wanted an upgraded version of the G-6. It did this while assuring the world that it was abiding by the terms of the embargo against the racist South Africans.

Embargoes delight arms merchants because the scarcities they create drive up the price of the items. When the United States and other traditional arms suppliers place embargoes on weapons they have previously exported, they create inducements for Third World nations to collaborate among themselves and for entrepreneurs like Cardoen, who already have the material or components, to manufacture and resell them elsewhere at sharply higher profit.

This is especially true of superweapon components. Although it is highly unlikely that any of the original nuclear weapons states would be so cynical, desperate, or stupid as to transfer finished superweapons to the Third World, they are far less scrupulous about transferring the components, the technology, or the exotic materials that go into such weapons. Seeing these cracks between the boards, the new technomercenaries work to establish niches within the cracks, getting the material and then rerouting it to their customers for considerable financial gain. Virtually every weapons embargo, therefore, lines the pockets of some individual or institution, be it Carlos Cardoen, an Israeli government-owned arms manufacturer, or the Chinese People's Liberation Army.

Industrias Cardoen, in fact, was born as a direct result of U.S. congressional displeasure with Augusto Pinochet's oppressive ultraright dictatorship, specifically with the killing of Orlando Letellier. The former Chilean foreign minister, an outspoken expatriate who hated Pinochet, was assassinated in 1978 when his car was blown up on Massachusetts Avenue in Washington. The brazen attack, coupled with human rights violations and other unseemly political developments in Chile, prompted Congress to slap an arms embargo on the Pinochet regime.* At the same time, however, Chile and Argentina were posturing menacingly at each other in one of those periodic temperamental machismo confrontations traditionally used by South American generals to show civilians why their armies are necessary. Pinochet therefore reacted to the arms embargo by determining that his country needed to be as self-sufficient as possible in weapons production.

Cardoen couldn't have agreed more. "Chile didn't have any arms to defend itself with because of the U.S. embargo. Don't forget also that our militaries had been, up to that time, based on supplies coming only from the United States," he recalled in an interview more than a decade later. "I was at that time part of the solution of the problem, which ended in the development of a new industry, a new effort, new engineering, new technologies, new capacities that we didn't even realize at the time we were able to put together." And that capability, Carlos Cardoen emphasized, was a direct result of Yankee foreign policy. "I think the circumstances that were produced in Chile by the embargo imposed by Senator [Edward] Kennedy certainly helped developing industries and efforts which we didn't know before we were able to cope with or [were] capable

*More than 2,000 Chileans were either killed or "disappeared" during Pinochet's seventeen-year rule. ("Pinochet Is 'My Franco,' Chile's Chief Says, Going His Own Way (Carefully)," *The New York Times*, April 30, 1992.)

of developing." (Kennedy was at the time chairman of the Senate Judiciary Committee, which initiated the embargo.)

Carlos Cardoen was therefore effectively made in America. He would be unmade and remade there, too. During the next ten years, he would evolve from being an unknown, but prosperous, manufacturer of mining explosives to Saddam Hussein's favorite weapons provider. As a direct consequence of his intimate relationship with both Pinochet and the Iraqi leader, he would also be reputed to be the second wealthiest man in Chile.

At its zenith, Cardoen's empire would be a conglomeration of companies—Explosivos Cardoen, S.A., Cardoen International Marketing, S.A., Swissco Management Group and Development Company, Inc., Defense Systems, Inc., Financial Management International, Inc., and others—that operated a diversified business whose chief product during the Iran-Iraq war was weapons and related technology. As the war wound down, the savvy Chilean would diversify into fruit exports, lumber production, a hotel, and even a little banking. But there was always really only one company—Industrias Cardoen—and a group of corporate alter egos. Industrias Cardoen's world headquarters was in the Santiago skyscraper. There were branch offices on five continents, plus weapons factories in Pontecho, Chile, and at a site outside Athens. Elviemek, the Greek facility—the only private arms plant in that country—produced high-altitude explosives and a variety of small arms and grenades. It was also used to reroute South African weapons to Iraq.

Cardoen got his first big break when the Chilean government advanced him $4.9 million for the armored vehicles. Before long, the product line expanded to include a variety of land mines, hand grenades, demolition charges, and cluster bombs. The last, in particular, were a source of pride and considerable revenue for Cardoen. At one point he controlled about half of the world cluster bomb market. Asked whether he had sold $100 million worth of the weapons to Iraq, Cardoen answered with unconcealed exuberance, "Hah! More than that." More indeed. Saddam Hussein bought more than $200 million worth of the deadly weapons, which release explosive bomblets over a wide area.*

---

*Depending on the quantity ordered, Cardoen's 500-pound cluster bombs cost Iraq between $5,980 and $7,230 apiece. The French equivalent cost $26,000. The difference in cost was directly related to the far cheaper labor in Chile, where workers were paid as little as $3 a day. (*Nasser Beydoun v. Carlos Cardoen, Augusto Giangrande et al.*, Eleventh Judicial Circuit, Dade County, Florida, September 4, 1990, pp. 7, 9, 10, and "Chilean Arms Maker No Stranger to Controversy," *Financial Times*, September 6, 1990.)

More important, Baghdad bought several turnkey plants from Cardoen, including one that produced fuses for chemical weapons. The last, named April 7, employed 120 Chilean technicians who worked side-by-side with Iraqis on precision machinery supplied by Matrix-Churchill. While making a point of saying that all of his activities were aboveboard, Cardoen also occasionally took steps to camouflage some of them. He told the U.S. ambassador to Chile, for example, that a plant complex he was building in Iraq was intended to turn mountains of brass artillery casings into bathroom fixtures. Safa al-Habobi's Technology Development Group in London had already bought a controlling interest in the British firm specifically to guarantee that superweapon tools would be available in Iraq when needed. Cardoen, who was ostensibly Matrix-Churchill's biggest customer, was buying precision machine tools from it and outfitting the plant in Iraq with them. As British investigators subsequently learned, Cardoen was in effect fronting for the Ministry of Industry and Military Industrialization by importing the equipment from Matrix-Churchill and installing it in Iraq. The April 7 and other factories would give Saddam Hussein the indigenous weapons producing and exporting capability he sought. Equally important, such factories gave Iraq invaluable experience running its own arms industry. Many were blown up during Desert Storm.

A lot of the material for the factories came from two old weapons plants in the United States, one of them capable of producing bombs. Cardoen convinced U.S. Customs that the equipment was scrap metal. The audacious scheme worked, with the result that valuable presses for making bomb casings were sent to Chile and then on to Iraq.

Cardoen also tried to buy a complete American turnkey steel pipe mill for Saddam Hussein in 1988. The plant, located in Aliquippa, Pennsylvania, was owned by LTV and would have required extensive, and costly, refitting. In the end the deal, which was one of several with potential backing by BNL-Atlanta, did not go through. Carlos Cardoen had evolved into much more than an arms technology provider to Saddam Hussein by the last year of the war with Iran.

"We are presently in the effort of improving technologies and offering to the world, hopefully, products that are cheaper, that are easier to use, and that have more than anything a multirole capacity," Cardoen said. "Third World countries cannot afford to have products that are highly specialized in defense," he continued.

For example, he saw a niche in the attack helicopter sector: a "vacuum in the gunship spectrum that needs to be filled to provide countries that are on a lean defense budget." The idea was to sell them helicopters that were cheaper than the U.S. AH-64 Apache and its French and Soviet rivals, the AS-332 Puma and the MI-24, which NATO called the "Hind." The answer was a modified version of the U.S. Bell Helicopter Textron 206L Long Ranger civilian model, which Cardoen turned into a one-man attack chopper that could carry a belly-mounted machine gun and 1,200 pounds of rockets. It was called the Cardoen Bell 206L-III Attack Helicopter.

Cardoen insisted that the 206L-III would be exported to fill several potential requirements, including "transport, for helping the civilian population, for helping during big national tragedies—say, a flood or an earthquake—or for emergency purposes." The picture was appealing, but disingenuous. Given the 206L-III's relatively small size and one-man crew, flood and earthquake victims would have to all but hang from its skids with their bare hands in order to be rescued. The machine's intended role was as an attack helicopter, a fact that Industrias Cardoen itself noted on a sales brochure. Cardoen, himself, made a point of telling Bell that Iraq would be an ideal customer for such a chopper. His other story— that the machine was ideal for spraying pesticides—would be turned into sick humor by Saddam, himself, who used the pesticide cover story to develop poison gas.

If Cardoen was lining up customers for his attack helicopter, and he almost certainly was, he was keeping their identities to himself. One who apparently found out, however, died with the secret. On the morning of March 31, as the Fidae 90 arms show was wearing down, a maid at the Hotel Carrera in Santiago walked into room 1406 and found a British journalist named Jonathan Moyle hanging in the closet with one of his own shirts tied tightly around his neck. Moyle, a twenty-eight-year-old former RAF helicopter pilot, was the editor of *Defence Helicopter World* and was in town for the arms show.

Chilean judges eventually termed the death a murder (overruling the Santiago police, who had called it a suicide despite a great deal of obvious evidence to the contrary) and issued a warrant for a pair of Iraqi suspects. Although the crime has never been solved, evidence suggests that Moyle was hit because he discovered that Industrias Cardoen and Iraq had concluded a deal involving the 206L-IIIs. Before he left for Chile, Moyle told at least one colleague that he believed fifty unarmed versions of the helicopter were being sold by Cardoen to Iraq. The deal would have been worth about $100 million. The other journalist recalled that Moyle had been excited because it sounded like "a good story."

Meanwhile, Industrias Cardoen cluster bombs were going to Ethiopia. In 1989 Pinochet authorized Cardoen to ship up to 1,680 of them in monthly installments to Mengistu Haile Mariam, the country's Marxist dictator. Cardoen's bombs were then used so savagely against civilians in the rebel-held northern part of the country that human rights groups complained to the Ethiopian government.

Pinochet was replaced by the civilian democratic government of Patricio Aylwin in March 1990. The new president, embarrassed by the sales, ordered the shipments suspended by the following September. (He would have been even more embarrassed, however, had it been made public that Cardoen contributed about $1 million to his campaign chest.) In any case, some observers in Santiago believed that Cardoen himself wanted to end the cluster bomb business with Ethiopia. This was because Iraq, his biggest customer, was one of several Arab nations that were unhappy that the insurgents that Ethiopia's Marxist regime was bombing were Muslims. Furthermore, Baghdad suspected (correctly) that Israel was partly financing the cluster bomb shipments to prevent the rebels from creating a new Islamic state, Eritrea, along the Red Sea.

Whatever the casualties among those who were caught in cluster bomb explosions, there were probably few or none among the ground crews who loaded them onto the attack aircraft or among the pilots who actually dropped them. That is because Industrias Cardoen had used its "imagination and talent" to devise a "safer and simpler" bomb that did not require costly and dangerous explosives to release the bomblets in the most effective pattern. Cardoen's engineers instead came up with a way to use the force of the air rushing past the plane to disperse the deadly bomblets. The invention was so clever that the Ministry of Industry and Military Industrialization was soon turning out safer and simpler cluster bombs by the hundreds. Washington even awarded it a patent (No. 4,744,301 on May 17, 1988).

By 1990, Cardoen had expanded his operation to include super-weapons elements, and the evidence suggests that there was no moral or qualitative ceiling on the endeavor. In fact, a report by the Pentagon's Defense Technology Security Administration a month before the start of the war in the Gulf detailed the ways in which Cardoen had helped Saddam's superweapon programs. It noted that Cardoen either had built or was planning to build factories for fuses, including three types used for chemical weapons, plus others to manufacture HMX and RDX, and still others to produce cluster bombs, fuel-air explosives, midget submarines, and sea mines. Furthermore, the report continued, "Cardoen's Baghdad office may have acquired precursor chemicals for Iraq's CW [chemical weapons] program" and "Cardoen has attempted to acquire nuclear technology on behalf of Iraq." The nuclear technology was said to include machine tools and high-quality oscilloscopes for measuring shock waves during detonation.

Carlos Cardoen's success, a model for the industry, came from sharply focusing his attributes into a self-sustaining operation that could circumvent the traditional arms and weapons technology system by selling almost state-of-the-art weapons at bargain prices, factories at high prices, and superweapon technology at incredible prices. And having become an expert at all this, he then managed to sell himself as a consultant and confidant to a megalomaniac whose hunger for weapons was fast outstripping his ability to pay for them. The debonair engineer's attributes included luck (the U.S. arms embargo on Chile), an affable disposition that even made him enjoy talking to reporters, audacity, and a flair for making adroit business moves and cultivating important people.

Cardoen built his empire on profits he made from selling murderous weapons, chiefly to Saddam Hussein, with the quiet but implicit encouragement of both the Reagan and Bush White Houses. Both administrations quietly and cynically armed both sides for the usual reason: to keep the region "balanced" (read stable). Iran's weapons were supplied for the release of hostages in Lebanon, while Iraq's were sold for use against Iran. Later, after Desert Storm, the Bush administration indicted Cardoen for alleged violation of U.S. export laws. In reality, the Department of Justice went after him for pure political expediency—for the crime of helping to arm a friend who had turned foe. Cardoen, caught in a political wind shift, came down with terminal legal pneumonia.

About $120 million of the Iraqi money—which had been in the account of a Cardoen-owned Panamanian company, Zodiac Enterprises, with an account in the Royal Bank of Canada's Geneva branch—was invested in enterprises at seven locations in the Miami, Ft. Lauderdale, and Orlando areas. One of them, virtually around the corner from Cardoen's own home, was run by Augusto Giangrandi, another Chilean and Cardoen's closest associate. It was called the Swissco Management Group and its job was to act as the U.S. shipping agent for Cardoen's arms.

Cardoen's American residence, a small mansion at 16141 Aberdeen Way, Miami Lakes, Florida, was bought from then Governor, later Senator, and Mrs. Robert Graham in January 1986 for $575,000, when cluster bomb money was pouring in from Iraq. The Florida Democrat's family was the original owner of the Miami Lakes district and is part of the dynasty that owns *The Washington Post*. Graham himself became a member of the Senate Banking, Housing, and Urban Affairs Committee, which oversees export controls. There is no evidence that Cardoen paid more for the house than its market value. The purchase, however, provided an excellent opportunity for the weapons dealer to try to cross an important political threshold as well as a habitable one.

On August 7, Anthony Mijares, Jr., president of the company that managed Cardoen's Florida holdings, held a fund-raising party for Graham that netted $50,000. Cardoen, Mijares, Giangrandi, and their lawyer, Abbey Kaplan, collectively contributed $12,000 to Graham's campaign. Cardoen duly became a member of the Friends of Bob Graham and was eventually invited to attend a private inaugural reception for the senator in Washington. Graham maintains that he never did anything for Cardoen. But, the wily Chilean must have known from long experience that such a relationship conceivably could bear fruit in unexpected ways.

Cardoen even managed to hire a retired U.S. Air Force lieutenant colonel and a former U.S. ambassador to Chile to open doors for him in Washington. The airman was Lieutenant Colonel Carlos Ricardson. The ambassador, James Theberge, went to work heading the Swissco Management Group's Washington office in the autumn of 1985, shortly after he left the diplomatic service, and remained there until February 1987. He died in January 1988. As is common inside the Beltway, Theberge's apparent job was to use his contacts to facilitate Cardoen's business activities by opening the right doors. What is less common, however, is the fact that Theberge also worked for the CIA for the last year to year and a half of his life, serving as a member of its Senior Review Panel. The panel's job is to advise the director of Central Intelligence. This means that Theberge either worked for Cardoen and the CIA simultaneously or he went directly from one to the other. Either way, it strains credulity to believe that he failed to inform the agency about Cardoen's nefarious enterprises.

Cardoen's undoing began with the nuclear trigger sting in a London suburb, which sounded the first loud alarm about Saddam Hussein's nuclear weapons ambition, and progressed relentlessly through the Persian Gulf War. The triggers (krytrons) were shipped from California and were en route to Iraq when they were intercepted because of a tip by the suspicious manufacturer to the U.S. Customs Service. The sting and events leading to it were photographed and aired by NBC News.* Cardoen was not involved in the krytron operation, but the resulting publicity drew sudden attention to Iraq's burgeoning arms buildup and he got caught in it.

By the time the smoke had cleared, the provider of weapons to the coalition's vanquished foe was himself in the U.S. government's sights. On March 27, 1991, a year after the Fidae show, Customs agents seized Cardoen's modified $4.7 million Bell 206L-III in a hangar at the Dallas airport. The action came after a five-month investigation, a Customs Service press release noted before denouncing Cardoen as "a documented international arms merchant believed responsible for providing arms and technology to the government of Iraq." By March 1992, five grand juries had heard evidence relating to his activities and his Florida property had been impounded.

Cardoen, fully understanding that Washington's previously blind eye suddenly had a menacing glare to it, went to the U.S. embassy in Santiago on July 16 to complain. He categorically denied a story on ABC News's "Nightline" earlier that month asserting that he and former CIA Deputy Director Gates had met in the 1980s to coordinate the transfer of arms and technology to Iraq. The CIA denied it, too.

More to the point, Cardoen angrily denounced the U.S. government's actions as a "witch hunt" and asserted that he had kept Washington informed of his dealings with Saddam Hussein through the embassy's military attaches and had invited them to visit his factory and other facilities. Claiming that the United States had at one time "applauded" his sales to Iraq, Cardoen handed Ambassador Charles Gillespie a letter protesting the new turn of events. It quickly whittled the situation, as seen by Carlos Cardoen, to a fine point: "It is a public fact that I have revealed all the pertinent circumstances at my disposal in order to expose the truth and defend myself from what I consider a true persecution that, in short, was intended to deflect the potential responsibilities that other

*Details of the operation are in Chapter 6.

interests had in the military fortification of Iraq, and to limit the creation and development of a defense industry in a Third World country such as Chile."

Cardoen was less than honest about his prior revelations and about limiting the Third World defense industry. The reference to deflecting potential responsibilities for the arming of Iraq, however, was on the mark. Those responsibilities, as he had good reason to know, rested in large measure in the White House.

By early 1993, Carlos Cardoen looked as though he would have the last laugh, however. On the night of February 12, after business hours, the CIA faxed a simple but top secret message to the U.S. Customs Service in Miami. It contained an oh-so-sorry message for the agents who had labored for two grueling years, working twelve-hour days, to nail down Cardoen's far-flung network. The message confirmed what Carlos Cardoen had repeatedly told news reporters and others for years: his activities as a weapons and technology procurer for Iraq had been done with the CIA's approval.

The news was devastating for the Customs agents. They had spent months going through records seized at Cardoen's Miami office, as well as other companies in New Jersey, Pennsylvania, and Oregon. They had cultivated sources in Chile and Germany. They had even traveled to Jamaica to meet with the arms dealer. The case they had developed was so good that they and the U.S. Attorney's office planned to announce Cardoen's indictment on February 18. But it all evaporated, at least temporarily, with receipt of the fax. What especially galled the Customs agents was that they had asked the CIA four times if there was anything in the files showing U.S. government approval of his activities, and four times the answer had come back negative. One agent closed the case with two words: "This stinks."

Cardoen was more realistic. In February 1993 he was asked by a Santiago reporter whether he was concerned about his "bad" image. "Well, I am not Julio Iglesias," he answered, referring to the popular Latin American singer. "The public image is not my business. If I were worried about my public image, I would have been a movie actor or a singer." In May 1993, Cardoen was indicted for smuggling chemical fuse technology right up to the day the Gulf War began. A trial, however, is unlikely. Cardoen has said he won't return to Miami.

•   •   •

Gerald Vincent Bull at first wanted to become a physician. But that changed abruptly when he discovered that the sight of blood made him sick. He therefore decided instead to make a career in the bloodless world of physics. Bull's particular interest (and the subject of his doctorate at the University of Toronto) was aerophysics: the science of how objects behave when they move through the atmosphere. And within that specialty he showed a particular aptitude—some would say a genius—for ballistics: for how projectiles behave when they fly. Very large guns and the objects that are fired from them soon became Gerald Bull's passion. He evolved into an artillery nut. And that suited him perfectly. Because of the distances involved in firing their big guns, artillerymen never see the blood of those they kill.

Some say that Bull's tempestuous personality emerged at a very early age. He was born in 1928 in North Bay, Ontario, the ninth of ten children. His father was an English-speaking lawyer who grieved for his French-Canadian wife after she died and then proceeded to remarry and abandon all of his offspring. Gerald, then three, was separated from all but two of his siblings and farmed out to a kindly uncle and a nasty, reproachful aunt. "In a sense he was an orphan, and that affected his personality a lot," said Charles H. Murphy, a close friend and colleague of Bull's and himself a respected U.S. Army ballistics expert. "He wanted people to like him, and he felt hurt and rejection keenly."

Bull's abandonment by his father and treatment at the hands of a cruel foster mother seem to have had two profound effects on him. He always felt financially vulnerable and therefore developed into a forceful purveyor of his own talent, an inventor whose penchant for selling his services to the highest bidder would eventually bubble to the surface in a fury. That impulse grew in proportion to his professional frustration. What is more, rejection, betrayal, and the perception of persecution turned an already stormy soul into an abidingly vengeful one. Both of those deep currents—a hunger for money and a passion for revenge—very nearly got Saddam Hussein the mother of all guns. They also got Jerry Bull killed.

His early motivation was pure enough. In 1951, after receiving his doctorate at the University of Toronto's Institute of Aeronautics—at twenty-two, he became the youngest Ph.D. in Canada—he took a job as a research scientist at the Canadian Armament and Research Development Establishment (CARDE) near Valcartier in Quebec. He soon became fascinated by all forms of military artillery and, specifically, by how they could be adapted to purposes other than war.

Bull left CARDE at the end of the 1950s to become a professor of engineering at McGill University in Montreal. Secreted deep within McGill's massive dark-gray granite walls, nestling protectively against Mont Royal, the prodigy of ballistics conceived plans for a gun that would challenge the sky itself. By the mid-1960s, he had become fixated on the huge Paris Gun that the Germans used in World War I to bombard the French capital from a distance of some seventy-five miles. Bull even went so far as to track down a cache of papers belonging to Dr. Fritz Rausen-berger, who had designed the gun for Krupp. The young Canadian then constructed a computer model of Rausenberger's complex formulas. He was delighted to see that he and his predecessor of fifty years ago had thought along startlingly similar lines.* He also knew a little about the V-3, a 500-foot-long monster cannon that Germany had almost completed at Pas de Calais in 1944 before it was destroyed by Allied bombardment. The weapon, a lineal descendant of the Paris Gun, was intended to pound the south of England.

The idea that sparked the work that was to preoccupy Bull for the rest of his life was that there was no theoretical limit to a gun's range. Given the right design, he concluded, gigantic guns—larger, refined versions of the Paris Gun and the V-3—would be able to propel satellites and other objects into orbit far more cheaply than multistage rockets.

Bull used his years of research at Valcartier to start the High Altitude Research Program, or HARP, at McGill during the 1959–60 academic year. HARP's purpose was to develop large-caliber guns that could fire small research vehicles into the upper atmosphere and space. This was to be done initially by using small rocket-propelled missiles that carried instruments in their noses. The missiles would have fins that folded inside special sleeves called sabots while they were inside the gun. Once a missile roared out of the gun's muzzle, the sabot would fall away, allowing

---

*Bull was so captivated by the Paris Gun that he and Murphy wrote a 246-page book titled *Paris Kanonen—the Paris Guns (Wilhelmgeschutze) and Project HARP* (Hereford and Bonn: Verlag E.S. Mittler & Sohn GmbH, 1988). The book not only detailed the World War I weapon, but went on to show in considerable technical detail how Bull would improve on it. By that time, the Chinese had become so interested in Bull's artillery work that they had given him a sizable contract to produce weapons for them. *Paris Kanonen* was even translated into Chinese, no doubt with considerable difficulty. (James Adams, *Bull's Eye*, New York: Times Books, 1992, p. 215.)

the fins to pop up for stabilization.* In an effort to persuade McGill to fund the project, Bull even decided to call the missiles Martlets, after the three red heraldic birds that appear on the university's coat of arms. He dreamed that specially instrumented, three-stage Martlets with pop-out fins, fired from hundreds of giant guns around the world, would one day give both rich and poor nations a reliable, accurate, and relatively inexpensive way to fling small satellites into Earth orbit. The cheapest sounding rockets cost about $75,000 each, not counting support services; the cost of a Martlet launch was estimated at only about $5,000.

The HARP program was at first funded solely by the university itself. But then the military became interested in the project. Soon, McGill's financial aid was supplanted by the U.S. Army's Ballistic Research Laboratories at the Aberdeen Proving Ground in Maryland. Then the Canadian Department of Defense Production bought into the project. In common with Wernher von Braun, Robert Goddard, and others whose dreams of sending rockets to space outstripped their pocketbooks, Bull accepted military money for his avowedly peaceful program.† There was enough funding by January 1962 so that HARP was able to test several surplus guns that were donated by the U.S. Navy. The largest of these had a bore that was more than sixteen inches. The tests were conducted at HARP's own site on Barbados. By November, rocket-projectiles fired from the guns were reaching altitudes of 215,000 feet, in the process proving that their electronic innards could withstand severe acceleration.

HARP proved to be largely successful. More than 500 shots were fired downrange into the Caribbean and South Atlantic during the rest of

---

*Bull was an early champion of powered projectiles fired from guns, but others followed with their own innovations. One feasible idea called for ramjet propulsion. (A. Hertzberg, A. P. Bruckner, and D. W. Bogdanoff, "Ram Accelerator: A New Chemical Method for Accelerating Projectiles to Ultrahigh Velocities," *AIAA Journal*, February 1988, pp. 195–203.) It is worth noting that this article, among thousands of others in fields from missile guidance to nuclear weapons detonation, is available to anyone who cares to subscribe to the journal or visit a library. No developing nation is at present likely to want to develop ramjet-accelerated projectiles for use in "tubes" (to use the authors' word). Yet such scientific papers can make valuable additions to specialized libraries in countries such as Brazil, China, India, Israel, and Japan.
†There was at least one military application that Bull considered for his big HARP gun: ballistic missile defense. He theorized that the guns could fire projectiles high into the atmosphere and then explode into dense clouds of shrapnel in the path of incoming ICBM warheads, destroying them. Tests, however, showed that hundreds of projectiles would have to be fired simultaneously in order to work, so the idea was abandoned. It was nonetheless the precursor of the so-called Brilliant Pebbles defense proposed more than twenty years later by proponents of the Star Wars program. One former associate of Bull's who was familiar with the idea called it "Dumb Pebbles." (James Adams, *Bull's Eye*, New York: Times Books, 1992, pp. 76–77.)

the 1960s, some of them actually arcing into space; the record was 112 miles. Soon, almost half of the world's database on upper atmospheric conditions was derived from HARP. The program proved that firing rocket-powered missiles with pop-up fins from guns was entirely feasible. HARP also developed and conducted the first serious studies on transmitting data from gun-fired objects. Both would eventually find military applications in such missiles as the U.S. Army's Copperhead. Bull's undeviating objective, however, was to use very big guns to get Canada into the space race.

"Bull was part of a great sea change in human affairs," one writer explained. "Bull was a heretic. He was an individualist in a technical era that, for all the blathering about the importance of freedom to the inventive and developmental process, demands a collectivist mind-set. His mind belonged in a past when individual, mercurial thought and disturbed brilliance still had a place in Western affairs."

HARP's end and Bull's reembrace of military artillery came abruptly in June 1967 when the U.S. and Canadian militaries stopped funding the program. The ostensible reason was that both Canada and the United States believed that space research was better conducted by rockets than by a logistically unwieldy collection of colossal cannons. But part of the reason had to do with Bull's abrasiveness and contempt for all bureaucrats and many colleagues. His funders and others did not relish being called "morons" and "the lowest form of life on Earth."

Whatever the reason, the demise of HARP, which Bull fathered and lovingly nurtured and by which he was nurtured in return, infuriated him. Dependence on fickle grant-givers had made HARP vulnerable, however noble its purpose, and had finally killed it. So Bull resolved that he would never again be in such a position. He decided to go into the only business in which his expertise in big guns would be rewarded with fat profits: the arms business.

The Space Research Corporation (SRC), as he called his new company, was established at HARP's 20,000-acre test site at Highwater, just on the Quebec side of the border with Vermont. (SRC bought all of HARP's assets, including the Barbados test facility, at salvage prices.)

It won $9 million in contracts from the U.S. military to produce excellent nuclear-capable artillery shells that had a range of twenty-five miles. The shells were so good that Israel bought 50,000 of them in 1973 for use in its American-made field artillery. Bull's contribution to Israel's—and America's—security was in turn rewarded. Senator Barry

Goldwater sponsored a bill that not only retroactively made him a U.S. citizen of ten years' standing, but gave him a high-level nuclear security clearance.

But Gerald Bull had much more on his mind than producing high-performance artillery shells. He had visions of magnificent field artillery pieces, the best in the world. And he could not get the gun with the meter-wide bore—the super Paris Gun—out of his head. Such a gun would be able to lob a 400-pound multistage Martlet 2,500 miles. One carrying a 200-pound warhead would fly more than twice that distance. It would even be able to propel guided Martlets into polar orbit.

Bull's problem, however, was that the U.S. government ammunition contracts would not cover the research that was necessary to perfect such weapons. He therefore started Space Research Corporation International in Brussels in 1976 with the encouragement of Poudreries Réunies de Belgique, a Belgian munitions firm that bought in for 38 percent of the business.

The additional capital allowed Bull to develop what was by all odds the most formidable standard artillery piece in the world. It was a 155-millimeter towed howitzer whose extra-long barrel allowed it to fire shells weighing twice as much as ordinary shells over a distance of twenty-five miles with considerable accuracy. Other 155s had ranges of no more than eighteen miles. The seven-mile difference was more than esoteric. In addition to keeping one's own soldiers away from the poison gas they shot at the enemy, an attribute that both Cardoen and Saddam Hussein appreciated, they also allowed their users to pummel the enemy while staying safely out of range of the enemy's own artillery.* And that is precisely what the South African Army did with the weapon after it outbid others for licensing and production rights. The howitzer was so good that it almost replaced air cover. Bull called it the GC-45 ("GC" for gun caliber). South Africa, which sold it to Saddam, called it the G-5. Carlos Cardoen, who would assemble it for shipment elsewhere in the Middle East, called it the CC-45 ("CC" for Carlos Cardoen).

By 1976, South Africa was looking at a deteriorating military situation in Angola, where Soviet-backed leftist Angolan and Cuban troops were using 122-millimeter Katyusha rockets with devastating effect against

---

*The numbers apply equally well to missiles, which are an extended form of artillery. As previously noted, the Iraqis worked furiously to extend the range of their Scuds because Baghdad was much closer to the Iranian border than Teheran was to the Iraqi border. Until Al Abbas and Al Hussein were ready, Scuds fired from Iran could hit Baghdad while Scuds fired from the Iraqi side of the frontier fell far short of Teheran.

the National Front for the Liberation of Angola and the National Union for the Total Independence of Angola, both of which fought for an avowedly independent government. Pretoria was worried that if the former Portuguese colony became a bastion of leftists, the stage would be set for the southward march of liberation movements that would eventually end on its own territory. Accordingly, it determined to get GC-45s and the extended-range ammunition that went with them.

Washington's relationship with Pretoria at the time was ambivalent. Officially, the United States supported the U.N. arms embargo that had been placed on South Africa in 1963 because of apartheid. In fact, the CIA was covertly supporting South African operations in Angola in a program code-named Feature. It therefore quietly encouraged a flow of advanced weaponry to South Africa, some of it through Israel, a close but quiet ally, and some directly. The gun running was orchestrated by an arms-dealing, sometime CIA contact named John "Jack" Frost, Major John Clancy III of the Joint Chiefs of Staff, John Stockwell of the CIA, and others in an operation that foreshadowed Iran-Contra. Stockwell's job was to tell South Africa where to find the weapons it needed and to covertly facilitate the transfers.

Bull was therefore unofficially but enthusiastically encouraged, particularly by Frost, to sell his full line to Pretoria. At the same time, he was officially encouraged by the Department of State's Office of Munitions Control to sell only "unfinished" ammunition to South Africa: rounds that were not fused or loaded with explosives. At one point, when U.S. Customs officials tried to investigate Bull, the CIA refused to share information about him, virtually ending the probe. It was clear that a cabinet-level decision had been made to quietly help the South Africans hold off the Marxists and that Bull was part of the effort.

Accordingly, he agreed in 1976 to supply Pretoria with what it needed. During the next two years, SRC shipped 60,000 fully usable 155-millimeter extended-range rounds, at least four 155-millimeter guns (three of which were advanced G-5s), and the technology and expertise that allowed Armscor to produce the weapons and ammunition itself. It turned out that the G-5 was more than a gun—even a superb gun—to South Africa. It made the country one of the world's leading arms exporters within only ten years.

When news of the deal was made public in 1980, a disbelieving Gerald Bull was charged with and convicted of violating the U.N. arms embargo. The CIA, now under congressional scrutiny, abandoned him.

After pleading guilty, he spent six months in the Allenwood, Pennsylvania, Prison Camp, a federal minimum security prison. The only friend he made during that time was Bosko Radonojic, a Yugoslavian exile who had been jailed for commandeering a TWA airliner and using it to drop anti-Tito propaganda over Chicago. Radonojic would eventually steer his friend to arms contracts in Yugoslavia. He himself was indicted in 1992 for bribing a juror in the trial of the mobster John Gotti.

The prosecution of Gerald Bull fit a pattern that pervades U.S. involvement in weapons proliferation. The United States has consistently promoted the spread of weapons and related technology by individuals when doing so was considered necessary to advance a particular agenda. When the agenda was met or abandoned, however, expediency dictated that these individuals be disavowed and betrayed. Such was the case with Saddam Hussein, Carlos Cardoen, and Gerald Bull.

Bull's conviction and sentence, particularly ironic in view of his having been honored with U.S. citizenship only seven years earlier, filled him with wrath for the United States. He remained convinced for the rest of his life that he had been betrayed and scapegoated by the Carter administration out of misplaced ideology and sheer political expedience. Space Research Corporation of Quebec went bankrupt. The country of his birth had deserted him, and his adopted country had jailed him. Bull, detesting North America, moved to Brussels to head the SRC office there. He would not recross the Atlantic for two years and vehemently insisted until his death that he was owed a pardon.

While in prison, Bull received a letter from the Chinese government that led to a contract for his long-range artillery. Six months after his release Bull, now all but broke, went to Beijing with his wife, Noemie (or Mimi). There, he was treated with a degree of respect bordering on veneration by officials who had read the translated version of *Paris Kanonen*. He was also offered a $25 million contract for chemical or nuclear-capable guns that could reach farther than their Soviet counterparts, which the Chinese faced along their common border. A $500,000 advance saved Space Research Corporation International from bankruptcy, which had been the fate of the Quebec operation.

SRC soon had offices or subsidiaries in Austria, Greece, China, Yugoslavia, Spain, Switzerland, England, Lichtenstein, Canada, and the Channel Islands, besides its headquarters in Belgium.

The Chinese bought plans for a complete manufacturing plant for both guns and ammunition so they, too, could turn out enough weapons to export the surplus. They called their version the WA 021 and first displayed it at the Asian Defense Exhibition in Beijing in 1987. The Yugoslavs got Bull's unique method of modifying their obsolescent Soviet 130-millimeter M-46 guns to fire 155-millimeter rounds. The South Africans got the G-6 "Kalahari Ferrari" (or "Rhino") self-propelled howitzer, which owed its speed and ruggedness to the fact that Bull managed to mount the gun itself on an adapted commercial crane chassis. The turret ring of the gun that blasted Cuban mercenaries in Angola turned on the same large steel ball that supported the towering cranes laboring peacefully at Canadian construction sites.

But with the exception of the ill-fated monster gun for Iraq, the weapon idea that undoubtedly most piqued Gerald Bull's imagination came from the U.S. Navy. It was a 1,000-mile-range cannon, carried by a submarine, that would fire projectiles guided to their targets with extreme precision by NAVSTAR Global Positioning System navigation satellites. The conventionally armed missile would sprout wings after being shot out of the gun, skip over the atmosphere, and then plunge onto its target with pinpoint accuracy. The Office of Naval Research (ONR) thought of it as a weapon that could be used to attack Moscow from the North Sea. The Pentagon's Defense Advanced Research Projects Agency thought of it as a "silo-buster": as a weapon that could destroy ICBMs in their underground launch tubes. Other possible uses considered by the Department of Defense included attacks on tank columns and airfields, and so-called decapitating strikes aimed at killing the Soviet leaders in their command bunkers and control centers. The weapons would be so accurate, thanks to satellite-assisted navigation, that there would be no need to arm them with nuclear warheads.

Despite the grudge he still held against the United States, Bull readily accepted an invitation to give a paper on "HARP and Subsequent Gun Technology" at the International Cannon and Orbiter Technology Workshop in Arlington, Virginia, in early November 1985. "Wild horses could not keep him away," according to Fred Quelle of ONR, who ran the meeting. After recounting the history of HARP and big guns, Bull went on to discuss his plan for a gun-launched orbiter, or GLO, that would meet the Navy's specifications. Afterward, he was asked to send a formal proposal to the Pentagon, which he soon did. The prospect of working on such a weapon excited Bull, and so did the possibility that it would finally bring him a pardon. But the Pentagon soon lost interest in the idea, partly because attention had shifted to space-based electromagnetic rail guns that were on the drawing boards for the Star Wars program, and partly because of Bull's own checkered career. There were others, however, who would take the GLO and Bull's other gigantic guns far more seriously.

Bull's most notorious relationship, with Iraq, got off to a rocky start in 1981, when Sarkis Soghanalian flew him to Baghdad in the mistaken belief that he produced big guns in addition to designing them. Soghanalian, a corpulent character who looked as if he had stepped out of the pages of a Graham Greene story, was a Lebanese-born arms merchant of the old school. He worked out of an office at the Miami International Airport doing standard deals—notably with Iraq and, by his account, with the knowledge of the CIA—for tanks, armored personnel carriers, howitzers, and the like.* He claimed in 1990 to have sold $2 billion in arms to Saddam Hussein and that information about the sales "went straight to the White House." A nearby photograph, autographed "With best wishes, Ronald Reagan," lent credence to his claim. At any rate, the first deal between Bull and Saddam went nowhere.

Six years later, however, Bull and the Ministry of Industry and Military Industrialization were engaged in a variety of programs, the scope of which even Carlos Cardoen would have admired. However happy Bull's relationship with China, it was Iraq that held the most allure. Bull believed, erroneously, that Iraq was virtually floating on oil revenues in 1987 and 1988. He therefore entered into the last major deal of his life with Hussein Kamel. For Bull, who privately called the Iraqis bastards, the relationship not only allowed him to profit by providing a wide range of services, but made it possible for him to realize his old dream of building the supergun. The Iraqis, mindful that the 500 superb howitzers they bought from Voest-Alpine, Austria's state munitions company, and from Armscor had been conceived by Bull, wanted to avail themselves of whatever else he could provide.

One Iraqi weapon, the Al Majnoon, was a self-propelled 155-millimeter howitzer designed by Bull in Brussels, built with French and German components, assembled in Spain, and flown to Baghdad in a Soviet transport. Another, Al Fao (both guns were named after battles in the Iran-Iraq War), had a 210-millimeter bore, making it the largest field artillery piece in the world. It could fire four rounds a minute at a range of more than thirty-five miles. In a frenzy of activity beginning in 1987, Bull also worked to supply Iraq with a fuse plant—an installation later

*Cardoen's relationship with the CIA lends credibility to the statement.

completed by Cardoen—machine tools for its munitions industry, and engineering advice for the nation's missile program. As a precaution, Bull's son Michel, who was in business with his father, at one point visited the Department of State's Office of Munitions Control to detail SRC's help to Iraq. The company was not selling weapons to Saddam Hussein, Michel Bull was careful to explain, only engineering. Relations between Washington and Baghdad being as cordial as they were in 1988 and the years immediately following, OMC had no apparent objection. It was the South Africa story all over again.

What the Iraqis wanted beyond standard artillery were guns they could train on the entire Middle East and even beyond: guns that could reach Tel Aviv to counterbalance Israel's renowned air force, and guns that could be trained on Teheran. The attempt to get such weapons began in November 1987, when MIMI's Hussein Kamel told Bull in Baghdad that Iraq wanted any new artillery Bull could invent. The following May, Bull hired a British engineer named Christopher Cowley to help design two colossal cannons. One, named Baby Babylon, would be a horizontally used test model having a bore of 350 millimeters and a length of 171 feet. The other, Big Babylon, was to be Gerald Bull's dream satellite launcher. It would have a 510-foot-long barrel, a 1,000-millimeter bore (a gaping mouth nearly forty inches across), stand 350 feet high, and weigh 2,100 tons. A propellant charge more than twenty feet long would hurl a 1,320-pound projectile 435 miles. A three-stage, self-propelled missile like Martlet could theoretically be shot into orbit. The Iraqi supergun came from the very proposal, then gathering dust, that Bull had made to the Pentagon two years earlier: a proposal which the military itself had requested after the conference in Virginia. While its designer may have thought of Big Babylon as a satellite launcher, its purchasers had other ideas; they wanted it as an artillery weapon.

At the same time, Saddam Hussein also wanted a space capability, and here, too, Bull was only too willing to help. In 1988, he put together a "Preliminary Proposal for Satellite Launcher Using Clustered Sadam [sic] Rockets." In it, Bull suggested clustering the same rocket engines used in Scuds to hurl satellites into orbit. (Brazil's Hugo Piva was then working on the spy satellite for his Iraqi patron.) Bull suggested four clustered configurations of five, six, seven, or eight rockets. Each combination could have sent a one-ton payload either into orbit or into downtown Tel Aviv or Teheran. Saddam chose the most powerful cluster. On December 5, 1989, a ripple of apprehension went through Western intelligence agencies and other groups of analysts when Al Abid ("the Worshipper") was launched. The rocket matched in every detail the drawings Bull had submitted more than a year earlier. Although it was only a test of the first stage, lasting sixty-five seconds, it unnerved Israel, which had only sent up its first space launch vehicle in September 1988.

U.S. intelligence analysts soon concluded that Big Babylon, the monster cannon, was intended for use against Iran, and Al Abid, or its successor, was for an attack on Israel. Scuds had been used successfully against Iran, but they were relatively expensive and in short supply. No more than 200 of the missiles had been fired at Iran during the eight-year war, 135 of them at Teheran. Expense was a limiting factor.

If war broke out with Iran again—and some analysts believed that to be inevitable—Saddam planned a full-blown barrage attack against Iranian cities modeled after the World War I sieges. They could be pounded cheaply and continuously from a safe distance by superguns that were protected by antiaircraft installations and the Iraqi air force. Only this time, the ammunition would most likely consist of binary chemicals as well as high explosives. "This is what led them to Bull and the big gun," one intelligence analyst concluded. "The big gun could launch smaller, cheaper, and perhaps more accurate rockets . . . if it worked. The gun represents a far greater threat as a terror weapon than the missiles."

Big Babylon's range notwithstanding, its fixed position was a serious shortcoming. Its breeches were to be sunk in a concrete-filled pit more than 100 feet deep so that it would point in only one direction and have a single, permanent elevation. Steerable projectiles and varying amounts of propellant would offset the problem to some extent, but the area covered by the gun was nonetheless severely restricted. The Iraqis therefore also wanted superguns that could be trained on various targets the way normal guns could.

Bull responded by designing two other guns while he, his assistant Christopher Cowley, and SRC's other engineers, most of them British, were laying out Baby Babylon. The first had a 350-millimeter bore and a 100-foot-long barrel; the second had a 600-millimeter bore and a 200-foot-long barrel. Like the Babylons, both of the military guns would have barrels made in sections that could be welded together. The smaller of the two was to have a range of 280 miles; the larger, 267 miles. Both would therefore be capable of hitting targets throughout Israel, in most of Syria, and in much of Iran and Saudi Arabia with standard ordnance carrying conventional, chemical, or biological warheads. (Nuclear warheads were considered too heavy.) Single- or dual-stage Martlets would increase that range dramatically.

For his part, Cowley thought the Iraqi research facilities, particularly Sa'ad-16, which he visited in 1988 and 1989, were "absolutely brilliant." "I had never seen anything in Europe that compared with that particular research facility. I'd never seen any university in Europe, and specifically in England, have such superb equipment," he said, adding that the building in which he worked was "absolutely ideal." And also fabulously expensive to build, equip, and operate. "We were talking about billions of pounds, and every European country wanted their share of that take," Cowley concluded.

Whatever, if anything, the mullahs in Teheran thought about the supergun, the Israelis would have been deeply alarmed about the Al Abid test and what it portended. The concern became even greater when in early 1990—not long after the Al Abid launch—Bull returned to China to seek a third-stage rocket for Saddam. The Chinese refused, but the Israelis found out about the attempt anyway. Knowing that Israel would be vulnerable to Al Abid, the two huge military guns, and perhaps to Big Babylon as well, the Mossad threatened Bull with "harsh action" on a number of occasions after it learned he was working on all his weapons projects, which by the spring of 1990 included not only guns and the Al Abid, but a multiple launch rocket system capable of firing chemical warheads, and an antitactical missile system that would spray tiny pellets in the path of an Israeli Jericho or an Iranian Scud. He was a tempting target because, unlike large design teams, he was almost solely responsible for the superweapons. To stop him would therefore be to stop the weapons.

"Carrying all his knowledge with him and not cooperating with too many people definitely was a key strategic point; that if you take him out, you (the Iraqis) lose control of the entire system," General Avraham Bar-David, the former chief of Israeli artillery, explained. Bull told friends about the warnings, but he disregarded them.*

---

*The warnings could be subtle yet terrifying. Bull told a coworker that he had seen half of a rented film on his VCR one night when he was called to the telephone for a long conversation about Chinese artillery. Since he wanted to watch the second half the following night, he turned the machine off with the tape stopped where it was when the phone rang. When he returned home the following evening, he saw that the tape had been rewound and placed back in its box, which was then on a side table. Bull determined that neither the cleaning lady nor either of the other two people who were supposed to have keys to the apartment had entered it. He interpreted the event as having been designed to frighten him. It did. (William Lowther, *Arms and the Man*, Toronto: Doubleday Canada, Ltd., 1991, p. 3.)

Like MIMI itself, Bull spread his net wide to produce his guns. SRC developed close ties with firms in England, Switzerland, Spain, Belgium, the Netherlands, and Italy.*

Nearly a year after warnings by the managing director of the British steel manufacturer Walter Somers that he was suspicious about the "petroleum" pipes his company was making, and six months after another executive notified the British Ministry of Defense about a huge amount of propellant allegedly going to Jordan, the net dropped on Babylon and the military guns.† On April 10, 1990, British customs officers uncrated eight wooden cylinders marked for shipment to "Republic of Iraq, Ministry for Industry and Minerals, Petrochemical Project, Baghdad, Iraq." Each was twenty-five feet long and three feet wide and contained a smooth-bore barrel that had been made to fit into one of the other barrels. All of the crates were seized, prompting Iraq's Foreign Minister, Tariq Aziz, to angrily tell reporters in Mosul: "Even if we bought a box of chocolates from Britain, they would say Iraq will use it to produce an atom bomb." Ten days later, a truck carrying Forgemasters' 350-millimeter tubes was stopped in Greece heading south, while another carrying Somers' tubes was intercepted in Turkey. Still more hardware was captured the following month in raids in West Germany, Switzerland, and Italy.

In 1989, while the Ministry of Defense and British Intelligence slept despite growing indications of what Bull was up to, Baby Babylon and an SRC-built scale model of its big brother had actually made it to Iraq. The gun itself was set up at a secret site at Jabal Hamrayn, ninety miles north of Baghdad, and test-fired three times (the seals between the tubes blew apart under the pressure of the first firing).

There were other problems as well, as U.N. inspectors were to report in the summer of 1991 when they returned from their first visit to the Jabal Hamrayn test range. "Technical problems" had eventually caused the Iraqis to abandon the idea of firing rockets from the big gun and to go instead to simple shells. The inspectors saw, however, that there was a parking lot full of components for Bull's huge cannon. These included

---

*Several of the firms that worked on the guns either paid kickbacks to the Iraqis or agreed to do so. They included Walter Somers, Sheffield Forgemasters, and Società della Fuccini. (Alan George, "Codename: Babylon," *The Middle East*, June 1991, p. 15.)

†The executive was David James, who told a government board of inquiry in London in June 1993 that he felt a "considerable sense of disquiet" about the giant tubes and notified British intelligence accordingly. He added that he provided an agent known to him as "Mr. Z" with descriptions of the tubes, company records, and a letter of credit guaranteeing payment by Iraq. ("Briton Says He Foiled Supergun Parts Sale to Iraq," *The New York Times*, July 1, 1993.)

forty-four steel tubes for the barrel of the 1,000-millimeter gun, as well as heavy equipment for the 350-millimeter model. There were also four hydraulic shock absorbers, six steel tubes and a steel breech for the 350-millimeter gun, and tons of propellant for Big Babylon. And they found a nine-page list of firms and countries that had been involved in the project. The cache was proof of Saddam's commitment to the supergun program and the extent to which it had advanced when the Gulf War came. All of the material in the parking lot, plus the test gun itself, was missed by U.S. reconnaissance satellites. As a consequence, it all survived the war without a scratch and had to be destroyed by the U.N team afterward.

The tabletop model was displayed at the military exhibition in Baghdad between April 28 and May 2, 1989. It might well have been seen by two American bankers who happened to be there at the time, as well as by a Chilean arms manufacturer who had a nearby exhibit.


Gerald Bull did not live to see his model transformed into the real thing. As he was fumbling for the key to his sixth-floor apartment in the Brussels suburb of Uccle early on the evening of March 22, 1990, a professional killer stepped up behind him and fired five bullets into him with a 7.65-millimeter automatic equipped with a silencer. He was dead before he hit the floor, with two slugs in his head and three more in his back. About $20,000 in cash was found in his pocket when the police arrived. The money and Bull's other possessions were evidently left behind because his assassin wanted to make it clear that he had been executed for political reasons, not murdered for money. There was a lot of blood.

# MARKETING
# MAYHEM

—

# 6

# LOOTING
# THE STOREHOUSE OF
# KNOWLEDGE

**R**elations between Iraq and Israel in the late summer of 1989 were terrible. Saddam Hussein, with growing foreboding, watched the stream of Jews emigrating from the Soviet Union to settlements that spread on the West Bank and elsewhere. But he did not watch passively. Although he had made a point of ostensibly expelling the Palestinian terrorist Abu Nidal five years earlier in order to open diplomatic channels to Washington and facilitate his arms buildup, he continued to quietly help Abu Abbas's Palestine Liberation Front and other anti-Israeli groups. The 1985 hijacking of a TWA jet and then that of the *Achille Lauro* cruise ship by Arab terrorists were two dramatic results of Hussein's coziness with the fanatics. And his massive armaments program was aimed, at least publicly, at defending Palestinians and other Arabs against Zionist expansion. Hussein warned that the Zionists wanted nothing less than a Jewish state that stretched from the Mediterranean to the Euphrates and vowed that they would not have it.

For their part, the Israelis followed Hussein's menacing gestures with growing apprehension. Iraq's positioning of enhanced-range Scuds in its far western desert and its large stock of poison gas were only two of many developments that were rightly taken to be deeply dangerous.

Given the level of tension that existed between the two heavily armed antagonists, then, it was not surprising that they avoided each other beyond their borders whenever possible.

Yet for five days during that summer of 1989, representatives of both countries did come together under one roof to collect information and perhaps intelligence that each considered so important it transcended their mutual animosity. And they weren't the only ones. Other rivals such as Japan, South Korea, China, and the Soviet Union also joined in the learning experience.

The nation that succeeded in bringing them together, in Portland, Oregon, was the United States. The occasion was the Ninth International Symposium on Detonation. Those who attended the meeting, by invitation only, represented a substrata of science and engineering: people who specialize in making devices that explode. Friend and foe sat together for five days and listened to more than 100 scholarly papers on the latest techniques for blowing things to smithereens with both conventional high explosives and nuclear bombs. And they did it with the encouragement of the United States, a self-professed world leader in arms control.

The event, which is held every four years at a different location, was jointly sponsored by America's preeminent military weapons research facilities, including the Office of Naval Research, the Naval Surface Weapons Center, the Army Ballistic Research Laboratory, the Army Armament Research and Development Center, and the Air Force Armament Laboratory. It was also underwritten by all three of the civilian national laboratories that do research on nuclear weapons: Lawrence Livermore in California and the Los Alamos and Sandia laboratories in New Mexico. The labs are operated for the Department of Energy, which is ultimately responsible for designing and producing the nation's nuclear armaments. About half of the more than 100 papers had to do with nuclear detonation in one form or another.

Some 500 scientists and engineers from twenty-one countries met at the Red Lion Inn on Hayden Island, in the Columbia River. The vast majority of those who attended the unclassified meeting were Americans from universities, companies, and the nation's preeminent civilian and military weapons research facilities. But there were also Spaniards, Swedes, Frenchmen, Dutchmen, West Germans, Canadians, Australians, Britons, Indians, and at least one South African, besides the Iraqis, Israelis, Chinese, and Soviets. Two of the Koreans represented their country's Agency for Defense Development. Four of the Israelis were from the Rafael Ballistic Center in Haifa, where missiles and nuclear weapons are designed, and one was from Israel Military Industries. Yehuda Partom, one of Israel's ranking nuclear weapons designers, even coauthored a paper with Jerry Wackerle, a friend and fellow big-bomb designer from the Los Alamos National Laboratory. Partom had visited the nuclear weapons research facility in New Mexico twice—once for a year—to do research with its powerful Cray supercomputers (access to which is severely restricted) and to collaborate on studies of high explosives specifically used in nuclear weapons applications.

Among the papers delivered by the Chinese, one—"Experimental Studies on the Detonation of an Explosive by Multi-Point Initiation"— concerned compressing fissile material to supercriticality, as happens in an atomic explosion. Were the Chinese giving away secrets? Certainly. But not to the nations that already had mastered the intricacies of nuclear weaponry. They were showing all the "have-nots" that they, too, possessed the technology. In fact, they were bragging about it. China, after all, was emerging as one of the world's most prolific suppliers of superweapons and related technology. Showing potential customers some of their wares, therefore, made good business sense.

Meanwhile, the host government was working its own double standard. Even as the Iraqi scientists were being encouraged by the United States to collect data on detonating nuclear weapons, a U.S. Customs agent named Daniel Supnick had only recently returned from London, where he risked his life in the famous sting operation that kept detonators that could have been used to trigger an atomic bomb out of Iraq's clutches.

Taken together, the two events reflect a U.S. weapons technology export policy that was, and remains, plagued by contradiction, confusion, hypocrisy, greed, and the self-serving machinations of petty bureaucrats and shortsighted politicians and military officers. Back in 1967, for example, a group of young Iraqi military officers was taken on a tour of all U.S. chemical weapons development centers, including the Aberdeen Proving Ground in Maryland. It was essentially a course on the manufacture and effectiveness of chemical weapons. One of the young officers was named Saddam Hussein.

To the credit of the United States, the vast spectrum of information and equipment—collectively called superweapon technology—that could be used to create weapons of mass destruction has been defined with great, if not perfect, precision and put into fat books by category and device or substance. In addition, a spate of carefully crafted laws are on the books that prohibit the distribution or export of most of it. The laws translate to voluminous lists of rules and regulations that are supposed to be followed by every federal agency involved in weapons, potential weapons, and technology that can be used to make weapons. The Department of Commerce, for example, is required by law to oversee all U.S. exports. It is also required to notify other federal departments when license requests are made for material on which they have expertise and with which another nation could acquire weapons of mass destruction.

Similarly, the Departments of Defense, Energy, and State are supposed to figure prominently in the regulatory process. So are the Central Intelligence Agency and the Defense Intelligence Agency. The entire system of lists and laws, cross-checks and multiple accountability, reflects an intelligence and sense of ethics that do credit to the republic that produced it. On paper, the system is leakproof. In practice, however, it is leaky: a victim of the very democratic process that created it.

The federal agencies that are involved in the export of weapons technology often work at contradictory purposes. The Department of Defense, for example, doesn't want U.S. weapons technology to fall into hostile or potentially hostile hands because it doesn't want American military personnel to have to face those weapons in combat or the United States to be exposed to them. This doesn't mean that the Pentagon is against *all* weapons technology exports, however. It does promote the sale of weapons and related technology, provided they are headed for friendly arsenals.

The Department of Commerce, on the other hand, exists to promote U.S. manufacturing, and it therefore wants to export as many products as possible that carry the "Made in the USA" label. Commerce therefore favors shipments to nations whose motives for buying them can be dubious at best, shipments that would never gain Pentagon approval. When the system works as it should, experts at the Department of Defense are informed about the nature of the item being exported and have the right to veto its sale. Yet both the Department of Defense and the intelligence agencies, which want to stay abreast of weapons technology exports, are routinely cut out of the information distribution process by Commerce on the grounds of protecting the proprietary rights of firms it thinks of as clients.

So the spymasters at CIA headquarters in Langley, Virginia, get even. They refuse to share their background information on foreign scientists and engineers who visit the United States seeking weapons data because they feel they must protect the sources and methods they use to collect the information.

And the laws governing the export of weapons technology are themselves fundamentally contradictory. Some, for example, prohibit the Department of Energy from sharing certain kinds of nonclassified but potentially valuable information developed by its weapons laboratories with so-called sensitive nations. Yet other laws say exactly the opposite: that not only should the information be widely disseminated but scientists at the those labs and elsewhere should, whenever possible, work in collaboration with their opposite numbers in other countries. The Freedom of Information Act also opens a reservoir of useful information to anyone who cares to take the time and trouble to use it, as Iraq's weapons designers learned before the Persian Gulf War.

It is in the nature of a system as open as that of the United States that a great deal of useful technology is freely available for the asking. Conservatives wailed for years that the old Soviet Union never needed as extensive an espionage system as the United States because so many of our secrets really weren't secret at all. While that is an oversimplification, it is true that many Western agents lost their lives trying to pry information out of the U.S.S.R. while their KGB counterparts were collecting it in perfect safety.

Furthermore, most of the data and material used to make super-weapons is so-called dual-use technology (or, in the case of chemical and biological warfare agents, dual-use chemistry and biology). This means that the stuff is so ambiguous that, taken by itself, it either doesn't relate to weapons at all or else can be used for peaceful as well as military purposes. Computers, machine tools, gyroscopes, certain kinds of explosives, rocket engines, and radars are only six obvious examples. Who can determine with certainty that the complicated rocket engine for which a single component is being bought is going to push a ballistic missile instead of launch a vehicle for carrying weather and communication satellites to space?

The Centers for Disease Control in Atlanta shipped a variety of deadly agents to several sensitive nations throughout the 1980s, ostensibly so the recipients could devise vaccines or countermeasures. It made eight shipments of Ebola, Marburg, and Rift Valley microbes to South Africa in 1984, for example: the same year the U.N. accused Pretoria of having a biological weapons program. The following year, the CDC rushed three batches of the Israeli strain of West Nile fever virus to Iraq by express mail. And in 1988, it violated federal law by sending St. Louis encephalitis virus to the Institute for Tropical Medicine in Havana by messenger. Asked who at the institute requested the deadly microorganisms, a CDC spokeswoman said that she didn't know and couldn't find out because the CDC "doesn't keep records" of such things. It's done "informally," she added. The procedure was clearly flawed. It was not the CDC's intention to help spread the wherewithal to wage biological warfare when it made the shipments, yet that was probably the result because of slipshod export procedures.

Not to be outdone by the civilians, the U.S. Army's Medical Research Institute of Infectious Diseases regularly opened its doors to nations with biological weapons programs. It shared data with Israel, China, and Taiwan, as well as taught scientists from India about several deadly diseases, including anthrax. The institute, at Fort Detrick, Maryland, is limited to defensive research by the Biological Weapons Convention. But Israeli scientists have no such constraint, since their country is not a party to the agreement. And the fact that representatives of three antagonists—India, Taiwan, and China—studied together under U.S. auspices was another example of Washington's cynicism where spreading knowledge of the deadly arts was concerned.

Finally, the United States, in common with the other nations, rewards its friends as it punishes its enemies. That, too, is permitted by law. Rewarding friends by selling them weapons or the essential technology to create them is also encouraged. The Department of Commerce favors such transfers because they help business. The Department of State likes them because they help solidify relations with the recipients. The Pentagon knows that sharing weapons and technology with friendly forces not only strengthens alliances but keeps defense contractors healthy. The intelligence agencies like such transfers because they open collaborative opportunities with their counterparts in the recipient countries. France and Israel, to take two more examples, have both benefited from U.S. help in their nuclear programs and have shared intelligence in return.

But when nuclear technology is involved, there is no practical way to prevent friendly nations from surreptitiously passing the knowledge on to third parties, however stringent the transfer agreements. And that has happened more than once. France not only sold much of what it had learned to Iraq and Israel—two mortal enemies—but even built reactors with which they could extract nuclear-weapons-grade uranium at Osirak (Iraq) and Dimona (Israel). Meanwhile, Israel itself passed on what it knew to South Africa, a beleaguered nation with which it developed a symbiotic relationship. And it threw in ballistic missiles as well.

No one at the 1989 Portland symposium seemed to have a problem with the presence of the Iraqis—M. Ahadd, S. Ibrahim, and H. Mahd of the Al Qaqaa State Establishment—since their nation had only the year before ended its war with Iran (which, not coincidentally, was not represented at the symposium). But the Iraqis' presence was significant. Mahd had a brand-new doctorate in nuclear physics. And "State Establishment" was a typically deceptive way of describing Al Qaqaa. Located just south of Baghdad, Al Qaqaa was one of MIMI's divisions. Its specialty was research in nuclear explosive devices. This meant its scientists and engineers studied and tested nonnuclear components of nuclear weapons: components such as the high explosives that make atomic bombs go off and the detonators, or triggers, that touch off the explosives with perfect symmetry. That is why Ahadd, Ibrahim, and Mahd made a point of repeatedly questioning others at the symposium about krytrons—the very type of trigger that Dan Supnick had successfully intercepted—and about computer detonation design codes. Their incessant efforts to collect data on the tiny devices made "a lot of people nervous," a weapons analyst from one of the three labs recalled. "If you're going to let an Iraqi listen to that," he added, referring to the papers that concerned nuclear detonation, "that's pretty stupid." Nor, he added ruefully, was the Portland meeting the first time it happened. The same thing had occurred at a Soviet detonation conference the previous year.

Ironically, twelve days before the detonation conference began, Al Qaqaa itself was partly detonated. Several hundred workers were killed in a massive explosion. The substance believed to have caused the disaster was cyclotrimethylenetrinitramine, or RDX (rapid detonation explosive) an explosive so effective at squeezing nuclear fuel cores to the point at which they blow up that its export in quantities of more than 2 percent of another explosive is prohibited by the Department of Defense. But the Iraqis didn't get their RDX from an American supplier. They got it from Carlos Cardoen. And it was the blast at Al Qaqaa, which the Iraqis claimed was a petroleum depot explosion, that drew Farzad Bazoft, an Iranian-born journalist on assignment from a British newspaper, *The Observer*. The Iraqis hanged Bazoft as a spy the following March.*

At any rate the Iraqis, among others, were learning how to detonate a variety of high explosives and were picking up related nuclear information courtesy of the Department of Defense and the trio of Department of Energy laboratories that design the most dangerous weapons in the world. But it didn't end there. The designs of detonators and other nuclear weapon components, as well as hundreds of specific techniques for increasing the weapons' performance, were contained in thousands of unclassified reports produced by all three laboratories. In one eighteen-month period in 1986 and 1987 that was studied by Congress, for example, they issued about 39,000 such reports.

Some laws prohibit the labs from providing many of their studies to so-called sensitive nations. These have traditionally included those that were communist, those that were suspected of developing nuclear weapons, and those that were considered to threaten U.S. national security for other reasons. There were fifty-seven of them as of June 1989, when the invitations to the detonation conference went out. Yet other legislation makes most of the research material, including the sensitive variety, available to those nations just for the asking. To further complicate matters, both sets of laws overlap in a large gray area that is subject to wide swings of interpretation.

Starting in 1974, a series of laws have required that even unclassified nuclear information be withheld from sensitive nations when, in the judgment of experts, it could help them to get nuclear weapons. The Atomic Energy Act, for example, puts controls over unclassified data that could help weapons production. The Nuclear Non-Proliferation Act does the same. The Export Administration Act specifically calls for safeguards against the transfer of unclassified technologies that could significantly contribute to the military posture of other nations.

But the situation is clouded because of other laws that require exactly

---

*Bazoft was executed despite a plea for clemency by British Prime Minister Margaret Thatcher. "Mrs. Thatcher wanted him alive," Iraqi Information Minister Latif Nassif Jassem was quoted as saying. "We gave her the body." The exchange, which echoed profound cultural as well as political differences, was one of the drumbeats that signaled the approach of the coming war. Another was young Bazoft himself. He really was a spy whose job was to collect a soil sample in the blast area so it could be analyzed to determine what kind of weapon had been tested. (Jassem's remark is from "Denying Pleas, Iraq Hangs British-Based Reporter," *The New York Times*, March 16, 1990. Bazoft's role as an agent is from Simon Henderson, *Instant Empire: Saddam Hussein's Ambition for Iraq*, San Francisco: Mercury House, 1991, pp. 207–8.)

the opposite. There is legislation, for example, that mandates the Department of Energy and its laboratories to collaborate with industry to disseminate unclassified research results. This is so American companies can benefit from an invigorating exchange of scientific and technical data. But the concept of free access goes even beyond that. The Freedom of Information Act specifically calls for the department to make such data available to anyone, U.S. citizen or foreigner, who asks for it.

Obtaining most of the weapons laboratories' reports is, therefore, only a little more difficult than shopping in a supermarket. In fact, the federal government facilitates the process by making more than 60 percent of the reports available through its own distribution center. When the General Accounting Office selected 30 out of 1,000 such reports and tracked inquiries on them, it found that 68 percent were from overseas. Three sensitive countries—Iraq, Israel, and Pakistan—requested and received six of the same reports. These dealt with modifying high explosives; improving ultrafast cameras that are used to study the effects of a nuclear detonation; improving a detonator that is used in most U.S. nuclear weapons; and shaping, machining, and setting off high explosives. Although the reports contained basic science, all could have helped nations develop or advance nuclear weapons programs.

The Sandia, Livermore, and Los Alamos labs even respond to mail inquiries. Between October 1985 and December 1987, they received more than 2,000 requests for nuclear research data. Almost 1,700 of such inquiries were answered. The main reason for not answering the others was that no record could be found of the information that was requested. Who was making the requests? That's difficult to say because the DOE does not require the labs to track either the requests or the information they provide. Sandia nevertheless did develop a system to track direct requests as late as 1986. Los Alamos began to provide information about requests it receives to Sandia two years later. But Livermore still has no accurate way of keeping track of who is asking for what information about its nuclear weapons research.

Then there are the computer codes that are sold to foreigners every year by the National Energy Software Center at Argonne, Illinois. The NESC is the Department of Energy's central facility for collecting and selling computer software. All three national weapons laboratories develop unclassified basic research and development computer codes, as well as more advanced ones to design, model, and test simulated nuclear explosions. Many of these have been bought by France, Japan, Pakistan, and

Belgium. They cost between $50 and $4,500 each. At those prices, they are a steal. And anyone can walk into the Brookhaven National Laboratory on Long Island and buy copies of the blueprints of the graphite reactor that was used to produce plutonium.

A report prepared by the General Accounting Office in 1988 found that all of the laboratories admit a stream of foreign visitors without conducting adequate background checks. The result is a security officer's nightmare. From January 1986 to September 1987, for example, 897 scientists and engineers from communist and sensitive nations visited the three weapons labs. These included 118 from China, 57 from the U.S.S.R., 18 from Argentina, 32 from Brazil, 149 from India, 25 from Iran, 2 from Iraq, 188 from Israel, 11 from Pakistan, 17 from South Africa, and 51 from Taiwan.

The same study revealed that of 637 visitors from sensitive countries, including India, Israel, and Pakistan, the Department of Energy required background checks for only 77. And it received information about only 14 of those. DOE officials explained to the GAO investigators that their agency got no background data on 46 of the visitors because doing so would have taken too long. Furthermore, information on the remaining 17 came only after their visits had begun. More ominously, about 10 percent of those 637 visitors came from countries that were on the Energy Department's classified Watch List: countries with organizations suspected of conducting nuclear weapons activities. Despite this, no background data on those individuals was requested.

The GAO blamed sloppy administration for most of the security lapses. In some instances, for example, visit and lab assignment approvals were made at too low a level. Other times, approvals were a fait accompli because the visitor was already on the premises. A requirement that field offices send postvisit reports to headquarters so Washington can assess what kind of data was provided to the foreigners was complied with after only 89 of 248 visits.

Iraqis were also admitted to Oak Ridge National Laboratory in Tennessee at least from 1979. While Oak Ridge does not do weapons research per se, it is the lab that developed EMIS, the electromagnetic isotope separation method for enriching uranium that became the model for Iraq's baghdatrons. In 1979, one Iraqi was admitted to Oak Ridge as an "alien guest" so he could do research in atomic physics, specifically on heavy ion-induced atomic collisions: precisely the basic science used in the baghdatrons. Another, who was completing his doctorate in nuclear physics at the Virginia Polytechnic Institute, spent 1982 and 1983 investigating nuclei that are "far from stability." That subject spoke to larger matters than the study of sub-atomic particles.

Scientists who work at the national laboratories are required to keep secrets for the sake of national security. But as members of an international community that thrives on the free exchange of information, they also have an understandable urge to share their discoveries with their colleagues at home and abroad. And in many instances the U.S. scientists collaborate with their foreign counterparts. But whatever the reason, thousands of visiting scientists from more than 100 nations, many of them on the sensitive list, passed through Livermore, Los Alamos, Sandia, Oak Ridge, and other facilities every year in what amounted to a virtual open admissions policy before Congress became involved in 1989. That year, the lawmakers saw to it that several of the procedures were tightened. But even when entrance is denied, friends in the right places can surmount guarded gates in suitably ingenious ways.

In the autumn of 1988, for example, Yehuda Partom and two colleagues, Noam Sack and Ehud Ganani, were denied permission to enter Los Alamos by the Department of Energy after one DOE official described them as "unacceptable." Another baldly called them "a weapons team."

Sack never reached the United States. But Partom and Ganani, thanks to the Los Alamos weapons scientists who "hosted" and worked with them, managed to get access to the lab from the other side of the security fence. Partom was set up in the offices of Jomar Systems, at the edge of downtown Los Alamos, and was provided with a telephone and a computer terminal. With them and an access code belonging to his host, Jerry Wackerle (with whom he collaborated on the paper given at the 1989 detonation symposium), he plugged into one of the laboratory's unclassified Cray supercomputers.*

Ganani worked out of his host's garage, though not, apparently, with a federal supercomputer. In helping them, neither of the Americans with whom they worked broke the law, since both Israelis remained outside of the Los Alamos lab itself. Furthermore, there is no evidence that they were spies in the accepted sense of the word. Yet the Americans made it possible for the two Israelis to collect (as well as provide) valuable

---

*Wackerle did not give Partom his computer password and ID number, according to a DOE official who testified about the episode at a congressional hearing. Instead, he did the dialing himself. (*U.S. Senate, Committee on Governmental Affairs, "Security Weaknesses at the Nuclear Weapons Laboratories,"* 100th Congress, 2nd Sess., October 11, 1988, p. 30.)

research data on nuclear weaponry. And they carried home what they collected. Partom's access to the Cray inside Los Alamos from an office several miles away betrayed a sophisticated technique that was even more disquieting than anything he may have learned. "We provided a service without intending to," observed Richard A. Du Val of the DOE, "and we now are entering into what I guess is the interesting area of electronic visits from outside the fence."

Yet other material, far more sensitive than that obtained by Partom and Ganani, has been physically stolen on the spot. During the 1980s, Chinese scientists visiting Livermore walked off with a considerable amount of highly classified nuclear weapons data. The theft is thought to have resulted in the successful testing of a neutron bomb in China in 1988. Meanwhile, the Chinese sold some of the other material they had collected over the years to Pakistan so it could build a bomb to counter India's.

Nor does the collector of information about superweapons have to be a scientist or a spy. The National Air and Space Museum's Archive Storage and Research Facility at Suitland, Maryland, has the plans for the World War II German V-2 and the U.S. Jupiter Intermediate Range Ballistic Missile that grew out of it. The V-2 was a rocket that could carry a ton of explosives more than 200 miles. It was therefore the world's first operational ballistic missile and the model for all that followed. Jupiter was America's first IRBM: a rocket that could fling a one-and-a-half-megaton warhead 1,700 miles into the Soviet Union from bases in Italy and Turkey. It was retired after the Cuban missile crisis of 1962 because intercontinental ballistic missiles, which could be kept at home, made it obsolete.

Both rockets' plans are available to anyone who has $5,500, which is what the Archive Storage and Research Facility charges to copy them. While it is unlikely that anyone would want to recreate V-2s or Jupiters, the $5,500 or a part of it would buy a pile of useful engineering data on solving problems that apply to all missiles: problems, for example, having to do with the design of the turbopumps and injectors that squirt propellant into the rocket engine's combustion chamber.* "I wouldn't build a Jupiter from those blueprints," said Peter Zimmerman, a physicist and weapons expert who was a member of the Strategic Arms Limitation Treaty's ne-

---

*The $5,500 fee is based on buying all the reels of microfilm that cover Jupiter. Buying only reels that contain specific material would be less expensive.

gotiating team. "But the big help that you would get, the leg up, is that you'd know how somebody solved kinds of problems, various kinds of problems, which will keep coming up. You'd know not only that somebody else had solved it, but this particular solution worked, and worked well enough to go into a production missile."

Just as information about weapons flows freely out of the United States and into sensitive hands, so too does the component hardware. Twelve nations on the sensitive list, for example, submitted some 1,160 export license requests in 1987 for dual-use nuclear hardware; all but 23 were approved by Commerce. And nearly 300 of the approved requests involved material that was shipped to facilities in countries suspected of having nuclear weapons development programs.

Like Brazil, Pakistan, Iran, and some of the other countries on the sensitive list, Iraq needed a wide variety of equipment for its embryonic nuclear weapons program. How it went about assembling what it needed, and the results that came from it, said almost as much about U.S. export control policy as it did about Iraqi guile. Even calling it a policy is a misnomer.

Because it sees its role as fostering foreign sales in support of American business, the Department of Commerce has consistently allowed equipment out of the country that is useful for military purposes. As noted, the law requires that Commerce notify appropriate government agencies when it receives export license requests for sensitive technology. A great deal of such equipment is defined by the Department of Defense, which periodically issues a fat, highly detailed list of technologies that it thinks are "crucial" to the military capabilities of all countries and are of "significant value" to potential adversaries of the United States. All four nuclear-related high explosives, for example—HMX, RDX, TATB, and PETN—are listed. (The first three were the subjects of six papers delivered at the detonation symposium in Portland.)

But many export items represent dual-use technology, for which the call sometimes goes the wrong way for the sake of making a sale—even when there is little doubt about the use for which the equipment is intended. One such case involved an advanced computer bound for Iraq. While it could have been used for peaceful purposes, according to Stephen Bryen, who was deputy undersecretary of defense in the Reagan administration, there was little doubt about its real purpose. "Its primary value is in missiles, and that's where most of them, I believe, have been sold," Bryen explained. "Our own army uses these computers at the White Sands Proving Grounds, and uses them extensively. It's an unusual computer because it's an analogue and digital computer wrapped into a single box. And that sort of machine is very specialized. It's not the kind of thing you would see in a normal business or even in a normal industrial setting."

Computers, in fact, topped the list of dual-use technology imported into Iraq from the United States. While Baghdad preferred German equipment for their meat and potatoes industrial needs, they correctly figured that the United States was the best place to shop for advanced computers. Between 1985 and 1990, Commerce issued hundreds of licenses for "electronic" computing equipment (as opposed to abacuses) valued at more than $96 million. Virtually every U.S. computer manufacturer sold its wares to Baghdad. Hewlett-Packard led with fifty-seven licenses. Unisys obtained only twenty licenses during that period, but it set the sales record: $30.2 million. Other computers that went to Sa'ad-16, the Nasser State Establishment's vast munitions plant at Taji, the Iraq Atomic Energy Commission, and elsewhere came from IBM, Sun Microsystems, Digital, Bull, NEC, Siemens, and International Computers Systems, a Digital distributor with offices in suburban London.

In fact, a great deal of weapons-related equipment was approved for sale to Iraq with the blessing of the Department of Commerce between 1985 and the eve of the Persian Gulf War. Besides computers, 771 export licenses provided software used by the Iraqi secret police to update dossiers; laser systems for jet engine repair; photographic equipment for "scientific research on projectile behavior and terminal ballistics"; $10 million for furnaces that could be used to make spheres of nuclear fuel; machine tools and lasers to turn Scud Bs into extended-range Al Husseins and Al Abbases; and quartz crystals to Salah Al Din, where electronics for nuclear weapons were designed and manufactured. This process—of aggressively promoting U.S. exports and even protecting them from interference by other agencies—has often been done with the blessings of the Department of State. Traditionally, Commerce and State have had a strong mutual interest in shipping U.S. products around the world.

Commerce has insisted that as many as two-thirds of the licenses that allowed weapons components to go to Iraq and elsewhere were approved by the DOE or the Pentagon, or both, which is true. But it doesn't describe the true dimension of the situation. In many instances, Commerce never even notified the Pentagon, DOE, or the intelligence agencies that orders had been placed for potentially dangerous material. In order to avoid as much as possible getting ensnared in disputes with other agencies like the Departments of Defense, Energy, and State, or the CIA—red tape that could slow or even stop the stream of products going abroad—Commerce often just cut them out of the process altogether.

"There were two kinds of difficulty," Bryen said. "The first involved cases for export to countries we thought might be involved in missile proliferation: that we saw. And the second involved those cases that we did not see, but we heard about, and that we wanted to pursue. For those that we saw, we had constant arguments, trying to make the point that we should not export some of these goods." Other times, he continued, the Department of Defense never even got to see what was being sent abroad. "When we sought the assistance of the Commerce Department, we really had to fight tooth and nail to get any information at all. And what we got was inadequate."

In other cases, Commerce not only approved licenses over the strongest possible objections from the Department of Defense, but even rebuffed requests for information from the Pentagon and its Defense Intelligence Agency. In at least one instance, a license was granted even after the manufacturer warned that the equipment had potentially dangerous military uses. The battle that ensued between Commerce and State, on the one hand, and Defense, on the other, became so rancorous that it had to be sent to the White House—to the National Security Council—for adjudication. This was the nuclear furnace episode.

Early in 1989 a Rancocas, New Jersey, firm called Consarc received an $11 million order for three custom-built furnaces that Iraq claimed it wanted in order to make titanium hip and knee joints for disabled veterans of the war with Iran. After Consarc's president, Raymond J. Roberts, got the order, he told the Department of Commerce by telephone and letter that the furnaces could also be used for nuclear weapons development. ". . . while this equipment is for titanium medical prostheses (this is what the customer has told us) there is nothing to stop them from melting zirconium, the main use of which is a cladding material for nuclear fuel rods," Roberts told a Commerce official by telephone in February 1989.

Yet Commerce didn't seem to want to think about the weapons angle, even though the shipment was to be made to Karbala, Iraq, a nuclear weapons research facility. According to one Pentagon official, the place was "across the street" from Al Qaqaa. But Iraq's Ministry of Industry and Military Industrialization, which placed the order, pointedly noted that the furnaces would neither be reexported to a third country "nor used for nuclear applications." Commerce, apparently preferring to think about helping crippled Iraqi war veterans, gave permission to send the furnaces to Iraq. Commerce lives by Calvin Coolidge's enduring advice: the business of America is business.

Whatever the stringent requirements of all of the laws governing sensitive material to Third World nations, and however comprehensive the Pentagon's list of militarily critical technologies, the system of safeguards broke down where it always seems to: in the bureaucratic trenches. Having been warned by the Customs Service that the furnaces were being prepared for shipment to Iraq with the approval of the Department of Commerce, the Pentagon asked Commerce to rescind its approval. Commerce refused. Defense insisted. Commerce dug in its heels. Finally, someone in the Pentagon alerted the White House, which decided to block the deal. Customs issued a "detention" order on June 27, 1990. On July 5—twenty-eight days before Iraq invaded Kuwait—President Bush had to intervene to kill the deal.

"It was clear to us that the purpose of the furnaces' going to Iraq was to assist them in their nuclear program; in manufacturing components of nuclear weapons by casting them in these furnaces," said Bryen. He was so upset by the furnace sale that he decided to fight it even after he left office. Bryen, after all, had a wealth of experience contesting Commerce's licensing decisions. Commerce's ignoring the Pentagon, he added, "was a signal to every operator in the world that the Defense Department had been cut out, and therefore the chances of slipping something through were very good. So it made every crook in the world happy." It is "their business to promote trade, so you don't expect too much of them," Bryen said. "But in the case of the State Department, we expect a lot more," he added with disgust.

Yet Commerce's handling of the furnace deal was particularly exasperating for Bryen. "To be told something of this sort by the company up front," he said, "and clearly that's well-documented—and in one case in writing—and never to look into the matter . . . It's a scandal."

Commerce officially maintained that Roberts's warning was not explicit enough (as though its licensing criteria depended on exporters evaluating the possible military uses of their own products). But Michael Manning, of the department's International Trade Office in Trenton, got right to the heart of the matter. Manning saw his role as trying to shepherd the sale—protect it—through a morass of impediments. After assuring

Consarc that it would have no trouble exporting the furnaces, only to see Customs override him, Manning telephoned a Customs special agent from Consarc's own office. He angrily pointed out that Consarc was losing money because the shipment was being held up, that the firm was a major employer in the South Jersey area, and that he (Manning) enjoyed "an excellent reputation with the parent company!" The last was no doubt absolutely true. Manning and his agency couldn't have been bigger Consarc boosters if they had been on the company's payroll. Customs became so concerned about his relationship with Consarc, in fact, that it warned him to lie low or risk being called by the firm as a defense witness in case the furnace dispute went to court.*

Commerce has even deliberately misled Congress. One internal report, for instance, showed approval for $139,535 worth of Hewlett-Packard equipment for calibrating, adjusting, and testing surveillance radar. The hardware was bound for the Salah Al Din Establishment, the document noted, adding that "according to our information the end-user is involved in military matters." That wasn't the half of it. Salah Al Din built the radar and most of the electronics used for tracking the ballistic missiles developed at Sa'ad-16. It also made the electronic systems for nuclear weapons. But when Commerce issued an extensive report to Congress listing all sales to Iraq between 1985 and the eve of the invasion of Kuwait in August 1990, it omitted both the manufacturer of the equipment and the end-user. Asked about the omission, Mildred Cooper, a spokeswoman for Commerce's Bureau of Export Administration, noted that the Export Administration Act prohibits disclosure to the public of proprietary information, including the name of an applicant for an export license. While she was technically correct, the action betrayed more sensitivity to business requirements than to national security, since such information could have been shared with the Department of Defense.

Commerce employees, including Dennis Kloske, the former Secretary for Export Administration, testified before Congress that while officials prepared printouts on exports for a congressional oversight committee, information regarding sixty-six export licenses for equipment bought by Iraq was doctored. Chevrolet Blazers that had been modified

*Consarc employed about 100 people. It was therefore in no sense a major employer in the area. There was also a branch in Bellshill, Scotland. The parent company, also based in New Jersey, was Inductotherm International. Manning's remarks and the interchange with Customs are from a U.S. Customs Service Memorandum, "Michael Manning Conversations Re: Induction Skull Melting Furnace (ISM) and Iraq," of July 13, 1990.

by a company called Gateway International were originally described as "vehicles designed for military use." But by the time word of their export reached the House's Subcommittee on Commerce, Consumer, and Monetary Affairs, they had been turned into "commercial utility cargo trucks."

During January and February 1988, both Commerce and the Department of Energy approved the export of $1.4 million in machine tools and lasers for use in lengthening the Scud B to increase its range. The company, Leybold, was German but it exported from the United States. Despite this potential use, the machine tool and laser license applications were referred to neither Defense nor State for review. For their part, the Iraqis were relatively straightforward about the deal, claiming they wanted the equipment for "General military repair applications such as jet engines, *rocketcases*, etc." (italics added). One of those extended-range Scuds demolished a U.S. barracks outside of Dhahran, Saudi Arabia, during the closing hours of Desert Storm, killing twenty-seven American soldiers and wounding ninety-eight others.

In some instances, cooperation between the federal agencies has been reduced to such a minimum that the result has taken on farcical overtones. Commerce maintains information about thousands of companies and individuals about which it has serious misgivings. But State has not been able to apply the data to those who approach its commercial attachés. In one case, Foggy Bottom approved 325 export licenses for a company that had been denied the same privileges by Commerce. The evidence suggests that State simply didn't want to use Commerce's records. But even if it had wanted to, the transfer of information would have been almost futile. Until 1989, State's Office of Defense Trade Control did not own a computer.

Commerce's Office of Export Intelligence Review fared little better. In May 1989, it received about 500 names of foreign individuals and firms linked to missile technology. Yet only about 100 of the names were entered into Commerce's screening process because the computer that handled screening had a limited capacity.

Disparities between Commerce and the Pentagon's figures are even more ludicrous. A General Accounting Office study found that during the first twenty-nine months of the Missile Technology Control Regime, Commerce identified 128 license applications for sale to thirteen countries as being subject to MTCR restrictions. During the same period, the Department of Defense identified 1,450 applications for sale to more than seventy countries as coming under the control regime's guidelines. "In other words," the House Committee on Government Operations noted, "whether the U.S. Government allows a missile related export to a Third World country can depend on which government agency is in charge of licensing the sale!"

Even the Nuclear Regulatory Commission has gotten into the act. The NRC approved the sale of nearly forty pounds of weapons-grade uranium to Romania in 1989. The Romanians maintained that the material was fuel for a research reactor. But alarmed NRC staff members objected to the sale on two grounds. They noted that Romanian military officers had bragged that their country could build nuclear weapons. In addition, they pointed out that Norway had filed a protest with Romania, claiming that a previous delivery of Norwegian nuclear materials had been diverted to a third nation, believed to be either Israel or India.

Cold war politics led directly to massive weapons technology exports and globe-girdling alliance systems such as NATO, SEATO, CENTO, and the Warsaw Pact. These military relationships led, in turn, to a universal weapons subculture among the officer class and the civilian strategists and arms specialists of the various signatories. Permanent, standing international brotherhoods of warriors who standardized weapons, conducted joint maneuvers, shared naval, air, and ground installations, and co-designed strategies came into existence.

Arms sales abroad not only directly benefited the companies that produced America's weapons systems by keeping them healthy, but also often lowered the unit cost of the Pentagon's own hardware because of extended production runs. The Soviets, in turn, sold their weapons to help support a chronically shaky economy in an effort that seemed to be as desperate as it was endless. The Soviet paradox was that its economy was enfeebled by the dizzying cost of the very weapons that were being produced to protect it. This was Catch-22 on the grandest of scales.

Both sides peddled their wares with profound cynicism and naïveté. The United States, for example, helped Israel to acquire the key elements of virtually all of its weapons systems, including military aircraft, ballistic missiles, nuclear weapons, and chemical and biological warfare agents. Yet it was simultaneously pumping weapons into Egypt and Saudi Arabia, two of Israel's adversaries, and looking the other way while France and Brazil performed the same service for Iraq. It sold the Shah of Iran all manner of high-tech weapons in order to block any possible Soviet move against its vital oil interests in Saudi Arabia and elsewhere in the region. It did the same with Pakistan in an effort to offset huge Soviet sales to India and the Soviet invasion of Afghanistan. It did it with South Korea to counter a North Korea that was also the recipient of Soviet weaponry, and with Taiwan, which faced a Soviet-armed China. Under the rubric of the North Atlantic Treaty Organization, and acting with an impartiality that would make Carlos Cardoen smile knowingly, it even provided fighter aircraft and other weapons of equal lethality to both Greece and Turkey, who were and remain traditional rivals. Where the Department of Defense and the Central Intelligence Agency were concerned, the old French axiom (often wrongly attributed to the Arabs) applied: Your enemy's enemy is your friend.

But ultimately, it is the weapons producer that generates arms for friend and foe alike. And the motive is always profit. In the netherworld of illicit or irresponsible weapons sales, subterfuge and deceit, or merely looking the other way, are the paths to that profit. Occasionally, there is a whistle-blower whose conscience causes him to alert either his own company or the authorities to the perfidious, deadly business that is transpiring. But they are the rare exceptions.

In early March 1984, a Swiss company named IFAT, or Institute for Advanced Technology, asked Honeywell Control Systems, Ltd., a British subsidiary of the Honeywell Corporation, to do missile studies for $100,000. The studies were to determine the feasibility of using fuel-air explosives on a ballistic missile. A fuel-air explosive, or FAE, releases a highly combustible fuel such as kerosene, gasoline, or JP-4 jet fuel into the air in the form of a potentially explosive cloud. The vapor is then ignited. Done incorrectly, the cloud simply burns. But done perfectly, it explodes with a heavily pressurized blast that sends out a fiery shock wave over troops, buildings, and other "soft" targets that is reminiscent of a miniature nuclear explosion. FAEs were used by the United States at least as far back as the Vietnam war, and the U.S. Air Force currently stocks the weapon.

Honeywell knew that IFAT represented the Egyptian government, which wanted to put FAEs on the warhead of a ballistic missile it was building in partnership with Argentina and Iraq and with $1 billion of Saudi money. It got this information from Keith G. Smith, a Honeywell Control Systems consultant and a managing director of IFAT. In trying to persuade Honeywell to do the studies, Smith explained that the missile was being designed to hit "high-value fixed targets such as cities, ports, oil refineries, and air bases." But, he assured representatives of Honeywell's Defense Systems Division in Minnetonka, Minnesota, at the end of March 1984, the weapon would probably "never be fired in anger." Rather, he explained, Cairo just wanted it as a "deterrent."

What Smith had every reason to know, but what he seems to have left out of his presentation, was that IFAT was part of the Consen Group of Zug, Switzerland. And the missile for which IFAT/Consen was trying to get fuel-air explosive capability was therefore none other than Condor-2, which was also being bankrolled by Baghdad for design and assembly inside a mountain in Argentina. When a Honeywell official present at the meeting noted that some fuel-air explosive technology was classified, Smith deftly replied that the study could be "sanitized" and that he was certain no FAE warhead would ever actually be mounted on the Egyptian missile anyway. In any case, he added, by the time the report landed on an Egyptian desk, all Honeywell logos and corporate symbols would have been removed.

Within a week of Smith's presentation, a member of Honeywell's Mission Analysis Division had studied the presentation, itself, and found it deceitful. But his warning was not enough to head off the two Honeywell divisions that were asked to do the study. In December 1984, they delivered their 141-page *FAE Warhead Analysis Final Report* to IFAT.

"Multiple fuel clouds could be created by dividing the warhead into several independently dispersed bomblets," the American engineers taught their foreign counterparts on page 71. "Cube root scaling laws suggest an increased kill area advantage by doing this."

"The most significant differences between conventional high explosives and the others is that TNT and similar explosives produce very high peak overpressures from very nearly a point source, while nuclear and FAE produce peak overpressures over an extended region," they explained on page 80.

"Detonation of multiple smaller FAE canisters containing a fixed total amount of fuel will cover a greater area with a minimum specified overpressure than can be covered by the detonation of the same amount of fuel in a single large canister," they went on to advise on page 91. It was a calculus of death. IFAT's Austrian and German engineers were the beneficiaries of a fine report obtained at a bargain price. And while Condor-2 was finally grounded, if only temporarily, those engineers and the copies of Honeywell's fuel-air explosive report are still out there somewhere.

•  •  •

Then there was Alcolac International, a small Baltimore chemical manufacturer which gained the dubious distinction of supplying thiodiglycol, a key constituent of mustard gas, to both sides in the Iran-Iraq war. Thiodiglycol is a quintessential example of the dual-use item. It is a common solvent widely used to make textile dyes and ballpoint pen ink. But it is also a so-called precursor chemical. Mixed with hydrochloric acid, another commonly used chemical, it becomes mustard gas. With the exception of shipments to eighteen countries, most of them in NATO, exporters of thiodiglycol must therefore obtain a license and supply records to Customs, Commerce, and State that identify all of its end users. Yet the rules for exporting thiodiglycol, like hundreds of other chemicals, are easily evaded because they depend on voluntary compliance by companies and on a Customs Service that is severely stretched in other directions.

And so it was that Frans van Anraat, a Dutch wheeler-dealer who owned two Panamanian companies in Switzerland and homes in Lugano and Milan, worked to beat the system while acting as a middleman to provide thiodiglycol to Iraq. Between 1984 and 1986, van Anraat and a Japanese colleague named Charles Tanaka arranged to have fifteen large shipments of the chemical sent to Iraq, mostly from Japan. But when their Japanese source began to run out, and obtaining it from a California supplier proved too expensive and complicated, they turned to a longstanding friend of Tanaka's, a New York businessman named Harold Greenberg, to find a new source.

Greenberg and his own partner then turned to Alcolac. In October 1987 they bought as much as 130 tons of thiodiglycol from Alcolac through a front company in Brooklyn and then had it consigned to one of van Anraat's Swiss firms. When the first of several shipments was made, a freight forwarder acting for Alcolac filed a customs form saying that the shipment was destined for Antwerp and listing van Anraat's company as the end user. But eight days after the ship carrying the mustard gas precursor sailed out of Philadelphia, van Anraat instructed Alcolac to write a new bill of lading that showed the chemical to merely be "goods in transit." Alcolac's export manager, Leslie Hinkleman, obliged. With a document showing no end-user location, van Anraat was then able to convince Belgian authorities to let him transship the thiodiglycol to Jordan. It eventually arrived in Aqaba for shipment by road to Iraq.

Delighted by the ease with which the shipment evaded the authorities, van Anraat and Tanaka flew to Baltimore and concluded a deal with Alcolac to provide as much as 3,000 tons of thiodiglycol. Alcolac would bill one of Greenberg's subsidiary companies for the chemical. The funds to pay for it would come from the Central Bank of Iraq. Van Anraat would transfer that money to the Banque Continentale du Luxembourg. The Luxembourg bank would in turn instruct a New York bank to pay Alcolac. The money laundering was analogous to the sleight of hand used to move the actual shipments, themselves, and further helped cover everyone's tracks. Meanwhile, van Anraat had Greenberg's subsidiary company delete all references to thiodyglycol from its invoices and instead call it Kromfax, Alcolac's perfectly ambiguous brand name for the chemical. He also persuaded Alcolac to put "goods in transit" (with western Europe as the destination) on all invoices and bills of lading. This was blatantly illegal.

Meanwhile, Peter Walaschek, a Czech-born sales representative of Colimex GmbH & Company, a West German pharmaceutical product importer and exporter, was performing the same service for Iran. Walaschek told Alcolac to ship his thiodiglycol to Cy Savas Oikonomidis E. E., a Greek textile firm that had secretly agreed to send it on to Bandar Abbas in Iran. Other shipments went to a phony company in Singapore, and then through Hong Kong and Pakistan before reaching Iran. Like van Anraat, Walaschek told Alcolac to make the shipping documents say that transshipping was permitted and that the chemical was bound for "the Far East." When Alcolac's freight forwarding company refused to take part in the deceit, Alcolac did the job itself.

Eventually, an alert Customs agent spotted "Kromfax" instead of the chemical's generic name on a shipping document and became suspicious. This led to an elaborate sting in which 430 drums of water were substituted for the thiodiglycol in the port of Norfolk, Virginia, in the dead of night. They were soon sent on their way to Karachi and then to Bandar Abbas. Customs agents meanwhile raided Alcolac's office and seized dozens of documents that implicated the company in the Iraqi and Iranian connections. All of the principals pleaded guilty to violations of U.S. export law. The company itself, which insisted that it knew nothing about the diversions, was fined $430,000. Leslie Hinkleman, the export manager who falsified documents, was charged and convicted. She received eighteen months' probation. Greenberg got two years' probation and was fined $27,000 (he made $90,000 in his capacity as a middleman). Tanaka was sentenced to twenty-seven months in prison and fined $6,000 (he also made $90,000). Walaschek was arrested, jumped bail, and surfaced in West Germany. But Bonn refused to allow his extradition.

Van Anraat was arrested in Milan and fought extradition from a jail cell in Italy. He won after convincing a local judge that he was wanted for a political crime in the United States. The Dutchman was duly released. But when a higher court reversed the ruling, van Anraat fled from Italy. He is still a fugitive.

"We thought we were doing business with reputable people in Europe," said Fred von Rein, Alcolac's vice-president for operations. Von Rein maintained that the huge amount of thiodiglycol being shipped abroad merely reflected market conditions. "Companies either buy or sell a commodity based on the strength of the dollar," he said, adding that the dollar was weak when the orders came in. But Breckenridge Willcox, the U.S. Attorney for Maryland who prosecuted Alcolac, wasn't buying it. "They were supplying an amount of product that would have satisfied legitimate European needs for decades," he asserted.

Given the number of legal loopholes, the backbiting and self-serving attitudes at the Departments of Commerce, Defense, Energy, and State, and the greed, duplicity, and convenient naïveté of many of the manufacturers, it has fallen to the Customs Service to carry a disproportionate share of the burden of slowing down the arms flow. It is as if Customs were playing deep safety on a football team—the position ultimately responsible for preventing the other team from scoring—while everyone else on the defensive unit was arguing over strategy or trying to increase the value of a contract. But if the analogy is appropriate, then Customs is certainly a single safety. It is out there all by itself. Besides preventing illegal exports, Customs is "involved in the drug war, interdiction, money laundering, fraud, and the investigation of commodities imported in the United States," Donald Turnbaugh explained. He was the head of the Customs office in Baltimore when the Alcolac sting was staged. "We have a lot of responsibilities with a limited staff. That's about as kindly as I can say it."

The limited staff did well enough in March 1990, though, when Customs inflicted its greatest sting on the Iraqis who were trying to smuggle the high-voltage capacitors and krytrons back home through Euromac, MIMI's frozen French-fry front company in Thames-Ditton.

That operation began in the autumn of 1988 when CSI Technologies, a San Marcos, California, electronics manufacturer, received an inquiry about capacitors. The firm wanting the information was Euromac (for European Manufacturing Center), Ltd. The inquiry was not about capacitors in general, however, but about a very special kind of capacitor. Euromac was interested in buying very small capacitors whose specifications, the president of CSI deduced, were most applicable to military activities, and particularly to detonating a nuclear weapon.* Jerold D. Kowalsky therefore told the U.S. Customs Service about the request. And he, in turn, was told to submit a low bid and then fill the resulting order.

During the months that followed, telexes were exchanged with Euromac in which design specifications were laid out, prices were quoted, and quantities were set. Kowalsky even went to London in September 1989 to meet with Euromac representatives at the Cavendish Hotel. He was accompanied by a man whom he introduced to his potential customers as Dan Saunders, his "manager for finance and export." Saunders was really Dan Supnick, the U.S. Customs Service special agent who had been involved in several other sting operations, including one in which military equipment was headed for the Ayatollah Khomeini's armed forces. The Euromac representatives were Ali Ashour Daghir, Euromac's director; Jeanine Speckman, the front company's export manager; and two Iraqi engineers who identified themselves as representatives of Al Qaqaa, the rocket research facility. It was Daghir who was identified as the importer of French fries. The Iraqis told Kowalsky and Supnick that the capacitors were for laser research. A $10,500 order was signed on the spot. The next day, Ms. Speckman phoned the two Americans and suggested that the capacitors be described as air-conditioning components on the export documents.

A few days after the meeting, a Milan newspaper broke the story that Euromac's Italian office was a front to acquire military equipment for Iraq, including components for cluster bombs. As the winter of 1989–90 wore on, telexes continued to cross the Atlantic. Daghir added a batch of krytrons to the original order for eighty-five capacitors and said that he wanted everything sent directly to Baghdad. Supnick rejected the proposal and instead tried to trick the Iraqis into coming to California to

---

*The capacitors the Iraqis wanted CSI to make were virtually identical with those used in the warhead of the Midgetman ballistic missile.

pick them up. But the wary Daghir would have no part of that. Finally, it was agreed that the capacitors and krytrons would be shipped to London on TWA and then rerouted to Baghdad on Iraqi Air.

Meanwhile, Euromac's office was put under surveillance by British Customs agents posing as street surveyors. In a car parked beside a nearby duck pond sat two NBC newsmen who had been tipped about the sting. The American journalists were even able to photograph the crate of capacitors and krytrons as it went up a conveyor and disappeared into the belly of TWA Flight 760 at Los Angeles International on March 19, 1990. Inside a warehouse at Heathrow, the crate was turned over to American agents, and a crate containing useless capacitors made especially for the operation was substituted. The switch was the same basic procedure that had worked so successfully against Frans van Anraat and his confederates in the thiodiglycol bust. On March 28, as the bogus crate sat inside an Iraqi Boeing 747, detectives from Scotland Yard raided Euromac's office, seizing boxloads of documents and computer records and arresting six people, including Daghir and Speckman. The bust was duly recorded by the television crew from across the street.

The Iraqis were therefore denied the capacitors and krytrons they needed to detonate their atomic bomb by an alert and conscientious American businessman working a long and dangerous sting with a skilled Customs agent. But the Iraqis knew how to use the equipment because the Department of Energy had seen to that in Portland, Oregon, the previous summer. And as U.N. inspectors later found, Iraq had used its own brain power to upgrade commercial capacitors and to get around its inability to buy krytons.

On January 31, 1991—while coalition bombs and cruise missiles were exploding across Iraq—a blue ribbon panel of the National Academies of Sciences and Engineering and the Institute of Medicine published its recommendations for a new approach to export controls in the post-cold-war era in a report called *Finding Common Ground*. The group's twenty-two members were sufficiently alarmed to call for a subtle, but meaningful, shift in the way superweapon proliferation is considered by the United States government. It recommended that proliferation be treated, not as a foreign policy problem, but as an explicit element of national security.

Essentially, the panel called for a more systematic effort to curtail superweapon proliferation by greatly increasing cooperation among the agencies involved in export controls; "harmonizing" various agencies' control lists to minimize overlapping and discrepancies; developing clear standards for weapons and dual-use items; removing export controls on dual-use items when their purely civilian use can be verified; getting business more involved; and developing formal policy mechanisms.

Export controls, the panel went on, should be administered by only one agency: the Department of Commerce's Bureau of Export Administration. *Commerce?*

John Ellicott, a high-powered, buttoned-down veteran Washington lawyer who was on the panel, and who therefore spent a great deal of time sorting out the motives of the various agencies involved in export control, said he believed that Commerce got "a bum rap." A week earlier Representative Henry Gonzalez, continuing his crusade against the Bush administration's role in the arming of Iraq and attendant coverups, had lambasted the agency on the floor of the House for what he alleged to be its failed export control policy. Ellicott said he agreed with much that the Texas Democrat said. But the real culprit, he maintained, was higher up than the head of the Department of Commerce or of any of the other squabbling departments. "The White House set the policy for Iraq," Ellicott asserted.

# 7

# GERMANY:
# EXPORTS ÜBER ALLES

In 1987, as West German companies culminated their relentless drive to make their nation the world's leading exporter, one of the country's grand old men was honored. Hermann Schlosser, then ninety-six and retired from the board of directors of the Degussa conglomerate, was awarded the German Federal Merit Cross for his services to industry. Schlosser's career had spanned his then-still-divided nation's most troubled times, from war to reconstruction to economic vigor.

The Second World War had been a painful time for Schlosser. He had watched his company's plants come under devastating attack from the U.S. Eighth Air Force by day and Britain's Royal Air Force by night. It was testimony to the firm's robustness that despite the bombing of its hydrogen cyanide plant in March 1944, it continued to fulfill what was an important, even critical, government contract. Six months later, more bombs knocked out another of his firm's plants, this one a Frankfurt operation that was working on another special contract. Undaunted and supremely patriotic, with the Fatherland crumbling under siege, Schlosser even managed to contribute 45,000 gold Reichmarks in 1945 to save an elite military unit.

When the war was over, Hermann Schlosser began resurrecting his company. He spent the next forty years first establishing a manufacturing base and markets in West Germany and then, like so many other corporate leaders, pushing industrial exports, many of them to the Third World. The foreign adventures undertaken by Germany's renowned generals gave way to a small army of equally aggressive industrialists and their salesmen. To be sure, rebuilding the economy, which included an embryonic nuclear industry, was financially lucrative. But it was more than that. It was a widely shared way of reasserting sovereignty in the absence of the more traditional way: possession of an army.

A tenacious, imaginative, and thoroughly dedicated entrepreneur, Schlosser remained on Degussa's board until 1980, by which time the company had become a world leader in metallurgy, chemicals, and engineering. From a business standpoint, Schlosser's life was an unmitigated success, a fact to which the Federal Merit Cross attested.

Left unsaid in the awards ceremony was the fact that Degussa, based in the industrial city of Hanau, near Frankfurt, not only had been involved in the most horrific crimes of the Nazi era, but was even then trying to help other countries with their own barbaric agendas.

Degussa is an acronym for *Deutsche Gold und Silber Schnedeanstalt*, or the German Gold and Silver Extracting Company. That name does not appear in any of the directories or corporate literature, however, and for very good reason. Officials of the extracting company are mindful of the fact that beginning in 1938—when smashed windows signaled the official beginning of the "special treatment" Jews were to be given by the Nazis— their firm had a lucrative contract with the SS to reprocess gold and silver jewelry that was forcibly extracted by the storm troopers from Jews in Lodz, Pasenice, and perhaps other Polish ghettoes. The proceeds were used to support the war. Nor was it the first time Schlosser's firm had wrung handsome profits from Hitler's anti-Jewish laws. Degussa had been the beneficiary of the Third Reich's largesse earlier that decade, when it was permitted to buy at cut-rate prices the bullion companies Jews were being forced to sell.

Corporate records are not meant to be social histories. But if they were, Degussa's would be soaked with blood and tears, with unspeakable suffering, mass murder, and other atrocities, all of it driven by remorseless greed.

Some of the revenue that accrued from the Jews' gold and silver might even have been spent on Zyklon B, the deadly hydrogen cyanide gas that hissed out of the showerheads at Auschwitz and other German death camps, killing millions of Jews and others. If that was the case, then Degussa would have realized a double return on its investment; it also invented Zyklon B and was its only supplier. It manufactured the pesticide through another firm known as Degesch, or *Deutsche Gesellschaft für Schadlingsbekampfung*, the German Vermin-Combating Corporation. Degesch was almost wholly owned by Degussa and I. G. Farben, another manufacturing giant that flourished under the Nazis but which, unlike Degussa, was closed down by the Allies after the war. No one from Degussa or Degesch was so much as tried for war crimes.

Even in 1945, as the Third Reich disintegrated under the air assault, Degussa bent to the task of providing raw uranium oxide for Berlin's embryonic atomic bomb program. The uranium eventually found its way to the U.S.S.R., where it was used in that country's first atomic bomb.

Schlosser's award was not for his considerable efforts to help Nazism. It was for steering Degussa, first as chairman and then as director, to the point where it had become a model of international corporate prowess: a solid, prudently managed company of the old school that was also an integral part of the nation's economy. Impressively diversified, Degussa dealt in precious and special metals, organic and inorganic compounds, pharmaceuticals, technochemical and metallurgic products, and technical equipment and installation. Leybold AG, also of Hanau, was a wholly owned subsidiary that manufactured vacuum pumps and components for vacuum pump technology. Their combined revenues were counted in the billions, their employees in the tens of thousands.

At the very moment the old Teuton was accepting his award, Degussa and Leybold had become the world leaders in superweapon proliferation, at least in recklessness and scope, if not in revenue. Their expertise in metallurgy, chemistry, and engineering had won major contracts in the Iraqi missile and nuclear weapons programs. They were also involved in nuclear arms projects in Pakistan, India, North Korea, Argentina, Brazil, and South Africa. Even Israel's nuclear scientists and engineers were valued customers.

Degussa symbolized postwar Germany's darkest secret. Some of the very companies whose products and equipment had been used to exterminate Jews and other undesirables, whose managers had gladly used slave labor, and who had contributed handsomely to Hitler's reign of death and destruction, were at it again. Forty years after the most rabid regime in modern history had been consumed in a firestorm, its provisioners were again plying their wares to new dictators, this time in the Third World.

The men of Schlosser's generation had excused themselves by telling their inquisitors that they were just following orders. Those who succeeded them in the directors' suites and board rooms invented a new excuse for the same attitude: they were just *filling* orders.

Degussa was by no means alone. But because of its extraordinary history and the incredible scope of its nefarious transactions, it was the leader in its class. It apparently would sell nuclear weapon and advanced ballistic missile technology to almost any developing nation that would pay for them. And there were many.

In 1984 and 1985, it reexported more than 210 pounds of U.S.-origin beryllium to India even though it knew, or should have known, that the element was on the Department of Commerce's controlled list. Beryllium is hydrogen bomb fuel. It can be used either to double the explosive capacity of plutonium in the weapon or, alternatively, to allow the bomb maker to use half as much plutonium. CIA Director William Webster maintained in 1989 that the sale was a clear indicator that India was working on a hydrogen bomb. Once caught, Degussa admitted that the beryllium's final destination was the Bhabha Atomic Research Center at Trombay, India's atomic bomb factory, but added lamely that it had been assured by its customers that the material would not be used in India's weapons program.*

In 1986 and 1987 Degussa repeated the process, this time re-exporting U.S.-origin zirconium from West Germany to North Korea. Zirconium is used as cladding to encase fuel rods in nuclear reactors. It acts as a "moderator" that slows the flight of neutrons from one rod to another. In the process, the rods themselves collect plutonium as part of the chain reaction. The plutonium can then be extracted and shaped into weapons material. North Korea was at the time building its nuclear reactor at Yongbyon, which U.S. intelligence subsequently identified as the probable home of the country's nuclear weapons program.

After a threat by Commerce to revoke its right to export to the United States, Degussa agreed to pay an $800,000 fine, the largest ever levied by Commerce's Bureau of Export Administration. It also agreed to allow

---

*The Indian order did in fact claim that the 99 percent pure beryllium metal lumps would be used to study "vacuum induction melting and casting para-motors for obtained fine grain defect free castings." But that amounted to necessary engineering jargon, a fact that could hardly have gone over the heads of Degussa's salesmen. (Certificate of Application and end use for beryllium lumps against order no. DPS/BARC/MTL/6065/PO/10185/FE/OGL, Government of India, Department of Atomic Energy, September 14, 1983, and marked "Secret.")

unannounced inspection visits to its special metals facilities by Department of Commerce agents. Given the level of Degussa's business, however, the fine amounted to a slap on the wrist.

From the late 1970s to 1992, Degussa's machine tool subsidiary, Leybold-Heraeus, was also on the prowl for business in nuclear weapons states. First it systematically transferred classified blueprints and other technology related to the manufacture of uranium melting furnaces, or autoclaves, from URENCO, an international consortium of companies involved in uranium research, to Metallwerke Buchs AG, or MWB, of Buchs, Switzerland.* MWB actually manufactured the autoclaves under the supervision of Leybold-Heraeus's avowedly capitalistic engineers. Leybold-Heraeus then tested them. When the firm was later confronted with the "misappropriation" of classified documents, it returned them and arranged an elaborate cover-up involving a fictitious source. Meanwhile, other parts of the autoclaves—specialized copper parts and valves—were made by a Leybold-Heraeus affiliate and shipped to the Middle East via a circuitous route that involved a company in Liechtenstein. Throughout, the furnaces were referred to as "containers," as both Leybold-Heraeus and MWB tried to conceal their real activities, minimize open contact, maintain tight plant security, and use deception in the handling and shipment of the components. German and U.S. officials are convinced that the furnaces wound up in A. Q. Khan's nuclear weapons operation in Pakistan.†

The blueprints themselves eventually found their way from Pakistan to Iraq and may even have been passed to nuclear weapons programs in Brazil and North Korea, according to the BND, Germany's equivalent of the CIA, and the Federal Republic's customs intelligence organization.

During the 1970s, Leybold-Heraeus was also involved in the development and supply of jet nozzles that enriched uranium for South Africa's six atomic bombs.

In July 1991, Leybold—by now a wholly owned Degussa subsidiary—delivered a vacuum induction annealing and smelting furnace to Fritz Werner Industrie-Ausrustungen GmbH, a company that had previously helped equip missile research and development facilities in Iraq and worked on other weapons projects for Burma's military dictatorship.

*Leybold was at the time called Leybold-Heraeus and was 33 percent owned by Degussa.
†Not long afterward, Pakistan began trying to purchase other melting furnaces from Consarc, the U.S. firm located in New Jersey, at a price of about $3 million each. It was not successful.

Leybold insisted that the furnace, which was sent to the port of Hamburg in ten boxes before being seized by German customs agents, was for the smelting of aluminum domestically. Such furnaces are actually used for the production of super-hard metal alloys of the type used in guided missiles and nuclear weapons. An internal memorandum circulated among Leybold's management on June 27, 1991, helped clarify the situation. It provided details about how the delivery was in fact to be camouflaged and sent to an outfit called Maktab el Buhut Attacknia, which was a cover for Libya's ballistic missile research facility in Tripoli. Libya was at that time trying to develop a ballistic missile of its own, Al-Fatah ("The Warrior"), which was to have a 600-mile range. Freelancing German engineers were in Libya, actually working on the project.

By 1992, the Hamburg Prosecutor's Office had the furnace case under investigation. The government's case was impeded, however, by Leybold's pointing out—correctly—that a change in German export regulations the previous April had freed the company to export this type of furnace wherever it wanted.

Leybold's tentacles also extended to Iraq's superweapon program. Its long-held denials of helping any Third World nation acquire nuclear weapons technology fell apart when U.N. inspectors began to disclose what they had found in places like Iraq's Taji weapons complex and in Baghdad's Nuclear Research Center.

In August 1991 the inspectors recovered 25,000 documents, 600 pages of which showed that both Leybold and Degussa had provided equipment to manufacture the uranium gas centrifuges that would have been crucial for producing enough enriched uranium to make nuclear weapons in large numbers.

By December, U.N. analysts had determined that an electron beam welder and laser cutter provided by Leybold and Degussa were two of the eight items of those deemed critical to the centrifuge process. The analysts, experts in nuclear weaponry, made it clear that the companies that had supplied the centrifuge-making hardware knew what its end use was to be. The usual protestations of ignorance would not do this time. "While much of the equipment is multi-purpose in the sense of being useful in a number of manufacturing processes," the U.N. report concluded, "the presence of applications-specific fixtures removes most doubt as to the intended use."

Even more damning was Degussa's and Leybold's involvement with the Al Atheer nuclear weapons development facility south of Baghdad.

One room, contemptuously described by a Department of Defense technical expert as the "Leybold Suite," contained the hot and cold isostatic presses necessary for making the shaped charges that implode on the enriched uranium, causing it to explode.

The purchase of the presses and vacuum furnaces may very well have been arranged at the Iraqi Embassy in Bonn on August 14 and 17, 1987, even as Baghdad and Teheran were slugging it out like two punch-drunk fighters seven years into their match. There, in the capital of the Federal Republic, Degussa's executive director and a representative of Leybold-Heraeus met with Ali Abdul Mutalib Ali, Iraq's economic attaché. Ali's Industrial Projects Company ran Iraq's nuclear procurement network in Germany. Most of Degussa's and Leybold's weapons technology exports to Iraq came after the two meetings.

Leybold tried to fend off critics of the furnace and press transaction by insisting that the equipment was "standard" and intended only for "general military repair." But experts in the Pentagon, like those at the U.N., took strong exception. The only realistic use for such precision equipment, purchased in the precise combination sought by Iraq, could be the manufacturing of centrifuges.

The firm countered by pointing out that some of the equipment—the carbon dioxide laser cutter and the electron beam welder—may have come from its Enfield, Connecticut, plant. Leybold couldn't really be sure, since they had shipped three electron beam welders to Iraqi military enterprises. One definitely had been shipped to the facility where Scud missiles had been made. Another had gone to the nuclear weapons establishment. The third . . . they didn't really know what had happened to it. They were sure, however, that one had been duly approved for export by the Department of Commerce. This was true. The company's Washington lawyer, Werner Hein, had pushed high-ranking Commerce officials to approve the export of the equipment even though analysts in the department's own Office of Export Intelligence Review objected to the sale. Upper management in Commerce's Bureau of Export Administration ultimately approved the licenses without bothering to alert the Department of Defense. Hein denies pressuring anyone.

"U.S. export officials transferred sensitive U.S.-origin equipment directly into the hands of Iraq's bomb and missile makers, and did it on behalf of an exporter that was already notorious for nuclear smuggling," the House Committee on Government Operations would later note, sourly. "The export went out at top speed even though there was a bad seller, a bad buyer, and a bad end use." Stephen Bryen, then Deputy Undersecretary of Defense for Technology Security, maintained with characteristic anger and frustration that Leybold's application would never have left his desk had it landed there.

Not long after this episode, Leybold officials visited the offices of several senators and congressmen. Its newly hired public relations men assured their listeners that the company would no longer deal with any Third World nation that had failed to sign the nuclear Non-Proliferation Treaty. And to prove that it had fundamentally changed course, Leybold produced some telling correspondence between it and two of its old customers: the atomic energy agencies of India and Israel.

A letter from K. Balu of the Indian Department of Atomic Energy's Directorate of Purchases and Stores complained that Leybold would neither install nor commission the installation of a vacuum arc remelting furnace it had already delivered. U.S. experts knew that such a furnace had several nuclear end-uses, including the fabrication of bomb cores, so they had asked Leybold not to install it. That sort of request had previously fallen on deaf ears. But now, after so much Leybold and Degussa equipment had been found in Iraq, the companies would become models of cooperation. What Balu's letter really showed, however, was the devil-be-damned attitude of Leybold's atomic salesmen. It also showed that listening to the Americans, even nominally, could save Leybold some money, since it could renege on its promise to set up its equipment. Balu, noting "our sense of shock," complained bitterly that Leybold had cashed the Indian letter of credit without completing the terms of the contract. If he didn't like it, Leybold no doubt told Balu, he could blame the Americans.

In another letter, Michal Berman, the Israeli Atomic Energy Commission's foreign purchasing manager, claimed to be "astonished" at the company's decision not to sell spare parts for the Soreq Nuclear Research Center, Israel's Los Alamos. The facility, Berman noted, had been a good customer of Leybold's for twenty years and was now in difficulty because it was unable to find compatible spare parts for "about 100 Leybold's [sic] pumps" it had installed.

Leybold offered the letters as proof that it was taking its new responsibilities as a good citizen seriously. But they only proved to incredulous congressional aides that Degussa and Leybold had for years spread nuclear technology around the world with an apparent lack of concern that bordered on abandon.

• • • •

**D**egussa and its corporate appendages peddle their wares in a crowded field. The competition includes a spate of the nation's leading industrial giants. But there are also many low-profile, middle-rung, workaday firms that aren't big enough to make the famous directories. (One of them, in fact, had only three employees.)

H & H Metalform, a medium-size but aggressive firm in Drenstein-furt, Germany, was half-owned by Iraq. By the time Iraq invaded Kuwait, H & H and Matrix-Churchill were its two most important nuclear weapons technology suppliers. H & H's two other owners, Peter Huetten and Dietrich Hinze, called themselves "specialists worldwide in aviation parts and cooking parts." If that sounded boring, it was precisely the idea.

Huetten, however, was anything but boring. In fact, he would have made an engrossing comic opera arms supplier if his business hadn't been so deadly. He dismissed Saddam Hussein's poison gassing of the Kurds and causing a million deaths in his war with Iran as something that was not for him, Huetten, to judge. Instead, he preferred to see Saddam's nobler side.

"He's forged a people, the Iraqi people. He's created infrastructures. He's built housing. He's done a great deal in the social area," Huetten proclaimed with unintended ambiguity. So apparently taken was he with Saddam Hussein, that he landed the contract to build the famous gigantic crossed-sword victory monument that towers more than 200 yards across and 100 high in Baghdad, and which commemorates Iraq's "victory" over Iran. The swords are held by impressions of Saddam's hands enlarged forty times. The swords themselves are hung with thousands of Iranian helmets.

But H & H's contracts soon called for creations that went well beyond the symbolic. They extended to supplying machine tools for making air-plane drop tanks that held poison gas and flow-forming machines to make thick metal thin enough so it could be used in centrifuges, missile parts, and other dangerous equipment. On its export application form, which was approved without incident, H & H blithely explained that the flow-forming machines were for use in making dairy equipment and street lamps. U.N. inspectors poking through the remnants of Saddam Hussein's war machine a few years later would not be so generous. They labeled some of the equipment "application-specific," meaning that it was un-doubtedly weapon-related. "One must assume that the accused knew that the alleged end-use [lamp posts] was false," one of the inspectors, a

German, wrote. The real uses were for centrifuges and rocket combustion chambers, the U.N. contended, adding that there was evidence that the same equipment was also sent to Brazil.

H & H also supplied nuclear experts to both Brazil and Iraq . . . specifically engineers who had designed centrifuges for the URENCO complex in the Netherlands. It was H & H's Dietrich Hinze who placed the engineers in jobs with the Brazilian Naval Commission, the Brazilian entity at the center of that nation's nuclear program. Then, later, he helped the same men set up contacts in Iraq.

Whatever else he was, Peter Huetten was the death merchant's death merchant laid bare; a man with dark visceral instincts that were seemingly unencumbered by moral nuance. Toward the end of 1987, for example, he learned that the Iraqi Army had barraged the Iranians with 6,000 of his rocket casings, some carrying poison gas, in one night. The weapons caused unspeakable carnage and made new widows, orphans, and child-less couples in Iran. On the other hand, since the rocket casings sold for $2,500 each, it had been a $15 million night for H & H. That many casings represented three months' production. Heutten was was so gleeful that he threw an impromptu champagne party to celebrate.

When articles about H & H's weapons trafficking in *Der Spiegel* in late 1989 drew a Thames Television crew from England to the front of his red brick office building, Heutten showed his wrathful side. As the video crew tried to set up its camera, a speeding Mercedes suddenly appeared on the sidewalk, heading right at the group. The startled Britons scattered, but not before their camera was knocked over. Heutten, like a bull charging at a matador's cape, repeated the attack each time the camera was set up. "If you keep on filming," the enraged German snarled through the automobile's open window, "I'll knock the camera into a thousand pieces." The confrontation ended in a fist fight and a protest by the Britons to their embassy. In 1992, following the U.N. revelations, the burly Westphalian and Hinze were arrested by their embarrassed government and held for trial.

When their indictment was handed up in March 1993, the charges were truly startling even by German standards. In addition to supplying gas centrifuge technology, Heutten and Hinze were alleged to have sold Iraq 27,436 parts for Scud B missiles and their Iraqi derivatives. They were also charged with selling machinery to produce other missiles. And if that weren't enough, the German prosecutors said that after the invasion of Kuwait ended those sales, H & H found a new outlet for its rocket combustion chambers: Libya. Between them, the two Arab countries had paid Heutten and Hinze more than $30 million. They have denied the charges.

Large and small firms alike work in the industrial world's gray area—its back streets and alleys—quietly filling orders for the otherwise unrelated chemicals, electronics, metals, fine and heavy machinery, and construction and engineering expertise that, taken together, constitute the Third World's collective arsenal of superweapons.

Like Degussa, many of them had been willing participants in the brutality of the Nazi era. That fact is only relevant because it reflected a cold-blooded business ethic that survived the war, an ethic that called for profit at any cost. No strategy was too devious, no amount of human suffering too great, no danger of conflagration too worrisome to dissuade those who worshipped at the altar of the Deutschmark.

"We have historical documentation which shows that many of these firms did request slave laborers to be sent to work for them," said Thomas Lutz, an archivist with a Berlin evangelical church justice organization. His allegation was borne out during war crimes trials in 1947, when piles of documents were used to show that Siemens and others actively recruited slave labor from France, Poland, and other captive countries and that the workers were treated with exceptional cruelty. The reason, as usual, was to maximize profit.* About 30,000 inmates of Auschwitz were killed building a nearby factory for Farben. Many were literally worked to death. Those who managed to survive the brutal ordeal were returned to the death camp for gassing.

Siemens was up to a great deal more than using slave labor to produce parts for planes, submarines, and missiles during World War II, however. Like Degussa, it was directly involved with the death camps. According to Bruno Baum, a concentration camp inmate and electrician who went on to become a member of the Berlin city council, Siemens had a monopoly on the electrical equipment in the gas chambers. Baum recounted at the 1947 trials that some of the most novel and ingenious devices came from Siemens. One, in particular, was a ventilation system that was so efficient

---

*Arms manufacturing cartels like Krupp and Farben also scrutinized the technical press and had their overseas representatives look and listen for information that was of commercial value. Much of this concerned military materiel. The firms not only used some of what they learned on the assembly line, but ingratiated themselves to the military by passing much of it along in that direction as well. (David Kahn, *Hitler's Spies*, New York: Macmillan, 1978, p. 63.) British and no doubt U.S. firms did the same thing.

at expelling used Zyklon B and drawing in a fresh supply that up to 10,000 people could be exterminated in twenty-four hours.

Speaking through an interpreter a half century later, Trudy Blass, a former slave laborer, said that Siemens's corporate memory should extend back to the war and to the work it did for the war. Some people, she said, have told her that the managers are different now. "But they are the same, you know," the elderly woman added. "They are the same managers in . . . I mean . . . how they behave."

Norbert Gansel, a member of the Bundestag and the leading critic of his country's more excessive business practices, agrees. "These companies served Hitler and the Wehrmacht because they were part of the arms industry. After the war, they converted to civil industry, but they kept their personnel and they kept their know-how," the legislator explained. "And so, after the rearmament of the Federal Republic, they returned, partially, to arms development and arms production again. But this is not enough to explain that sort of phenomenon," he added, referring to the fervor with which some German companies sell weapons technology. "Sometimes I have the feeling that there is something like a bad evil in special places, in special companies, in special personnel and special branches."

"There is an old tradition in many corporations, and it's particularly true in German corporations, of being apolitical," observed Peter Hayes, a historian at Northwestern University who specializes in modern European history. Hayes said that German firms ought to be especially conscious of their social and political responsibilities in light of the Nazi experience. "After all, they were brought into close proximity with murderous political policies that had terribly damaging effects on millions of people. Thus, they are more aware than most people are that business is not just business, that it can have tremendous political consequences."

Certainly no one would accuse Siemens of harboring Nazi sentiments, of using slave labor, or even of abusing its workers today. To the contrary, the huge multinational prospered during Germany's postwar economic miracle by adequately compensating its work force while attempting to be as competitive as possible.* Competition, after all, is the

---

*With profits of $1.6 billion on a turnover of more than $37 billion, Siemens was listed by the *Financial Times* as being the ninth largest firm in Europe in 1991. And with 373,000 workers, it was also the second largest employer. ("Europe's Top 500," *Financial Times*, January 13, 1992.)

essence of a free market economy. Yet Siemens's health, like Degussa's and the others', derives from a particularly tough-minded corporate mentality. Under such circumstances, ethics and morality are relegated to church on Sunday morning. During the rest of the week, they are buried under the bottom line in an unending search for new markets. During the mid-1980s, for example, two-thirds of Leybold's and 55 percent of Siemens's business depended on exports. No wonder the Third World market was, and remains, so important. Therefore, almost anything goes.

Siemens, which has run television commercials in the United States bragging about its "precision thinking," is a case in point. The leader of Germany's electronics industry has sold precision hardware, software, know-how, and training to nations around the world that are clamoring for nuclear weapons and poison gas technology.

At one point in the late 1980s, for instance, Washington pointedly asked the Foreign Ministry to determine why Siemens had sold an electronic control system for mixing heavy water to a plant at Hazira, India. The Indian heavy water facility happened to be the largest of its kind in the Third World and was a prime component of New Delhi's nuclear weapons program. Siemens maintained that the Indians duped it into making the sale by claiming that the equipment was for an ammonia plant. But the firm never had to defend itself because, despite Washington's demarche, the ministry did not pursue the matter. Somewhat belatedly, however, Bonn did order the mixing equipment to be put on the export control list.

The German Technology Ministry reported in 1987 that Siemens sold critical uranium enrichment technology, as well as other nuclear technology and expertise, to Brazil with the controls mandated by the IAEA. The Bundesamt fur Wirtschaft, or BAW (the Economics Ministry) agreed to the transfer only on condition that the controls be enforced. Yet they weren't. It later turned out that although the hardware and instructional material were technically for Brazil's commercial nuclear industry, they somehow "wandered" into the country's nuclear weapons program. Siemens was therefore pressed by the IAEA for details of the transaction. But it refused to cooperate, saying that as far as it was concerned, the matter was closed. The Economics Ministry, which singlemindedly saw its role as promoting German exports, no doubt rooted for Siemens.

Reports in 1989 and 1990 by the BND and the Finance and Foreign Ministries detailed a dark deal between a wholly owned Siemens subsidiary named Interatom and Iraq's nuclear weapons procurement network.

This one picked up exactly where Degussa and Leybold left off in the nuclear arming of Iraq. Once Baghdad was confident that it could get the Degussa and Leybold equipment it needed to manufacture critical components for its centrifuges, it began looking for a company to build an actual production facility and train technicians to run it. That was Siemens and Interatom.

Interatom agreed to provide a clean room, which is necessary for centrifuge construction, and training for twenty-three scientists at one of its facilities outside Cologne. The Iraqis' own clean room was identified in Interatom documents as BO 1, to be located at Al Furat, about twenty miles south of Baghdad. Siemens later claimed that the room was to be used as part of an oil pipeline construction project. But when U.N. inspectors visited the site where the Iraqi clean room was to be installed, Iraqi nuclear weapons scientists told them that the facility was in reality going to be Saddam's first centrifuge factory. BO 1 was intended to be the workshop where the centrifuges were to be tested before being turned over to Saddam's bomb makers. It was clearly not intended to test pipes.

Even more incredibly, Siemens claimed that it was training twenty-three Iraqis only in technologies that had to do with the pipes and petroleum transportation. Yet even Enzio von Kuehlmann-Stumm, a PR man for Siemens, admitted that those same technologies had clear value for the operation of the centrifuges.

And there were other incongruities. Forty-three weeks of instruction had been completed before the company even filed for the necessary licenses with the Economics Minister, for example. Not by mere coincidence, the head of Interatom's Advanced Reactor Program happened to be in Baghdad for purposes related to the clean room project when the Iraqis overran Kuwait.*

Despite all these dangers, Interatom evidently believed that the potential benefit—the project was worth $10 million—was worth the risk. It even clung to that belief during the summer of 1990, when it knew that it was under investigation by the ZKI: the German Customs Criminal Institute. The deal finally fell apart, however, within hours of the Iraqi Army's rolling into Kuwait. In a letter dated that day, August 2, 1990, Dr. Joachim Jahnke, the head of BAW's export control division, advised

---

*He was permitted to leave Baghdad with Willy Brandt, the former German prime minister, on December 5: ten days after all other Siemens employees departed. A source claimed that Bonn feared that Iraq would hold the Interatom manager hostage in order to get advanced reactor technology.

Interatom that its "international reputation" would suffer if it continued working with its "Iraqi partner." Only then did Interatom decide to sever its ties with Saddam Hussein.

Any ambiguity that lingered over the German companies' arming of Iraq ended when the U.N. inspectors began gathering documents after the Persian Gulf War. Inspectors found unambiguous evidence that Germans had been there. In fact, the Iraqis had turned to the Germans first for their superweapon technology needs.

The inspectors saw that Karl Kolb had delivered no fewer than five complete poison gas plants. Thyssen had set up a biological weapons research facility at Salman Pak. Thyssen, MBB, and Gildemeister were proved beyond doubt to have participated in the ballistic missile program. Thyssen's involvement was ironic. Fritz Thyssen, one of the company's leading lights in the 1930s, had been an early and enthusiastic supporter of Hitler because of the Fuhrer's antisemitism. A half century later, the firm had helped refine missiles that rained down on Israel.

Nowhere, however, was the trail more distinct than in the nuclear weapons area. Numbers alone did not tell the whole story, but they told enough to embarrass Germany. Twenty of the forty-eight firms identified by the IAEA inspectors as having supplied technology for Jafar Jafar's "Mechanism" were German. Of the 602 machine tools found by the inspectors at Iraqi nuclear weapons plants, 242 had been made in Germany. Most of the forty-seven machines that were designated as "key" originated in Germany. Of those, all thirteen that were labeled "Level 1" (indispensable) by the inspectors were German, as well as ten that were put in the "Level 2" category. The "Level 1" equipment was used to make parts for the baghdatrons, centrifuges, and other components.

For months, the IAEA had been turning over damning documents to the German embassy in Vienna. Now, still smarting from the renowned poison gas episode in Libya three years earlier—"Auschwitz in the sand," as the press called it—the Federal Republic decided to act decisively. In July 1992, 420 federal officers raided nine firms, with Degussa and Leybold heading the list, and recovered evidence showing that tens of thousands of items had been exported to Saddam Hussein's superweapon machine. "We have found the tomb of the Pharaoh," said one of the customs agents who took part in the bust.

•   •   •

The seeds of the July 1992 crackdown and subsequent efforts to overhaul Germany's export laws were planted not in Iraqi sand, but in Libyan.

Germany's other important Arab customer was Colonel Muammar el-Qaddafi and his notorious poison gas plant at Rabta, forty miles southwest of Tripoli. As was the case with Sa'ad-16 and Project 395, a bevy of German firms—forty-two of them—combined into a superweapon consortium. Overall responsibility for the project went to Imhausen-Chemie AG, a large chemical concern which signed a contract with Libya in 1984, allegedly to deliver a pharmaceutical plant.

Imhausen, too, had a Nazi history. In the 1930s, the company developed a synthetic fat substitute from Germany's ample coal resources in a contract with the SS. After years of testing on unwilling victims in Heinrich Himmler's concentration camps, the project was finally abandoned. Along the way, Imhausen's president and founder, Arthur Imhausen, had been made an honorary Aryan despite having some Jewish blood. Now it was his son's turn to make his mark. Jurgen Hippensteil-Imhausen assured his suppliers that he was merely helping Libya to build up its drug industry. In fact, as was clear from the beginning, the sprawling facility was supposed to provide Libya with chemical bombs, artillery shells, and rocket and missile warheads in large quantities.

The installation was designed in two parts. One, masterminded by Imhausen, was to be responsible for producing the poison gases themselves. The other, called the "Metal Works," was to weaponize the deadly chemicals. It in turn consisted of three plants: one to make artillery shells, one to make bombs, and one to make rockets. That part of the complex was designed and built by the Japanese at a total estimated cost of $3 billion. Construction was arranged by C. Itoh, the big Japanese trading organization. Japan Steel Works, a division of Mitsui, was the general contractor. Two other Japanese firms are also suspected by U.S. intelligence of providing precision machine tools and the installation's power plant. When the United States complained to Japan about its companies' role at Rabta and headlines began to appear, the technicians were hurriedly sent home and both Japan Steel Works and Toshiba abandoned the project.

Similar, repeated complaints to Bonn were systematically ignored. Indeed, scores of richly detailed reports by the Federal Republic's own intelligence organization not only were ignored but also on more than one occasion were actually lost.

Like similar clandestine operations in Iraq and elsewhere, deception and secrecy played central roles at Rabta. That is why it was located so far from the capital; why it carried the ambiguous code name "Pharma 150"; why the plans to the complex did not bear the designer's name; why it was surrounded by barbed wire and guards; and why most of the material that went into it was addressed to the Pen Tsao Material Medica, a Hong Kong company for which Imhausen was building a chemical plant.

None of those measures would have been necessary had the facility really been designed to manufacture drugs, a point Washington heatedly made to Bonn several times in the mid-and late-1980s to no avail. CIA analysts, whose curiosity was piqued by the large facility going up in the Libyan desert, followed its progress on imagery collected by KH-11 photo-reconnaissance satellites. The spacecraft delivered their "take" in near-real time so the photointerpreters could watch the concrete being poured almost as it was happening. The pictures, as well as information collected on the ground, left no doubt as to what Pharma 150 was.

It is likely that one of the reasons the German government hesitated as long as possible to take up the Rabta issue was that the plant was built to Imhausen's specifications by Salzgitter Industriebau GmbH, or SIG, a subsidiary of Salzgitter AG, which was owned by none other than the Federal Republic itself. This meant that Bonn had, in effect, contracted to build a poison gas factory for an unstable North African despot who was known to menace his neighbors and harbor and finance terrorists. On the other hand, many in the government were mindful that SIG was paid a little more than $4 million just for the 200 looseleaf binders full of highly detailed blueprints that it prepared in close consultation with Imhausen. Another likely reason for the foot-dragging had to do with unpleasant associations between the poison gas factory and the killing chambers in the concentration camps.

Imhausen itself, which collected $150 million from Qaddafi for over-all planning, gave SIG's designers specific requirements for the size of the facility and the equipment it would hold.

Siemens played a crucial role in the Rabta operation as well. On December 16, 1986, the freighter *Roubini II* left the port of Antwerp with a cargo that included one of the company's "Teleperm M" systems. The freight documents stated that the equipment weighed 10.5 tons, was valued at $1.4 million, and was headed for the other side of the world: to the Pen Tsao Material Medica. But Teleperm M's real destination was only three hours' flying time from Siemens's headquarters in Munich: the port of Tripoli.

Teleperm M was not purchased to make cough medicine. It was a highly advanced, computer-controlled apparatus that would automatically mix the precise amounts of precursor chemicals for poison gas. More than two years later, in the summer of 1988, Siemens sent another shipment that ended up in Rabta. This one contained electrical control panels, computers, and six "field multiplexers." The last are measuring devices that electronically monitor and control the flow of chemicals. The number of them, six, is particularly interesting since the nerve gas tabun is made from six chemicals.

In 1987, the CIA, which was watching Rabta's construction and providing the administration with reports whose findings were passed on to Bonn to no avail, went public. It leaked news of the chemical weapons facility to *The New York Times*, which ran the story on page one on December 24. It was *The Times*'s columnist, William Safire, who would later call Rabta "Auschwitz in the sand" because of Qaddafi's vociferous anti-Israel stance.

When German involvement in Rabta was reported in detail by that country's aggressive investigative reporters during the winter of 1988–89, naming several companies that included Siemens, the firm's public relations office swung into action, stubbornly maintaining that the company was innocent. It contended that Siemens had no idea that the Teleperm M hardware was bound for Libya; that having worked with Imhausen for twenty years, it took the company at its word when it said that Teleperm M was destined for Hong Kong.

Volker Schmidt-Wellenburg, the Senior Director for Corporate Business Guidelines—Siemens's export ethicist—maintained that his firm made every effort to obey German law and keep potential weapons out of the hands of other nations. He even cited a computer-driven export control system that is used to monitor the 500,000 products Siemens exports from Germany, plus another 350,000 it manufactures in the United States, as proof of his firm's ethical responsibility.

Like any number of other weapons proliferators, Siemens was and remains particularly wary of such homegrown investigative news organizations as the magazines *Der Spiegel* and *Stern*, which they consider to be staffed by meddling scandalmongers. It was *Stern* that broke the story about Siemens's supplying some German submarine plans to South Africa and that dug its way into the Rabta scheme.

If Germany abounded with corporate scoundrels in the 1980s and beyond, it also produced a tough cadre of investigative reporters, environmental activists, and liberal parliamentarians like Gansel who tenaciously exposed their skullduggery. Hans Leyendecker of *Der Spiegel* ("The Mirror") and Egmont Koch, a reporter with *Der Spiegel* television, doggedly pursued the proliferators. Like Gansel, the two journalists were children of the sixties who took a far more enlightened path than many of their elders. As a result, both were wary of their country's corporations. As the Düsseldorf bureau chief of *Der Spiegel*, Leyendecker exposed Germany's role in the Rabta chemical complex in Libya, the Iraqi nuclear and missile programs, Pakistan's nuclear program, and a long list of other escapades going all the way to North Korea. They and other reporters were only too aware of their country's lingering reputation from the Holocaust and other atrocities.

So was Harald Müller, a dedicated proliferation specialist with the Frankfurt Peace Research Institute. "This 'Auschwitz in the sand,' I mean it was a nasty article, but it stuck. It was not only a PR question, but for many of us. . . . Don't underrate the feeling of people of my generation who are sitting in the Bundestag. It hurts. I mean, we really want to get over that, to have a distance between us and that insane . . . It's conscience."*

Siemens and the other corporations were also deeply concerned about their images, though to judge by their proliferation record, for different reasons. They knew that in a capitalist economy, image—how the company is perceived by potential customers—is crucial to success. Siemens's concern for its image, in fact, has played as least as much of a role in whatever it does to reduce weapons proliferation as any apparent moral compunctions.

"We are certainly very much concerned about possible effects on our image," Volker Schmidt-Wellenburg explained. "And this is especially true in the United States, because we know that the U.S. public is very sensitive indeed about such issues."

But no amount of public relations could convince one longtime Washington proliferation specialist that Siemens and the other companies involved in Sa'ad-16, Rabta, and the other projects simply did not know

*Müller recalled in 1992 that he used the Auschwitz-in-the-sand argument to rally members of the Bundestag against the Rabta project by asking them how they thought it would look if poison gas that landed in Israel came from Germany. (Interview by Burrows in Washington on March 19, 1992.)

what they were doing for their customers. "The FRG [Federal Republic of Germany] is hanging Imhausen for the Rabta deal and claiming that the other 100 German firms which were involved there were 'misled' by Imhausen," he said. "To say that the FRG's flagship electronics firm [Siemens] was misled in Libya, misled in Iraq, misled in Pakistan and misled in South Africa raises questions of management competency," he added with undisguised contempt.

The Rabta situation finally came to a head during the winter and spring of 1990 following a year of scandals that were continuously investigated by the West German news media. In early March, the Bush administration leaked reports to *The New York Times* and ABC News that, after a one-year hiatus caused by protests to Bonn from Washington, the Libyans were once again manufacturing some mustard gas at the isolated facility. More ominously, the Defense Intelligence Agency concluded that Rabta was moving toward full-scale production.

Washington therefore turned up the heat. This resulted in a plan hatched by Hans-Dietrich Genscher, the German Foreign Minister, for Libya to open Rabta to international inspection. But Reginald Bartholomew, the Department of State's ranking official on chemical weapons proliferation, called in the West German ambassador, Juergen Ruhfus, to say that the United States rejected Genscher's proposal out of hand because it was wholly inadequate. State's Bureau of Intelligence and Research no doubt reasoned, correctly, that Rabta could have been made to look like the pharmaceutical plant Qaddafi claimed it was, or even a shoe factory for that matter, in plenty of time for the inspectors' visit.

Even before Genscher made his proposal, however, West German media stories spotlighting those who designed, built, and fitted Rabta, together with American protests, had finally prompted a reluctant but embarrassed German Government to launch a serious investigation.* This

---

*Although the Rabta complex was designed, constructed, and fitted primarily by German companies, other nations were involved as well. The nearby metalworking plant, for example, was built with the assistance of Japanese firms and is believed by U.S. intelligence experts to manufacture the bomb canisters and warheads that carry the poison gas. In addition, 270 Thai nationals, including engineers, were working at Rabta in 1989. One U.S. official with considerable knowledge about the facility said, contemptuously, that the Libyans even needed foreign help to install and putty-in the facility's windows. ("U.S. Hints at Chemical Arms Bunker in Libya," *The New York Times*, March 7, 1991, and "U.S. Fails to Oust Thais at Libya Plant," *The Washington Post*, June 1, 1989.) In Senate testimony on January 24, 1989 CIA Director Webster named the Japanese as being "involved" in the facility adjacent to the chemical weapons plant. (See the Senate Committee on Foreign Relations hearings on the "Chemical and Biological Weapons Threat," March 1, 1989, p. 40.)

resulted in the arrest of Jurgen Hippenstiel-Imhausen, the owner and manager of Imhausen-Chemie, on May 10, 1989. Nearly a year later, on March 22, 1990, he was charged with violating West German export law by providing Colonel Qaddafi with the poison gas factory. To compound the offense, Hippenstiel-Imhausen had also failed to cut the Federal Republic in on the profit from the sale; he was therefore additionally charged with failure to pay $9.5 million in taxes. (What he had not failed to do, however, was get rid of some of the evidence against him. In the spring of 1988, alarmed by the story about Rabta that appeared in *The New York Times* the previous December, Hippenstiel-Imhausen rectified the situation by having some of his employees move company records to "a neighboring country," according to German intelligence.)

Although the prosecutor's office made a point of announcing that Salzgitter was also under investigation, nothing came of it. As the mystery writer Dashiell Hammett might have put it, the hapless Hippenstiel-Imhausen was going to take the fall for Rabta all by himself.

Facing a maximum prison sentence of thirteen years, the chemical executive subsequently changed his plea from innocent to guilty in an apparent effort get a reduced sentence. And it worked. On June 27, 1990, Jurgen Hippenstiel-Imhausen was sentenced to five years in prison, thus becoming the only participant in the Rabta scheme to go to jail. The company, however, was allowed to keep the $60 million in profits it made on the deal since the prosecution never even mentioned confiscating the money. (The prosecutor was nonetheless reassigned after being told that he had been "overly persistent" in his investigation.)

While Hippenstiel-Imhausen's trial was still going on, the mercurial Colonel Qaddafi reacted to the anger in Washington and the furor in Germany by pretending to incinerate his own pharmaceutical factory. Having been bombed once by the United States for committing terrorism, the Colonel most likely had no wish to provoke another attack because he was manufacturing poison gas. On March 14 the facility was therefore reported by the Libyan press agency to be blazing. Tunisians almost simultaneously told officials in Washington that they had seen a pillar of smoke rising over the complex. Next, Libya variously blamed the purported conflagration on the United States, on Israel, and particularly on West Germany. The Germans, now on the defensive, felt obliged to deny that they were trying to destroy the evidence of their complicity in the project even as 2,000 residents of Tripoli obediently took to the streets with signs that denounced them as "spies." That same day Qaddafi went on television to warn that "If the current investigations prove that West German intelligence is involved in any act inside Libya, then Germany's economic presence inside Libya will be eliminated."

Within two weeks, however, intelligence reports suggesting that the fire had been an elaborately staged hoax and that poison gas was still being produced at Rabta began filtering into Washington. By mid-June, there was no almost no doubt about it. Some imagery interpreters concluded that all the smoke had come from the burning of truckloads of old tires, while the facility itself had been generously doused with black paint so as to appear charred to the spy satellites' powerful cameras. Meanwhile, production at Rabta continued. The CIA was to estimate in early 1992 that the facility had produced as much as 100 tons of chemical agents.

Furthermore, the Libyan government had by then planned a second chemical weapons factory on the Rabta design, though somewhat smaller. This one was to be located at Sebha, a place Qaddafi no doubt hoped was so remote—a Saharan oasis 400 miles south of Tripoli—that it would not have to suffer the sort of exposure that was inflicted on Rabta.

But it did anyway. On August 10, 1990, the U.S. consulate in Stuttgart sent a cable to Washington saying that a TV and radio station in Baden-Baden, SWF, had reported the existence of plans for a second Libyan poison gas factory. That was interesting enough. But the American consular officers were so astonished by the name of the new project and its developer that they could hardly believe it. The Sebha facility was called "Pharma 200." And its developer was Imhausen-Chemie.

Incredibly, Imhausen had hatched the new plan between December 1988 and January 1989 *while* the Mannheim prosecutor's office was investigating the company's role at Rabta. In addition, the consulate's cable continued, Imhausen was also under investigation in connection with $11.5 million in Federal Republic research funds that were intended for use in studying coal liquefication. Hippenstiel-Imhausen was alleged to have padded the number of people and personnel costs in the liquefication project and then pumped the funds he received for them into the "Pharma 200" project. Ironically, news of the Sebha connection broke within eight weeks of his being found guilty and sentenced because of the Rabta affair.

"Planning a second poison gas plant while the first one is already under investigation shows a degree of cold-bloodedness (or stupidity) in which extenuating circumstances play no part," the cable from Stuttgart concluded.

Whatever Imhausen's and other German firms' involvement in the

Sebha project in 1990, they seemed to have evaporated by the winter of 1992, at least in the opinion of the CIA. Robert M. Gates, the agency's director, told a Senate committee in January of that year that Colonel Qaddafi was being "forced to go to less trustworthy sources in the gray and black markets in the developing world" to create his new poison gas facility. Evidently, the profits were no longer worth the price, even for Imhausen and some of the others.

These Iraqi and Libyan escapades sent shock waves through Germany and forced a change in basic philosophy, which went from " 'Do everything for exports' to 'Control exports for the sake of national security: global security,' " Harald Müller, the proliferation expert, recalled.

In the 1980s, during its nadir, the Economics Ministry's Export Licensing Division employed only two professionals, one of them a teacher, in the nuclear controls office to process some 120,000 applications a year. While Siemens and other exporters used high-speed computers for record-keeping, the two individuals who were responsible for monitoring their license requests kept their records in cardboard boxes. Asked by the Bundestag why that was so, the director of the Department of Export Control responded by saying that his organization also had the enormous responsibility of controlling textile quotas. "We cannot afford to have more manpower in such an exotic sector as nuclear licensing," Müller quoted him as answering. It explained where the priorities were. The entire export control sector had no more than fifty professionals in those days. By 1992, the figure had jumped to five times that many.

In addition, the number of computers Export Control had in 1988 was substantially increased within the next four years. It was planned to use the new computers in a modern communication system in which customs, the nation's intelligence agencies, and other organizations would exchange data. Beyond that, according to Müller, a new group of young, alert, and interested legislators had moved into Parliament with an agenda that included serious export control. And the specialist-journalists were playing an important role, too, he maintained. "Not everything they write is correct," Müller said, "but that doesn't matter as long as they keep up the tension."

The leaky laws have been plugged, too, so they require tighter and more accurate procedures and call for stiffer penalties for convictions: up from five years to as many as fifteen. There is now an independent Federal Export Office, and the law allows the government to confiscate gross earnings. Perhaps the most revealing part of the new law is a provision that permits the Customs Investigative Institute to tap telephones and intercept mail. That provision was bitterly debated in a country that has placed special emphasis on privacy in the wake of the Hitler years. The new legislation's most novel proviso is one requiring that every corporation involved in international trade have one member on its board of directors who is designated to go to jail if it loses a court case and a sentence is warranted.

Whatever Germany's intentions, and the evidence was unmistakable by 1992 that they were serious, the high-stakes chess game between the proliferators and the watchdogs continued. On March 12, 1992, Leybold issued a twelve-page press release, "Corporate Principles Governing Internal Export Controls on Nuclear Non-Proliferation," which came complete with an eight-part declaration to exceed the export law's requirements. It also contained screening criteria and sample forms to be filled out by salespeople to help determine possible transgressions ("Examination Criteria for New Customers/Not Yet Examined Customers/Endusers"). "Leybold gives clear and unambiguous priority to the goal of nonproliferation of nuclear weapons and suitable delivery systems over commercial interests," the document solemnly declared.

Yet later that spring, another Leybold high-temperature furnace was seized in Rotterdam as it was heading for Tripoli, allegedly for use in Qaddafi's Al Fatah ballistic missile program. The furnace was not shipped directly by Leybold but, as had been the case the year before, through Fritz Werner. It was also believed that Leybold first sold the furnace to Heraeus, yet another firm, which in turn sold it to Fritz Werner. Still another furnace reportedly went to Pakistan's nuclear weapons program that same spring.

One company, smaller than many of the others, was in a class by itself. It was the notorious Alfred Hempel GmbH, which had the dubious distinction of supplying heavy water to two enemies at the same time—India and Pakistan—beginning in the 1970s. The Düsseldorf firm was founded by the man whose name it bears—a man so nostalgic about the war years and so devoted to the German military that he used a photograph of himself in a Wehrmacht uniform, replete with medals that included the Iron Cross, on Christmas cards that said "Season's Greetings" in German, English, and French.

Hempel, who died in 1989, was an arms broker's arms broker; a soul mate of Peter Huetten's who was totally lacking in scruples. Although he was to the far right politically, he made millions off the two largest Communist countries in the world. In 1982 and 1983, for example, Hempel delivered sixty tons of Chinese heavy water to Bombay for about $25 million. Then he provided the same service to the Indians with Soviet heavy water. The substance is vital for the control of fission in reactors that use natural uranium. Since the heavy water never passed through Germany, Hempel knew, no German law was broken. Hempel also sold heavy water to Argentina, a haven for unrehabilitated Nazis, and to Israel, the Nazis' arch foes. Hempel was not in business during the Nazi years, but had he been, he undoubtedly would have enjoyed it immensely.

# 8

# THE YARD SALE
# AT THE
# END OF HISTORY

The International Chetek Corporation of Moscow is located at 15 Varvarka Ulitsa, two blocks south of Red Square, and around the corner from the Central Committee's locked headquarters. It is ironic that the business nestles in a place that, for more than seventy years, was the capital of virulent anticapitalism, for it is the all-out quest for capital that drives Chetek.

Number 15 is a dreary two-story building of unrelieved angularity that suggests an ecclesiastical office. Its red bricks were laid before the Bolsheviks seized power. It has therefore borne mute witness to Lenin's cold-blooded harangues, Stalin's stony gaze and murderous vendettas, Khrushchev's bombast and flirtation with catastrophe in Cuba, Brezhnev's ruinous arms buildup and rape of Afghanistan, Gorbachev's bare-knuckled duels with his own intransigent Politburo, and Boris Yeltsin's impassioned call for national unity and progress as he stood on a tank that was his iron podium—an island in a sea of cheering patriots.

For thirty-four Novembers, 15 Varvarka Ulitsa also felt the rumble of olive-colored trucks pulling ballistic missiles past Lenin's squat tomb in lines so neat they could have been choreographed at the Bolshoi Ballet. Overhead, waves of bombers would also pass in review, rattling the old building's windows and sending shivers down its beams. Many of the missiles would carry atomic and thermonuclear explosives. All of the planes could have been loaded to do the same.

Now the annual parade trumpeting the glory of Marxism-Leninism and the triumph of the proletariat, a massive celebration of weaponry calculated to pacify citizens, impress friends, and intimidate foes, has abandoned Red Square to three goose-stepping soldiers who change the guard at the tomb on the hour. The tactical missiles have been called home for dismemberment. The big ones—308 intercontinental killers like the SS-18 "Satan," each of which could turn ten cities the size of Boston into smoldering ruins—are being phased out, at least in Russia itself. Most of the bombers are immobilized for lack of funds and lack of mission, their deadly cargoes stacked in bunkers guarded by demoralized privates.

The old Soviet Union's land, sea, and air forces are in a virtual stand-down because of the renunciation of communism and because of the East-West reconciliation. The end of more than four decades of armed confrontation, of the ceaseless production of ever more advanced weapons that went mostly unused, has left Western armies and the arms industries that supported and fed off them somewhat weakened and disoriented. But it has left their counterparts in the Warsaw Pact in utter shambles.*

Weapons and weapon systems by the many thousands—tanks, planes, ships of all kinds, missiles, rocket launchers, satellites, radars, command and control facilities, artillery, whole bases—are suddenly cold war surplus. Basic conventional weapons technologies that have been improved both quantitatively and qualitatively since the Nazi invasion in 1941 are for the most part idle and effectively unusable. So are the vast quantities of nuclear weapons, the reactors that produce the plutonium that goes into them, and very large quantities of the raw plutonium itself, which sit in storage. And so too are the thousands of scientists and technicians who designed, built, and serviced all of it. They are now all but unusable by Russia, the rest of the Commonwealth of Independent States, and eastern Europe. Unusable but not useless.

That is where the new corporation comes in. Chetek, which emulates classic capitalist innovation and aggressiveness to a fault, was convinced that it had found a use for the nukes and for many of the people who

*It also allegedly defeated the communist ideology, in the process ending what was perhaps the last great ideological conflict that stimulated creative social and scientific processes, according to Francis Fukuyama in *The End of History and the Last Man* (New York: Free Press, 1992).

accompany them. For a considerable fee—$300 to $1,200 for 2.2 pounds, depending on the waste's toxicity—and in the professed cause of ecology and the well-being of mankind, Chetek wanted to incinerate toxins (chemical, biological), nuclear weapons, radioactive materials including discarded reactors, and other deadly stuff in underground nuclear explosions by the hundred. It also came up with a scheme to put out oil well fires, such as those started by Iraqi soldiers retreating from Kuwait in 1991, the same way: by nuking the wells themselves. All of this allegedly could be done using private capital and working under the auspices of the Russian Ministry for Atomic Energy, commonly called Minatom. The scheme, which would violate the test ban moratorium, reflects the sheer economic desperation that struck at Russia in the wake of perestroika and the desperate measures that are being hatched to stave off the system's total collapse. Chetek is the corporate personification of the shady characters who prowled the back alleys and dank bars of every city in central and eastern Europe after World War II selling anything—cigarettes, chocolate, nylon stockings, drugs, forged papers, and even themselves—just to stay alive.

By the winter of 1992, its grasp on stability almost gone, Russia was slipping into a frightening Dostoyevskian netherworld in which expedience overwhelmed shame and morality was widely abandoned for survival. Women from decent families entertained foreign visitors for wages that would have been insulting elsewhere. Gangs of Russians roamed Moscow's streets and controlled much of what commerce there was, while Gypsies hunted in packs, diverting tourists and then stealing their wallets, watches, and handbags. Middle-class men and women huddled in freezing underpasses all day for the possibility of selling a puppy or kitten. The police, militia, and customs service were pervasively corrupt and adept at shakedowns. People were careful not to tell their neighbors that they were leaving town for fear of being burglarized.

"Bread, land, and peace"—the three staples of Lenin's idealized society—had given way to a simpler but stark mechanism: hard currency. And the devil take traditional values; these were not traditional times. One Muscovite, married to an accomplished geophysicist and coming from a good family that went back to the Czars, could find only one word to describe her society: "vulgar."

Yuri Gagarin's portrait, with his perpetually boyish face, once set above the artifacts of a proud space program in Moscow's space museum, now presided over a small fleet of used American cars that waited to bring fat profits from the relatively few Muscovites who could afford capitalist luxuries. Most of the spacecraft, like the victims of Stalin's purges, quietly disappeared from the long museum hall, perhaps never to return. The number two Sputnik, an officially designated backup for the one that made history on the night of October 4, 1957, lay on the floor in a dusty corner near a plaster bust of Lenin, its four antennas badly bent. The spacecraft was waiting, unguarded, to be stored in some warehouse or perhaps even to be sent to the scrap heap. Thirty-five years earlier it had been ready to carry a nation's dreams to space; now it was pushed aside to make room for a used Pontiac.

Chetek, like the discarded spacecraft, symbolizes the moral squalor that was compromising a once formidable national technology. The company's very existence is symptomatic of the problems besetting a military-industrial complex that is being auctioned off in a frightening political and economic whirlwind, in a system teetering dangerously on the brink of chaos. To be sure, every piece of military hardware, from belt buckles to aircraft carriers, is on the block. But more ominously, the elusive and potentially more destructive technology itself is also moving. And the technology is much more difficult to stop.

In a letter to the Deputy Secretary General of the U.N. in September 1991, Chetek claimed that "underground peaceful N-blasts are aimed at global demilitarization, better world environment and that is their fundamental distinction from routine N-weapon tests." The letter went on to suggest that company representatives would be more than willing to bring their nuclear explosives to Iraq and other Third World countries for the "complete annihilation of war chemical arsenals" and to Kuwait to "extinguish oil fires by underground N-blasts."

Trying to sell nuclear explosions is by no means the only enterprise in which Chetek is engaged. The company was formed even before the Soviet Union disintegrated to market all manner of Russian science and technology for profit. Like many of their fellow citizens, the scientists, engineers, and technocrats in the defense business were horrified to find themselves trapped in a collapsing economy as the 1980s drew to a close. With meager prospects for employment in the nation's eviscerated defense and allied industries, a small group of scientists and managers decided in the autumn of 1990 to bring their specialized abilities to bear early in the new capitalist process so that they would be able to establish a firm foothold with foreign funding.

The reasoning was sound enough. Theirs was a country that was second to none in nuclear weapons technology (nuclear reactor technology being an altogether different matter). The former Soviet Union was a leader in space science and technology, having produced the most powerful and dependable boosters in the world, conducted more annual launches than all other countries combined, and orbited the only permanently manned station. Its engineers produced first-rate ships, rockets, and aircraft. The MIG-29, for example, had a look-down-shoot-down fire control system, a top speed two and a half times that of sound, and fine maneuverability. It was as good as any fighter in the West. The SU-27, its equally advanced fighter-bomber cousin, was ideal for dropping nuclear or chemical weapons. Both aircraft were not only put on the world market but competitively priced: a MIG-29 brought about $20 million, or about two-thirds of what its American F-15 counterpart cost.

"We can sell at ten percent of the price of our competitors and there will still be a profit," said Mikhail Maley, Boris Yeltsin's defense adviser, referring to arms sales. "Just compare the salary of a Soviet [sic] worker and an American; the exchange [rate] between the ruble and the dollar. You will have an answer. Our workers make $4 a month."

That being the case, the disaffected scientists and technocrats concluded, they didn't have to make a living on the street, peddling amber necklaces, army wristwatches, old Soviet flags, fur hats, used KGB uniforms, and matrushka dolls for hard currency. (The whole country seemed to be a matrushka doll, with one reality concealed inside another.) What they had to do was organize their own fraternity so it could sell its wares in a competitive international market. Accordingly, twenty major research centers and institutes and a few production facilities, led by nuclear weapons scientists, formed a consortium, a joint stock company, with Minatom's blessing and support. The idea was to raise start-up capital, pool their resources, and with them produce products and services that would earn still more money. The corporation's name was an acronym of its motto: *Chelovek, Tecknologia, Kapital*, or "Man, Technology, Capital." It officially came into being on December 20, 1990.

Chetek's infrastructure and facilities began to coalesce early the following year. It either issued its stock to scientists or paid them directly for the exclusive right to market the results of their research. A flier promoting the nuclear waste disposal plan said that Chetek was the "sole proprietor of the technology of guaranteed and ecologically pure liquidation of highly toxic chemical materials and industrial wastes using underground thermonuclear explosion energy." A share of Chetek was worth 12,000 rubles, or about $7,000 at the time (the ruble subsequently plunged). It claimed to have 250 million rubles ($150 million) of working capital that year, much of it raised from former members of the powerful Central Committee and the military-industrial complex, according to sources in the Foreign Ministry. Chetek soon opened eight offices around the country (one of them near the Krasnoyarsk reactor and plutonium reprocessing complex and military industrial area in Siberia), took over the former Council of Ministers sanitarium at Sosni and some of its executive jets, and acquired a fleet of Zil limousines.

Before long, there were plans for a Global Space System—a large orbiting satellite—that would provide a range of communication functions into the twenty-first century and facilities that would reprocess aluminum, copper, and magnesium chips, make exceptionally tiny diamonds for industrial purposes, produce aluminum "bottlenecked drums" for use as fire extinguishers and food storage, electronic beam generators for medical use and for the sterilization of food, and quite a bit more, including genetic engineering.

Chetek's earliest ties with the nuclear sector, however, were ominous. It acknowledged—boasted—that its partners in the underground bomb project were both the Ministry for Atomic Power and Industry and the All-Union Research Institute for Experimental Physics at Sarova, near Gorky. Minatom was responsible for Russia's civilian and military nuclear energy programs (and therefore controlled warhead and bomb production and is responsible for the nation's far-flung reactors, including the four at Chernobyl).

It is no coincidence that Viktor N. Mikhailov, a leading bomb designer and Minatom's deputy minister in charge of nuclear weapons design and manufacture, was one of the two men who signed Chetek's solicitation letter to the U.N. (He went on to head the ministry itself.) Mikhailov, a nervous-looking chain-smoker who favors droopy, checkered socks, most likely has his own financial stake in the company. While visiting Washington in the waning days of the Soviet Union, he waxed eloquent about the prospects for Minatom's dealing with Chetek, not just on peaceful nuclear explosives, but in other nuclear areas. "I think in the future, the scope of the questions under mutual discussion will be getting wider," he said. "We will be enlarging our contact with this company."

The All-Union Institute, like its counterparts in Russia and elsewhere around the world, is better known by its post office address: Arzamas-16. The cover is for security reasons. Arzamas-16 is where the

Soviet Union's first atomic bomb was designed.* Yuliy Khariton, Yakov Zeldovich, Yuri Trutnev, Andrei Sakharov, and others developed the U.S.S.R.'s hydrogen bomb there in the late 1940s and early 1950s. Improvements in the weapon were made continuously at Arzamas-16 for most of the following three decades. It is the equivalent of the U.S. Los Alamos National Laboratory. Chetek, in fact, was conceived at Arzamas-16.

With the specter of disarmament and consequent unemployment looming, a group of about ten important weapons designers went to the defense and trade bureaucracies in a desperate effort to find other markets for their talents. They had a unique problem. Elsewhere in the country, military aircraft designers were turning to the creation of civil aircraft, while many defense plants were retooling to manufacture consumer products. But hydrogen bombs can't be reconfigured as power boats or milking machines. They are explosion-specific; all they can do is blow up. If their basic function was by definition unalterable, however, the use to which that function was put could at least be altered. The weapons designers therefore decided to turn their attention to a different kind of bomb: one that would create peaceful nuclear explosions, so-called PNEs, for broadly defined "ecological" purposes. Chetek was initially conceived to sell PNEs and provides as neat an example as any of how social disarray and financial fear can drive weapons scientists to consider even the most harebrained schemes. Several top nuclear weapon scientists, including Trutnev, who worked with Sakharov, and Igor Andrushin, the head of Arzamas-16, became shareholders.

The concept of harnessing nukes for nature was first described in a scientific paper published in Russia in February 1991. It was then quietly unveiled at an international scientific conference in Moscow two months later. But it exploded at an environmental conference in Ottawa at the end of April. The meeting, a symposium on nuclear tests in the Arctic, was sponsored by the Canadian Centre for Arms Control and Disarmament. Viktor Mikhailov was invited to attend by virtue of his position in Minatom. He not only accepted the invitation but asked whether he could bring along three people who would pay their own way and who represented a company that had an interesting proposal to make on nuclear weapons. The Canadians enthusiastically agreed.

*That bomb was assembled at the All-Union Institute of Technical Physics, or Chelyabinsk-70, just east of the Urals. It was tested at Semipalatinsk on August 29, 1949. (Thomas B. Cochran and Robert Standish Norris, *Soviet Nuclear Warhead Production*, Washington: Natural Resources Defense Council, February 14, 1991, pp. 7–8.)

On the first day of the meeting Vladimir Borisovich Dmitriev, who served briefly as Chetek's president, gave a short talk that revealed the nature of the company and its most important immediate project. Neither his presentation nor one that followed had been shared with the meeting's organizers in advance.

Dmitriev, gray-haired and in his early fifties, had the purposeful but controlled bearing of a military officer or an intelligence agent. "My company has the right of commercial use of 'know-how' technologies of ecologically safe destruction of chemical weapons and highly toxic industrial wastes using the underground thermonuclear explosion energy," Dmitriev explained. Such explosions would turn what they blew up into "safe neutral plasma" with "no harm or even risk to people." They were planned for Novaya Zemlya, an arctic archipelago that curves away from continental Russia into the Berents Sea. This was the area where the Soviet Union tested its most powerful nuclear weapons. The viability of such a system would have to be proven in a special experiment to be conducted under international supervision. He went on to indicate that the experiment—a test—would only be a formality designed more to put the international community at ease than to prove the concept. It was "self-evident," he explained to his audience, which was by then incredulous, that exploding H-bombs in shafts 3,000 feet or more underground could be fully justified on grounds of both "total safety" and efficiency.

Dmitriev was followed by Dr. Alexandr Chernyshev, another former bomb designer, who expounded on the benefits of the plan in an illustrated lecture titled, "Underground Nuclear Explosions for Ecology." Meanwhile, Mikhailov watched the audience intently, trying to gauge its response. That was not difficult. The crowd, mainly environmentalists, was aghast. "Frankly, everyone in the room thought [the Chetek representatives] were crazy," John Lamb, the Centre's executive director, later recalled. During a break, one Centre official said, Chernyshev launched a frenzied discussion of the need for small nuclear weapons. He rhapsodized over the value of mini-nukes, which he said Minatom should be allowed to continue developing.

The Canadians' incredulity turned to anger six months later when one of their officers picked up a flier inside 15 Varvarka Ulitsa stating that their center and others had "discussed and approved" the plan. The group emphatically demanded that Chetek remove the reference to its having endorsed the use of nuclear explosions for ecological purposes.

Chetek's own resolve could be measured by the fact that in addition to its eight regional offices, it had hired representatives in western Europe and North America. The North American salesman was Danny Wolfson, an aggressive agent for Chetek at Ph.D. International Trading, Inc., of Montreal. Wolfson's resolve matched that of his employer. "We're willing to entertain all ideas," he asserted. "It doesn't matter who, where, or when. We have all the technologies and they're going to be used." Those words would be echoed by many people in many places behind the former Iron Curtain as the economy continued to sour. Some of them would be old KGB types who slid into businesses like Chetek's, bringing their technology with them, after their security service was technically terminated.*

Chetek's econukes pose several immediate dangers, dangers that the Canadian Centre for Arms Control and Disarmament, among others, was quick to note. There is the environmental danger, ill-defined but no less probable, with nuclear blasts going off underground and radiation undoubtedly leaking into water tables, the ocean, and the atmosphere over long periods and slowly contaminating them. Fear of such contamination is what stopped the U.S. Peaceful Nuclear Explosives program in its infancy in the 1970s.

There is also the possibility that one or more of the devices, as is the case with many of the former Soviet Union's more than 40,000 actual nuclear weapons, could end up in the possession of terrorists or hostile governments through theft, robbery, or diversion and covert sale.

Chetek was only the most visible element in the still-fragmenting former Soviet Union. There were other less visible, even invisible, elements that frightened Westerners and even citizens of the fifteen restive nations that now stretched across Eurasia. If Chetek's founders could be so bold as to publicize their audacious plans, what were the other, less responsible elements in that desperate land up to? What were the thousands of nuclear weapons scientists capable of doing, or the germ warfare specialists who had been trying to develop a "superplague" before communism's sudden demise sprang open under them like a trap door, or the Scud-missile-armed warlords who battled along the border between the Central Asian

---

*By the winter of 1992 rumors abounded that the core of the KGB remained intact in the shadows, waiting to see whether Yeltsin and the experiment in democracy and capitalism would survive as he envisioned or whether the nation's course would be altered enough to warrant their return to power.

states and Afghanistan? Since no superpower had ever disintegrated before, no one could predict what would happen.

The Commonwealth of Independent States is the wild card in the marketing of mayhem. It can provide everything—fissile material, technology, equipment, scientists and technicians, germ warfare expertise, complete delivery systems, and even the finished bombs themselves—to willing buyers. The prospect of "loose nukes," as the phenomenon is called by Western intelligence, is the most sensational part of any discussion of the former Soviet Union. But there are other, more likely scenarios.

"Much less attention has been paid to the more immediate dangers of nuclear bomb material and associated hardware being smuggled across the now porous borders of the collapsing empire," U.N. inspector David Kay has written. The greatest barrier to Iraq's nuclear ambitions was not any lack of technical skills, which it acquired from the West overtly or otherwise, but the fissile material itself. Buying bomb-grade uranium or plutonium from Russians, Kazakhs, or Ukrainians would have been both faster and cheaper than assembling and using baghdatrons and centrifuges.

Although an environmental threat can exist anywhere, it is especially likely to be tolerated in the former Soviet Union, where Marxist production imperatives have left a pernicious legacy of waste and destruction in the name of progress. Using underground nuclear explosions to mask the refining of warheads or selling the PNEs themselves to anyone who can meet the price is a particularly plausible scenario in Russia.

"Our economy, subordinated for decades to the strategic and military interests of the former Soviet Union, was a one-way street: It was directed toward production growth, regardless of the quality and marketability of products, energy consumption or effects on the environment," Vaclav Havel has written. He referred to Czechoslovakia but his words could as easily be applied to the old Soviet Union. "The then ruling regime took the per capita output of cement and steel as evidence of its own indispensability, as a symptom of prosperity and social development. That system, based on ruthless exploitation of the past and the future at the expense of the present, ingeniously took advantage of the fact that environmental consciousness was nonexistent or suppressed and consigned to the periphery of public concern. The main thing was to give the people decent wages and enough to eat in order to keep them from rebelling."

One of the worst horror stories to emerge from the veil of the cold war concerns the Novaya Zemlya. In 1992 and 1993 the Russians themselves disclosed that for years the Soviet military used the waters on both sides of the three islands as a dumping ground for eighteen nuclear reactors from atomic submarines and ice-breakers despite a three-decade ban on such activities. Eight of the devices contained hot fuel laden with cesium-137 when they were dropped into the water. And they lied about it throughout. The Soviets also conducted underwater nuclear bomb tests in the area and disposed of uncountable canisters of nuclear waste. The navy even sank an entire nuclear sub—a prototype powered by a liquid metal cooled reactor—off the east coast of Novaya Zemlya after an accident in May 1968. The radioactive mess haunts Norwegian and Alaskan fishermen who fear that their catches will become dangerously contaminated.

By 1990 the carcasses of 890 expended first stages of missiles, most of which began leaking unused fuel as soon as they hit the ground, littered a wide area to the east of the large space launch facility at Tyuratam, near the devastated Aral Sea in Kazakhstan. "Tell me," a writer-politician from the region asked the Soviet Congress of People's Deputies in May 1989, "is there another state in the world which permits its own population to be poisoned?"

The infamous secret cities, a vast conglomeration of nuclear weapons design, production, testing and storage sites, as well as facilities dedicated to other arms development deep within the motherland itself, bear testimony to the scope and effect of the Soviet superweapons enterprise. Many, like Arzamas-16 and Chelyabinsk-70, bore only postal numbers.* Until recently, all were forbidden to foreigners and others who weren't cleared. Many didn't even appear on maps. Soviet plutonium and tritium production for weapons, for example, took place at Chelyabinsk-40 near Kyshtym; at Tomsk-7, the Siberian Atomic Power Station ten miles north-

*The cities that are or were involved in nuclear weapons, their postal names, and populations are Seversk (Tomsk-7: 107,700); Zherzunogorsk (Krasnoyarsk-26: 90,300); Ozhorsk (Chelyabinsk-65: 83,500); Kyshtym (Chelyabinsk-40: unknown); Kremryuv (Arzamas-16: 80,300); Novouralsk (Sverdlovsk-45: 63,300); Rusnoy (also Sverdlovsk-45: 54,700); Zernogorsk (Krasnoyarsk-45: 63,300); Sunezkinsk (Chelyabinsk-70: 46,300); Zarchinuy (Penza-10: 61,400); Torifugornuy (Zlatoust-36: 29,800). (" 'Classified' Nuclear Facilities List Obtained," *Yomiuri Shimbun*, Tokyo, November 17, 1991.)

west of Tomsk; and at a mining-chemical combine on the Yenisey River thirty-five miles northeast of Krasnoyarsk, also in Siberia. Before 1987, there were as many as fourteen reactors at the three sites, all producing weapons-grade plutonium and tritium from uranium. Together, the maze of secret cities held 755,800 employees and their families, dwarfing the number of their American counterparts. Some 100,000 of those people held and continue to hold nuclear security badges; the equivalent of the top-secret U.S. "Q" clearance.

The secret cities were built by slave laborers from Stalin's and his successors' gulags, who were exploited the way the rest of the environment was. They were memorialized by Aleksandr Solzhenitsyn in *The Gulag Archipelago*:

"And so it was that Chebotaryov served out his second term at Chupin. But to his misfortune his last camp was a top-secret one, one of that group of atomic projects—Moscow-10, Tura-38, Sverdlovsk-39, and Chelyabinsk-40. They were engaged in separating uranium-radium ores, and construction was proceeding according to Kurchatov's plans, and the construction chief was Lieutenant General Tkachenko, who was subordinate only to Stalin and Beria. Every quarter the zeks had to renew their pledges of 'nondisclosure.' But this was not the real trouble—the real trouble was that those released were not allowed to return home. The 'released' prisoners were sent off in a large group in September, 1950— to the Kolmya! Only there were they relieved of convoy and declared to be *a particularly dangerous special contingent!* They were dangerous because they had helped make the atomic bomb! (How can one really keep up with all this and describe it? Chapters and chapters are necessary!) There were tens of thousands of similar ones scattered all over the Kolmya!! (Look through the Constitution! Look through the codes! What do they say about *special contingents??*)" In other words, whatever the limitations of their original sentences, anyone unlucky enough to work at constructing one of the secret cities got an automatic life sentence for security reasons. Untold thousands perished in the process.

Nor was life much better for those who had to work at the completed sites, whether that involved refining uranium ore, operating the reactors and reprocessing equipment, or building the weapons themselves. Workers at the A-reactor and chemical separation plant at Chelyabinsk-40 in 1949–51, for example, received radiation doses eighty times the current standard. It wasn't that the Ministry of Medium Machine Building (Minatom's old name) didn't set radiation standards; dose-response levels were well understood by then. It's just that plutonium production was so high a priority because of the needs of the H-bomb then under hurried development that the standards were ignored.

Many of the secret cities were and are Chernobyls in slow motion, though unlike the dramatic reactor accident, the appalling damage they inflicted on the environment was as cloaked in secrecy as the weapons they produced. For years, all high-level radioactive waste discharge from Chelyabinsk-40 was poured directly into the Techa River. Some of it was found as far away as the Arctic Ocean. It was also dumped into Lake Karachay, which has no outlet, and which eventually accumulated 120 million curies of long-lived cesium-137 and strontium-90. Chernobyl, by comparison, released 1.22 million curies of the deadly radionuclides. In 1957, high-level waste solutions stored in a concrete tank submerged in water at Kyshtym heated and exploded, blowing off a yard-thick concrete lid and releasing seventy to eighty metric tons of waste into the atmosphere. Some 217 towns and villages in the area with a combined population of 270,000 were heavily contaminated, including their water supplies. People were still being evacuated from the area nineteen months after the explosion.

"We have finally begun to realize lately how ruthless we have been in relation to nature and, consequently, to ourselves, the more so our children and grandchildren. The feeling of the inexhaustability of the natural wealth of 'our immense Motherland,' in no way justified, has led to its thoughtless and rapacious destruction. And today these accumulated and carefully muffled problems have risen up before an economically exhausted society in all their urgency, a society that does not know how, or with what, to patch the countless ecological 'holes' that are facing it."

The sentiment, unthinkable coming from a Russian scientist even a few years ago, reflects the most insidious part of the country's dilemma. It would not only be touching, but highly promising, were it not for the fact that it was written by three Russian scientists as the prelude to that first paper justifying and describing Chetek's econukes.

If the specter of proliferating PNEs wasn't bad enough, there are some 40,000 finished nuclear weapons spread across Russia and the Commonwealth of Independent States. The combination of a disintegrating social and military structure and wrenching poverty and unemployment do not bode well for keeping them where they belong. It is often said that stealing or capturing nuclear weapons in chaotic situations is a main proliferation danger. One scenario involves a breakaway republic seizing ICBMs on its territory. Another has to do with rogue officers using nuclear weapons to blackmail the central authority. A third involves commando-type action by ethnic minorities or even outsiders. But these are not the biggest worries. Nuclear weapons would be virtually useless to the uninitiated because of the complex codes and special handling needed to detonate them.

The more likely scenario involves a direct sale by those who know the codes and arming procedures. Selling just one operable missile, bomb, or warhead and then fleeing the country could turn three or four impoverished colonels into rich men, particularly by Russian standards.

In fact, such a transfer almost happened in 1991, though not for profit. A Lutheran minister in eastern Germany befriended a twenty-eight-year-old senior lieutenant in the Special Troops of the Soviet General Staff: the men assigned to guard the nuclear weapons.

The lieutenant was the commander of a guard unit protecting Scud warheads that had been removed from various launch sites around eastern Germany the year after the country's reunification. The warheads had been shipped to the lieutenant's base at Alten-Grabow, about an hour south of Berlin, where several hundred of them were stored in overcrowded and undermanned bunkers.

Like so many Soviets, the disintegration of his country and its guiding principles had left the young officer foundering in a moral swill. The Marxist god had not only failed, it had evaporated. To make matters worse, he and his small detachment were protecting weapons that the Foreign Minister, Aleksandr Bessmertnykh, had told the world had been removed from German soil. This added shame to confusion.

In those circumstances, it was natural for the young Russian to befriend a Lutheran minister who lived near the weapons site. And soon after he did so, he startled the minister by making an incredible proposal. The lieutenant asked to be put in touch with Greenpeace, the international environmental action organization, because he wanted to sell it one of the Scud warheads for 500,000 deutschmarks: about $320,000.

The minister contacted Greenpeace, which in turn notified William Arkin, its American nuclear weapons expert. Arkin was widely known to be the foremost nuclear weapons analyst outside government. He had already begun to hear rumors about the disenchantment that was spreading inside the Soviet Army when he got the call from Germany.

"It was in late 1990 that we started to hear rumors coming out of East Germany, of a lot of Soviet soldiers defecting, of a lot of weapons being available for sale," Arkin later recalled. "There was even a rumor that the deputy commander of Soviet forces in East Germany was dismissed because of a lack of discipline among Soviet units left in the country. It was at that point, ironically—when we were monitoring the situation in East Germany—that we were contacted by someone who had access to a Soviet soldier. And it seemed to us at first a fantastic idea, that one could actually undertake to lay one's hands on a Soviet nuclear weapon," he added.

Over the next eight months, Arkin communicated with the lieutenant, whom he would not publicly name. This was done very cautiously through a series of intermediaries, including the minister. During that time, Arkin and the young officer exchanged about a dozen letters, with the American putting questions to the Russian, and the minister relaying them. Arkin, understandably sensitive to the possibility that Greenpeace was being enticed into a hoax or a sting, asked for detailed information about the lieutenant's unit, about the type, size, and shape of the warhead, and about what the Russian required in return for handing it over. It was possible that the KGB or GRU, Soviet military intelligence, was conducting an elaborate sting to see what the market was for nuclear weapons.

Arkin had coauthored a book on Soviet nuclear warheads for the Natural Resources Defense Council and knew a great deal about the Scud version. The one the lieutenant described checked out perfectly. It was nine feet long, six feet wide, and weighed 1,500 pounds. Furthermore, Arkin knew, this was no firecracker of an atomic bomb. It was a city-buster that could do more damage than the bombs dropped on Japan. Used against, say, Hamburg, it would gut the heart of the city and leave hundreds of thousands dead.

The young Russian provided Arkin not only with abundant details about the warhead but, equally important, with security arrangements at Alten-Grabow. "He knew enough about what was going on," Arkin said. "He was able to describe with enough detail what type of weapons were in the base, how many there were, and what the security and guard procedures were. And he had a very specific claim, which was that there was a window—a time period—when he thought he would be able to gain access to the nuclear weapon and remove it from the base." Finally, the soldier named his price and insisted on being given asylum in a third country. Not only would he need to be spirited to Sweden or Switzerland or some other nation, but so, too, would those of his comrades who helped him get the warhead out.

Satisfied that the soldier was real and the deal was serious, William Arkin went to his colleagues in Greenpeace to hash over some fundamental questions. "What would we do with a nuclear weapon once we got our hands on one?" he asked. "And then, how would we get rid of it once we had our hands on it?" And there was more. If only some members of the unit were in on the operation, what would happen to those who were innocent and left behind? Would they be shot, killed, for the sake of preserving security? What if a group of terrorists or gangsters stumbled onto the plan and hijacked the warhead after Greenpeace got it out of eastern Germany? The organization finally concluded that the benefit of snatching an atomic warhead was worth the risk of having something go horribly wrong.

"For the next six months," Arkin remembered, "we began to plan an operation." It was an operation that involved smuggling a 1,500-pound device out of a fortified garrison, moving it safely to a neutral location, showing it to the news media, and then getting rid of it. Showing it to reporters was the point of it all. Civilians unveiling a nuke at a news conference, perhaps pulling a shroud off it like they do in commercials for next year's car, would demonstrate in the most dramatic way that the things were really out there and were for sale.

Now it was time to meet the Russian and his minister. That was helped by a stroke of luck. Greenpeace had for some time wanted to visit a Soviet weapons base in the former East Germany, size up the security system, and get a clear sense of what such a facility looked like. By coincidence, the organization's office in Germany was given just such an opportunity at that moment. It had arranged with local authorities to inspect a hastily abandoned Soviet warhead storage site in a town north of Berlin.

During the second week of June 1991, Arkin and two other Greenpeace activists visited the deserted storage site, photographing and videotaping it extensively. That same weekend, Arkin set up what was to be his only meeting with the mysterious lieutenant. It took place in the apartment of another peace activist, though not a member of Greenpeace, near the Mexicoplatz S-Bahn stop on West Berlin's subway.

The meeting got off awkwardly. The soldier, clearly wary that *he*, himself, was the subject of a sting, would not accept any of Arkin's identification cards. The lieutenant only relented when Arkin gave him his Greenpeace business card. In return, he offered his own army ID. He was an ethnic Russian, a graduate of the Soviet military academy, and an engineer. He had served with the Special Troops of the General Staff for five years, he told Arkin, most of them guarding nuclear weapons in East Germany. The lieutenant appeared to Arkin to be serious, humorless, and a true believer who had abruptly switched belief systems.

They talked for about two hours, mostly about the money the Russian wanted and exactly how the warhead was to be smuggled off the base. The money, William Arkin told the Russian, could be a sizable problem. It wasn't that it couldn't be gotten. But accepting it in return for handing over the warhead would reduce him to the status of a mercenary or even a pariah in the eyes of the world. What nation, Arkin asked, would provide asylum to someone who made a killing by betraying his country? It was a problem the lieutenant said he would think about.

The technical end of pulling off what would be the theft of the century was certainly feasible. The officer seemed to be in charge of the shifts of guards who protected the installation's perimeter. What Arkin learned from inspecting the abandoned warhead storage site was that the outer perimeter was really all the protection the place had. Twelve soldiers guarded the perimeter at night, Arkin learned, and his lieutenant, who had access to the bunkers where the warheads were stored, was the man in charge of their shift.

"He told me that he had figured out a way of gaining access to the warheads, themselves, during the transition from one shift to another: during the time when one platoon hands over its responsibilities to another. And it was at that point that he believed he would have access to the keys, and access to all of the necessary alarm codes, that would enable him to get into the bunker," Arkin said. "Then, using the assistance of two of his subordinate enlisted men, he was going to load this 1,500-pound nuclear weapon onto a truck and, basically, just drive it out of the base.

"I know it sounds fantastic on a certain level," Arkin continued. "But in fact the level of security, the orientation of security in the Soviet Army, was very heavily weighted toward defending against a NATO attack. It was not heavily weighted toward protesters, or public intervention, or terrorists." At the end of the meeting, Arkin gave the soldier a list of technical problems requiring solutions and arranged to meet again.

Now plans had to be made for getting the Scud warhead into Berlin. The organization's local chapter was assigned to take care of that problem.

Essentially, the plan called for the Russians to drive their truck to a site well away from the base, where they would be met by Greenpeace representatives in their own truck. The warhead would then be transferred from one vehicle to the other and taken to a barge dock on a canal near Alten-Grabow. It would then be loaded onto a barge and moved to Berlin, where another truck would take it to its final stop. It would then immediately be examined by nuclear experts assembled by Arkin. The next day, according to the plan, it would be presented to hastily assembled reporters. Meanwhile, another Greenpeace team would spirit the defectors first to a safe house and then to the border of whatever country had agreed to accept them. Finally, while every newspaper in the world carried banner headlines proclaiming that a nuke had been successfully stolen, the Russians would be called and told where to pick up their warhead. The operation was even given a code name: Loose Cannon.

Arkin had contact twice more with the lieutenant, both times through the minister. He finally agreed to accept asylum without the deutschmarks after Arkin told him that likely book and movie contracts would more than make up for an upfront payoff. More technical information was exchanged, and a time and date were set for the transfer: midmorning on September 7, 1991.

Toward the end of July, however, the lieutenant abruptly vanished. "Our intermediary lost contact with him and was quite worried," Arkin recalled. It was clear that something was happening at the Soviet base. "Our intermediary said to us, the security of the base has been shifted. A change has been undertaken. And we became concerned that perhaps we had compromised our source, or we had made a mistake somewhere in our activity."

The four-day coup in which Gorbachev was put under house arrest happened a week later. It became clear to Arkin and the others that there was considerable upheaval inside the Soviet armed forces: upheaval that would explain the sudden change in security procedures at the warhead base.

In any case, the disappearance of the lieutenant meant that Greenpeace had to abandon Loose Cannon. Arkin later learned that the Russians withdrew the last of the warheads during the week of August 17, and he concluded that his senior lieutenant had been withdrawn with them.

Whatever its outcome, the experience alarmed Arkin. What he drew from the episode, he said, was a stark realization that the traditional indoctrination and allegiances of the keepers of the former Soviet Union's nuclear arsenal had dangerously eroded. However positive the lieutenant's motives, Arkin added, he was living proof that the notion of keeping nuclear weapons secure was more myth than reality.

But Arkin was far from the only knowledgeable person who fretted over the atomic arsenal that remained in the rubble of the collapsed Soviet system.

"If the Soviets [sic] do an excellent job at retaining control over their stockpile of nuclear weapons," then U.S. Secretary of Defense Richard Cheney observed, citing a 25,000–30,000 figure, "and they are ninety-nine percent successful, that would mean you could still have as many as 250 that they were not able to control." In fact, the Soviet Union's nuclear arsenal peaked at 45,000 warheads in 1986, according to Mikhailov. That was substantially higher than Western estimates and called intelligence analysis into question. All of them are potentially salable.

And to make matters worse, about one-third of the weapons in the nuclear arsenal can, like the Scud warhead, be handled by as few as three men. A sixth of the weapons—as many as 5,000 of them—could be carried off by a single individual. The latter include nuclear artillery shells, short-range missile warheads, small nuclear bombs, nuclear land mines and torpedo warheads, and even so-called backpack or suitcase nukes that were designed to be carried by atomic commandos. Any of them could, under the right circumstances, be taken out of the country and smuggled to a buyer. And at least one important buyer is actively searching for such weapons. Then CIA Director Robert M. Gates said flatly in December 1992 that "Iran is *out shopping* for nuclear weapons. . . . Russia is an obvious target, and Russian instability gives us concern in this regard." (Italics added.)

Also of concern are more than 125 metric tons of bomb-grade plutonium that are stored at Chelyabinsk and Tomsk. This means that the stockpile contains enough bomb-grade material to make more than 15,000 more weapons. Some of the plutonium is raw; some has already been machined into cores. In addition, 1,000 more metric tons of highly enriched uranium is stashed at four locations around the motherland: probably at uranium enrichment facilities at Sverdlovsk, Angarsk, Krasnoyarsk, and Tomsk. That works out to 45,000 more bombs. Evgeniy Mikirin, who was in charge of the nuclear fuel cycle, noted in the spring of 1992 that there was "a problem in storage and utilization of the growing stockpile" of highly enriched uranium. One of the main problems, he added, was the lack of a central storage facility. This means that as Russia continues to move deeper into social, political, and economic chaos, it will do so with many thousands of at-the-ready nuclear weapons and the key ingredient for 60,000 more scattered across its length and breadth.

The United States tried to ease that problem in the summer of 1992 when it agreed to help build an enormous central depository at Tomsk for the storage of nuclear weapons material. The preliminary design for the facility not only showed the extent of the problem but reflected the Russians' well-known penchant for designing gargantuan structures. The sixty-acre underground facility would have fifty two-story halls, each seventy-five yards long. Each hall would hold 2,000 containers, each of which in turn held up to eleven pounds of plutonium or twice that much of highly enriched, bomb-grade uranium. Trains running aboveground would deliver the containers to elevators at both ends of the facility, which would lower them for permanent subterranean storage.

The biggest swords-into-plowshares agreement of the post-cold-war era calls for the United States to buy bomb-grade uranium from Russia's dismantled nuclear warheads for use in commercial nuclear power plants. Under the terms of the agreement, which President Bush announced in the summer of 1992, the Russians would sell their fissile material for hard currency, part of which would go to make badly needed repairs on their own power reactors.

But Russia is only one of four countries of the former Soviet Union possessing nukes. Kazakhstan, Ukraine, and Belarus have their own arsenals. Kazakhstan, for example, had 1,410 nuclear weapons in 1992, including 1,040 mounted on SS-18s and 370 stored in bunkers for use on forty Bear H bombers. The country also has large deposits of uranium ore. Like the others, Ukraine agreed to relinquish its nuclear weapons in the spring of 1992 in deference to the nuclear Non-Proliferation and Strategic Arms Reduction Treaties. Indeed, many of the 4,000 nuclear weapons that had been on Ukrainian soil during the cold war were duly returned to Russia for destruction. But they were tactical, not strategic, weapons. Kiev was careful at first to retain 176 ICBMs plus more than 600 cruise missiles and bombs for fourteen nuclear-armed Bear and sixteen Blackjack bombers. The latter are equivalent to the U.S. supersonic B-1B. Counting the missiles' multiple warheads, Ukraine had more than 1,650 nuclear warheads, Kazakhstan had 1,410, and Belarus had 81.

The total was therefore at least 3,141 warheads outside Russian territory. One hopeful sign was that the Belarusian parliament voted in late February 1993 to return all of its warheads to Russia for destruction. Another was the decision by Ukraine five months later to begin dismantling its 130 SS-19s, the largest of the ICBMs turned out by the U.S.S.R. Each missile carries ten warheads. The decision was made after prodding by the Clinton Administration and promises to help fund the dismantling operation and increase cooperation between the two nations. Faced with a worsening economic crisis and a large debt to Russia for gas and oil, Ukrainian President Leonid M. Kravchuk decided in September 1993 to dismantle all of his country's warheads and use their uranium for power reactors. He also agreed to sell Russia the Ukrainian half of the disputed Black Sea fleet. But the Ukrainian parliament, calling the plan treasonous, vowed to fight it, causing a disgusted Russian government to kill the deal.

Beyond the weapons in the former republics was the issue of whether atomic bombs or warheads were stored in areas of Russia itself where ancient rivalries had been reignited since the collapse of the Soviet Union. Russian officials assured their American counterparts that there were no problems, but there was no way to verify that claim.

However worrisome Ukraine's infighting appeared to be, Washington was taking consolation in the belief that positive control of the weapons— the various enabling codes required to arm, launch, and send targeting information to the missiles—was securely in Kremlin hands. But by the end of 1992, increasingly apprehensive Russian and Ukrainian defense experts were acknowledging in private that the Kremlin had lost confidence that Ukraine's nuclear forces would obey orders from Moscow. The Russians may have had positive control of the weapons, but the Ukrainians were exercising "administrative control." They did this by paying the salaries and providing housing and other social services for the missiles' crews. Kiev dramatically demonstrated its physical control of the weapons by preventing Russian specialists from servicing both the warheads and missiles, an action that alarmed Moscow because it increased the risk of an accident.

Even more ominously, work was going on at a top-secret research institute in Kharkov to determine if Ukraine could break the enabling codes or develop substitutes that would allow the Ukrainians themselves to use the weapons if they choose. The Russians had taken the codes but not the weapons. Scientists at the institute were also concentrating on developing new codes for the strategic bombers' gravity bombs and short-range missiles. These are the weapons that Ukraine could use as a deterrent against a new wave of Russian expansion.

The Kharkov facility, built by Moscow to conduct training as well as research and development for the Soviet strategic rocket forces, had been taken over by Ukraine "lock, stock, and barrel," according to a highly knowledgeable source. Russian experts think it will be several years before Ukraine could develop its own enabling codes and even longer before it masters complex targeting procedures that took a great deal of time to refine. Yet the Russians are worried. First, and most obviously, there was a long-term strategic problem because Ukraine could become a nuclear power in its own right. But there is also a potentially deadly short-term problem. Any attempt to use enabling codes not authorized by Moscow could set off a disabling system in a warhead that produces a chemical explosion and perhaps a serious radiation leak. It would also set off alarm bells in underground bunkers throughout Moscow.

Arming the gravity bombs and as many as 670 air-launched cruise missiles, many or all of them nuclear, would be quite a bit easier. The Russians have told U.S. officials that they took the weapons' enabling codes with them when they left Ukraine, but coming up with new codes for these relatively simple devices would not present the problem that comes getting ballistic missiles in operable condition.

Many Ukrainian politicians and soldiers remain undaunted by the obstacles and convinced that independence from Russia and the other former Soviet republics depends on using Soviet hardware to their own advantage. That was why they tried to pirate the Black Sea fleet during the first days of the breakup of the empire. And it is also why they grabbed the SS-19s, SS-24s, and bombers as well. On November 5, 1992, Igor Yukhnovsky, Ukraine's first vice prime minister, threatened to sell his country's entire force of 176 ICBMs if it so chose. "We can sell these nuclear warheads to the highest bidder . . . to nuclear states. That means Russia first of all, or maybe another state, depending on which pays most," he said coyly. Whatever the ethics of trying to sell Russia its own missiles, Ukraine was clearly serving notice that it intended to use the weapons to enhance its status as an independent entity. There was no doubt about that where Vlodymyr Tolubko, a former senior officer in the Soviet Strategic Rocket Forces turned adamant nationalist Ukrainian parliamentarian, was concerned. "Do you know the word 'idiots'?" he asked rhetorically in the spring of 1993. "Idiots are people who give up their nuclear weapons."

Ukraine was committed to becoming a nuclear-free state, the politician explained several days later, but its more important imperative was salvation. "But perhaps that will not apply if somebody doesn't want to buy this wretched stuff," he added, animatedly. "You cannot push to the wall a state that is trying to rise to its feet. The United States and Russia are rich; they must help Ukraine in this terrible situation. We know that what we have is a treasure, and on this we will insist."

The Ukrainians have also felt belittled by the West, particularly by the United States, which, they feel, treats them like mischievous children. George Perkovich, a U.S. disarmament specialist, participated in a blue ribbon two-day workshop in Moscow in the summer of 1992 and reported both Russian and Ukrainian frustration with the nuclear arms reduction process. The Russians were reluctant to give up the SS-18, complained about Boris Yeltsin's agreeing to give up more strategic missiles than the United States, and whined about the high cost of dismantling their arsenal (for which they wanted U.S. aid), Perkovich reported.

The Ukrainians, on the other hand, dwelled on the humanistic side of the proliferation problem. "In a cognac-imbued late-night dinner, I asked the Ukrainian Colonel [Astakhov] what was really the issue," Perkovich recalled. "His response, and that of his English-speaking colleague, was illuminating, if vague. It was mostly about Respect—the human dimension of relations. He said, 'Why do you Americans trust the Russians and not us? Why do you press us so hard about nuclear weapons, but accept the fact that the Russians will keep thousands of them? History should tell you that it is the Russians you have to worry about.' These were proud representatives of a proud people and they feel as if they are being treated as a lowly Third World country. Not surprisingly they hang onto the one symbol of stature they have, their nuclear potential." Vice Prime Minister Yukhnovsky's bizarre threat, however, belied the colonel's view of his own country's maturity. But whatever else Ukraine was, it was very well armed.*

The more serious proliferation threat, however, comes more from the insidious sale of nuclear-related dual-use technology than from passing

*In the split-up of the old Red Army, Ukraine marshaled 500,000 to 600,000 troops. Ukraine ended up with 4,080 main battle tanks, 5,050 armored fighting vehicles, 4,040 artillery pieces, 1,090 combat aircraft, and 330 combat helicopters. It also controls some 50 percent of the former Soviet airlift capacity and a half share in the 380-ship Black Sea naval fleet, giving it the second largest military force in Europe. It has more troops and equipment than France, Britain, or Germany. Only Russia has more. ("What's Happening to the Red Army? A Lot," *The Wall Street Journal*, August 17, 1992.)

around whole missiles or even their warheads. This is particularly true in Russia, Kazakhstan, Ukraine, and even tiny Estonia. Of the four, only Russia signed an agreement in April 1992 with the Nuclear Supplier Group to control the export of sixty-five dual-use items. Estonia, Kazakhstan and Ukraine, wary of incursions on their independence, refused to enter the accord. Even Russia, while holding the line in several other areas, has violated both the suppliers group agreement and the Non-Proliferation Treaty by continuing to ship unsafeguarded nuclear fuel to Kazakhstan and Ukraine.

Kazakhstan itself owns the Ulbinsky Metallurgy Plant at Ust-Kamenogorsk, the old Soviet Union's largest producer of the zirconium and beryllium metals used in power reactors and nuclear weapons and of the uranium fuel pellets used in reactors. Since the uranium in the pellets is already partially enriched, it would be particularly attractive to prospective customers like Iraq, Pakistan, Israel, Brazil, or Argentina, all of which have uranium enrichment technology that could use the pellets. In fact, U.S. intelligence had determined that by late 1992 the Kazakhs who ran the plant had made their sale to an overseas customer: a load of beryllium, which has a variety of nuclear weapons applications, that went to Iran.

Dneprodzerzhinsk, until recently a closed military production center in Ukraine, is the site of the Pridneprovsky Chemical combine, one of the largest complexes for producing nuclear-related dual-use material, including heavy water, zirconium, beryllium, hafnium, and ion-exchange resins used in the uranium enrichment process. The installation also has a stockpile of 800 tons of unsafeguarded uranium oxide. An American company that bought part of a chemical plant at Dneprodzerzhinsk reported that its Ukrainian partner shipped forty-five tons of hafnium and beryllium to docks in Belgium and the Netherlands with no apparent idea about the elements' final destination. Not far away, the old SS-18 assembly line at Dnepropetrovsk turns out grain silos (made from hollow rocket cylinders), sausage making machines, and trolley buses. ("We built the best rockets in the world and we thought we were great," Yuri Alekseev, the factory's chief engineer recalled nostalgically. "But when we built our first thirty sausage machines they fell apart. We had to go back to the drawing board.") And U.S. officials fear that it may be going back into the missile business, like so much of the former Soviet Union's and eastern Europe's arms industry, which also was eminently more successful at building weapons than sausage stuffers.

1　　　　　　　　　　　　　　　　　　　　　　　　　　　　　　2

Left, Jafar Dhia Jafar, the man Saddam chose to develop the Iraqi atomic bomb. Right, Amir Hammoudi al-Saadi, the organizational genius behind the Iraqi superweapons program, who played Albert Speer to Saddam's Hitler. Western-educated like so many of Iraq's scientists, he speaks fluent English and German, and worked in the Czech, East German, and Yugoslavian weapons industries.

A U.N. inspector walks through the partially destroyed hall of Iraq's uranium enrichment plant at Tarmiyah, north of Baghdad. The Tarmiyah complex contained nearly 400 buildings, but the United States did not know its nuclear role until a defector crossed into Turkey after the war ended and revealed what Iraq had been planning.

A vacuum pump used to enrich uranium sits on the back of a truck after U.N. officials succeeded in getting Iraq to show them what it had tried to hide during the first series of U.N. inspections of the Iraqi nuclear weapons program.

4

5

A bulldozer crushes empty Iraqi chemical weapons at the Al Multhanna weapons facility near Baghdad. Iraq built at least 150,000 chemical weapons of all kinds from land mines to missile warheads.

FOUNDED IN 1801 BY ALEXANDER HAMILTON

# NEW YORK POST

METRO EDITION

FRIDAY, JANUARY 18, 1991 / Partly cloudy, near 40 today; cloudy, mid 20s tonight / Details, Page 2          R R R   40¢ in New York City 50¢ elsewhere

# MISSILES HIT ISRAEL

*Journalists wear gas masks while working in Jerusalem shortly before Iraqi missiles landed in Tel Aviv and Haifa yesterday.*

Agence France Presse

■ *Iraqi SCUDs rip Tel Aviv & Haifa*
■ *Report Israeli jets striking back*

GULF WAR EXPLODES; COVERAGE BEGINS ON PAGES 2 and 3

6

The moment Israel long feared came the second night of the Gulf War. Although Iraq had thirty chemical warheads for its Scuds, none was ever fired at Israel. Pentagon officials believed the Iraqis feared nuclear annihilation. (As one said, "You do not gas Jews.")

7                                                                              8

Left, Benazir Bhutto—brilliant, charismatic, beautiful. But when it came to discussions of nuclear war, she was left out in spite of her positions as Prime Minister and Defense Minister of Pakistan. Right, Dr. A. Q. Khan, director of Pakistan's nuclear weapons program and a man who held strong anti-Western and antisemitic views.

9

Its canopy and air intake protected against the vagaries of desert air, an F-16 intended for the Pakistani Air Force sits on a temporary tarmac at a U.S. Air Force base outside Tucson, Arizona. The United States refused to deliver the fighter-bombers to Pakistan after it finally determined that Pakistan had acquired nuclear weapons and might use the F-16s to drop them on Indian cities.

10

This souvenir snapshot would have yielded an intelligence bonanza when it was taken in 1989. Christopher P. Drogoul (right) was illegally channeling more than $5 billion to Saddam Hussein in the biggest bank fraud in U.S. history. Zuhair Abbas (left) managed Project 395, the umbrella organization that constructed facilities for Iraq's combined nuclear weapon and Condor-2 ballistic missile programs. Fadel Kadhum (center) was counsel to Iraq's superweapon procurement program and was himself a top intelligence official. Behind them is the excavation for the Badush Dam, which was to generate electricity for the production of nuclear weapons.

Left, Saddam Hussein and his favorite arms dealer, Carlos Cardoen, at Saddam's palace during the Iran-Iraq War. Cardoen claimed his work for Saddam had CIA sanction. Right, Gerald Bull dealt with Iraq not only on the supergun but a wide range of projects, including an ICBM and an antiballistic missile.

What British customs missed: The first shipment of parts for Gerald Bull's supergun sits in a parking lot near the city of Mussayib, Iraq. Although Her Majesty's Customs Service intercepted one shipment of supergun parts disguised as oil pipes, this one had gotten through earlier—and was not bombed during the war.

14

This 350-millimeter long-range cannon, situated 125 miles north of Baghdad, could have fired artillery rounds at Teheran. Designed by Bull, it was the forerunner of a larger model that was supposed to fire objects into Earth orbit. Incredibly, the gun went unseen by the U.S. reconnaissance satellites and survived the Persian Gulf War intact. U.N. inspectors examined it during their post-war investigations.

15

Antennas and satellite domes dominate this Bavarian landscape outside Bad Aibling, Germany. Here, U.S. intelligence listens for communications that will give advance warning of weapons programs being developed throughout the Middle East.

Left, the cover of a Russian brochure advertising the BN-800 breeder reactor, capable of producing enough plutonium for thirty bombs every year. The reactor was being offered to both China and India by early 1993. Right, Greenpeace's nuclear weapons guru, William Arkin, inside an abandoned Soviet nuclear weapons bunker north of Berlin in June 1991. Two dozen hydrogen bomb warheads were once stored here. The next day Arkin met with a Soviet lieutenant offering to sell Greenpeace a nuclear missile warhead.

For sale: A scale model of the Russian nuclear reactor complex being built in Cuba. The same type of reactor has been sold to Iran and has been offered to China, India, Pakistan, and Brazil. All but China have refused to sign the Nuclear Non-Proliferation Treaty.

19  20

Left, Shimon Peres, Israeli patriot, committed international Socialist, and the father of the Israeli nuclear bomb program. At virtually every juncture in the development of the Israeli bomb, Peres played a critical role in moving the program forward. Right, Israel's "Dr. Strangelove," Yu'val Ne'eman. Ne'eman not only once ran the country's nuclear weapons program but also developed its first spy satellite.

21

Above a favorite beach south of Tel Aviv sits the range safety building for the Palmikim missile test range. Officers at the facility would destroy any errant Israeli missiles if they endangered populated areas near the site. They have never had to act.

Israel's Arrow missile streaks skyward on its way toward intercepting a tactical missile during a 1992 test. U.S. intelligence believed that the missile, financed mainly by U.S. taxpayers, was one of several weapons systems where the Israelis shared technology with the South Africans and the Chinese.

22

23

The bio-bomb, a tiny bomblet three inches across containing deadly bacteria or viruses. Israel fears that Iran is developing bombs like this one, which was built by the United States. Hundreds of these bombs could be clustered in a ballistic missile warhead and then burst over a populated target such as Tel Aviv.

The abandoned streets of Pripyat, a mile and a half from the Chernobyl nuclear reactor. The disaster caused by the explosion at Chernobyl has inspired some Third World countries—including Libya—to explore the possibility of radiological bombs, bombs that would disperse radioactive materials such as cobalt or cesium over wide areas, making them—like Pripyat—uninhabitable.

24

The historic launch pad where the first Sputnik was launched and Yuri Gagarin began man's ascent into space. The Baikonur Cosmodrome is now the property of Kazakhstan, one of a dozen important Soviet defense sites in the hands of Muslim states that used to be part of the Soviet Union.

25

Japanese protest the arrival of the *Akatsuki-Maru*, a plutonium-carrying ship, as it entered the port of Tokai. The ship was transporting plutonium from France for Japan's fast-breeder reactor, but the protesters knew the same plutonium could be used to fuel at least 150 atomic bombs.

26

Japan's homegrown H-2 rocket, capable of launching heavy payloads into space—or warheads at an enemy. In spite of its pacifist constitution, Japan has developed a variety of dual-use technologies, such as advanced rocketry and plutonium reprocessing, that make it a stand-by superpower.

A Chinese Silkworm missile streaks toward a target during a 1980s test. The Chinese used profits from sales of the sea-skimming antiship missile to advance other longer range missiles both for its own military and those of its Third World clients.

The Hollywood Connection: Arnon Milchan (second from right) is one of moviedom's hottest producers. Milchan has also served as a conduit for the transfer of sensitive American technology to Israel's nuclear and missile programs. With him at the Hollywood premiere of *Sommersby* were (left to right): Terry Semel, chief executive officer of Warner Brothers, with whom Milchan has a $600 million movie production deal; Richard Gere, Jodie Foster, and Steve Reuther, his partner in New Regency Enterprises.

THE MINISTER OF DEFENCE

Tel-Aviv, November 22, 1974

TOP SECRET

Dear Dr. Rhoodie,

    Allow me to thank you most sincerely for the great efforts you employed to ensure the success of the meetings which took place in Pretoria on the 13th and 14th of this month.

    I am looking forward very much to meeting you again during your next visit to Israel.

    With warm personal regards, I am,

Sincerely yours,

Shimon Peres
Minister of Defence

Dr. E.M. Rhoodie,
Secretary for Information,
Pretoria,
The Republic of South Africa
-------------------------

Shimon Peres's top secret 1974 letter to the Secretary of Information of South Africa, Dr. Eschel Rhoodie, thanking him for opening up strategic cooperation between Israel and South Africa. This cooperation led to joint efforts in nuclear weapons and missile technology.

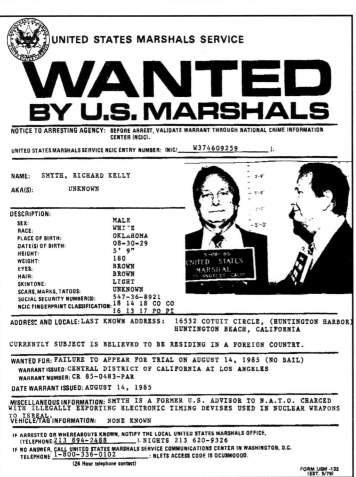

Wanted poster for Richard Kelly Smyth, a California scientist and defense contractor, who supplied 810 nuclear triggers to Israel and then disappeared just before trial. Smyth, who was in business with Arnon Milchan, is believed to be living in a Tel Aviv suburb.

Arthur Biehl, once director of H-bomb research at Lawrence Livermore National Laboratories, went to the FBI after Milchan arranged for him to meet with a top Israeli official at the Beverly Hills Polo Lounge.

32

The Overberg Test Range in Arniston, South Africa. Built to Israeli specifications, it was the home of a nuclear-capable missile the Israelis helped the apartheid regime build in record time.

33

Missile in a mountain: Far away from prying Israeli eyes, Argentina built Iraq a long-range, nuclear-capable missile deep inside this mountain near the Argentine town of Falda del Carmen. The billion-dollar project was financed by Saudi Arabia.

From these offices in the Swiss town of Zug, German and Austrian engineers fanned out to sites in Argentina, Egypt, and Iraq, where they worked on the Condor-2 missiles.

---

$200\,^\circ C$ properties

EPon 828 from shell ........... 50% by wt.

(1) Versamide 140 from general mills (Henckel) ........... 50% by wt.

(2) mix very good at ambient

(3) Pre Cut the C-C cloth

(4) Preimpregnate the cloth and keep at ref.

~~(5) layup the cloth on the parts~~

(4) sandblast the parts

(5) degreasing.

(6) apply thin coat (0.02 to 0.03 inch) of the mix

(7) Cure at Room Temp. or at little elevated Temp.

(8) apply the preimpreg. cloth at R. Temp or little elevated Temp while applying low pressure to keep material on

(9) Repeat for 4-5 plys.

These handwritten notes, retrieved from the garbage can of missile designer Abdelkader Helmy, provide simple instructions on how to prepare the carbon-carbon material needed for Condor-2 missile reentry vehicles.

37

Advena Laboratories, Pretoria, South Africa: Each of the vaults contained an atomic bomb that the Afrikaaner regime was prepared to use against black South Africans.

38

In this lone building in the middle of South Africa's Kalahari Desert is the test hole where the apartheid regime intended to detonate its first atomic bomb. The plan called for the test to take place only if South Africa felt its very existence threatened. Then, the white leaders believed, the United States would be faced with a horrible dilemma: Either save the white government or watch as the next bomb incinerated black soldiers.

Even little Estonia is in the dual-use business. In one case, a shipment of four tons of zirconium that was to be sent from Russia to Estonia, allegedly for jewelry production, was evidently headed for a third country. Russian export control officials, suspicious because the grade and quantity of the metal was incompatible with its stated end use, could not get the Tallin government to say where exactly the shipment was destined, so they blocked the export. They also admitted that large quantities of dual-use metals are apparently finding their way from Estonia to countries with ambitious nuclear weapons programs.

Estonia is also the home of the Baltiets machine tool factory, where machine tools used in the Soviet nuclear weapons program were produced, according to a study by the Monterey Institute of International studies. It also has two 25-megawatt submarine training reactors, a uranium milling operation, and an export firm suspected of exporting radioactive materials.

The metals came from a plant just on the other side of the Russian-Estonian border. *Izvestia* reported in November 1992 that the facility, the Phosphorit chemical factory, had found that huge blocks of cesium-137 were missing. The element, along with strontium-90 and cobalt-60, is ideal for use in what nuclear terrorism experts call "radioactive dispersal devices" or radiological bombs. The deadly material could be wrapped around conventional explosives and then detonated, dispersing lethal doses of radioactivity over a wide area.

"Cesium shoots out an invisible beam of deadly gamma-quantum rays that pierces right through ferro-concrete and steel walls," *Izvestia* reported. "In essence, the stolen material is a radiation weapon that can kill 30 and even 60 years from now." The article blamed the smuggling on an "atomic mafia" and noted that there were more than 5,000 enterprises in the St. Petersburg region that used such isotopes.

The study found Estonia's facilities typical of those of the former Soviet states. While only four of the former Soviet republics had nuclear weapons on their soil in 1992, six had research reactors useful for weapons development; five had nuclear research centers; four produced heavy water that countries like India and Israel need for their weapons reactors; and seven had uranium mines (including the world's largest, at Murantau in Uzbekistan).

Overall, the study concluded, Russia has all the facilities needed to build nuclear weapons; Ukraine has 75 percent of them; Kazakhstan has 40 percent, and the rest have much smaller percentages. But by combining their capabilities into consortiums—with nations inside or outside the new states of the former U.S.S.R.—they could become key proliferators, if not nuclear weapons states themselves.

Do-it-yourself nuclear bomb makers can buy at least three kinds of Russian reactors and probably the experts to go with them. Two reactors, the VVER-440 and VVER-1000, are water-cooled and water-moderated power models designed for civilian commercial applications. But as is the case with other power reactors, they produce plutonium residue that can be separated and reprocessed until it is bomb-grade. A nation that imported one or more of the reactors, however, would also need reprocessing facilities. The VVER-440 is the type that was being built in Cuba. It is also the reactor that Russia contracted to sell to Iran in August 1992 while the highly competitive Chinese negotiated with Teheran for their own reactor sale. The Iranians, intent on becoming a dominating power in the Middle East and arming themselves accordingly, played the Russians and Chinese off against each other in order to get the price down. And it worked. Moscow agreed to reduce the price of the two VVER-440 Model 213s, along with an option for two more, from $4 billion to $2 billion rather than lose the sale to Beijing.* The main concern here, according to U.S. officials, was not that the reactor fuel would be turned into bombs, but that the Iranians or any other Third World customers would gain experience in the handling of nuclear materials, a crucial first step in the development of weaponry. The third type is the notorious fast breeder, which is designed specifically to turn uranium into plutonium.

The question of what will be done with the Iranian reactors' spent fuel does not seem to have crossed the minds of the Russian salesmen, at least in their recollection of the negotiations. After learning of the fifteen-year agreement, an unhappy Department of State asked Moscow to at least collect the used fuel rods and ship them home. David Kyd, a spokesman for the International Atomic Energy Agency, reported that the American request seemed to have surprised the Russians, who claimed that they hadn't even thought about what would happen to the used fuel rods. Kyd added that there are no guarantees that Iran will return them to their country of origin.

*The Russian deal, however, was better in the short run. Russia produced all of the components needed for the reactors. The Chinese, on the other hand, had licensed much of their technology from European and Japanese suppliers, and were therefore unlikely to permit reexport of that technology to Iran. (Interview with a U.S. Department of State official on September 4, 1992.)

Nor are the Russians ignoring their own backyard. Moscow has quietly agreed to provide Kazakhstan with soup-to-nuts nuclear technology—the entire fuel cycle, from mining and enriching uranium to reprocessing plutonium—in exchange for Kazakhstan's continuing to send Russia up to 220 pounds a year of the plutonium it extracts from a fast breeder at Aktau. Kazakhstan's ostensible reason for wanting nuclear independence is to conserve its oil reserves for export. Although the idea has a certain amount of validity, at least for energy-hungry Kazakhs, the fact remains that such a system could also be made to yield bomb-quality uranium and plutonium. And since Kazakhstan is not yet a party to the NPT, there are no safeguards against its doing just that.

Meanwhile, India wanted one of the powerful VVER-1000s. Other potential customers for Russian reactors included Pakistan, Israel, Brazil, and China itself. What stood in the way of many of these and other sales was a shortage of hard currency. In December 1985, for example, the Soviet Union agreed to sell North Korea four VVER-440s, but the deal collapsed because of the $3 billion price (and because Pyongyang refused to let IAEA representatives inspect its other nuclear facilities). Failure to sell North Korea the reactors, however, broke a tradition. Moscow had trained hundreds of North Korean scientists and technicians for their nation's "peaceful" nuclear program, including reprocessing technology. The Russians had refused to deliver blueprints for a reprocessing plant in the 1970s, when North Korea's nuclear weapons program was in its infancy, but the training served its purpose. Pyongyang had its plant in full operation by 1992.

As the decade wore on, India emerged as a hot prospect for Russian power reactors. India, in fact, has been one of the chief beneficiaries of the old tradition of assisting comradely nations. As was the case with North Korea, the Soviet nuclear weapons establishment worked at the edges of the Non-Proliferation Treaty where India was concerned.

During the 1980s, while the United States was helping Pakistan by looking the other way on nuclear issues, the Soviet Union was doing a great deal more for its own south Asian ally. India had chosen a natural uranium-fed reactor to produce its bomb-grade material. Natural uranium was, of course, abundant. But natural uranium reactors require heavy water, which is not easy to produce. So Techsnabexport, the Soviets' uranium exporting enterprise, agreed to sell India tons of the stuff. Since the NPT requires official notice when shipments of a metric ton or more of heavy water cross borders, the crafty Soviets shipped it in consignments of 990 kilograms.

In 1991, Techsnabexport became a private enterprise and its bureaucrats entrepreneurs. The past was not something they wanted to hear about. Albert Shishkin, the operations director, agreed that the intermediary in the Indian heavy water deal was the notorious Alfred Hempel, the right-wing German nuclear technology dealer. But Shishkin angrily denied that Techsnabexport or anyone else in Moscow had known that the water was being rerouted to India by Hempel. He limply explained that the arrangement with Hempel was "like an April Fool's Day joke," in that his old enterprise had been given phony end-use documents supplied by Hempel's front company. "This is like a trial, like the election of your Supreme Court judge, the one who told dirty jokes to his secretary," Shishkin said, referring to the Clarence Thomas confirmation hearings, which were then on television in Moscow. "You have your documents," Shishkin added, "and we have ours."

The prize for anyone wanting to produce his own plutonium, however, would be a $500 million BN-800 fast breeder. That reactor, designed by the Soviet nuclear weapons establishment for its own use, was made superfluous by the end of the cold war. But since it could produce more than 500 pounds of plutonium a year, or enough for roughly thirty bombs, it would be a real prize for India. New Delhi therefore wanted one of these, too. Evgeniy Mikirin has denied that BN-800s have been built, let alone marketed. While they may not have been built, one was indeed advertised at a trade show in Lyons, France, in 1990 and at another in Birmingham, England, in 1993. It was featured in a brochure, "REACTOR BN-800," at least one of which was immediately collected by a U.S. intelligence agent. The Russians were also marketing a smaller fast-breeder, called the BN-350, to Israel, with both sides insisting that its main purpose was to provide electricity for the sweetening, or desalinating, of sea water. The BN-350 could produce enough plutonium for twelve bombs a year. The capability to produce such devices, given the right incentive, is clearly there.

All of this, plus the prospect of a brain drain in which the most talented Russian and other former Soviet nuclear and rocket scientists and engineers simply took off for greener pastures, so deeply concerned the United

States by early 1992 that a series of measures were taken to defuse the situation.

That February, Representative George Brown, a California Democrat and the Chairman of the House Committee on Science, Space, and Technology, announced that he planned to introduce legislation to create a U.S.-Russian Science & Technology Foundation to fund joint projects in both countries with start-up funding of not less than $200 million.

By March, one American company had hired Boris A. Babayan, the scientist who created the supercomputers used by the Soviet space program and by its nuclear weapons designers. Babayan was described as the Seymour R. Cray of his country. An American businessman had, in the meantime, come up with the idea of hiring unemployed Russian scientists, engineers, and technicians to "close the research and development gap with Japan."

The Department of Energy then weighed in with its own plan to hire 116 Russian scientists to do fusion research at the Kurchatov Institute of Atomic Energy in Moscow for a total of $90,000, or $65 a month per scientist. While that sum was a pittance to their American counterparts, it amounted to seven times the unofficial national average monthly wage. The Russians had done pioneering work in the elusive attempt to harness hydrogen as an unlimited energy source.

Nine days after the DOE announcement, the prestigious National Academy of Sciences publicly called on the federal government to act "immediately and aggressively" to help reorient basic science and technology in the former Soviet Union. Its recommendations included a call for using $400 million in an existing Department of Defense budget line covering the dismantling of former Soviet weapons for new research opportunities among its scientists. The plan crystalized in the Nunn-Lugar amendment, originally passed by Congress in 1991 with the $400 million appropriation, and then doubled the following year. The idea, sponsored by Senators Sam Nunn and Richard Lugar, was to pay U.S. companies to dismantle the nukes. Yet by the summer of 1993, only $31 million had been formally obligated and even less spent. This was the result of reluctance on the part of the Pentagon and the Department of Energy to spend their dwindling resources on the former Soviet Union rather than on their own weapons, on the cumbersome nature of their bureaucracy, and on the confused and occasionally hostile reception the idea received in Russia and Ukraine, respectively.

The Academy also called for additional support for an International Science and Technology Center in Moscow, which was to be established by the United States, Russia, Japan, and the European Community. A second center, sponsored by the United States, Canada, and Sweden, was suggested for Kiev. Both centers were supposed to serve as clearinghouses and liaison offices for nonweapons-related projects that would provide professionally rewarding alternative employment to former Soviet weapons designers. Most of the projects would take place inside the old Soviet Union. The idea was sound enough, but a year later, it had yet to be implemented.

Although it was not seen as an immediate problem, the potential brain drain of former Soviet weapons scientists and engineers was very worrisome to Robert Gallucci, the Department of State official who was overseeing the development of the International Science and Technology Centers. "Most of them still live and work in relatively closed facilities, and they have limited access to foreign recruiters," he noted. "So I don't think that they represent a problem right now. If we succeed, however, in opening up Russian society, they might get around. If we haven't done any better in replacing their weapons design work with more peaceful projects, we will have made a big mistake."

The Russians themselves estimated that there were between 1,000 and 2,000 scientists who could design nuclear weapons and 3,000 to 5,000 more who could design and operate uranium enrichment or plutonium reprocessing facilities. All in all, the Defense Intelligence Agency estimates that there were one million weapons scientists in the former Soviet Union when the cold war ended.

But there were no plans whatever for the 100,000 scientists and technicians with knowledge of how to put a missile program together, or the 25,000 who had worked for Biopreparat, the covert germ warfare program before it was terminated in 1991. Some U.S. intelligence analysts feared that program even more than its nuclear counterpart. Just before it was shut down, Biopreparat scientists had been working on the "super-plague" bomb, one of which could have killed half the population of a medium-sized city.

The dire situation of the ex-Soviet nuclear weapons fraternity was not lost on others who were covetous of its potential for bomb designing and manufacturing and who had money to offer. These included Libya, Syria,

Iraq, China, and probably Algeria, which was getting a reactor of its own from China. Israel's active nuclear weapons program would also have much to gain from disaffected Russian Jewish scientists (though many scientists in other disciplines who have immigrated there are collecting garbage and driving taxis because of a glutted labor market).

Most Russian scientists, like their American counterparts, give no indication of wanting to leave their country. Yet several have been asked and some have succumbed. The countries of choice are, respectively, South Africa, Australia, Canada, the United States, and Israel. But offers from these five, who have enough nuclear scientists and engineers, are rare.

The Third World, as might be expected, offers more fruitful prospects. Viktor Mironov, a sixty-year-old expert on plutonium processing, claimed that Iraq had offered him $100,000 in 1990 to work in its nuclear program. He declined, he added, but "a young specialist did go, and there are a lot of cases like that." In December 1991 a senior scientist at the Kurchatov Institute reported that at least two of his colleagues turned down offers of $2,000 a month from Libyan head-hunters. Libya and Algeria *have* imported some engineers and technicians. But rather than being weapons scientists, they are experts in small research reactors. Libya wanted them to restart its ten-megawatt research reactor at Tajoura, while Algeria needed them to help train technicians to work on a much larger Chinese-supplied research reactor, which was itself a knockoff of a 1950s Soviet model. One packed off to China for a year-long stint in that country's nuclear program; another, who specialized in Tokamac-type fusion reactors, headed for North Korea (loaded down with a suitcase full of food that had been painstakingly collected by the wife he left behind).

Which of their better-qualified countrymen would follow depended on how prospects went in their homelands. By the summer of 1992, those prospects looked very dim, at least to analysts in the West. In congressional testimony that June, CIA and DIA analysts sketched a picture of a rapidly disintegrating military-industrial complex, with many defense plants either bankrupt or nearing it, and with weapons sales expected to plunge 60 to 80 percent through the rest of the year. The ratio of military spending to overall economic output had dropped from 15 to 17 percent during the cold war to between 4 and 6 percent because of 40 percent reductions in the purchase of weapons for the ground forces, 50 percent for the air force, and about one-third for the navy. This mirrored the near-collapse of nuclear weapons research, testing, and production.

Seen in this light, the coming glut of conventional weapons to be dumped on the world market is only the proverbial tip of the iceberg. But it is a huge tip.

Everything in the space program, including the capability to use SL-13, Proton, and other boosters to launch military reconnaissance and communication satellites for Third World countries, is now available for a price. "There are no more secrets," said Vladimir Lobachev, the director of the mission control center in a Moscow suburb, with disarming honesty. "We will sell anything, in any form, which will make a profit." That includes the use of transonic wind tunnels, computers, specially made scale models, and actual flight testing at the Bor flight test complex to perfect new aircraft or missiles.

It also includes a mountain of first-line weaponry that the old Soviet Union kept for itself during the cold war against the day when it would have to be used against the West. One glaring example among many is the AS-16 air-to-surface missile, a weapon so new that Western intelligence only learned about its capabilities from a slick brochure picked up at a Moscow arms show. The weapon has a range of close to 100 miles, is extremely accurate, nuclear-capable, and can be carried in multiple numbers by the same type of Backfire bomber being bought by Iran and China. "From the point of view of a Third World country faced with U.S. naval air power," one respected journal has noted, "the Backfire/AS-16 combination must be enormously attractive."

NPO Energomash of Moscow, founded in the 1950s by Valentine P. Glushko, one of the great Soviet space pioneers, is Russia's preeminent rocket engine design facility. It has provided engines for almost everything from the booster that carried Sputnik-1 to the 6.6-million-pound-thrust array of engines that power Energia, the world's most powerful launcher (its services, too, are for sale). Now, strapped for cash and mired in a space program so anemic that it was forced to carry the logo of a sanitary napkin company on the booster that carried a Japanese journalist to space in December 1990, NPO Energomash is selling several types of engines.* The most powerful of these, the RD-170, is the same engine that powers Energia. An NPO Energomash sales brochure notes that the engine would be useful for any nation that wanted to build a space station or embark on a mission to Mars. There aren't many of those around anymore. There

---

*The reporter, Toyohiro Akiyama, racked up charges of $1.5 million a day during the eight-day flight.

are any number of nations, however, that could use such an engine in the first stage of an ICBM.

In 1991, the Indian Space Research Organization bought a rocket engine and related technology from Glavkosmos, the Russian civilian space agency. Following an angry protest by the United States, the Indian embassy in Washington issued a press release asserting that the engine was intended strictly to send civilian communication satellites to geosynchronous orbit, 22,300 miles above the equator. India, the release went on, wants to build its own geosynchronous launch capability rather than be dependent on the United States, France, and Russia, as had previously been the case. It explicitly denied that the rocket would be used for military purposes. The statement neglected to note that communication satellites in geosynchronous orbit would play a crucial role in any warfighting situation and, further, that ballistic missile early warning satellites, which are supposed to provide instant warning of a surprise missile attack, also inhabit that altitude.

Two years later, Boris Yeltsin compounded Washington's irritation by proclaiming not only that he remained committed to supplying the Indians with all the rocket engines they wanted, but that his attitude signaled a sea change in Moscow's policy. Describing his country as a "Euro-Asian power" during his first visit to India, the Russian President made a point of saying that he was "moving away from a pro-Western emphasis" to a "purposeful Eastern policy." The $250 million rocket deal was a clear violation of the Missile Technology Control Regime, which Russia promised to respect without signing. The embattled Russian undoubtedly reflected that workers in his country's collapsing space industry could not eat agreements. Adherence to documents was a prerogative of the rich and powerful.

The United States, however, was unrelenting. In June 1993, after a year of quiet arm-twisting, word was leaked to the news media that Washington was putting heavy pressure on Moscow not only to halt the Indian rocket deal but to abandon the sale of rocket fuel to Libya. Early in July, President Clinton used the carrot and stick on Yeltsin in an economic summit meeting in Tokyo, threatening economic sanctions if the transfers were consumated and promising increased aid and participation in lucrative joint space proejcts if they were abandoned. The result was instructive. The Russians announced a week later that they were backing out of the deal with India, the more worrisome of the two. The Indians reacted by claiming that a similar deal could be cut with other nations and that, in any case, they would press on with their own research. Analysts did not doubt it, and calculated that India could come up with a comparable rocket in five to seven years.

"Nobody ever contemplated that the Soviet military-industrial complex would end up in Chapter 11," said Russell Seitz, an associate at the Olin Center for Strategic Studies at Harvard (and novelist Tom Clancy's technical adviser). "It's the yard sale at the end of history."*

The sale includes MIG-29 and SU-27 fighters that U.S. intelligence would have spent a small fortune to obtain only a few years ago, but which are no longer of interest except as trade items to other countries.

Mindful of Yeltsin's precarious position in a nation whose economy has been gutted, the United States has been careful not to criticize Russian arms sales too harshly, lest it create a conservative backlash in the Kremlin and in the Congress of People's Deputies. Yet the weapons exports remained nettlesome. "Anybody can sell arms," one senior Western diplomat said in Moscow. "But Russia's list of buyers is essentially our list of nasties."

For their part, the Russians bridle at being rebuked for their efforts, particularly by Americans. They often point out that more than half of the world market in conventional arms is controlled by the United States. "If we sell SU-27s to China—and it's our legal business—the United States objects," said Pyotr G. Litavrin, head of export control for the Foreign Ministry. "Then they sell F-16s to Taiwan: 150 aircraft. And then they say it's their response! It's ridiculous: two dozen SU-27s versus 150 F-16s!"

Ironically, the Chinese became the biggest customers of the Russian aerospace and nuclear industries, much like the owners of a surviving store buying merchandise from a competitor that has gone bankrupt. Decades of ideological sniping, name-calling, undisguised contempt, and even border skirmishes that on at least one occasion looked like near-war, dissolved during the yard sale. Beijing agreed to buy an entire Backfire bomber factory and a uranium centrifuge complex capable of making bomb-grade uranium. (China had never mastered the process, largely relying instead on plutonium for its weapons.) It also agreed to purchase complete military laboratories for the development of high-tech conventional weapons. The labs would be dismantled and shipped to China.

*He referred to Fukuyama's *The End of History and the Last Man*.

266

One senior Russian Defense Ministry official claimed in 1993 that as many as 2,000 defense scientists had gone to China during the past two years—many for short visits—to help transfer advanced weapons systems to their former enemies. That did not include scores of Russians who were quietly recruited by Beijing to stay for a long duration. At the same time, 300 to 400 Chinese defense specialists were working at four key Russian aerospace research installations. Yeltsin himself admitted that China bought $1.8 billion worth of arms from his country in 1992 alone, even as negotiations were underway for the transfer of another $1.5 billion worth of S-300 advanced air defense missiles that could be used against cruise and possibly ballistic missiles. Indeed, the Russians were so captivated by potential sales to China that in May 1993, they moved a pavillion full of advanced fighters and other weapons directly from an arms exhibition in Abu Dhabi to a private show at Nankou, just north of Beijing.

Nor were the Chinese the only bargain hunters. Iran was Russia's other new big post-cold-war customer. By the summer of 1992, it was working out details on at least four major deals with the Russians—the sale of the reactors; 112 top-of-the-line Russian military aircraft, including a dozen Backfires and forty-eight MIG-29s; a minimum of three and maximum of five Kiloclass diesel submarines; and even a complete MIG factory. The total bill, payable in hard currency, could be $6 billion, depending on the number of reactors and subs that are actually sold. As is often the case, Russian technicians would accompany the equipment for the purpose of training their Iranian counterparts, something Iran wanted even more than the weapons themselves.

In the autumn of 1991, a couple of MIG-29s were even sent on an old-fashioned barnstorming tour of several U.S. cities. While the Russians hardly believed that ordinary citizens at air shows would want to buy their top-of-the-line dogfighter, they did sell several ten-minute joy rides for $1,000 a minute.* They also picked up a little extra cash peddling MIG-29 T-shirts, a clear sign that they were catching on to Western-style

*It wasn't top-of-the-line for long, though. Even as the tour got under way, an advanced MIG-29, renamed the MIG-33, was being designed. It was tested in June 1992 and sent to the Farnborough Air Show in Great Britain three months later in a clear effort to stimulate export sales.

marketing techniques.* Not to be outdone, Ukraine sent two of its own MIG-29s, resplendent in blue and orange paint, on a twenty-city North American tour the following spring. The price for a ride was competitive with the Russian price.

The Ukrainians even outdid the Russians when they put an entire, unfinished nuclear-capable aircraft carrier on the block. The ship had an interesting background. In 1984, publication of three highly classified KH-11 satellite photographs in *Jane's Defence Weekly*, a respected British publication, created a sensation in the intelligence community by revealing the spy satellite's capabilities. This resulted in the jailing of the U.S. Naval Intelligence analyst who sent them to England. The subject of the pictures was the Soviet Union's first nuclear-powered carrier, code-named Black Com 2 by NATO and ultimately named the *Admiral Kuznetsov* by the Soviet Navy. Eight years later, the Navy and CIA analysts who had scrutinized the pictures could have walked into the Nikolaiev yard where the ship was built and bought its sister ship, the *Varyag*.†

The *Admiral Kuznetsov* sailed out of the Black Sea the day before Ukraine voted for independence in December 1991 (after which it claimed the whole Black Sea fleet as its own). It was sent to join the North Sea fleet at Severomorsk. At 65,000 tons, the *Varyag* was to be identical with the *Admiral Kuznetsov*, and 30,000 tons lighter than most U.S. super-carriers. But it was nevertheless a world-class carrier, substantially larger than the four 43,000–ton *Kiev* class carriers that also came out of this particular yard.

In the spring of 1992, with all of its hull and 80 percent of its superstructure and propulsion system complete, the asking price for the *Varyag* was $1 billion as it was, $2 billion finished, and $4 billion with the all-important extras: sixty-five fighters, strike aircraft, and supporting helicopters. The *Varyag*'s broker was Ole-Yakov Libaek, a flamboyant

---

*Not one to let any threat go unused, Lockheed, Boeing, and General Dynamics—the consortium that was building the F-22 Advanced Tactical Fighter that suddenly didn't have an enemy—took an advertisement in a trade journal to warn that sale of the MIGs to Third World nations also constituted a threat to the United States. ". . . as Third World countries acquire sophisticated fighters and air defense systems, geopolitical instability will increase. So, too, will the likelihood that our tactical fighters may encounter high-technology Soviet fighters outside of Europe." ("For Sale," *Aviation Week & Space Technology*, June 18, 1990, no page number.)

†Counting the total cost of building, launching, and operating a KH-11, they could have bought either of the carriers for what it cost to take their pictures. And ironically, even the Kremlin's own spy satellite imagery, which the CIA would have paid a fortune to acquire only a few years earlier, was being sold to anyone with a few thousand dollars. One of the images that went on the market was of the Pentagon, shot straight down.

Oslo entrepreneur. By the autumn of 1992 China and Ukraine were deep in negotiations for the carrier.

A completed deal would mean that China owned a superweapon of immense prestige and capability. It would possess a floating air base that could carry attack aircraft virtually anywhere, including to the disputed Spratly Islands, whose large oil reserve China covets. The *Varyag* is a fleet admiral's dream. But it is also an accountant's nightmare. In the first place, aircraft carriers (and submarines) are immensely expensive to operate in and of themselves and also because they require enormous support structures in naval ministries and elsewhere. And given the state of technology of relatively cheap ship-killing missiles like Exocet and Silkworm, no carrier can sail unprotected by escort vessels. As IBM's Richard Garwin once said in another context, a high-tech automobile can easily be put out of action by a low-tech rock. A carrier is as tempting a target as it is a formidable weapon. It therefore requires a protective phalanx of other ships, and that multiplies the expense enormously. "Let them buy it and see how expensive an aircraft carrier is to operate," one American defense analyst quipped when asked about the sale of the *Varyag*. In the end, the Chinese apparently came to the same conclusion and backed out of the deal, leaving the carrier to be sold for scrap metal.

Ole-Yakov Libaek was far from the only dealer in ex-Soviet arms. Even Eduard Shevardnadze, the great peacemaker, hawked the Sukhoi fighter-bombers made in his hometown of Tblisi when he visited Iran in January 1993.

**A** group of individuals in the Russian government began making some effort to stem the flow of many weapons out of the country. In the spring of 1992, a feeble clampdown on "adventurers" who were illegally exporting arms by bribing high officials got under way when the Supreme Soviet's Industry and Energetics Committee drafted legislation that created a commission that would have stronger control over the licensing of arms exports. "Currently, you are supposed to buy a license for exports," said Youri F. Tarasiuk, a member of the legislature and the man in charge of the conversion of military production to civilian. "Adventurers use private channels to get approval from high-ranking government individuals, and maybe they are tipped" (i.e., bribed). The military procurement budget's being cut by about 85 percent during the first quarter of 1992 was too much, he added, and left child care and some other social services as the only activities at some factories. "This is too much of a cut," he complained.

Many ordinary Russians agree. Closing down weapons factories has created deep-seated anger because of the way it has destroyed the standard of living. "They go out onto the street and start sort of a campaign on their own, organized in a military way," Vitaly Shlekov, the Russian's Deputy Minister of Defense observed. "They're practically running lots of towns and even cities. In Moscow alone you have more than one million people employed by the defense industry. Try to stop that."

The most astounding experience in Dieter Sommerfeld's life occurred quite unexpectedly in December 1990. Sommerfeld was the newly elected mayor of Lychen, a resort community fifty miles north of Berlin in the former East Germany. That bitter day, he had an unexpected visitor: a colonel named Soltaganov who was the commander of an important and mysterious Russian military base three miles outside town. The Russians had virtually no contact with the people of Lychen for the twenty-three years in which they manned the secret facility. Now, Soltaganov explained to Sommerfeld drily, his unit was abandoning the place in two weeks. Just after Christmas, the Russian colonel gave the German mayor a tour of the facility. Asked what the base had been used for, Soltaganov, unable to contain a laugh, replied that it had been "a storage site." On January 5, 1991, he blithely turned the keys to the installation over to the incredulous mayor, climbed into a staff car, and drove home.

Dieter Sommerfeld held the keys to a pair of adjoining underground bunkers that were protected by tons of concrete and earth and six rows of security fences, two of them electrified, in addition to guard towers and a pill box with slits for machine guns. Timber-reinforced trenches and earthworks had been dug just within the innermost fence to provide a final obstacle for approaching NATO troops. Three years earlier, two local boys, aged eight and fourteen, had been shot to death for wandering too close to the outermost perimeter of a nearby, similar base. Inside, heavy double black-and-yellow blast doors protected a subterranean weapons den lined in concrete and painted with glossy hues of light tan and gray, making its chambers glare harshly under the wire-protected ceiling lights. The glossy paint made the warhead warren easier to keep clean. (Such efficiency even extended to a lone, coverless toilet, which was mounted on raised concrete like a throne, to make swabbing around its base easier.)

The mayor was wandering through the remains of VK79 Extra, a unit that had been composed of 200 to 300 elite Soviet Army and Special Troops of the General Staff. The weapons storage areas, now so quiet and empty that footsteps echoed in them, had held between 50 and 100 nuclear warheads for advanced short-range missiles called SS-23s, missiles that had been targeted to destroy virtually all of the major population centers in the eastern part of West Germany, from Hamburg to Frankfurt.

All of the warheads had been carefully evacuated. Yet everything else remained exactly as it had been before the withdrawal, which had clearly been done hastily. It was as if the soldiers had suddenly been spirited away by aliens, leaving the moment of departure and their petty artifacts frozen in time. Double bunks were unmade, the electricity was left on, fuel remained in tanks, and the ceiling cranes used to move the warheads were operable. The barracks were fully furnished with chairs and desks. Chemical weapons gear, including suits and goggled masks, was strewn on the floor and piled on shelves, along with helmets, jackets, belts, and canteens. A poster on the wall illustrated the procedure for putting on the poison gas clothing. A large handpainted wooden map even showed where the missile brigade was supposed to deploy for its attack.

"It looked as if they had been driven from the table and jumped out of their beds . . . that's what it looked like," Sommerfeld recalled in amazement. "There were plates and everything still on some tables."

The bunkers, barracks, and defense perimeter were a nuclear ghost town, a doomsday museum that still resonated with the existence and deadly purpose of those who had just hurriedly departed. The young soldiers could have annihilated half of Germany.

Two years earlier, access to the bunkers at Lychen would have amounted to a major Western intelligence coup. But on that winter day in 1991, with the Russians routed and the cold war over, no one really cared anymore. On the face of it, the facility had become a mere curiosity, a historic relic. But it was really more than that. The deserted bunkers outside of Lychen were a symbol of the pathological disarray, bordering on anarchy, into which their previous owner had plunged.

# TOUR DE FORCE

—

# 9

# ISRAEL:

# ATOMIC SOVEREIGNTY

At five o'clock on the afternoon of Sunday, June 7, 1981, eight F-16s and six F-15s roared off Etzion air base's baking, tire-blackened runway with their afterburners blazing. Etzion was on the eastern edge of the Sinai, not far from the parched, trackless desert that T. E. Lawrence described as "an ominous land, incapable of life, hostile even to the passing of life." Others called it the "Sun's Anvil."

The heat at Etzion made the air less dense and therefore less able than cool air to support the fighters' wings. And the loads the aircraft carried only made matters worse. Each of the F-16s, relatively small and dainty-looking attack aircraft, carried a pair of 2,000-pound Mk 84 high-explosive bombs, three drop tanks filled with 1,040 gallons of fuel, and a deadly AIM-9L Sidewinder air-to-air missile on its wing tips. The F-15s were also heavily loaded with extra fuel to extend their range and with braces of high-explosive Shafrir heat-seeking air-to-air missiles and radar-guided AIM-7 Sparrows. The fuel supply for this mission was so precious that all of the planes had been topped off while their pilots went through the preflight checklists with engines revving.

After struggling into the air with their heavy loads and joining up for a "running rendezvous," the fourteen fighters flew twenty-five miles south at an altitude of 350 feet and then banked left on an easterly heading. This quickly took them down valleys that cut through the craggy mountains separating the Negev from the Gulf of Aqaba. Appropriately, the port of Aqaba had itself been the site of a daring surprise attack by Lawrence of Arabia more than sixty years earlier.

The fighters came out of the mountains over water, skimming the eight miles between the Sinai and the Arabian Peninsula at 230 feet. Still flying "on the deck"—a particularly dangerous thing to do on a hot day with full fuel and heavy weapons—the F-16s and F-15s quickly entered Saudi airspace and pressed on, making certain to stay just on the Saudi side of the border with Jordan. The mission's planners had precisely calculated every aspect of the operation. They knew, for example, that if the attackers hugged the desert, no search radar beyond twelve miles from their flight path would pick them up.

The F-16s flew in two waves of four, with one wave 12,000 feet behind the other. They were shepherded by a pair of F-15s on either side and by two more covering the rear. The F-15s were along to protect the bomb-laden fighter-bombers from any enemy fighters that tried to pounce on them. Instead of being strung out, fighters and fighter-bombers were bunched tightly because that, too, would lessen the possibility of one of them straying onto an enemy radar screen. Flying close together also allowed the pilots to communicate by hand signal rather than use the radio. When they did speak, it was to give or acknowledge information in short, staccato sentences. That, too, reduced the chance of being discovered.

The pilots nursed the fuel in their unmarked jets by flying under 400 miles an hour along the Saudi leg of the mission. After taking a heading parallel to the Jordanian border for seventy-five miles, the combat planes abruptly banked to the northeast, following the border, and then, throttles pushed forward, streaked right for their target at almost 575 miles an hour and at a height never greater than 500 feet nor lower than 350. As they approached Lake Bahr Al Milh on the outskirts of Baghdad, two pairs of F-15s quickly climbed to 20,000 feet. The other pair went up to 25,000 feet. From that lofty perch, they circled as a protective umbrella, prepared to stop any Iraqi MIGs that came up from bases in the area to threaten the F-16s.

When they were a little more than four miles from the Osirak nuclear reactor, one F-16 after another swung into a stomach-wrenching climbing turn to 8,000 feet and rolled over on its back so the pilot could keep his eyes on the target. Each then plunged into the bomb run upside down, only righting itself when it was into the dive. The gravitational pressure, or G force, on the pilots' bodies was so great that they could hear themselves grunting through their oxygen masks and radios. The pilot of the lead F-16 went into his inverted dive pulling more than eight and a half Gs, meaning that he was being pushed into his ejection seat by a force eight and a half times his own body weight. It felt like turning to stone.

The attack went exactly as it had been practiced for months. Fire from the ground, including surface-to-air missiles, was thick but inaccurate. Not only did the Iraqis have insufficient time to warm up their radar, but the attackers came from due west, right out of the late-day sun.

All of the pilots knew exactly what the reactor looked like from above, very high above. They had studied photographs of it taken by a U.S. KH-11 reconnaissance satellite. KH-11s sent their pictures down from 100 or so miles in near-real-time. This meant the images came in as though they were on television. The intelligence on Osirak had been fresh. Even better, the resolution of the images—the smallest objects that could be discerned—was on the order of five or six inches. As a consequence, every meaningful detail of the reactor had been scrutinized before the pilots left Etzion. Although U.S. intelligence sometimes shared space reconnaissance imagery with allies, it almost always fuzzed the pictures so the object being photographed was clear enough to recognize while the true quality of the cameras that took them remained secret. This time, however, it was different. The pilots on "Operation Babylon," as the mission was called, had gotten the same clear, three-dimensional pictures as the CIA's and Department of Defense's own interpreters. The imagery was so good, in fact, that the fliers could have shot it themselves through the transparent Head Up Displays through which they now peered at their target.

The F-16s released their bombs from under 4,000 feet with extraordinary accuracy. Fifteen of the sixteen 2,000-pounders slammed through the reactor's dome and continued into its control room and core area. The bombs' fuses were set to delay the explosions long enough so they penetrated deep into the heart of the installation before going off. All but one of the fifteen exploded perfectly (the one that didn't was a dud). The sixteenth went off in a nearby hall. With its supporting structure blown outward, Osirak's dome collapsed onto its core, which was itself blasted to twisted rubble.*

The Osirak attack took 100 minutes from takeoff to bomb release and amounted to a textbook "surgical strike." Not only had the pilots practiced repeatedly on a mock-up in the Sinai, constructed with the help of the KH-11 imagery, but they even knew precisely what damage their bombs would do. That may have been because two Israeli engineers from Haifa's Technion had paid a visit to the Nuclear Regulatory Commission in Washington the previous October 9, just after the mission was conceived, and had asked NRC experts to describe in detail what precisely delivered 2,000-pounders would do to a reactor like Osirak. Technion was and remains Israel's preeminent institute of technology and specializes in military research. The engineers were rewarded with a detailed answer, which ultimately may have figured in the decision to use delayed fuses to maximize the effects of the blast.†

When the visit became known publicly two weeks after the attack, Frank Ingram, an NRC spokesman, claimed ignorance of the Israelis' motives. "We had no idea" that such an attack was being planned, he said. Avi Pazner, a spokesman at the Israeli embassy in Washington, also professed ignorance. The PR man maintained that the visit didn't have "the slightest connection" with the raid: "absolutely nothing to do with it." Instead, Pazner lamely asserted, Israel had been considering buying an American reactor since 1976 and had only sent the engineers to the NRC to find out what sort of destruction an attack against it would do.

---

*The attack was the first on a nuclear reactor, albeit one that had not yet gone on line. In the U.S. attack on Tuwaitha during the Gulf War, another precedent would be set: an attack on an operating nuclear reactor. The Iraqis themselves tried to hit Dimona, the Israeli reactor, with three Scuds during the closing days of the war, one of them reportedly coming close. Other attacks were threatened. A Cuban MIG-23 pilot who defected to the United States told of a Castro plan to attack Florida's Turkey Point commercial reactor if the U.S. invaded Cuba. In August 1992, the Serbs threatened to fly suicide missions against reactors elsewhere in Europe if United Nations troops used force to interfere with their "ethnic cleansing." The president of the breakaway Russian republic of Chechnya threatened to attack Russian reactors, and the Pakistanis claimed to be prepared to do the same thing to reactors in India.
†There could be no meaningful answer unless the thickness and composition of the containment and the arrangement of the reactor beneath it were known. There are two ways the Israelis could to have learned that. French engineers who worked on Osirak and who were sympathetic to their cause could have provided blueprints or diagrams. More likely, the mission's planners were shown KH-11 pictures that were successively taken as the reactor's foundation was dug, its walls went up, and it was filled with equipment, including the core. Such procedures were old hat by 1980. In fact, the Israelis' own nuclear weapons reactor at Dimona was photographed by CIA U-2s while its concrete was being poured in 1958 or 1959.

At any rate, with Saddam Hussein's French-built reactor—the heart of his ambitious nuclear weapons program—a smoldering shambles, the F-16s banked hard left, dropped down to 175 feet, and sped home. Fifty miles out, they climbed to 40,000 feet to conserve fuel and, still under the watchful eyes of the F-15 pilots, raced straight for Israel through Jordanian airspace. All returned safely but with only fifteen minutes' of fuel in their tanks.

The Osirak raid soon took its place beside Entebbe and other storied feats of Israeli heroism and daring. The audacious attack compounded Saddam Hussein's problems in developing his own nuclear weapons, set that program back considerably, and in the process guaranteed that Israel would continue to have a monopoly on atomic arms among Middle Eastern nations for several more years. (The attack's embarrassing success also taught the Iraqi dictator the virtue of spreading out, concealing, and hardening his nuclear, missile, and other research facilities. Attackers a decade later would therefore not do so thorough a job as the Israelis.) One exuberant former Israeli journalist and adviser to Prime Minister Menachem Begin wrote in his own account of the episode that the de-struction of Osirak brought Iraq's nuclear program "to a resounding halt."

It did nothing of the kind, as the leader of the attack himself was to explain several years later. "We expected them to regain their nuclear capability much faster than they did," said Colonel Ze'ev Raz. "We knew that we were only delaying them and that delay was much longer than we thought."

The attack on Osirak, which was also known as Tammuz-1, only increased Saddam Hussein's resolve to get nuclear weapons at any cost. It thereby had the effect of upping the ante. It also further convinced the deeply humiliated Arab (if he needed more convincing) that the only way he was ever going to be able to offset Israel's far-reaching strike capability was with ballistic missiles like Al Abbas, Al Hussein, and Condor-2 and the deadly chemical and biological agents and atomic warheads to go with them. Saddam was well along in realizing both of those goals when U.S. Air Force F-15s and F-16s were called upon in the Gulf War nearly a decade later to do what their Israeli predecessors had done: take out Iraqi reactors and other, more important facilities, yet again.

The night the first Scuds fell was the occasion for the third Israeli nuclear alert, the first having taken place ten days before the Six-Day

War in 1967, when Israel armed its first two bombs, the second during the night in 1973 when Israel feared for its very existence during the fourth Arab-Israeli war. Israel was prepared to use its nuclear weapons against Iraq if the Iraqis used poison gas in the Scuds they fired in 1991 at Tel Aviv and Haifa. No chemical-tipped Scuds were fired at Israel, of course, but the Iraqis admitted to U.N. inspectors after the war that they had at least thirty chemical-filled warheads for the enhanced Scuds. Israeli intelligence had claimed that the warheads had only been tested for the first time during the weeks before the war started, but U.N. inspectors found no evidence to verify that claim.

The Osirak episode was no less a watershed for Israel than it was for Iraq. The elimination of the reactor was cause for relief and for an outpouring of pride in Israel. But the fact that the device was there in the first place was taken as a dangerous omen. A popular saying among displaced Palestinians in the 1950s and 1960s was that if every Arab spat on Israel, it would drown. The expression was as far-fetched as it was wistful. But it did reflect the Arabs' twenty-five-to-one population advantage over the Jews, and also the fact of the tiny country's impossible land ratio and its precarious geographical position: surrounded by hostile neighbors and with its back to the sea. It didn't take a von Clausewitz to figure out that Israel needed a colossal advantage in weapons technology to offset those liabilities. The ultimate such weapon, Israeli strategists concluded, was nuclear.

Israel's future leaders believed as far back as the birth of the atomic age itself—before there was an Israel—that if their new state was to survive, it would require its own atomic bombs. The weapons would force the big powers to take Israel seriously, and they would also hold the Arab hordes at bay or, failing that, vaporize them. The founders of the Jewish state believed that the Arabs would readily finish what Hitler started if they thought they could do so. But the Israelis were resolutely determined that there would be no second Holocaust.

"If there was a genocide in Biafra—irrespective of the political issues involved—it was because the Biafrans failed to secure the arms they needed, while the Nigerians received planes and guns from Russia and Egypt," then Israeli Defense Minister Shimon Peres explained in a memoir in 1970. "Israel was saved from this fate because she managed to acquire some of the armaments she needed. Israelis were naturally sensitive to this problem, with the memory still fresh of six million Jews who were crushed and murdered by the Nazis in Europe."

And no leader of Israel knew more about its nuclear weapons program than Peres. The dour technocrat's presence ran through the Israeli nuclear weapons program like an unbroken thread. While he and others credit the two scientists who developed the bomb, it was Peres, who espoused "atomic sovereignty," who fathered it. As director-general of the Israeli Defense Ministry during the late 1950s, Peres negotiated the purchase of Dimona, Israel's top-secret weapons reactor from France, managed its construction in spite of wide opposition on financial as well as moral grounds, and set up LAKAM, the nuclear espionage procurement network. It was he who guided the morally outrageous nuclear alliance with South Africa when he was defense minister in the mid-1970s and, as prime minister a decade later, who approved the most massive nuclear weapons buildup in the Third World.

And if a bomb can have a grandfather, it was surely David Ben-Gurion, the founder of the State of Israel and the man who chose Peres for the historic role he would play trying to counter the enemy's over-whelming advantage in size with fission weapons. "What is Israel?" Ben-Gurion, the nation's first prime minister and defense minister, mused. "Only a spot. One dot. How can it survive in this Arab world?"

Ernst David Bergmann, a brilliant chemist who most have credited with being the father of Israel's bomb, never doubted the answer. "I am convinced . . . that the State of Israel needs a defense research program of its own," he wrote, alluding to the creation of nuclear weapons, "so that we shall never again be as lambs led to the slaughter."

Israel therefore bent to the task of acquiring nuclear and chemical weapons, together with the means to deliver them over very long distances: an assured strike capability of fearsome proportion. In doing so, it made up in guile, deception, ingenuity, and often sheer genius what it lacked in the kind of resources the superpowers had. But it did more than that. Slowly at first, then with increasing momentum as the 1980s began and progressed, Israel spawned a galaxy of weapons and related systems—defensive as well as offensive—that were based on often extraordinary technology spread across a spectrum whose dimension was out of all proportion to the size of the country and its population. It did this by literally every means possible: by poking into every likely place where there might be a benefit to be gained, financially, politically, scientifically, or technologically. The Non-Proliferation Treaty, which would have hampered the effort, was studiously ignored. So, too, was the Missile Technology Control Regime.*

What could not be ignored was history.

And on September 13, 1993, as he affixed his signature to the Principles of Palestinian Self-Rule, Peres had to believe that his strategy of atomic sovereignty had paid off. Forty-five years of nuclear weapons work was worth it, in spite of the risks, the three nuclear alerts that could have led to nuclear war, the alliances with the pariahs of the world, the rocky relations with the United States. To Peres, the bomb had delivered unto Israel a guarantee of nationhood . . . no matter what weapons the Arabs had devised. The irony that the father of the Israeli atomic bomb was also its chief peacemaker was something every Third World proponent of nuclear weapons could understand. By making peace, Peres was making the idea of nuclear weapons acceptable to a whole world full of aspiring politicians seeking similar guarantees. Israel, after all, was not the only nation that could be hypnotized by the idea of atomic sovereignty.

Peres was proud of his role. One week after he had signed the Palestinian accords, Peres was called on to defend them. As a member of the Likud bloc questioned his patriotism, Peres jabbed his finger at his accuser and shouted, "Did you build Dimona? Did you do Entebbe? Did you buy weapons? You empty head!"

There was an even deeper irony, however. The accords signed that day and those to be signed later with Jordan and Syria were in effect treaties to end the Six-Day War, when Israeli fighter-bombers destroyed the Arab air forces on the ground and swept into the West Bank, Gaza, the Golan, and the Sinai. That war, the Israeli leaders gathered at the White House knew, was a war that had been begun to protect Israel's then nascent nuclear capability.

On May 26, 1967, two Egyptian MIG-21s swept over the Dimona nuclear reactor at 52,000 feet. Attempts to shoot them down with surface-to-air and air-to-air missiles failed. There could be no doubt as to their mission: It was a reconnaissance run to prepare for a bombing raid on the reactor, perhaps as early as the next day. The news deeply troubled then Chief of Staff Yitzhak Rabin and his deputy, Ezer Weizmann, who until then believed Egypt was not serious about a war. No bombers ma-

---

*After a series of reports on Israeli–South African missile cooperation aired on "NBC Nightly News" in October 1989, the U.S. pressured Israel to agree to abide by the MTCR, which it did reluctantly.

terialized the next day, but preparations for the preemptive attack that decided the war began in earnest. More ominously, Prime Minister Levi Eshkol ordered the arming of Israel's first two nuclear weapons. By the time Israeli jets streaked across the Sinai ten days later to begin the Six-Day War, the bombs were ready.

And so a war that had been begun to protect Israel's nuclear capability was finally ending. It was as if Israel was asking its atomic bombs to protect its old age just as Israel had protected their infancy twenty-seven years before.

**A**lthough no Israeli military planner ever doubted that the Arabs (or, more precisely, the Muslims, when they counted Iran and Pakistan) would themselves try to acquire nuclear weapons, Osirak brought the point home most forcefully. The reactor's existence made the prospect of an Islamic bomb loom increasingly large. Until 1973, mutual annihilation was the worst-case scenario in Israel's war-fighting doctrine. During the Yom Kippur War, when Israel readied its short-range (260-mile) missiles in response to a two-front assault and heavy casualties, Israel's strategists envisioned the final act as a kind of Middle Eastern Little Big Horn, with them as the Seventh Cavalry. If every man, woman, and child in Israel was to fall under the Arab sword, they would at least inflict ferocious punishment on their enemies. It was the equivalent of Mutual Assured Destruction. After the war, Israel wanted a whole range of tactical weapons: small warheads, artillery shells, and atomic land mines.

But as the Reagan administration shifted strategy in the 1980s from MAD to an implicit belief that one side could in fact come out of an all-out nuclear exchange with some semblance of its civilization intact, so did Israel as a consequence of Osirak. Presuming that they would face nuclear armed opponents no later than 1995, the Israelis decided that survival would still be possible if they could increase their technological lead.

Accordingly, the strategy of slugging it out to the last man gave way to a more sophisticated doctrine that required "the bomb" to be the centerpiece of a large, independent, technically advanced, and highly integrated strategic and tactical nuclear weapons system: a version of the Single Integrated Operational Plan, or SIOP, that comprised America's entire nuclear war-fighting machinery. Israel wanted the same kind of system the big boys had.

This meant it had to acquire a full range of nuclear weapons in several sizes and configurations. It needed dispersed and redundant delivery systems that included attack aircraft, submarines, and both short-range and long-range missiles—the triad used by the superpowers themselves. It still required tactical weapons: nuclear land mines that could be planted in deep holes at the edge of the Golan Heights to obliterate Syrian or Iraqi tank columns as they crossed into Israel. It needed neutron bombs to fight a nuclear war on its own soil if necessary, reducing the radiation threat to its own citizens while devastating enemy troops and equipment.

In short, Israel was telling its enemies that it had a complete list of responses ready for any occasion. While on the one hand asserting that it would never "introduce" nuclear weapons to the region and denying that it had finished weapons, Israeli officials made a point of insisting that they intended to do whatever was required to preserve their country, as any nation would. The denial, of course, was semantics. Israel was a screwdriver's turn away from arming its weapons: a turn that U.S. officials knew would take no longer than six hours.

If the Arabs or the Iranians tried to annihilate Israel with a first strike, as Saddam Hussein threatened to do with chemicals before the war in the Gulf, they would do so at their peril. Israel had enough medium-range missiles tipped with boosted fission or perhaps even thermonuclear warheads, H-bombs, to cause what strategic planners call a "death spasm." If the Arabs were prepared to wage limited nuclear war, it would be answered with gravity bombs, air-to-ground missiles, nuclear artillery rounds, and short-range ballistic missiles. If they tried swarming over the Golan Heights, they would do so over the atomic mines and under the neutron bombs.

And if they banked on the support of a distant ally, like Pakistan, that ally would know beforehand that Israel's long-range strike capability could wreak havoc on it as well. Similarly, poison gas attacks would lead to ferocious reprisal. One Pentagon analyst, asked in the early days of Desert Storm to gauge the Israeli response to such an attack, answered succinctly: "You do not gas Jews."

It was vital that the Arabs and Iranians not miscalculate. They had to know implicitly that attacking Israel, whether with conventional forces or superweapons, would lead to a massive, society-smashing defeat. And while their enemies were filled with wonder at the prospect of getting nukes as simple equalizers, Israel understood that there were gradations to the game. For their part, the Arab states and every other Third World nation had to be jealous of the Israeli superweapon program. By the 1990s, several of them had even mimicked it by developing their own indigenous capacities to produce atomic warheads and the missiles that went with them. One of those nations was Iraq.

As important as the weapons were, Israel also had to have the infrastructure to manage an all-out war: an infrastructure carefully scattered around the tiny nation and often protected by double barbed wire, mines, and tethered attack dogs.

Being about the size of Massachusetts and having a population of just over five million, 30 percent of it clustered in a few large cities, Israel is especially vulnerable to being overrun or crippled by even two nuclear weapons dropped on Tel Aviv and Haifa (Jerusalem has an effective nuclear missile shield: it holds hostage irreplaceable and deeply revered historical sites belonging to Judaism, Christianity, and Islam).* That is why Israel, alone among nations outside the United States, is fixated by layered ballistic missile defense and has worked closely with the United States on Star Wars research. Having a defense to protect its cities and other strategic assets was an important element in any war-fighting doctrine. But it is multiple strike capability, not missile defense, that steers Israel's strategic planning and shapes its new doctrine.

The "Bor," which is located under Tel Aviv, is Israel's equivalent of the National Military Command Center in the Pentagon. There is a larger subterranean command post at Nevatim Air Base at the edge of the Negev. Its U.S. counterpart is the Strategic Command bunker in Omaha, the headquarters of the old Strategic Air Command. The nuclear weapons fuel reactor at Dimona combines the missions of the Department of Energy's facilities at Savannah River, Georgia, and Hanford, Washington. The nuclear weapons laboratories at Nahal Soreq, south of Tel Aviv, are, in the words of one former U.S. nuclear weapons designer, "the equivalent of our Los Alamos, Lawrence Livermore, and Oak Ridge National Laboratories." Just down the road from Soreq, and near a favorite beach of bronzed, bikini-clad civilians, is Yavne, the missile test range version of

---

*As of 1977, about 20 percent of Israel's total population of 3.6 million lived in Tel Aviv and Haifa (30 percent counting Jerusalem). While the Arab states were far larger, their cities, too, were hostage to population-killing nuclear attacks. Twenty-five percent of Egypt's 39 million people lived in Cairo, Alexandria, Giza, and Aswan; 28 percent of Syrians lived in Damascus, Aleppo, and Homs; 23 percent of Iraqis lived in Baghdad, Basra, and Mosul; 38 percent of Jordanians lived in Amman, Zarka, and Irbig; 41 percent of Libyans lived in Tripoli and Bengazi. (Shai Feldman, *Israeli Nuclear Deterrence*, New York: Columbia University Press, 1982, p. 55.)

Vandenberg Air Force Base in California. Nearby is Be'er Yaakov, where the Jericho missiles are manufactured in an underground factory. At Rafael, outside Haifa, there is a nuclear weapons design lab known as Division 20 and a nearby missile development lab called Division 48. Rafael, like Pantex in Texas, is also the place where Israel's nuclear weapons—more of them than are owned by Great Britain—have been put together since late 1966, the dawn of Israel's atomic age. Technion, the national science institute in Tel Aviv, does a great deal of military research. And the biggest strategic assets of all are the nuclear weapons bunkers at Tel Nof Air Base in the Negev and the Jericho long-range missiles. The bunkers hold the seventy nuclear bombs that Israel's Black Squadrons would drop on long-distance raids against Arab allies. The Jerichos, hidden in bunkers cut into the Judean hills just west of the town of Zekharyeh, are for the same purpose.

There is also a chemical weapons production facility built five stories below ground at Dimona and a biological weapons facility at Nes Zionya, south of Tel Aviv.

The most important of these facilities fill a strategic corridor between the Mediterranean and Jerusalem. The missile test fields at Palmikhim, the reactor and research center at Soreq, the home of the black squadrons at Tel Nof, and the Jericho-1 and -2 missile fields in the Judean Hills are all only a few miles away from each other.

Strategically, this is the heart of Israel, where any final battle would occur, from where Israel could best defend itself. As seen from space, the area is a patchwork of security zones, villages, airfields, and farmland. It is a corridor no more than twenty miles long, but within it, unknown to most Israelis, is the guarantor of their survival as a nation . . . weapons so terrifying in their ferocity and flexibility that no one would dare attack them.

The most important of all is just south of the Tel Aviv–Jerusalem rail line's intersection with one of Israel's main north-south highways. There, say analysts, near the village of Tirosh on Route 302 near the western edge of the missile field, sit the bunkers where many of Israel's nuclear weapons are stored. A five-minute drive from the black squadrons and the Jerichos, they would be mated with those delivery systems in a time of crisis and dispersed.

The development of the Jerichos, in fact, showed just how far Israel had advanced in twenty years since the 1973 war, when it had a few primitive French-designed missiles in the field, their 260-mile range just barely enough to strike Egypt's military headquarters outside Cairo. By 1993, bunkers for as many as fifty Jerichos were visible in even commercial satellite photos. There were Jericho-1s, with a 700-mile range, capable of striking Baghdad or Teheran's outer suburbs, and Jericho-2s, with an 1,100-mile range, capable of holding virtually every Arab capital—or oil field—hostage.

By the 1990s, Israel had also developed most of the nerves and connective tissue that held it all together: a command, control, communication, and technical intelligence apparatus that would allow it to execute its nuclear doctrine.

Israeli war planners understood that multimillion-dollar spy satellites like its Offeq were vital for selecting targets. The KH-11 could do that job, as it had at Osirak, but in the final analysis the big reconnaissance satellite belonged to a foreign power. This meant its considerable capability could be denied to Israel because of even a moderate change in U.S. policy.

The nation required communication satellites like Amos, which would ensure that the commanders of its missiles, bombers, and submarines could coordinate their strikes; airborne blue-green lasers to penetrate the ocean with instructions to the cruise-missile-carrying submarines; and antimissiles like Patriot and Israel's own Arrow to stave off enemy missiles, even, if necessary, after an Israeli first strike.

It is the array of integrated systems, built on a comprehensive doctrine, that distinguishes Israel's war-fighting structure from others in the Third World. Getting the bomb, as India and Pakistan had done, was one thing. But working out an intricate and highly coordinated multidimensional strategy for using it was quite another. When Israel came to believe that it could no longer defend itself with a simple "bomb in the basement," it fully wired itself for nuclear war. It was a system that Israel's enemies could not counter or match. Indeed, they could barely comprehend its complexity.

This served Israel in two ways. First, and most subtly, it sent the same message to its many Muslim enemies that the United States had sent to the old Soviet Union: brainpower, high-tech innovation, would overcome swollen defense budgets and masses of troops. Brains beat brawn. If the Arabs could be made to understand that fact, it was believed, they would eventually come to the peace table; and peace, not merely arms control, would dictate Israel's own weapons requirements. This strategy culminated in the accord with the PLO. Second, and this was anything but subtle, was the implicit fact that any surprise nuclear attack against Israel would have to totally overwhelm the scattered, dug-in, heavily protected, multitiered nuclear force to bring victory. An atomic bomb dropped on Tel Aviv, or even several of them striking targets around the country, would cripple Israel but not forestall certain, reflexive, horrifying reprisal by the nation's surviving forces. Israel has therefore achieved what strategic analysts call "escalation superiority": the ability to control the pace of a conflict by being able to guarantee that its attackers will be obliterated.

It is also important to note that the integration of Israel's weapons reflects an integration of the people who produce them. Many of the founders of Israel came from places where they could not own land and where, therefore, a great premium was placed on the protective effects of education and fluid wealth: money. Education led to the professions, which insulated against the tyranny of property. Money could occasionally stave off danger and be moved quickly if necessary. Although shades of the Jewish faith developed over time, persecution was a constant that bonded all Jews and made relations among them cohesive. This has manifested itself in the weapons area just as in any other, and probably more so because, ultimately, Israel's existence is guaranteed only by the force of its own arms.

The infrastructure that is currently developing the integrated weapon systems is therefore as integrated as the weapons themselves. Those who labor at Technion, at Dimona, and at Israel Aircraft Industries, to take only three examples, are bonded in unspoken ways by a common endeavor borne out of a common fear: that of being abandoned. Collectively, they constitute a freely functioning force which takes it as an article of faith that the drive for unsurpassable weaponry requires money, dedication, cohesion, and the exploitation of the world around them for the highest stake imaginable: survival.

Abandoning MAD and embracing war-fighting, of which Star Wars is one component, grew directly out of the extremely close relationship that was established by President Reagan and Prime Minister Begin, immediately after Reagan took office in January 1981. Reagan was building on Jimmy Carter's deal with the Egyptians and the Israelis. In return for agreeing to the Camp David accords, Israel received more money, more technology, and more encouragement for its military machine. But that was merely mechanical, the result of a political deal. The Reagan-Begin alliance was one of ideological soul mates. In return for Begin's staunchly anti-Soviet policy in the Middle East, Reagan reversed the Carter administration, giving Israel a free hand in the occupied territories and with the Palestinians in general. By the end of the Begin era, Israel was receiving $4.3 billion from the United States annually, or exactly 10 percent of its gross domestic product. Most of that came as direct and indirect grants. Israel also received unprecedented help acquiring weapons, weapons technology, and classified technical data.

Nor were U.S. presidents Israel's only political benefactors. It has also received substantial help in Congress. One particularly insidious form of help came through exemptions from requirements related to all manner of proliferation. Two laws passed in the wake of revelations about Iraq's missile and nuclear programs provide good examples.

One law required the President to report to Congress on global missile proliferation but excluded indigenous developments in eighteen countries. The other required inclusive reporting on nuclear, chemical, and biological weapons development as well as missiles. There was a notable exemption in the second piece of legislation, however.

The device used by the bill's sponsors, who included then Senator Al Gore, was to exempt two categories of allies: NATO allies and "non-NATO allies." The latter consisted of only three nations: Australia, Japan, and Israel. This was like promulgating a law to curb dangerous wild cats but excluding lions and tigers. Even more stringent legislation, requiring some sanctions against nuclear weapons states, was scuttled in 1992 when pro-Israel Representative Sam Gejdenson of Connecticut held up the bill until Israel was excluded from it as well. Staff members from two congressional committees involved in wrangling with Gejdenson over the matter were convinced that the congressman's staff counsel, John Scheibel, was the true force behind the weakened legislation. And they suspected that whatever other motivation Scheibel had for not holding Israel to the same proliferation standard as most other Third World nations, one of them was likely connubial. His wife, Esther Katz, was the political director of AIPAC, the powerful pro-Israel political action committee. In Washington, those are the sort of ties that truly bind.

So by 1992, with the tacit encouragement of Ronald Reagan and a spate of politicians and their apparatchiks, most of Israel's nuclear war-fighting capability—technology and equipment—had "Made in the USA" stamped on it. While Washington did not actively endorse Israel's nuclear strategy, it provided assistance that its own strategic planners had to know would lead to a quantum improvement in nuclear capability. They had to know because Israel was following the U.S. war-fighting strategy.

U.S. officials who studied the Israeli weapons program were not surprised by the decision to follow American strategic policy. "Mimicking is too mild a word," said one strategic analyst. "They absorbed it because they were part of it. The public simply doesn't realize how close the two nations are operationally. We don't have to speculate on their nuclear doctrine. It's ours. They have all the documents; they've studied them all." The U.S.-Israeli cooperation on strategic matters carried other dangers. When it came to Israel, U.S. military scientists seemed to forget that their country had a nonproliferation policy.

There is no better example of U.S.-Israeli strategic weapons intimacy than the Arrow. The problem-riddled antimissile missile—it had failed five out of six tests by July 1993—was largely funded by the United States. More incredibly, it was built in the same complex as the Jericho, leading many to conclude that an exchange of data was taking place between the two engineering teams. Even if that was not the case, which would have been amazing, the Arrow had a second mission that would prove extremely helpful to Jericho's developers anyway. It was designed so that it could mimic an incoming missile. This meant it had to have some of a ballistic missile's characteristics. But since Arrow was a "defensive" missile, it was exempt from the Missile Technology Control Regime. There were some in the U.S. government who were appalled at the Reagan administration's duplicity in the Arrow operation, especially since even hinting of a similar technology transfer to an Arab state would explode into a major scandal.

The blue-green laser, developed by a scientist at the Negev Institute (which is closely affiliated with Dimona), was viewed so positively by his American counterparts that he—identified only as S. Rosenwaks—was allowed into Livermore to do more research. In fact, scores of other weapons scientists roamed around the Los Alamos and Sandia labs as well. So while the United States was not giving finished atomic bombs to Israel, it was helping the Israelis in almost all ways possible to assemble the weapon's strategic components. Arab frustration at this spectacle was understandable.

Israel was also the beneficiary of unprecedented cooperation with

U.S. intelligence, part of which resulted in the sharing of the KH-11 imagery, which was valuable not only as an intelligence tool but for pinpointing targets. In 1983, the two countries concluded an intelligence pact that was described as "the most comprehensive agreement ever signed between the CIA and a foreign intelligence service."

There were also other strategic concerns. Israeli strategists have traditionally felt that their nation needed ballistic missiles that could reach not only the capital of every antagonist in the Middle East but the old Soviet empire as well. It was the Kremlin that fed the Arabs the weapons, including missiles, that constituted the unending threat to Israel's survival. It would therefore be useful for the men in the Kremlin to know that their own country would not escape attack in an all-out war while their Arab proxies were being devastated.

By marrying atomic bombs first to long-range aircraft in the Black Squadrons and ultimately to intercontinental ballistic missiles, Israel became the first Third World country to pose a strategic threat to a superpower. That development was not lost on the Kremlin. Following the test in September 1989 of an advanced Jericho-2 ballistic missile, whose range covered the oil fields at Baku and could possibly reach the port of Odessa as well, a Soviet Foreign Ministry spokesman said that "Israel is known to possess a technological basis necessary for the creation of nuclear weapons. The availability of delivery systems makes Israel a source of danger, far exceeding the boundaries of the Middle East region."*

Far, indeed. It was fundamental to Israeli strategy that all the world understood that the nation had a reach as long as, and proportionate to, its collective memory; that after Hitler, no serious threat would go unpunished. The reach could abduct Adolf Eichmann, assassinate Gerald Bull, pulverize guerrilla bases in Lebanon, avenge the murder of Olympic athletes, land commandos in Uganda, blow up Palestine Liberation Organization headquarters in Tunisia, wipe out reactors in Iraq, steal patrol boats in France, and turn cities from Cairo to Kiev into radioactive wastelands. Israel's reach had to be global if it was to be credible. Such capacity can deter only if adversaries know it exists.

And so it needed a Dr. Strangelove to subtly weave the fear of an Israeli-engineered apocalypse into the fabric of Middle Eastern life. Just

---

*The Israelis, however, were balancing the books. On November 5, 1956, six days after the Suez invasion, Bulganin sent a message to Israel seeking to protect his endangered Egyptian clients. It pointed out that the U.S.S.R. had missiles capable of reaching any point in the world. (Shimon Peres, *David's Sling*, London: Weidenfeld and Nicolson, 1970, pp. 210–11.)

as Henry Kissinger used the image of a slightly deranged Richard Nixon to wring agreements from recalcitrant but nervous friends and foes, Israeli leaders like Peres used the image of Yuval Ne'eman straining at his leash to intimidate opponents.

While Bergmann established the science that led to Israel's bomb, it was Ne'eman who made the science real. Then, later, it was he who made the most outrageous statements about the weapon. While never fully revealing its existence, he hinted darkly that his country had a super slingshot that could obliterate any Goliath. If Israel's enemies saw Yuval Ne'eman as a mad scientist, his background made the image credible.

Originally a protégé of Ben-Gurion and Peres, Ne'eman served as a freedom fighter in the Hagana underground during Israel's war of independence and then moved on to spy, professor, nuclear weapons scientist, politician, and strategic thinker. His career mirrored Israel's own multifaceted military history. It even provided the model for an adventure novel in which an Israeli scientist named Yuval Newman thwarts a Libyan-Pakistani plot to destroy Israel.*

Ne'eman's own curriculum vitae accurately, if somewhat immodestly, describes him as a "world renown [sic] nuclear physicist," "architect of Israel's atomic energy capability," and "father of the Offeq [spy] satellite." It also notes that from 1973 on, he held a series of jobs whose power belied their unassuming titles. He was strategic adviser to Defense Minister Moshe Dayan during the Yom Kippur War, indicating that he played a pivotal role in the decision to arm his country's nuclear arsenal. Later, he first became Peres's adviser when he assumed the defense minister's job after the war, and then "chief scientist" at the ministry, meaning that he was in charge of Israel's nuclear weapons program. That was the position Bergmann had held when the nuclear weapons program began.

At one time or another, in fact, Ne'eman held virtually every job of any consequence in Israel's strategic programs. He was the deputy director of military operations; scientific director and chairman of the Israeli Atomic Energy Commission; minister of science and development; chairman of the National Commission for High Energy Physics; president of Tel Aviv University; and chairman of the Israel Space Agency. He also founded and headed the ultranationalist Techniya Party and was a close friend of Edward Teller, the guiding light behind the American hydrogen bomb and the prototypical Dr. Strangelove.

*It was Steve Shagan's *Pillars of Fire*, published in 1992.

So when Yuval Ne'eman spoke, Arabs listened. And what he said could be frightening. He made references to targeting as many as eighty sites in the Arab world and about the conditions Israel had to set for "nuclear suicide." He talked about the value of having nuclear weapons on submarines so that his country could launch a guaranteed "second strike from the depths of the sea" should any opponent miscalculate to the point of making a serious attack on his country.

Although Israel has less than one percent of China's population and land mass, it is fast approaching China's status as a nuclear power. Only Israel among Third World nations can come close to matching the superpowers' destructive capability. India and Pakistan could destroy each other's cities and create a radioactive nightmare. India might even successfully lob a couple of warheads across the Himalayas at China. But Israel poses a threat to a wide swath of the world. It has already fixed its cross hairs on between sixty and eighty targets, including the Persian Gulf oil fields, some of the world's oldest cities—Damascus, Baghdad, Cairo, Teheran, and Tripoli—and superweapon facilities as far away as Ain Oussera in Algeria and Kahuta in Pakistan. In terms of nuclear weapons and the means to deliver them, Israel is therefore already a de facto superpower.

The road to this point was neither easy nor cheap, with some analysts estimating its total cost at more than $5 billion.

As is the case elsewhere, Israel's status as a superweapon superpower has depended on huge amounts of money. Unlike most of the others in the club, however, it had the additional expense that came with a sophisticated command and control system and it has not been able to skim profits off natural resources or a vast manufacturing base to feed its weapons appetite. The weapons buildup was therefore financed in three basic ways. One, unique in all the world, involved the solicitation of sympathetic Jews. This ran the gamut from coupon collections by pro-Israel organizations to bond sales to outright contributions by wealthy patrons. Most of the latter were American (Baron Edmund de Rothschild of France being a notable exception). According to U.S. intelligence estimates, Israel collects hundreds of millions of dollars a year from its rich supporters, much of it from campaigns. In 1960, a Committee of Thirty (Jewish millionaires) was asked to quietly raise funds for the nuclear weapons project. It collected $40 million for the construction of the reactor and the adjoining, fabulously expensive, underground plutonium separation plant at Dimona.

A second source of weapons funding came directly from the annual U.S. loan and grant package. Between 1949 and 1991, Israel received an estimated $53 billion in U.S. loans and grants, much of it for military equipment. Between 1974 and 1989, for example, Tel Aviv received $16.4 billion in military "loans." Except they weren't really loans at all; they were outright grants that were only called loans because loans don't require congressional oversight, while grants do. And although much of the money was used to purchase American weaponry such as F-15s, $1.8 billion a year went straight into an amorphous—and virtually unaudited—account set up for discretionary weapons spending.

Finally, Israel, like China, has sold military equipment at the lower end of the technical scale to help raise funds for the nerves of war, most notably superweapons. It has sent Chile and South Africa Boeing 707 Phalcon early warning aircraft, which could have helped the Afrikaaners' nuclear war-fighting system. It has sold both countries upgrade packages for their Mirage fighters, Reshef guided missile boats, and electronic warfare equipment produced in its own turnkey plants. There has also been speculation that the three countries have shared submarine technology. Israeli exhibits at arms shows around the world offer Galil rifles, gas masks, artillery pieces, fighter upgrade packages: the stuff of conventional battles. It has even trained legions of presidential bodyguards for African despots, from Ethiopia's Haile Mengistu to Liberia's Samuel Doe.

But beginning in the mid-1970s, when the need for a more sophisticated arsenal first arose, Israel's biggest source of income (aside from the United States government) has come from evolving and often overlapping relationships with pariah states. The strategy has been as brilliant as it was opportunistic. Although funding from Washington is vital for a variety of weapons and technology acquisition, the United States will not directly finance nuclear weapons and related delivery systems. Furthermore, there is usually some kind of string attached to whatever aid it does give. Israel has therefore chased large sums of capital with no strings attached.

Since the 1973 war, for example, it has forged partnerships or deals with the Shah's Iran, then with Botha's South Africa, Pinochet's Chile, and lastly with Li Peng's China. Each had something Israel wanted: cash to build its modern, strategic war-fighting complex. And Israel had something to offer each of them: high technology that was beyond their ability to create, but not beyond their ability to use.

Furthermore, Israel found that each trading partner shared some of its own insecurities and sometimes some of its enemies, as well. It shared a hatred of Arabs with Iran; a fear of being overrun by Marxists with South Africa and Chile; and a deep enmity toward the Soviet Union with China.

Morality was absent in all of the arrangements, but that was not readily discernible because they were carefully kept low-key. The arms deal with Iran coincided with the Savak's torturing of dissidents. South Africa, Chile, and China not only had brutally repressive regimes, but at the time of their deals with Israel were themselves the subjects of U.S. arms embargoes because of their sorry humanitarian conditions.* While Israel claimed that its aid to South Africa would help protect that country's 110,000 Jews, many of them Holocaust survivors and their children, it had good reason to know that it was also helping to prop up apartheid in all of its hideous manifestations. If all-out war came to southern Africa, the bombs would incinerate millions of blacks in another Holocaust.

The Iranian connection began in the wake of the war in 1973 and continued until the Shah fled from the radical clerics in 1979. Both nations had two important things in common: they were not Arab in a part of the world that was overwhelmingly Arab, and they were stalwarts in the U.S. military and political sphere of influence.† They were to cooperate on six separate weapons, involving a 155-millimeter gun, codevelopment of gun boats and, biggest of all, the inertially guided Jericho-2 ballistic missile. Jericho was planned but ultimately not developed or produced with Iranian money.

The South African connection was the most important of all. South Africa, many in U.S. intelligence believed, had quite simply financed Israel's war-fighting strategy. The major element of the strategy, the Jericho-2, was paid for with South African rand. In fact, the missiles' 1,100-mile

---

*Both the South African and Iranian secret police were trained by Israel. (The South African connection is from a Windrem interview on March 9, 1990, with a U.S. congressman who wished to remain anonymous. The Iranian connection is from "Allon at the Court of the Shah," *Tel Aviv Davar*, May 20, 1980.)

†There were listening posts in Iran, to take only one example, where huge antennas tracked Soviet missiles that were test fired from Tyuratam to the Pacific. The facilities were judged to be so important in assessing the capabilities of Soviet missiles that, following the revolution, they were replaced by billions of dollars' worth of eavesdropping satellites like Rhyolite, Magnum, and Vortex and the placing of new antennas in western China.

range was not as much an Israeli requirement as it was South African. Other projects financed by South Africa included the Offeq spy satellite, the airborne command post, and the Lavi fighter-bomber that was eventually canceled.

The China connection was established in the late 1970s and has remained one of the most enduring, and enigmatic, of Israel's relationships. Initial exchanges seem to have been started when a mysterious Israeli billionaire and arms merchant named Shaul Eisenberg began shepherding both superweapon and conventional technology eastward.* By 1993, Israel had sold to China "several billion dollars" worth of arms technology, according to the CIA. Israel exported guidance technology for at least one Chinese missile, the sea-skimming Silkworm, and reportedly for the CSS-2 "East Wind" IRBM as well. Another transfer to China involved the U.S.-designed Sparrow air-to-air missile, which Israel improved and sold to China. The Chinese then turned it into their own version, the PL-8, and sold it to Iraq. Had Israeli fighter pilots attacked Iraq during the Persian Gulf War, then they most likely would have had to face what was essentially their own missile. And Israel was ready to sell technology by its biggest benefactor to gain the hard currency it needed to keep its strategic program going.

The single most bizarre transfer of U.S. technology to China may have been that of the very missile that stood in the way of the Scuds Iraq fired at Saudi Arabia and Israel itself during the war in the Gulf: the Raytheon-built Patriot.

In March 1992 an internal debate raged in the U.S. intelligence community over whether Israel had, in fact, sold the weapon's technology to China. Both the CIA and the DIA were convinced that Israel had transferred Patriot technology to the Chinese in a deal that would give cynicism a new meaning. Under the scenario worked out by the intelligence agencies, Patriot data went east in exchange for Chinese data on the M-9 and M-11 ballistic missiles that China was trying to sell to Pakistan, Iran, and Syria.

Then Defense Minister Moshe Arens insisted that the allegation was untrue. "I'm denying your suggestion," he told NBC's Tom Brokaw in 1992, "or the suggestion of the unidentified people who are floating this accusation."

---

*The CIA reported than an Eisenberg company, URDAN, served as the company for the transfer of Israeli missile technology, a charge URDAN has denied.

The Department of State said it believed Arens, but neither the CIA nor the DIA was persuaded. Where they were concerned, the question was not whether the information had been passed, but whether it was done by the Israeli government itself or, as someone suggested, in a "rogue" Mossad operation. The notion that one of the world's most disciplined, loyal, and insightful intelligence organizations would willfully pass secrets vital to national security to a foreign power without the knowledge of the prime minister, defense minister, or other high-ranking officials strained credulity.

However it happened, the Patriot episode left many U.S. officials furious, particularly since sixty-four of the weapons had been hurriedly dispatched to Israel to protect it against the Scuds.* "By knowing how the Patriot works, China is going to be able to configure its own missiles to avoid it," said Gary Milhollin, who noted that Pakistan, Syria, and Iran had paid large sums of money for M-series ballistic technology.

The transfer of Arrow technology to China is even more worrisome. By June 1993, Congress's General Accounting Office (GAO) had drafted a classified report questioning whether Israel could be trusted to keep the technology to itself and concluding that the United States should "heighten" its concern over the possible misuse of Arrow technology. The GAO used several Department of Defense and intelligence community reports to prepare its own, some of which led it to assert that Israel "may continue" to peddle American technology, including Arrow, elsewhere to help its own economy. The other reports also conclude that Israel is "increasing measures" to "conceal transactions that risk U.S. sanctions." The GAO study added that the United States was exercising "inadequate control" over Arrow's finances, even though U.S. taxpayers were contributing nearly all of its $528 million research cost.

Finally, the ultrapragmatic Israelis also were establishing close ties with China's enemy, India, even as the GAO report was being prepared. The reason was not hard to fathom: both nations faced implacable Muslim

---

*Israel wrung concessions out of the U.S. in return for not attacking Iraq directly, an event that would very likely have cost the coalition its Arab members. Israel was permitted to "nominate" more than 100 targets for U.S. warplanes and cruise missiles to hit. These included railroad and highway junctions, industrial facilities, power plants, and storage bunkers in western Iraq. Destruction of many of the targets ensured that Iraq would not be able to launch a conventional war against Israel for many years. In addition, Secretary of Defense Richard Cheney also promised to reestablish an early warning satellite downlink such as the one that warned of the Scuds in the event of another war, and further agreed to ensure Israel's "technical parity" with Saudi jet fighters.

opponents. With the South African connection disintegrating because of Pretoria's swing in political direction toward relative liberalism, Israel was evidently looking around for a new soul mate. And the fact that New Delhi was a huge nuclear power only made the arrangement more attractive: what Peres called a "natural bond" in an interview in India in June 1993. The bond, he maintained, was both countries' ancient origins, love of democracy, and the terrorists each faced.

Israel had learned the ways of foreign procurement from a master: France. The French, whose enduring contribution to Israeli national security was undoubtedly the reactor and reprocessing facility they built at Dimona, were not strange bedfellows at all. Possibly because of the large number of Jews in France who suffered antisemitism from the time of Gobineau to the Vichy government's deportations to Germany in World War II, France favored a strong Israeli military from the day Israel was born. Referring to Arab hostility toward the French in North Africa and to Israel, French Defense Minister Maurice Bourges-Maunoury told Shimon Peres in the autumn of 1955 that the two countries faced similar foes and challenges and that there ought to be quick and open cooperation. "There is the same regularity in the ebb and flow of the Mediterranean tides which wash the shores of both France and Israel," he said. "We must not let its troublesome waters reach our coasts."

Two developments convinced France to provide Israel with a "research" reactor and accompanying reprocessing facility. First, Canada did India the same favor in September 1955, and that was publicly known. The French were persuaded on that basis alone that they could help Israel without setting an immoral precedent.

But any lingering doubts were set aside following the British, French, and Israeli invasion of Suez in October and early November 1956, when the French and British abandoned Israel because of rocket-rattling by Nikolai Bulganin and arm-twisting by Eisenhower. Ike was not afraid of the Soviets. But he did believe, correctly, that the British and French had launched the attack in a pathetic and futile attempt to maintain some dignity while their colonial empires disintegrated. For its part, however, France was deeply embarrassed by its forced withdrawal and became doubly resolved that Israel needed to be insulated as much as possible from such vagaries. The Israelis, of course, couldn't have agreed more.

The betrayal at Suez, like the Soviet cutoff of military aid to Iraq during the first two years of the Iran-Iraq war a quarter of a century later, further convinced Israel that it floated alone on a sea of expedience, a captive of political winds and tides it could not then control.* The Israelis were upset with the French and British for abandoning them. But they were absolutely enraged at Eisenhower. "You Americans screwed us," one former Israeli government official said many years later. "If you hadn't intervened, Nasser would have been toppled and the arms race in the Middle East would have been delayed."

Ben-Gurion and Peres, suddenly aware that American Jews could not provide Israel's salvation by political means, resolved to push ahead with the nuclear weapons program as a first priority. However Eisenhower "screwed" Israel at Suez, he at least had to be given credit for helping start the nation's atomic weapons program, however unintentionally. Israel acquired its first reactor, a small five-megawatt research model, during the mid-1950s under Ike's "Atoms for Peace" program. Although the device was closely monitored by U.S. scientists and, in any case, was too small to be of direct help in the weapons program, it was invaluable for training Israeli scientists in reactor design and operation. Meanwhile, other Israeli scientists were working at Saclay, outside of Versailles, where France's national atomic energy center had its own small research reactor. A decade later, their places would be taken by Jafar's studious disciples.

The French-supplied reactor and reprocessing facility were virtually identical to those built by Saint-Gobain at Marcoule, in the southern Rhône Valley. The only foreigners present at Marcoule in those days, in fact, were Israelis.

The installation in Israel itself would at first be called a textile factory, then a laboratory for the "University of the South." By 1960, when many Israelis knew there was a nuclear reactor at Dimona, Ben-Gurion was still insisting that its purpose was benign; he even lied about

*If they needed more convincing, the Israelis had only to think about the arms embargoes that were slapped on them throughout their history. As far back as 1929, just after Arab anti-Jewish riots, Jews were not allowed to obtain weapons, while the Arabs were permitted to get them from a number of regional sources. A regional arms quarantine that was begun by the U.S., Britain, and France before the 1948 war was extended after it, yet Britain continued to supply equipment and training to Egypt and Iraq. After the Six-Day War, France imposed its own arms embargo on Israel, while Britain suspended negotiations for the sale of Chieftain tanks in the 1970s because of Arab oil pressure. Israelis therefore took it as an article of faith that true safety required the "liberation of Jews from the dependence on Gentiles." (Gerald M. Steinberg, "Israel: High-Technology Roulette," in Michael Brzoska and Thomas Ohlson, eds., *Arms Production in the Third World*, Stockholm International Peace Research Institute, London: Taylor & Francis, 1986, pp. 163–64.)

it unabashedly to his own parliament. On December 21 of that year he told the Knesset that Dimona would "serve the needs of industry, agriculture, medicine, and science and prepare Israeli scientific and technical personnel for the construction of a nuclear power station in the future, which we assume will be in ten to fifteen years' time. Like the American reactor, this one too is designed solely for peaceful purposes and has been built under the direction of Israeli experts. It resembles the reactor that the Canadian government helped install in India, though ours has a smaller output." The Knesset, most Israeli citizens, and Israel's supporters in the United States and elsewhere may have believed the old man, but the French knew better. And so did Washington.

Work on the Dimona complex, technically the Negev Nuclear Research Center, began early in 1958 under the eyes of CIA U-2s and in front of its agents. So, too, did work on Rafael. By late 1958 or early 1959, U-2 imagery clearly showed the plutonium reprocessing plant being dug and concrete for the reactor being poured in a swarm of hundreds of French and Israeli workers and their earth-moving and construction equipment.* The snooping was continued by U.S. reconnaissance satellites after they went into operation during the summer of 1960, as well as by their Soviet counterparts two years later.

The National Security Council was duly briefed by the CIA's photointerpreters. Unlike other briefings, however, those relating to Dimona in 1959 and afterward, by the same specialists who would be praised for their work during the Cuban Missile Crisis in the autumn of 1962, were not pursued. No pointed questions were asked by the President or his cabinet secretaries. No requests for follow-up flights were made.

Although official correspondence (which is still classified) was exchanged between the White House and the Israeli government, the apparent level of inaction by most succeeding U.S. administrations has led

---

*The reason for siting the reprocessing facility underground, a tremendously expensive process, was to thwart overhead snooping. But when photographed progressively as the work took place, the dimensions of the excavation, position relative to the reactor, shape of the rooms, pouring of the concrete, size and position of electrical and waste facilities, and other factors told photointerpreters who were knowledgeable about such facilities what they were looking at. The site was originally discovered by a U-2 that was looking for evidence that the Israelis were practicing using cluster bombs for the defense of Lebanon against a threatened attack by the Egyptian-Syrian United Arab Republic. The imagery revealed that a fifteen-foot-thick concrete floor and walls were being poured exactly as they had been at Marcoule, according to Dino Brugioni, a well-known former CIA photointerpreter. When work on the subterranean facility was finished, he added, the contractor tried to camouflage it with sod, but to no avail. "That was it," Brugioni said, triumphantly. (Burrows interview with Brugioni on April 30, 1993.)

many observers to conclude that the United States turned a blind eye to, or, to use another frequent metaphor, winked at, the development of the Israeli atomic weapons program. Although Washington denied Israel off-the-shelf nuclear weapons, it did almost everything else possible to ensure that the Israelis developed exactly what they needed. This was particularly true during the Johnson and Reagan administrations. Naïveté was never a factor.*

Within eighteen months of Dimona's going operational, in late 1963, for example, the U.S. chargé d'affaires in Tel Aviv sent a secret telegram to State that drew undeniable conclusions about Israel's atomic energy program. The diplomat, William N. Dale, divided the amount of money several of Israel's scientific research institutions cost during the fifteen years between 1950 and 1965 by the number of scientists working at them. The result, in each case, was an expression of what it cost in equipment and services—laboratories, libraries, and so on—to keep one scientist supported at each facility during that time.

Aside from Dimona, the highest equipment-and-services-to-scientist ratio was at the Weizmann Institute—"with facilities as good as any in the world"—which cost $25 million and employed 280 scientists and engineers. That, Dale calculated, meant that each person represented an investment of a little less than $100,000 in facilities and services.† By the same measure, Dimona's roughly $60 million price tag could be justified only by hiring a staff of 600 scientists and engineers. Given the fact that there were only 2,100 scientists and engineers in the whole country at the time, that only 200 specialized in nucleonics, and that roughly 40 of those were at Dimona, there was a clear anomaly. A staff of 40 would push the equipment and services figure all the way up to

*By 1965, two eminent American scientists, I. I. Rabi, a Nobel laureate from Columbia University, and Jerome Wiesner of MIT, had urgently warned the Israeli government against developing nuclear weapons, of the "overwhelming danger in which Israel would place itself if it were to make any moves toward the introduction of nuclear weapons in the Near East." (Secret airgram A-955, sent to the Department of State by William N. Dale on May 19, 1965.) It is fair to conclude that President Kennedy knew what the Israelis were up to since Wiesner was his science adviser.

†The airgram, which went to Washington in a diplomatic pouch, gave the following investments and services relative to staff during the same period: Hebrew University, $16 million, or $80,000 per scientist; Technion (the Israel Institute of Technology), $69,000 per scientist; and the Israel Atomic Energy Commission's Soreq Research Establishment, about $75,000 per scientist. In 1965, Dale claims, the 200 nuclear scientists and engineers, less the 40 at Dimona, were distributed as follows: 93 at Soreq; 55 at Weizmann; 10 at Technion; and 5 at Hebrew University. (Secret airgram A-742 from William N. Dale to the Department of State, "Current Status of the Dimona Reactor," April 9, 1965, p. 3.)

$1.5 million per scientist, an extraordinary sum to spend on mundane research. More significantly, the $60 million put into Dimona was more than the entire $58 million Israel had spent on all of its other scientific research facilities combined since the nation came into being.

Whereas Israel had been contented to buy jet aircraft, steam turbines, locomotives, and other major hardware from the West, thereby letting other countries "sweat out the development costs," Dale went on, it had gone strictly on its own in the nuclear field. If Israel was pouring an enormous amount of its precious resources into a nuclear power project, the Foreign Service officer continued, it was an economic "blunder" because at least four countries—the United States, Britain, Canada, and France—were anxious to sell Israel proven, and therefore much more economical, power reactors for electricity.

Dimona was therefore an incredibly wasteful investment, he concluded, unless . . . *unless* "the Israelis have been deliberately developing their nuclear potential with national security in mind." Dale ended his appraisal by surmising that the Israelis would begin replacing Dimona's French uranium with very-high-quality amounts of the local (unmonitored) variety that year; that the plutonium separation plant would begin operating in 1967; and that Israel's first atomic bomb would be assembled for possible testing in 1968.

The timetable was off by two years. The evidence suggests that Israel indeed had a workable bomb by the end of 1966 and two in time for the 1967 war. Six years later, when the Arabs and Israelis next went to war, they had twenty atomic warheads mounted on Jericho-1s and had even miniaturized one type to fit into a suitcase.*

Dimona certainly was not wasteful. As Peres noted when he resigned

---

*Some CIA analysts believed Israel had the bomb in 1968. Other knowledgeable sources have suggested it had "five or six" of the weapons by 1969. On July 7, 1970, CIA Director Richard Helms told Congress that Israel then had the means to build an atomic bomb. (Peter Pry, *Israel's Nuclear Arsenal*, Boulder: Westview Press, 1984, p. 29.) In September 1974 James G. Poor, the Director of the Atomic Energy Commission's Division of International Security Affairs, reported to his superiors that his analysts believed that Israel had already produced nuclear weapons and was embarked on accommodating them for use on a variety of delivery systems, including aircraft and the Jericho. The report was accompanied by material from the national intelligence officer at the CIA who specialized in the Israeli nuclear program ("Prospects for Further Proliferation of Nuclear Weapons," Washington: Atomic Energy Commission, September 4, 1974).

The Mossad wasted no time in passing news of the laptop A-bomb on to the KGB. It wanted Brezhnev to understand that even if Black Squadron F-4s carrying nuclear bombs were beaten back during all-out war in the Middle East, a "carpet salesman" could accomplish the same thing by leaving his suitcase near the Kremlin Wall.

as deputy defense minister in 1965, after eighteen years on the job, every shekel was worth it. "Today, Dimona is Dimona. No one has gone bankrupt, and the other prophesies of doom have not come true," he told the newspaper *Ma'ariv*. "The Dimona reactor is today one of the state's greatest technological achievements, with important scientific and technological applications for the future."

The United States also knew early on that the American-supplied Soreq Nuclear Reactor and Research Center was part of the weapons complex. The facility, which is near the coast between Tel Aviv and Ashdod, houses the five-megawatt reactor obtained from Eisenhower. Soreq is the Israeli equivalent of a U.S. national weapons laboratory like Lawrence Livermore or Los Alamos. Research at Soreq runs the gamut from detonation to the effects of nuclear explosions. By the mid-1980s, its scientists were well on the way to developing computer codes for hydrogen bombs.

Only in 1986, when a disgruntled Moroccan Jew named Mordecai Vanunu described to British journalists and a nuclear weapons expert what he had seen deep inside Dimona while working as a technician with high clearances, was the world let in on the secret. Israeli agents lured Vanunu from his refuge in London in September 1986. He turned up in Israel several weeks later and on March 27, 1988, was given an eighteen-year prison sentence for aggravated espionage and aiding an enemy in wartime.

Vanunu's revelations, which appeared in the London *Sunday Times* complete with pictures he took secretly inside Dimona, enabled experts to estimate that the facility was generating about eighty-eight pounds of plutonium a year, or enough for ten bombs. It could achieve such high output because its power capacity was secretly increased over the years from 26 megawatts to 70, and possibly to as much as 150.

Whatever Israel accomplished by itself, it has depended from the beginning not only on its own computers but on vastly more powerful ones in the United States. It has been estimated that a team of nuclear weapons designers using the calculators of the 1940s would take five years to solve what it takes a Cray supercomputer one second to accomplish. Computers greatly refine and speed up the advanced weapons design process by eliminating impractical theories at the beginning and by simulating all of the factors that affect the explosion. And the faster they are, the less critical testing becomes. Supercomputers therefore become increasingly important in direct proportion to increased limits on testing.

Very-high-speed computers have therefore been crucial for Israel, which formally requested to buy Cray 2s in 1988 for its research facility at Technion. While the National Security Council and other interested organizations considered the matter, the Greater Washington D.C. Chapter of the American Society for Technion tried to raise funds to buy the machines in a special Supercomputer Project. How this was done illustrates the way Israel's U.S. support base mobilizes to provide it with whatever it requires.

Sophisticated computers like the Cray 2 were "indispensable for undergraduate teaching as well as graduate and staff research," one of the Supercomputer Project's fliers stated before listing six categories of pledges (the highest of which, at $100,000 or more, made the giver a benefactor). The project raised at least $509,000, according to a program that was distributed at a banquet at the Washington Hilton in September 1989 to honor Max M. Kampelman, the chief U.S. negotiator at the arms control talks in Geneva.* Cray 2s at that time cost about $13 million each.

But the money went to Bristol, England, not to Minnesota, where Crays are built. After two years of heated debate, the U.S. government failed to resolve the matter one way or the other. Technion therefore ordered a pair of lesser supercomputers from Meiko Scientific, Ltd., of Bristol, for $1.2 million, and took delivery in December 1991.

The closeness between the United States and Israel has been reflected in thousands of visits by Israeli scientists to the United States over the years, many of them to collect data that Washington officially denies supplying. LAKAM personnel have for years been sent to Israeli embassies in the U.S. and other Western nations as science attachés who are responsible for collecting any data, secret or otherwise, considered useful. LAKAM, or the Science and Liaison Bureau, was invented by Peres to procure anything the nation's scientists needed by any means necessary. They collect all relevant scientific papers and publications and make extensive social and professional connections with scientists in the countries where they are posted. Israeli scientists working abroad are en-

*The program listed Kenneth Adelman, former director of the Arms Control and Disarmament Agency, Lawrence Eagleburger, Deputy Secretary of State, Moshe Arad, the Israeli Ambassador, Richard Perle, a former Assistant Secretary of Defense, George Shultz, former Secretary of State, Henry Kissinger, another former Secretary of State, and others as being members of the Honorary Committee.

couraged to do the same thing when participating in foreign research projects.

The U.S. government insists that allowing Israelis and other foreigners to participate in unclassified research does not help their weapons development programs. That is absurd. Weapons development always derives from basic research, as Iraq and Pakistan know so well, and often in areas that have no apparent military value. The basic principles of rocket propulsion and guidance or of electromagnetic isotope separation are the same regardless of the application. They are infinitely adaptable but they do not bend.

Not only were scientists from civilian research centers arriving regularly at the labs, but others from Israel's nuclear weapons programs at Technion, Soreq, and Dimona were welcomed as well. During the late 1980s, six scientists from Dimona and Soreq visited Los Alamos and at least three others headed for Livermore. While the research might appear innocuous, close analysis says otherwise. Two scientists from the Israeli weapons program attended a conference on electromagnetic isotope separation—the same method used by Iraq in its baghdatrons—in 1986, not long after Israel began using the process to enrich uranium for its bomb program. And Dimona's electrochemistry group leader put in six weeks at Los Alamos studying an area that had to do with his specialty back home: plutonium reprocessing. The Dimona scientists at Livermore duly published in *Physical Review*, their discipline's most prestigious journal, noting that their research in the United States had been paid for by the Department of Energy.

Meanwhile, scores of others worked closely with their American counterparts, soaking up invaluable data in the process. During a twenty-month period in the late 1980s, as Israel's strategic upgrade was peaking, seventy-five Israeli scientists of all stripes visited Livermore, sixty visited Los Alamos, and fifty-three went to Sandia, all of them nuclear weapons labs. In fact, many came under the auspices of a five-year agreement between the Department of Energy and Israel's Ministry of Science and Development that was signed in 1987. The agreement—the most comprehensive the DOE has with any nation—called for "cooperative activities" in nuclear physics, fusion, material sciences, and other areas vital for the development of advanced nuclear weapons.* Considering that Israel

---

*The document was No. W-7405–Eng-48: "Current Energy R&D Bilateral Agreements as of July 1987 with U.S. Department of Energy Involvement."

has never produced so much as a single commercial watt of nuclear energy, the Department of Energy's not knowing that it was directly helping Israel's nuclear weapon program surpasses comprehension.

Whatever reading the Department of Energy took on these people, there could have been no doubt about the reason Dr. Yehuda Partom and his wife, Ilya, each spent fifty-seven weeks at Los Alamos and other national labs between 1985 and 1990 as "guest scientists." Yehuda was one of Israel's nuclear weapons designers; Ilya directed a vital part of Israel's Jericho development program at Rafael. Her work was so vital that some U.S. officials credited her with directing the entire program. Together, they amounted to Israel's First Family of Mass Destruction.

Mrs. Partom's request to visit Los Alamos in June 1988—her second visit there—listed research in unsaturated zone hydrology as her interest. The work would benefit Department of Energy projects to study the storage of nuclear wastes, according to Dr. Partom's American host and coworker at Los Alamos. Interestingly, her research topic involved the hydro-dynamic characteristics of fluids in tubes, a subject not unrelated to the performance of missile fuels. Her work, too, involved many hours on the lab's supercomputers. Otherwise there was no apparent cause for anyone to be suspicious about Dr. Partom, who, in any case, was supposed to be kept away from classified material. Robert S. Vrooman, the laboratory's international security officer, claimed uncategorically that there was "nothing in her conduct to suggest a security problem."

Indeed, Ilya Partom's individualized "security plan" stated that she was not to have access to "any classified or secure equipment, material, or information," that she was to be briefed about where she could not go and about what routes she had to take to get to where she could go (complete with a map). It even stipulated that she was to have lunch every day from 12 to 1 P.M. in Building SM-261, the Otowi Cafeteria. Her husband had his own security plan.

But nothing in Yehuda Partom's plan prevented him and another Israeli scientist, Ehud Ganani, from gaining access to a Cray 2 used by an American colleague at Los Alamos and accessing designs for nuclear weapon detonators and the effects of nuclear explosions in space during the 1988 visit.

Nor did Ilya Partom's plan later prevent her from trying to get Ronald J. Hoffman, the president of a Los Angeles firm called Plume Technology, Inc., to sell Israel parts of a highly sophisticated computer program called CONTAM III. The "plume" in the firm's name had to do with the heat plumes that ballistic missiles make when they are fired. Among several other uses, CONTAM III is the software that allows U.S. Defense Support Program satellites to track the heat plumes of ballistic missiles. Intercepting warheads is impossible unless the trajectories of the missiles that release them can be precisely tracked. It is therefore intimately related to Star Wars research and also potentially valuable for Israel's own missile design program.

Hoffman had begun negotiating with Rafael for the sale of several CONTAM III codes at least by the end of 1986 and was on such close terms with Arnold Segal, an officer who worked with Mrs. Partom at Rafael, that he ended one letter expressing "Love to Henia and your boys." Hoffman also assured Segal in the letter: "Export licenses or approval of Technical Assistance Agreements will not be a problem, as long as we identify a commercial satellite project as the requirement driving the technology need." If it occurred to Hoffman that there was a clear discrepancy in selling Israel's Ministry of Defense software for a civilian satellite, it went unrecorded.

By May 1990, however, Ilya Partom was apparently trying to speed things along. Preparatory to buying the software from Hoffman, she sent him a letter inviting him to give a one-hour talk on the subject at Technion's Space Research Center. She also told him that she wanted to set up a meeting to discuss the specific CONTAM III codes Israel wanted to buy. Hoffman's asking price for the software and a course of instruction on how to use it was $423,000.

Hoffman went to Israel on May 29 and returned on June 10. What happened there is not known. Four days after his return, however, he was arrested by two Customs Service agents posing as brokers for South Africans who were interested in buying CONTAM III and who paid him $150,000. On realizing that he was being stung, Hoffman boasted in an evident attempt to impress his captors that his clients included the head of Israel's missile program. The revelation did not help. He was eventually convicted on nine counts of violating the Arms Export Control Act.

Decades of persistently collecting every scrap of useful scientific and military data, overtly when possible and covertly when necessary, have paid off handsomely. The Israel Space Agency, a small organization established in 1983 and chaired by the ubiquitous Yuval Ne'eman, has benefited from cooperation with NASA and access to the American Institute of Aeronautics and Astronautics and similar professional organizations that have specialized subgroups for rocket propulsion, guidance, telemetry, thermodynamics, and other areas. This helped produce the Shavit rocket and at least two satellites with military applications.

The net result of the entire collection process, as well as close cooperation with other nations in both dual-use and dedicated weapons technology, has been to give Israel an extraordinarily potent force structure.* That structure, in turn, rests on diverse technology so advanced that it is in many respects better than its counterparts in the United States. The government of Israel talks about this as little as possible for at least two reasons. First, and most obviously, it makes no sense to give its many enemies a clear idea of its military strength. Second, it makes no sense to give its many friends a clear idea, either. Admitting that it could incinerate every major city in the Middle East is no way to sell Israel bonds or collect money for Technion.†

But such is the case. By 1992, Israel not only had more than 200 atomic bombs—up from twenty in 1973 and 100 in 1985—and was getting close to developing a thermonuclear one, but possessed most of the infrastructure to develop the necessarily advanced and highly integrated command, control, communication, and intelligence system to go with them.‡ Israel's infrastructure was so good, in fact, that an Institute for Defense Analysis study prepared for the Department of Defense in April 1987 rated it "in some instances more advanced than in the United States." No document in the public realm better explained Israel's commitment to nuclear-war fighting.

The Israelis won particularly high grades in three basic areas: extrapolating from U.S. equipment and ideas, rapidly developing and fielding equipment, and the quality of their research. The study noted that much Israeli electronic warfare and communication equipment in the field was "ahead of U.S. fielded equipment." It listed scores of innovative weapons or weapons-related systems either being researched or actually

---

*South Africa, to take only one example, poured substantial funding into Shavit, Jericho, the Phalcon airborne early warning and control system, the now-abandoned Lavi fighter, a couple of kinds of short-range missiles, and a great deal more.

†On the other hand, Israeli leaders have studiously hinted by oblique means—usually by saying that their country would not be the first to use nuclear weapons in the Middle East—that Israel possessed the weapons. This was meant to cause the most intimidation while sustaining the least damage.

‡It has actually produced 300 nuclear weapons but has retired many of the older ones.

in production. These included directed-energy weapons like the nuclear-pumped x-ray and chemical lasers under development by the Strategic Defense Initiative Office (SDIO) for the Star Wars ballistic missile defense program. "The capability of Soreq to support SDIO and nuclear technologies is almost an exact parallel of the capability currently existing at our National Laboratories," the report said.* It should be noted, it continued, that "the Israelis are developing the kind of codes which will enable them to make hydrogen bombs."

Soreq was also reported to be conducting advanced laboratory research using an electrothermal gun to perfect the ablative material that protects nose cones when they speed down through the atmosphere; research on short-wavelength chemical lasers that would be used to communicate with submerged submarines; hypervelocity guided missiles for air defense; a unique, "in the world" computerized vision system involving eye-brain function for fighter pilots targeting enemy aircraft (when the pilot sees an enemy and thinks "shoot," the plane shoots); missile defense technology involving propulsion systems, structures, warheads, and fuses; hollow-charge warheads with self-forging fragments ("totally revolutionary technology"); rotating solid rockets; and spaced armor that could stop armor penetrators by using small explosive charges ("U.S. urgently needs this technology").

Israel Aircraft Industries, the nation's largest company with annual sales of $900 million and 20,000 employees, was cited for its work in air defense suppression, air defense and attack aircraft, missiles and other guided weapons systems, airborne radars, secure communication systems, tactical and strategic intelligence systems integrated into command, control, and communication hardware and software, jammers, active electronic countermeasures, synthetic aperture and inverse synthetic aperture radar—ideal for radar imaging satellites capable of seeing through clouds or at night—and a good deal more.

Although the stars of the Israel Defense Force are its assorted nuclear and chemical weapons and ballistic missiles, there is also a growing supporting cast of dazzling new space-based weapons based on the nation's formidable technology.

---

*The nuclear-pumped x-ray laser, pioneered at Lawrence Livermore, was never satisfactorily tested and was abandoned as unworkable in 1992.

The most important support system is the colossally expensive re-connaissance satellite named Offeq, or Horizon, which is officially (and ambiguously) called a "scientific" spacecraft. It, too, is one of top scientist Yuval Ne'eman's pet projects. Although Offeq was long in the works before the war in the Persian Gulf, its mission gained importance in the minds of many Israelis who berated both the government and military intelligence for not predicting Iraq's invasion of Kuwait and for overly relying on U.S. intelligence and on the protection of France and other Western nations.

"In matters of our own basic security," Yuval Ne'eman once said to justify the Osirak raid, "how can we put our trust in any foreign country, or in any international organization?" The statement, however, had a far broader context. "What would the French do [if Iraq developed an atomic bomb]? They would send some pretty blonde to charm, and she would report back and say everything's fine, there's no problem. Are we really supposed to trust that?"

Offeq-1 was launched on September 19, 1988, on a Shavit booster, making Israel only the eighth nation to send a satellite into earth orbit.* Offeq-2 went up on April 3, 1990, the day after Saddam threatened to destroy "half of Israel" with his binary chemicals if it became involved in an attack against Iraq. The timing was hardly coincidental. While Ne'eman, speaking on behalf of the space agency, dutifully lied by pro-claiming that Offeq was "not designed for military purposes," other Israeli leaders pointed out that Shavit could also reach any target in Iraq as well

---

*Its orbital characteristics included a perigee, or lowest altitude, of 155 miles and an inclination to the equator of 142.9 degrees. Such a low altitude allows high-resolution pictures to be taken. The inclination, or flight path, took it over every nation between 37 degrees north and south latitude, which includes all of the Arab nations and Iran. A polar, or near polar, orbit is the usual route for reconnaissance satellites. But launching Offeq in that direction would have meant that Shavit and its payload might have passed over unfriendly countries soon after lift-off. A malfunction at that time could have put booster and satellite in Arab hands. Instead, the launch angle took them high over the Mediterranean and Europe.

Two days after the launch, George Shultz cabled congratulations to Prime Minister Yitzhak Shamir. "This impressive technological achievement reflects your national commitment to scientific excellence," Shultz said. The Secretary of State probably knew better. At any rate, by January 1992, with an Offeq-3 launch in the offing, even Defense Minister Moshe Arens pointed out that Israel urgently needed a "military spy satellite" in the wake of the Persian Gulf War. ("Ofeq-3 Satellite to Be Launched 'Soon,' " FBIS-NES-92–010, January 15, 1992, p. 42.) For a sound political and technical explanation of Israeli photointelligence requirements and plans, as well as the origin of the Shavit launch vehicle, see John Simp-son, Philip Actor, and Simon Crowe, "The Israeli Satellite Launch," Space Policy, May 1989, pp. 117–28.

as propel a spacecraft into orbit. The satellite's lowest altitude, only 129 miles, was near-perfect for taking pictures. Offeqs or their successors, all with twelve-inch or better resolution, will be used for real-time intelligence collecting, early warning, and targeting.

Offeq's rocket booster was itself of prime interest to U.S. intelligence, which didn't need to be told by Israelis that it could reach targets in Iraq and beyond. Shavit's performance indicated just how far Jericho's technology had advanced. They are, after all, the same rocket. Three weeks after the first launch, an analyst at Livermore laid out Shavit's ballistic missile capabilities in a paper titled "Israeli Missile Capabilities: A Few Numbers to Think About." With a 1,650-pound (750-kilogram) nuclear warhead, the author calculated, the Shavit had a range of 3,600 miles. Since the Israelis had told their then-allies, the Iranians, in 1977 that they had the 1,650-pounder, the 3,600 figure had to be Shavit's minimum range. If Israel had been able to reduce the size of its warheads to 650 pounds—which was clearly possible if it could make others that were portable—then Shavit's maximum range was 5,500 miles. That capability put all of Europe and Africa, as well as all of Asia except for parts of the Russian Far East and Indonesia, within its striking range.

Israel's other active satellite program involves the $300 million communications platform named Amos. Scheduled for launch in late 1994 or early 1995 on a French Ariane launch vehicle, Amos will be parked in geosynchronous orbit 22,300 miles over Zaire, from where it will relay military and communication traffic. It will be parked next to at least two Arab League communication satellites, or Arabsats, and presumably will eavesdrop on them as well as relay messages to Israel's ground and air forces and to a pair of cruise-missile-carrying submarines.*

The subs, Dolphin Type 800s built in West Germany at a price variously estimated at between $530 million and $600 million, guarantee Israel a second strike capability in the unlikely event that its planes and

---

*Blue-green chemical lasers, another area in which Israel is doing advanced research, would also be used to communicate with the subs in so-called bellringer operations. In situations in which war was imminent or had actually started, deployable rockets carrying the lasers would be fired to send the submarines a signal to come to periscope depth for further orders. Blue-green lasers can penetrate to 3,000 feet over a range of 6,200 square miles. (Edwin S. Townsley and Clarence A. Robinson, "Critical Technology Assessments in Israel and NATO Nations," Alexandria, VA: Institute for Defense Analysis, April 1987, p. II–1.)

land-based missiles are knocked out in a first strike.* The cruise missiles carried by these boats would come from Israel Aircraft Industries and would probably look like a shorter-range version of the U.S. Navy's 1,600-mile-range Tomahawk.

Like the missile-carrying submarines, the Arrow antitactical ballistic missile program clearly reflects Israel's belief that it can survive a nuclear war. And as is also the case with the subs, Arrow is at once technically complicated and heavily subsidized by the United States. The ultimate cost of the missile shield has been estimated at between $2 billion and $5 billion, with 80 percent of the still undetermined R & D costs coming from the United States. Although U.S.-Israeli cooperation on the project started in 1985 under the Strategic Defense Initiative, it gained great impetus during the Persian Gulf War, when thirty-nine Scuds landed on Israeli territory, severely shaking Israel's confidence that U.S. Patriots or any foreign system could protect it. It was the first time since 1948 that Israelis well inside their own country were bombarded.

Arrow has had a particularly tumultuous history. Its first three tests were essentially failures, prompting Washington to question whether the project was viable. In addition, Arrow's foes in Israel repeatedly pointed out that since the country is so small, the system would have to be 99.9 percent effective to work at all. Its proponents have said that such results are possible. The opposition has dismissed such optimism as "chutzpah."

By the end of 1992, despite all of its help over four decades, the United States wanted Israel to drop plutonium production and come clean as its ally, South Africa, did that year. American diplomats quietly warned about Dimona's age and about how a fire at the thirty-year-old facility the year before had caused panic. They cautioned that its safety systems, whose life had been precariously extended by sharing U.S. safety procedures and data, could not be trusted.

---

*The United States agreed to pay about half of the total cost. When it became known that the Israelis wanted to use electronic systems in the subs made by Krupp Atlas, a German firm, and Loral Corp. of Ohio, Senator Claiborne Pell protested vigorously. The Rhode Island Democrat demanded that the equipment come from his own state's Submarine Signal, a division of Raytheon, and ordered the General Accounting Office to study the matter. The deal was worth $95 million. ("Senator Insists Israel Use Military Aid Funds in U.S.," *The Jerusalem Post*, July 13, 1990.) As it was, Raytheon was at the time installing similar equipment on 1950s-vintage Egyptian subs. The boats, called "Whiskey class" by NATO, were the first postwar Soviet types. The Kremlin sold seven directly to Egypt; others were eventually bought from China, which copied them from two it received from the U.S.S.R.

Some in Israel were moved by the plea to brake and even reduc
the dependence on nuclear weapons. But most were not. The Scuds th
hit Tel Aviv and Haifa during the first night of the war and narrowly misse
Dimona on the last night, and the threats to "fire" half of their countr
with poison gas barely hinted at what mortal enemies like Saddam Hussei
would do to them unless they could answer with devastating effect. "Nevε
again" had renewed meaning, as a poll conducted by the Center fc
Strategic Studies at Tel Aviv University soon after the Scuds rained dow
showed. Ninety-one percent of those questioned said that Israel shoul
develop nuclear weapons, up from 78 percent four years earlier. And i
another "astonishing rise," 88 percent said that their consciences woul
be clear if their country used atomic bombs. Only 53 percent of thos
polled in 1987 believed that it was morally acceptable to incinerate mil
lions of civilians. The nuclear threshold had therefore gone up in ever
sense.

# 10

## THE CRESCENT
## OF CRISIS: PLOWSHARES
## INTO SWORDS

In January 1961, weary of years of bloodshed and frustration, the people of France voted overwhelmingly to end the rebellion in Algeria and heed Charles de Gaulle's call for its independence. But having already been ejected from Vietnam after the bitter defeat at Dien Bien Phu seven years earlier, and feeling particularly rooted to a place their fathers and grandfathers had nurtured for 130 years, members of the French officer corps in Algeria vowed to fight the decision. That April, General Maurice Challe, the former commander-in-chief of French forces in Algeria, organized a "Revolt of the Generals" in a full-blown military rebellion whose purpose was to hold on to Algeria at all costs.

As it happened, French scientists were at that moment preparing to set off France's fourth atomic explosion at a test site at Reganne, 400 miles south of Algiers in the Sahara. When word of the revolt reached Paris, however, emergency orders were sent to the physicists at Reganne to detonate the bomb as quickly as possible, regardless of whether they had time to get the science return they wanted (a higher yield). Headquarters' fear was not misplaced. The order was immediately countermanded by the general in charge of Reganne, a friend of Challe's, and was only carried out by the scientists after what was undoubtedly a most forceful communication from the capital. The explosion was "optimized," according to a high-level official at the Commissariat à l'Energie Atomique, to get rid of the bomb as unambiguously and irrevocably as possible so it would not fall into the mutineers' hands. De Gaulle was clearly worried that Challe and his confederates would seize the weapon and use it for their own political ends.

Six years later, it was China's turn to face atomic anarchy. The location was Xingjiang Province, the far western region that formed a long frontier with the Soviet Union. The trouble began when the province's military and party boss, Wang Enmao, had a serious falling-out with Chairman Mao Tse-tung, Marshal Lin Piao, and the Red Guards, who were at the time carrying out a ferocious cultural revolution across the country. Wang, a former Hunanese peasant who had been appointed to his post by Mao himself, was more than an irksome renegade. He was a warlord who commanded the loyalty of eight army divisions and the overwhelming majority of Muslims among the province's five million people. The followers of the Prophet Muhammad had no intention of submitting to the Red Guard's heathenism and renowned cruelty. Knowing this, Wang supported the Muslims and got their fidelity in return.

From Beijing's perspective, Wang's rebellion threatened catastrophe. Because Xingjiang was so remote, isolated, and sparsely populated, it had been selected as China's nuclear and missile development and test center. Lop Nor, at the northern edge of the desolate Tarim Basin, was established in 1959 and remains the country's only nuclear test site. China's first fission device was exploded there on October 16, 1964. Seven months later, a weaponized version—a bomb—was successfully dropped from an airplane and exploded. Production began immediately, with all manufacturing and a great deal of storage also taking place in Xingjiang. By 1967, the province had also sprouted ballistic missile test facilities.

Mindful of all this, the wily warlord decided to tell Chairman Mao to keep the Red Guards out of Xingjiang or he would seize what was essentially China's entire nuclear development, production, and weapons storage system. Wang was holding Mao's own gun to his head and the Chairman knew it. Not only could nuclear weapons in the "revisionist independent kingdom" (as Mao called it) be used against the rest of the country, but their removal from Beijing's control would also strengthen the Soviet hand in the region, perhaps calamitously.

Mao certainly would have understood that Muslims in Xingjiang had more in common with Muslims in neighboring Kazakhstan than they did with Han Chinese Marxists in far-off Beijing. He therefore backed down early in 1967, ordering Lin Piao to suspend the cultural revolution in Xingjiang and keep the Red Guards on a tight leash. "Peaceful coexistence" was the new order of the day. Or, as Mao himself might have put it in the old, more liberal days, Wang was one thorny flower that had to be allowed to bloom.

The two incidents, widely separated by time and place, are intimately connected by circumstance. They are early examples of what can happen when political hatred and instability combine with superweapons to form a potentially critical mass.

The revolts of the generals occurred at opposite ends of a 6,000-mile-long zone of upheaval that starts in Mauritania and extends eastward through the Maghreb and Egypt, then up into Syria, Iraq, Iran, and Turkey, and finally wends its way east again, along the old silk and spice routes, through Armenia, Azerbaijan, Kazakhstan, and the other former Soviet republics in Central Asia, and ends in the Xingjiang Autonomous Region. It is an area that stretches a third of the way around the world, a crescent of turmoil, seething with restive, newly liberated peoples.

Liberation has suddenly freed the peoples of the crescent to settle old ethnic scores in blood feuds and murderous vendettas of annihilation, spread Islam through the purifying medium of holy war, overthrow their own or foreign governments by assassination, rebellion, or invasion, and commit unspeakable atrocities in the service of God or his anointed representative of the moment. And always near at hand, or soon to be there, are the wonder weapons that are the lasting legacy of the departed western European and communist imperialists. Saladin's new sword is being forged. It is an atomic bomb or a canister of deadly chemicals riding on a pillar of fire.

The witch's brew of fragmentation, religious zealotry, ethnic hatred, and unprecedentedly dangerous weapons makes this the most volatile and potentially perilous place on Earth.

Militant Islamic revivalism, or "fundamentalism," as it is usually called, is by far the most pervasive and serious of the crescent's many unique dangers.* There are more than a half billion Muslims between the Atlantic and Xingjiang. A growing number of revivalists among them believe that the West long ago ended their civilization's golden age, ostensibly by colonization, but more insidiously through moral pollution. They feel contempt for all outsiders, including Russians, who they believe have subverted their culture to the point where it is mired in poverty, subservience, and humiliation. At best, the foreign infidels are seen as carriers of corruption; at worst, they are taken to be the enemies of God. Like Christian fundamentalists, they see Marxists in particular as the devil's handmaidens. Yet ironically, in their implacable monotheism, rigid dogma, and absolute belief in the justification of brutal means to achieve their ends, they resemble nothing so much as the old Bolsheviks themselves. Militant Islam has become communism's replacement.

As far away as Malaysia, an imam exhorts the faithful to throw off their shackles and rally to the just cause. "Islam is the only force capable of filling the spiritual vacuum in the West," he declares, "so [Westerners] are afraid of the great Islamic revival. . . . For this reason they are slaughtering children . . . in Yugoslavia and Burma and Eritrea and Kashmir. We must arise . . . so that the Muslim generation that will liberate the Islamic world can break out from its prison of assault by culture, Christian proselytisation, secularization, economics and politics. . . ."

But it is not only outsiders they hold in contempt. There is a special loathing for those among their own nationalist leaders who emulate the infidels, also in alleged defiance of the law of God and to the detriment of their own victimized societies. Turmoil is therefore more likely to erupt within the crescent itself than beyond its sphere of influence, as fiercely competing sects and ethnic groups clash over supremacy. Iran and Iraq spent more than $100 billion, not to destroy Israel, but to decisively

---

*In a sense, the term "Islamic fundamentalism" is redundant. It was invented in the West to describe ultraconservative Muslims as if they were the equivalent of the born-again Protestants who take the Bible to be the literal truth. But there are no shades of belief in Islam, as there are in Christianity and Judaism. It is therefore per se fundamentalist. All Muslims accept the fact that every circumstance of life is contained in the Koran, their equivalent of the Bible; in the *Sunna*, the collected sayings and actions of Muhammad; and the *Sharia*, or code of law. Muslims who drink alcohol or eat pork, for example, are not religious liberals; they do so in defiance of their religion's precepts. In Islam, there is no fundamental separation between mosque and state.

cripple each other once and for all. Their eight-year war of attrition had an effect that extended well beyond the combatants themselves because it prompted other nations in the region to choose a side, in effect creating two camps whose mutual hostility survived the war. Iran was backed by Syria and Libya, while Egypt, Algeria, and the Gulf sheikdoms supported Saddam Hussein, whom they took to be the lesser of two evils compared with Teheran's fierce mullahs.

Iran's Pahlavi dynasty, taken to be lackeys of the United States, was overthrown by those holy men in 1979 and replaced by a Revolutionary Council that was responsible for ensuring strict adherence to Islamic principles in all phases of life. Two years later, Anwar al-Sadat paid with his life for making peace with Israel. He was gunned down by Islamic militants in the army who could not contain their rage at what they took to be his betrayal of God.

Exactly ten years after the revolution in Iran, one took place in Sudan. The Islamic military government that seized the dreadfully impoverished country set out to do immediately what its Muslim predecessors had done in the seventh to eleventh centuries: spread Islam beyond their own borders, particularly to other Arab nations like Egypt and the Maghreb: Libya, Algeria, Morocco, and Tunisia. "The mission it has embarked upon," one diplomat said of the new government in Khartoum, "includes the imposition of Arabic and Islam throughout the country, including the south, and the subversion of the secular Arab and African governments in the region."

For their part, Arab secular leaders have struck back at the revivalists, often ferociously. Saddam Hussein has relentlessly attacked radical Shiite rebels in the Basra region of Iraq and elsewhere. Syria's President, Hafez al-Assad, has slaughtered more than 20,000 members of the Muslim Brotherhood and other militants. The Brotherhood, founded in Egypt in 1928, is barred from participating in Syrian politics. In Libya, hundreds of members of radical Islamic groups have been thrown in jail by Colonel Qaddafi.

Tunisia's radical Ennahdha (Renaissance) Party has been repressed and some of its members jailed after repeated clashes with the police and the discovery of plans for an "Islamic revolution." Diplomats in Tunis reported in 1992 that at least 7,000 revivalists had been arrested and questioned during the preceding two years; the radicals themselves charged that as many as 30,000 of their brethren had been detained, questioned, and tortured during the same period.

Algeria's Islamic Liberation Front (FIS), finally legalized in 1989, won 55 percent of the national vote that year and 49 percent of the first round of the general election in 1991. The government responded by canceling the second round, banning the party, and arresting and jailing most FIS leaders. So ended the Algerian experiment in democracy. It was the same in Morocco, where the leader of Justice and Welfare, the largest of the radical groups, was put under house arrest while several of his lieutenants were jailed.

Yasir Arafat has warned Hamas, the largest of the revivalist factions in the Gaza Strip and the West Bank, that continued acts of violence against Palestinians in an effort to gain control over them will bring retaliation.

The ties that bind are more than religious. The crescent's eastern half, from Azerbaijan to Xingjiang, is bound culturally as well. As was the case with maps drawn by Europeans throughout Africa without regard for the more than 800 tribes that lived there, those imposed in the Middle East and Central Asia ignored close ethnic relations. Farsi, Iran's language, is widely spoken in western Afghanistan and Tajikistan. Northern Central Asia was historically a mostly Turkic world—the entire region was known as Turkistan as late as the early part of this century—and with the redrawing of the Soviet map, it is realigning to that more natural state. With scant exceptions, a traveler fluent in Turkish could communicate with everyone he or she encountered along a route stretching from the Balkans to 1,000 miles inside China.

Politically and economically, however, the upheaval zone is more aptly described as a cauldron than a crescent. When Moscow withdrew from its former Central Asian republics, it took its money with it, leaving them poor and disoriented. The end of enforced communist harmony also allowed ancient and obscure blood feuds to surface, as when the Armenian majority in Nagorno-Karabakh, an enclave in Azerbaijan, demanded autonomy in 1988 and instead touched off a bloody war. Armenia, a Christian stronghold surrounded on three sides by Islamic states—Turkey, Azerbaijan, and Iran—is the Israel of Central Asia. And like Israel, it is a flashpoint that could create a large explosion. When Turkish Prime Minister Suleyman Demirel said publicly that he was under heavy pressure at home to help his country's Turkic cousins in Azerbaijan, for example, Russia, a mostly Christian nation like Armenia, warned the Turks to stay out of the dispute or risk attack.* Armenia's stated intention to restart its two Soviet-made power reactors, for example, prompted some concerned officials in the nuclear community in Moscow to fear that it had embarked on a long-term nuclear weapons development program.

Elsewhere in the Caucasus the end of Soviet rule was producing miniconflicts between long-repressed Islamic groups by the fall of 1992. Farther south, there remained the festering relations between Iraq, the pariah of the Persian Gulf, and its various Iranian and Arab enemies; between the Iranians and the Arabs; and between Egypt and Libya, Egypt and Sudan, and Sudan and all four nations of the Maghreb. Alarmed that Iran was trying to exert its revivalist influence among Central Asia's Muslims, for example, Saudi Arabia quickly tried to check the move by establishing diplomatic relations with Uzbekistan. This is the rough-and-tumble world of the Islamic crescent in the waning years of the twentieth century. The search for power in the ashes of old empires is causing dizzying realignments in a world convulsing with religious zealotry, territorial ambition, jealousy, and endless, often murderous intrigue.

Then there is the weapons factor. In 1973, when the Yom Kippur War was fought, Islamic superweapons were only a seductive fantasy. Twenty years later they were a reality. Two Muslim nations, Pakistan and Kazakhstan, possess nuclear weapons. And Kazakhstan's arsenal is guarded by restive, resentful Russians. Five other nations—Iraq, Iran, Syria, Algeria, and Libya—are pursuing nuclear weapons with varying degrees of fervor and success. Iraq's effort, which may still be under way, has been well documented. Five—Iraq, Iran, Egypt, Syria, and Libya—have or are trying to acquire biological weapons. Six—Iraq, Iran, Syria, Egypt, Libya, and Pakistan—have or are trying to get chemical weapons. Ten—Iraq, Iran, Syria, Libya, Egypt, Saudi Arabia, Yemen, Pakistan, Kazakhstan, and Afghanistan—have ballistic missiles of various ranges. Nine—Iraq, Iran, Syria, Algeria, Libya, Saudi Arabia, Kuwait, Pakistan, and Turkey—have long-range fighter-bombers. Six—Iran, Syria, Algeria, Libya, Egypt, and Turkey—have submarines.

---

*Typically for the region, Turkish-Armenian hostility goes back at least to World War I, when the Ottomans allegedly massacred 1.5 million Armenians in eastern Turkey in a territorial dispute.

More important, the weapons technology for the nuclear warheads, chemical and biological agents, missiles, and even submarines is increasingly being developed at home and then passed around in exchange for hard currency. Egypt, Iraq, Iran, Pakistan, Syria, and Libya have developed vigorous weapons industries. Turkey is actively engaged in F-16 production and, thanks to a coproduction agreement with Germany's HDW, submarine building. The Turks are so good at constructing subs, in fact, that they design their own versions of a German import. The crescent bristles with weapons.

The Islamic Republic of Mauritania is the crescent's left tip. Standard guidebooks say that 80 percent of the military dictatorship's two million people are of Arab-Berber stock, that Arabic and French are the official languages, that it is three times the size of Arizona, and that its major products are dates, grains, and iron ore. But a proliferation guide would add that U.S. reconnaissance satellites spotted Iraqi fixed missile launching equipment at several remote airfields in the Mauritanian desert in the spring of 1990. Although the imagery did not turn up missiles, it did reveal metal rails and related equipment used to move large missile launchers. At the same time, more than a dozen Iraqi military technicians turned up in Mauritania. American intelligence officials concluded that the Iraqis wanted the facility because Mauritania's 400,000 square miles and 350-mile-long ocean front not only provided plenty of room for long-range missile testing, but did so far from Israeli intelligence collectors. Mauritania said there were no such facilities. Iraq said nothing. The launchers would have been used to test either the mysterious Tammuz 1 (an Iraqi Scud topped by an SA-2 upper stage) or the problem-plagued Al Abid, or both. Mauritania's flirtation with Iraq's missileers ended with the invasion of Kuwait, however.

In mid-April 1991, a terse Foreign Office statement issued to the news media in London said that Group Captain William Cross, the British military attaché in Algeria, had been recalled "for operational reasons." It added that "as far as we're concerned, he didn't do anything that we would consider incompatible with his status." While the statement was suitably ambiguous, it was also perfectly true. Before he left Algiers, Cross had been engaging in a practice long an integral part of his status, as well as that of military attachés from other countries. The diplomat, a former RAF pilot, had been spying for the Crown and had been thrown out of Algeria after being caught the previous February.

Cross's subject was a nuclear facility near Ain Oussera, about 165 miles south of Algiers in the foothills of the Atlas Mountains. The Algerians, no slouches themselves in the fine art of the ambiguous press release, were shortly to proclaim that their Chinese-supplied Es Salam ("Peace") reactor and related equipment were being built "with the sole aim of mastering the application of nuclear energy in the framework of development." No mention was made of what, exactly, was to be developed.

Whatever the Algerian government said, however, there does not seem to have been much doubt in Cross's mind, nor in the minds of CIA, MI 6, or Russian Intelligence Service analysts, about the real nature of the plant at Ain Oussera. It was situated in a military exclusion zone near an air base and a Soviet-built SA-5 antiaircraft missile battery and was protected by a high fence and armed soldiers. A sign on the fence warned in French and Arabic against taking pictures. The Algerians called all this a "research compound."*

When Cross was caught, his camera was confiscated and its film removed, as happens to other "tourists" who venture into forbidden locales. But there were other pictures of the place that could not be confiscated. They came from a U.S. KH-11 reconnaissance satellite, which had imaged the facility the previous January. The week that Operation Desert Storm began 4,000 miles to the east, CIA analysts studying the imagery noted the facility's desolate location and its defenses. They also saw that the complex seemed to comprise a reactor hall and possibly even a reprocessing plant. The size of the reactor's cooling towers indicated that it would have a capacity of forty megawatts or more. That would be far more than a simple research reactor required. And use of the reactor for power generation also seemed to be out of the question. "There are no electrical power generation facilities at the reactor and no electrical power transmission lines nearby. This is clearly a military nuclear reactor for weapons production," one analyst concluded. It would be about right for turning some of Algeria's huge stockpile of low-grade uranium into

---

*They had previously bought a small reactor from Argentina which went into operation outside of Algiers in 1989. It was operated under International Atomic Energy Agency safeguards. It was used for educational and research purposes by the country's 300 nuclear scientists and technicians.

enough plutonium to produce one bomb core a year, with the first possibly being ready by 1998—with some outside help. The information was undoubtedly passed on to British intelligence, which is how Group Captain Cross came to make the inauspicious drive over the high Atlas with his own camera in the first place.

Following Cross's expulsion, news about Ain Oussera was quickly leaked to American and British newspapers, and was accompanied by even more alarming reports that the Chinese were also helping their Algerian customers to adapt nuclear warheads to the country's various aerial and missile delivery systems. These included three MIG fighter-bomber squadrons, two Sukhoi ground attack squadrons, and Frog tactical missiles with a range of forty-five miles.

Algeria reacted to public disclosure of its large nuclear facility within three weeks. The state radio said that Cross had been expelled after being picked up near the "imaginary nuclear plant south of Algiers" and that his report amounted to "hysterical and unfounded fantasies." For good measure, the broadcast ended on a note similar to those heard in India, Pakistan, and other nations with nuclear weapons programs. The United States, it said, wanted to "impose on the world and to subjugate it to what the Algerian foreign minister has called a world dictatorship based on material power."

Algeria agreed in February 1992 to allow International Atomic Energy Agency inspectors access to Es Salam. As Iraq proved, however, diversion was still possible; the safeguarding of reactors depended squarely on their owners' honesty. The decision to grant access to the reactor was made two months after the revivalists won a stunning 49 percent of the first round in Algeria's first democratic general election. The second round, set for January 1992, was abruptly canceled by the government, which promptly threw most FIS leaders in jail.

Having won an election fairly, only to see it taken away from them, the Islamic militants reacted with fury. If the system denied them the power that was rightfully theirs, the system would have to be changed. As was happening in other Muslim countries, the militants fomented chaos in order to weaken and embarrass the government, to shake it until it fell. This was done according to tradition: by shedding blood.

That summer homemade bombs exploded almost every day in public places throughout the country. Telephone and electrical lines were blown up. At the end of August, a bomb went off at the Air France counter at

Houari Boumedienne Airport with such force that one of the nine people killed stuck to the terminal's ceiling. More ominously, armed men on motorcycles or in cars shot and killed soldiers and policemen with increasing frequency and with weapons which themselves had been stolen from police stations and barracks. They even tried to assassinate Mohammed Tolba, the nation's security minister. Some of the killers, like those in Iran, Sudan, and elsewhere, had fought with the Islamic Mujahedeen against the Soviets in Afghanistan and returned home infected with the belief that only deadly violence could protect their religion.* The government responded by cracking down on the militants and unleashing not only the army but hooded antiterrorist brigades, vigilantes, to mount an increasingly fierce antiguerrilla campaign. By the spring of 1993, however, the insurgency had escalated from hit-and-run attacks to gun battles lasting for up to two days. This betrayed the fact that many previously isolated revivalist groups were coordinating to form a single disciplined command structure. Both sides seemed to be headed toward a murderous and, in the view of the revivalists, a cleansing civil war.

Meanwhile, on Algeria's eastern border, Colonel Qaddafi was expanding his chemical weapons arsenal. The poison gas capability was itself only a consolation prize—a "poor man's atomic bomb"—that had been acquired because he could not get a rich man's atomic bomb: a real one. As far back as the late 1970s, the Libyan dictator was so fixated by the dream of owning atomic bombs that he allegedly offered to pay India the equivalent of its national debt—nearly $18 billion—for the technology. It was one of the first instances in which a Third World nation tried to acquire nuclear weapons from another while bypassing superpowers. No one, it seems—not even debt-ridden India—was willing to gamble that the wildly bombastic, mercurial, and rueful Colonel Qaddafi would be able to contain himself once nuclear weapons were at his fingertip.

In 1980, the strongman therefore opted for chemical agents as the next best thing. He paid Imhausen-Chemie and the other European

*Mujahedeen veterans of Afghanistan were fighting against Serbs in Bosnia-Herzegovina. ("Muslims From Abroad Join in War Against Serbs," *The New York Times*, November 14, 1992.)

and Japanese companies many millions of dollars to provide him with a capability he was unable to acquire on his own. In addition, U.S. intelligence suspected that Iran had independently supplied Libya with chemical weapons in exchange for mines that it used in the war against Iraq.

Qaddafi was determined to arm his country with strategic weapons. Recalling the U.S. air attacks on Tripoli and Benghazi in April 1986 in retaliation for Libyan terrorist activity in Europe, he told university students four years later that only superweapons and Arab hegemony could hold America and other threatening nations at bay.

"If they [the Americans] know that you have a deterrent force capable of hitting the United States, they would not be able to hit you. Because if we had possessed a deterrent—missiles that could reach New York—we would have hit it in the same moment. Consequently, we should build this force so that they and others will no longer think [about an attack]. Whether at the level of Libya or at the level of the Arab homeland, in the coming twenty years, this revolution should achieve the unity of the Arab nation. . . . This should become one homeland, the whole of it, possessing missiles and even nuclear bombs," Qaddafi said before calling for "reciprocal" treatment of the Arabs and the West. "The world has a nuclear bomb," he growled, "*we* should have a nuclear bomb."

However unlikely it was that Qaddafi would acquire such a bomb, along with a compatible missile whose 4,000-mile range would put it within striking distance of Washington, he was nevertheless intent on building a serious strategic missile capability. Also in 1980, Libya invited a West German firm, OTRAG, to build a missile test facility near Sebha in the Sahara and test what it called an inexpensive "satellite launcher." The firm had tried to do the same thing in Zaire four years earlier, but abandoned the project after neighboring countries questioned Zaire's commitment to a space program and charged that, instead, it was a thinly disguised ballistic and cruise missile development operation. It was the same in Libya, though this time Lutz Kayser, the company's president, asserted that Europe needed the "easily processed Libyan oil" as much as Libya needed German rockets.

Morocco, another of Qaddafi's nervous neighbors, was among the first to sound the alarm. The government press agency issued a statement in March 1981 saying that the "medium-range missiles" developed by the Germans would be able to carry nuclear warheads that were being simultaneously developed in Libya (which was nonsense). Following reports by agents in Germany confirming the deal, and then photographs of the budding facility sent back by U.S. reconnaissance satellites, Bonn persuaded the Munich firm to abandon the project.

By 1993, Libya joined a growing list of outlaw nations that had turned their attention away from traditional European suppliers to the black and gray markets of East Asia. U.S. intelligence had found that a Thai company had designed and built tunnels for nerve gas production near the town of Tarhuna, about forty miles southeast of Tripoli.

At the same time, Western intelligence discovered yet a third plant, this one at Benghazi, Libya's second city. This facility was not for the production of chemical weapons, but for the manufacture of the precursors needed for the deadly brews at Rabta and Tarhuna. The discovery was ominous because it indicated that Libya no longer would have to depend on outside sources for the precursors.

Qaddafi, in the meantime, bought a slew of Scud Bs from the Soviet Union, many of which he transferred to Iran in 1985 in a show of solidarity with the Ayatollah in his war with Saddam (prompting Saddam to tell the Kremlin that it ought to clamp down on its own reexport rules). He also tried to buy CSS-2 "East Wind" long-range ballistic missiles from China, but was rebuffed. Similar attempts to buy Brazilian and Soviet advanced long-range missiles also went nowhere (in the first instance, because of intense U.S. pressure).

By then, however, still other German engineers, as well as Poles bearing wind tunnel designs, were back in Libya. Throughout the rest of the decade, representatives of several firms and freelancers were understood to be working on still another ballistic missile, Al-Fatah. A German who claimed to have been a manager at the secret missile site at Tauwiwa, in the Sahara, told the German magazine *Stern* in 1987 that he and his colleagues believed the rocket was for high-altitude research "because we wanted to believe it. For another thing, we earned a lot of money, and money helps overcome any doubts one may have." He added that Al-Fatah had by then been tested and was in early production. U.S. intelligence disputed this at the time, saying that a prototype of the missile had only just been built and was ready for flight testing at the air base at Sebha. If that didn't work, the CIA noted, Qaddafi had taken the precaution of ordering 650-mile-range missiles, Scud Ds, from North Korea.

While Qaddafi continued to try desperately to get the elusive ballistic missiles, he took a time-honored intermediate step. In the winter of 1989, Moscow confounded Middle East arms controllers by selling Libya between twelve and fifteen SU-24D swing-wing ground attack aircraft. With all-weather capability and a round-trip strike range of 800 miles, chemical weapon-laden SU-24s could now strike Egypt, Israel, or almost any U.S. force in the Mediterranean. In addition, the Russians agreed in April 1989 to turn a Libyan IL-76 transport into an airborne refueler, increasing the SU-24's range by 50 percent. Less than a year later, the Libyans themselves were testing the same concept with a U.S.-built C-130 Hercules transport and a French-supplied Mirage F-1 fighter-bomber. The two aircraft connected on four of six attempts, U.S. intelligence told *The New York Times*, thereby publicly warning Qaddafi that it was on to him while showing off its own powers of observation.

Farther east, Egypt continued to look warily at Libya and also at its ancient rivals Iraq and Iran. A moderate among Arab nations and a stalwart in the peace process with Israel begun by Jimmy Carter, Egypt entered the 1990s beset by dangers borne out of the enmity of radicals both within the country and without.

Egypt has no known plans to acquire nuclear weapons. But in 1992, after the United States forgave its $7 billion in military debts, it went on a nuclear shopping spree. First, there was an agreement with India to revamp and upgrade its thirty-year-old Soviet research reactor. This was followed by an agreement with Argentina to buy a 22-megawatt research reactor perfectly sized for nuclear weapons research. The Egyptians also ordered a cyclotron accelerator, useful for gaining experience with enrichment technologies, from the Russians. In January 1993, the Russian Foreign Intelligence Service noted that Egypt had begun building a facility at its Inshas El-Rami research center, which "in its design features and engineering protection could in the future be used to obtain weapons grade plutonium from the uranium irradiated in the research reactors." The facility was strictly off-limits to foreigners.

Whatever its nuclear weapons intention, Cairo is trying to assemble a huge inventory of conventional weapons, plus some supers as well. By the beginning of the decade, it had long possessed stocks of chemical and biological weapons.* It also had a force of creaky Soviet-supplied TU-16 jet bombers, plus two Soviet subs, six Chinese subs, and a pair from Great Britain. Furthermore, it had a brace of Scud Bs, the standard-issue ballistic missile for Soviet clients, which had been delivered at the time of the war with Israel, in 1973. Not content with the old, inaccurate missiles, however, Egypt eventually joined forces with Iraq and Argentina to produce the Condor-2 and with North Korea to develop Scud Cs and Ds. It dropped out of the Condor project in 1989 under intense pressure from the United States and right after an embarrassing episode in which an Egyptian-born aerospace engineer named Abdelkader Helmy was arrested and pleaded guilty to a charge of illegally trying to export carbon phenolic cloth to Cairo. The material is used in missile nose cones and in stealth aircraft to reduce their radar image. Egypt's Condor development facilities are now involved in another international project, this one to build an improved version of the Scud factory at Heliopolis with North Korea. The irony is that Egyptian missile technology has in the process been transferred to Iraq, Egypt's adversary.

Egypt has had a particularly virulent bout of revivalism that is being championed by three groups with sometimes close ties: the Muslim Brotherhood, the Islamic Group, and Holy War. Following Sadat's assassination by Holy War in 1981, the revivalist movement grew until, four years later, enormous pressure was being exerted on President Hosni Mubarak to implement strict Islamic law. His government resisted by calling into force a 1981 law that put all mosques under the control of the minister for religious endowments. Forty-five prominent Islamic radicals were arrested almost simultaneously.

In February 1990, headlines around the world carried pictures of an Israeli tour bus that was ambushed between Cairo and Ismailia, killing nine Israelis and wounding seventeen others. Eight months after the bus attack, Dr. Rif'at al-Mahgoub, the moderate Speaker of the People's Assembly, was murdered by Holy War, Sadat's killers. In 1992, intimi-

---

*A Russian Foreign Intelligence Service report of January 28, 1993, asserted that Egypt's biological weapons program had close ties to U.S. programs, especially with pathogenic microorganisms. It said that an American "naval military-medical laboratory for the study and development of means of combating particularly dangerous infectious diseases is also known." The report added that the laboratory is a leading medical-biological center in the region, is staffed by "highly qualified American specialists," and is "strictly classified." (Foreign Broadcast Information Service, JPRS Report, *Proliferation Issues: Russian Foreign Intelligence Service Report: Proliferation of Weapons of Mass Destruction*, April 4, 1993, p. 47.)

dation and death stalked all of Egypt's Christians and Jews. In Asyut Province, halfway between Cairo and Luxor, thirty people—including thirteen Copts who were massacred by Islamic militants—were murdered between April and June. Following the shooting of the local militant leader by security forces that June, sixty-four Christian homes and shops were burned. Several police and government officials were also murdered, including Faraq Foda, a leading intellectual who openly criticized the revivalists, two Coptic priests and, in April 1993, Brigadier General Mohammed al-Shaimi, the senior police official in southern Egypt. The attacks and a wave of terror against tourists have begun to set off alarm bells in Washington. "The question," one Middle East analyst at the Pentagon wondered, "is how long Egypt will remain Egypt and not become Iran."

By the winter of 1992 Iran and Sudan were being seen by several Arab intelligence services as more than just instigators of revivalist violence. Tunisia, Algeria, Egypt, and Saudi Arabia had become so concerned by what they saw as carefully orchestrated violence that they put aside differences to coordinate intelligence and policy. Some intelligence officers told *The New York Times* that Iran was training, arming, and financing militants out to prevent an Arab-Israeli peace agreement and was bent on fomenting rebellions in the area so that Islamic republics modeled on Iran would come to power. Meanwhile, Sudan's Muslim leader, Hassan al-Turabi, was applauding the breakup of the Soviet Union, saying it would free up nuclear technology for Islamic use. A senior Jordanian official described Iranian backing of the revivalists as part of "a very big plan which we are all treating as an actual war being waged from Teheran." Other Arab security officials said that Iran's operation was run by "minders" from the Foreign Ministry, the Revolutionary Guard Corps, and the Islamic Guidance Ministry. The Foreign Ministry was said to have a division to manage revivalists that was headed by President Rafsanjani's younger brother. "This is an attack being waged from inside our countries, which is not as easy to stop as, say, an Iranian invasion of the Gulf," another official explained.

Across the Red Sea, in Saudi Arabia, the conservative Wahhabi regime enforces the *Sharia* by beheading murderers, traitors, and adulterers, and amputating the hands of thieves. But that isn't conservative enough for several underground radical groups that want to end the monarchy's ties with the United States and its tacit live-and-let-live attitude toward Israel. On November 20, 1979, militants made headlines around the world by taking over the Grand Mosque in Mecca, the birthplace of Muhammad and therefore the holiest place in Islam. The attack touched off fear that the royal family itself was in danger. King Khalid proved that he was in command of the situation by having sixty-three people decapitated for their role in the affair.

Yet revivalist pressure has been relentless. Pro-Iranian Shiite terrorists were believed responsible for bombing a Saudi embassy vehicle in Ankara in January 1990 and for the murder of three Saudi diplomats in Bangkok the following month. The attacks were part of a vendetta following the execution of sixteen Kuwaitis in 1989 for their involvement in bombings that took place in Mecca during that year's religious pilgrimage.

If revivalists ever do stage a successful coup in Saudi Arabia, they will inherit a country well stocked with modern arms. Riyadh's price for an open oil spigot, allegiance to the West, and opposition to Saddam Hussein and the mullahs in Teheran has been access to up-to-date weapons. With one very important exception, all of them have been supplied by the West. The exception, though, is an extremely important one: the CSS-2. Unlike Libya, Saudi Arabia was able to buy thirty of the weapons from China. With a range of up to 2,200 miles, CSS-2s would make attractive prizes for militants who staged a successful coup and who wanted to attack Israel, Turkey, or Egypt. The missiles are attended by Chinese technicians. There are also persistent rumors that nuclear warheads, also supplied by China, could be flown into nearby bunkers but kept under Chinese lock and key.

As important as the missiles are, their reported $3 billion price tag was small compared with the whole defense bill run up by the kingdom during the Iran-Iraq war: $44.3 billion, or almost $2 billion more than even Saddam Hussein spent. Most of it went to buy not only the CSS-2s, but also 8 frigates and a support ship from France, 318 fighters, trainers, and helicopters from Great Britain, 187 antiship missiles from Italy, and 3 AWACS and 60 F-15s from the United States. There would be a follow-up order for 72 more F-15s, plus $7.2 billion for Panavia Tornado strike fighters, Hawk trainers, and helicopters.

But by far the biggest Saudi expenditure went for the quiet construction of what amounts to an advanced, surrogate U.S. military facility that is so tailored to meet U.S. requirements that American aircraft staged from it with no trouble during Desert Shield and Desert Storm. In return for letting the Saudis buy the AWACS, they agreed to provide the United States with an elaborate, state-of-the-art forward base holding scattered but highly integrated air, missile, naval, and command facilities that replicated, and in some cases surpassed, the prototypes at home. King Khalid Military City, built in secret in the desert, is a huge military oasis complete with missile silos and nuclear-bomb-proof underground command bunkers.

The quiet conservatism used by the Saudis to acquire their weapons was matched by the way they used oil revenues to project their influence. In Afghanistan, for example, Riyadh backed at least one victorious Islamic guerrilla army, the Sunni Ittehad-i-Islami, in its fight to control Kabul. An opposing faction, the Shiite Hezb-i-Wahadat, was bankrolled by Teheran. To take another example, it also bowed to U.S. prodding by discreetly paying Syria about $2 billion for the armored division Damascus sent to fight Iraq in the Persian Gulf War.

The Saudis, in fact, had become the banker for several Muslim superweapon purchases. They lavished $26 billion on Iraq, including more than $1 billion for the Condor-2 program. They also financed the early stages of Pakistan's nuclear weapons program.


Saddam Hussein, bloodied but not beaten in his war with the coalition, emerged from the conflict determined to pick up where he left off before the hostilities began, at least in the view of the CIA. "Saddam still has significant residual programs in all four areas of weapons of mass destruction," Robert Gates told the Comstock Club in Sacramento, California, in December 1992. "And he will continue to pursue these programs regardless of the expense and regardless of the state of U.N. sanctions and inspections." The CIA Director went on to say that U.N. inspectors had forced the Iraqis to admit to having at least 150,000 chemical warfare munitions, not the 20,000 originally claimed by Baghdad, and that it had nuclear scientists and technicians "more than enough to reconstitute a weapons program." Gates added that Iraq may have enough fissile material to make a nuclear weapon in five to seven years if U.N. inspections and sanctions end. Other estimates had it that it would take Iraq only a matter of weeks to produce some biological weapons and months to field chemical weapons.

What lay in back of Gates's mind was an understanding that, irrespective of how much of Iraq's superweapon equipment had been neutralized by coalition bombs and U.N. blowtorches, the knowledge of how to reconstitute the programs—collect more pieces and put them together again—would remain after the last inspector had departed.

Western hopes to the contrary, several of Saddam's neighbors came out of the conflict with deeply ambivalent feelings about the dictator. While he had made an egregious mistake by invading Kuwait, and was certainly a source of constant worry for some of them, he also emerged from the conflict in some degree as a hero. It was hard to feel sorry for the sybaritic Kuwaitis. But beyond that, whatever destruction the invasion had caused Saddam, it remained that he had been the one to stand up to the West as an independent Arab. He had had the courage to push for an all-out effort to get the only weapons the West truly respected. And, when all was said and done, the only ballistic missiles ever to strike Tel Aviv and Haifa had been his. No wonder that in January 1993, even Egypt responded to George Bush's Tomahawk missile attack against the Zaafaraniya nuclear equipment plant in Baghdad by indicating that it amounted to an unnecessary and gratuitous whipping of an Arab who was already on his knees. In fact, several Arab leaders, including those with relatively close ties to the United States, worried that the attack and the continued bleeding of Iraq by U.N. sanctions would only make a hero out of Saddam in the eyes of the revivalists. Yet being on his knees is exactly where at least two of Saddam Hussein's immediate neighbors wanted him.

Since the entire Syrian Army could be run for a year on a lot less than the $2 billion Damascus was given from the Wahhabi war chest during the Gulf War, it is reasonable to suppose that Hafez al-Assad put the excess funds into still more weaponry for an already swollen war machine. Given Syria's ancient animosity toward Iraq and its hatred for Israel, that would not have displeased King Fahd and his council of ministers.

On war day, Hafez al-Assad's conventional forces consisted of an estimated 404,000 troops, 4,350 tanks, 558 combat aircraft, and a dozen deep-water naval vessels, five of which were diesel submarines. The Syrian 9th Armored Division, which was dispatched to Saudi Arabia, used the same T-72 main battle tanks that its Iraqi opponents had, since both nations had been clients of the Kremlin. With the exception of more than sixty French Gazelle helicopters, the entire arsenal was provided by the

Soviet Union, Czechoslovakia, Poland, and China. Not content with hand-me-downs, however, the Syrians bought thirty-eight new high-speed, high-altitude MIG-25 interceptor and reconnaissance aircraft from the Soviets in 1980 and, starting in 1987, between sixty and eighty MIG-29s. They also owned a minimum of 200 surface-to-surface tactical missiles, including Frogs, Scud Bs and Cs, and Sepal cruise missiles.

But Assad, who tacitly believed—incorrectly—that Israel would never come to terms with the Arabs unless they could match it qualitatively, also pursued higher-tech conventional weapons and some that were highly unconventional. In 1988, his attempt to buy 300-mile-range SS-23 ballistic missiles from the Soviet Union on credit was turned down by a cash-hungry Kremlin. A year later, requests for other sophisticated arms, including SA-10 and SA-11 antiaircraft missiles, ran headlong into Gorbachev's efforts to shed his country's pariah status in the West and seek political and economic support there.

China, however, had no such compunctions, and neither did North Korea. In July 1988, Beijing agreed to sell Syria at least twenty-four of its newly developed M-9 ballistic missiles, causing deep apprehension in Israel. The M-9 has a range of 375 miles, which covers all of Israel and most of Iraq. It is also twice as accurate as any Scud and, because it is propelled by solid fuel, can be erected and fired in half an hour. Although $280 million of the M-9's development cost had been advanced by Damascus, vigorous U.S. opposition to the sale seemed at least to delay the arrival of the finished goods, but not the technology to build it. In November 1991, for example, Secretary of State James Baker returned from Beijing to announce that "clear gains in the fields of proliferation and trade" had been made as a result of pressure put on the Chinese. This, he added, meant that no M-9s would be sent to Syria. M-9 tractor-erector-launchers were subsequently spotted in Syria, but the missiles themselves could not be found by U.S. spy satellites. Since the vehicles are useless without their deadly cargoes, however, it was reasonable to suppose that one way or another the missiles would eventually make it to their launchers. One plausible way would be for China to sell Syria the technical wherewithal—software—to make the missiles themselves, thereby living up to the letter of its agreement with the United States while effectively making the sale anyway.

At the same time, North Korea reportedly sold Syria the hard stuff: 120 homemade, 360-mile-range Scud Cs, at an estimated cost of $500 million (or 25 percent of the Saudi gift). While inferior to the M-9, the advanced Scud still makes an attractive terror weapon for use against large population centers. A first installment was shipped to Syria in February 1992 through Iran's port at Bandar Abbas and then by air. The freighter carrying the missiles, the *Dae Hung Ho*, managed to evade reconnaissance satellites and slip through a net of U.S. Navy F-14 fighters and P-3 reconnaissance aircraft, helicopters, and surface vessels. If there was ever a doubt about what the *Dae Hung Ho* carried, it was dispelled that August when two of the Scud Cs were tested. Both China and North Korea have also helped the Syrians set up two of their own missile production factories, one outside Hama, the other near Aleppo.*

Chemical agents, a likely payload for Syrian missiles, are abundant. Damascus received its first chemical weapons, in the form of artillery shells, from Egypt in the early 1970s when both countries were allied against Israel. By the mid-1980s it was receiving precursors and related technology from the usual suspects: Germany, France, Austria, Switzerland, and the Netherlands. Many of the chemical brokerage houses that helped the Syrians start their own "pesticide" and "pharmaceutical" operations performed the identical service for the Iraqis.

France, which had a special relationship with the Levant through the colonial period and then under a League of Nations mandate, has been Syria's chief supplier. It has generally adhered to the guidelines of the Missile Technology Control Regime and the Nuclear Suppliers Group, which was started in 1978 to control the export of nuclear "trigger" technology.† But there was no such international agreement on the prohibition of chemical precursors until the so-called Australia Group finalized a list of them in late 1991 and ratified it the following June (after stiff opposition from France and Great Britain).‡ In the mean-

---

*At the time the Scud Cs were shipped to Syria, North Korea was putting the finishing touches on a missile with nearly twice the Scud's range: a 600-mile-range IRBM code-named Nodong-1. Early indications were that Libya, for one, was interested in the weapon. ("North Korea Ready to Begin Flight Testing New Ballistic Missile," *Aerospace Daily*, March 16, 1992, and "Libya May Buy N. Korean Missiles," *The Washington Times*, June 4, 1991.)
†The NSG, or the London Suppliers Group, as it is also called, was Belgium, Canada, Czechoslovakia, France, Germany, Italy, Japan, the Netherlands, Poland, Sweden, Switzerland, the United States, the United Kingdom, and the Soviet Union.
‡The Australia Group was started to identify and curtail chemical precursors that could be significant for weapons development and to limit their export. Twenty nations were signatories to the agreement, which was itself meant only as an interim measure until a Chemical Weapons Convention could be signed. That happened late in 1992. The signatories were Australia, Austria, Belgium, Canada, Denmark, France, Germany, Greece, Ireland, Italy, Japan, Luxembourg, the Netherlands, New Zealand, Norway, Portugal, Spain, Switzerland, the United Kingdom, and the United States.

time, France turned a blind eye to the export of chemical precursors to Syria because it didn't want to act unilaterally and in the process lose a lucrative market. As was the case with German exports to Iraq, salesmen and licensing officials in France who knew where their products were going simply chose to look the other way and think happy thoughts.*

"Every day I sign off on export licenses and I wonder whether I have not just signed my resignation," one French licensing official admitted. "In the area of chemical weapons manufacturing equipment, it is totally impossible to distinguish between civilian and military end-use. The equipment is strictly identical."

Syria is now believed to have at least three chemical and one biological warfare production sites. They are located, respectively, just north of Damascus, near Homs, in Hama, and at Cerin. The chemical facilities can make several tons of chemical agents a year, including mustard gas, sarin, tabun, and the even more lethal VX agents. Israeli intelligence has estimated that Damascus has several thousand standard iron bombs filled mostly with sarin and up to 100 such warheads for use on its ballistic missiles. Some of these are in at least two underground storage facilities: one near Safiyah in the northeast, and another along the Damascus–Homs road.

Like Iraq, Syria has had no qualms about using its deadly chemical weapons at home, though it did so against Islamic militants rather than Kurds. Following violent demonstrations sparked by the Muslim Brotherhood in Hama in January and February 1982, Syrian Army units sealed off the city. Seventy rebels were reported to have been collectively executed outside the municipal hospital. Meanwhile, other army units apparently went to every house suspected of holding insurgents and pumped in cyanide gas, killing all of the occupants the way exterminators fumigate insects. On February 22, the government broadcast a report saying that security forces had taken fierce reprisals against the Brotherhood and its sympathizers "which stopped them breathing

---

*Moscow, on the other hand, seems to have steadfastly refused to provide chemical warfare equipment. This crystallized in March 1988 when Colonel General Vladimir Pikalov, the commander of Soviet chemical warfare forces, was asked in Damascus for SS-23 missiles that were to be specifically loaded with chemical agents. Pikalov returned three months later and not only rejected the request for the missiles but sternly rebuked the Syrians, saying that his country was not in the business of proliferating chemical weapons. (Kenneth R. Timmerman, "Weapons of Mass Destruction: The Cases of Iran, Syria, and Libya," Los Angeles: Simon Wiesenthal Center, 1992, p. 60.)

forever." That was Hafez al-Assad's way of dealing with revival-ists.*

There have also been indications that Syria is working on its own nascent nuclear weapons program, partly through the kind of patient networking used by Iraq, but also with direct support from China. In February 1992 it signed a nuclear safeguards agreement with the International Atomic Energy Agency, paving the way for it to buy two 24-megawatt research reactors from China. As usual, the package included the training of Syrian scientists, engineers, and technicians on Chinese reactors. The purchase was subsequently postponed. Yet Assad remains interested in nuclear weapons and in providing his scientists with the long-term wherewithal to produce them, either alone or with an ally.

If Syria itself isn't cause enough for deep concern in Israel and the West because of Assad's political and military ambitions, its close relationship with Iran is doubly vexing. Syria backed Iran in its war with Iraq. It has also allowed large caches of Iranian small arms and ammunition to be delivered to Teheran-backed Hezbollah terrorists in Lebanon. And Iran has repaid the favors. It is believed to have facilitated the passage of, and perhaps even paid for, the North Korean–built Scud Cs to Syria.

The odd affinity between secular Syrian Sunnis and revivalist Iranian Shiites, between stringently secular politicians and revolutionary revivalists, is potentially the most dangerous in the Middle East. By the time the smoke settled in the Persian Gulf War, Syria and Iran were showing unmistakable signs of political and military collaboration. Like a worldly suitor pursuing a marriage of convenience, relatively powerful Iran was courting ambitious Syria with promises on a grand order. And the indications were that it could make good on its word since China and Pakistan were Iran's major benefactors.

---

*If Assad has been willing to exterminate opponents at home, he has been equally willing to do so abroad. Syria has been implicated in the attack on the U.S. Marine barracks in Beirut in 1983, which resulted in 241 deaths; in the Rome and Vienna airport attacks two years later in which 23 were killed; and in the motorized hang glider incident in Israel the same year in which an Israeli Army captain was killed. In addition, Assad has sheltered and nurtured a viper's nest of murderous extremist groups, both in Syria itself and in Lebanon. They have included the Popular Front for the Liberation of Palestine, General Command; the Abu Nidal Organization; the Popular Struggle Front; the Kurdish Workers Party (which commits murder and mayhem in Iraq); the Armenian Secret Army for the Liberation of Armenia; the Japanese Red Army; and the Palestine Islamic Jihad (which claimed responsibility for attacking the Israeli tour bus in Egypt).

Iran's way of trying to protect itself from the United States and Turkey—it sees the government in Ankara not only as an old adversary but as Washington's Muslim toady—is to forge an Islamic shield across Central Asia, the northern edge of the Persian empire's traditional sphere of influence. The "Caspian Council," which Iran started after the breakup of the Soviet Union, links it with Turkmenia, Kazakhstan, Azerbaijan, and Russia in a clear attempt to cut out Turkey. This was followed by an agreement with the Afghan Mujahedeen and Farsi-speaking Tajikistanis to set up an association to "expand Farsi in the Asian states." Teheran also opened an embassy in Tajikistan and upgraded its mission to Azerbaijan. Syria's role in this is evidently to help protect Iran's western front against Israel and Iraq while the mullahs concentrate on the east. But the clerics in Teheran, led by the redoubtable Ali Akhbar Hashemi Rafsanjani, have a good deal more in mind than menacing Israel, fending off the United States and Turkey, and influencing other Muslim nations in the region. They are convinced that by virtue of their nation's size, location, history, resources, and the purity of its religion, it ought to be a major force within the entire Third World.

Rafsanjani is pursuing that course with a deftness that borders on brilliance. While maintaining strict adherence to the tenets of Islam, for example, he has liberalized life in the capital just enough so as not to make the place forbidding to foreigners, particularly to businessmen. The idea is to portray Iran as a country that adheres to its moralistic religious code while still maintaining an enlightened and growth-oriented political and economic atmosphere, as befits a great power.

Compared with the wrathful and vindictive Ayatollah Ruhollah Khomeini, who ruled by issuing streams of fearsome decrees from deep inside his secluded lair, Rafsanjani is a man of the world. He had his international coming-out party on September 1, 1992, when he flew to Jakarta in order to upstage other Third World leaders at the Non-Aligned Summit meeting. His pro-family, antifeminist speeches did not have the desired effect, however. He had a more receptive audience in Islamabad, where his visit occasioned the announcement of a strategic alliance between Iran and Pakistan in which the former would consider any attempt to destabilize the latter as an attack on itself and would act accordingly. This was greeted by cheering crowds and a barrage of flowers. Western observers, some of whom would shortly send detailed reports to intelligence services, also noted that the Iranian party included Akbar Torgan, the Defense Minister; Reza Amrollahi, the First Deputy President and head of the Atomic Energy Organization of Iran; five other officials from the agency, which is responsible for both the civilian and military nuclear programs; Major General Ali Shahbazi, head of the Joint Chiefs of Staff; and other high-ranking military men. Rafsanjani's comments to the Pakistani National Assembly, echoing vintage macho Islam, brought cheers and thumping.

Next, the Iranian Boeing 707 flew over the Himalayas to Beijing, where Rafsanjani again attracted world attention by signing an agreement with Premier Li Peng for the purchase of a 300-megawatt power reactor. Although the machine would take some time to deliver because several of its key components would have to be manufactured in Germany, Japan, and elsewhere, the deal was taken as another dangerous sign by an increasingly apprehensive United States.

Weapons, especially superweapons, are the critical element in Teheran's foreign policy equation because Iran cannot project its influence over such a large area without being able to use considerable force. The government emerged from its debilitating war with Iraq determined to rearm as quickly as possible. No sooner had the fighting stopped than Iran went on a massive weapons-buying binge, according to both French and Saudi intelligence sources. Between 1988 and 1992, it quietly committed more than $7 billion in rising oil revenues to stocking up on fighters, missiles, tanks, and nuclear weapons technology from China, Russia, eastern Europe, and North Korea.

China supplied seventy-two jet fighters and 200 T-72 tanks. It also negotiated for the sale of advanced M-9 missiles and shorter-range M-11s. North Korea sold the Iranians Scud Cs and offered Scud Ds. Russia and some former members of the Warsaw Pact contracted to ship the Iranians MIGs, Sukhois, and Backfire bombers as well as SAM-5, SAM-11, and SAM-13 advanced antiaircraft missiles that could be used to protect their other purchases from air attack. Much to the consternation of the United States, the Russians also contracted to sell Iran Kilo-class submarines for $250 million each. During the "Tanker War" in the mid-1980s Iran used mines and gunboats in an effort to interrupt the flow of Arab oil. They were not especially effective. But submarines are a different matter. The Russian subs, which are diesel-powered, quiet, and easy to operate, could have a decisive effect in stopping vessels carrying Arab oil or in attacking enemy warships. "A sub like that one can't be swept away as easily as a mine field," noted James A. McCoy, a former Royal

Navy frigate commander. "It changes the equation very significantly."*

Whatever else was in the overall equation, monetary concerns began to figure prominently. By August 1992, Iranian currency reserves were so stretched that one western European country recommended that letters of credit no longer be opened for Iranian businesses. Shades of Iraq.

In addition to the equipment being bought around the world during the beginning of the 1990s, there was already a mountain of conventional arms, in varying states of repair, left over from the Shah's own extensive acquisition program. By 1992, Iran owned more than 800 combat aircraft, including at least 100 that were among 132 planes of all types flown from Iraq to Iran for safekeeping during the Persian Gulf War and not returned. The American contributions included F-4E Phantoms and whatever was left of eighty F-14A Tomcats that were delivered just before the coup.† There were also four British-built frigates; a large number of U.S.-supplied antiaircraft missiles, and whatever remains of forty Chinese-made Scuds, many of which were used against Iraq. The nation's entire weapons bill was estimated by the CIA in 1992 to be $2 billion a year. That same year, however, Iran's parliament allocated almost $6 billion to rebuilding the nation's defenses alone.

But Iran's leaders believe that only superweapons can maintain their revolution and extend its influence. "We have learned," Rafsanjani said in 1991, "that preserving our independence and survival in this unsuitable international climate is not possible without science, technology, and the necessary tools." The tools, as usual, are poison gas, long-range ballistic missiles, and atomic bombs.

Iran has good reason to know how effective chemical weapons can

---

*Boris Yeltsin announced during a visit to Seoul in November 1992 that construction of nuclear submarines would end in Russia within three years. Although this was encouraging news, it was not quite all it seemed, since his country had scores of usable nuclear subs that were in mothballs. The statement also omitted the sort of diesels that were bought by Iran. ("Yeltsin Plans End to A-Sub Program," *The New York Times*, November 20, 1992.)

†Most of the Iraqi military planes were MIGs and Sukhoi fighter-bombers. They also might have included some Mirage F-1s and one or more of the dozen TU-16 bombers that were delivered beginning in 1973. The total also included several European and American airliners, which were incorporated into Iran's civil air system. All of the aircraft were valued at $1.2 billion and were confiscated, Teheran said, as reparations from the war with Iraq. ("Teheran to Seize the Planes Iraq Sent to Iran for Safety," *The New York Times*, July 31, 1992.)

Of the original number of Tomcats, two were lost in crashes and one was at Grumman for repairs at the time of the coup and was therefore not returned. At least seventeen of the remaining seventy-seven were cannibalized for parts to keep the other sixty flying. Tomcats rely on sophisticated avionics and are difficult to keep working properly.

be; it has been on the receiving end of poison gas attacks. Its untrained and unprotected irregulars and Revolutionary Guard Militia were hit by bombardments of chemical weapons during the war with Iraq. The army is also aware that chemical weapons can be effective psychologically as well as physically.* It has therefore produced limited quantities of its own chemical weapons—mainly mustard gas, the usual nerve agents, and hydrogen cyanide, at secret locations at Qazun, Al Razi, Bahshwir, and Damghan, east of Teheran. According to one British report, Damghan produces about five tons of nerve gas a month, some of which is then fitted into Scud B warheads. The Iranians also twice tried to buy biological agents without success.†

The Iranians also have firsthand experience with ballistic missiles as both targeteers and targets. They used substantial numbers of Russian- and Chinese-supplied Scud As and Bs against Iraq during the war of the cities and were reportedly producing their own version, called Iran-130, within a year of the end of hostilities. And not all of the Scud Cs they purchased from North Korea have gone to Syria. Iran is believed to have a substantial inventory of the weapons and tested one as late as the spring of 1991. The increasingly cordial relationship with China also led to discussions about buying M-9 technology, although there is no evidence that a deal was concluded.

China, in fact, was constantly pushing technological fixes rather than hardware on Iran. For one thing, it didn't want to get caught violating the Missile Technology Control Regime. For another, selling technology was more profitable than selling equipment. Combined, they led China to make a series of unconventional deals. China supplied Iran with several of its HQ-2 antiaircraft missiles along with a kit that converted them to short-range ballistic missiles. It also sold Iran two CSS-2s for "test and

---

*In *The Death Lobby*, Kenneth R. Timmerman described an Iranian video team's photographing the grisly effect of the attack on Halabja for use in training soldiers. The intention was to show them how despicable their opponents were. But the tape had a decidedly negative effect. "Instead of inciting young recruits to hate Saddam, it instilled in them a fear from which they never recovered. This was the awesome power of the Iraqi dictator. Confront him ye who dare." (Boston: Houghton Mifflin, 1991, p. 294.)

†They have shown a reluctance to use such weapons, however. Following a complaint by Iraq that Iran used chemical weapons against them, a U.N. inspection team visited the area in question in April and May 1987. It found no conclusive evidence that Iranian forces gassed the Iraqis and, to the contrary, reported that it suspected the Iraqis had been hit by their own mustard gas after a sudden shift in the wind direction. ("Weapons of Mass Destruction," p. 28.)

development" purposes that allowed the Iranians to familiarize themselves with the powerful missiles in preparation for component sales.

The warhead of choice for Iran's eventual long-range ballistic missile is atomic: the Islamic bomb. The search for nuclear arms was begun in the 1960s by the Shah, who planned to spend as much as $30 billion by the end of the century on twenty nuclear power plants that could have yielded plutonium for weapons. A large nuclear power plant near Bushehr, in the south, was started by a Siemens subsidiary in 1975 and abandoned four years later, when the revolutionary mullahs decided that nuclear energy was un-Islamic. Leaving nothing to chance, however, Iraq attacked the facility by air at least six times in 1987. The war with Iraq had in the meantime changed Iranian leaders' minds about the uses of atomic energy for both peace and war. "Iran cannot ignore the reality of nuclear power in the modern world," Rafsanjani noted in 1989.

No indeed. An intelligence analyst studying Iranian efforts to acquire nuclear-related equipment and technology around the world might liken the task to watching a pattern emerge after enough dots are connected on a stick picture. Pakistan was asked for uranium gas ultracentrifuge technology. South Africa was approached for hundreds of tons of uranium yellowcake feedstock and a small amount of low-enriched uranium. A uranium dioxide conversion plant, a fuel fabrication plant, a heavy water pilot plant, and fuel cells for reprocessing plutonium were ordered from Argentina. India was asked for a 10-megawatt research reactor. China was contacted for calutrons, for 27- and 30-megawatt research reactors, and for the power reactor. Russia was offered a contract for four of its own VVER-440 power reactors. Cuba was asked to sign a VVER-440 reactor technology agreement by which it would share data with Iran. And Germany, Spain, and Brazil were asked to complete Bushehr. The pattern leaves no doubt that Iran is determined to establish its own uranium fuel cycle in order to produce a bomb.

Understanding Iranian intentions, several nations declined such lucrative deals, evidently because unfavorable publicity was not worth the money. A request that Siemens restart construction of the two huge 1,300–megawatt reactors at Bushehr, for instance, was rejected by Germany. An offer to buy enriched uranium from France was also turned down. Brazil refused to sell Iran nuclear technology it had developed with Siemens. Argentina decided not to sell Iran the $18 million worth of nuclear equipment after the United States conveyed its displeasure over the deals and offered its own financial incentives. Even India, bending to intense U.S. pressure, withdrew an offer to sell Iran a research reactor.

The tenacious Iranians therefore looked elsewhere and found not only reactors but, more important, a willingness to help them learn the nuclear arts. The Chinese and Russians had no apparent qualms about selling that vital component to Iran, and neither did Pakistan. In 1990, China and Iran signed a ten-year nuclear cooperation agreement in which Beijing agreed not only to build the research reactors and supply calutrons but to teach the Iranians how to operate them. Much of that training would go on at Iran's nuclear fuel cycle research center at Isfahan. This was followed two years later by the sale of the promised power reactor and yet another technology-sharing pact. The Iranians, banking on everyone's having a price, also entered into a nuclear cooperation agreement with Moscow in 1991; one that brought reactors to Iran and Iranian scientists to Russia. And as part of a wide-ranging agreement for scientific cooperation, Pakistan has agreed to train Iranian nuclear physicists at its Institute for Nuclear Science and Technology.

According to the People's Mojahedin of Iran (PMI), a leading organization opposed to the country's Islamic government, there is already a growing nuclear cadre of 3,000 personnel at work at Isfahan. A second, top-secret center is located at Moallem Kelaieh, near the Caspian Sea. This is a weapons design center run by the nuclear unit of the Revolutionary Guards on a $200-million-a-year budget. The Defense Ministry contains its own nuclear weapons division. All three organizations are under the direct control of Rafsanjani's office. In 1987, the Atomic Energy Organization's budget was $20 million, according to a PMI spokesman. Its 1992 budget, he added, was at least $240 million. While U.S. intelligence would provide no such data, at least publicly, it did conclude in a National Intelligence Estimate in 1991 that Iran's interest in nuclear energy went well beyond peaceful purposes. Particularly disquieting were remarks by Deputy President Ataollah Mohajerani calling for an Islamic bomb. "Because the enemy [Israel] has nuclear facilities, the Muslim states, too, should be equipped with the same capacity. I am not talking about one Muslim country," he added, "but, rather, the entirety of Muslim states."

At least one other Muslim state, Iran's deadly enemy, Iraq, has also helped Teheran's nuclear weapons program, however inadvertently. During the coalition air attacks against Iraq in January 1991, Hussain al Sharistani, the nuclear physicist who was jailed and tortured for alleged "cooperation" with Iran, managed to escape and later turned up in Iran. He no doubt found a job.

All of the media attention paid to Iran's nuclear efforts finally led to an IAEA inspection in February 1992 and to yet another embarrassment for the atomic watchdogs. That month four senior staff members led by Jon Jannekens, the agency's top inspector, spent less than a week in Iran. At the end of the short visit Jannekens came to a sweeping conclusion. He blamed rumors of Iran's chase after nuclear weapons on sloppy news reporting. "We have reviewed some of the media coverage of the activities alleged to take place in Iran," he said, "and we are very pleased to confirm that there doesn't seem to be a shred of evidence of any of these misleading representations." Period. Unfortunately, it was Jannekens, not the press, who had been misled. The site the team had been allowed to inspect "with no restriction, no limitations on access" turned out not to be the site they had asked to see.

Iran's latest Islamic nemesis, Turkey, is also looking covetously to the east, where it sees more than fifty million Turkic-speaking and ethnically related peoples spread from the Golden Horn to the Gobi Desert.

So while Koran-toting Iranian evangelists ply the region to spread Islam in the traditional way—by building small mosques, reciting stories from the life of Muhammad, and exhorting the faithful to pray—the Turks plan to launch a satellite called Turksat, which is designed to broadcast Turkish television from the Adriatic to China. While Saudi Arabia donates a million copies of the holy book to the area, TRT, the Turkish state communication network, plans to use an existing satellite, Intelsat VI, to beam eighty-nine hours of news and entertainment a week directly at the six former Soviet republics it feels closest to: Azerbaijan, Turkmenistan, Uzbekistan, Tajikistan, Kirghizstan, and Kazakhstan. Although these were never part of the Ottoman Empire, schoolchildren in Turkey are taught that all Turks come from the plains of Central Asia—from where modern Turks emigrated more than 1,000 years ago. Seen in that light, the artificial frontiers erected by Stalin were merely temporary barriers.

"We are at an intersection of great regional events, including conflict and opposing tendencies in the new world order," said a Turkish Foreign Ministry official. "The disintegration of communism has brought a greater threat of Islamic fundamentalism [to Central Asia]." Ataturk abolished the caliphate in 1924 and Turkey has strictly separated mosque and state ever since. The Turks, determined to keep it that way throughout what they see as the eastern segment of their new sphere of influence, are therefore on a collision course with Iran.*

With 647,000 men under arms, more than 3,700 tanks, nearly 500 modern, mostly U.S. combat aircraft, and a growing fleet of indigenously built German submarines and other modern naval vessels, and with its own F-16 plant and German U-209 submarine manufacturing facility, Turkey is one of the most powerful and best-equipped nations in the area.

The Kremlin's de facto abandonment of its six former Islamic republics has left a vast, volatile region filled with unsophisticated peoples who now own some of the most sophisticated, and certainly the deadliest, weapons in the world. Nomads and their camels, wanderers across the steppes for untold centuries, pass within sight of laser complexes that could bounce beams of directed energy off the moon. Cheese, live chickens, and melons are still sold, as they have always been, in oblasts that now contain ballistic missile silos and tunnels for testing atomic bombs.

The arms and the systems that support them are the coin of the realm in an area convulsing with suddenly unrestrained political, religious, and ethnic animosity. To be sure, the weapons and facilities are attractive prizes for would-be buyers from far-off places. But they are most likely to be used to settle old scores or create new ones closer to home as old-guard Communists clash with their Muslim rivals, battles for regional independence erupt, and borders are adjusted and readjusted.

Although Afghanistan is anything but a part of the former Soviet Union, it illustrates the true nature of the situation. In 1979, Soviet tanks rolled over the frontier toward Kabul, dismissing the Communist-led Afghan army as being incapable of battling rebel forces. Ten years later, the same mountain men earned the distinction of becoming the world's most prolific missile launchers by firing 1,540 Scuds at their own countrymen during the civil war that followed the Soviet departure. That is about as many V-2s as Hitler fired at England.

Whatever else the old Soviet Union left behind when it evacuated

*The western segment consists of the so-called Black Sea nations. In the spring of 1992, Turkey succeeded in getting Azerbaijan, Armenia, Russia, Ukraine, Moldavia, Bulgaria, and Romania to agree to participate in a regional economic plan in which it seemed destined to play a central role.

its southern Islamic belt, there was an abundance of major weapons facilities and installations to support or complement them.

Siting weapons development and test centers far from population centers (including the capitals where the politicians themselves lived) seemed prudent when the atomic age began. No one wanted a runaway chain reaction, an accidental detonation, or an errant ICBM to kill hundreds or thousands of the citizens the weapons were supposed to protect. Besides, secluded facilities in far-off places were considered easier to keep secret than those in areas swarming with people. That is why the United States tested nuclear weapons in the Pacific atolls when it could and still tests missiles in the vast reaches of the Pacific. It is why the Soviet Union used the barren reaches of Semipalatinsk to test its own warheads and fired its long-range missiles from Tyuratam in Kazakhstan to the Sea of Okhotsk and Kamchatka. France used both the Sahara and the Pacific for its nuclear tests and China used and continues to use Xingjiang.

In addition, finished weapons were dispersed to outlying areas, not only to have them closer to their targets, but also to spread them out enough so they would not all fall victim to a single localized attack. Aside from overhead spying, the occasional penetration by an agent, or the divulging of data by a disaffected insider, the system worked reasonably well so long as tight control was kept over the far-flung sites.

But the dispersal system contained a paradox. The very factor that kept civilians safe and the sites relatively secret—their remoteness— also made them particularly vulnerable to seizure when control was loose or lost altogether. Loose control is what could have done in the French in Algeria and the Chinese in Xingjiang. Absolute loss of political and military control by the former Soviet Union in the fractured regions along its southern flank, from Irkutsk to Novokazalinsk, created the dangerous vacuum that Iran, Saudi Arabia, Turkey, and a slew of local despots and terrorists want to fill. Missile manufacturing centers and test sites, power and research reactors, a fast breeder, chemical weapons production and storage facilities, a plutonium storage plant, and assorted biological and nuclear weapons facilities that had been secure in the Soviet Union were suddenly exposed to large belligerent groups that coveted them for the advantage they would bring in wars that seemed inevitable. This, together with outright arms sales, has turned a key instrument of national security into a major source of international insecurity.

And while Moscow is justifiably concerned about Central Asia's volatility, it is also convinced that the three Slav republics—Russia, Ukraine, and Belarus—will be far better able to recover from their economic devastation without "the crushing burden" of Alexander II's everneedy Islamic acquisitions. Alexander Solzhenitsyn went so far as to say that if the non-Slav republics don't secede from the Commonwealth of Independent States on their own, they should in effect be shown the door. By 1990, when he made that suggestion, ethnic tensions were already running high from one end of Central Asia to the other. Racial animosity in the autonomous republic of Tuva, on the Mongolian border, sent Russians packing. Crimean Tatars accomplished the same thing by retaking from the Russians land they had long considered their own.

But if the ethnic Russians considered the Islamic republics to be a drain on their resources, the republics had their own smoldering grievances: persistent bigotry and economic repression. In 1988, on the eve of the great Soviet upheaval, the six Islamic republics had the lowest per capita income among all fifteen federated republics. This, too, created a deep hatred for the northerners. Whereas millions of Russians in Ukraine and Belarus are difficult to distinguish from the locals, they stand out in the Central Asian republics as a privileged, almost colonial elite the way the French stood apart in Indochina, North Africa, and the Levant. There has been little intermarriage and only a tiny minority of Russians speak local languages. Less than 1 percent of Russians speak Kazakh, for example, while 62 percent of Kazakhs speak Russian.

For their part, Slavs throughout the area have long since gotten the message, especially given animosities that linger from the days when the Soviet Army brutally fought Afghan Muslims. Since 1985, 800,000 people, most of them Russians, have left Uzbekistan. In 1992, at least 90,000 others fled Tajikistan, while 185,000 others pulled out of Kirghizstan between 1989 and 1992. The percentage of Slavs in all of the Islamic republics dropped steadily between 1979 and 1989. "When empires collapse," *The Economist* observed, "pity those children of the imperial power left under the falling masonry." The departing children were leaving a strategic black hole.

There were 104 SS-18s loaded with 1,040 warheads at two bases in Kazakhstan at the end of 1992. Just across the border with Russia, at Dombriatovskiy, there were 64 others, carrying 640 more warheads. Dombriatovskiy is so isolated that it can only be entered by passing through Kazakh territory. Tyuratam, also in Kazakhstan, is the size of Delaware and is therefore the largest space launch and missile test facility on Earth. It is the place where the Strategic Rocket Forces tested all of the country's ballistic missiles and trained missile crews. Tyuratam at one time employed 99,000 people, with the lowliest jobs—construction and maintenance—going to Central Asians. Not far from Tyuratam are the Dzhusaly and Novo-Kazalinsk missile and satellite tracking stations, both of which would be invaluable to any Muslim nation wanting to know when U.S., European, or Israeli reconnaissance satellites were passing overhead.

Sary Shagan, the antiballistic missile, laser, and early warning radar test center, is also in Kazakhstan. So is Semipalatinsk, the former Soviet Union's main nuclear weapons test site and the home of a nuclear weapon research center. Vozrozhdeniya Island, in what is left of the Aral Sea, and Akau are old biological warfare test sites.

Andreyevka, about fifty miles from the Chinese border near the Dzungarian Gate, is thought to be a major military intelligence station that can intercept satellite communication and maneuver spacecraft. The Russian Navy's own communication intercept facility is at nearby Niko-layevka. Ust-Kamenogorsk, in the same region, is the home of the Ul-binskiy Metallurgical Kombinat, which supplied beryllium and zirconium to the old Soviet nuclear weapons and nuclear power complex. A fire and explosion there in 1990, which caused widespread pollution, set off mass demonstrations by the inhabitants of the area and demands that eastern Kazakhstan be declared an "ecological disaster zone." Aktau, called Shev-chenko in the Soviet era, is the site of the Prikaspiy uranium mining facil-ity, an experimental fast-breeder reactor, and even a plutonium stockpile.

In January 1992, following a demand by Yeltsin that all former Soviet military personnel swear allegiance to Moscow, Kazakh President Nursultan Nazarbayev threatened to form an independent armed force, while one of his deputies announced plans to sell some of the republic's arms abroad. The previous summer, he had also made it clear that he considered the Tyuratam rocket facility a "great asset for us," meaning for Kazakhstan. In February 1992, 2,000 soldiers rioted for three days at Tyuratam over poor food and working conditions, burning barracks in which four soldiers perished. A new draft policy that stopped recruiting from areas outside Kazakhstan was started immediately.

Xingjiang is part of the Urumqi Military Region, which includes all of Xingjiang and western Tibet. The province contains the Haiyan nuclear plant at Koko Nor, which has developed and assembled 400 to 500 nuclear weapons. It also has the 62,000-square-mile Lop Nor nuclear weapons test facility—the largest such site on Earth—and Urumqi itself, where uranium is enriched and shaped for weapons use. Beijing is so concerned about a Muslim revisionist independent kingdom that it has relocated substantial numbers of Han Chinese soldiers to the area and has made a real effort to promote Turkic Chinese into the officer corps.

The effort has had mixed results at best. Turkic officers are referred to as "jackals" by their neighbors and a persistent ethnic war of independence rumbles along, sometimes violently. Suspected Muslim separatists blew up a bus during the February 1992 Lunar New Year festival, killing as many as six people. Both Muslims and Han Chinese in Urumqi speak openly about how the disintegration of the Soviet Union and the consequent liberation of its Central Asian republics have given heart to the area's radical Turkic Uighurs, who want to break away from China.

"This is East Turkistan, not China," one Uighur insisted. "China is Beijing, Shanghai, Hangzhou. But Xingjiang is East Turkistan."

"We're all one big family," said another, referring to Xingjiang and Kazakhstan, Kirghizstan, and Tajikistan, with which it shares a fluid border. "We should stick together."

The members of the Islamic family share something else besides religion, cultural identity, and increasingly militant nationalism. They now know how to make atomic bombs and, between them, easily have the wherewithal to do so. And like their counterparts from the Maghreb to Mosul, they will eventually have delivery systems as well.

By the summer of 1992, it began to dawn on Spanish, French, and Italian defense officials that, for the first time, their cities were within striking range of bombers and missiles coming from a new direction: North Africa and the Middle East. They were so apprehensive about the potential for an attack from those directions, in fact, that they began to quietly create a European ballistic missile defense strategy that would be linked to the region's new air defense system. A possible missile attack from Iran, Iraq, or Syria, or an attack by air-refueled Libyan fighter-bombers crossing the Mediterranean to hit targets in the south of France, was particularly worrisome. It would not have escaped the generals who were responsible for protecting France against a Libyan bombing raid that the attacking planes, Mirage 5Ds, were made in France.

# 11

## INDIA AND PAKISTAN:
## OUR GOD
## CAN LICK YOUR GOD

In mid-October 1984, ten years after India startled the world by exploding an atomic bomb, Pakistani intelligence learned—perhaps from its great friend CIA Director William Casey—that India was about to launch a surprise attack against Pakistan's own nuclear research facility at Kahuta. The installation is situated in the rugged foothills of the Himalayas just to the east of Islamabad in an area that was called the Northwest Frontier Agency when Pakistan was part of India and India was under British rule. The region is a large arrowhead pointed at the belly of the Central Asian steppes, Russia, and far western China. Afghanistan and the fabled Khyber Pass lie to the west and Kashmir to the east. This geography makes the area ripe for turbulence and intrigue.

The activities at Kahuta are driven by Pakistan's long, secret, almost frenzied pursuit of atomic weapons to offset India's early lead. The effort has involved intense research, widespread and precisely orchestrated smuggling, vast sums of money, and help from a variety of nefarious suppliers, some of them nations. Without its own nuclear weapons to offset India's, the reasoning has gone, Pakistan would forever be at its rival's mercy. Every disagreement, every border incident, every clash for whatever reason—and certainly the disputed Kashmir region is always an excuse for such confrontations—would happen in the shadow of India's ultimate weapon: nuclear bombs. That was intolerable. And so Kahuta, the nuclear Shangri-La, had to be protected at all costs.

Pakistan therefore sent an explicit message to New Delhi through diplomatic channels to then Prime Minister Indira Gandhi. If India attacked Kahuta on October 21 as planned, the Pakistanis warned, there would be a reprisal that would cost them dearly. Fighter-bombers would strike every nuclear installation in India, civilian as well as military. These included five power reactors that generated electricity, four research reactors used in India's nuclear weapons program, and a spent-fuel reprocessing facility. All ten installations were near the heavily populated cities of Bombay and Madras and along the Ganges River. Most of them were in Bombay's northern suburbs, at the Bhabha Atomic Research Center. The consequences of such an attack were readily apparent to the Indians. Massive amounts of radiation pouring out of shattered reactors and nuclear storage sites would contaminate vast areas. Indians would die by the thousands. Others would suffer the effects of radiation poisoning for years, if not for untold generations. The Indians backed down.*

Nor would 1984 be the final chapter in the saga. Over the next eight years, either outright nuclear competition or tensions over Hindu-Muslim flare-ups, first in Kashmir and then throughout India and Pakistan, would sound the nuclear alarm. Even in the months after Indira Gandhi reined in her military, there were rumors of yet another raid. The rumors were spurred by Mrs. Gandhi's assertion that Pakistan's nuclear weapons program required that a "new dimension" be added to India's defense posture. Her own assassination at the hands of Sikh extremists and her bodyguard provided only a short respite. In 1985, Mrs. Gandhi's son and successor, Rajiv, hinted several times at new developments in India's nuclear arsenal. Tit followed tat that year. In June, Rajiv told a Paris interviewer that India might have already made components for nuclear weapons. In July, ABC and NBC News reported on ominous developments in the Pakistani weapons program, including reports that it had tested the conventional explosives necessary to detonate a bomb.

In August, the Indian Atomic Energy Commission chairman an-

---

*Ironically, they got a taste of the consequences of such an attack when poison chemicals were inadvertently released at the Union Carbide pesticide plant at Bhopal that December. More than 2,000 people died in neighborhoods near the factory, while an estimated 200,000 were injured, many of them critically.

nounced the start-up of a huge 100-megawatt research reactor at the Bhabha center with a none-too-subtle declaration that the reactor could produce plutonium. Attempts to lessen the tension ultimately led to an agreement in December between Gandhi and Zia ül-Haq, Pakistan's President, that they would not attack each other's nuclear facilities. (The document would not be formalized until 1991.)

Meanwhile, one close call followed another. In November 1986, half of the Indian Army went on maneuvers called Operation Brass Tacks. Fearing that the hour of final conflict was at hand, the jittery Pakistanis launched their own massive mobilization. And to up the ante, they "cold tested" a nuclear device to assure themselves it would work if the Indians attacked. The following March, with the near-war fresh in his mind, Zia ul-Haq appeared to confirm that Pakistan had all the components needed for nuclear weapons. Both nations moved to the brink again in the spring of 1990, again over Kashmir, and yet again in December 1992, when the sacking of the Ayoda temple by Indian Hindu militants followed news reports that Pakistan had planned to use nuclear weapons against India in 1990.

The Indian subcontinent is the most dangerous place on Earth. It is the incubator of racial and religious hatred that is more virulent and persistent than any biological epidemic (though it, too, could be unleashed in a war). The slum of every city of consequence is a purgatory in which rampaging Hindu and Muslim fundamentalists search for their opposite number and kill them. The race for superweapons is therefore driven as much by sheer hatred as by geopolitical considerations. While both sides have invented elaborate excuses for developing nuclear weapons—strategic deterrence, for example—their real purpose is genocide. The Indians and the Pakistanis fundamentally despise each other. The mutual contempt is so deep that even television programming is affected. In March 1993, a thirty-nine-part series on the Bible running on Indian television was interrupted after the ninth episode by death threats made against television station employees. Muslim militants issued the warnings because they believe that mortals should not play the roles of revered biblical figures like Moses and Jesus. The series eventually resumed. The Bharatiya Janata Party, which preaches hatred of Muslims and favors India's formally declaring itself a nuclear-weapons state for reasons of prestige, has gone from near obscurity to threatening the long-ruling Congress Party itself. And far from harboring only Indian rednecks, it attracts large numbers of middle-class professionals. "A dirty fish in a big pond can dirty the water," one BJP supporter said of the Muslim minority. Even in the polite salons along Washington's Embassy Row, the diplomats who represent both nations make remarks that betray the depth of their hatred. Pakistani Ambassador Abida Hussain asks guests what the difference is between India and Pakistan. "In Pakistan, we worship one God," she answers rhetorically. "In India, they worship many gods, some with nine arms and legs."

At the same time, the intensely emotional religious animosity has a hard-edged political component. Had the Indians done to Kahuta what the Israelis had done to the Osirak reactor at Tuwaitha in 1981, and had Islamabad retaliated as it threatened, pressure on the Gandhis to finish off Pakistan with nuclear weapons once and for all would have been enormous. And if the subcontinent had become the scene of the planet's first nuclear war—whether in 1984, 1986, or 1990—it would have been caused by politico-military currents that went even deeper than the mutual hatred of the combatants themselves. It was contentious geopolitics on a grand scale that got both nations their superweapons in the first place.

India's and Pakistan's race to arm with nuclear weapons encompasses all aspects of proliferation. It has to do with coveting the weapons as trophies of national prestige; with technology transfer, in terms of both knowledge and hardware, until self-sufficiency was achieved; and with the tone of the larger proliferation that was struck by East-West rivalry during the cold war. But most of all, it has to do with the role of patriots—their countrymen would call them visionaries—who were driven by the single-minded goal of making their respective nations so powerful that none would dare challenge their sovereignty. So fierce was their determination to bring nuclear weapons home that, in the words of one leading Pakistani politician, they were fully prepared to see their own people "eat grass" if that's what it took to realize their ultimate goal.

Indeed, 1984—the year India purportedly planned to attack Kahuta—was itself a critical time in Pakistan's drive for atomic warheads. It was the year Pakistani scientists finally put on line a gas centrifuge cascade that enriched uranium until it was bomb-grade. Although the creation of an actual atomic warhead was still six years away, the start-up of the cascade was by all odds the single most crucial element of the Pakistani program. Whether or not Pakistani nervousness about the Indians was justified, it was at least understandable, since India had a long head start.

. . .

India entered the nuclear club on the morning of May 18, 1974, when it detonated a twelve-kiloton bomb—almost exactly the size of the Hiroshima one—in the Rajasthan Desert, southwest of Delhi and very near the Pakistan border. The event was a disillusioning experience for many of those who observed India closely and who looked to it as a paradigm of peace and order. "The shock waves shattered all the standard images," two of those observers have written. "India was the world's largest democracy, the land of Nehru and Mahatma Gandhi, the altar of nonviolence and nonalignment and pious calls for universal nuclear disarmament. It was also the home of the desperately poor and diseased and yet, of all the poor and backward lands, the one that had most pinned its hopes for the future on nuclear power and the promise of the supposedly peaceful atom. And now this same India was also the first of the less-developed countries to test a nuclear device."

The Indians, however, were just as mindful of their pacifistic image as were outsiders. They therefore seized upon the old dream of nuclear scientists and engineers—to harness atomic explosions for massive civil engineering projects such as diverting rivers and leveling mountains—and adapted it to their new weapon. They called it a PNE, or peaceful nuclear explosion, and blithely told the rest of the world that it would be used for such colossal enterprises as moving huge tracts of earth. The Pakistanis, who had already clashed with New Delhi over Kashmir in 1948 and 1965 and over the creation of Bangladesh out of East Pakistan in 1971, could only hope that the huge tracts of land the Indians wanted to move were not inside their borders.

Besides proclaiming that their bomb was a strictly peaceful one, which was as stunningly hypocritical as it was brazen,* New Delhi also boasted that "Not a single thing in it was foreign." While that may have been true where the weapon's actual design and components were concerned, it was another bald-faced lie in spirit. India's atomic bomb came from Canada, France, and the United States. And it was developed as a direct consequence, not just of some "traditional rivalry" with Pakistan,

---

*Indian leaders were explicit about the possible military uses of their nuclear weapons, even before the weapons were available. In a speech in Bombay in the spring of 1946, Nehru said, "I hope Indian scientists will use the atomic force for constructive purposes. But if India is threatened, she will inevitably try to defend herself by all means at her disposal." (Steve Weissman and Herbert Krosney, *The Islamic Bomb*, New York: Times Books, 1981, p. 132.)

but also of a deep fear and hatred of China. India's bomb mushroomed out of three seemingly unrelated events: unrelated except where India was concerned.

First, there was the battle with China over Tibet in 1950. When the smoke cleared, Buddhism's picturesque mountain stronghold, long an important buffer between the world's two most populous countries, was overrun by the People's Liberation Army. It was soon one of Beijing's "autonomous" republics. Then there was the humiliating defeat by China in a border war in 1962. The rout remains embedded in the Indian psyche and has done the most to transform the Indian military from a pathetic postcolonial weakling into the fourth-largest institution of its type in the world. And two years later, in 1964, China's own inaugural nuclear explosion left no doubt within India's civilian and military leadership that China had become a long-term menace of fearful proportion.

India's nuclear energy program, from which the first bomb and its several descendants evolved, was started in 1945—even before independence— with the creation of the Institute for Fundamental Research. The IFR was headed by an enthusiastic Cambridge-educated physicist, Homi Bhabha, who shaped nuclear research for war and peace and, in the process, saw to it that the Indian program always moved toward self-sufficiency. At Bhabha's instigation, India built an extensive uranium mining industry, fuel fabrication facilities, heavy water plants, and even two small research reactors at Trombay, just north of Bombay. More important, he convinced Canada, France, and the United States to prime India's nuclear pump.

The Canadians contributed Cirus, a large and sophisticated heavy water research reactor fueled by natural uranium, as part of the Colombo Plan to aid former British colonies in south Asia. It was similar to the reactor France sold to Israel. And like the Dimona reactor, Cirus's fission process produced an important by-product: bomb-grade plutonium. Canada also helped start a heavy water plant and a nuclear fuel complex. The heavy water facility was as critical as the reactor. Although the reactor used plentiful natural uranium, it needed the heavy water to moderate the heavy neutron flux as the chain reaction took place.* Heavy water

---

*Be it ordinary water, heavy water, or graphite, the moderator's job is to keep the neutrons from colliding and fissioning—splitting—at an excessive rate. Unmoderated, the chain reaction would go from critical, which is what is supposed to happen, to supercritical in a matter of seconds. A supercritical chain reaction, in which the neutrons were fissioning out of control, would essentially turn the reactor into a bomb. That is what happened during Chernobyl's "power excursion." It took forty-one seconds to explode.

would therefore become a critical commodity for the Indians. Those who could obtain it would become, and in fact *did* become, heroes.

The French signed a nuclear cooperation agreement with India in 1951 that called for the always critical personnel exchanges and the training of Indian technicians in the then arcane realm of nuclear energy. French scientists also taught Indian scientists how to extract plutonium from spent nuclear fuel, a process that is fundamental to plutonium-fueled bombs. There could be no illusions about the end result of the extraction process. Dr. Bertrand Goldschmidt, who headed the French Atomic Energy Commission's international relations division (and who also helped Iraq's, South Africa's, and Israel's nuclear weapon programs), recalled years later that Homi Bhabha's plans had certainly included nuclear weapons. "Bhabha always wanted the bomb," Goldschmidt recalled matter-of-factly. Whatever moral problems there may have been in ingratiating themselves with the Indian nuclear science community, it made very good business sense for the French. Getting a foot in the door, they knew, could mean lucrative reactor sales later.

Typically, the United States outdid its cohorts in generosity. It subsidized loans and research grants for 1,300 Indian scientists and technicians to study at nuclear facilities in the United States.* It provided two complete light water power reactors (built by General Electric for $118 million and largely paid for by the Agency for International Development). Most important, where the development of the bomb was concerned, it helped to build a small reprocessing plant at Trombay with which the Indians could learn how to extract the plutonium that grew on Cirus's fuel rods. The facility was built from declassified plans of the Purex solvent extraction process developed by the United States at Hanford, Washington. At least twenty-four Indians were trained to operate the plant.

Indians trained in the West would ultimately include the two most critical figures in the weapons program: Raja Ramanna and P. K. Iyengar. Ramanna was the young nuclear scientist most responsible for making the "Buddha smile"—the code words that told Indira Gandhi in 1974 that she was the second woman, after Golda Meir, to have her finger on the

*By 1993, 6,000 scientists were working in the Indian Defense Science Organization alone. Their Pakistani counterparts numbered 50.

nuclear button.* Iyengar, who was also part of the nuclear weapon team, was almost certainly responsible for the importing of heavy water during the 1980s. Like Israel before it, and Iraq after it, India realized the value of a good Western education. But it also understood the importance of indigenous supply lines and facilities. Both Ramanna and Iyengar later rose to become chairmen of the Indian Atomic Energy Commission. In addition Ramanna, a nuclear hawk, became Minister of State for Defense.

No one in authority ever doubted that, however many beggars there were in Bombay, caged prostitutes on the Calcutta waterfront, and children being born and dying in the squalid alleys of New Delhi, India would somehow come up with the money for a bomb. And it did. Between 1954, when its Department of Atomic Energy was established, and 1991, India pumped about $2.3 billion (in 1991 dollars) into its nuclear weapon program. Much of that was spent on purchasing or building reactors and the infrastructure that went with them. Perhaps it was a good investment after all. By 1991, India would be manufacturing its own reactors and trying to export them to Cuba, Argentina, Egypt, Iran, and Syria. That, after all, was the traditional way to gain a decent return on investment.

Finally, Washington helped India to go nuclear in a rather negative way. The Nixon administration cynically ignored atrocities committed by Pakistan against secessionists, including Hindus, during its brutal invasion of East Pakistan in March 1971. Since Nixon was using Pakistan as a conduit to improve relations with China, he failed to condemn his ally for genocide. The rampage, which may have caused up to three million casualties, led to India's intervention and the birth of Bangladesh. While America's support for Pakistan did not in itself compel India to push for nuclear weapons, it certainly convinced Indian policy makers that their course was correct.

The Pakistanis often made veiled references to their relatively modest but efficient program in order to stave off the Indians. "In view of the disparity that had developed in the conventional areas between the two countries," one leading Pakistani strategist publicly observed, "and India's achieving a nuclear power status, it became imperative for Pakistan to acquire nuclear technology. Pakistan is left with no choice but to create

*During each of the three times Third World nations almost resorted to using nuclear weapons, a woman ran one of the governments involved. The third, Benazir Bhutto, was Prime Minister of Pakistan when it almost went to war with India in the spring of 1990. She had limited knowledge of her country's nuclear capability, however. Meir's crisis came during the 1973 war with the Arabs.

a nuclear deterrent, whether by bluff or by possession. For a poor country like us, a conscious policy of ambiguity is highly effective to keep the enemy at bay." It was David drawing attention to himself and waving his slingshot at Goliath.

The giant, on the other hand, let his size speak for itself. But even India's size belied the extent of its colossal arsenal and a remarkable indigenous capability to stock that arsenal. While they loudly professed their peace-loving nature throughout the 1980s, the Indians were in fact embarked on an all-out armament binge of astounding proportions. And since they neither did it openly nor bragged about it, the West remained largely ignorant of the program's true dimension.

During that decade, India designed and built—not imported—five power reactors, each larger than 200 megawatts and each a potential plutonium producer. It constructed a uranium purification and conversion plant and a laboratory needed to enrich the metal to bomb-grade. It also set up three heavy water facilities, a fuel fabrication plant, and three separate research reactors. At 100 megawatts, one of the research reactors was the largest such plant in the world. The Indians even set up their own small fast-breeder in preparation for a much larger one they ordered from the Russians.

And while the dozen or so nuclear weapons were the crown jewels of their national defense system, they were set among many others. That decade saw the development and the first serial production of the Prithvi, a Scud-like mobile missile, and the successful testing of Agni. The Indians were also manufacturing their own MIG-29s under license from the Russians and diesel submarines under license from the Germans. No fewer than five facilities worked on biological weapons. They also bought two aircraft carriers from the British and began designing their own. India, after all, had the world's third-largest pool of technically trained personnel. It was no accident that a nation that produced the best microchip designers in the world at Intel also produced missiles and nuclear weapons and the computers to create them.

But even beyond the immense indigenous infrastructure that produced all of that, there was a substratum of foreign equipment that made India the largest arms importer in the Third World.

And what they could neither develop nor import legally, they smuggled. Throughout the 1970s and into the 1980s, for example, India smuggled hundreds of tons of heavy water from Europe, the Soviet Union, and China even as it struggled to build its own production facilities at Hazira.

The complex itself was designed to produce 110 tons of heavy water a year.

Most of the biggest Western firms claimed to have been deceived. Siemens sold India a Teleperm computerized fluid mixing system for the heavy water manufacturing process: the same system it sold to Libya for mixing poison gas at Rabta. Siemens says there were many other Western components as well. The software to run the Teleperms came from two companies: Imperial Chemical Industries of Great Britain and MTI of New Jersey. The minicomputers on which the software ran came from the Digital Equipment Corporation, the American computer giant. The entire system was managed by another U.S. company, Kellogg USA, a management company, Siemens claimed.

Asked about the role Siemens played at Hazira, its public relations man said that India had made vague reference to an ammonia plant. "The consumer never tells details of the process to the supplier of the system," he said. "That would be similar to revealing the Coca-Cola formula." Coca-Cola, however, cannot turn Beijing or Islamabad into a radioactive wasteland. There is no evidence that the companies actually knew the intended use. But if any of them did know what use the Indians intended to make of their equipment, Gary Milhollin noted, it would have been in violation of the nuclear Non-Proliferation Treaty. The treaty prohibits the export of heavy water production equipment without safeguards. "Hazira is not safeguarded," he said, "so it can supply heavy water to reactors making plutonium for bombs."

Much of the illicit heavy water was to end up at Bhabha, the most modern and complete nuclear weapons development complex in the Third World. Not even Israel and North Korea, and certainly not Pakistan, had such an impressive facility.

As is the case at Los Alamos and other places where devices are designed to incinerate whole cities, Bhabha is physically sumptuous. The complex, situated in Trombay, is set off by palm trees and abundant, monsoon-fed gardens that are carefully manicured. It is as if the lush surroundings, bursting with natural beauty, were intended to tranquilize those who work at their deadly business inside the buildings. It is a place vastly different from Dhravia, one of Bombay's southern suburbs, where miserably poor Muslims were hounded and murdered by fanatical Hindu nationalists in January 1993 during the worst wave of sectarian violence to hit India since the partition in 1947.

Trombay and Dhravia are dramatic manifestations of *Maha Bharata*, the Hindu nationalists' persistent dream of a greater India in which Muslims have finally been vanquished, leaving the entire subcontinent and the ocean into which it protrudes ruled by Hindus.

Pakistan found out about the secret work that was going on in India's nuclear weapon program as early as the 1960s and became understandably alarmed.* Its response, also understandable, was twofold. It tried to convince the countries supplying India with expertise and equipment to stop doing so. It also simultaneously bent to the task of getting its own bomb. The first strategy failed. In 1971, for example, efforts to convince Pierre Elliott Trudeau to stop helping India were of no avail. The Canadian Prime Minister, who like Mohandas Gandhi and Jawaharlal Nehru was a self-professed apostle of peace, assured a Pakistani Atomic Energy Commission official that there was "nothing to worry about" where India's motives were concerned. Yet Trudeau was not so sanguine as he let on. His effort to get Indira Gandhi to renounce the use of plutonium from the Cirus reactor for weapons was categorically rebuffed. There was no mention of prohibiting the development of peaceful nuclear explosives in the original agreement between her nation and Canada, she sternly told Trudeau, and changing the agreement after the fact would be "discriminatory."

Pakistan's own nuclear bomb program was both pragmatic and visionary. The immediate impetus for acquiring nuclear weapons was, of course, to counter India's. "If India builds the bomb, we will eat grass or leaves—even go hungry. But we will get one of our own," the militant Zulfikar Ali Bhutto threatened in 1965. "We have no alternative."

Yet there was more to it than that. Pakistan, whose Muslim religion has been forged by incessant friction and occasional wars with its mostly Hindu neighbor, also became determined not just to fend off India, but to lead all of Islam in technical virtuosity. That, Islamabad decided, included developing nuclear arms. Its nuclear arsenal would therefore be more than Pakistani: it would be Islamic.

Ali Bhutto told Henry Kissinger as much when the Secretary of

*As early as 1964, Homi Bhabha bragged that India could produce a nuclear weapon in 18 months and had already started a "Subterranean Nuclear Explosion Project." A year and a half later, however, he was killed in an airplane accident. The project was therefore slowed. (Introduction, by K. Subrahmanyan, to Sreedhar, *Pakistan's Bomb: A Documentary Study*, New Delhi: ABC Publishing House, 1986, p. ix.)

State visited him in the summer of 1976 to urge against developing an atomic bomb. All of the other great civilizations—Christians, Jews, Hindus, and Communists—had nuclear weapons, Bhutto claimed to have told Kissinger, and "the Islamic civilization" would therefore have them as well. Ten years later General Zia ul-Haq, who overthrew Bhutto and then had him hanged for murder, left no doubt as to where he stood on the subject. "It is our right to obtain the technology," he told an Arab journalist. "And when we acquire this technology, the entire Islamic world will possess it with us." Pakistan would ultimately acquire nuclear weapons capability through a variety of difficult, surreptitious means. It would then try to pass on much of what it learned to other Islamic states for a shared "Islamic bomb."

It is difficult to determine just how successful Bhutto was in creating an Islamic bomb network. But whatever the plan's shortcomings, it was not for lack of trying. Pursuit of the atomic genie actually began with the encouragement of the United States in 1955, the year before Pakistan changed its status from a dominion of the British Commonwealth to that of a fully independent Islamic republic. That year the old U.S. Atomic Energy Commission, bursting with what it saw as its proselytizing role in spreading the wonders of atomic energy under Dwight Eisenhower's Atoms for Peace program, concluded an agreement to cooperate on nuclear research with the newly created Pakistan Atomic Energy Commission. What better way to help underdeveloped nations, the thinking went, than to provide them with a source of energy that one day would be too cheap to meter? Between then and January 1972, a handful of Pakistani scientists attended conferences on reactor technology at the Argonne National Laboratory and elsewhere in an effort to deliver atomic energy to their country to meet its growing power needs.

Although Pakistan's nuclear program was for the most part peaceful, Pakistanis remained mindful enough of the Indian weapons program to keep their options open. That meant taking their first, tentative steps toward forging their own nuclear arms capability.

Like the colossus with which it shared the subcontinent, Pakistan studiously avoided signing the Non-Proliferation Treaty. The NPT was signed by the United States, the United Kingdom, and the Soviet Union in 1968 and came into effect two years later. It explicitly prohibits nations that have nuclear weapons from passing them on to those that do not. Furthermore, the agreement stipulates that no nonnuclear weapon state that becomes a party to it can acquire or manufacture nuclear weapons.

The NPT empowers the IAEA to do safeguarding checks. The NPT's framers also anticipated the ploy of calling nuclear weapons "peaceful," and specifically prohibited the sham. No wonder the Indians, who were working on their own "peaceful" bomb even as the NPT was signed, refused to be party to it.

Pakistan's low-keyed work on nuclear weapons was transformed overnight into a crash program when the country's army suffered its ignominious defeat at the hands of the Indians during the war over East Pakistan in March 1971. That stinging defeat did to Ali Bhutto what China's defeat of India in 1962 had done to Nehru, and what the Israeli obliteration of the Osirak reactor at Tuwaitha in 1981 would do to Saddam Hussein. It showed Bhutto in the most dramatic way how vulnerable his country was to a better-armed opponent. And, as Saddam Hussein came to believe implicitly, Bhutto became convinced that nuclear weapons would prove to be the great equalizer.

Accordingly, Ali Bhutto flew fifty of his nation's top scientists to the town of Multan, near the Indian border, in January 1972. There, under a brightly colored tent on the lawn of a stately colonial mansion, he ordered them to make him an atomic bomb.

Bhutto, the atomic evangelist, began by working his captivated audience slowly. He recounted the humiliating defeat by India and vowed that Pakistan's honor had to be vindicated. He insisted that he had always wanted their country to have nuclear weapons but that he had been ignored. Now, he added, the moment was at hand. Pakistan was going to have the bomb. He wanted it. The people wanted it. And the scientists—newly minted Ph.D.s in nuclear physics and some of the discipline's most respected old hands—were going to provide it. The scientists under the candy-striped tent reacted with unbridled, almost giddy enthusiasm. "Can you give it to me?" the evangelist exhorted his parishioners. "Oh, yes, yes, yes. You can have it. You can have it," the enthusiastic physicists answered.

"How long will it take?" Pakistan's Prime Minister wanted to know. That question produced disagreement and debate. Finally, one scientist said that a bomb could be delivered in five years. Bhutto held up three fingers. "Three years," he said. "I want it in three years." After further discussion, some of it heated, the group agreed that it could provide the country with an atomic bomb if it got the necessary resources and facilities. "I shall find you the resources and I shall find you the facilities," Zulfakir Ali Bhutto promised. And he was as good as his word.

For the remainder of Bhutto's regime and throughout those that followed, Pakistan pursued nuclear weapons by all means possible. But the relentless drive to acquire the bomb was always insulated by continuing official denial that any such program existed and by disingenuous offers to renounce nuclear weapons if India did the same.

In 1972, even as the scientists were getting down to the business mandated by their Prime Minister, another Pakistani was settling into work of a slightly different sort very far from home. Dr. Abdul Qadeer Khan, a short, chubby metallurgist with a new doctorate from the Catholic University of Leuven in Belgium, was hired by the Physical Dynamics Research Laboratory, or FDO, in Amsterdam. FDO was a subsidiary of a Dutch firm, Verenigde Machine-Fabrieken, and worked closely with one of western Europe's most important nuclear facilities: URENCO. Because they were unwilling to rely on U.S. nuclear fuel for their power reactors, Great Britain, West Germany, and the Netherlands had created URENCO in 1970 to guarantee their own supply of enriched uranium. The enrichment plant was located in the town of Almelo, Holland, and used highly classified ultracentrifuge technology to separate scarce, highly fissionable U-235 from abundant U-238 by spinning the two isotopes at up to 100,000 revolutions a minute. FDO was a URENCO subcontractor and consultant. Its personnel, including A. Q. Khan, were therefore technically subject to tight security controls.

Khan, a thoroughly likable fellow who made friends wherever he went, was enthusiastically recommended to URENCO for a clearance by FDO, which noted that he had lived in the West for eleven years and was married to a Dutch national. The Dutch security service, or BVD, then ran a background check on Khan. The investigation was as leaky as those conducted by the Department of Energy's nuclear weapons laboratories in the United States. The BVD neglected to find out, for example, that Mrs. Khan was not Dutch at all, but rather was a Dutch-speaking South African who carried a British passport. At any rate Khan, duly cleared, began to fit right into FDO, URENCO, and his neighborhood, which was near Schiphol Airport. He plied the secretaries in the office with candy and cookies, gamely went out for volleyball with his neighbors, and took his wife and two daughters to the seaside or into the Ardennes on weekends when the weather permitted.

FDO, a typical Dutch office, was relaxed, free-spirited, and jovial.

Within a week or so of being hired, Khan was sent over to the enrichment facility at Almelo. It was the first of many trips he would make to the factory. Khan was also made responsible for translating technical documents, which he often took home with FDO's blessing. As the months passed, A. Q. Khan became thoroughly familiar not only with all of the design plans at Almelo but with those belonging to the companies that supplied parts for the ultracentrifuges.

Khan's most important foray to Almelo was made in the autumn of 1974, when he spent sixteen days in the plant's most secret area. His assignment was to translate a highly classified report on a breakthrough in centrifuge technology from German to Dutch. During that sixteen days, the delightful young Pakistani popped up everywhere. Asked by one colleague why he was writing in a foreign script, Khan replied that it was only a letter to his family back home. Another noticed that he continually roamed around the facility, notebook in hand, but thought nothing of it.

No one seems to know for certain when A. Q. Khan began committing espionage for Pakistan. He certainly would have been an ideal choice as a spy. He came from a family of patriots. His father was a teacher; his grandfather and great-grandfather were military officers. Most important, his joviality masked a bitter past. He had been born in Bhopal during the British raj. But his family, like so many millions of other Muslims, had been forced to flee to Pakistan during the partition of India. He therefore often remarked, as Israelis did, that "everybody kicks those who do not have a country of their own." And, he added, "We have to safeguard this country of the pure more than our own lives!"*

A subsequent investigation by the Dutch turned up no evidence that he was sent to the Netherlands as a spy. Nor is it clear whether he approached his government, or the other way around. Whatever the case, it seems that he began pulling secrets out of URENCO and transmitting them to Islamabad only after India exploded its peaceful bomb, and the stint inside Almelo was the finale to his career in espionage.

In January 1976, A. Q. Khan and his family suddenly left Holland and turned up in Pakistan. His wife wrote to her former neighbors that they were on vacation and that her husband had fallen ill. Soon afterward, Khan himself sent a letter of resignation to FDO, effective that March. It was all nice, neat, and pleasant. Smiling A. Q. Khan apparently managed

---

*"Pakistan" is derived from two Persian words: *pak*, meaning "pure," and *stan*, meaning "country."

to steal secrets from the west Europeans which, together with the pains-
taking collection of the right equipment by other Pakistanis, would guarantee that his country finally got its own atomic bomb.* The others were
S. A. Butt, who handled the European procurement, and a retired Pakistani brigadier, Inam ul-Haq, who was the driving force behind the
North American network. Until the scandal broke back in Amsterdam,
Khan's unsuspecting Dutch friends, neighbors, and colleagues loved the
man. They probably still do.

While A. Q. Khan was appropriating uranium enrichment technology
in the Netherlands and his colleagues were doing so elsewhere—and six
months after the Indian test—Islamabad signed an agreement with the
ubiquitous Saint-Gobain Techniques Nouvelles to build a reprocessing
plant at Chashma. The facility would remove bomb-grade plutonium from
used uranium fuel rods. The aggressive French firm was well qualified
for the assignment. It had previously built reprocessing facilities at Dimona under much more secret circumstances.

The French connection deeply upset the White House, which dispatched Henry Kissinger to Pakistan to warn Bhutto that economic and
military aid would be cut off unless the project was abandoned. If it were
stopped, Kissinger added, the United States would open its huge weapons
chest to Pakistan. Specifically, Kissinger said, the Pentagon would supply
Pakistan with more than 100 A-7 Corsair II fighter-bombers and other
military hardware. The A-7 was an attack aircraft used by both the U.S.
Navy and Air Force in Vietnam. It could carry nuclear weapons up to
450 miles. Bhutto, however, would not back down. No aircraft or any
number of them could equate with an atomic arsenal.

Having failed with a carrot, Kissinger tried a stick. If Bhutto refused
to go along, the Secretary of State threatened, the United States would
"make a horrible example" of him. That taken care of, Kissinger continued
on to Paris in hopes of derailing the deal there. Any hopes he had of
squelching the arrangement, however, were short-lived. The Quai d'Orsay
reacted angrily to what it correctly perceived as blatant American meddling in a deal that not only would benefit France economically but would
enhance its reputation as a world leader in nuclear technology. But Kis-

*A 1979 Dutch government investigation concluded that it was reasonable to assume that Khan
obtained classified information. However, Dutch officials state that Khan was not prosecuted
because it was impossible to prove what information he might have taken. A. Q Khan has
repeatedly denied that he engaged in any illegal conduct and notes that no criminal charges
were brought against him.

singer saw a broader picture than the one involving France and Pakistan and fretted over its dimension. France was also known to be negotiating with Iraq to build the Osirak reactor, while West Germany had just concluded a deal with the generals in the Brazilian junta for a massive infusion of nuclear technology of all kinds.

In the end, Kissinger managed to convince Valéry Giscard d'Estaing that the reprocessing plant represented an unacceptable potential danger. The French president soon hit upon a way of getting out of the deal while saving the easily bruised Gallic countenance. He decided that his country would drag its feet in honoring the terms of the Chashma contract, hopefully with the result that the exasperated Pakistanis would finally break it themselves. But Pakistan would have none of it. Ultimately, France therefore had to unilaterally abrogate the contract while holding out the possibility of providing Pakistan with power reactors that could be used only to create energy.

Yet François-Xavier Poincet, the disgruntled director of Saint-Gobain Techniques Nouvelles, saw more jealousy than altruism in Washington's manipulation of his government and therefore of his company. "It's devilish, you know," he told two journalists. "The Americans are backward in reprocessing. They cannot bear to see the world market taken over by another country before they are ready. They believe they have a God-given right to tell others what to do, but their real God is American business. It's absolutely devilish."

But it wasn't really all that devilish. Pakistan was now working in a number of areas, overt and covert, to get its bomb. If it couldn't buy a complete factory, it would build one. Its agents, directed by the relentless Dr. Khan, prowled Europe to obtain, by any means necessary, the thousands of items that were needed to produce nuclear weapons. The shopping list was extensive. It included the hundreds of specialized pieces of equipment that not only were necessary to operate the centrifuge cascade that enriched uranium, but would provide redundancy to compensate for breakdowns and other failures. The search went on for years. It is still going on.

In more than twenty letters written to the network of Pakistani agents who smuggled centrifuge parts out of Canada during the late 1970s, Khan laid out the successes and failures of his teams. He described the travels of key operatives, the role of such companies as Siemens, Union Carbide, and others in building Kahuta, and even the technical papers he was ordering from the U.S. Department of Commerce with no more trouble than he would have had requesting data on wheat production.

Pakistan's network was so efficient that it was later massively copied, with less ultimate success, by Iraq. Similarities in operating technique were so striking, in fact, that they led Congress and elements of the U.S. intelligence community to suspect that Pakistan, or at any rate some Pakistanis, were helping the Iraqis.

In any event, from 1976 to 1979, companies in the Netherlands, West Germany, and Great Britain—the members of URENCO—illegally exported gas centrifuge hardware and technology to Pakistan. By 1988, the equipment had been used to enrich uranium to 90 percent for bomb production.

As far back as April 1980, two Dutch companies sent bomb-making equipment to Pakistan, including 6,200 tubes made of special steel. The same month, a Norwegian government-owned firm sold Islamabad zirconium tubes, which hold stacks of uranium pellets in reactor cores. The following month it was reported that the Pakistan Atomic Energy Commission (modeled after its U.S. namesake) contracted with a Spanish company for the first phase of a design for a new nuclear power plant. In June, French firms sold Pakistan equipment for potential use in reprocessing plants. In September, it was reported that the Swiss government refused to stop exports of sophisticated nuclear technology to Pakistan despite U.S. objections. At the same time, there was a report that Swiss firms supplied Pakistan with equipment for possible use in uranium enrichment. The year closed with Canada charging three men with illegally exporting restricted items to Pakistan. At the same time, an Italian subsidiary of Saint-Gobain Techniques Nouvelles reported supplying special steel vessels with reprocessing applications. There was also a report that British companies sold thirty-one electrical inverters and a metal finishing plant to Pakistan. All of the material had nuclear applications. It seemed that the Pakistanis never slept.

As the decade continued, events moved ever more quickly. In the beginning of 1988, there was a report that Pakistan was preparing a nuclear test site, followed by another saying that Saudi Arabia had offered Pakistan $800 million to help make a hydrogen bomb. The reported offer came with a condition, though. The Saudis did not want the resulting technology to get into Saddam Hussein's hands. In March a Swiss company, Cora Engineering, stopped shipping equipment to Pakistan that was to be used for uranium enrichment after threats were made against the firm and one of its executives suffered a bomb attack. In May the magazine *Nucleonics Week* reported that the Soviet Union, which was already supporting India's nuclear research program, had offered to provide the same service to Pakistan. The next month, the U.S. embassy in Ankara formally urged the Turkish government to stop the secret shipment to Pakistan of electrical inverters and other equipment that could be used for bomb triggers and for uranium enrichment. That same month, however, Washington and Pakistan concluded a $3.2 billion aid agreement that included forty F-16s. In July it became known that West German firms had supplied aluminum rods, vacuum pumps, and other nuclear-related material to Pakistan. Two months later, U.S. arms control and intelligence officials and IAEA inspectors reported "suspicious" activities at Pakistan's Candu reactor at Karachi, one of the original reactors supplied by Canadian General Electric in the mid-1960s (it started up in 1972).*

"Look, as a soldier, if you have to fight with a man—if he has a stick—and I'm without a stick," explained Brigadier Inam ul-Haq, said to be the driving force behind Pakistan's procurement effort in North America, "I would like to have a stick myself."

The following months and years saw more of the same. Responding to a leaked CIA charge that Pakistan would be able to explode an atomic bomb within three years, President Zia ul-Haq assured the world that his country had absolutely no intention of acquiring a nuclear arsenal and that it had neither the capacity nor the intention of producing nuclear arms. He gave the same assurance to President Reagan. And A. Q. Khan was quoted by a Lahore newspaper as saying that Pakistan could enrich uranium and produce an atomic bomb "if necessary." China, meanwhile, had begun to provide Pakistan with nuclear weapon design technology and enriched uranium.

**K**han himself had by then became a national hero: a scientist-manager on a par with Jafar Jafar and Yuval Ne'eman. He was rewarded for his

---

*IAEA inspectors were involved because the reactor was subject to partial safeguards. Although the Candu (for *Cana*dian *deuterium uranium* reactor) was strictly a civilian power reactor, it was attractive to nations intent on making nuclear weapons for at least three reasons. It used fuel made from natural uranium, which eliminated the expensive enrichment process. It could be refueled while operating, rather than having to be shut down, which made it harder for inspectors to know how much fuel had been burned and for how long. And it produced bomb-grade plutonium as a waste by-product of the fission process. (Steve Weissman and Herbert Krosney, *The Islamic Bomb*, New York: Times Books, 1981, p. 67.)

patriotism by being made the head of a research institute that was named after him: the A. Q. Khan Research Laboratories at Kahuta. Although he was portrayed as a superspy by the European press after his feat was made public, he himself not only avoided reference to it but denied that Pakistan had received any technical help, clandestine or otherwise, from other nations. "All the research work [at Kahuta] was the result of our innovation and struggle," he told an audience of librarians in Lahore in 1990. "We did not receive any technical know-how from abroad, but we can't reject the use of books, magazines and research papers in this connection."

On one occasion—his receiving a gold medal from the Pakistan Institute of National Affairs—Khan boasted that Kahuta had put Pakistan "on the world nuclear map." And he added that his long stay in Europe and "intimate knowledge of various countries and their manufacturing firms was an asset." That was putting it mildly.

Beneath Khan's apparently serene, almost self-effacing demeanor, there beat the heart of a dedicated Muslim scientist. Indeed, he often seemed conflicted by the requirements of strict secrecy about his country's nuclear weapons program, on the one hand, and an irresistible urge to brag about it—to flout it in the face of the West—on the other.

"Western countries had never imagined that a poor and backward country like Pakistan would finish their monopoly [on uranium enrichment] in such a short time," he told a Rawalpindi journalist in February 1984. "As soon as they realized that Pakistan had dashed their dreams, they pounced at Pakistan like hungry jackals and began attacking us with all kinds of accusations and falsehoods. You see yourself . . . how could they tolerate a Muslim country becoming their equal in this field?

"All Western countries, including Israel, are the enemies not only of Pakistan," he continued, showing unmitigated anger, "but in fact of Islam. Had any other Muslim country instead of Pakistan made this progress, they would have conducted the same poisonous and false propaganda about it. The examples of Iraq and Libya are before you."

**U**.S. intelligence services often grumble, with some justification, that their blunders receive worldwide attention while their triumphs necessarily go unheralded. That was the case in 1983, when the CIA penetrated the Pakistani nuclear program so thoroughly that at least one of its representatives saw and copied the plans for the Islamic bomb. The plans had come from China. The agent even obtained the catalog numbers of some of the parts the Pakistanis were buying from foreign suppliers. The agency sent the plans to physicists at one or more of the nation's three weapons laboratories who, in turn, created a scale model of the bomb.

Its core was about the size of a soccer ball and had multiple detonators precisely spaced around its surface. In fact, it was the same simple design that had been tested by China on October 27, 1966, when an intermediate-range ballistic missile—itself a derivative of the large Soviet SS-4—was fired from the Shuang Chenge Tse test range at the Lop Nor nuclear test site. The resulting explosion, equivalent to 20,000 tons of TNT, was about the size of the weapon that had struck Nagasaki two decades earlier. While its destructive power was small by superpower standards, it was great enough to kill hundreds of thousands of residents in India's tightly packed cities. And because of the proximity of the two nations, the Pakistanis would not even need a ballistic missile to deliver their weapons. They could use a C-130 transport plane.

The physicists reported that the bomb was so good it would work every time, even with small manufacturing errors. The model was eventually presented to Benazir Bhutto and Pakistani diplomats in Washington to prove that the United States knew what their own physicists back home were up to.

The Indians and the Pakistanis dueled over long-range delivery systems as well, and again India came in first. On the morning of May 22, 1989, it forced its way into the long-range ballistic missile club by successfully test-firing an intermediate-range missile. The weapon, named Agni, lifted off from the Interim Test Range on India's northeast coast and arced 620 miles before its dummy warhead splashed into the Bay of Bengal. In fact, the test shot was conservative, since the three-stage missile was designed to lob a one-ton warhead 1,500 miles.

The nation reacted jubilantly to the news. "For India, Agni represents a quantum leap in strategic capability," crowed *India Today*, a respected national magazine. "Already, with the Pokharan explosion of 1974, India had demonstrated its ability to make a nuclear bomb. In 1980, the SLV-3 rocket launched the country into the space age. All that was missing was the vital third leg of the triad—a potent medium-range ballistic missile capable of carrying a warhead over long distances." Nor did the article omit the likely targets at the ends of those distances. "Agni, deployed operationally and with a conventional warhead, could destroy a major military installation anywhere in Pakistan, in fact, in most of south Asia including Afghanistan." But then the writers raised their sights to the more important target. "For India, the greater strategic impact is that it can reach major targets in southern and central China. But of more vital import is its deterrent factor. Armed with a nuclear warhead, Agni offers the potential to put India on a par with China as far as military deterrence is concerned."

Avul Pakir Jainulabuddin Abdul Kalam, the fifty-eight-year-old doyen of India's space program, couched the triumph in less prosaic terms. He was to Agni what A. Q. Khan was to the Pakistani bomb program and what Dr. Frankenstein was to the renowned monster. It was Kalam who conceived Agni many years before. It was he who had in effect assembled the thing and breathed life into it. And it was he who fully understood its several purposes. "It gives us the confidence that we are capable of designing any kind of missile," he was to explain. "We are now self-sufficient both in design and in missile technology. It is a technological strength," he went on. "Strength respects strength. Weaklings are not honored. So we should be strong."

Whatever India's level of self-sufficiency in the art of missile development in 1989, Agni and the series of lesser rockets that preceded it derived from foreign designs and technology, much of it dual-use.* In fact, Agni's earliest ancestor was designed at NASA's Langley Research Center and flown out of its Wallops Island launch facility, both of them in Virginia. Its name was Scout. Kalam knew a great deal about Scout because he had studied its plans, seen it put together, and watched it fly.

Scout was designed at the end of the 1950s as a low-cost way of getting small research satellites into orbit. The four-stage, solid-propellant rocket was first launched in 1960. Three years later India invited the United States, France, Great Britain, and the Soviet Union to help it start an ostensibly civilian space program. All four responded enthusiastically. Between 1963 and 1975, more than 350 of those nations' scientific rockets blasted off from the new Thumba test range, which the United States had helped to design.

---

*India's earlier surface-to-surface missile was called Prithvi (earth). It could carry a 2,000-pound warhead about 150 miles with considerable accuracy. Akash (sky) was a medium-range surface-to-air missile. Nag (cobra) was a short-range antitank missile with a highly advanced "fire-and-forget" capability. The SLV-3 was a civilian booster designed into carry satellites into orbit.

Meanwhile, Kalam spent four months in 1963 and 1964 at both Langley and Wallops Island becoming intimately acquainted with Scout. It would have been clear to the Indian that a larger and more powerful version of the rocket could carry a warhead deep into China. Given what the Chinese had done to his country in 1962, the notion of being able to strike back over long distances—high over the heads of the People's Liberation Army—would have been sorely tempting. And it was in 1962 that the National Committee for Space Research was founded and placed under India's Atomic Energy Commission. The committee was headed by none other than Homi Bhabha, who, of course, was feverishly working on an atomic bomb. Scientific space research was to be undertaken by the Indian Space Research Organization (ISRO).

In 1965, with Kalam's tutorial complete, India asked NASA for financial and technical information about acquiring Scouts of its own. NASA answered that while the rocket was unclassified owing to the purely scientific nature of its work, and was therefore available for purchase, the Department of State would have the ultimate say. NASA nonetheless proceeded to send technical reports on Scout's design to the man who requested them. His name was Homi Bhabha.* This pattern—of sending specialists abroad to gather supposedly peaceful technology while acquiring the means to turn it into weapons surreptitiously—would be used by Israel, Iraq, Pakistan, and other nations more than a decade later.

Under Kalam's exhaustive efforts, Scout became Space Launch Vehicle 3, or SLV-3, India's first satellite launcher. Both rockets are seventy-five feet high, both use four solid-fuel stages, and both can put a ninety-pound satellite into orbit. SLV-3's first stage and Agni's are virtually identical.

The United States was not the only nation to help India develop ballistic missiles. The Soviets and the French stayed on after the Thumba days, while the British left and were effectively replaced by the West Germans. While the first stage of the Agni was derived from the Scout, the second stage had an even more mundane origin. It consisted of two rockets derived largely from the Soviets' standard surface-to-air missile,

*While NASA was communicating vital data for developing nuclear delivery systems to the Indian Atomic Energy Commission, the Johnson White House was trying to convince the Indians that such development was too expensive. (A secret National Security Action Memorandum, No. 355: "The Indian Nuclear Weapons Problem," August 6, 1966.)

the SA-2, or Guideline as it was called in NATO.* Agni was therefore a true superpower hybrid.

The Soviets further contributed to India's space program mostly by letting the Indians build a variety of short-range missiles under license while helping them to develop their own satellites. With the launching of the Rohini satellite in 1980, India became the seventh nation to send an indigenous spacecraft into orbit. The French gave India liquid-fuel rocket technology in the form of the Viking engine used to propel the European Space Agency's Ariane launch vehicle. Viking is the same engine France was going to sell to Brazil until the United States vigorously protested. India's version of Viking is used in Prithvi, its short-range missile.

True to form, the Germans were the most helpful of all. Beginning in 1976, West Germany's Aerospace Research Establishment, DFVLR, sent experts to help the Indians with guidance systems.† They also were instrumental in teaching the Indians about the intricacies of navigation systems, including an "autonomous payload control system"—an inertial navigation system—that could be used to guide either satellites or warheads without using signals from the ground. They taught the Indians how to perform high-altitude rocket simulation tests, helped construct rocket test facilities, arranged delivery of electronics and other equipment from German firms, conducted wind tunnel tests in Germany of the SLV-3, sold rocket motor segment rings, codeveloped and tested computers for rocket payload guidance, and provided DFVLR-developed software for satellite orbital analysis.

Finally, the Germans provided extensive help with carbon composites: materials so light but strong that they are used for rocket nozzles and, more ominously, as ablative heat shielding for the nose cones of ballistic missiles that must plunge through the Earth's dense atmosphere before exploding. DFVLR's contribution, including plans for a precision filament-winding machine that India began using in 1985–86, ultimately allowed the country to manufacture its own nozzles and nose cones. The

---

*The SA-2 was a two-stage, thirty-five-foot-long interceptor missile having a solid-fuel booster and a liquid sustainer. It gained prominence on May Day, 1960, when one or more of them brought down Francis Gary Powers's U-2. Two years later, SA-2s deployed in Cuba provided the first indication that the Kremlin was sending ballistic missiles there. The Soviet derivation of the Agni is from a conversation with a U.S. official in August 1991.

†DFVLR, or Deutsche Forschungs und Versuchsanstalt für Luft und Raumfahrt, has about 4,000 employees and is funded mainly by the German government.

late Prime Minister Rajiv Gandhi noted cryptically that the carbon composites produced by the machine would be for "atmospheric reentry." But some of his subordinates were more to the point. They said that the end result would be a "domestically developed heat shield."

And what would the shield shield? In 1983, New Delhi established the Integrated Guided Missile Development Program under its Defense Research and Development Organization. IGMDP currently uses nineteen laboratories and is supported by fourteen academic institutes and government facilities and twenty-seven industrial firms. It is charged with creating a coherent, indigenous, surface-to-surface missile program whose products would use any appropriate explosive technology. As Pakistan elevated A. Q. Khan to head its nuclear weapons research program, India eventually moved Kalam from the civilian Space Research Organization to head IGMDP. Although Agni (and a 3,000-mile-range follow-on) should ultimately be able to carry conventional warheads, it will be capable of carrying far more powerful stuff.

For one thing, India has been experimenting with fuel-air explosives. While these are extremely difficult to use on ballistic missiles, the task (as Honeywell engineers demonstrated for Condor-2) is not impossible. But in the end, there can be little doubt that the nuclear and ballistic missile programs will be brought together. "Implicit in the IGMDP programme, though never acknowledged officially, has been the instruction for proving a whole range of technologies that relate to an IRBM/ICBM system," the *Jane's Defence Weekly* correspondent in New Delhi wrote in reporting the Agni test. "The ambiguity in the mandate parallels that of the nuclear weapons programme because the existence of an effort in the IRBM/ICBM area minus the nuclear weapons component would not be credible." Indeed, in a manner of speaking, they were made for each other.

The Indian ballistic missile program had become so ambitious and specialized by 1990 that New Delhi could select particular missiles to match separate targeting requirements the way a golfer chooses the right iron for a particular shot. Agni could be trained on Beijing and other Chinese targets. Prithvi, which was Agni's first stage rewired and topped with a warhead, was a Scud-like missile with a range to match. That meant it could be used against Pakistani ground forces or against Karachi, Islamabad, Rawalpindi, or Lahore. So could a new air-launched cruise missile then under development.

On August 18, 1992, just before the Indian and Pakistani foreign secretaries conferred on "reducing tension" over Kashmir, India indulged itself in some classic missile diplomacy: It tested one of its Prithvis. Whatever else was on the missile, it certainly carried a message.

But India's long-range plans extend well beyond even the mating of atomic or thermonuclear warheads and IRBMs. It sees itself as both a great culture and as the regional superpower responsible for the subcontinent and ocean that bear its name. Accordingly, New Delhi now possesses the world's fourth-largest army and navy. But even that isn't quite enough. Ultimately, the Indian military establishment intends to put hydrogen warheads on intercontinental ballistic missiles with ranges of up to 5,000 miles.

As early as May 1989, Director of Central Intelligence William H. Webster warned that "indicators" showed that New Delhi was working hard to develop H-bombs. That, he added, would touch off a full-blown nuclear arms race on the subcontinent. India's purchase of beryllium, which is used to enhance fission reactions, was one of the indicators. The beryllium was supplied by Degussa with authorization by Bonn's economic office. Typically, India rejected Webster's assertion as "baseless." The pro-government *National Herald* denounced the CIA's "infinite capacity to weave fantasy out of supposition and surmise and to make improbables look like probables." Nevertheless, both Robert Gates and R. James Woolsey concurred with their predecessor.

The delivery vehicle for India's hydrogen bomb is to be an ICBM whose range would extend over most of Central Asia, Russia, the Indian Ocean, all of China, and as far as the Philippine Sea and Australia. Agni's true importance is not its role as an intermediate-range missile. It is really a proof-of-concept vehicle that needs only to be scaled up and given an improved guidance system to turn into an ICBM. This, as one Indian defense official put it, is "the next logical step." And that step, as usual, points to China. "As long as China can reach New Delhi with its ICBMs, India will remain in a weak position. India's self-defense demands a strategic reach to Beijing. Anything less than that will not be acceptable." Agni, he continued proudly, "is a manifestation of India's self-reliance and a reiteration of faith in our capabilities. In no way is it an expression of aggression. China can reach our territory at any time. Can any self-respecting country accept that?" If the official was asked how Pakistan would feel under similar circumstances, his answer went unrecorded.

•　•　•

If the Indian-Pakistani relationship reflects almost unprecedented mutual hatred, it also reflects pervasive and cynical big-power manipulation. The dynamics of the region have been profoundly affected not only by relations between India and Pakistan, but by the falling-out of China and the Soviet Union in 1959 because of ideological differences and by the way each, as well as the United States and some of its NATO cohorts, played off that falling-out.

Relations between the two Communist behemoths became so strained after their parting of the ways that border clashes took place and a war almost broke out. It was therefore understandable that Moscow courted India and cultivated it as a military client. And if the Soviet Union was an ardent suitor—supplying factories to build late-model MIGs, bombers, tanks, and later even a nuclear-powered submarine—India was an equally willing recipient of the attention because of its problems with China.

It was ironic that Pakistan decided that it needed nuclear weapons after it was routed by India in 1971. This was nuclear dominoes, given the fact that India had come to the same conclusion after China got the bomb, and the Chinese felt compelled to get theirs because of the Soviet threat. Furthermore, the cozy Soviet-Indian relationship—both united in their hostility toward China—made Beijing a natural ally of Pakistan. The Chinese felt the same way. A special relationship between the two countries therefore developed during the 1960s. So two sets of belligerents emerged during the 1970s: the Soviet Union and India versus the People's Republic of China and Pakistan.

But there was an added complication. Starting in 1969, the Nixon administration began using Pakistan (and Romania) to backchannel communications with China in an attempt to normalize relations. Bringing China in from the cold was Nixon-Kissinger realpolitik: a shrewd way to squeeze the Soviet Union from two and a half sides (east, west, and Iran). Washington therefore decided to accommodate Pakistan, its conduit to China. Furthermore, when the Soviet Army rolled into Afghanistan ten years later, effectively extending its frontier (and military presence) with Iran, the United States decided to counter the occupation by using Pakistan as a staging area, supply point, and refuge for anticommunist Afghan guerrillas. It was therefore important for Washington to make certain concessions to Pakistan.

The most important of the concessions had to do with arms proliferation policy. Politics as played by Washington are recounted in some detail in the last chapter. Suffice it to say, succeeding administrations alternately tried to stop nuclear weapons proliferation in Pakistan (as happened when Kissinger warned off the French and Ali Bhutto himself) or merely decided to look the other way while Islamabad scrambled for superweapons to offset India's. That is what happened during the Carter, Reagan, and Bush administrations. Besides pumping advanced weaponry into Pakistan, presidents from Carter on did little or nothing to discourage Islamabad's push for nuclear warheads and the missiles to carry them.

Jimmy Carter's response to the invasion of Afghanistan, in fact, was to offer General Zia $400 million in aid. But the crafty general dismissed it as inadequate. So in 1981 Reagan asked Congress to approve a six-year, $3.2 billion aid package. Zia found the raised ante acceptable.

Yet the legislators went even further. They granted Pakistan a six-year waiver from the provisions of the Symington Amendment, which prohibited aid to nonnuclear weapons countries that imported unsafeguarded enrichment technologies (as was the case at Kahuta). Both administrations and Congress therefore purposely deluded themselves (at least for the record) into believing that sending large quantities of conventional arms to Pakistan would make the Pakistanis so confident in their military ability that they would forgo nuclear weapons.

In identical letters to Speaker of the House Jim Wright in 1987 and 1988, Reagan asserted that U.S. military assistance to Pakistan "remains extremely important in reducing the risk that Pakistan will develop and ultimately possess such a [nuclear] device. I am convinced that our security relationship and assistance program are the most effective means available for us for dissuading Pakistan from acquiring nuclear explosive devices." He added that the assistance would reduce incentives and create disincentives for Islamabad to produce nuclear weapons. This was tantamount to believing in the tooth fairy. But as late as October 5, 1989, George Bush also signed off on Pakistan's being nuclear weapons clean. In a memorandum to Senator Claiborne Pell, Chairman of the Foreign Relations Committee, Bush, like Reagan, expressed deep concern about Pakistan's nuclear weapons program. But he also justified his decision that Islamabad did not have a nuclear weapon on "information available to the United States government."

In fact, as is now clear, Pakistan had every intention of developing an atomic bomb no matter what Washington did. Threats did not work, and neither did the influx of conventional weapons. What might have been effective—a serious clampdown on technology transfer and a serious effort to help calm tensions in Kashmir—fell victim to political expediency, as usual.

If there was one area in which the Indians and Pakistanis were in agreement, it was in the open disdain of First World finger-wagging about the evils of superweapon proliferation. As A. Q. Khan forcefully put it, they and other Third World nations see such preaching, as well as the supposed benefits of IAEA safeguarding, as hypocritical attempts to maintain the status quo.*

That is why Pakistan developed nuclear weapons irrespective of what the United States said or did. It was finally able to machine seven nuclear warheads during the spring and summer of 1990. If it mattered in a religious context, and it did, Islam finally had the atomic bomb. Pakistan's possession of such weapons created a situation in the region that was as unique as it was potentially dangerous. The area became the only place on Earth where five nuclear powers—Russia, Kazakhstan, China, India, and Pakistan—effectively converged.

K. Subrahmanyan, Director of the Institute for Defense Studies and Analysis in New Delhi, was almost sanguine about his country exchanging atomic or even thermonuclear salvos with Pakistan or even with China. His thoughts, in fact, were eerily reminiscent of those in the American far right who believed in the 1980s that their countrymen could ride out and survive a nuclear war with the Soviet Union by hiding in trenches in their backyards that had been covered with doors and dirt:

"Even the failure of deterrence will cause vast, but still finite damage, considering the kind of arsenal the two sides are likely to have for a long time to come, with the advantage being in favor of India if India were to exercise its option [to arm with nuclear weapons]. It will not mean nuclear winter, rapid escalation involving the use of hundreds of warheads and loss of control over the war. It will be analogous to the situation between the superpowers in the early fifties. *That situation will still be preferable to one of India remaining non-nuclear, facing the threat of humiliation, defeat and disintegration*" (italics added).

---

*Many Third World nations believe that the superpowers have hypocritically tried to stop "horizontal" proliferation—many states acquiring nuclear weapons and delivery systems— while fostering their own "vertical" variety. In addition, proliferation literature, particularly American, has been interpreted as "talking down" to developing nations. One critic described the gist of American thoughts on the matter as coming down to the notion that "younger countries simply could not be trusted to know what was good for them, nor were they yet fully responsible, so nuclear weapons in their hands would be more dangerous than in ours." (Brahma Chellaney, "South Asia's Passage to Nuclear Power," *International Security*, Summer 1991, pp. 46–47.)

# 12

## THE REAL CHINA
## SYNDROME

**S**ince Norway and Sweden sit on the same continental plate as the Xingjiang Autonomous Republic, vibrations from the underground "event" that took place at Lop Nor on May 21, 1992, traveled to the two Scandinavian countries with no interruption and little distortion. While scientists at Hong Kong's Royal Observatory were fooled into thinking their seismographs had picked up an earthquake, the Norwegians and Swedes immediately took the distant rumble for what it was: the signature of an underground nuclear explosion. That was not surprising because many Chinese underground thermonuclear weapons tests had been detected over the years.

What was surprising was the magnitude of the blast: one megaton, or the equivalent of a million tons of TNT. "When I saw the reading this morning, I said to myself, 'This is incredible,' " said Klaus Meyer of the Uppsala University Seismological Department. "It was one of the world's biggest underground nuclear bombs since underground testing started." It was in fact China's largest-ever underground nuclear explosion.*

*The largest Soviet underground test, between 2.8 and 4 megatons, occurred at Semipalatinsk on October 27, 1973. The United States broke the record in this category on November 6, 1971, when it exploded a 5-megaton warhead in Alaska.

What the Swedish geologist had no way of knowing, however, was that the Chinese nuclear test was only one incredible development among several that took place that month. Taken together, they were even more incredible than they were individually.

The day before the Chinese test, India scored its first major space triumph when one of its Augmented Space Launch Vehicles lifted off from the Sriharikota Launch Range north of Madras and sent a sixty-six-pound scientific satellite into low Earth orbit. The Indians steadfastly—and correctly—maintained that the ASLV was a civilian launch vehicle. Similarly, its cargo was a small spacecraft carrying only a gamma-ray detector and an atmospheric experiment. They were correct but they were also typically disingenuous. As was clear to everyone else in the international space community, including the Chinese, the same ASLV that could loft a satellite into orbit could also carry a warhead to any place in China.

Furthermore, the satellite launch was a precursor to the planned polar orbiting of a one-ton Indian remote sensing spacecraft in 1993. (That launch was to fail.) With a space reconnaissance program of their own, the Chinese were aware that the "remote sensing" satellite could also do double duty in reconnaissance and targeting. Nor would Chinese apprehension have been eased by knowing that the spacecraft's polar orbit would provide coverage of all of China, while its ten-meter resolution would send the images down in significant detail.

The megaton blast at Lop Nor was therefore intended to send a forceful message to New Delhi: China would not be intimidated by shows of long-range rocket capability. It had the wherewithal to devastate India. Such demonstrations and counterdemonstrations of power are not rare in the relations between nations. But this one was set off while the President of India was in China on a "goodwill" visit.

India did not protest the blatant insult. Instead, it answered eight days later with the second successful firing of an Agni from Balasore far into the Bay of Bengal. The IRBM's 1,500-mile-plus range put half of China, including all of Xingjiang, within reach of Indian missileers. And India sent Beijing another message. For the first time, it allowed two of its naval vessels on an exercise with two ships from the U.S. Navy. It did so despite the fact that Washington had earlier announced a ban on the sale of rocket technology to India because New Delhi had refused to cancel an agreement with a Russian space company to develop an engine capable of firing payloads into deep space.

China would not have been happy about the joint exercise. Yet there would have been some grim solace in the fact that a ceremony had been held in Islamabad four days earlier—on May 25—to mark the rededication of a U.S.-supplied Pakistani research reactor that China had been only too happy to upgrade.*

A dynamic was at work in these events that went far in explaining why China was and remains the single most cynical and remorseless superweapon proliferator. It combines xenophobia, greed, and an unshakable belief that China's history, culture, and geography make it the rightful leader of the Third World.

It was Mao himself who created the concept of the "three worlds," as described by Deng Xiaoping in a speech at the United Nations in 1974. The first consisted of the United States and the Soviet Union. The second grouped Japan and all of Europe. The third placed China with Africa, the Middle East, southeast Asia, and other formerly colonial (i.e., suppressed and exploited) lands.

Ironically, almost two decades later, China's own neighbors—several of them members of the Third World itself—felt threatened by China. The People's Republic not only is the world's third-largest country (after Canada and Russia) and its most populous, but also has the most neighbors: Russia, North Korea, Taiwan, North Vietnam, Hong Kong, Laos, Myanmar, Bhutan, Nepal, India, Pakistan, Afghanistan, Kazakhstan, Tajikistan, Kirghizstan, and Mongolia.

None of them need to be reminded that, Deng's lofty speech about the essential unity of the victims of imperialist oppression notwithstanding, China has invaded India and Vietnam, grabbed Tibet, tried to subvert Indonesia, threatened to invade Taiwan and fought artillery duels with the islands of Quemoy and Matsu, and engaged in border battles with the U.S.S.R. that at one point threatened to turn nuclear. In addition, China harbors a lingering hatred of Japan—an old score to settle—because of atrocities committed during the Japanese occupation in the 1930s and 1940s. It also no doubt has twinges of jealousy because of the economic miracle that has taken place in Japan since World War II.

There is no illusion about the reasons such widespread Chinese aggression, actual and threatened, has taken place. China is bent on not only becoming the dominant power in east Asia, but the acknowledged

---

*Appropriately, President Ghulam Ishaq Khan took the occasion to note that 1992 was the fiftieth anniversary of the Manhattan Project. He contrasted that weapon with what he called Pakistan's "peaceful" nuclear program. ("Khan on Need to Exploit Nuclear Energy," FBIS-NES-92-103, May 28, 1992, p. 53.)

leader of the Third World itself. Given its size and billion-plus population, Beijing believes it is entitled to no less, and it is arming accordingly. Having already mastered the four staples of superweaponry, China was by the start of the 1990s adjusting its strategic forces for regional conflict. It wants to project its power beyond its shores, particularly in the South China Sea, where it claims sovereignty over a huge region that includes the Nan Sha (Spratly) and Paracel Islands. Besides being strategically located between Vietnam, Malaysia, and the Philippines and along Japan's oil route to the Middle East, the Spratlys are thought to contain large oil reserves. They have therefore been claimed by China, Brunei, Malaysia, the Philippines, Taiwan, and Vietnam. China, ever mindful that it is precariously energy deficient, went so far as to literally stake them out: it planted markers on several of the islands and enacted a law claiming them. And in order to avoid any possibility of misunderstanding, biological weapons were stored near the markers.

Having what it considers to be the ultimate military fallbacks— chemical and biological weapons, missiles and the nukes to go with them—China is therefore concentrating on the acquisition of more practical weapons suitable to the kind of force it wants to project in its region. It is developing ballistic missiles called DF-25s with two-ton high-explosive warheads (Scuds carry 500-pounders). It is also buying Iranian air-to-air refueling capability to extend the range of the fighters and bombers it is acquiring in the Kremlin's basement sale. And it is assembling a navy that will almost definitely include the region's first aircraft carrier, the purchase of which the Communist Party in Beijing has approved.

"One cold war has ended—two more cold wars have begun," a Chinese foreign policy document warned in 1992. The two new cold wars the Chinese seemed to be referring to were the contest between capitalism and the remaining Communist countries and the growing friction within the Western alliance itself. "We're going to exploit the divisions among Western countries, strengthen ourselves, and focus our efforts on the Asia-Pacific region and the nations along our border," the statement went on to declare. With the exception of Taiwan, China does not seem to be contemplating the acquisition of an entire nation, as Saddam Hussein tried to do with Kuwait. Yet memories linger of an older, larger empire that existed a century and a half ago that included Nepal, half of Bangladesh, Myanmar, Thailand, Malaysia, Indochina, Taiwan, North and South Korea, Mongolia, and large tracts of Russia, Kazakhstan, Kirghizstan, and Tajikstan.

Understandably, the very notion of Chinese suzerainty has unsettled some of its neighbors. One of its immediate effects has been to propel Taiwan into beefing up its own air and sea forces. Less immediately, but ultimately more importantly, China's eye on the South China Sea may help to turn Japan's Self-Defense Force into an offensive force with superweapon capabilities to match its superpower status. The reemergence of Japan in such a role will set off alarms throughout east Asia. The fears China's xenophobic leaders have as they peer out at a seemingly threatening world are matched by similar worries among the ring of neighbors that look in at them.

In January 1984, Premier Zhao Ziyang delivered a toast at a White House dinner in which he declared that the Chinese do not "engage in nuclear proliferation ourselves, nor do we help other countries to develop nuclear weapons." In an interview with the official Chinese news agency a year later, then Vice Premier Li Peng echoed his boss. "I wish to reiterate that China has no intention, either at present or in the future, to help non-nuclear countries develop nuclear weapons. . . . China's nuclear cooperation with other countries . . . is confined to peaceful purposes alone." Li's remarks could have been prepared by the very Pakistani leaders to whom his country was at that moment supplying the wherewithal for atomic bombs with full knowledge of what they were doing. The Chinese Foreign Ministry followed suit. "We by no means favor nuclear proliferation, nor do we engage in such proliferation by helping other countries to develop nuclear weapons," a Foreign Ministry spokesman insisted in June 1984.

Seven years later, in August 1991, Li Peng, who had in the meantime become premier, went so far as to announce at a meeting in Beijing with his Japanese counterpart that China had decided "in principle" to support the Non-Proliferation Treaty. At that moment, the People's Republic of China was thought to have 400-plus nuclear weapons, including land- and sea-based ballistic missiles, bombs, mines, and artillery shells.*

---

*The timing of the announcement was doubly ironic. Li was hosting a politician whose own country had a vast "defensive" capability and mounds of plutonium and other ingredients necessary to make nuclear weapons in short order. Furthermore, his remarks coincided with the release in Washington of a congressional report showing that, for the first time since 1983, the United States had surpassed the former Soviet Union as the biggest arms supplier to the Third World, including the Middle East. ("U.S. Ranked No. 1 in Weapons Sales," *The New York Times*, August 11, 1991.)

But China's repeated sale of ballistic missile technology and nuclear war-making equipment and technology belied its leaders' dovish pronouncements. Even as Li spoke, Chinese scientists, engineers, and technicians were fulfilling a secret 1983 agreement to provide Algeria with its reactor and, reportedly, with detailed advice on how to adapt the plutonium warheads that would eventually come from it to various delivery systems.

China's other customers included Argentina (heavy water and enriched uranium); Brazil (enriched uranium); India (heavy water); Iran (training technicians, the sale of reactor technology, and the sale of an entire research reactor); Iraq (allegedly violating the U.N. trade embargo in 1990 by selling lithium hydride for possible use in nuclear weapons); and North Korea (training nuclear scientists). Worse, it also sold Pakistan a reliable bomb design, uranium hexafluoride feedstock, tritium gas for boosting fission bomb yields, and centrifuge magnets, as well as accepting an order for a 300-megawatt power station, training a small army of its nuclear weapons scientists, and even regularly inviting officials to nuclear tests at Lop Nor. South Africa bought sixty tons of enriched uranium from China. In addition, China unabashedly spread short-, medium-, and long-range Silkworm, M-9, M-11, and CSS-2 technology and related technology around the world, only occasionally backing down in the face of sporadic pressure from Washington. Its actual or potential customers included Argentina, Brazil, Iran, Iraq, North Korea, Pakistan, Saudi Arabia, and Syria.

If the Chinese seem two-faced where proliferation is concerned it is because, politically and militarily, they are. China proliferates and denounces proliferation simultaneously and with equal conviction because, where arms exports are concerned, it does not speak with one voice.

China may be the world's largest avowedly Communist country, but the heart of its military organization and weapons procurement, development, and export operation is strictly a family business, and a profit-oriented one at that.

On paper, the nation's military is run by the Ministry of National Defense. In fact, the ministry is merely a facade that was created to deal with its foreign counterparts. The real power lies in the Central Military Commission, or rather with its half-dozen virtually autonomous, almost feudal subgroups: the General Staff Department; the General Political Department; the Commission of Science, Technology and Industry for

National Defense (COSTIND); the General Logistics Department; the National Defense University; and the Academy of Military Science. Each is responsible for its own plans and budgets.

The first four are, in turn, run by power centers, many of which were formed decades ago around individual revolutionary leaders and which are dominated by family networks that look out for themselves regardless of who controls the government. The networks quietly steer operations in a way that is reminiscent of organized crime. In 1992 COSTIND, to take only one example, was dominated by its deputy director, Major General Nie Li. She was the daughter of China's last living marshal and its undisputed nuclear guru, Nie Rongzhen. Her husband, Lieutenant General Ding Henaggao, was COSTIND's chairman. President Yang Shangkun's eldest son was reported to be another COSTIND official, as was Zhang Pin, a son of former Defense Minister Zhang Aiping. Deng himself at one time denounced the networks, saying that they represented "a lingering clan mentality," a vestige of the nation's feudal past. Former U.S. ambassador to China James Lilly called them a "decaying dynasty." Others call them Communist aristocrats. The leaders of the Central Military Commission—the heads of the six subgroups—communicate through the family network. Even the Communist Party state leadership has only limited control over these subgroups and no veto power over their actions.

China's arms trade, both imports and exports, is largely handled by two major organizations: the China North Industries Corporation (NORINCO), which operates under the aegis of the New Era Corporation and which is controlled by the General Staff Department and COSTIND, and Poly Technologies, an arms trading company run by the General Staff Department's Equipment and Technology Department. NORINCO and Poly Technologies are intense business competitors. New Era, an administrative body, has other affiliates besides NORINCO. They include the China Precision Machinery Import-Export Corporation, which peddles tactical missiles at arms shows; CSSC, the State Shipbuilding Corporation, which manufactures naval vessels; the Great Wall Corporation, which handles space launch services; and more than a dozen other companies. Poly Technologies, which also exports missiles, as well as every type of conventional weapon, is the more influential of the two. None of these companies are secretive. Poly Technologies even has a brand-new headquarters in downtown Beijing, its gleaming twin towers festooned with the Chinese characters that spell its name.

The generals who run both organizations, and who are therefore responsible for all foreign weapons sales, know that the proceeds of those sales go directly to improving the quality of their own armies' weapons. That is because Deng Xiaoping decreed it so in 1984.

Fed up with a bloated military and embarrassed by the army's poor performance against Vietnam five years earlier, Deng resolved to streamline the military by cutting one million of its four million troops. More important, he also told the officer corps that, like an adult offspring who lives at home, it was going to have to stop free-loading and start helping pay some of the bills. If it wanted the most modern weapons, Deng said, it was going to have to devise ways to earn them. The People's Liberation Army (PLA), which includes all three traditional services, was thereby given no choice but to come up with hardheaded ways of earning foreign currency or see its capability slowly atrophy.* The PLA did as it was told, with results that were to have far-reaching consequences throughout the world.

Conventional arms sales became one staple. Between 1988 and 1991, China sold $1.2 billion worth of long-range guns, ammunition, F-6 fighters (export versions of the J-6, which was, in turn, a knockoff of the MIG-19), and patrol boats to Myanmar's state "law and order council," or SLORC, a military dictatorship that blocked a democratically elected government from taking office. China was so driven by the need to export weapons that as late as the 1980s, it was selling J-6s out of its own air force's inventory to Egypt, Iran, Iraq, North Korea, Pakistan, Somalia, Tanzania, and Zambia. The J-6 was replaced by the J-7 (the Chinese version of the venerable MIG-21), but it, too, was exported in quantity to Albania, Egypt, Iraq, Tanzania, Burma, Bangladesh, Iran, Thailand, and Zimbabwe.

---

*Its business is not confined to weapons exports, however. The People's Liberation Army also owns part of the five-star Palace Hotel in Beijing and the Cathay in Guangzhou. It produces a wide variety of civilian goods, including pianos, home appliances, and civil aircraft. In 1989, it produced civilian products worth $4 billion. ("The Army That Makes Money," *The Economist,* October 5, 1991, p. 38.)

The PLA even set up a military amusement park, the China North International Shooting Range, thirty-eight miles outside of Beijing on the road that leads to the Great Wall. For 150 yuan, or about $27 a round, tourists could fire mortars toward the nearby hills. Light and heavy machine guns, a variety of sidearms, and AK-47 assault rifles were also available, as were 14.5-millimeter antiaircraft guns (aircraft not included). One Japanese group spent $500 in an hour in 1992 and proudly had its picture taken next to the weapons it had used. ("Army's Business Sideline: These Guns for Fun," *The New York Times,* September 28, 1992.)

By 1992, arms exports accounted for 50 percent of the money used to modernize the PLA. Deng's decree catapulted China into a distant, but still significant, number three position among arms exporters to the Third World during the 1980s (after the Soviet Union and the United States). Its drive to supply a wide variety of basic weapons, cheaply and in quantity, earned it as much as $5 billion in 1987—largely because of the Iran-Iraq War—and an average of about half that during the rest of the 1980s.

More important, the decree created a sales strategy which had consequences that reached far beyond China itself. The idea of selling weapons and weapons technology to procure still newer weapons and technology in a kind of self-reinforcing financial cycle became a model for other Third World countries like Argentina, Brazil, India, Iran, South Africa, and Taiwan.* That, in turn, set the basis for the current situation, in which Third World countries are engaged in a thriving arms trade among themselves, in many cases skirting involvement with traditional suppliers altogether. Pakistani aid to Iran's nuclear program, Israel's helping South Africa to acquire a long-range ballistic missile, and Brazil's sales of nuclear, missile, rocket, and space technology to Iraq are only three cases among scores.

Although they are supposed to consult the Ministry of Foreign Affairs before overseas arms sales are concluded, the generals reserve for themselves the final word on whether or not deals are made. The civilians in the Foreign Ministry have carried the nonproliferation banner with considerable zeal, cautioning the military to pay more attention to how arms sales impact on China's subtle diplomatic relations with other nations. The ministry has no stake in the weapons the generals sell, yet it has to deal with the political consequences of the sales: unending protests from the United States and other nations. It has therefore urged Poly Technologies, in particular, to be more prudent in transferring sophisticated weapons and superweapon technology to potentially turbulent regions.

---

*This is not to say that some of these nations did not have export-oriented arms industries before Deng's order. Brazil's plans to export conventional weapons go back to the 1960s; sales exceeded $1 billion by 1980 and had more than doubled by 1984, when Deng issued his ultimatum. But it is clear from studying the pattern of such exports in several nations that the Chinese model was increasingly followed. (See Michael Brzoska and Thomas Ohlson, eds., *Arms Production in the Third World*, London: Taylor & Francis, 1986, passim.)

Poly Technologies has reacted to that relatively pious advice with unconcealed scorn. "We are determined to devote ourselves to raising funds for promoting the four modernizations of China," one Poly Technologies officer snapped. "This is a glorious mission that should claim precedence over all others. Right now, the Ministry of Foreign Affairs should review how to serve this mission. . . . It is wrong to sacrifice the number one mission for the sake of foreign [diplomatic] affairs."

In common with some of their Russian counterparts, the generals have also been angered by what they see as the ministry's caving in to high-handed, hypocritical chastising by the United States. When Washington protested the pending sale of a submarine to Pakistan for $100 million (at a profit of $60 million), the ministry urged the generals to abandon the deal. Angry Poly Technologies officials countered by telling the ministry that it had to learn to cope with the Americans. And, for good measure, they asked the ministry why it had not criticized the United States for failing to protest when the Soviet Union leased a nuclear-powered sub to India.

And here they had an ally in Deng himself, who was at least as interested in profits from arms exports as his generals. A Foreign Ministry objection to the sale of the CSS-2 missiles to Saudi Arabia in the mid-1980s eventually landed on the old man's desk. The Premier summoned a Poly Technologies official to ask one question:

"How much money did you make?"

"Two billion dollars," the official answered.

"Not a little," Deng reflected aloud, evidently pleased. That is where the dispute ended. The Foreign Ministry had lost again.*

China did more than simply hawk off-the-shelf hardware, however. Some of its sales were distinctly creative. The M-9 and M-11 deals with Iran, Syria, Libya, and Pakistan are cases in point. Like any aggressive sales team, Precision Machinery Import-Export began pushing the M-9 and M-11 missiles years before they went into production. In November 1986—even before all of its design work had been completed—a model of the M-9 was displayed at the Asian Defense Exposition in Beijing. A year

*U.S. intelligence analysts and others have calculated that the deal was worth $3 billion in then-current dollars.

later, China began negotiating with Syria, Pakistan, Iran, and Libya for development funds—up-front money—for the weapon.* Besides Pakistan, Syria, which had old Scuds, also kicked in start-up funding for the project.

By the summer of 1988—even before Chinese units received M-9s—development deals for them were beginning to be cut from Pakistan to Libya, all the while with Beijing denying that anything was amiss. In February 1989, China was reliably reported to be trying to sell them to Iran. Three months later, U.S. intelligence reported that Syria and China had actually signed an agreement for M-9s. Within days, word was leaked that Libya had agreed to contribute $170 million toward the Syrian M-9 purchase, provided it got 60 of the 140 missiles that were ordered. In August, a Chinese Foreign Ministry spokesman denied that any such contract had been signed. In December 1990, after the Saudis had paid Syria the $2 billion to join the anti-Iraq coalition, the CIA reported that thirty M-9 launchers and an unspecified number of missiles had been ordered by Syria, with Saudi Arabia footing $285 million worth of the bill. At the same time it was reported that Iran and China had signed a ten-year technology transfer agreement which included production of both M-9s and M-11s in Iran. In January 1991, a concerned Israeli official with obvious intelligence connections asserted that the Syrian M-9 purchase would cost $300 million.

By March 1991, China had delivered M-11 launchers to Pakistan, along with dummy missile frames for practice launches: the first return on its $300 million investment. The Department of State reacted by urging the White House to suspend high-tech exports to China. In April, intelligence reports showed that mobile launchers for the M-11 were under construction and that Pakistani Air Force technicians were in China, training to use the weapons. In May, a secret Defense Intelligence Agency study concluded that Beijing's public statements denying it had sold ballistic missiles in the Middle East were lies. It added that the Pakistani

*The creation of missiles was not the only joint deal cut by China. It and Pakistan codeveloped the Karakoram K-8 jet trainer in the early 1990s and planned to market it in the United States. "The equipment is made in the U.S. and the aircraft is very economical," said Shi Ping, the plane's chief designer. "We want to talk to U.S. companies about selling it there." The name Karakoram comes from a mountain range between China and Pakistan and symbolizes the friendship between the two countries. ("Karakoram K-8 Trainer Makes Air Show Debut," *Aviation Week & Space Technology*, March 9, 1992, pp. 42–43.) Later, Iran expressed an interest in the project, as well.

deal violated a pledge made by the Chinese in 1988 that they would do no such thing.

In June, China's ambassador to the United States, Zhu Qizhen, admitted to reporters at the National Press Club in Washington that his country had sold "some conventional weapons to Pakistan, including tiny amounts of short-range tactical missiles. I think here you call it M-111 [sic]." That same month, a Chinese freighter was tracked carrying M-9s from a factory in China to Cyprus, with Syria as their destination. By January 1992, there was hard evidence that China had also sent the Pakistanis up to thirty tons of solid-fuel chemicals for the M-11s, as well as guidance systems for the missiles. By December, missile components had arrived in Karachi, causing consternation at the CIA.

The sale of technology and components rather than finished missiles was calculated to protect China from accusations of violating the Missile Technology Control Regime when the weapons came on line. While the Pakistani missiles would have M-series technology at their core, they would not carry a "Made in China" label. Similarly, Pakistan's Hatf missiles were hybrids of both M-11 and French sounding rocket technology.

Throughout, pro-China White House policy impeded efforts to stop Beijing's proliferation. Two years earlier, for example, U.S. intelligence turned up evidence that the PLA was prepared to sell the Libyans about 10,000 tons of poison gas precursors for their second chemical weapons plant at Sebha as well as M-series missiles. China has extensive chemical and biological warfare programs, both geared to spread toxic agents, not combat them. Being the only country to have undergone attack by biological agents—at the hands of the Japanese—the Chinese are especially well versed in their effect.

At any rate, word of the chemical weapons shipment to Libya was promptly passed to the Department of State, which tried to persuade Beijing not to go through with the deal. But State's protest came right after the White House granted China most-favored-nation status. During congressional testimony in which the chemical weapons agreement was made public, an exasperated senator vented his frustration over what he called a failed Executive Branch policy toward China. "You certainly can't defend China on trade," said Joseph R. Biden, Jr., a Delaware Democrat. "You can't begin to defend them on human rights. You can't begin to defend them on their handling of the situation since Tiananmen Square."

A month later, having received the U.S. protest and then been pushed into the international spotlight by the testimony in Congress, China stopped the shipment from a chemical factory on its coast. At the same time, according to leaked intelligence, a second chemical manufacturer in China agreed to send the precursors to Libya. That, apparently, was where the intelligence trail went cold.

The disintegration of the Soviet Union and the end of the war against Iraq boded ill for the People's Liberation Army and for the Chinese government as a whole. Washington's courting of Beijing in order to flank Moscow, beginning in the Nixon presidency, had given China a degree of international importance it had not had before. When the Soviet Union and its militant anti-Westernism began to unravel at the end of the 1980s, however, China's importance as a counterbalance also diminished.

The war against Iraq only made matters worse. The unprecedented cooperation between the United States and the Commonwealth of Independent States, plus U.S. dominance of the coalition, further underscored the former Soviet Union's reduced status as a world power and therefore of China's status as a counterweight to it. In addition, the war effectively closed a lucrative conventional arms market, already mostly dried up, that had existed during the Iran-Iraq war. For China, the slaughter that took place on both sides amounted to an economic windfall, and one in which Beijing itself remained impartial. China Precision Machinery Import-Export, for example, had managed to sell Silkworms to both sides. Finally, the apparent effectiveness of Western high-tech weapons made them the envy of all of the onlookers, including the People's Liberation Army. New upscale arms buyers no longer wanted to settle for obsolete, if low-cost, Chinese weapons.* Nor did the PLA itself.

One appreciative Chinese government strategist offered his own interpretation of the Gulf War as a vision of the future. "As a result of the extensive use of such high-tech equipment as military satellites, attack nuclear submarines, aircraft carriers, high-performance combat aircraft and cruise missiles, the battlefield of the Gulf War stretched out horizontally hundreds of miles and even thousands of miles, and vertically

---

*By 1992, China's profit from arms sales has plummeted 80 percent from 1988. A CIA report to Congress blamed a glut of more advanced Western and ex-Soviet equipment on the world market. ("Over the Cliff," *Aviation Week & Space Technology*, August 3, 1992, p. 19.)

from space to high altitude, medium altitude, low altitude, ultra-low altitude, the ground, sea surface and even the underwater areas, forming a high-tech battlefield with unprecedented depths and dimensions."

That being the case, China began to use the foreign exchange it earned from weapon sales to restock its own arsenal with highly advanced arms. The national defense budget rose 12 percent in 1991, to $6.4 billion, and by 13.8 percent in 1992, to more than $7 billion. It easily outstripped the budget increases for agriculture (increased by 7.2 percent), education (11.3 percent), and science (7.4 percent). Although Deng had made the one-million-man cut in PLA personnel by 1992, he favored infusing the services with modern arms backed by cutting-edge science. The ICBM force bristled with CSS-3 missiles with 4,350-mile ranges and larger CSS-X4s that could strike targets 6,200 miles away. Plans called for the creation of a deep-water navy, including an extended fleet of submarines, two of which already carried ballistic missiles. They also called for sophisticated radars, computers, navigational equipment, and command and control systems.

Furthermore, China spared almost no expense on its nuclear weapons facilities. A huge secret weapons production complex, most of it underground to protect it from spaceborne reconnaissance, was built in Sichuan Province. The installation, called the "Third Line," is so large that it even dwarfs the U.S. and Soviet weapons facilities built after World War II. In addition, a closely held plan, the "863 High Technology Plan for Energy," calls for China to build three types of experimental reactors, including a fast breeder, by the year 2000.

If its traditional suppliers were going to restrict weapons sales to China after the Soviet Union collapsed, the Chinese decided to go to their former opponent for the weapons they wanted. Chinese scientists and weapons buyers were therefore prominent among those attending the former Soviet Union's ongoing yard sale in the early 1990s.

In March 1992, Beijing announced that it planned to negotiate science and technology cooperation agreements with Russia, Kazakhstan, Ukraine, Belarus, and Uzbekistan. Meanwhile, it picked up as many as sixty SU-27s, the first dozen of which were delivered in 1991, and made plans to produce its own version of the powerful MIG-31 fighter using 1,500 Russian engineers and technicians. The idea, Western analysts concluded, was to use the MIGs as mini-airborne warning and control planes to direct the SU-27s and other strike aircraft in combat.

China's air generals also bought air-to-air refueling capability from Iran (which got it from the United States during the reign of the Shah) and their own IL-76s from Russia. In exchange for air-to-air refueling kits for their fighters and refueling pods for some of their tanker aircraft, the Chinese agreed to provide Iran with nuclear reactor technology and the means to manufacture both the M-9 and M-11 missiles. They wanted the four-jet, swept-wing Il-76s for use as both aerial refuelers and AWACS.

Faced with these expenses, the leadership in Beijing responded in the classic capitalistic manner; it tried to give its current customers what they wanted and in the process create new ones. It was a policy that was as arrogant as it was cynical. The apparent idea, used effectively in the Middle East by France, was to ingratiate themselves to customers and make political inroads by offering weapons and services that were not readily available elsewhere.

China had done that before. This time, however, the stakes were going up. In common with other proliferators, the Chinese began to learn that old and new customers alike hungered for increasingly sophisticated weapons, not merely discards or "export items." A glaring example of this occurred when China allowed Pakistani scientists to use the nuclear weapons facility at Lop Nor and permitted both scientists and generals to observe China's own tests there over a period of ten years.

The first harbinger of China's new direction had actually developed in July 1985—five years before the Persian Gulf War—when Poly Technologies and Prince Bandar bin Sultan of Saudi Arabia struck the $3 billion deal for CSS-2s. The Saudis only went to the Chinese in the first place because the U.S. Congress, responding to Israeli pressure, temporarily turned down a request by Riyadh for short-range Lance missiles and F-15E Strike Eagle fighter-bombers. Saudi Arabia thereby made the transition from conventional to superweapons to spite their otherwise reliable benefactor and petroleum customer.*

When news of the ballistic missile transfer broke in the news media in the spring of 1988, straight-faced Chinese Foreign Minister Wu Xueqian obediently told reporters that Beijing had only concluded the deal because it was "conducive to stability" in the Middle East. The first missiles were

---

*They got the F-15s and the AWACS starting in 1987 and contracted for a second batch of seventy-two of the fighters five years later.

delivered, apparently undetected by U.S. intelligence, in late 1987 and were deployed on unprotected launch pads at Al Joffer, 60 miles south of Riyadh, and at Al Sulaiyil, 400 miles farther south. The sites were deep in the "Empty Quarter," which helped protect them from Iraqi and Iranian Scuds, an Israeli commando raid, or an Osirak-type air assault.* The Saudi monarchy let it be known that it purchased the missiles to hold Iran's fanatical mullahs in check.

Ironically, it was the Saudi sheiks' fear of Iranian revivalism that prompted them to support Iraq with substantial amounts of money. Saddam Hussein would repay the gesture on August 2, 1990, in his own inimitable way.

Meanwhile, the United States discovered the presence of CSS-2s in Saudi Arabia in March 1988 only after a truck carrying one of the missiles went off a road and became stuck in sand. Keyhole satellites had been photographing Chinese ships unloading at a Saudi port for months. The weapons coming out of the holds were assumed to be bound only for Iraq. What the analysts saw, however, was only the equipment that was taken off the ships during daylight hours. After sunset, when the reconnaissance satellites could not see clearly, the CSS-2s were unloaded and put on trucks and driven inland. One night, however, a vehicle carrying a CSS-2 strayed into the desert and got bogged down in sand. It was spotted, helplessly stuck like a debilitated bug, by an alert photointerpreter who scrutinized pictures of the area taken the following day. Once it became apparent that the truck was carrying a large missile, full coverage of the Arabian peninsula was ordered, and the CSS-2 missile fields were soon discovered.

What followed was a crisis that occurred 5,000 miles from China but which the Chinese, themselves, had fueled. As word spread, first in intelligence circles and then in the media, Israel indeed began to plan an Osirak-style attack with its F-15s. Within days, and unknown to the world at large, another potential explosion loomed in the Middle East. As U.S.-made F-15s went on alert in both Israel and Saudi Arabia, Secretary of State George Shultz had to mediate between the two countries, extracting promises from the Arabs that their long-range missiles would

---

*The missiles were unprotected in the sense that they were not housed in silos. They were undoubtedly well guarded. Israel had successfully tested its own long-range ballistic missile, Jericho-2, the previous year. That, in fact, may have been another reason for the Saudis to order CSS-2s.

not be targeted at Israel. That having been done, the nervous Israelis were persuaded to, in effect, take their thumbs off their fighters' arming switches.

The story about the CSS-2s erupted in the U.S. news media just before Wu Xueqian arrived in Washington to discuss closer technological ties between the two countries, a situation George Bush, like Ronald Reagan, favored. Shultz raised the matter of the Saudi missiles with Wu, but received no "satisfactory" response. Subsequent appeals for restraint in other missile sales by Secretary of Defense Frank Carlucci, Assistant Secretary of State H. Allen Holmes, Deputy Secretary of State Lawrence Eagleburger, and National Security Adviser Brent Scowcroft prompted bland assurances from the men inside the Forbidden City that they intended to act in a "responsible" way. If they further defined that term, it was not publicized.

Beijing's superweapon machinations bedeviled the Reagan and Bush administrations. Both were determined to exploit China economically and politically by selling it U.S. goods and services while simultaneously continuing Nixon's policy of using it to flank and counterbalance the Soviets. Ideally, this meant granting the Chinese most-favored-nation status so that sensitive high-tech equipment—the stuff the generals in Beijing were really after—could be sold to them. But China's record on human rights, which was a condition of most-favored-nation status, was always problematical.

It was problematical, that is, until the Tiananmen Square massacre on June 3–4, 1989, when it suddenly turned horrific. An estimated 5,000 people were killed by soldiers during prodemocracy demonstrations, and twice that number were wounded. Yet in the face of continuing evidence that the Chinese were proliferating superweapons, including submarines and nerve agents, and committing persistent human rights violations, Bush took the position that dealing with China would be more productive than isolating it. "We want to advance the cause of freedom," he told a Yale graduating class on May 27, 1991, "not simply profess our purity."

One of the restrictive measures it was prepared to take, the White House announced that day, was to block the sale to China of U.S. high-speed computers used for missile testing. This, in turn, led to a situation similar to the one Leybold got into when it tried to persuade the German government that it was obeying export laws and in the process unwittingly uncovered deals the government had not known about. Saying publicly that he was going to stop the sale of the computers was also an announcement that until then the sale had actually been planned. The fact that Bush had been prepared to transfer to Beijing computers used to produce advanced ballistic missiles, particularly while reproaching the Chinese for their missile exports, was in itself remarkable. China policy "is not made in this building," a frustrated Department of State official complained. "It is made in the Oval Office. All of our China policy has been personalized by the President."

At any rate, discovery of the CSS-2s caused some concern within the U.S. intelligence community, not merely because the intermediate-range missiles were there, but for a more arcane reason. Whatever they had in range—up to 2,200 miles in their most improved version—they lacked in accuracy. The CSS-2 was a twenty-year-old design by the time it arrived in Saudi Arabia, and whatever improvements may have been made in the meantime, it was considered so inaccurate at full range that carrying a standard high-explosive warhead would be all but useless.

"You can't make that [missile] accurate enough to be useful" with a conventional warhead, one U.S. expert said. Its accuracy would be far less critical, on the other hand, if it carried chemical, biological, or nuclear weapons. Despite the fact that the Saudis had recently signed the Non-Proliferation Treaty, speculation continued that some secret deal had been worked out in which a number of nuclear warheads were kept on Saudi soil and guarded by Chinese. The Saudis would not let Americans or other coalition partners anywhere near the two missile installations to see for themselves.

From Washington's point of view, the bad news about the CSS-2s was that they helped to destabilize the Middle East, probably spurring the Israelis on even more in their own long-range missile buildup (as if they needed spurring on). The good news was that Saudi Arabia was at least a Western bulwark with close but low-keyed relations with the United States. Whatever maneuvering had to be done in Congress to accommodate Israel's sharp-eyed lobbyists, planners understood that the Saudis walked a tightrope; they had to show a certain amount of hostility to Israel to pacify the Arab League while remaining firmly committed to those who paid their bills: chiefly their petroleum customers in the West. Appearances to the contrary, strategists in Washington and Riyadh understand that both nations are entwined in an intimate, unholy alliance; that if the oil stops flowing westward for whatever reason, the United States and western Europe will be plunged into politico-economic calamity, one of the effects of which would be the drying up and blowing away of Saudi Arabia and the other sheikdoms.

The Chinese went even beyond Arabia to sell missiles. In 1984, a delegation of ballistic missile experts went to Argentina and Brazil to try to sell DF-5s to both countries for use in their "space" programs. Their intended customers would have been aware that the rocket was the ICBM version of the civilian Long March 2 launch vehicle, which was never actually produced. The fact that the Chinese tried to sell a ballistic missile for use as a space launcher, rather than the space launcher itself—say, the refined Long March 3—was typically shrewd. Buying the DF-5, the salesmen undoubtedly explained in their pitch, would have given both countries two systems for the price of one. Neither Argentina nor Brazil had enough hard currency to afford DF-5s, however, so they declined the offer. But nine years later, in 1993, Chinese technicians were back in Brazil, this time selling missile technology rather than full-up systems.

China's most pernicious trade has been in nuclear weapons. It exploded its first atomic bomb, a twenty-five-kiloton device, on top of a tower at Lop Nor on October 16, 1964. It was code-named CHIC-1 by those in Washington who evaluated it with the help of seismic data, air sampling, and other intelligence. On June 17, 1967, only thirty-two months later, a full-yield hydrogen bomb was successfully tested by being dropped out of an airplane. CHIC-6, as it was called, yielded 3.3 megatons, or 231 times that of the Hiroshima blast.

China's nuclear program dates at least from 1951, when the country signed a secret agreement with Moscow through which the Chinese sent uranium ore westward in exchange for Soviet technical assistance. By 1953, working under the guise of developing peaceful uses for nuclear energy, the Chinese were hard at work on weapons design. Before the final rupture with the Soviet Union in 1959, Moscow provided China with an experimental reactor, uranium processing facilities, a cyclotron, and equipment for a gaseous diffusion plant. Khrushchev drew the line on handing over bombs, however. He did promise to provide Mao Tse-tung with his own sample atomic bomb but then quietly reneged in 1959. Worsening relations between the two nations was the ostensible reason, but there was very likely a personal one as well.

That year, Mao told Andrei Gromyko, the Soviet Foreign Minister, that in the event of war with the United States, the Russians should allow American troops to penetrate deep into Chinese territory. "Only when the Americans are right in the central provinces," Mao added, "should you give them everything you've got." It is interesting to speculate about what the ever-inscrutable Andrei Gromyko was thinking as he listened to the Chinese leader. Whatever it was, he related the discussion to Khrushchev. The thought of Mao's allowing Soviet H-bombs to incinerate millions of Chinese for the sake of destroying Americans evidently rattled Khrushchev, who concluded that Mao was a "lunatic on a throne."

By 1991, China had tested nuclear and thermonuclear weapons thirty-six times. Its weapons were divided into the same kind of missile-bomber-submarine "triad" used by the United States and the old Soviet Union. When fighting broke out along the Sino-Soviet border in 1969, the Chinese retargeted their ICBMs from the U.S. to the U.S.S.R. They have remained that way ever since.

Between the 1950s and 1991, no reactor in the People's Republic of China produced so much as a watt of commercial electricity. The first power plant went on line at Qinshan, along the southeast coast, in December 1991. Another was under construction at Daya Bay, near the Hong Kong border. All of the others were strictly dedicated to research and weapons production.

Yet starting in the 1950s, when they began training North Korean scientists in nuclear technology, the Chinese have repeatedly claimed that their product was strictly peaceful. The idea has been to cloud the true nature of what they were doing by selling dual-use technology or heavy equipment. The glaring exception was Pakistan.

It is a measure of Chinese avarice that they also exported heavy water to India, which was Pakistan's implacable enemy and China's chief nemesis as well. Between 1982 and 1987, China sold 130–150 tons of it to India through Alfred Hempel, the late German arms broker. Like the Russians who used Hempel to transfer heavy water to India, the Chinese claimed that their knowledge of its destination ended on Hempel's bill of lading. But the Chinese were as disingenuous as their Communist rivals. Since that quantity of heavy water is only usable in reactors, and since only Indian reactors needed large quantities of it at that time, there could have been little doubt where the water was headed.

The Chinese have also done well in the Middle East. In 1986, they did a feasibility study for Iraq which showed they could build a complete nuclear power plant for it by 1990. Since the Iraqis stipulated that the facility was to be camouflaged so as not to be seen by reconnaissance satellites, it could have no other purpose than the clandestine production of plutonium for weapons. China never built the plant and called reports of the study a "sheer fabrication." In 1989, though, the Chinese did help Iraq manufacture special magnets for stabilizing the ultrahigh-speed centrifuges that were used to enrich uranium. The following year they agreed to sell seven tons of lithium hydride, which was almost certainly intended for Baghdad's nuclear weapons program, despite a U.N. embargo. With sales of conventional weapons drying up after the end of the war with Iran, the Chinese were anxious to open new avenues of export.

They therefore went to Iran as well. In the 1980s, Beijing sold Teheran an electromagnetic separator—what the Iraqis called a baghdatron—and what it termed a "mini-type" research reactor. Stung by U.S. goading because of its nuclear weapons exports, the Foreign Ministry issued a statement explaining that the facilities would be used "for nuclear medical diagnosis and nuclear physics research, isotope production, education and personnel training. Guided by the internationally observed regulations," the statement went on, "China has requested the IAEA to enforce safeguards before these facilities were shipped." Left unexplained was the sale of calutron equipment worth millions of dollars that could be used to electromagnetically enrich uranium.

Nor did the Foreign Ministry explain why China had been training fifteen Iranian nuclear engineers since 1988 under a clandestine agreement that was signed during the war with Iraq. One of the Iranians said that the group was working under a secret cooperation agreement, but he would provide no further details.

Two months later, Iranian government sources announced, with evident pride and a trace of spite, that China would replace Germany and France as the builder of yet another reactor that the two European countries stopped constructing when the Shah was overthrown. In concluding remarks on the last day of his visit to Iran, Prime Minister Li Peng said he had agreed to provide the Muslim nation with "the necessary expertise and technology for the completion of the Iranian nuclear reactor in accordance with a comprehensive agreement that will make the PRC Iran's biggest trading partner and arms supplier." An Iranian source said that the two nations had agreed to increase the volume of their trade exchanges in 1992 to $5 billion. Meanwhile, a Chinese Foreign Ministry spokesman dismissed as "sheer fabrication" reports that his country was helping Iran in its nuclear weapons program. Wu Jianmin, the official who had used the same term to deny the Iraqi nuclear feasibility study, evidently found something resonant about it.

Syria bought a small reactor from China in 1991. A Chinese Foreign Ministry spokesman called it a "miniature neutron source reactor with the power of thirty kilowatts used for neutron activation analysis and isotope production." It will nevertheless be useful for training scientists and engineers in the basics of nuclear physics and reactor operation. They will be training to use a much larger, twenty-four-megawatt research reactor, which may be provided in a follow-up sale.

Algeria's reactor was very much another matter. Although China promised in 1984 that it would export only nuclear technology that was under international safeguards, it nonetheless secretly contracted with Algeria to build a power reactor at about the same time. Following a CIA leak about its existence in April 1991, together with informed observations that the facility was too large for basic research and too small to produce power, and that it was heavily protected and carefully secluded, Algeria hurriedly announced that it would sign the NPT. China, also under the spotlight, did the same.

The Algerian reactor episode said more about U.S. policy toward China than it did about Chinese policy toward Algeria and other nuclear weapons clients. As early as 1988, the CIA had clear evidence that China had sold a potentially dangerous reactor to Algeria. It was also aware of persistent reports that Iraqi scientists and uranium had found their way to Algeria.

From the CIA's standpoint, China was less of a problem than was the Department of State, particularly Richard T. Kennedy, State's special ambassador on nonproliferation matters. The intelligence specialists informed Kennedy in 1988 about the reactor. Yet Kennedy, whose belief in nuclear trading between the United States and China coalesced perfectly with his president's determination to allow China to enjoy most-favored-nation status, sat on the information for two years. In March 1991, the CIA briefed a congressional committee on amorphous "nuclear weapons" aid the Chinese were giving to the Algerians. The following month, it leaked more of the same to *The Washington Times*, a favorite repository of intelligence storm warnings. That November the CIA, aware of the fact that effective action to head off construction of the reactor might have been taken during the previous three years, became so frustrated by the

White House's bottleneck that it leaked specific information about the reactor and let it be known that it had unambiguous photoreconnaissance imagery to prove what it said.

By 1991, China had established itself as a rogue nation, and a brutal one at that. Intelligence reports of persistent weapons proliferation, conventional and unconventional, multiplied almost daily. The Chinese refused to participate in international discussions to prevent missile proliferation; they used slave laborers to manufacture weapons and other export items; they supported the murderous Khmer Rouge in Cambodia; they perpetrated the massacre at Tiananmen Square and dealt harshly with the surviving dissident leaders from the 1989 demonstrations. They even baldly stole nuclear weapons data from the Lawrence Livermore National Laboratory during the 1980s, either deliberately doing the computer-age equivalent of picking locks, or else simply taking advantage of lapses in security. However it was done, it was espionage, and it led to China's own neutron bomb.*

Why, then, the determination of two succeeding Republican administrations to reward them with most-favored-nation status while playing down their moral transgressions? Because whatever Mao's definition of the term, China's real great leap forward got under way with Deng's economic reforms, beginning in 1979. While not abandoning the socialist path altogether, Deng allowed some "coastal open cities" and "special economic zones," especially along the coast, to flirt with capitalism. The result was an economic explosion that is still cresting, as the end of the century approaches, in a kind of economic miracle that has left the nation's rural interior dour and poor by comparison. (The Tiananmen Square demonstrators mistakenly believed that the economic reforms portended trickle-down democracy.)†

*The number of Chinese nationals studying high-energy physics, particularly lasers, at Lawrence Livermore during the 1980s and early 1990s was stunning for the way it paralleled Israeli visits. An FOIA request for unclassified visit or assignment forms yielded thirty-two approvals between 1986 and 1990. On September 21, 1987, to take only one example, Zhou Quangzhao, the president of the Chinese Academy of Sciences, requested permission to visit Livermore. He listed his research interest as an ambiguous "Various activities," while his sponsor explained that the purpose of the day trip was "Familiarization with LLNL's unclassified fusion research programs." Another was interested in learning about satellite laser ranging; still another in streak and framing cameras, which have nuclear weapons test applications. (For the espionage, see "Chinese Atom-Arms Spying in U.S. Reported," *The New York Times*, November 22, 1990, and "China's Neutron Bomb Blamed on Espionage at Livermore Lab," *The Washington Times*, November 23, 1990.)

†See, for example, "Entrepreneurial Energy Sets Off a Chinese Boom," *The New York Times*, February 14, 1993.

South Korean, Japanese, American, and western European firms rushed into the breach to sell their wares and, in turn, to buy Chinese products in unprecedented numbers. It also resulted in inflation, some budget deficits, falling productivity, and, in some cases, increasing foreign debt. A retrenchment was therefore begun that year which, among other things, called for increased exports and austerity at home.

Whatever China's foreign debt problem was with other countries, it had no such problem with the United States. America imported a great deal more from China than it exported. In 1990, the U.S. trade deficit with China was $10.6 billion, or $4.2 billion higher than the previous year. China exported $15.4 billion worth of goods to the United States in 1990, while only $4.8 billion in merchandise went the other way.

So here was the reason for going easy on the Chinese in the weapons and technology transfer area: the Bush administration, like its predecessor, saw a placated China as a long-term, potentially fat market for beleaguered American exporters. More immediately, George Bush desperately wanted to climb out of the deficit hole because of a stubborn recession that was more threatening to Republican control of the White House than any other issue since Ronald Reagan was sworn in. China seemed destined to be a major economic power well into the twenty-first century, and it was therefore taken to be in the best interest of the United States to maintain a solid trading relationship with Beijing. It wasn't put quite that way to the world at large, however. The administration explained repeatedly that China would never be brought into the fold by isolating, reprimanding, and humiliating it. Rather, the thing was to keep channels open and provide the material it needed, including conventional weapons and high-tech dual-use items, to show it that it would be rewarded even for taking good behavior seriously. As though that had worked with Iraq.

Bush saw his job as having to reprimand the Chinese enough to convince a Democratic Congress and naive journalists that he was serious about curtailing superweapon proliferation, while not seriously angering Deng and his subordinates, the keepers of the world's most populous and fastest-growing market. But while the Bush administration counseled patience with the Chinese, it had to abandon much of the playing field to determined opponents of its policy. These included John Glenn, head of the Senate Committee on Governmental Affairs, Jesse Helms on the Senate Foreign Relations Committee, the CIA and DIA, stubborn investigative reporters, and a small but determined band of well-connected proliferation experts such as Gary Milhollin and Leonard S. Spector.

Whatever the protestations of innocence, being caught in the spotlight repeatedly finally persuaded the Chinese to abruptly adopt both the Non-Proliferation Treaty and the Missile Technology Control Regime in 1992. It is possible, though unlikely, that the White House's policy worked. More likely, one public revelation after another about its grim activities finally convinced Beijing that there was more to be gained by reducing some dual-use exports and ending others. Headlines and television exposés had done a great deal to curb French and German exports following the Persian Gulf War and had helped further tighten the lid on American exports as well.

But China couldn't please everyone. At least one writer, a Bangladeshi named Gowner Rizvi, took it to task for caving in to the West and betraying the Third World in the process. "The acquisition of nuclear weapons was a means to an end: to strengthen the negotiating position of the Third World and ultimately end the subservient status of the newly emergent and developing states. The stonewalling of demands for a new international economic order," Rizvi asserted, "confirmed opinion in the Third World that the only way to get rid of economic dependence was to alter the balance of power." China had served as a valuable means to that end by proliferating superweapons, he added, but in the end it had sold out. "For the West, China's accession is part of a strategy to uncouple China from the Third World and co-opt it into the Western bloc." This, Rizvi concluded in evident anguish, would make the achievement of nuclear weapons capabilities by other developing countries "difficult, if not impossible." But Rizvi was forgetting that the Chinese had already uncoupled from the Third World, becoming gung ho capitalists of their own volition. Capitalism, more than any antiquated ideology, would keep them in the weapons business for a long time.

# 13

# EAST ASIA:
# THE OTHER RING OF FIRE

In ordinary circumstances, Chang Hsien-yi's defection would not have been especially notable, particularly given the number of other defections that occurred during the cold war. One day in January 1988, Chang, his wife, and their three children simply boarded an airplane at a former U.S. air base in a remote part of the Republic of China (Taiwan) and disappeared into thin air.

Yet Chang's unauthorized flight was taken with the utmost seriousness by the Taiwanese government, which fired him from his job and issued a warrant for his arrest as soon as it became known that he was gone. It also promised to punish anyone who had anything to do with the incident. The government's consternation arose from the fact that Chang Hsien-yi was a colonel in the Taiwanese military, a nuclear scientist, and the deputy director of the Nuclear Energy Research Center at the military's Chungshan Institute of Science and Technology. Most galling of all, and humiliating, it became apparent in the days following the forty-five-year-old scientist's departure that he was also a spy for the CIA. During the furor that erupted in Taiwan when Chang's defection became known to the public, one newspaper accused the American spy agency of having committed an "ungentlemanlike action." That wasn't the half of it.

Chang's "action" was apparently to provide startling details about the Taiwanese nuclear weapons program, specifically about its forty-megawatt research reactor at Lung Tan, twenty miles southwest of Taipei. Both the reactor and the Chungshan Institute are in a walled compound. The Lung Tan reactor, the largest of four such reactors in Taiwan, was sold to Taipei by Canada in 1969 and was similar to the one used by India to produce plutonium for its weapons program.

If Taiwan was consternated because of Chang's revelations, the United States was equally consternated because of what amounted to a Taiwanese reprise in its long search for nuclear weapons. It had all been played before. Looking across the ninety-mile-wide Taiwan Strait at a sworn enemy that had a four-million-man army, nuclear weapons, and a fixation about "liberating" their island, Chiang Kai-shek and his Kuomintang colleagues had decided at least as early as the mid-1960s that they had better acquire their own nuclear arsenal as a counterforce.

Taipei therefore asked the United States for a reprocessing plant in 1969 and was turned down by the Nixon administration.* The Nationalists then did what everybody else seemed to be doing; they turned to France. An agreement was soon worked out in which Saint-Gobain Techniques Nouvelle would provide a plant that could reprocess 100 tons of used fuel a year.† But the Nixon White House quickly killed that deal, infuriating the French in the process, by threatening to cut off military and economic aid. Yet the Taiwanese were persistent. The CIA said in a September 1974 assessment that Taiwan was conducting "a small nuclear program with a weapon option clearly in mind; and it will be in a position to fabricate a nuclear device after five years or so."

In June 1976, IAEA inspectors visiting a Taiwanese research reactor found that ten barrels of used fuel containing 500 grams (one pound) of plutonium were missing. Two months later, U.S. government officials told *The Washington Post* that intelligence indicated that Taiwan had been

---

*Besides the obvious wish to limit nuclear weapon proliferation in the area for its own sake, the United States was also mindful of warnings from the People's Republic of China that it would invade Taiwan if the latter acquired nuclear weapons. Having to abandon the opening of China—the jewel of the Nixon administration's foreign policy—to support Taiwan against an invasion by the PLA would have been Nixon's and Henry Kissinger's worst nightmare.
†This was the same-size plant that SGN wanted to help Pakistan build at Chashma and Israel build at Dimona. (Steve Weissman and Herbert Krosney, *The Islamic Bomb*, New York: Times Books, 1981, p. 152, and Seymour M. Hersh, *The Samson Option*, New York: Random House, 1991, p. 29, respectively.)

secretly reprocessing nuclear fuel into weapons-grade plutonium for some time. That leak was the prelude to another crackdown.

Washington was so determined to keep nuclear weapons out of Taiwan's hands that it forced the Taiwanese to dismantle some of their equipment and return much of the rest to the United States, where it came from. It also extracted a pledge from Taipei that research in any area having nuclear weapons implications would be abandoned. "After the Americans got through with us," one Taiwanese scientist remarked, "we wouldn't have even been able to teach physics here on Taiwan."

Its pledge notwithstanding, Taiwan had apparently accumulated enough plutonium-bearing spent fuel from the Lung Tan reactor by 1988 for more than ten weapons. It was also making a secret reprocessing facility and had even begun shaping bomb cores. Colonel Chang undoubtedly passed on information about the spent fuel and the secret facility to the CIA. That February—the month after the colonel arrived in the United States and was "debriefed"—a delegation from the Department of State went to Taipei and extracted another pledge: that the research reactor would be shut down once and for all and work on the reprocessing facility would end.

As is customary, Chang Hsien-yi was given a new name and moved with his family to a location the CIA would not disclose. A Taiwanese newspaper reported in February 1988 that Chang's daughter, Pei-fen, wrote from Georgia to a former classmate, though there was no return address on the envelope. The United States had swallowed another nuclear defector and put out another fire.


The tenacious but abortive Taiwanese nuclear weapons program had a counterpart in South Korea. Yet there, too, the United States had to use its considerable clout—and physical presence in 1979—to prevent Seoul's pursuit of nuclear weapons. General Park Chung Hee, a repressive demagogue who became president in 1961, had vivid recollections of Chinese "human-wave" attacks during the Korean War. He therefore flirted with the notion of acquiring atomic bombs. But matters never went beyond that because Washington kept Seoul on a tight leash. It provided a great deal of economic aid, built South Korea's armed forces to 600,000 men, and assured Park and his cronies that nuclear weapons in the United States were all that was needed for its protection.

• • •

Japan was different. And it was the same. The nation that emerged from World War II as stridently pacifistic was turned by the United States into the Far East's major bastion against militant communism. The dichotomy between a pacifistic people whose constitution prohibited a standing army and their assigned role as the area's primary defender of the capitalistic-democratic faith resulted in considerable political ambiguity and an ongoing identity crisis. There *is* no army, for example. But there is a Self-Defense Force whose weapons are the qualitative counterpart to Japanese automobiles and whose quantity is huge, given the size of the country. The United States turned its chief Asian proxy into the military equivalent of a football team having only a defensive unit, but one so latently powerful that it could push opposing offensive units all the way back to their own goal line.

This has caused the identity crisis. Militarily speaking, the Japanese are hard-pressed to know who they are, and that has led to a deep inner instability.

Japan, for example, is the only nation outside of the United States that is allowed to make F-15s, arguably the world's finest attack fighters. Yet Japanese F-15s are configured as interceptors for defense only. Similarly its F-16s, designed by General Dynamics primarily as scrappy fighter-bombers, are also slated to be used only for defense; that is, to attack invaders of the home islands. The FSX, the twenty-first century's F-16, is also purportedly for defensive close air support only.

Japan has been encouraged to build launch vehicles powerful enough to propel spacecraft to the moon, but it is strictly prohibited by its own constitution from lowering their trajectories to the point at which they become ballistic missiles. Its nuclear technology and plutonium stockpile are among the most formidable on Earth, yet the creation or possession of atomic weapons is strictly forbidden. After pressing it to extend its defensive perimeter to 1,000 miles, the United States denied Japan the right to do so with its own aircraft carrier. Japan was not prohibited from building many other weapons, however, including Patriot and tactical missiles, tanks, submarines, and reprocessing facilities.

By the time the cold war ended, the United States had helped Japan to become a standby superpower whose military and industrial might had grown to immense proportions under the protection of America's nuclear umbrella. But it adapted to that awkward role with understandable confusion, as a giant encouraged to develop its muscles, but only for very limited use. After all, Japan had a powerful big brother who would take care of the rough stuff if the need arose.

The United States maintained an economically dominant relationship throughout the Pacific rim during the cold war, protected by the Seventh Fleet and a string of military bases from the Philippines to Taiwan, South Korea, Japan, and the Aleutians. While the mainland Chinese railed at Taiwan, North Korea threatened South Korea, and Communist Hukbalahap guerrillas terrorized the Philippines, American industry thrived in the region because of low wages and lingering political fealty to Washington. Like the traders and trappers who were protected by cavalry outposts on the American frontier, those of their descendants who went even farther west a century later worked under the watchful eyes of carrier task forces and bomber squadrons that stretched across the region. Many of these units were and remain nuclear-ready.

All American forces in the Pacific come under the U.S. Pacific Command, or USPACOM, which technically is responsible for protecting 100 million square miles of land and sea extending from the West Coast to Africa and from the Arctic to the Antarctic. In point of fact, the overwhelming majority of American land, sea, and air forces are positioned in the shape of a bow and arrow within that region. The bow stretches along the Pacific rim from the Philippines to Alaska. The arrow is a line that goes from Pearl Harbor through Guam to Taiwan. As the 1990s began, with the last embers of the cold war all but extinguished, the United States had 516,388 military and civilian personnel and their dependents stationed in the Pacific theater.* There were also 218 ships and submarines and 1,454 aircraft. The total cost of keeping that operation going was more than $16 billion annually, not counting $2.3 billion contributed by Japan and some financial support from South Korea.

Not surprisingly, a $4 trillion national debt that was rising at a rate of almost $400 billion a year, a persistent recession that was crippling or terminally ending many industries, and the end of the Soviet threat combined to force a reduction of America's armed presence in the far Pacific. In 1992, a nation that was beginning to doubt itself for the first time in its modern history wanted jobs and a healthy economy far more than it

---

*There were 297,987 soldiers, sailors, airmen, and marines; 36,410 civilian employees of the Department of Defense; and 181,991 dependents of both groups. ("Military Presence: U.S. Personnel in the Pacific Theater," GAO/NSLAD-91–192, Washington: General Accounting Office, August 1991, p. 26.)

wanted a role as the planet's policeman. U.S. forces in Japan were therefore slated for an initial cut of 10 percent, and military personnel in Korea, too, were to be reduced. The Philippines simultaneously decided it no longer wanted an American presence at the huge installations at Subic Bay and Clark Air Base.

Congress meanwhile mandated that the Pentagon reassess its missions, its force structure, and the location of its forces in South Korea and east Asia generally. It also called on both Korea and Japan to bear more responsibility for their own security and to pay direct costs for whatever U.S. forces were required to protect them. Uncle Sam was partly closing his umbrella.

With one important exception, the withdrawal was similar to that staged by the British a century earlier. The Royal Navy protected the United States throughout most of the nineteenth century, allowing the young nation to concentrate on commerce and to thrive economically. When the Crown withdrew its protection at the turn of the century, America had no choice but to build its own navy, a force that eventually became second to none. The exception, however, was critical. The United States had made no vengeful enemies before the British men-of-war departed. The Japan that was protected by the United States, on the other hand, faced a semicircle of nations it had raped and plundered before and during World War II, nations whose memories were long and vivid.

The Pacific rim is often called the Ring of Fire because of its volcanic activity. But lava is far from the only thing that has erupted in the region. Where ethnic and nationalistic animosities are concerned, the western Pacific of the twentieth century almost makes Europe look tranquil. Here is where the Japanese and Imperial Russian navies clashed in 1905 and where most of the fighting in the Pacific boiled over during World War II. Here is where Russia bases its Far Eastern fleet and much of its nuclear defense force; where the ballistic missiles test-fired from Tyuratam slammed back into the Kamchatka Peninsula; and where KAL 007 met its tragic end. Here is where China and Taiwan continue to stare angrily at each other (while engaging in surreptitious trade); where the U.N.'s first "police action" started in 1950; and where the French were routed by the Viet Minh in 1954 and the Americans, after an exhausting and traumatic war, by the Vietcong two decades later. Here is where Imperial

Japan's voracious generals and reluctant but stoic admirals launched the Greater East Asia Co-Prosperity Sphere in the 1930s, a scheme that rationalized pillaging the entire rim, from Mandalay to Manchuria, and led to the bloody showdown with the United States. It was a showdown bracketed by a notorious surprise attack and the only use of nuclear weapons in war. Atrocities were committed, including the stocking of army brothels with thousands of abducted Korean and Chinese women and the use of bacteriological warfare, which remain deeply ingrained in the collective psyche of most of the nations in the area. Hatred of Japan is widespread in the lands it conquered. Like eastern Europe, the Middle East, and Central Asia, there are many old grievances, jealousies, and ambitions along the Ring of Fire.

Yet there are no common security structures to anchor prosperity and promote stability. There is no equivalent in Asia of NATO, the old Warsaw Pact, or the Helsinki Accords. There are no treaties proscribing certain weapons and no agreements about human rights. SEATO, the Southeast Asia Treaty Organization started in 1954 by the United States, Great Britain, France, Australia, New Zealand, Pakistan, the Philippines, and Thailand to shore up defenses after the fall of North Vietnam, is a faded memory.

And there is another basic difference between Europe and the Pacific. By cold war's end, much of the rim was bursting with prosperity derived from industrialization, not only because of inherent growth but because there was no eastern Europe to pump capital into as a survival measure. China, Taiwan, Japan, South Korea, Hong Kong, Singapore, and Indonesia were riding a wave of hard work, ingenuity, foreign investment, and uneasy peace. In 1992, China had hard currency reserves of $45 billion. Japan had $70 billion. Taiwan had the largest hard currency hoard in the world: $85 billion. And tiny Singapore, the Lion City-State, had $34 billion in foreign exchange reserves and was richer than New Zealand. Average life expectancy in Singapore was seventy-six years, and nine of every ten citizens owned their own home.

The wealth, combined with relentless animosity and greed, also made the Pacific rim a fertile ground for weapons sales. Unlike Algeria, Egypt, Iraq, Afghanistan, and the other beads on the Islamic string, most of the nations that formed the rim had vigorous science and technology research capabilities and robust manufacturing operations. These were the building blocks of serious proliferation. It was therefore not surprising that by 1992 European and American corporations that had been burned by the sale of critical weapons technology to Iraq and Pakistan were calling on east Asian nations from China to Malaysia for new sales orders.

The Asians, however, were themselves increasingly active competitors. The Japanese economic miracle following the Second World War was fueled by cheap, skilled, and disciplined workers and aggressive managers who scoured the world in search of new markets for their high-quality, innovative products. Like the United Kingdom, another island nation with limited natural resources, Japan understood that it had to trade or die. The trading included weapon technology. During the 1980s, Japan's Toshiba Machine Company sold not only secret submarine propulsion technology to the Soviets but a sophisticated electron beam welding machine to China for its missile program. NEC, another corporate giant, was found guilty of selling missile technology to Iran.

Now, with the United States pulling back and only the ghost of the Soviet Union remaining, a vacuum is building along the Pacific rim as Japan and the others eye each other warily and hedge their bets on the future with both conventional and unconventional weaponry.

Japan scrutinizes every move North Korea makes in nuclear weapons research. For its part, Pyongyang harbors the gnawing suspicion that Tokyo is stockpiling plutonium, not only for reactor fuel but for bomb fuel as well; that with the United States in retreat, Japan's old imperialist urge will return. The corporate barons of Seoul and their opposite number in Tokyo compete to win markets with a mutual cultural contempt so strong it is almost palpable. Taiwan takes on both of them and China, too. Whatever the result of the Korean War, North Korea continues to treat its cousins south of the 38th parallel with an ambivalent mixture of envy and contempt.

Nor is India as far off as maps suggest. New Delhi's testing of the Agni missile, development of a deep-water navy, and brazen establishment of its largest naval base only fifty miles from the nearest Indonesian island has propelled the Indonesians into their own military buildup. It includes missile and nuclear research programs, the latter aided by a cadre of Pakistani scientists. Indonesian postcards conjure lush rubber plantations, coconut palms and coffee groves, tigers, and "Bali Hai." None show drawings of the rocket launch center that is planned to go up at Biak in the eastern Celebes; of Serpong, the nuclear research center outside of Jakarta; or the thirty-nine former East German warships sold to Indonesia in July 1992. Serpong's reactor, made by Siemens, went critical in 1991.

Jakarta's purchase of the ships—one of the largest mass sales of naval vessels in modern history—was a textbook response to India's plans for the new naval base and to its overall power projection in the Indian Ocean. The deal included fully armed 16,908-ton Parchim-class corvettes, nine Kondor-class fast-patrol minesweepers, and a dozen landing craft. The prospect of the world's fourth most populous state (and the world's most populous Islamic state) having nuclear weapons, long-range missiles, and modern warships sends tremors all the way to Australia, where many people still recall that they were on Japan's invasion list in World War II. Australians still fear the yellow peril.

An Indian-Japanese alliance would help both of those nations' economies, guarantee a Japanese trade route from Singapore to the Straits of Hormuz, and flank China. This, too, would unsettle the Australians, not to mention the Chinese.

Even Singapore, which is smaller than New York City, has an air force that not only uses F-16s (parts for which are locally made in an agreement with General Dynamics), but which even has an aerial demonstration team. It also holds arms bazaars. Singapore, like most of the others, is well-heeled.

But far from making the powers in the region feel fat, flush, and secure, much of the new money itself has gone into buying enough weapons to protect what is left. China's fear and loathing of Japan, for example, is one of the forces driving its own expensive, and persistently frustrating, weapons modernization program.

Although Taiwan's nuclear ambitions have been temporarily thwarted, it began arming in earnest with conventional weapons as the 1990s started, and also accelerating its long-range missile and space programs and chemical and even biological weapons programs. That is because the Taiwanese, like others, perceived that the superpowers' backing off from confrontation meant they were less in need of allies. And that, in the vernacular of the street, meant it was now every man for himself.

That much was readily apparent to at least one U.S. defense analyst. "Taiwan is uneasy," he said. "This nice bipolar world of the cold war is over. From Taiwan, you look across the straits and you see Sino-Soviet relations relaxing. Where are the Chinese going to put those troops that were stationed along the northern borders? You look south, and the Chinese and Vietnamese are talking. Where are those Chinese troops in the south going to go?"

Where, for that matter, were the twenty-four SU-27s the Chinese bought for more than $1 billion in 1991 during the Russian yard sale? It turned out that the first dozen, delivered the following year, were stationed seventy-five miles south of Shanghai. Plans called for their eventual deployment farther south along the coast, where they would cover Taiwan and, more importantly, the South China Sea, including the hotly contested Spratly and Paracel Islands. This did nothing to ease Taiwanese fears about the colossus it faced on the other side of the Taiwan Strait.

By then, weapons merchants were coming from all points of the compass to carry away chunks of Taiwan's swollen foreign currency reserve. "Arms dealers from Europe to Africa are active in Taipei," said John Bih, editor of the respected *Defense Technology Monthly*. "They know Taiwan needs more weapons to deter an invader who may be tempted by this island's new wealth to take it over."

Relations with the United States did nothing to soothe the Taiwanese, since Washington had treated them ambivalently. In 1953, during the worst of times between Washington and Beijing, the Seventh Fleet was positioned in the Formosa (Taiwan) Strait to prevent Mao from invading and overrunning the island. A quarter of a century later, in 1979, the United States recognized China and simultaneously broke off formal diplomatic relations with Taiwan (abrogating a defense treaty in the process). In 1982 it agreed to Chinese demands to freeze weapons exports to Taiwan at that year's level, $700 million, and then gradually reduce them over an indefinite period.

By 1990, however, Washington was still selling Taiwan $620 million worth of weapons a year. Two years later the Bush administration quietly agreed to sell Taiwan components for Patriot missiles, rather than the entire weapon. "It would be as good as a Patriot," one senior U.S. defense official observed wryly, "sort of their own version of a Patriot." Nonetheless, the policy of the Bush administration, like the one it replaced, clearly tilted toward China.

Accordingly, Taipei has spent lavishly on its navy and air force, an island nation's first line of defense. It agreed in the autumn of 1991 to buy six fully armed submarines from the Netherlands for $3 billion. That deal followed the $750 million purchase of two other Dutch-built subs, the *Sea Dragon* and *Sea Tiger*, which were delivered in 1987 and 1988. And within a week of announcing the newest submarine sale, it was also made public that Taiwan was buying as many as sixteen Lafayette-class frigates from France for $4.8 billion more. The Taiwanese Defense Ministry would not comment on the purchases.

Seeing that China was buying the SU-27s from Russia and staking claim to the Spratlys—and realizing that an indigenous effort to build its own fighter had stalled—the Taiwanese also began casting about for a foreign dogfighter that could clear the sky of the fine Russian fighter-bombers. They considered the U.S. F-16, the Swedish Grippen, the French Mirage 2000, the Russian MIG-29, and the Israeli Kfir.*

They considered the U.S. F-16 quite a bit, but the U.S. did not consider them, at least until the summer of 1992. That August, however, President Bush reversed the policy of not providing Taiwan with first-magnitude weapon systems. He decided to sell Taiwan 150 F-16s for $6 billion. "This sale of F-16s to Taiwan will help maintain peace and stability in an area of great concern to us," Bush said at the F-16 plant in Fort Worth on September 2. East Asia wasn't Bush's only area of concern, though. He might just as well have been referring to the plant in which he stood, where 5,800 of 20,000 workers were threatened with layoffs because of shrinking orders. Bush was badly trailing Arkansas Governor Bill Clinton in the polls just two months before the presidential election. His most pressing concern was therefore not Beijing but Dallas-Fort Worth.†

For his part, François Mitterrand shared Bush's sentiments exactly. Following a year of negotiations, Dassault landed a $3.8 billion contract to deliver sixty Mirage 2000-5 multipurpose advanced combat jets to Taiwan. It was the jet's first overseas sale and, mirroring the situation in Texas, came at a time when the large aircraft manufacturer had just laid off 3,200 workers.

The range of Taiwan's missiles has increased substantially since its first indigenous weapon, Hornet, debuted on National Day in October 1978. A tactical ballistic missile similar to the U.S. Army's Honest John, Hornet's twenty-mile range wouldn't even have gotten it across the strait, let alone to PLA targets. But it was a start. The development of the Hornet and the missiles that came after it, including the Sky Bow antiaircraft missile and a sea-skimming cruise missile, was at least in part helped by the Massachusetts Institute of Technology, which began training Tai-

---

*Fighters weren't their only frustration. After Taiwan Aerospace Corporation announced in 1991 that it planned to buy 40 percent of McDonnell Douglas's commercial aircraft business for $2 billion, Washington pressured the St. Louis–based company to back out of the deal.
†At about the same time, Bush approved the $5 billion sale of seventy-two F-15s to Saudi Arabia over Israeli protests. The jets were made by McDonnell Douglas, which was also experiencing layoffs.

wanese engineers in missile guidance technology in 1974 under a
$917,000 contract. The Department of State abruptly stopped the program
in June 1976. Hornet was followed three years later by the Green Bee,
whose range was sixty-five miles. The Green Bee was eventually scuttled,
partly because of pressure from the United States. No matter. Scientists
at Chungshan were by then working on Sky Horse, a missile whose 600-
mile range made it suitable for either reaching cities and other targets on
the mainland or putting satellites into orbit.

A Japanese policy maker following China's menacing moves around the
Spratlys and the Paracels—China was spending $4 million just to build
a freshwater supply system on one of the Paracels, evidently in preparation
for a permanent military base there—would have had cause for concern.
The maneuvering would have seemed to herald the specter of a vague,
distant danger for Japan. As the citizen of an island nation dependent on
seaborne commerce for its survival, and knowing that tankers carrying
petroleum from the Middle East to Japan pass the Paracels, the thought
of their being controlled by far-ranging Chinese aircraft and naval vessels
would have brought apprehension. He would have been well aware that
China wanted hegemony in the region. He also would have known that
either a North Korea with nuclear weapons and missiles or a united Korean
peninsula with one huge army was another potentially perilous possibility.
And he would have known that they all, in addition to the Philippines,
Singapore, Thailand, Malaya, Indonesia, Taiwan, Myanmar, and what had
been Indochina, recalled the brutal Japanese occupation before and during
World War II with abiding bitterness.*
    What he might not have known—what very few of even the oldest

*As is the case in the Netherlands, Poland, and other European nations where memories of
the Nazi occupation linger, hatred for the Japanese is felt more than articulated. One notable
exception, however, occurred in 1991 when the so-called comfort women case was made public.
It involved Japan's use of thousands of Korean, Chinese, and other women from occupied
countries in government-run military brothels against their will and in appalling conditions.
Smoldering hatred over the forced prostitution program erupted in January 1992, when Japanese
Prime Minister Kiichi Miyazawa visited South Korea. "The Japanese treat their dogs better
than they treated us," said Hwang Kum Joo, a sixty-nine-year-old former comfort woman, after
the visit. "When I saw Miyazawa in Korea, I wanted to hurt him physically. He's just like all
the Japanese. He wants us all to die out so there will be no one left to tell the truth." Meanwhile,
in Singapore, schoolchildren were being herded through an exhibit at the national museum
which showed graphic images of Japanese atrocities during the occupation a half century earlier.
("South Koreans Express Pent-Up Anger at Japan," *The New York Times*, February 23, 1992,
and "Tokyo in the New Epoch: Heady Future, with Fear," *The New York Times*, May 5, 1992.)

hands in government knew because it was the nation's most closely guarded military secret—was that Japan had also used its own super-weapon in World War II: bacterial agents. After the cholera, dysentery, typhoid, plague, anthrax, and paratyphoid agents had been tested on Americans, Britons, Chinese, and other "human guinea pigs," they were used ferociously against Chinese and Russian forces by a special group known as Unit 731.*

Japan's articulated military policy was spelled out in Article IX of the 1947 Constitution: "Aspiring sincerely to an international peace based on justice and order, the Japanese people forever renounce war as a sovereign right of the nation and the threat or use of force as a means of settling international disputes." In order to accomplish that lofty aim, the document continued, "land, sea, and air forces will never be maintained. The right of belligerency will never be maintained."

Forty-five years later, Japan's $33 billion defense budget was the world's third largest, after that of the United States and Russia. Between 1986 and 1990, Japan's total weapons imports came to $10.97 billion, putting it behind only India among Second and Third World countries. In 1990 alone, Japan moved ahead of India, spending a little more than $2 billion to India's $1.54 billion, and trailing Saudi Arabia by only about $500 million. Japan's arms expenditures rarely raise eyebrows because they are a far smaller percentage of gross domestic product than are those of India and Saudi Arabia (0.6 percent in 1990 versus 16.7 percent for India and 14.9 percent for the Saudis). In addition, 80 percent of Japan's weapons purchases were in the form of licensing agreements paid to foreign companies like McDonnell Douglas, General Dynamics, and Raytheon

---

*In the summer of 1942 alone, Unit 731 contaminated Chekiang Province in China by spreading all of those agents. Flasks full of deadly bacteria were emptied into wells, rivers, and reservoirs, tossed into houses, and even dropped from planes. Some 3,000 Chinese military prisoners in two camps were carefully photographed being handed rolls to eat by their humane-looking guards. Then, in a display of almost unbelievable magnanimity, the prisoners were photographed as they were released. It in fact *was* unbelievable. The rolls had been injected with typhoid and paratyphoid, which the newly repatriated soldiers unknowingly took back to their own lines. In return for handing over Unit 731's detailed records and sharing data with U.S. intelligence, no member of the group was prosecuted for war crimes and the episode was quietly dropped. "The value to the U.S. of Japanese BW data is of such importance to national security," an investigating board declared, "as to far outweigh the value accruing from 'war crimes' prosecution." (Peter Williams and David Wallace, *Unit 731*, London: Hodder & Stoughton, 1989. See pp. 69–70 for the prisoner release tactic and p. 210 for the U.S. attitude.) As was the case with Wernher von Braun, developer of the V-2 rockets that were fired at civilian targets in London, Paris, Antwerp, and elsewhere during World War II, it was judged more important to acquire the weapon than punish its creator.

so the Japanese, themselves, could manufacture F-15s, F-16s, and Patriots.

But the huge budget translates into the twenty-fifth largest armed force on Earth. While 250,000 men and women under arms is not especially large, their equipment is extraordinary, a reflection of the cutting-edge technology that flows in other sectors. There were thirteen fighter squadrons with 430 tactical aircraft in Japan in 1990, including specially adapted F-15Js with synthetic aperture radar, plus reconnaissance, transport, and early warning units. There were also sixteen antisubmarine squadrons with 220 aircraft, four destroyer squadrons having almost as many "cans" in the Pacific as the U.S. Navy, and six submarine groups.

The contradiction between the number and quality of men, women, and weapons and the constitutional prohibition against land, sea, and air forces is reconciled by one word: defense. The organizations are not called "armed forces," but "Self-Defense Forces." As was the case when the U.S. War Department became the Department of Defense in 1947, "defense" sounds less threatening than "armed force" and therefore has more public relations value. But in the case of Japan, public relations is not the main reason for the use of "self-defense." The Japanese people have been stridently against a national military force and foreign adventures since their defeat and the near-annihilation of two of their major cities.

At the same time, the imperative of Japan's being able to defend itself was recognized as early as the late 1940s, when General Douglas MacArthur proclaimed that the country was not to be denied that capability. The nation's Supreme Court supported MacArthur's manifesto in 1959, ruling that "the pacifism advanced in our Constitution was never intended to mean defenselessness or non-resistance." That is ostensibly why the Self-Defense Forces exist. And strictly speaking, they are forces that are conventionally armed.

Yet if the potential for quickly turning superweapon technology into the finished weapons themselves means anything, then Japan is also unconventionally armed: armed with its super-high technology. And since much of that technology is dual-use, the seeds that blossomed into Japan's highly unconventional economic miracle also sprouted highly unconventional protective thorns: superthorns. Flower and thorn are inseparable.

The plutonium stockpile is a case in point. Japan decided during the oil crisis of the 1970s that it wanted to be as self-sufficient in energy as possible. Nuclear power seemed to be a logical alternative to petroleum, but since uranium was expensive at that time, Japan decided to leapfrog ordinary power reactors (though it would have forty-one of them in service by 1992) and go instead to so-called fast breeders. Fast-breeder reactors do not breed fast, but they are able to burn plutonium to produce electricity while generating—breeding—still more plutonium in a kind of nuclear alchemy.

Japan therefore signed a $4 billion contract allowing it to send expended uranium from its power reactors to La Hague in France and Sellafield in Great Britain, where it would be reprocessed into plutonium and returned to Japan over a 17,000-mile sea route. The Japanese also planned to build their own huge reprocessing facility at Rokkasho in the northern part of the country so they could eventually reprocess their own uranium into plutonium and then into pellets for burning in the $4.5 billion breeder.

Meanwhile, the first shipment of a little more than a ton left Cherbourg on November 7, 1992, on the 324-foot freighter *Akatsuki Maru,* but only after about 100 Greenpeace protesters tried to block the convoy of trucks carrying the fissile material to the dock, and then tried to block the freighter itself. Riot police and French Navy frogmen and commandos broke up a violent demonstration.

The ship left Cherbourg's military harbor under the temporary protection of French warships, while the U.S. Department of Defense maintained that it would be monitored throughout its two-month voyage by American warships, aircraft, and military intelligence, presumably including reconnaissance satellites. The *Akatsuki Maru* was also escorted for most of its trip by a 6,500-ton, light-cannon- and machine-gun-equipped vessel named *Shikishima* which was operated by the Maritime Safety Agency, the Japanese coast guard. The *Akatsuki Maru* docked safely at Tokai early on the morning of January 5, 1993, with enough plutonium to make 120 atomic bombs.

As large as the other projected shipments were, however, they would in themselves only add to an already existing stockpile of incredible size. Early in 1992, Japan had ten tons of plutonium in storage. As much as 150 more tons were to be reprocessed in Europe. Combined with what Japan itself planned to reprocess, that would give the country 400 tons of plutonium by 2020, or enough for 50,000 bombs! Until the *Akatsuki Maru* sailed, the Japanese government maintained that it had no intention of stockpiling plutonium, that it would keep only as much of the element on hand as it could burn. That changed when it was discovered that technical problems in fabricating the plutonium into fuel would delay the start-up of the reactor. The plutonium would therefore have to be stored until the problem was solved.

During 1992, economic and environmental concerns began to militate against the massive plutonium buildup, or what had been referred to for years as a "plutonium economy." For one thing, the world oil market was stable. For another, uranium hexachloride—raw reactor fuel—was then relatively cheap. For still another, there was the dangerous world glut in plutonium, much of it in the former Soviet Union (that summer, Japan was considering converting plutonium in Russian warheads to reactor fuel). Finally, there was ceaseless pressure from Greenpeace and other environmental groups at home and abroad to abandon plutonium altogether.* There were obvious environmental dangers from an accident at sea, the environmentalists contended, as well as the possibility of the plutonium's falling prey to pirates who were, or who were working for, terrorists of other nations. The route from Europe to Japan is therefore a closely guarded secret, though the receiving port is near Yokohama.

Nor would the gigantic quantities of plutonium on land be easy to protect against diversion.† One shipment, the first to be sent to the new fast breeder, which is located at Monju, was brought to a standstill in rush-hour gridlock on a Tokyo expressway on the evening of July 6, 1992. The trucks, which carried 375 pounds of the fissile material—enough to make thirty bombs—were separated from each other by motorists trying to get home. The ease with which some of the material could have been hijacked was appalling.

Still, Japan remained determined to convert its uranium to plutonium and use the open seas to get it home. Tokyo pressed on with encouragement from its uranium supplier. "If the complaints continue," one U.S. congressman who was involved in foreign policy murmured, "we may decide to provide naval escorts as well, or to get help from other navies." And that was pretty much it.

As matters stood, Japanese science and industry would be sitting on a massive pile of bomb-quality plutonium by the end of the century. All Japan would need to turn the plutonium into nuclear weapons was

---

*The Citizens' Nuclear Information Center in Tokyo, for example, lobbied against plutonium proliferation, published a regular bimonthly newsletter in English, *Nuke Info*, and ran a three-day International Conference on Plutonium in 1991.

†In April 1992, the IAEA quietly warned that Japan's plans to store huge quantities of plutonium could pose "political and security problems" in the region and urged that the stockpiles be kept under international custody. There was no immediate response. ("Japan Is Cautioned on Plan to Store Tons of Plutonium," *The New York Times*, April 13, 1992.)

appropriate technology. And relatively speaking, Japan has even more technology than plutonium.

Unlike the Israelis and Pakistanis, who had a "bomb in the basement"—actual weapons kept secret—Japan has a "capability in the basement." It has one of the world's most advanced nuclear engineering infrastructures and a formidable scientific, industrial, and financial base. A nation that can develop a sixty-four-bit microchip would have no trouble mastering 1940s nuclear weapons technology.* Asked how long it would take Japan to produce a finished nuclear weapon, one knowledgeable Japanese answered that it would be "N minus six months" of a political decision to do so. Perhaps having only the potential to develop nuclear weapons, however, will be enough to guarantee Japan's security.

Japan has also decided that its status as an emerging superpower requires it to be in space. It was only the third nation after the United States and the Soviet Union to reach the moon (with a pair of small lunar orbiters in January 1990). The point was to demonstrate that, while any nation with sound astronautical technology could get a missile to go 1,000 miles, only a world-class power could reach the moon.

By way of expressing the full scope of their seriousness about being a presence in space, the Japanese have also signed on as participants in the U.S. space station, sent a spacecraft out to welcome Halley's Comet (Sakigake in 1985), got a television reporter named Toyohiro Akiyama onto Mir (thereby getting the first Japanese and the first journalist into space), sent three scientists to Houston for astronaut training (one of whom, a chemist named Mamoru Mohri, went into space on the *Endeavour* orbiter in September 1992), signed an agreement with Russia to cooperate in space research and allow the Japanese to use Russian facilities, and even designed their own small, unmanned space shuttle. Japan's seriousness about going to and staying in space can be judged by the fact that it has created a massive spaceport on Tanegashima, a beautiful island off the southeast tip of Kyushu, while its Shimizu Corporation, the largest construction company in the world, has a space project office that assigned twenty-five engineers to design a lunar base and other space concepts.

All of this requires powerful computing capability, excellent guid-

*In September 1992, Fujitsu Ltd. announced that it had created the world's fastest supercomputer. The machine, which linked 222 custom processors, was said to be able to perform 355.2 billion calculations a second. It was slated to sell for $125 million and be suitable for simulating wind tunnel operation. ("Fujitsu Says Its Computer Will Be the World's Fastest," *The New York Times*, September 10, 1992.)

ance and control systems, a large support structure, and rockets with enormous lifting capacity: the same elements that are needed for a world-class ballistic missile program. The quality of the computers and the guidance and control equipment is a long-established fact. The National Space Development Agency and its sister organization, the Institute for Space and Astronautical Science, together constitute Japan's NASA. And both have evolved into excellent, highly motivated organizations.

After some initial difficulty the rockets, too, have proved their mettle. Developed with the help of Rocketdyne, Thiokol, and other U.S. firms, the seventy-five-foot-high H-1 can carry a 7,100-pound object into Earth orbit. The H-2, a strictly indigenous booster which looks like the massive U.S. Titan 34D, was designed to carry heavy satellites into orbit and lunar and planetary explorers to the moon and beyond. The H-2's primary contractor, Mitsubishi, also happens to be so heavily involved in weapons production that by itself it amounts to a shadow Ministry of Defense. A third rocket, the J-1, was being developed in 1992 as a reliable, low-cost, solid-fuel booster to get one-ton payloads into orbit. All three are convertible to ballistic missiles, the first two with intercontinental range. Because it will be solid-fueled, the J-1 will, in addition, be suitable as a quick-response weapon. Conversions would be relatively easy.

Japanese scientists and engineers have also provided their country with an impressive array of Earth satellites. By 1991, NEC, Toshiba, and the ubiquitous Mitsubishi had launched about a dozen communication satellites, all with heavy American involvement. In fact, Japan successfully launched fifty-one of its own spacecraft between 1970 and 1990, most of them for scientific research. In addition, Hughes Aircraft Company built a series of geostationary weather satellites for Japan.

What was most interesting, however, was Japan's diverse and accelerated Earth observation program. Despite the country's relatively small size and the availability of three other "remote sensing" programs— America's Landsat, France's SPOT, and Russia's Soyuzcarta—the Japanese felt compelled to develop four programs of their own. The first, Japan's Earth Resources Satellite (JERS), was equipped with infrared optical sensors and synthetic aperture radar so it could differentiate objects by their temperature and see them through clouds and at night. The second, the Japanese Polar Orbiting Earth Observation System (JPOPS), is intended for polar surveillance (that orbit is the same as is used by U.S. electro-optical spy satellites) in 1999. The third, an Advanced Earth

Observing Satellite (ADEOS), was designed to supplant the fourth type of observation spacecraft, the Marine Observation Satellite (MOS). Again, like U.S. imaging reconnaissance satellites, ADEOS was designed to be used in a so-called sun-synchronous orbit, where objects' shadows remain the same length on every orbit. This makes change or movement on the ground easier to spot by intelligence analysts.

While Japan's fleet of satellites has been designed ostensibly for peaceful purposes, there is no doubt that, like India's and Israel's, they amount to proof-of-concept technology with obvious military applications. As is true with the plutonium, the space launchers, and the entire scientific and technical base, having satellites with potential military capability moves Japan steadily closer to military independence. And military independence appears to be the international sine qua non of the highly technologized twenty-first century.

Every policy maker in the world, certainly including those in Japan, knows from hard experience what beginning students of international relations learn early in their academic careers: there are no "friends" among nations, only allies. They also know that allies are patricentric, self-absorbed, and fickle, and that alliances are therefore forever shifting like sand in a relentless surf. Iraq, Iran, and Pakistan have also learned this lesson at first hand.

Although Japan needed no single episode to illustrate the importance of its being able to take care of itself militarily, the clarifying moment came during the debate in the United States over sharing FSX fighter technology, a debate that took place against the broader backdrop of loudly expressed U.S. anger over Japan's economic success relative to the United States.* While administrations before George Bush's were able to separate military and economic policies, the collapse of the Soviet Union and the

---

*It also learned the lesson from NASA through participation in the space station project and in its own first space lab mission, though the space agency's problems had to do with domestic economic and political machinations, not with international rivalry. The station's ongoing re-configuration, caused by unending political battles in Washington, caused consternation bordering on disbelief in Japan, whose own involvement was disrupted and made more costly through no fault of its own. "The continuing slippage and descoping of the Space Station Freedom program are viewed as emblems of declining U.S. commitment and capability," in the words of one report. The European Space Agency, ESA, had the same problem participating in the Ulysses solar-polar mission with the United States. Both programs taught America's partners that it was highly unreliable. (The report is Mark R. Oderman and Hiroshi Yoshida, "U.S.-Japanese Cooperation in Civil Space Programs: A Review of Past Cooperative Efforts and a Consideration of Future Opportunities," 4th Space Technology, Commerce & Communications Conference, Washington D.C., January 10, 1991, p. 9.)

worsening economy in the United States during his presidency combined to turn economics itself into a major national security issue.

By 1989, with the U.S. economy stagnating, Japan's successes made it a target for shrill attacks in Congress and by industry. The evils of technology transfer—inventing television, computers, VCRs, and the rest and then "giving it" to Japan so the Japanese could beat the Americans at their own game—became a war cry. The malaise in Congress focused on the FSX (Fighter Support Experimental), a high-tech, souped-up derivative of the F-16 which was designed for coproduction in Japan and which the Reagan administration had promised to sell to Japan as cutting-edge technology. But Congress suddenly became reluctant to supply the plane, charging in bitter terms that technology was flowing to Japan and that providing the Japanese aerospace industry with still more knowledge would eventually further undermine U.S. industry.

The FSX impasse was eventually resolved by somewhat scaling back the fighter's technology, chiefly in radar and important software. This gave the Japanese problems they would not otherwise have had. Efforts to work things out on their own created extra expenses and delays for both Mitsubishi and General Dynamics, which were to coproduce the fighter.

Although efforts were already well under way to make Japan self-sufficient in all manner of conventional weaponry when the FSX controversy erupted, the anti-Japanese angst in the United States during the debate and Japan's clear vulnerability to Washington's vicissitudes amounted to a watershed. U.S. policy was suddenly seen as being arbitrary, protectionist, and even racist. "We still do not have a clear idea of whether to depend on the U.S., or to do as much as we can ourselves," said Jiro Hagi, chief of planning for the Self-Defense Force. "But I think that whenever we can, we are going our own way."

Japan's own way follows four routes, three of them legal: buying high-tech off-the-shelf equipment; making and improving existing weapons under license; and pushing research and development for future weapons, both conventional and unconventional.

Japan prefers to coproduce or solely produce existing weapons under license in order to gain experience not only in manufacturing but in improving them. That was the point of wanting to turn out an undiminished FSX. Putting together all of the aircraft's components and then integrating them into a single airframe would have enhanced Mitsubishi's assembly line skills while simultaneously infusing its technology bank with state-of-the-art knowledge. Japan decided to build its own F-15Js ("J" for Japan) at $65 million apiece rather than buy them off the shelf from McDonnell Douglas for $25 million. The additional expense was worth it to the Japanese because making the planes from scratch meant that the aircraft's manufacturer, Mitsubishi, gained valuable production experience. It also allowed the company to integrate indigenous components, such as phased-array radar, computers (the fighter's brains), and an air-to-air missile, the Mitsubishi AAM-3 (which is said to be superior to its U.S. counterpart, the AIM-9L Sidewinder). This also had the effect of providing work for Japan's electronics and other subcontractors. Although the F-15J was U.S.-designed, it was a Japanese fighter in every other important sense of the term.*

Ryozo Tsutsui, director general of the Japan Self-Defense Forces' Technical Research and Development Institute, where much of the country's advanced weapons work goes on, has left no doubt where his nation stands on long-term programs. "We realize that no country can obtain perfect self-sufficiency," he said in a 1989 interview. But "I believe Japan should keep to the highest state of the art in military technology as a deterrent."

This has translated not only into plutonium stockpiling, the array of missiles, and the various satellites, but into a spate of other high-tech weapons, some of them dual-use. One such project involves an engine that could propel an aircraft five times the speed of sound. Japan decided in 1992 to invest $330 million in initial work on the engine. Sensitive to criticism that it takes technology without giving in return, Japan invited four Western jet engine manufacturers to share 25 percent of the program. There is no doubt that such an engine could propel an airliner. It could as easily propel a stealth bomber, an aircraft carrying an orbit-bound satellite piggyback, a reconnaissance plane, or a long-range fighter-interceptor for fleet or home island defense.

Other programs, several of them closer to fruition, include the Yamato-1, a 100-foot-long naval surface craft built by Mitsubishi Heavy Industries that uses superconducting electromagnetic propulsion—magnets and powerful electric currents instead of screws—to produce a powerful "silent drive." Used underwater, the technology could make nuclear-

---

*Coproduced weapons include the Patriot, Hawk (surface-to-surface), Sparrow, Sidewinder, and TOW missiles, the P-3 naval patrol aircraft, and the Chinook, Huey, and Cobra helicopters.

powered submarines obsolete. Although the demonstration vessel was designed as a prototype for oceangoing ferries and cargo vessels, it got its name from the Imperial Navy's World War II flagship.

A fourth means of weapons technology transfer—the illegal kind—was best illustrated in June 1990 when it came to light that Ronald J. Hoffman, president of Plume Technology, Inc., a tiny California engineering firm, illegally sold software that can be used for designing rockets for Star Wars systems. The program, similar to the one he wanted to sell to Israel, was designed to track the exhaust plumes of ballistic missiles so they can be intercepted, a potentially valuable capability for a nation that could come under such attack from China, the Korean peninsula, or elsewhere in the region. Three of Japan's leading defense firms were the buyers. Hoffman was convicted in 1992 of selling the software to Nissan in 1986, Toshiba in 1986 and 1987, and Mitsubishi in 1989, for a total of $542,343. He was given a two-and-a-half-year jail sentence, four more on probation, and fined $225,000. The three companies denied any wrongdoing, claiming they were unaware that the sale violated the U.S. Export Control Act and that they relied on Hoffman. That Mitsubishi, to take one example, would pay $335,160 for obviously sensitive software without the customary export license raised a question, however, in the context of its legendary caution. No charges were brought against the three companies.

Warnings in the United States about Japan's quest for a new empire and an ensuing war with the United States are farfetched.* At the same time, Japan's leaders are looking uneasily to the day when their neighbors begin to edge into the power vacuum left by the U.S. and former U.S.S.R. along the Pacific rim and throughout the western Pacific. Whatever the genuine sentiments for pacifism felt by the average Japanese—and they remain strong—it is clear that the leaders in both government and industry are preparing for the day when confrontations develop in the area and challenges have to be answered.

Accordingly, restraints that were acceptable under America's umbrella no longer are. Although Japanese companies are constitutionally prohibited from selling weapons overseas, for example, there is growing internal pressure to reverse the law and find lucrative markets for home-made weapons. Some knowledgeable U.S. officials note that there has

*See, for example, George Friedman and Meredith Lebard, *The Coming War with Japan*, New York: St. Martin's Press, 1991.

already been "nibbling at the edges"—selling classified submarine propeller technology to the former Soviet Union, navigation and air-to-air missile parts to Iran, specialty computer chip-making factories set up in China, and the poison gas casing factory at Rabta, for instance—and that in the end the pressure to export weapons will, in the words of one expert, be "too great to resist." Illegal transfers reflect a desire by the most aggressive companies in the defense industry to expand their business to markets other than Japan's.

The military itself nibbled, too. In 1992, Japan bowed to international pressure by sending soldiers far from home for the first time since World War II. It dispatched a 600-man army peacekeeping force to war-ravaged Cambodia. The decision, which reversed a policy set after the Second World War that prohibited Japanese troops from going to other countries, came only after a rancorous debate in which all 137 Socialist lawmakers announced that they would quit the 512-member lower house of Parliament. (Their colleagues rejected their resignations and the bill passed, 329 to 17.) While the armed soldiers were forbidden to perform any duties except such peacekeeping functions as providing food, restoring communications, and rebuilding hospitals, there was no doubt in Japan, nor in any of its anxious neighbors, as to what the decision meant. "Even with the [peacekeeping] amendments attached, we consider this a quantum leap from what public opinion used to be," a senior Foreign Ministry official admitted. "The concept is in place."

So it was. Less than four months later, the Foreign Minister himself called for changes in the law that would expand the Self-Defense Forces' peacekeeping role to a global one. Although Michio Watanabe's remarks in early January 1993 were called mere trial balloons by some analysts, they were seen by others as presaging a constitutional review that could end in an expansion of the military's sphere of operations. "From now on, one of the roles of the Self-Defense Forces should be to maintain global peace and order under the leadership of the United Nations," Watanabe asserted. Taking him up on the offer, U.N. Secretary General Boutros Boutros-Ghali suggested a year later that Japan amend its constitution for just that purpose. Even as Prime Minister Kiichi Miyazawa's government rejected the proposal, it was making tentative plans to send a second military contingent to Mozambique if the U.N. requested it. Other officials were in the meantime calling for the purchase of long-range ships and planes, ostensibly to carry out Watanabe's long-range plan.

It was yet another precedent—a clear road marker—on the way to a cloudy but disturbing destiny. That destiny would, in turn, be shaped in very large part by events taking place only a few hundred miles due west.

The "hermit kingdom" got its name because of the extraordinary isolation, secrecy, and self-sufficiency imposed on it by its xenophobic leaders from its birth in 1945. While all Communist countries were "denied territory" to the United States and its allies during the cold war, the People's Democratic Republic of Korea, North Korea, was undoubtedly among the most denied territories of all. That is why its nuclear weapons and other programs, along with its aggressive strategy to sell anything it could produce, took a long time to understand. But reconnaissance satellites were invented to make certain that no territory could be completely denied. It was primarily the prying eyes of KH-11s that first pulled back the shroud covering North Korea's intensive effort to develop its own nuclear weapons. Prying eyes and, as in Taiwan, a defector.

Yongbyon, sixty miles northeast of Pyongyang, had interested CIA and Pentagon photointerpreters and analysts for years. The first satellite imagery of the area, hard by the Kuryong River, showed a small, two-to-four-megawatt research reactor that had been sold to North Korea by the Russians in 1965.* A succession of satellite photos that started to come in during the mid-1970s, however, showed that Yongbyon was spreading out as new facilities, including a research installation, roads, railroad tracks, power grids, housing, and storage areas, were added. North Korea had embarked on an intensive nuclear weapons development program on an assumption—incorrect as it turned out—that South Korea would be allowed to produce its own atomic bombs with the encouragement of the United States.

In 1980—the year after South Korea's nascent program ended—one of the satellites returned unambiguous evidence that a new reactor was also going up at Yongbyon. It was an especially interesting reactor, too, as progressive photos of it during the next few years showed. It was a thirty-megawatt, graphite-moderated, gas-cooled machine that burned natural uranium, which North Korea had in abundance (the primary mine, just north of Pyongsan, was also photographed from space and its output

*It was subsequently upgraded to eight megawatts.

carefully measured). Ominously, while the North Korean reactor was modeled after a French G-1 military reactor whose plans were public, it was mostly homemade, suggesting an incredible investment that reflected a determination to be independent of outside suppliers.* More ominously, the reactor's size and design suggested to CIA and DIA specialists that its purpose was to produce plutonium.

That is where matters stood until early 1989, when another reconnaissance satellite that was tasked to rephotograph Yongbyon returned even more unsettling intelligence.† The new imagery clearly showed that the North Koreans were making important additions to the place. These included a new research center, a housing complex, a nuclear detonation test site, a third reactor with a capacity of between 50 and 200 megawatts, and a reprocessing facility which, according to one expert, was "the size of an aircraft carrier." Some of the facility was underground, like Dimona. The new reactor's construction site was seen in the high-resolution photos to be protected by antiaircraft guns. As was true of the Algerian reactor, this one was far too large to be used for research and was not connected for generating power. The detonation site, which was found later on the shore of the Kuryong, seemed to be used for testing technologies for imploding nuclear cores.

At the time the detonation site was discovered, an export official at EG&G, America's premier nuclear trigger supplier, approached the Department of Commerce's enforcement arm in Boston. In September 1990, a company executive named Stephen Barry told special agent Ken Crossen that a Korean named Hee Young Chae had the month before inquired about buying four krytrons and a hydrogen thyratron. Both devices are nuclear triggers that would be useful for setting off the implosion packages that would be tested along the Kuryong River. EG&G krytrons had been smuggled to Israel and Pakistan in the 1980s, so the firm was especially wary of the problem. Barry told Crossen that the Korean, who lived in the Los Angeles suburb of Granada Hills, had at first admitted that he wanted to ship the triggers to North Korea but changed his story after

---

*Some material did come from the West, however. In 1990, Degussa was fined $800,000 for illegally reexporting U.S.-made zirconium to North Korea. The material was used as cladding for uranium fuel rods.

†It is very likely that air sampling to find trace elements was also done by U-2 aircraft flying out of SAM range over the Yellow Sea and the Sea of Japan. In addition, SR-71 reconnaissance aircraft made many runs along the North Korean coast during the 1970s and 1980s and at least once drew a SAM, which missed. ("U.S. Expresses 'Serious Concern' Over Firing of North Korean Missile," *The New York Times*, August 28, 1981.)

being told that he needed an export license to do so. That was when EG&G decided to go to Commerce.

The feds in turn decided to sting Chae. Two months later EG&G shipped him the triggers, minus a few critical components, together with packing slips noting that a valid export license was required if they were to be forwarded to North Korea or other countries on the U.S. enemies list. Meanwhile, the North Korean agent was placed under continuous surveillance. Not long afterward, he shipped the triggers to Singapore, which the Commerce agents believed to be nothing more than a stopover on the way to Yongbyon. "If the supposed end-user in Singapore complained that the krytrons didn't work, then it would stand that they were a legitimate customer," an agent explained. "If not, then we had a pretty good indication Chae had shipped them to North Korea." There was no complaint, leading Commerce to believe that it had uncovered yet another nuclear weapon smuggling operation. The case was still under investigation in late 1993.

If they needed any more proof of what North Korea was up to—and they didn't—it came from Ko Young Hwan, a thirty-eight-year-old North Korean diplomat who defected in the summer of 1991. Ko revealed the existence of an underground research facility at Bakchon, sixty miles north of Pyongyang, which apparently had gone undetected by the spy satellites. That error would soon be corrected. Ko, who said he abandoned his country because he was disenchanted with Pyongyang's hard-line communism, claimed that North Korea was within two years of making its first atomic bomb.

That estimate jibed with the CIA's. The following February, CIA Director Gates shocked the House Foreign Affairs Committee when he told it that his agency's best guess was that North Korea would have a nuclear capability in between "a few months to as much as a couple of years." The third reactor was expected to go on line in 1992 and produce sixty-two pounds of plutonium a year by 1995, enough for three bombs. Meanwhile, Gates's analysts had calculated that North Korea could have enough fissile material from the thirty-megawatt reactor for six to eight bombs.

In February 1993, Gates's successor, R. James Woolsey, left open the possibility that North Korea may already have had enough plutonium for a bomb. And former Secretary of State Lawrence Eagleburger, who had been privy to the most sensitive intelligence during the final months of the Bush administration, went even further. The redoubtable diplomat said he believed that the Koreans already had the finished product.

Whatever the precise timetable, North Korea's swiftly approaching status as a nuclear power so unnerved Lee Jong-koo, South Korea's Defense Minister, that one day he unexpectedly threatened to launch an "Entebbe-style" commando raid against Yongbyon unless Pyongyang signed nuclear safeguard treaties. Within minutes of the statement's going out on the South Korean news agency's wire, however, cooler heads prevailed; the commando reference was excised from later stories. "The ministry cancels this portion of the minister's remarks as nonexistent," an oxymoronic Defense Ministry statement said bluntly.* (An Entebbe-style attack was ruled out by those who patented the original, however, most likely because the targets were well out of range and dispersed. Fearful that North Korea would arm Iran with 600-mile-plus-range Nodong-1 ballistic missiles that could reach their country, the Israelis offered to invest at least $1 billion in North Korea. One Israeli described the North Koreans as "eager negotiators" but said discussions were ongoing. In fact, they soon fell apart.)

Lee was upset because he had seen the pictures and been briefed, along with other senior South Korean and Japanese officials, by the CIA in an attempt to increase regional pressure on Pyongyang to abandon its atomic dream. While both South Korea and Japan were gravely disturbed by the evidence, Seoul was especially rattled. The South Korean capital is so close to North Korea—fifty miles—that the government at one point decided against buying Patriots because it wouldn't have time to use them in an attack. It eventually changed its mind.

Meanwhile, South Korea, Japan, and the United States played politics. In October 1991, the United States announced that it would withdraw all of its nuclear weapons from South Korea—estimated to be forty nuclear-tipped artillery rounds and sixty bombs—and reduce its troop strength from 43,000 to 36,000 and eventually down to 30,000 or less. The

---

*Lee's slip of the tongue caused explosions in both Seoul and Pyongyang. South Korean opposition parties demanded that he be fired immediately, not only because the remark was "fatal to inter-Korea relations," but because it might have given the North an excuse to launch a surprise attack. For its part, the North denounced the hapless minister for committing "an unpardonable military provocation" that had brought the peninsula to the brink of war. ("Opposition Demands Defense Minister Ouster Over Commando Raid Comment," AP, April 13, 1991, and "North Korean Newspaper Says Seoul Commando Threat Risks War," Reuters, April 16, 1991.)

following month, South Korean President Roh Tae Woo declared that his country would no longer have U.S. or any other nuclear weapons on its soil and called on North Korea to abandon its nuclear weapons program.

Turning up the heat still further, South Korea and the United States announced a month later that the North Koreans would be allowed to inspect South Korean civilian and military sites for nuclear weapons if they opened their own facilities to U.N. inspection. In December, Roh declared that his country possessed not one nuclear weapon. "As I speak," he pledged solemnly on national television, "there do not exist any nuclear weapons whatsoever, anywhere in the Republic of Korea." The successive actions were designed to provide North Korea's aged Kim Il Sung, the world's longest-ruling Communist, a face-saving way to abandon his program.

The Americans and Japanese also had parts to play. While Gates was testifying before open sessions of Congress, the Department of State was leaking a stream of information about North Korea's high jinks to the news media ("North Korea Digs Tunnels for Nuclear Arms," *The Washington Times* reported in February 1992, to take only one example among dozens).

But the Japanese did even better than that. They asserted, as they had before, that they would neither recognize North Korea diplomatically nor send it aid or war reparations until it dismantled its reprocessing facility and allowed IAEA inspectors to look over the complex. (North Korea had signed the NPT in 1985 but insisted that it would not permit a safeguards agreement allowing on-site inspection until Washington removed South Korea from under its nuclear umbrella. That had now been done.) The Japanese also made public French SPOT imagery of Yongbyon taken from more than 500 miles overhead which, according to a professor named Toshibumi Sakata, clearly showed "a nuclear reactor with a fuel facility in the south and a research facility to the north." The space imagery expert also noted that the North Koreans were "scattering" their plutonium separation facilities.

Pyongyang had traditionally insisted that its nuclear program was strictly peaceful, that it had neither "the need nor the capacity" to develop nuclear weapons. Yet it had tenaciously maintained that whatever program it did have was no nation's business but its own. Now, however, the pressure seemed to be forcing change. It had been relatively easy for North Korea to be "self-sufficient" when aid was coming from China and the Soviet Union. But China had ceased giving aid and the Soviet Union had ceased, period. By the winter of 1991, the hermit kingdom was isolated and quaking economically, and no amount of Scud sales was going to change that.* Kim Il Sung gave evidence of understanding that bravado would no longer work.

By the end of 1991, North Korea was squirming in a difficult situation, one whose convolutions reflected turmoil within the highest levels of the Pyongyang regime. It apparently decided to have the proverbial cake and eat it too, just as the Iraqis had tried to do.

On December 31, North and South Korea agreed in principle that neither country would "test, manufacture, produce, accept, possess, store, deploy, or use nuclear weapons." The following month, Pyongyang signed the NPT's nuclear safeguards accord and promised ratification later in the year. In May, it gave the IAEA a 100-page document describing a web of previously unknown nuclear-related facilities (plus the huge reprocessing plant at Yongbyon, which it called a "research laboratory"). It also admitted that it had produced a tiny bit of plutonium in the "laboratory," insisting it was for peaceful purposes, and provided some of it to the IAEA for analysis. Neither IAEA Director Hans Blix, who was finally allowed to tour the facility at about the same time, nor U.S. intelligence analysts could fathom why a research laboratory required a 600-foot-long building with concrete walls up to six feet thick.

But what looked like a promising situation abruptly turned sour in January 1993. A U.S. reconnaissance satellite had by then returned imagery of two nuclear waste storage buildings near the Kuryong, where the North Koreans had tested their core implosion charges. CIA analysts deduced from the digital pictures that the waste in the buildings would show that a good deal more plutonium had been turned out at Yongbyon than its owners admitted. The intelligence was sent to IAEA headquarters in Vienna.

Nor were the waste sites the only indicators that Pyongyang had quite a bit more plutonium than it was letting on. The CIA was also convinced that a second reprocessing plant was out there somewhere, along with equipment that had been evacuated before the IAEA people arrived. During the early spring of 1992, convoys of trucks had been

---

*Comparative figures for North and South Korea in 1990 were startling. Respectively, their populations were 21,720,000 and 42,793,000; gross domestic product per capita was $1,064 and $5,569; the real growth rate was −3.7 percent and 9.0 percent; military spending as a percent of GDP was 21.5 percent and 4.1 percent; and total foreign trade was $4.6 billion and $134.9 billion. ("The Great and the Dear," *The Economist*, April 18, 1992, p. 32.)

spotted hauling machinery away from Yongbyon. Ko Young Hwan, the defector, apparently told the CIA that the bomb work had gone underground.

Hans Blix, whose agency had missed the Iraqi nuclear weapons program despite on-site inspections, was determined not to suffer such an embarrassment again. He therefore directed the inspectors, whom North Korea had already admitted into Yongbyon six times, to demand access to the waste sites. The IAEA people obediently told the North Koreans that they wanted to take samples from the buildings. They were immediately and firmly rebuffed. Nor were they allowed to take samples from the core of the thirty-megawatt reactor. Such samples could show how long the device had been in operation and were therefore another way of calculating plutonium production. At the same time, a North Korean delegation at IAEA headquarters was shown the deliberately fuzzed, but still unambiguous, satellite imagery and chemical evidence pointing to an elaborate effort to deceive the IAEA. The chemical evidence was drawn from the small plutonium sample that the Koreans had previously given the IAEA.

The North Koreans maintained that they were denying access to the facilities because of renewed joint U.S.-South Korean military maneuvers. It was an implausible excuse. More likely, U.N. and other experts believed, the North Koreans were stalling in order to gain enough time to move incriminating evidence out of the waste sites to another location or even to one of the myriad tunnels that were under Yongbyon itself. Meanwhile, they ranted about "never allowing anyone to violate the dignity of the nation" or "impose any unreasonable measure on us as regards the nuclear problem." Blix, out of patience, responded by demanding that the North Koreans open their doors to an unprecedented "special inspection," or suffer the consequences (one of which is economic pressure).

A week later, Pyongyang let loose a lengthy diatribe, again insisting that it had been pushed to its limit. Kim Il Sung, an octogenarian despot who was unaccustomed to having his word challenged, issued a statement accusing the United States of "trying to attain its sinister purpose" by manipulating the IAEA for purposes of espionage. If the U.N. pressed the matter, the "Great Leader" warned, his country would take an unspecified "countermeasure for self-defense."

"The allegation that we have 'suspicious facilities' related to the nuclear problem is a sheer lie. We have no other nuclear facilities than those we have reported to the International Atomic Energy Agency," a Korean Central News Agency report that carried his remarks added. "If we accepted inspection of 'suspicious objects' as demanded by the United States, it would be the beginning of the exposure of all our military objects and bases and would become a precedent of permission for the opening of military bases on all nonnuclear states."

The U.N. expected an atomic shell game to begin in North Korea, much like the one that took place in Iraq, with nuclear components hurriedly moved from one location to another just ahead of the inspectors. But the North Koreans had no intention of being chased around their own countryside by intrusive foreigners. Cornered and panicked, they startled the world by announcing on March 12 that they intended to renounce the Non-Proliferation Treaty, thereby becoming the first nation to do so.

"They realized that it was only a matter of time before their huge investment in this project would be shut down," one American analyst concluded. "It could not go forward with inspectors around. They felt they had no choice."

The decision was taken by the United States, the United Nations, and some of North Korea's neighbors as a de facto admission that it had decided to press on with its nuclear weapons program. As the winter of 1993 turned to spring, the intelligence community had two lingering problems with North Korea. If it really was working on clandestine nuclear weapons—and that was now taken to be a virtual certainty—South Korea and Japan would feel enormous pressure to follow suit. It would be atomic dominoes in east Asia. More insidiously, there was a very high probability that North Korea would sell its nuclear technology for desperately needed foreign exchange. "They have never made a weapon or developed a weapons technology that they didn't try to sell," one knowledgeable official observed. And by 1993, North Korea's marketable weapons also included biological and chemical weapons and the Nodong-1.

Then, in mid-June, Pyongyang reversed itself yet again, saying that it would "suspend" the treaty withdrawal, this time mere hours before the move was to take place, and agreed to discontinue plutonium production. This left matters where they stood before the withdrawal announcement. Mechanical monitors would be kept in place, but inspectors remained barred from the sensitive areas, pending negotiation.

Swerving all over the diplomatic road and reversing course in unprecedented ways left some observers with the impression that the North Koreans were stalling for time until they crossed the line in what they called a "cheat and retreat" strategy. If that was the case, more swerving could be expected.

By late 1993, however, the intelligence picture was a good deal clearer than the political one. North Korea was much further along in its nuclear weapons program than Iraq had been. Former Secretary of State Lawrence Eagleburger testified in June that he believed Pyongyang already had the bomb. His own department had concluded that North Korea had enough plutonium for one of the weapons, while the Defense Intelligence Agency surmised that it had as many as five. Furthermore, the plutonium that was already processed—however much it was—was turned from separated liquid to heavy metal. Nor were the U.S. intelligence and diplomatic communities happy to learn in July 1993 that Yongbyon's main reactor was due to be refueled, meaning that its spent fuel would be available for still more plutonium reprocessing.

Diplomatically speaking, the mercurial North Koreans were staging the shell game with extremely high stakes. While the diplomats on both sides continued the tortoiselike negotiating process, their leaders crowed for political effect. President Clinton, visiting South Korea that same month, warned that if North Korea developed and used an atomic weapon, "We would quickly and overwhelmingly retaliate." Oh, yeah, said the voices on the other side of the 38th parallel: "The United States must ponder over the fatal consequences that might arise from its rash act. If anyone dares to provoke us, we will immediately show him in practice what our bold decision is."

"North Korea," one knowledgeable congressional staff member mused in the spring of 1993, "is the only country that could still pull off a crisis like the Cuban missile crisis." The hermit kingdom, he added, could well surprise the international community with a superweapon fait accompli like Khrushchev and Castro had in 1962. In fact, a visit by a small group of high-ranking North Korean generals to Cuba in February 1991 underscored just that point. Their host was Fidelito Castro, son of the dictator and secretary of the Cuban Atomic Energy Commission, who hosted them at "Quark House." News of the visit disquieted North Korea watchers in the CIA and on Capitol Hill.

Far more disquieting is the possibility that the impoverished North Koreans will put their biological weapons expertise on the market or sell Scud Ds, whose 650-mile range puts Osaka within striking distance of the North Korean launch site at Nodong. Furthermore, the Japanese learned, an 800-mile-range missile, the Nodong-2, was on the drawing board. It could hit Tokyo. That threat is far more worrisome to Japan than the missile's appearance in the Middle East, which is where the headlines usually put it, and for good reason. The Japanese were so unnerved by the successful test firing of three Nodong-1s on May 29, 1993, for example, that for the first time they raised the possibility of arming themselves with nuclear weapons. North Korea wants to export 150 of the missiles to Iran in exchange for oil. Whatever Pyongyang's plans for the weapon, though, the Japanese were mindful that they were within its striking range and that was enough. They therefore decided to hedge their nuclear nonproliferation position by refusing to endorse an indefinite extension of the NPT, which expires in 1995. "We are thinking of a hypothetical situation in which Japan is alone, naked, with other countries having increasing nuclear capabilities and we face an increasing military threat," one Foreign Ministry official was frank to admit.

Perhaps the most disquieting factor of all is the nature of the personality whose finger is on North Korea's collective button. Kim Jung Il, son of the last leader installed by Joseph Stalin, is anything but a chip off the old block. Unlike his dour, octogenarian father, the new head of North Korea's National Defense Committee, its nuclear weapons and Scud programs, and the national armaments industry in general, is a "flaky" fatso in his early fifties who wears high heels and a pompadour to appear taller and who is addicted to cowboy movies and kinky sex (both of which he enjoys in a luxurious chalet overlooking Yongbyon).

As those who watch North Korea closely know, the "Dear Leader" offers two possibilities, though it is hard to say which is worse. He could be overthrown by disgruntled hard-line generals who accelerate their country's nuclear weaponization and overseas sales initiatives. Or he could remain in power, perhaps to live out the role of Clint Eastwood packing an atomic .44.

**A**s South Korea's leaders looked around them, caught in a historic political sea change, they confronted five inescapable facts. The United States had withdrawn nuclear weapons from their territory. It was also mostly withdrawing itself from the region.* North Korea was poor while their country was very well off. North Korea was probably going to get nuclear weapons one way or another. And North Korea had vowed to reunite the peninsula.

---

*The United States was also removing all 428 of its nuclear weapons from Guam and had never had them on Japanese soil. With the withdrawal from the Philippines, this meant that all U.S. nuclear weapons in the region were on carriers and submarines. ("Warheads Returning from Overseas," *The New York Times*, August 20, 1992.)

This posed a potentially serious problem for Seoul; it faced a poor but extraordinarily dangerous rogue regime on the other side of the 38th parallel. Seeing that their protector was slipping away, the South Koreans thought it prudent to find a replacement. It would be China.

South Korea's conventional military forces were robust at the start of the 1990s. Its arms industry, which comprised about eighty companies employing 45,000 people, was exporting about $100 million worth of munitions and light naval vessels a year, much of it indigenously designed. Like Japan, however, South Korea has enjoyed a variety of collaborative deals with U.S. firms, including the production of F-5s and F-16s, McDonnell Douglas's MD-500 helicopters, and General Electric's M-167A1 Vulcan antiaircraft gun. Korean industry spokesmen have made it clear that, like their Japanese competitors, they are using cooperation with American firms to fine-tune their own design and manufacturing processes.

U.S. military policy toward the country was formed in the cauldron of the Korean War, the low point of which came in the opening weeks, when rapidly advancing North Korean troops pushed the South Korean and U.S. armies into a defensive perimeter around the port of Pusan, which almost turned into another Dunkirk. Only MacArthur's brilliant flanking action, the invasion at Inchon, averted a victory for the North. From that point through the end of the 1980s, South Korea received an unending infusion of American weapons, technical know-how, industrial cooperation, and armed presence. While being cautious about sharing the latest technology, succeeding administrations through Reagan's encouraged the military buildup in South Korea, particularly as a market for arms that were made in America.* For their part, the South Koreans inventively upgraded the Honest John missile to make it more accurate,

---

*The economic plight of the United States during the Bush administration, however, softened the prohibition of high-tech weapons in order to help U.S. industry. During the Carter administration, for example, the transfer of F-16s to the South Korean Air Force was prohibited. By 1991, with the defense industry crippled because of domestic defense cuts, the Bush administration approved not just a weapon transfer, but a technology transfer, when it allowed a $2.52 billion deal for seventy-two of the fighters—still state-of-the-art—to be manufactured in South Korea. In fact, the whole deal called for a dozen F-16s to be purchased outright from General Dynamics, thirty-six more to be assembled in South Korea from kits, and then for the seventy-two to be made indigenously. The Pentagon justified the deal to Congress by explaining that it would add "an important force for political stability" in the region. It was hoped, of course, that the transfer would have the same effect on General Dynamics and on the economically beleaguered Bush administration itself. ("U.S. Announces Co-production Deal with South Korea for F-16 Fighter-Jets," Agence France Presse, July 8, 1991.)

turned the obsolete 1950s Nike-Hercules surface-to-air missile into a tactical ballistic missile, and twice successfully test-fired an indigenous surface-to-surface missile with an estimated range of perhaps 200 miles. If Scuds ever rained down on South Korea, they would be answered in kind. South Korea was also working on its own IRBM for the usual two reasons: to have a weapon that covered all of its rival's territory and to provide a launch vehicle to orbit satellites that could provide concomitant targeting information. Plans to launch an ambiguously named "observation" satellite were well underway in 1993.

And while South Korea continues to claim that it has no plans to develop nuclear weapons, Pyongyang's nuclear ambitions have somewhat altered the equation. Pressure in Seoul to respond in kind to the North Korean nuclear program developed within a week of the first NPT announcement when a vocal minority of hard-liners in the legislature denounced their government's decision to forgo the production of plutonium. "There is a lot of criticism that we have given up the right to reprocess and enrich nuclear fuel, our nuclear sovereignty," Han Sung Joo, South Korea's Foreign Minister, remarked. "We have stripped ourselves, while North Korea is getting the bomb, and Japan has all the nuclear material it needs and then some. There is something of a clamor to reconsider this."

One immediate solution, undertaken even before the North Korean announcement, was a rapprochement with China that broke almost forty years of enmity growing out of the Korean War.* The Chinese, after all, had tried to persuade North Korea not to develop nuclear weapons. The fact that Beijing was developing closer ties to their country, the men in Seoul reasoned, could put further pressure on North Korea to abandon its madcap race for the bomb. Whether it would work, or whether increasing isolation and U.N. sanctions would convince the hermit kingdom once and for all that only nuclear weapons would guarantee its salvation, remained one of the most important questions in the region and beyond.

Another solution was to set up a reprocessing plant of their own at the nuclear research facility outside Seoul. The ostensible reason for

---

*The pact was immediately denounced by Taiwan, which claimed to be the only legitimate China, as a violation of its trust and a trampling on international justice. At the same time, North Korea strongly opposed the new relationship, though it was clearly not prepared to break relations with its old benefactor. ("China and South Korea Planning to Establish Diplomatic Relations," *The New York Times*, August 23, 1992, and "Chinese and South Koreans Formally Establish Relations," *The New York Times*, August 24, 1992.)

building the plant, the South Koreans maintain, is the same as Japan's: to close their own fuel cycle to assure nuclear independence. The South Koreans were also pursuing plutonium-reprocessing contracts with both Britain and Russia that would permit them to retain tons of plutonium. Either would give them the potential to meet a threat from the north (or from Japan) without U.S. help, should that become necessary.

Whatever happens, the prospect of accelerated arms proliferation and an almost inevitable military clash hang heavy in the air. China, with no serious remaining military threat, is nonetheless stocking up on highly advanced weapons and, as noted, is claiming islands that straddle Japan's economic jugular vein.

The continued existence of two Koreas will inexorably raise tensions on both sides of the 38th parallel, particularly in the poor, paranoid, and perhaps nuclearized North. But a Korea that is brought together with or without nuclear weapons—largely out of a collective fear and hatred of both China and Japan—will in turn start Japan's own final metamorphosis into a superpower in possession of superweapons of dreadful capability.

As the North Korean nuclear crisis continued to evolve, in fact, rumors of a secret Japanese nuclear weapons program began circulating in both Japan and the United States. Antinuclear activists in Japan suggested that a nuclear weapons research program could well be under way. The rumor, they noted in the politest of whispers, is that the research is being done in the chemical section of the Defense Research Institute in Tokyo. The rumor in the United States moved, not among antinuclear groups, but within the national security system. Quiet talk about Japan's having a top-secret team of specialists who could assemble a bomb within a week from components that already exist was making the rounds. There was no evidence to support either rumor, but they were not all that farfetched in a region where the balance of power is shifting rapidly and unpredictably. The value of deterrence, after all, lies in uncertainty.

China, for one, will not find the prospect of nuclear weapons in either the Koreas or Japan bearable for long.

# PERIL AND POSSIBILITY

—

# 14

## THE
## WORLD MISSILE:
## TWO CASE HISTORIES

**A**bdelkader Helmy and Arnon Milchan would have made an odd couple. Both men were born in the Middle East, both lived in California during the 1980s, and both were attracted to big money. A casual observer might have concluded that the similarity ended there. After all, Helmy was an anonymous aerospace engineer, while Milchan was a movie mogul who produced *Pretty Woman, JFK, Memoirs of an Invisible Man, Under Siege, Sommersby, Falling Down,* and many other films. More fundamentally, Abdelkader Helmy was a Muslim who was intensely loyal to his native Egypt. Arnon Milchan, an Israeli-born Jew, was just as devoted to the land of his own birth. On the face of it, then, the only thing both men shared besides the region of their birth and the state in which they lived would have been a deep political and cultural animosity. It would have been fair to conclude that the similarity ended right there.

But it also would have been wrong. Helmy and Milchan shared something else: a single-minded endeavor that would very likely have caused each to understand and perhaps even appreciate the other, though they were implacable enemies. That is because both of them were also high-flying purchasing agents. And not only that, but they happened to be engaged in the same enterprise: acquiring long-range ballistic missiles for the countries from which they came. In the end, one would be forced to embarrass himself and his superiors before Congress after languishing in prison, while the other would become an international celebrity who hung out with movie stars in Cannes and in the Beverly Hills Hotel's famous Polo Lounge. On January 14, 1991—three days before the air war started over Iraq—Milchan concluded the deal of his life in Paris with Time Warner while his opposite number sat in the federal prison at Lompoc, California. And there was even a deeper irony. Their respective fates would exactly parallel those of their missiles.

The weapons themselves had various names, but were most widely known as Jericho-2 and Condor-2. They shared one strategic similarity— the capability to obliterate the other's territory—and a spate of technical ones. On the face of it, the missiles were roughly similar in design, had about the same range, were multiple-staged, mobile, used mostly solid fuel, and were designed to carry conventional, chemical, biological, or nuclear warheads. Condor, in addition, was also conceived to deliver fuel-air explosives. Less obviously, both were based on U.S. designs and technology. Still less obviously, both were the product of multinational programs, the shadowy handiwork of competing alliances of sworn political enemies and their corporate parasites who were willing to quietly contribute large sums of money, commit espionage, smuggle components and technology, and lend considerable technical expertise in order to perfect machines that could carry death to hapless populations many hundreds of miles away.

Knowing that their missiles would be as alarming as they were repugnant to North American and European nations, the competing consortia disguised the projects as best they could, doing most research, development, and testing south of the equator and therefore out of the limelight. Perhaps most insidiously, the projects became models for others. North Korea used Iranian and Libyan front money to produce Nodong-1, or Scud D, not for itself, but as a profitable export item. China did the same with the M-11 and M-9. It developed the missiles with Syrian and Pakistani financing as part of a consortium whose plan was to sell the finished weapons back to those who bankrolled them. The technique marked an ominous new dimension in proliferation because it showed the Third World that small groups of nations could cooperate successfully, synergize, for the development of their own superweapons without the participation of First World governments.

Condor and Jericho were conceived as terror weapons that would oppose each other. Condor was the product of a consortium representing Saudi Arabia, Iraq, Egypt, and Argentina which relied on shadowy Europeans for expertise. Jericho was jointly developed by Israel, South Africa, and, in an earlier era, imperial Iran. American engineering, technology, and materiel were generously sprinkled on both programs. The two main forces behind Condor and Jericho were Iraq and Israel, respectively. Yet in only one of the many ironies that haunted both programs—an irony played out in many other such undertakings—South Africa helped to fund a missile designed to obliterate Iraq with money it was paid by Iraq for artillery Saddam Hussein intended for use against Israel.

It is tempting to call the story of these two missiles a textbook case of how superweapons are created and then either stopped in time or allowed to take their places in the world's deadly arsenals. But "textbook" is not apt. The novel and the screenplay would be better suited to capture the intrigue, the ironies, and the knot of devious personalities enmeshed in these two extraordinary enterprises. In fact, the story of Condor and Jericho would make an excellent film for Arnon Milchan, who could not only produce it but could even play himself.

Helmy came to the United States in 1979 with a bachelor's degree in engineering, a master's in rocket propulsion, and a Ph.D., all of them from Cairo University. He started as a foreign-exchange scientist working at the Jet Propulsion Laboratory in Pasadena with a National Research Council grant. JPL contracts with NASA on a variety of space projects, most of them having to do with solar system exploration and, therefore, with rockets. Having decided that his job prospects were better in the United States than in Egypt, at least at that time, Helmy became a U.S. citizen in 1987. He had meanwhile been employed by Teledyne-Mc-Cormick-Selph and then by Aerojet Propulsion. Both companies were heavily involved in aerospace research. All three jobs, including the one at JPL, involved work on either the Space Shuttle, cruise missiles, or the Harpoon antiship missile. And in all three he blended in with his co-workers as a middle-class, workaday, earnest young professional and family man who lived inconspicuously in a cream-and-gray ranch house on St. Andrews Drive in the Sacramento suburb of El Dorado Hills and who wanted to make his mark in a country with apparently boundless opportunities in aerospace.

What was not readily apparent to those who worked with Abdelkader Helmy, however, was that he came from a very good family and was unusually well connected back in Cairo. He had worked at the Egyptian Rocket and Electronic Research Center there as a young engineer and was a close personal friend of Abdul Halim Abu Ghazala, the Minister of Defense, and others involved in military technology. He had even met President Hosni Mubarak on several occasions. So Helmy was well connected. But he kept a very low profile in order to protect what he did for those connections.

Arnon Milchan, on the other hand, had one of the highest profiles in California because he was one of the most successful movie producers in Hollywood. By 1992, at the height of his career, Milchan had production credits on at least twenty-four films. The eleven most successful grossed about $1 billion between 1989 and 1993. His friends included Barbra Streisand, Oliver Stone, Tom Cruise, Richard Dreyfuss, Robert De Niro, and Sydney Pollack. His surprisingly small office—Room 4 in the old music building on the Warner Bros. lot—held a picture of him in a tuxedo standing beside a similarly dressed George Bush and his wife, Barbara. In another, Tom Cruise had his arms around Milchan's two daughters. A small painting depicted a screaming man with screws tightening at his temples. The image was an obvious metaphor for the pressure Milchan felt from his work. The full extent of that work, however, extended well beyond Hollywood. It went all the way to Israel's missile fields.

Milchan's known residences were a 300-year-old farm outside of Paris, an apartment in Paris, a bungalow at the Beverly Hills Hotel, and a penthouse condominium at the Herzilya Heights complex in Herzilya Pitua, north of Tel Aviv. He was a citizen of both Israel and Monaco, was close to Labor Party officials in Israel—most of all, Shimon Peres—and was said to be worth close to $1 billion. In January 1991 Milchan's New Regency Enterprises made the deal with Time-Warner, French pay-TV giant Canal Plus, and Scriba & Deyhle, a German movie company, in the biggest American-European joint venture ever. The agreement gave Milchan a $900 million kitty to produce forty more films.

On the face of it, Arnon Milchan was an immensely ambitious and extraordinarily gifted wheeler-dealer: a man whose self-definition was described by money, power, and the need to mingle with the rich and famous. "The main kick for Milchan is the glamour aspect, getting to schmooze movie stars and power brokers, the 'starfucker' phenomenon," Steve Abbott, a former business partner, explained in Hollywood's studiously crass poolside argot. Yet he was also mysterious and enigmatic.

The contradictions start with accounts of his education. In 1986, for example, he told the *Jerusalem Post* that his stay at a proper British boys' school ended because of anti-Semitism. Seven years later, he told *Premiere* magazine that he was thrown out because he was sneaking out to pick up girls. Similarly, some profiles have him attending the London School of Economics, others the City College of London. And he told the *Jerusalem Post* he had also attended the University of Geneva. Yet, when a private investigator checked Milchan's curriculum vitae for a prospective partner in 1990, he found that there were no records of anyone with Milchan's name attending, let alone graduating from, the London School of Economics or the University of Geneva. "You just never know whether he was telling the truth or not. The kind of deals he was in, the level of finance and the way he operated, seemed to me like a world upside down. I felt we were dealing with a sort of dangerous, shady quality," observed Charles McKeown, a scriptwriter who knew Milchan. Shady wasn't the word for it. Out in the deep shadows, beyond the range of the lighted sound stages and the make-believe that is carefully packaged on them, another Arnon Milchan existed.


There was nothing out of the ordinary about Kosmos 2019's launch, at least at first. The 2,800-pound satellite, carried by a workhorse SL-4 Soyuz booster, rose smoothly into the sky above the Plesetsk Cosmodrome at 3:58 on the afternoon of May 5, 1989, and sailed into its designated orbit. Even before it reached orbit the Soviet spacecraft was picked up by large radars in Great Britain, Turkey, China, and Alaska. In addition, the SL-4's heat plume—the long comma of fire expelled by its engines— was precisely tracked by a U.S. Defense Support Program, or DSP, satellite that was parked 22,300 above the equator in an orbit that kept it over the same spot on Earth. All of the data were instantly relayed to the North American Aerospace Defense Command's worldwide missile tracking complex inside Cheyenne Mountain, just outside of Colorado Springs, where they were analyzed with the help of powerful computers. Within an hour, the computers had established that Kosmos 2019 was flying in a low orbit inclined 62.9 degrees relative to the equator. That made it a photoreconnaissance satellite on what appeared to be a routine surveillance flight.

Three days after the launch, however, the men and women inside Cheyenne Mountain were mystified to see the spacecraft begin radical changes in direction to alter its ground track, or the swath of land and sea over which it flew. When the maneuvering ended, on May 14, Kosmos 2019's orbit was taking it over a ribbon of Earth that included a 1,200-mile-long stretch of land and sea that began at Arniston, a fishing town 130 miles east of Cape Town, South Africa, and ended over Marion Island, almost halfway to Antarctica. The spacecraft's overall orbit was elliptical, with its lowest altitude—about ninety miles—coming along the Arniston-Marion stretch.* Since imaging spy satellites take pictures of their targets at the lowest possible altitudes for the sharpest results, the analysts concluded that whatever it had been assigned to photograph was in the vicinity of Arniston. Kosmos 2019 remained in that orbit for three days before being ordered on May 18 to return to Earth immediately with its exposed film. On June 1, it was replaced by Kosmos 2025, which flew a virtually identical mission. The second recon satellite did its dip on June 10 and was instructed to land under its parachute five days later.

The high cost and short duration of both flights convinced the Air Force that something the Soviets considered important and urgent was happening, or was about to happen, along the route between Arniston and Marion Island.

Arniston is one of the most beautiful places in a country renowned for its natural splendor. It is a white-washed fishing village whose rugged docks and brightly colored boats punctuate miles of some of the most spectacular beaches in the world. The sand is creamy and the water that laps at it is jade. It adjoins the De Hoop Nature Reserve, set in a vast, sparsely treed bowl that sustains wild flowers, impalas, springboks, ostriches, and the proprietors of a lodge that caters to tourists who never fail to be impressed by the beauty of the landscape. (They are less than impressed by the small shanties on the other side of Arniston, where the "colored" people live, however.) Above the open wooden boats, many of

*Its high point, or apogee, was 221 miles, while its perigee, or ordinary low point, was 116 miles. The dips down to 90 miles were special maneuvers not associated with its standard flight profile. (Nicholas L. Johnson, *The Soviet Year in Space: 1989*, Colorado Springs: Teledyne Brown Engineering, 1990, p.126.)

them propped up for minor repairs, there is a sky that would have inspired Matisse—a deep blue dome dappled by snow-and-gray gulls on an endless search for wayward fish and morsels discarded by the men who follow the fish.

Arniston's serenity would be complete except for the occasional, distant roar of a rocket engine being run up on a test stand at the nearby Overberg Test Range or the sight of a missile streaking under the dome and disappearing to the southeast, in the direction of Marion's attentive metal ears. The town's residents have seen almost all manner of missiles cleaving the sky near their village, but they deflect questions about them because they know that the nearby test range is off limits for both strangers and too much loose talk by locals. "Please don't ask," Jock Dichmont, a weather-treated wreck diver, occasional fisherman, and former lawyer, told NBC News. "This is a very high security area, and all we know is that occasionally we see a missile streaking across the sky."*

Kosmos 2019 and 2025 had come to watch the preparations for a particularly important launch. By July 5, when a ballistic missile finally roared away from Overberg and arced 500 miles out over the Indian Ocean toward Marion Island and its tracking antennas, a KH-11 had also been maneuvered to scout the situation. More important, the same DSP satellite that had followed the SL-4s that shoved the Soviet recon satellites into orbit used its infrared sensor to follow and measure the ballistic missile's heat wake as well. It immediately relayed the information to Cheyenne Mountain, whose computers compared the shape, temperature, density, and other elements of the missile's heat plume with those of other rockets they had stored in their memories. The computers said that the new South African missile's exhaust trail bore a striking resemblance to that of

---

*A brochure promoting Overberg as an excellent site for missile testing by other nations made the point that the facility benefits neighboring towns because of the "additional purchasing power, the increased number of pupils, the creation of new job opportunities and the participation of Overberg Test Range personnel and their families in community activities." But residents of the area tell a different story. Whenever a missile is tested, fishermen are prohibited from going to sea. There was so much activity at the range by the summer of 1989, according to a news account, that the community itself was threatened with extinction and many of its residents had to resort to burglary and petty crime to make ends meet. Dichmont told Windrem that Armscor, the weapons firm, prohibited fishing for twenty-one days that September, presumably because of missile tests, and that the ban had a "deleterious effect" on the fishermen. House break-ins by "desperate" fishermen were at an all-time high, he said. (Windrem interview with Dichmont in Arniston and "Weapon Tests Starve Fisherfolk," *Sunday Times* (Johannesburg), September 24, 1989.)

Jericho-1, a short-range ballistic missile that Israel had begun evolving in 1962. KH-11 imagery showed that the missile's tractor-erector-launcher was the same as used for Jericho-1.

Within hours, the Defense Intelligence Agency's Directorate for Current Intelligence had produced a Special Assessment which reported the launch, called the missile a probable SRBM, and went into considerable detail linking it directly to substantial Israeli "assistance." "Once an operational ballistic missile capability exists," the report predicated, "Pretoria will have acquired another means with which to intimidate its regional neighbors." The data both sides collected from their satellites, plus communication intercepts and previously collected information, gave them a very good idea of what sort of missile the South Africans had tested. Seeing that the launch was the subject of intense scrutiny, the South Africans themselves lamely called it a "booster rocket."

The missile was indeed an advanced derivative of Jericho-1, whose successor, the nuclear-capable Jericho-2, was at that moment being deployed in the Judean hills west of Jerusalem even as it was still being tested. Although the Arniston missile (as the CIA called it) rested squarely on Israeli, and therefore American, technology, it was strictly homemade.*
It and others were constructed by Armscor in Overberg's missile and rocket assembly building with the help of Israeli engineers and technicians. The Israeli connection went even beyond providing the weapon's technology, though. It went to the heart of South Africa's ballistic missile program itself. Overberg's assembly building, central control center, satellite checkout area, launch site, tracking towers, antennas, huge aircraft hangar, runway, and residential and recreational complexes were very similar to Israel's own missile test site at Palmichim, thirty-five miles south of Tel Aviv. Those who have seen both installations in satellite photographs say that they are virtual twins.† South Africa would become so dedicated to its ballistic and other missile programs that by 1990 Armscor was building a think tank for further missile development on a 1,250-acre site in the Lebanon State Forest near Houwhoek, on the Cape.

Israel's extraordinary closeness to South Africa and its weapons

*"Arniston" would not, of course, be South Africa's name for the missile. It was given that name by the CIA, which customarily assigns names to new missiles according to where they are first launched.
†Unlike Palmichim, where security is intense (see Chapter 9), security at Overberg is comparatively relaxed. There is a single fence and guard post and an occasional sign warning would-be trespassers away. Bredasdorp, a town set 1,200 feet up a nearby hillside, commands a view of almost the whole test range.

program had its genesis in 1974 when both nations, feeling desperately isolated and surrounded by implacable enemies, tentatively decided to cooperate in a number of scientific, economic, financial, and political areas. It was an alliance born of a shared desperation.

"We argued that at a time when the West (Free World) was lacking in strong and determined leadership, Israel and South Africa formed the two pillars supporting the Free World's strategic interest in Africa and the Middle East," Eschel Rhoodie, South Africa's Secretary of Information at the time and a prime instigator of the plan, has written. "We argued, further that Israel was surrounded by a hundred-million hostile Arabs and that South Africa was confronted by more than twice that number of Blacks, most of them politically hostile to South Africa and the West. Should one of Israel or South Africa succumb, the chances were great that the Black and Arab states would gang up against the remaining one with disastrous results either in the strategic Middle East or in the mineral rich Southern part of Africa. The Free World would, to our way of thinking, not survive a global Marxist onslaught if its two strategic pillars in Africa and the Middle East collapsed."*

It is highly unlikely that either Israel or South Africa would have collapsed—their acquisition of nuclear weapons, after all, was meant to forestall just such a possibility—much less that both nations' disintegration would have doomed the free world. Yet Rhoodie's apocalyptic vision of Arab-Black-Communist armies taking over the world, with the attendant slaughter of their enemies, provides stark insight on each nation's worldview and on the nature of the bonds that held them together. Each considered itself a beleaguered bastion of Jewish or Judeo-Christian civilization whose common cause was mutual survival in a world of remorselessly savage enemies preoccupied with their destruction.

In addition to deciding that close relations with Israel were imperative, Rhoodie, Information Minister Cornelius Mulder, former Prime Minister John Vorster, and another colleague decided to embark upon a far-reaching, veiled public relations campaign on behalf of their country

---

*Whatever else most residents of South Africa thought about their country in 1974, it was not as a pillar of the "Free World."

Rhoodie may have been somewhat paranoid, but he was also capable of political insight. Warned not to befriend the Israelis for fear of antagonizing "the Arabs, particularly Iran" (sic.), he observed that "Iran and Israel actually enjoyed extremely good (if well camouflaged) relations." The relations were so good that they included joint development of a number of weapons, including Jericho. (Eschel Rhoodie, *The Real Information Scandal*, Pretoria: Orbis SA (PTY) Ltd., 1983, p. 112.)

and its system of apartheid. This included using a $160 million slush fund to quietly attempt to buy, infiltrate, or otherwise influence African, Middle Eastern, and American newspapers, newsletters, magazines, and television programming. The escapade eventually turned into a major scandal called "Muldergate" when the Botha government charged Rhoodie and the others with hatching and carrying out the scheme without the knowledge of the government as a means of enriching themselves through fraud.* Rhoodie at one point asserted that in 1975 he gave almost $200,000 to an Israeli millionaire arms dealer to quietly buy *West Africa*, an influential magazine.† The dealer, he said, was named Arnon Milchan.

Rhoodie's view of the world was shared by many Israelis and South Africans, and none so much as Shimon Peres. Then defense minister, Peres wrote to Rhoodie in November 1974 to thank him for his "great efforts" in bringing the two nations together. After secret meetings with his opposite number in Pretoria earlier that month, Peres told Rhoodie that "a vitally important cooperation between our two countries has been initiated." There had been deals between the two nations before, but nothing like the scale being envisioned. "This cooperation," the letter continued, "is based not only on common interests and on the determination to resist equally our enemies, but also on the unshakable foundations of our common hatred of injustice and our refusal to submit to it." The letter was marked "top secret," and with good reason; brutality toward blacks was then at its height in South Africa, and the country's scientists had just begun their pursuit of the ultimate racial weapon. A common hatred of injustice indeed.

The two nations' siege mentality being what it was, first Israel and then South Africa sought weapons that would offset their overwhelming disadvantage in manpower. Jericho was developed to intimidate the enemy

*They denied the charge and Rhoodie even wrote a book, *The Real Information Scandal,* in which he countercharged that the Botha government knew full well what they were up to, but had made them scapegoats when news of the clandestine public relations campaign was made public. As for Milchan, he now downplays his involvement with South Africa.
†The London *Observer* and the now defunct *Washington Star* were on the shopping list but were never acquired. Television stations were also under consideration. There was even a secret plan to establish a black film industry in South Africa which would produce feature and news films to show that the government's policy of separate development worked. "This project was to give them a pride in their own customs, culture and history, not that of the White Man, and to promote the concept of law and order," Rhoodie wrote. *The Citizen,* a "middle of the road" newspaper designed to influence the South African and international business community, was specifically intended to take a "pro-Israeli line." (*The Real Information Scandal,* pp. 87 and 119.)

and, if that did not work, to annihilate it in staggering numbers. On October 8, 1973, for example, Golda Meir reportedly ordered Defense Minister Moshe Dayan to arm at least some Jericho-1s with nuclear warheads as Syrian forces pounded Israeli northern positions while 100,000 Egyptian soldiers and more than 1,000 tanks poured across the Suez Canal in an apparent race to the Israeli border. Given the number of Israelis fighting at close quarters with the Syrians and the mass of Egyptian men and armor moving across far-off Sinai, military headquarters in both countries' capitals would have been the more likely target. The missiles' relatively poor accuracy supports the theory that at least some of them would have been nuclear or chemically tipped. Dayan, who was said to have become deranged at the time—to have gone "batshit," in the words of a U.S. National Security Council official who followed the situation closely—was reliably reported to have warned Meir that the end of Israel was imminent unless something drastic was done. For the South Africans, missiles carrying conventional or atomic warheads would do to the black legions what steam locomotives pulling Gatling guns had done to their forebears a century earlier. That is why Israeli missile and nuclear weapon technology came to South Africa while large quantities of uranium and hard currency moved in the other direction.*

The deal was struck during meetings between Israeli Prime Minister Yitzhak Rabin and South African President John Vorster during the latter's state visit to Tel Aviv and Jerusalem in April 1976. The bargain with Vorster was a Faustian one. The man from Pretoria had been jailed by the British in World War II as a Nazi sympathizer.

A year later, the arrangement led to a dramatic tradeoff. Israel exchanged thirty grams of tritium, which is used to initiate nuclear explosions, for fifty tons of South African uranium. The tritium was flown to South Africa in twelve shipments of 2.5 grams each over an eighteen-month period. That amount would provide initiators for one bomb every six weeks. On the planes were people like Rhoodie and Benni Blumberg, the head of the secret LAKAM nuclear procurement network started by Peres. LAKAM and its South African counterpart, the Bureau of State Security (BOSS), ran the operations together. They even agreed on code names for the two commodities: tea leaves ("teeblare" in Afrikaans) for

---

*The advantage to South African money was that it came without strings attached. U.S. funds, on the contrary, were supposed to be directed for specific projects and programs which Washington wanted to monitor.

the tritium and mutton ("skape") for the uranium. The shipments were considered to be so important by both governments that then respective heads of government were notified as soon as a shipment had been completed.

And it was a perfect deal. Israel needed the uranium not only to fuel Dimona, its plutonium production reactor, but to feed its new uranium enrichment facilities. The Israelis had succeeded in varying degrees in enriching uranium by laser, calutron, centrifuge, and jet nozzle (the last being a process it developed with South Africa). Later, another shipment of fifty tons was made, followed by 500 more that South Africa sent north for safekeeping and eventually allowed Israel to use. Keeping the immense size of the shipments under wraps was of critical importance since disclosure would give away Israel's biggest nuclear secret: it had expanded Dimona fivefold since the 1950s. Similarly, the size of the tritium shipments heading south would betray the extent of South Africa's own atomic bomb program then just underway.

The arrangement with South Africa was not the only one that Peres and the rest of the Israeli leadership was working on during the early part of 1977, before Labor lost to Menachem Begin's Likud. There were parallel missile and nuclear deals with Taiwan and a missile deal with the Shah's Iran. In April of that year—the month the first shipment of tritium was flown to South Africa—Peres went to Teheran to sign six secret oil-for-arms agreements that included a missile component. Jericho was the key Israeli technology up for trading. Iran was then in the throes of an arms buildup like the one Saddam Hussein would initiate a decade later. In 1974, the United States had refused the Shah's request for Pershing-1 missiles and the next year refused an even more dangerous request, this one for four decommissioned Polaris ballistic-missile-firing submarines. So the Shah turned to the Israelis. They would be the Shah's back door to the storehouse of American military technology. Under the agreements, Iran made a down payment of $260 million worth of oil from Kharg Island, according to the Iranian general who negotiated the pact. In addition, Iran would make a substantial contribution to Israel's advanced military research. In return, the Shah was to get Jericho-1, which the Israelis were upgrading with contraband American technology: specifically, with U.S.-designed inertial guidance systems that Israel was forbidden to make available to other governments.

It was the same deal that would later be offered to South Africa. The missiles were to be transported through a Swiss intermediary, then assembled and tested in the Iranian desert. Iranian experts trained by the Israelis actually began work on the plant site. And on July 19, 1977, a high-ranking Iranian general watched with his Israeli counterparts as a Jericho was fired from a secret site south of Tel Aviv.

Although the Israelis did not offer the Shah nuclear weapons, top-secret minutes of a meeting of both sides make it clear that the Iranians were told that the missile they were supposed to get could easily accommodate atomic warheads. General Ezer Weizmann—who had succeeded Peres as defense minister only two months before—assured his Iranian opposite number that "all missiles can carry an atomic head, all missiles can carry a conventional head." He added, for good measure, that the Jericho could carry a 1,650-pound warhead: the same weight as Israel's nuclear warhead. The deal fell apart in 1979, however, when the Pahlavis fled before the Ayatollah's Islamic revolutionaries. So Israel needed a new partner if it was to develop its expensive new missile. The Israelis therefore turned to their new friends, the Afrikaaners.

Israel had first provided South Africa with the wherewithal to produce missiles during the late 1970s, when it gave the apartheid regime its own version of the Gabriel antiship missile, renamed Skorpion by its new owners. Ballistic missiles were the next logical step.

South African strategists grasped early on that the weapons topped with conventional or more deadly warheads were cheaper than squadrons of manned bombers and were far more difficult to stop. Pretoria also figured that its own version of Jericho would be considerably more accurate than the Scud and would therefore be a potentially lucrative item for Armscor to offer on the world market.

As was the case in Israel, nuclear arms were seen as the ideal weapons of last resort: the ultimate equalizers. And Israel, of course, knew that South Africa had an active nuclear weapons program. It was no coincidence that a joint Israeli–South African nuclear test in the Indian Ocean would take place within months of the Shah's departure.

On September 22, 1979, a U.S. VELA ballistic missile early warning satellite spotted a telltale double flash on the Indian Ocean near South Africa's Prince Edward Islands. Despite Israeli and South African denials, a detailed study made by U.S. intelligence eventually determined that the blast was caused by the testing of a neutron bomb in the three-kiloton range. This was the "enhanced radiation" weapon intended to stop Syrian troops from storming the Golan Heights. The September 22 "event" was the first in a series of such tests. One Israeli source claimed that three tests were actually conducted at that time, all supposedly under thick cloud cover. But "it was a fuck-up," he said. "There was a storm and we figured it would block VELA, but there was a gap in the weather—a window—and VELA got blinded by the flash."

At any rate, Rhoodie's frenzied nightmare of hordes of rampaging savages using an unending supply of Soviet weapons to wear down conventional forces was widely shared within both nations' leadership. Israel therefore played a crucial and cynical role in helping its white ally to develop and test nuclear weapons that could obliterate African blacks. Its "full-blown" partnership in the missile program, as one CIA report put it, paralleled the development of nuclear warheads to go on the missiles themselves.

U.S. intelligence seems never to have doubted otherwise. "Israelis have not only participated in certain South African nuclear research activities over the last few years, but they have also offered and transferred various sorts of advanced nonnuclear weapons technology to South Africa," an interagency report on the September 22, 1979, "event" concluded. A year later, a detailed CIA study entitled "South Africa: Defense Strategy in an Increasingly Hostile World" stated implicitly that Pretoria had a clandestine nuclear weapons program, though portions that almost undoubtedly related to Israeli cooperation were blacked out in a copy of the document released under the Freedom of Information Act. It is inconceivable that Israel did not know that the missile and nuclear programs it was transplanting to a neighboring continent were not only compatible but designed to be fully integrated.

Accordingly, Jericho-1 technology began moving south in the mid-1980s. In 1983, Armscor confiscated 400 square miles on Cape Agulhas, the southernmost point in Africa. There, over the protests of environmentalists, it erased a small village, fenced off a nature reserve, and filled the property with the same facilities—radars, a landing strip, a missile assembly building, a control center, and the cylindrical observation and tracking towers—that Israel had designed for itself and had offered to the Iranians. The Iranians' loss became the Afrikaaners' gain. And like the abortive Iranian deal, it was kept absolutely secret from Israel's closest ally and benefactor, the United States.

The July 5, 1989, launch of the South African missile, now called "Arniston" at the CIA, was followed by a second on November 19, 1990, and possibly a third the following year.

But there was a great deal more going on at Overberg than the test firing of the Arniston SRBM. Even before that first launch, the facility was used at least three times by Israel to test its more advanced, medium-range Jericho-2. South Africa got missile technology, including Jericho-1s, in part for helping Israel test even newer weapons. This followed the same pattern as the nuclear weapons technology transfer.

South Africa would eventually cloak its missile program in peaceful garb. It would announce in 1992 that it had embarked on a major program to enter the commercial space launch business. This mystified industry analysts and proliferation specialists alike. A Rand Corporation report done for the Pentagon noted that Brazil, the most advanced of all "emerging" space launch nations, could at best recoup only 40 percent of its investment because of stiff competition from Russia, China, and France, as well as the United States. "South Africa has absolutely no rationale for a space program," the proliferation expert said. "The testing it has done shows it's a ballistic missile program." The only conceivable use for ballistic missiles, other experts said, would be the old one: to use with nuclear warheads that were made before the country signed the NPT.

But those events were unanticipated during the previous decade, when the common threat fueled Israel's and South Africa's joint missile race. The three Jericho-2 tests at Overberg were accompanied by a spate of tests at Palmichim, the first occurring in May 1987. There were more test firings in November 1988, September 1989, January 1990, December 1990, and March 1992. There was even one from the operational site in the Judean hills in November 1990. All were successes.

The Bush administration had in the meantime turned up the heat on Israel to get it to enter into serious peace negotiations with the Arabs and to abandon the settlement of occupied Arab lands, two prospects that Yitzhak Shamir, the resolutely conservative Prime Minister, found detestable. During Bush's first year and a half as president, a behind-the-scenes guerrilla war therefore developed between the White House and Shamir. Among other time-tested tactics, Bush's subordinates leaked intelligence data to the news media revealing for the first time that Israel was helping South Africa's missile and other weapons programs. Citing "intelligence sources," for example, NBC News broke the story of the July 5 test on October 25. The story was widely quoted and was followed by a barrage of others, both on television and in print. One, in *The Washington Post*, quoted an "informed official" who claimed that U.S.

Ambassador Thomas Pickering had earlier been "rebuffed and told it was none of Washington's business" when he complained about the Israel–South African missile connection.

The Israelis responded by emphatically denying the charge and counterattacking: accusing the administration of spreading the information to pressure them to negotiate with the Arabs. The reports must have been all the more galling to the Israelis because they coincided with the Gaza and West Bank rebellions, in which rock-throwing Palestinian youths confronted Israeli occupation forces who shot tear gas, rubber bullets, and occasionally metal ones at them, while the world's TV cameras captured it all for the evening news. Responding to a public warning by Bush himself that Israeli transfers of U.S. weapons technology, and specifically a nuclear-capable intermediate-range missile to South Africa, were "taboo," Shamir shot back in a radio address on October 29 that such allegations were "baseless lies."

Meanwhile, the Department of State announced that it had "no indication" that Israel had transferred U.S. missile technology to South Africa. *U.S.* technology was the sticking point. Israel's unarticulated but clear position was that whatever it might or might not have transferred to South Africa was indigenously developed, not American. One Washington news story correctly asserted that Jericho-2 technology had reportedly been transferred to South Africa. But in the same paragraph it added that Israel had "developed the Jericho intermediate-range missile on its own." Wrong. And that was where men like Arnon Milchan came in.

It is said that during a tense moment in shuttle diplomacy during the Yom Kippur War, Henry Kissinger suddenly declared to Golda Meir, "First, I am an American; second, I am the Secretary of State of the United States of America; third, I am a Jew." The Prime Minister is said to have replied, without missing a beat: "That's all right, sonny, we read from right to left."

So does Arnon Milchan. "I know what the feelings are to have to defend the fact that you're born in a certain way, you know, you're born Jewish, Israeli, [and] there's nothing you can do about it," Milchan, a tenth-generation Palestinian-Israeli, told NBC News in 1992. "So, you learn how to grow up with saying, 'Wait a minute: I have the right to exist in peace.' My family's been there for 400 years and, really, it's second nature [to defend the country.] You have to survive honorably. At the end of the day, it's not just about being alive, it's about being alive and being able to look yourself in the mirror."

The image in the mirror is deceptively humble. It shows a man in his late forties whose plain talk, self-deprecating wit, studiously casual attire, and hatred of posing for pictures cloaks an uncompromising drive to be rich, powerful, and important. Milchan has harnessed an apparently easygoing charm, access to Israel's Old Boy network, deft social and business maneuvering, an eighteen-hour workday, and a relentless hunger for money to amass his own fortune and quietly play a vital role in the defense of Israel. The sporty movie mogul with Barbra Streisand or Jodie Foster clinging to his arm and the procurer of Israeli superweapons are so unlikely a combination that it would do justice to one of Israel's fabled intelligence operatives.

Whatever role Milchan played in Israel's quest for superpower status—he says he was merely a patriot—the record shows he was a great success.

When Milchan's father died in 1966, he left his son a small import business, Milchan Brothers, that was tottering on bankruptcy. But the twenty-two-year-old sabra and two colleagues soon developed a nutrient for iron-deficient fruit trees which he convinced Du Pont board chairman Irving Shapiro to manufacture. Milchan was and remains an exponent of the it's-not-what-you-know, it's-who-you-know school. So he befriended Shapiro and was soon selling the product for Du Pont in Israel, Turkey, and Iran. A decision to use technical people instead of salesmen to advise farmers led to a bonanza of orders, established the company's reputation, and brought in tens of millions of dollars annually in Iran alone. But Milchan's business acumen went far beyond tree food. According to the *Los Angeles Times*, he once claimed to have talked the Shah into building an airport even though he had never been involved in construction of any kind, let alone of airports. Milchan later denied the story, saying he only received a contract to pull up weeds from existing runways. Whatever the truth of the matter, Arnon Milchan was definitely casting about, looking to make a fortune almost any way he could.

His entrée into Peres's circle seems to have convinced him that the fortune lay in selling weapons. He therefore arranged to represent Raytheon, North American Rockwell, Magnavox, Bell helicopters, and Beechcraft in Israel "and elsewhere." By 1975, Milchan managed to make headlines because of an improper $300,000 commission paid to his company by a Raytheon subsidiary for the sale of Hawk missiles to Israel.

Milchan himself, who had in the meantime become close to Moshe Dayan and other political notables, was not accused of wrongdoing. He went on to make a series of adroit deals that soon made him one of the biggest arms merchants in Israel, if not *the* biggest. But Milchan eventually became bored with the business. He decided to stay in the weapons trade but to give up running it on a day-to-day basis in favor of living the life of a millionaire playboy in Hollywood, Cannes, and Tel Aviv. It was an obvious jump to the more glamorous world of movie-making.

His first introduction to the business of film and media came, not in Israel or in Hollywood, but in South Africa. And the man who got him started was none other than Eschel Rhoodie. The ubiquitous South African first met Milchan at a reception in Tel Aviv. Peres did the honor, informing Rhoodie that Milchan's father and brother, who owned Milchan Brothers, the Tel Aviv chemical business, had "done a great service on behalf of Israeli's national security." There was no further explanation. Another South African who was at the reception said that Peres's relationship with Milchan had apparently started in a business deal but had developed into a "warm friendship" despite a twenty-year age difference.

By 1977, with the Israeli–South African relationship moving forward, the two nations set up a joint secretariat to handle various matters, not the least of which was "propaganda and psychological warfare." That effort was an outgrowth of Rhoodie's use of the South African Information Ministry to wage the $100 million propaganda campaign on behalf of apartheid. Under the terms of the agreement, Israel would provide input into how to portray both countries' best side. South Africa would provide the money, with each country appointing a secretary to look after its interests.

By 1977, according to a high-ranking South African official, the two began an even more complicated relationship: Rhoodie was appointed the South African representative to the joint secretariat, while Milchan was named the Israeli representative.

The two men grew to become friends. Milchan bought Rhoodie's condominium in the exclusive all-white enclave of Plettenberg Bay (at a $15,000 profit for Rhoodie). More important, said the South African official, Milchan was given a special assignment by Rhoodie: "Operation Hollywood." According to the South African, this entailed the proposed use of South African cash to fund movie and television deals that would show the Pretoria regime to its most flattering advantage.

The South African said Milchan recommended that the apartheid regime actually penetrate the American movie business, making secret purchases of U.S. media organizations, including the UPI-TN and a San Francisco cable franchise. Although there is no evidence that anything came of these proposals, Milchan and Rhoodie used a South African Information Ministry safe house to discuss the proposed deals, according to the official. It wasn't in some dilapidated, nondescript neighborhood, however. It was in Cannes.

Milchan has been interviewed many times, but has at various points offered contradictory explanations of his role in South Africa, acknowledging to the *Jerusalem Post* his role as an Israeli "money man" for Rhoodie's operation. Then, in 1992, he gave three conflicting accounts of his South African dealings to the *Los Angeles Times*. First, he said that he spent only three days in South Africa although the South African Information Ministry "probably had plans for me." Then, he acknowledged that "I had worked with them, but I wasn't the 'money man,' " before finally categorically denying "any involvement in any organization in South Africa."

He noted that he had in fact pledged to "fight the rest of my life against racism and apartheid," and that, after all, he was the producer of the antiapartheid film *The Power of One*.

Richard Kelly Smyth, an aerospace scientist and computer expert, met Milchan in Israel at the start of the 1970s. Smyth worked for North American Rockwell as a chief engineer in its avionics division and went to Israel to set up a subsidiary. Affable, aggressive Arnon Milchan's intimate connections within the Israeli military, which were by then extensive, had already landed him the job of Rockwell's "point man" with the Israeli government. He and Smyth soon struck up so close a relationship that he was able to convince Smyth to leave Rockwell and go into the aerospace business for himself. Milchan's beginnings in the arms trade are fuzzy. He was only in his late twenties when he first emerged as a representative for Rockwell, Raytheon, and the others. Although he had been a hero in the 1967 war, those who knew him suspected that it was the Peres connection, not gallantry in combat, that landed the positions.

In January 1973, while still working for Rockwell, Smyth founded Milco International and a couple of other small firms, whose business was research and trading. Smyth later conceded that Milco was named after

Milchan, who in large part bankrolled it. Not surprisingly, the company was soon doing 80 percent of its business with Israel, with Milchan taking 60 percent of the earnings on those deals for himself. The U.S. government agents and lawyers who eventually investigated Smyth believed that during those formative months he was turned into an Israeli purchasing agent whose long-term assignment was to supply technology and materials for Israel's missile and nuclear weapons programs. They also came to believe that his recruiter was Arnon Milchan. Most, if not all, of the material that Milco exported to Israel went directly to Milchan Brothers or to Heli Trading Company of Tel Aviv, which Milchan either owned or co-owned even as he was getting started in the movie business. The theory gained credibility when the ultimate destination was factored in: LAKAM. The shadowy organization was not well known in the United States at that time, although it would gain considerable notoriety in 1985 when its best-known spy, Jonathan Pollard, was arrested and charged with selling top-secret files to Israel. Throughout most of the 1970s and well into the 1980s, in fact, Arnon Milchan led two lives simultaneously: film producer and arms merchant.

Between 1979 and 1985 Milco channeled a steady stream of missile and nuclear weapon equipment to Heli and Milchan Brothers. According to the U.S. Justice Department, the aspiring film-maker first ordered krytrons from Smyth in 1975, at the time when Israel was accelerating its missile and nuclear weapon programs. Smyth was warned by the U.S. intelligence agent who regularly debriefed him after overseas trips that the electrical devices were strictly controlled. He explained that to Milchan at the time and at least once more in a letter he wrote in 1977. The matter was dropped for two years. In 1979, however, Milchan again tried to get krytrons out of the United States. This time Smyth agreed to smuggle them to Heli and shipped at least 810 in fifteen batches between 1980 and 1982. Another 70 were on order when things began to get hot. Smyth told the Boston company that made the krytrons that they were going to be used domestically. He then declared on the export documents that they were "pentodes," or simple voltage amplifiers.

But there was much more to the Milchan-Smyth connection than nuclear triggers, as an examination of Milco's records would later reveal. As early as 1973 Milchan Brothers ordered $189,000 worth of chemicals for solid rocket fuel from the company. All told, millions of dollars worth of fuel and hardware was transferred from the United States to Israel's nuclear and ballistic missile programs between 1973 and 1980. The long list of materials that were transferred ranged from lasers to high-voltage condensers for nuclear weapons tests, and delay lines, which are used to separate a missile's stages. Some of the material was code-named: krytrons were "pinto"; radars were "Carl"; the oscilloscopes were "refrigerator"; and the inertial guidance system was "strapdown." There were also oscilloscopes especially suited to weapons testing and enough fuel for an entire Jericho missile battery.

"What this list shows is that Israel treated the United States like a nuclear and missile Kmart for many years," said Gary Milhollin, the proliferation specialist. "They simply swarmed over here for the blue light specials and took everything home that they weren't supposed to have. And it's not even clear that they stopped at the cash register."

"This is an advanced procurement effort," a weapons analyst who was well acquainted with Milco's activities explained. "You don't procure things like ammonium perchlorate to store it. Typically, you would be procuring a year or two before the missile went operational." Milchan's shopping list was similar to the one Abdelkader Helmy would soon carry for Condor-2.

As Arnon Milchan would have known only too well, however, his friend Smyth had over the years become a great deal more than a mere conduit for weapon components, exotic and otherwise, going to Israel. Smyth was not only a good scientist, but one who carried top secret clearances for a variety of advanced programs, including the FB-111 and the B-2 stealth bomber during its most secret phase, the MX missile, and the Advanced Tactical Fighter. In 1980—at about the time he was betraying his country by clandestinely sending devices to a foreign power that were intended to trigger its nuclear weapons—he was honored with an appointment to the prestigious U.S. Air Force Scientific Advisory Board. The board is a blue-ribbon group that advises the service on highly advanced weapons systems and whose members require White House approval.

Smyth soon persuaded two other board members, Arthur Biehl and Ivan Getting, not only to come on Milco's own board but to invest in the company. Both were world-class weapons scientists. Biehl had run the nuclear weapons design group at Livermore and specialized in miniaturizing nuclear weapons and designing plutonium production reactors, two areas that were of special interest to Israel. Ironically, he had also been the first director of Livermore's Group Z, which analyzes nuclear proliferation from a technical standpoint. Getting was a pioneer in the development of radar, a former vice-president for engineering at Raytheon, and the former president of the Aerospace Corporation, the Air Force's premier think tank. Believing that Milco's main business was with the Pentagon, Biehl and Getting in turn recruited Robert Mainhardt for the firm's board. Mainhardt had been a metallurgist at Los Alamos in 1943–45 and had designed nuclear weapons under Biehl at Livermore.

Before long, Arthur Biehl, the workaday scientist, was introduced to charming Arnon Milchan, the rising movie mogul. He was soon invited to an actor's home on the pretext that the actor was interested in some electronic work on a music project he was involved in and needed an expert. It was the first of several visits to the actor's home in an apparent effort to get the magic undertow to take hold, to get Biehl to succumb to hobnobbing with celebrities.

Then, one evening sometime in 1981 or 1982, the scene abruptly shifted to the Polo Lounge, a darkly paneled playpen for Hollywood's power brokers. There, Milchan and Smyth introduced Biehl to an Israeli named "Benny."

Biehl had already noted with growing concern that the vast majority of Milco's transactions were not with the Pentagon but with Israel. He had begun to worry that an uncomfortably large number of the items being exported were useful in nuclear weapons and missiles and had expressed that concern to Smyth. His and Getting's repeated questions about whether proper export licenses were being obtained were met with evasion. Now Biehl found himself sitting at a table in a plush, dimly lighted saloon with a man whom Smyth described as "maybe the third most powerful man in Israel." The mysterious "Benny" began by trying to reassure Biehl that there was nothing improper about Milco's sending materials directly to Israel, that it was simply more efficient than having to maneuver through the usual bureaucracies at both ends of the route. He also thanked Biehl for lending his expertise to the procurement effort for Israel, explaining that the Jewish state needed to be strong so there would never again be a Holocaust. While his country would not be the first to introduce nuclear weapons to the Middle East, "Benny" said in a well-worn line, it did need a stockpile of them. Benny was thought by several intelligence analysts to be a top-ranking Israeli agent.

If Israel wanted to recruit him as an agent, Arthur Biehl mused when he was alone, this was the way it would be done: gradually evoking sympathy for a great cause and, by expressing gratitude for the help he had given, convince him that he was already an accomplice anyway. "[You] never know," he said afterward. "I read James Bond every once in a while." Biehl decided to go to the FBI.

Ivan Getting had in the meantime also become suspicious, particularly after being asked to help Israel get missile range instrumentation radars by escorting two Israeli engineers to Raytheon and RCA. Although the Israelis would not share their entire parts list with Getting, what they *did* tell him they needed made him suspicious that the radar they had in mind was far more restricted than that used for range instrumentation. Both Biehl and Getting resigned from Milco on July 24, 1982.

Bob Mainhardt stayed on and, in the next few years, continued to work with Smyth and Milchan on sensitive projects. He said later that Milchan would get up at Milco board meetings and reel off a list of the material he needed for the following year. Mainhardt remembers that Milchan twice asked for material and technology Mainhardt thought was out of bounds. One was "greensalt," the solid form of uranium hexafluoride that constitutes the feedstock needed to enrich uranium to bomb-grade inside ultragas centrifuges. It can also be used to make armor-piercing depleted uranium artillery rounds from scratch: the stuff that can go through a tank's armor. Milchan also said he needed three million pounds of depleted uranium bars themselves. The greensalt export was not approved by the board, according to some of those on it, but the depleted uranium bars were okayed. They were duly code-named: "Sulphur." Finally, the producer pressed Mainhardt for specific information on an advanced nuclear reactor design.

Mainhardt's biggest problem with Milchan's list did not so much concern the two uranium deals, but the request for information on an advanced nuclear reactor. "That was it for me," Mainhardt said later. "I know espionage laws. I grew up in Los Alamos when we were putting together the first atomic bomb. Klaus Fuchs was my dorm-mate and David Greenglass was one of my best friends," he said of the men charged with spying for the Soviet Union. "So I know about espionage." He quit.

The smuggling operation began to unravel in January 1983, when Smyth notified the FBI that his Huntington Beach, California, office had been burglarized. He admitted on questioning that he had illegally exported "vacuum tubes" to Israel. The G-men in turn informed Customs, which raided Milco and carried off boxes of documents that not only showed the tubes to be krytrons but yielded records of most of the other items as well.

Two years later, after the krytron operation was made public, Milchan denied having had anything to do with it. "I don't know what the hell they were talking about," he said he recalled thinking when he was first told that the deal had been uncovered. "I guessed that there was one of the companies that I owned, was involved in ordering something." He knew whom to call when word of the case broke, however. His first call, he said, was to Shimon Peres. But the federal investigators who sifted the evidence in the boxes and elsewhere were not convinced. They concluded that the krytrons had, indeed, been ordered by Milchan "on behalf of the Israeli government."

On May 16, 1985, Smyth was indicted on thirty counts of smuggling and making false statements. On at least two occasions after that, his lawyers negotiated with federal prosecutors about a deal. Assistant U.S. Attorney William Fahey wanted Smyth to plead guilty to reduced charges and become a government witness because he was after a bigger fish.

On Wednesday, August 7, a week before he was scheduled to appear at a hearing, Smyth, his wife Emilie, and his mother visited Brian R. Carter, an old friend of Smyth's and another member of Milco's board. Smyth was deeply depressed, Carter remembered, because Milchan's lawyers had given U.S. Attorney Robert Bonner, who was to prosecute him, the letter he wrote to Milchan in 1977 saying that the krytrons needed an export license. The document was devastating because it proved that Smyth knowingly broke the law when he shipped them to Israel. Carter said that Smyth's lawyers had at that point advised their client to plead guilty because the letter made the case against him conclusive. "Milchan had screwed him. I think he felt betrayed," Carter said. "I read a lot about Israel after this stuff happened. The whole thing was like a Ludlum novel."

Two days later, on August 9, Richard and Emilie Smyth told family and friends that they were going away for the weekend. Smyth phoned his lawyer, Alan D. Croll, to say that he and his wife were sailing to Santa Catalina Island for the weekend but that he would appear in court for the hearing the following week. Richard and Emilie Smyth then drove off in their cream-colored Oldsmobile and never returned. They abandoned five grown children, a $600,000 waterfront house at Huntington Beach, and membership in a yacht club. Smyth, a fugitive, was later seen in Herzilya Pitua, the same Israeli town where Milchan has a residence.

At the very least, Smyth's disappearance saved Milchan a great deal of embarrassment. The very day Smyth drove off, the U.S. government served two sets of papers that would have revealed even more about the Smyth-Milchan relationship. Customs served a subpoena on Smyth's auditor seeking all records related to business dealings between Smyth and Milchan. Meanwhile, the Department of Justice requested that the Judiciary of Jerusalem take Milchan's sworn statement and provide the United States with "all business documents (including correspondence, orders, invoices, bank statements and the like) reflecting the purchase by Heli Trading of the krytrons and the importation of the krytrons into Israel." The request also noted that the Department of Justice was investigating "additional illegal exports." With Smyth gone, both requests became moot.

The case soon disappeared into the background of U.S.-Israeli relations, though it was resurrected a few months later when the Pollard scandal broke and news organizations felt the need to recount recent episodes that had tarnished the "special relationship" between the two countries.

Some 469 of the 810 krytrons were returned. The remainder, Israel claimed, were destroyed while testing conventional weapons. In an interview not long after the indictment Peres, by then prime minister, denied to Robin MacNeil of the "MacNeil/Lehrer News Hour" that he had any knowledge of the case. And a few months after that, the U.S. Customs Service intelligence unit suggested that not all of the krytrons ended up in Israel. Some, the intelligence analysts concluded, could well have been forwarded to South Africa.

By 1989, the Israeli–South African relationship had become an albatross for both nations. News reports of Israel's helping the South African ballistic missile program had tarnished the righteous image Israel had worked so hard to cultivate in the United States. South Africa had meanwhile cut a deal with the United States, the Soviet Union, and Cuba that ended the bloody stalemate in Angola. The usefulness of its small stockpile of six nuclear weapons had expired, although not before the weapons had been used politically if not militarily two years earlier. Faced with an increasingly effective Cuban-Angolan conventional force, the nuclear test site in the Kalahari was readied with the full knowledge that the ruckus would be seen and heard by U.S. and Soviet intelligence systems, just as Israel's arming of the Jerichos had been picked up in 1973. Pretoria's A-bomb rattling, at least in part, led to a settlement of the Angolan situation and a sharp reduction in tensions between South Africa and its neighbors. That, in turn, prompted South African President F. W. de Klerk to order the destruction of all six nuclear weapons. They were carted from their storage area in a Toyota van and taken to a place where their uranium cores were removed. All of the weapons' components were then destroyed, along with cabinet records showing Israel's role in their creation.

When the decision to destroy the bombs was revealed in March 1993, the secret of Israeli–South African cooperation in their development seemed safe. De Klerk simply lied when he told his parliament and the world beyond that the country had received no help with the project. Conveniently left out of the speech, however, was the fact that the laboratories outside of Pretoria where the weapons were built and stored remained usable. At the same time, de Klerk emphatically refused to kill the 700-mile range Arniston missile or the nation's Jericho-type "space launch vehicle" with its 1,100-mile range. Early in 1993, when the generals who had been so closely allied with Israel announced that they were severing those ties, they also revealed that they were looking for Arab business.

If Richard Kelly Smyth has ventured out of Israel at all, it would have been to go to Barcelona for the 1992 summer Olympics. A father's love and pride would have sent him searching for his son, Randy, who represented the United States in the sailboat competition. Young Smyth walked off with his second silver medal in Barcelona, having won the first in Los Angeles in 1984. If his father was there, he walked past the eyes of the Spanish federal police and a Paris-based customs agent who carried his picture and who scanned the crowds during the awards ceremony trying to find the face that matched it.

Condor-2, or DOT, or Project 395, or Badr-2000, or Vector (its various Argentine, German, Iraqi and Egyptian names), was well under way before Helmy began feeding it restricted U.S. technology. It was born out of frustration, military machismo, and economic necessity in Argentina in the late 1970s and early 1980s.

As early as 1977, Argentine Air Force generals were toying with the idea of developing their own ballistic missile program, possibly because of Brazilian advances in rocket design, and possibly because of a rancorous dispute with Chile over the Beagle Channel near Cape Horn. The ostensible vehicle for this was a "sounding" or "research" rocket that was eventually named Condor. Knowing that their country lacked the technology to produce the rocket on its own, the generals approached Messerschmitt Boelkow Blohm, the large West German aerospace firm, and asked for help. It would have been clear to the Germans even before they met the representatives of the Argentine junta that since air force officers do not ordinarily contract for civilian research rockets, the generals had more in mind than measuring the photon flux above the atmosphere. And that was precisely the case.

As conceived by the South American officers and MBB's technocrats, *Das Projekt Condor* would evolve into two rockets. The first, Condor-1, would indeed be a research rocket: a single-stage, solid-fuel sounding rocket capable of lifting 1,000 pounds to forty miles. But its research role would be military, not civilian. It would be the precursor to a much larger, highly advanced, intermediate-range ballistic missile called Condor-2. The Argentinians were very clear about Condor-1's role as a development vehicle for their killer missile. "The idea to manufacture the Condor came about in 1977–78 when the Air Force decided to develop the technology for a missile that would carry loads for a given distance," Air Force Chief of Staff Brigadier Jose Antonio Julia later remarked. "The idea [was] to place satellites into orbit, but with a change in the trajectory and the load, the missile could carry anything."

MBB initially worked on Condor-2 in-house. Since it was also working on an upgraded version of the U.S. Pershing-2 ballistic missile for West Germany, however, Washington quickly warned the Munich firm that a technology transfer could be avoided by its leaving Condor-2 alone. The company reacted cleverly. It furloughed some thirty senior managers and engineers to create a new firm specifically to develop Condor. And it put it in Zug, Switzerland, a neutral locale within commuting distance of Munich. The new company, named the Institute for Advanced Technology, or IFAT, was founded on August 5, 1983. As it happened, some of the MBB people had recently worked on a rocket fuel plant in Egypt, where a thriving tactical rocket industry was located. The Soviet arms cutoff to Iraq in 1980–82 had sent Saddam Hussein's weapons buyers to Egypt, where they established close relations and left huge sums of money. Since Egypt had signed the Camp David Accord four years earlier, it had been left with a mountain of weapons it no longer needed.

By the summer of 1983, a symbiotic relationship was developing that promised to benefit all of the participants in the embryonic Condor-2 program. The Argentinians, who had conceived of the missile in the first place, found a willing and highly knowledgeable management and design team at MBB. The Germans, who believed in the missile and who needed financing to develop it, went to their other clients, the Egyptians, and found not only anxious partners but a pile of Iraqi money. On February 15, 1984, IFAT and the Egyptian Ministry of Defense signed a contract to jointly develop Condor-2. The Iraqis themselves would quickly see the value of the new missile so clearly—as the "white knight" upon which to mount their nuclear warheads—that they would want to participate directly. Iraq would, in fact, become Condor's leading partner.

Within weeks of IFAT's coming into existence, it formed a second company, Consen SA, in Monaco. IFAT would be responsible for Condor-2's financing while Consen would handle contracting and overall management. Consen SA reported to the international business community that its main activity was engineering and that 95 percent of its products were imported from West Germany. That was true as far as it went, but there was a great deal more to the murky company than was publicly known.

Eventually, there would be an international spiderweb of sixteen companies in Monaco, Switzerland, Germany, Austria, the United Kingdom, and Argentina that worked on Condor-2, most of them wholly owned by a ghostly parent company called the Consen Group. It would be headed by Ekkehard Schrotz, a wealthy German engineer.

Other European corporate leaders, not a part of the Consen Group, would also be attracted to the Condor project as its momentum increased, and for very good reason. Condor-2 may have started as a Latin American fantasy, but in reality it was to be a Muslim missile aimed primarily at Israel, and that meant heavy Arab financial involvement. The Europeans, particularly the Germans, smelled big money. Some of them also seem to have smelled a satisfying way to make it and endanger Jews at the same time. Adolf Hammer, one of IFAT's five founding fathers, had worked on

a team that Messerschmitt sent to Egypt in 1959 to help build jets and
rockets to threaten Israel. Technical difficulties and Mossad letter bombs
convinced some of the scientists, including Hammer, to return to Germany.
Back home, he was soon climbing Messerschmitt's corporate ladder, and
kept doing so after it became the conglomerate MBB. Hammer was the
executive in charge of MBB's initial contribution to Condor-2. When MBB
shed the project under pressure from Washington, he went with it, settling
in a Consen subsidiary in Salzburg, Austria. Adolf Hammer eventually
received so many threats that, however dedicated he was to developing
rockets to point at Israel, he stopped commuting to work and hired twenty-
four-hour-a-day security guards.

Nor were there any illusions on Consen's part about what it was
really up to. Typically, the engineers and managers rationalized their work
by noting that others were doing it, too, and by turning a blind eye to
their product's purpose. "We are on a collision course with the mid-range
missile politics of the superpowers," said the president of Consen's board,
a tough Bern lawyer named Peter Bratschi. "We cannot tell the governments who give us contracts what they should do."

Condor-1 made its public debut at the Paris Air Show in 1985. It
was a single-stage, solid fuel, "multipurpose missile," the literature explained, which would be Argentina's "answer to the growing challenge
of the Space Age." The literature also noted that the research rocket came
out of MBB's Astronautics Division. Its successor, to which no reference
was made, was by then also being shaped at MBB. But it was not being
designed in Astronautics; it was being designed in the Defense Technology
Division.

The follow-on was an advanced, mobile, two-stage, solid fuel ballistic missile that could carry a half-ton warhead more than 600 miles.
By 1985 it was not only well along in development, but the centerpiece
of an international consortium. Two events had pushed work on Condor-
2 into high gear. First, British military technology had been decisive in
Argentina's humiliating defeat in the battle for the Falkland Islands in
1982.* The generals therefore wanted to lay claim to equally advanced
arms, specifically to a missile that could reach the British-occupied islands, some 500 miles off their coast. Second, and more important, Raul

---

*To underscore the point, their own single notable victory in the conflict, the destruction of
H.M.S. *Sheffield*, was accomplished by firing an advanced French Exocet missile at it.

Alfonsin's impressive victory over the Peronist Party in 1983 had been followed by a severe reduction in the military budget, forcing the more ambitious officers to look for outside sources of funding.

In a manner of speaking, Condor-2 had gotten off the ground the following year, 1984, when Egypt and Iraq signed on for what they took to be the creation of an Islamic missile whose capability would easily eclipse that of the Scud. Saddam Hussein, three years into his war with Iran and still stung by the Soviet weapons cutoff, would provide roughly $750 million and research facilities. Egypt, ostensibly Condor-2's most fervent Arab supporter, had been quick to approach Consen and the Argentinians as soon as word of the project reached Cairo. The Egyptians were supposed to add expertise gained from their own missile program and other research facilities. Meanwhile, the impassive, supremely cunning Saudi sheiks, following long custom, appeared to be unaware of or uninterested in the project while depositing another $1 billion into Swiss banks for its support. This no doubt threw Schrotz and his Consen colleagues into near-delirium. The strategy, as usual, was for the sons of the desert to cover at least two bases at a time. If Condor proved viable, they would be able to quietly influence the way it affected politics in the region. A missile that could be fired at Zionists in Israel, the Saudis no doubt reflected with grim pleasure, could also be fired at revivalists in Iran. And if the project came to nothing, they would at least get credit for having tried to realize an Islamic missile, and for what was to them a pittance.

The Germans responded to the largesse by going on a lavish procurement and hiring binge in which many MBB engineers and others "changed sides." Top recruits were given fat bonuses for signing on at salaries of up to $10,000 a month. But the moves were more apparent than real. From an engineering standpoint, Condor remained an MBB-developed weapon, with many of its designers simply trading one paycheck for another. Meanwhile, Consen's own employees spent weeks at a time in MBB's offices and engineering rooms collecting helpful data. Consen also placed orders with MBB for "special" rocket motor parts, missile steering elements, and other dual-use hardware, sometimes paying 400 times the standard market price. The Arabs, after all, were so rich it didn't matter. Condor-2 was going big-time.

What was not generally known, however, was that Condor-2 was being designed by engineers who were also working on another top-secret program: Germany's first indigenous ballistic missile since the V-2. It was called KOLAS, a German acronym for Complementary Air Attack System. This was nothing less than a replacement for the Pershings that were to be withdrawn from Germany in 1988 under the terms of the Intermediate Nuclear Forces Treaty. The INF concerned missiles with ranges of more than 300 miles. KOLAS, whose range was to be less than that, was planned as a means of attacking Warsaw Pact forward air bases in the event that a massive invasion of western Europe developed.

There were at least two aspects of the KOLAS program, however, that neither Bonn nor Washington wanted known. First, KOLAS was largely based on Pershing technology. It was one of the sweeteners Jimmy Carter offered West Germany to permit the stationing of the Pershing-2 on West German soil. The weapon's manufacturer, Martin Marietta, was working directly with MBB on the KOLAS design. "The INF Treaty cost the firm one-fifth of its production," one knowledgeable insider said. "Now, with the help of the Germans, Martin Marietta sees a way to keep marketing its Pershing technology, which was very costly to develop." Second, while KOLAS was to carry conventional warheads, including those with cluster bombs, it was also to be nuclear-capable, a fact that any number of Germany's neighbors would have found disquieting. KOLAS was scrapped when the Soviet empire collapsed in 1989. Its enduring contribution to weapons proliferation, however, would lie in the fact that it was the key link between advanced American nuclear missile technology and the dangerous expertise that came to bear in Condor-2. That expertise would survive not only KOLAS but Condor-2 as well.

At any rate, seeing that Condor was attracting world-class managers and engineers and, more important, heavy financing, the Alfonsin government issued two secret decrees in 1985 and 1987 that officially approved the missile's development. It also specifically granted the transfer of Condor-2 technology to Iraq in return for its investment. Initial plans seem to have called for the construction of ten missiles, five of them going to Iraq and five more going to Egypt. This was apparently to be followed by an additional 400, also divided between those nations, plus an unspecified number going to Argentina itself. One Israeli intelligence estimate put Condor-2's development cost alone at $2.4 billion and predicted that each finished missile would cost $8 million. "Because of the high cost of the missile," the report concluded, "it is highly probable that it will be fitted with a nonconventional warhead." It was a plausible analysis.

Nobody would spend $8 million on a missile that just blew up a building and made a hole in the ground.

From the highway, the buildings jutting out of a mountain in the Sierra Chica range, just north of the town of Falda del Carmen in Argentina's Cordoba Province, looked like a modest factory complex with cows grazing out in front. At first, the townspeople believed that preliminary work on a dam was in progress. Then word got around that the facility was an aircraft factory. The windsocks that billowed in front of the place, useful for helicopter and light plane operations, seemed to bear out that theory.

But how to explain the very high radio antenna, satellite dish, two guard towers, a double barbed wire fence that even ran up the brush-covered mountain behind the squat buildings, and checkpoints at the site's Alta Gracia and Villa Carlos Paz entrances that were manned by federal police and Argentine Air Force guards? How to explain the trucks loaded with sealed containers holding electrical equipment that began arriving at the site from the port of Buenos Aires in 1984, or the French, German, and Italian engineers who worked at the site. And how about the large Soviet-made Iraqi Il-86 cargo plane that made an emergency landing at Rosario in August 1988 and continued on to Cordoba the next day after its twelve crewmen were kept incommunicado in a local hotel by Argentine security police? How to explain the shrill sound of rocket engines that cut through the night and that seemed to come from deep within the mountain itself? Most Argentinians, and certainly the citizens of Falda del Carmen, knew that it was better not to try to explain too much.

In fact, the mountain itself had been hollowed out for use as a rocket test chamber that would muffle noise, provide maximum security, and conceal what was going on from U.S. and Soviet reconnaissance satellites. The high-tech cave was big enough to hold a foundry in which a large truck could turn around. As many as ten bunkers, most measuring thirty-six feet by forty-two feet, and all having two-foot-thick concrete walls, were built against the side of the mountain and then covered with earth to their roof lines. When the secret test and fabrication facility was finished, in 1983, it looked much like its counterpart at Sa'ad-16 would look three years later. As was the case with Palmichim and Overberg, there was no need to re-invent an installation for a second project that was the same as the first.

Meanwhile, Condor-2 development facilities were taking root in Egypt and Iraq. A fuel and test area was established at Abu Zaabal, northeast of Cairo, and a missile production plant was going up at Helwan, south of the capital.* The latter was called Factory 17. Egypt's part of the Condor-2 program was run by its Ballistic Missile Egypt office, or BME, which reported to Defense Minister Abu Ghazala. The point man between BME and Consen was Colonel Ahmed Khairat, who coordinated Condor development out of an office in Salzburg shared by both Consen and IFAT. The chief engineer was Fouad al-Gamal. Abu Ghazala and al-Gamal would figure prominently in Abdelkader Helmy's downfall.

Iraq built its own massive network of missile development and test facilities, the largest being Sa'ad-16 outside of Mosul, with tens of millions of dollars worth of equipment from western Europe and the United States. It also conducted research at at least three other sites near the towns of Mahmudiya, Habbaniya, and Sakhar, all within forty miles of Baghdad. The idea was to eventually become independent of both Argentina and Egypt and build its own Condors.

Even as engineering and site work continued through the mid and late 1980s, so did clandestine procurement and outright espionage. Some of the technology—the weapon's guidance system, for example—remained elusive.

So did a certain kind of warhead. In 1984 a devious British computer expert and arms dealer named Keith Smith persuaded Honeywell to sell him a detailed, specially researched, 300-page study on fuel-air explosives. FAE, as the weapon is called, spreads and then ignites gasoline vapor in an intense air burst that is reminiscent of an atomic explosion and that incinerates such "soft" targets as people, buildings, and parked aircraft. Smith, who had contacts at a Honeywell subsidiary in England, told them, correctly, that he was an IFAT representative working on behalf of Egypt. But he neglected to mention the fact that Consen was also involved in the project or, more importantly, that Iraq was a silent partner.

---

*Abu Zaabal was in part built by WTB International AG, the Swiss subsidiary of a large German construction company which, like Consen, was based in Zug. Kurt Stoeberlein, the firm's general manager, claimed in 1989, the year after the installation was finished, that "No one told us the purpose of the project" even though Consen itself had given WTB the contract. (Memorandum from Alan George, May 24, 1989.)

Over the objections of the Honeywell engineers who did the study—and who called the proposed sale "shady"—it was duly passed on to Smith for a measly $100,000.* The FAEs were planned for Condor-2.

However meticulously Consen's Teutonic technocrats structured the Condor program, nothing had prepared them for having to hold an Arab alliance together, particularly one involving two of the region's proudest and most ambitious nations. Condor's seams began to open in 1987–88. Iraq, which was footing a large chunk of Condor-2's development cost even as it fought a horrendously expensive war with Iran, became convinced that it was paying Egypt and Argentina separately to do the same work and was dealing with "bumblers and gyppos," as one observer put it. In addition, Baghdad considered the Egyptian Condor facilities and workmanship to be sloppy and dangerous. Egypt's grievance was with Argentina. The Egyptians prided themselves on their growing missile expertise, but they were not being allowed as much hands-on experience at Falda del Carmen as they wanted. The frustrated Arabs, who were supposed to make significant contributions to the missile's technical development, felt as though they were being forced to look over the Argentinians' shoulders. Iraq's scolding, complaining, and ill-concealed plans to go it alone on Condor, plus Argentina's secretiveness, eventually convinced Egypt that it would have to develop its own Condor-2. That's where Helmy entered the picture.

As the relationship with Iraq worsened during 1987, it became clear to Abu Ghazala, Egypt's Defense Minister, that his country would have to pursue Condor on its own. He therefore drew up a shopping list of material he needed for Badr-2000, as the Egyptian and Iraqi Condors

---

*Louis Lavoie, the Honeywell engineer who was chiefly responsible for the six-month study, deplored the sale after word of it was broken by NBC News six years later. While the study was not a "recipe" to build such a weapon, he said, the principles in the report could be translated for the task. ("Scientist Raps Honeywell on Iraq Bomb," *Pioneer Press*, St. Paul, MN, December 2, 1990, and "Iraq Bomb Linked to Honeywell," *Star Tribune*, Minneapolis/St. Paul, December 1, 1990.) Honeywell maintained that there was no evidence that the FAE study reached Egypt, let alone Iraq, and that it consisted of "previously published, unclassified information that was of little practical military value." (Honeywell News Release, "Honeywell and Alliant Techsystems Announce Results From Investigation Into Fuel-Air Explosive Study," February 15, 1991.) Western intelligence officials took a different view. They concluded that the information reached both Egypt and Iraq. (Simon Henderson, *Instant Empire*, San Francisco: Mercury House, 1991, p. 160.) Smith tried to make a similar deal with Martin Marietta, which rebuffed him. (Interviews with Martin Marietta engineers in December 1990.)

were called. This meant that both Iraq and Egypt were independently chasing much the same technology and materiel that Argentina had already accumulated at Falda del Carmen. All three nations were now working on identical versions of the Pershing-2 knockoff.

Helmy was recruited to help the Badr-2000 program by Abu Ghazala, his childhood friend, while he was back in Cairo on vacation in the late summer of 1987. The choice was perfect, since the new American citizen was a fine rocket scientist, knew his way around the U.S. space technocracy, and had in any case been quietly consulting on Condor-2 since 1984. Abu Ghazala persuaded Helmy that he could serve his native land and make a great deal of money himself if he helped to get important missile technology out of the United States. The list included carbon-carbon for nose cones, ablative carbon-carbon fabric for missile engine exhausts, chemicals that were needed for attaching the fabric to the exhausts, microwave antennas to aid tracking, and some of the key chemicals used to mix solid rocket fuel. Helmy later itemized the total cost of the materials at $614,128.

Beginning in December 1987 and continuing through the end of the following March, Helmy received a series of bank drafts from IFAT that totaled $1,030,000. That winter, working at home through his own Sciences and Technologies Applications company, Helmy spent $262,000 collecting the technology ordered by Abu Ghazala. He was helped by an old friend, James Huffman, who ordered much of the material through his own Ohio-based company, Mesa Associates. Huffman repackaged the items for routing to Egypt.

Abu Ghazala flew to Washington in late March 1988 for a meeting with his American opposite number, Secretary of Defense Frank Carlucci. The purpose of the trip was to sign a historic agreement elevating Egypt to the status of a NATO country where U.S. weapons purchases were concerned. There was nothing in the terms of the document, however, that permitted the transfer of advanced missile technology, let alone by clandestine means. While Abu Ghazala was in Washington, al-Gamal, the Egyptian Condor's chief engineer, flew to Sacramento under an alias, Fouad Mohamed, for a secret meeting with Helmy. That day, Helmy went to the Aerojet Solid Propulsion Company, where he worked with a secret clearance, and returned with two cardboard boxes. The next day—March 23, when Abu Ghazala and Carlucci met—Helmy and al-Gamal flew to Washington with the boxes, each of which was addressed to a nonexistent person, Foud Moha, in the office of the Egyptian Military Attache. From there, they were transferred to a drop point at 1821 T Street, NW, and then flown out of the country in diplomatic pouches. The boxes, which had a combined weight of 185 pounds, contained the carbon-carbon material and carbon ablative cloth needed for Condor's nose cone and exhaust nozzles. The U.S. Customs Service knew this because, suspicious of al-Gamal's jaunt from Cairo to Sacramento via Chicago, it had followed him straight to Helmy.

The engineer was therefore placed on constant surveillance on March 18. Not only was he followed wherever he went, but his trash was picked up and sifted late at night on a weekly basis, and both his home and office phones were tapped. Among other noteworthy items, the trash yielded scrawled notes on the chemicals, metals, and other materials needed for missile production, plus the names of likely sources: the Fiberite Corporation of Winona, Minnesota, and North Technica of Frankfurt, for example. One Aerojet official who saw the list of chemicals and other materials retrieved from Helmy's trash described it as "a complete package to build or upgrade a tactical missile system."*

Whatever his success, however, Helmy was urged by Abu Ghazala to work even harder. During the next three months he collected still more carbon-carbon, chemicals for solid propellant, and other materials, all the while being watched and, beginning in May, being wire-tapped as well.

It was during one such call, an international one with Khairat in Salzburg in late May, that Helmy learned about what happened to Ekkehard Schrotz.

"Did you know that certain people tried to do away with us?" Khairat asked. "They put something in the director of the company's car and it exploded with the driver in it."

"It happened where you are?" Helmy asked.

"No," Khairat replied solemnly, "in France."

It happened early on the morning of May 27 in the village of Grasse, outside of Monaco, where Schrotz had a villa. The Consen Group leader's

---

*Besides many scrawled notes listing several controlled items and references to the Scud B and the American Sparrow air-to-air missile, the trash search yielded an envelope from the Fiberite Corporation of Winona, Minnesota. Fiberite manufactured the heat-resistant ablative material Helmy was after. (Affidavit of David E. Burns, U.S. Customs Service, pp. 16–17, and U.S. Congress, House Committee on Ways and Means, Subcommittee on Oversight, *Administration and Enforcement of U.S. Export Control Programs*, 102–72, 102nd Cong., 1st sess., April 18 and May 1, 1991, p. 117.)

Peugeot was blown to bits, just as Khairat said. But by a fluke, Schrotz himself had not taken the car to work that morning and had therefore escaped unharmed. He got news of the bombing at his desk from his wife. The would-be assassins did not know that their intended victim escaped, however, and therefore called Agence France Presse within minutes of the explosion. Schrotz, the caller announced, had been "condemned to death because of his crimes in the service of Saddam Hussein. He built rockets for Saddam Hussein." The voice identified itself as a member of the "Protectors of Islam."

A few days later, lists of scientists and businessmen who worked on Condor and Consen's own organization charts and other documents were taken when its Zug office was expertly burglarized. Some of the material, linking Consen and MBB, eventually landed in news media mailboxes. Although there was some suspicion that Iranians were behind the bombing and burglary, both had the hallmarks of Mossad. Following a call threatening his and his family's "execution," Ekkehard Schrotz went into hiding.

On June 24, 1988, an Egyptian Air Force C-130 that was preparing to take off from Baltimore-Washington International Airport for its biweekly flight to Cairo was abruptly stopped and searched by U.S. Customs agents. Four-hundred and thirty more pounds of ablative carbon fabric were turned up and promptly confiscated. Helmy, Huffman, Khairat and al-Gamal were subsequently indicted for conspiracy, money laundering, and illegally exporting rocket and missile components to Egypt. The episode created a minor sensation on the international scene and a serious embarrassment for the Mubarak government. Khairat and al-Gamal held diplomatic immunity and therefore escaped prosecution. But Helmy and Huffman went to prison even as Condor unraveled.

The United States had watched Condor's progress through the late 1980s with growing unease; the missile itself had been a primary reason for the creation of the Missile Technology Control Regime in 1987. Even before the MTCR took effect, the Department of Defense and some of its foreign counterparts blocked a variety of the sort of dual-use items required to build the missile. (Abu Ghazala's apparent desperation to smuggle the material out of the United States is testimony to the embargo's effectiveness.)

Within four months of Helmy's arrest, the United States and its MTCR allies were putting considerable pressure on both Argentina and Egypt to abandon the project while simultaneously holding out economic incentives if they cooperated. Mubarak, embarrassed over the Helmy affair and growing increasingly wary of Iraq, fired Abu Ghazala in April 1989 and abandoned Badr-2000 at about the same time.

Matters did not go so smoothly in Argentina, however. Although Washington increased the pressure on Buenos Aires to drop Condor at least as early as the summer of 1988, apparently winning an agreement with President Carlos Saul Menem to at least mothball the project, Menem soon became locked in a battle with his military leaders over the missile's fate. He had so little control over Condor, in fact, that his own generals were able to prevent a team of U.S. observers from inspecting Falda del Carmen in May 1991 even though Menem had approved the visit.

"When they first went in, the air force told them that there was no Condor-2 project," one Western diplomat recalled. "Then they showed them some parts. But when the Americans asked about other parts they knew existed, the air force just denied they existed at all. It was a lot of stonewalling that left a bad taste in everyone's mouth," he added. The parts secreted at Falda del Carmen included fourteen completed first stages and a number of the all-important guidance systems, none of which the air force would allow outsiders to see. Still other parts of the rocket system were said to be unaccounted for. Worst of all, the original plans for the missile mysteriously disappeared from air force archives.

The impasse between the president and the generals seemed to end a few weeks later, when Antonio Erman Gonzalez, the Defense Minister, announced that Condor-2 was to be "deactivated, dismantled, reconverted and/or rendered unusable." All elements of the program, he continued grandly, would be "cancelled in a complete and irreversible manner."

Not quite. Argentina may have cancelled the program but, it seemed, it could not cancel the missiles themselves or their scattered components. A year later, government spokesmen explained that a plan for destroying the missiles in Falda del Carmen eluded them. Urged to simply blow them up, one high official explained, straight-faced, that the noise would be heard by more than a million people living around Cordoba, which was a stronghold of the political opposition at the time. "You can imagine that we don't want a series of explosions going off with everyone knowing about it and saying, 'Well, there goes the Condor.' "

In the end, a decision was made that seemed to satisfy everyone. Argentina agreed to turn seventeen rocket engines and fourteen missile bodies over to Spain's space agency, INTA, with an agreement that Argentina could join the space launch program. So on January 9, 1993, the missiles sailed out of Buenos Aires harbor to be destroyed in Spain, their technology to be subsumed in a supposedly peaceful rocket called Capricornio. On the morning of January 20—the Bush administration's last day—INTA was rewarded by the Department of State, which approved a spate of missile-related exports. Apparently unnoticed, however, was a Department of Defense report made a few months earlier concluding that Capricornio was more than just a potential space launch vehicle. INTA, it turned out, is responsible to the Spanish military, and its "scientific" space booster was also being developed as a ballistic missile that could threaten Muslim revivalists across the Mediterranean in Algeria. Phoenix would be an appropriate name for the missile.

Iraq never gave up on the missile, however. Fourteen Condor bodies and one mobile launcher were found in Iraq by U.N. inspectors after the Gulf War and destroyed.

Neither Jericho nor Condor was a technological transplant. Whatever technology and materials were extracted from the West, both weapons were developed by groups of nations working at a common task. As the international automobile, sewing machine, and hamburger have developed in the new world economy, so has the international missile. Jericho and Condor were created by dedicated consortiums working on their own and with no direct help from the owners of the best missiles on Earth: the five permanent members of the Security Council.

In addition, both were developed, not with the help of engineers who had defected, but by well-trained professionals who either were indigenously produced or were foreigners hired specifically for that task. And while key hardware had to be openly bought or smuggled, the most important element in the missile equation came from inside the heads of those who designed them. The heads are not subject to export restrictions, limitations imposed by the Missile Technology Control Regime, or erasure. Most missile designers are free to roam where they will, working for whom they please. As Cyrano wore his adornments—his medals—on his soul, the rocket scientist and engineer carries his professional ability within his mind. It follows that the wherewithal to develop ballistic missiles is not only freely available throughout the world, but can materialize as an innocent-looking civilian rocket. Indeed, it can *be* an innocent civilian rocket having the potential for dark uses.

Nor does ballistic missile technology ever really disappear. It can be reduced to the point of latency: it can be "quiescent," as one U.S. intelligence analyst put it. That is what happened to Condor-2. The missile was technically stopped, but it can no longer be erased like so many equations on a blackboard. It remains rooted in three countries and lies dormant, waiting to be awakened for a future crusade.

The Arniston, South Africa's version of the Jericho, survived because it was developed from the beginning as a clearly conceived, highly focused, closely managed, and extremely secret project. In addition, it existed with the tacit approval of Israel's powerful and generally benevolent benefactor, the United States. Not only was it the beneficiary of an incalculable amount of expertise picked up by every Israeli rocket scientist and engineer who prowled through America's universities, libraries, technical institutes, national laboratories and space facilities, but official efforts to stop it were always more apparent than real. The Arniston may be Israeli in most respects, but its patrons were successively sympathetic U.S. presidents and an extremely powerful lobby in Washington. In addition the United States shared a truly close working relationship with South Africa through most of its history.

The remarkable thing about Condor, on the other hand, was not that it was stopped but that it went as far as it did. It was conceived, financed and developed by a motley group of individuals who had widely differing motives and mores. With no real technology base of their own, Argentina, Egypt, and Iraq were forced to depend on European managers and engineers. Like all "hired guns," the Germans, Swiss, and the rest were motivated, not by altruism, but by sheer greed. IFAT, Consen, the MBB people, and other parasites overcharged the Arabs by as much as one-third for both parts and labor. The Iraqis and Egyptians, uncomfortable bedfellows at best, never really trusted each other. Meanwhile, the members of the Argentine junta scorned all of the Arabs, however much they contributed to the project. The disparities between the participants led to more than cheating and hostility; they led to a lot of press, most of it bad.

Finally, as the stream of news accounts and intelligence reports made their way north, the Bush administration took an increasingly tough line on Condor. By October 1989, warnings from Washington had gone not only to West Germany and MBB, but to Argentina as well. They prompted President Carlos Menem to publicly assure the world that his country's space program was entirely peaceful. But Bush was not convinced. Toward the end of that month, he met with Menem at a hemispheric summit in San Jose, Costa Rica. After a tennis match with Menem, the former captain of the Yale baseball team aired his concern about the missile program, specifically saying that he did not want the technology to "wind up in the hands of a dangerous madman like Saddam Hussein."*

It was in a response to a question at a news conference later that day that Bush said transferring "forbidden technology" to Israel was "taboo." The question came after NBC News aired the October 25 report linking Jericho with South Africa. But Bush's warning was also clearly intended for Menem, who would soon begin dismantling Condor in his own country.

Jericho was a very different matter, however. Two weeks later, Bush delivered approximately the same message to Yitzhak Shamir in the Oval Office, but with no apparent effect. Appearing on the "MacNeil/Lehrer News Hour" afterward, the Israeli Prime Minister not only asserted that the NBC story was untrue, but added that Bush accepted its falsehood as a fact. The only salient fact was that it no longer mattered what Bush thought. South Africa's missile was a fact.

---

*If Bush worried about his own country's and western Europe's contribution to Hussein's massive superweapon spree, it went unrecorded. A number of U.S. government agencies, including the CIA, had already expressed concern.

# 15

# THE
# TERRIFYING
# ALTERNATIVE

The explosion in a subterranean garage at the World Trade Center in New York on February 26, 1993, killing six and injuring scores of others, traumatized the city and stunned the rest of the nation. The terrorist attack was a wakeup call, telling Americans that deadly violence in Belfast, Beirut, Bosnia, and elsewhere was no longer an abstraction playing itself out on the evening news. Terrorists—and a bungling lot at that—used commonly available chemicals delivered in a panel truck to cause an explosion whose effect seemed horrendous. Yet relatively speaking, the blast amounted to a mere whisper of other, grimmer, possibilities.

Had the bombers used something called a "radiological dispersal device," or radiological bomb, for example, they would have caused not just a terrible explosion but a catastrophe. This weapon would consist of such commonly used nuclear material as cesium-137, strontium-90, or cobalt-60, each of which has common medical and industrial applications, and an aerosol that disperses them when the bomb goes off. Were such a weapon to be used in the Trade Center, the smoke pouring out of the blast area would be laced with deadly radioactivity. The chimney effect created by the tower's construction would draw the combination of fine

482

ash and minute particles of powdered oxide of cesium, strontium, or cobalt to every floor. Nothing—not the concrete and steel construction materials or the distance from the site of the explosion—would protect the thousands inside the structure and their would-be rescuers from the flux of gamma rays.

Many who could not escape quickly, such as the kindergarten class that was trapped in an elevator, would soon die horribly from internal bleeding while vomiting and defecating uncontrollably. Since they would be closest to the site of the explosion and spend the most time there, many of the firemen, policemen, and rescue workes would almost certainly perish within hours of their arrival. Those who survived would suffer the effects of radiation sickness, including diminished immunological defenses, for the rest of their lives. Bodies of the dead would begin to deteriorate in offices, elevators, and stairwells while enough radiation suits were rounded up to outfit those sent to collect them for autopsy and burial. The psychological stress on the survivors, their families, and the rescuers would be enormous. Most insidiously, no one would be able to tell in the first few hours that the explosion had been spiked with radioactive isotopes. There would be no mushroom cloud, no visual signature to tell the victims that they had been poisoned, perhaps fatally, until the nausea and diarrhea struck.

The twin towers themselves would have to be abandoned as uninhabitable radioactive shells for years, if not forever. The half-life of cesium-137—the time it takes half of it to decay—is more than thirty years, while the strontium would have half decayed in twenty-eight years and the cobalt in a little more than five years. And should the terrorists be lucky or persistent enough to get plutonium-239, which has a half-life of 24,000 years, both structures would have had to be torn down and buried as radioactive waste.

Biological weapons would have the same terminal effect on those targeted for them. Furthermore, they could be used with even more devastating effect when dumped into a reservoir or released in a subway. And finding the terrorists responsible would be almost impossible. Such are the consequences of letting superweapon technology and materials drift downward until simple men with murderous intent get hold of them.

The proliferation of superweapons is now the most dangerous specter facing this planet. It is more fearsome in the short term—the coming decade—than burgeoning population, assaults on the environment, and even the scourge of deadly epidemics. Indeed, the spread of chemical and biological weapons, nuclear bombs, and the systems that can speed them on their way constitutes the most pernicious "epidemic" of all time. To say that the problem is as unprecedented as it is dangerous is to succumb to banality. Yet it is true.

The new reality—the single most salient fact about the proliferation of superweapons—is that no one is safe from them; there is no place to hide. A "regional" nuclear war is a contradiction in terms unless the region is defined as the entire planet. Besides the distinct possibility that nations other than the principals would be drawn into such a conflict, the environmental effects of atomic or hydrogen warfare would be transnational, as even the relatively modest catastrophe at Chernobyl demonstrated. The Serbs who threatened to crash an airplane into a European nuclear reactor if outsiders intervened in their war against the Muslims, releasing a deadly cloud that respected neither borders nor blockades, understood that stark reality and so did the nations they threatened. If the proliferation of superweapons is fundamentally international, then so must be the attempts to reverse it. The effort will be a Herculean one if precedent means anything.

There must be a comprehensive system of control regimes, or what we think of as technical fixes. That is, international agreements have to be strengthened and adhered to with serious emphasis on cutting off technology that is vital to superweapon development. As we have tried to demonstrate on these pages, the system of technical fixes used by the industrialized nations in the 1980s was pathetically inadequate, and matters only grew worse as Third World nations increasingly went into the proliferation business on their own. Given the amount of technical knowledge and technological wherewithal that is already spread around the world, the prospect of the technical fixes succeeding is, in our estimation, not very good. But fixes are the easy part.

The hard part is political. No effective control regime is possible without an underlying political resolve to stop and even reverse superweapon proliferation. There are obvious ethical implications to the renunciation of such weapons. But more important, at least where real movement in the right direction is concerned, there are pragmatic reasons as well. It is imperative that all nations understand that superweapons, particularly nuclear ones and the force structures that go with them, are not only inherently dangerous but staggeringly expensive, worrisome, and ultimately useless.

A former U.S. chief of naval operations confided that his line officers hated having nuclear weapons on their ships. They knew that no one was going to fire nuclear weapons at them, he said, and therefore that they weren't going to fire theirs at anyone else. Yet the deadly devices had to be attended to—cared for with the kind of constant attention that is lavished on infants—lest an accident happen that would end a career ignominiously. And there was every reason to believe that the Americans' counterparts in the Soviet Navy felt the same way. Political institutions, like the officers who serve them, must conclude that nuclear weapons are far more trouble than they are worth. It cannot be said with enough emphasis: technical fixes depend squarely on political will.

Superweapons are the ultimate tools of nationalism, and, their owners believe, they therefore bring automatic respect because they guarantee survival. Israel's atomic arsenal and its complicated triad force structure are not fully understood by the Arabs. But the Arabs who came to the peace table in September 1993 to sign the historic peace accord with Israel at least understood that Tel Aviv's nuclear weapons guaranteed they would never succeed in pushing the Jewish state into the sea. Similarly, the serious nature of the Iraqi and Iranian nuclear programs and the existence of an Islamic bomb in Pakistan convinced Israel that it could not go on knocking out Osiraks forever and that long-term security required a political settlement.

So, telling the leaders of insecure nations that the cost of developing nuclear weapons will be enormous in political and economic terms won't work. Nothing has a higher priority in a vigorously nationalist state than the ultimate equalizer; it protects the motherland, calls attention to needs other nations should heed, and puts the country on a footing with the superpowers.

Nowhere is the bomb more the center of nationalist culture than in Pakistan, where it is treated like a second religion; the seven bombs are thought of as sacred stones that radiate a magic power protecting the nation. The theological element is not farfetched. A. Q. Khan, the bomb's creator, is treated like a mystical figure by much of the Pakistani press, which exaggerates his successes, derides his critics in the West, and even declaims his personal security (although he travels in bulletproof limousines and always has a pistol at the ready in his briefcase). The quasi-religious nature of the man, his organization, and the end product makes reversing the situation virtually impossible. It is the same where the bomb is still being sought.

India and Pakistan developed atomic weapons despite brutal poverty.

Israel and South Africa developed them despite international recriminations. North Korea developed them despite abject poverty and isolation. Iraq came chillingly close to developing them despite the destruction of its first nuclear research center, sabotage, and the crippling cost of the eight-year war with Iran.

Trying to rein in proliferation through traditional means alone—sanctions, trade embargoes, diplomacy—therefore cannot work. Such efforts are laudable because they delay weapons programs. Certainly individuals and corporations that willfully aid superweapons programs should be exposed and punished. In addition, the technical fixes outlined below are important ways to slow the process. But beyond that, the solution must be political. Argentina and Brazil put brakes on their race for missiles and the bomb when they realized that the respective threats to their sovereignty were overblown. Settlement of the Kashmir dispute would similarly help to defuse the most volatile of the atomic standoffs. Helping the two Koreas to find a common ground would cool the situation there. And nations that continue to preach violence and chase the bomb, like Iran, should be isolated and embarrassed.

But the crux of the matter is to grasp the new reality: Western arrogance aside, "ragheads" and others in the Third World are fully capable of producing superweapons on their own.

The successful control of dual-use technology does not require an unending list of prohibited items. To the contrary, the shorter and more precise the list, the better. This is not a contradiction in terms. "The Pershing-2 is the model for a lot of Third World projects," a Pentagon official with considerable experience in export control explained, citing only one superweapon system among hundreds. "It has 250,000 parts. The point is that you don't have to stop all 250,000 parts from being exported to stop the missile. You only have to stop several key parts: actually a small number." A missile's ablative nose cone, rocket motor, guidance system, pumps, and electronic stage separators are examples of key items that need to be prohibited from export. Without them a ballistic missile is a useless hulk. (But if a Third World nation wanted not the gold medal in the missile Olympics but a bronze, few of those components would be needed.)

This does not mean that given enough time, skill, and funding, the key parts can't be made indigenously. That is what India did when the maraging steel and solid fuel it needed for its PSLV—the Polar Satellite Launch Vehicle that wins the ICBM look-alike contest—was withheld by Missile Technology Control Regime members. The Indians simply manufactured their own steel and fuel. Similarly, when the United States refused to supply India with a Cray supercomputer, Indian missile designers improvised by linking 250 powerful personal computers that were the Cray's equal and then exported them.

Yet denying finished goods and key technology creates serious problems for the nation that wants the weapon system. "The key is delaying the project," the Pentagon expert continued. "In each of these countries, you have a finite amount of money, a finite amount of resources, and competing projects. If you have a missile program or a nuclear weapons program that is running late and over budget it becomes a target for the managers of competing projects. They point out the cost overruns and the delays to the political leadership in hopes of getting the missile or nuclear program slowed down."

Determining what the competing projects are is one of the many roles of intelligence. Once the projects have been identified, and provided they are relatively benign, they can be targeted for enough aid to ensure that they remain competitive with the missile, nuclear, or other superweapon program. Encouraging the development of conventional forces is one way to accomplish this, since they traditionally compete with such "cutting edge" groups as ballistic missileers for funding. Even within a single service like the air force there is always competition between aircraft and missile units for resources. As late as 1955, when the United States was far more advanced in strategic weaponry than all but a handful of Third World nations are today, the Air Staff still favored manufacturing B-52s over ballistic missiles. The bomber generals were so stubborn, in fact, that a Ballistic Missiles Committee had to be set up to bypass them.

Systems integration, at which Western nations excel, is another key proliferation chokepoint. European, Russian, and American engineers have crisscrossed the globe to show Third World clients how to integrate highly complex superweapon systems (as have their Third World counterparts from Brazil, China, and Israel). Major superweapon technology transfers almost invariably involve teams of engineers and technicians whose job it is to help the customer integrate the system being sold with all or part of the larger weapons apparatus. Long-range missiles, for example, are immensely complicated vehicles in which all of the essential components must either work together perfectly or fail completely. Withholding the expertise to get them to do that is yet another way to slow or stall missile proliferation.

It is fundamentally important that an export control regime be world-wide and highly integrated. This is not an impossible goal since relatively few nations want nuclear weapons and ballistic delivery systems in the first place. The vast majority of countries are not engaged in superweapon proliferation and have no apparent interest in the matter. For varying reasons, Canada, Switzerland, Italy, Spain, the Scandinavian and Benelux nations, and others that could have developed their own ballistic missiles and nuclear warheads chose not to do so. Some, like Italy, Norway, and the Netherlands, rejected the weapons because they were protected by the U.S. nuclear umbrella anyway. (Italy's eschewing nuclear weapons also grew out of its being governed by a succession of left-wing governments and its having the largest Communist Party in western Europe.) Others, like Sweden and Switzerland, concluded that their neutrality (and safety in the event of a major war) was best served by keeping nuclear weapons off their territory. Following the Cuban missile crisis in 1962, South and Central America declared themselves nuclear-free zones, and with the exception of Brazil's and Argentina's flirtation with atomic weapon research in the 1980s, they have remained nuclear-free. South Africa became the first nation to drop out of the nuclear club when it dismantled its six atomic bombs rather than chance their falling into the hands of a hostile black government. While that decision rested more on expediency than on ethics, it was nevertheless sensible.

It is obvious that no control regime can work without a serious commitment by the People's Republic of China, the nuclear weapons states in the former Soviet Union, Israel, and the two Indian subcontinent nations. Nor can it work without such nonnuclear industrialized states as Germany, Switzerland, and Italy reining in their dual technology. It is also clear that braking the spread of nuclear weapons depends on Brazil, South Africa, and even a renegade like North Korea withholding their knowledge and assistance, even in the face of relatively lucrative offers to do otherwise.

Less apparent, but no less important, is the increasingly worrisome situation along the Pacific rim. The nations that constitute that region are superweapon proliferation's most dangerous wild card. The unwelcome publicity that came with revelations about the arming of Libya and Iraq caused the most important European suppliers, most notably Germany, to toughen their export regimes. Bonn, which was particularly embarrassed, also enacted strict criminal codes that give real muscle to the export laws. But no such standard exists along Asia's new gold coast, where free trade, low wages, and high technology are the region's unofficial religion. No wonder that Japan, the Koreas, Taiwan, Indonesia, Hong Kong, and Singapore ("the new Switzerland," according to one proliferation expert) amount to a vast mall for customers who do not want to get caught shopping in Europe or in the United States. No control regime can work unless the rim nations agree to set and abide by international standards.

The standards must rest squarely on political will and on concomitant multinationalism. Chemical and biological agents, long-range missiles, and nuclear weapons have proliferated because the desire to stop them gave way to expedient and overriding political and economic imperatives: to the shortsighted establishment of alliances of convenience and fat contracts. The missile and nuclear weapons programs of Israel, Iraq, India, and Pakistan were consciously helped by nations that were parties not only to the nuclear Non-Proliferation Treaty, but to the Coordinating Committee for Multilateral Export Controls (CoCom) and the Missile Technology Control Regime (MTCR). The inescapable consequence of a shrinking planet is increasing interdependence, since geography no longer provides a buffer against catastrophe. General Charles A. Horner, the head of the U.S. Space Command, estimated in the spring of 1993 that the world had eight years before "launch vehicles" like India's became a permanent intercontinental ballistic missile threat.

A successful control regime also needs to be multilateral. Political resolve must manifest itself in a comprehensive nuclear test ban, the strengthening of nonproliferation agreements—chiefly the Non-Proliferation Treaty, but also CoCom, the MTCR, and the various chemical and biological weapons conventions, which are appallingly porous—and closer cooperation and communication among those who possess the technical wherewithal to spread superweapons. If nations that sign the NPT also adhere to a comprehensive ban on nuclear weapons testing, it will make cheating more difficult (though not impossible if weapons-hungry governments are willing to risk producing untested weapons or, like Pakistan, buy a proven design).

The IAEA needs strengthening. One apparent way to do this is by consolidating its ties to the Security Council, rather than having it continue to be a kind of appendage of the organization. Safeguarding also must be substantially strengthened. That begins with more aggressive monitoring which, in turn, should entail the use of American, Russian, and other nations' intelligence assets—including agents, signal intercepts, and re-connaissance satellites—on a cooperative basis to pinpoint transgres-sors.* The U.S. reconnaissance satellite data showing the Iraqis' desperate attempt to hide their nuclear equipment in the days following the Gulf War were shared with the IAEA to good effect; this serves as a model. The satellite intelligence was used like an unerring roadmap that led the inspectors to the carefully hidden research and production facilities. Space imagery, a powerful tool in the hands of skilled interpreters, also helped to unmask North Korea's clandestine nuclear weapons operation.

Armed with the intelligence, IAEA teams should be able to make unannounced site visits. A nation that refuses to admit the inspectors, cannot satisfactorily account for significant fissile material discrepancies, or is caught in possession of nuclear weapons development equipment should be subject to increasingly severe U.N.-administered coercive and immediate measures, including economic sanctions, political castigation, and armed intervention.

Economic penalties could include the loss of most-favored nation status with the United States, the raising of trade barriers generally, a loss of credit from the World Bank, International Monetary Fund, and other lending institutions, and even blockade. Transgressors would also be subject to extensive, and embarrassing, reportage by the world news media. Facing stiff sanctions and being branded a pariah would probably have the desired effect on many nations. Conversely, cooperation, in-cluding the abandonment of superweapon projects, should be rewarded. The carrot-and-stick strategy succeeded in convincing Argentina to aban-don Condor-2.

*There are precedents for such cooperation going back to at least 1977, when the Soviet Union relayed to the CIA intelligence on the preparation of a South African nuclear weapons test site in the Kalahari that was spotted by one of its Cosmos reconnaissance satellites. In 1977, a reconnaissance satellite was instructed to take a look, and with the Soviet sighting confirmed, Pretoria was warned to abandon the deep hole. President Bush repaid the favor at least once when he warned Mikhail Gorbachev about the coup that took place in August 1991. (The Kalahari data is from Jeffrey T. Richelson, *America's Secret Eyes in Space*, New York: Ballinger, 1990, p. 138. Also see "U.S. May Tell Soviets: Let's Share Some Secrets," and "Gorbachev Says Bush Called Him to Give Early Warning of a Coup," *The New York Times*, April 21, 1989, and November 13, 1991; "Soviets May Get Access to Missile Sensor Data," *Space News*, October 7–13, 1991; and Ray Cline, "Common Foe for KGB-CIA," from *The Washington Post* as reprinted in *The Sarasota Herald Tribune*, October 14, 1989.)

It also persuaded Moscow to end the rocket deal with New Delhi. Boris N. Yeltsin understood that his nation's future depended not on the Indian space agency but on support from the White House. The day after Yeltsin announced the dissolution of Parliament and that legislative body in turn dismissed him (in September 1993), the Clinton administration and key congressmen accelerated a $2.5 billion aid package to Moscow. While the show of support was by no means repayment only for breaking the contract with India, Yeltsin's action demonstrated that he and his advisers were sensitive to U.S. proliferation concerns. They were rewarded handsomely for playing the game, as the British might put it.

Conversely, the Clinton administration reacted—correctly—to the sale of M-11 technology to Pakistan by first leaking word of it to the news media to draw attention to the Chinese transgression and then by slapping a $1 billion high-tech export ban on the People's Republic, about half of it in satellite sales. A week earlier, the President publicly urged China to abandon an imminent underground nuclear test or suffer unspecified consequences. The public admonitions over the missiles and the test came at a time when Beijing was making its own all-out public relations blitz to get the International Olympic Committee to award it the 2000 summer games despite persistent civil rights abuses. Hosting the games would have brought great prestige to China, not to mention millions in hard currency. Beijing was so sensitive to its image that it released a well-known political prisoner and announced that it would beef up notoriously lax civil-aviation safety standards to get the games. The committee nevertheless awarded the games to Sydney, proving that it was more prepared than some governments to take a moral stand.

China's acute awareness that appearances count, which was similar to Germany's in the aftermath of the Libya and Iraq fiascos, shows that nations can be embarrassed into correcting roguish behavior and that repeatedly turning the media spotlight on them is a viable antiproliferation weapon.

Economics is in many respects proliferation's catalyst. As we have noted, economic desperation drives Russia and some of the former Warsaw Pact nations to peddle weapons and technology. The possibility of considerable profits or at least balanced international payments also prompts Third World countries like China, Brazil, and Israel to do the same. Economics, as well as such related issues as overpopulation, drive proliferation just as surely as do purely political motives. Unfortunately, that subject is beyond the scope of this book. Suffice it to say that, all things being equal, well-off, relatively secure societies like today's Japan are less likely to buy or sell superweapon technology than those that are insecure, needy, or desperate. Ultimately, solving economic problems, especially as they are driven by population pressure, is the surest way to defuse proliferation and enhance true national security.

A nation that could not be persuaded to abandon the quest for nuclear weapons by political and economic coercion and by international reprobation should face the possibility of military intervention by the United Nations. Officially at least, Iraq was punished, not for its hell-bent effort to get the entire panapoly of superweapons, but for aggression against Kuwait. The coalition's response served notice that molesting neighbors, particularly neighbors whose oil is indispensable to the West, is unacceptable. But its value as a deterrent to proliferation was problematical. In fact, as noted in Chapter 1, it had the unfortunate side effect of demonstrating the importance of high-tech weapons, from smart bombs to satellites. Had the coalition announced at the outset that the destruction of Saddam Hussein's superweapon technology was a major motivation for Desert Shield, however, it would have left itself open to embarrassing, perhaps even politically debilitating, questions about how he came to get that technology in the first place.

Military intervention would necessarily entail the highly selective destruction of nuclear weapons research and development sites from the air. The use of force is a particularly difficult area because it goes to the heart of the rationale for proliferation in the first place. Colonel Qaddafi spoke for many Arabs and others when he told Libyan students that the United States would not dare to attack their country if it had the means to strike New York with nuclear-armed missiles in retaliation. It is taken as gospel in the Third World that possession of nuclear weapons—equalizers—is ultimately the only way to stand up to the big boys. The use of force against Third World proliferators, especially as it is conducted by the industrialized northern countries, therefore carries the risk of being labeled as bullying. Coalition-style attacks on Third World superweapon seekers, particularly if spearheaded by the United States, would confirm the Third World's worst fears about northern chauvinism and racism and lead to a redoubling of efforts to acquire equalizers. As previously noted, while the Arab members of the coalition were delighted that the Iraqi threat to the region was decisively ended, at least temporarily, there was nonetheless residual grumbling from the same quarter about the humbling of fellow Arabs at the hands of Americans and Europeans. Military action would therefore have to be undertaken only by U.N. mandate.

Similarly, sharply reducing American, Russian, and other nuclear stockpiles is important not only from the standpoint of diminishing the prospect of war or diversion, but because it establishes those nations' credibility as opponents of proliferation and undercuts accusations that they are hypocritical. Trying to convince Third World nations that nuclear weapons are bad for them while maintaining large numbers of the devices is as effective as trying to persuade a young person not to use cigarettes while blowing smoke in his face.

It is also important to get Third World nations themselves involved in the nonproliferation process by giving them access to the control process rather than continuing to have all nonproliferation initiatives come from the north. This would help to break down the "rich man–poor man" relationship, often derided as patrimony by Third World nations, that now exists. It is therefore better to have the tenets of nonproliferation treaties, foremost among them the NPT, controlled regionally than by Europe and the United States. This could have three important advantages: reducing regional rivalries, tailoring agreements to meet local needs, and minimizing the presence of the United States and its European cohorts, which tends to antagonize the Third World.

As the only nation to have used nuclear weapons in war, and the sole remaining superpower, the United States has a special responsibility to lead the way. We do not believe that Washington should be the planet's policeman. Even if such a role could be undertaken—and we believe it would be ruinously expensive both politically and monetarily—it would be counterproductive. There is ample evidence that unilateral American pronouncements and pious declarations about ethics are really camouflage for a racist doctrine that calls for superweapons to remain exclusively in the hands of the United States and other white industrialized nations. Where India is concerned, to take only one example, finger-waving and admonitions have only hardened the resolve to acquire the forbidden fruit.

At the same time, the United States must, by virtue of its power, play a leading role in shaping the nonproliferation agenda by setting an unambiguous example for the rest of the world. That special responsibility will be abdicated with perilous consequences. Yet the challenge is formidable. What follows, again comprising a political dimension and a control regime, is meant not only to define what the United States ought to do, but to serve as a model for the community of nations as a whole.

America's proliferation record in the Third World has been characterized by subjectivity and shortsightedness. The old Machiavellian doctrine about rewarding friends and punishing enemies, a staple of Foreign Policy 101, has manifested itself in a highly subjective policy whose heart is the "tilt." This entailed favoring one nation or another in an effort to prevent or offset Communist encroachment in a given area or region through economic, military, and political support. It was a success because its goal was relatively simple and straightforward: stopping an ideologically monolithic and brutal opponent that frightened many democratically inclined Third World countries.

But tilting is not only unsuccessful in today's infinitely more complicated, fragmented world, it is counterproductive and dangerous. The United States and the Soviet Union competed throughout the cold war within a structured environment that they controlled by mutual, unofficial agreement. It was understood, for example, that neither side's proxies would control nuclear weapons. This worked because the respective proxies knew that their sovereignty was guaranteed by U.S. or Soviet military might. Except for an occasional test of wills on the order of the Berlin blockade and the invasion of South Korea, or an aberration like the Cuban missile crisis, the system eventually settled into a stable status quo. With the old Soviet Union gone, however, no nation on the wrong end of a U.S. tilt can seek help from a big brother. It must therefore look after itself. Superweapons are the most appealing way to do so.

Where tilting once created military stability because it continuously adjusted and readjusted a world battle line that was more or less fixed, it now creates instability, since almost all the proxies have become free lances who are forced to look after themselves in a much less certain world. In those circumstances, homemade weapons with foreign lineage are the ultimate guarantors of sovereignty, and the deadlier they are the better.

Every time the United States tilts toward a country by supplying arms and technology and looking the other way for the sake of expediency while a superweapon development program is occurring, which happened in Israel, Iraq, and Pakistan, it foments dangerous long-term instability.

Demarches aside, the United States effectively tilted toward Israel for a variety of reasons, toward Iraq because it was at war with Iran, and toward Pakistan because of its role in the Afghanistan war. Whatever the short-term benefits of such policy, the long-term result was to leave Iraq with the capability to produce nuclear weapons and Israel and Pakistan with potent stockpiles of ready-to-assemble atomic bomb components.

Iraq and Pakistan overcame a variety of technical obstacles by taking political advantage of a superpower that was willing to be duped in order to advance its own short-term goals. Both were able to import much of the equipment they required, not so much because the export laws they circumvented were seriously flawed (Germany aside), but because the United States and other nations on whose books the laws were written used them arbitrarily. In the case of Israel, the United States was not duped. It was willingly co-opted. This resulted in a policy that was and remains not only blatantly hypocritical but abidingly dangerous on two scores: it legitimizes the quest for superweapons by the enemies of those that have them and it extends our own dangerous technology to unintended and worrisome places.

The tilting is additionally dangerous because it automatically becomes a catalyst for the beneficiaries' neighbors to step up their own quest for superarms. Whatever Iran's motives for seeking nuclear weapons and missiles to carry them, and they are politically complex, there can be no doubt that knowing about Iraq's own latent capability in that area is another compelling reason to press on with the deadly business.

If India fears Pakistani nuclear weapons, and it ought to, it at least has the consolation of seeing the United States abandon Pakistan in order to tilt in its own direction. Although New Delhi is currently the beneficiary of Washington's political largesse, it will not be deluded into thinking that the mercurial Americans couldn't as easily tilt in some other direction if that proved attractive. The Indians will therefore continue to tend their ballistic missile and nuclear weapons programs and perhaps hope that when they, too, are abandoned by the Americans it will not be for trumped-up charges of terrorism.

By April 1993, the Clinton administration was considering adding Pakistan to its official list of nations that support terrorism because of its alleged support of guerrillas fighting to free Kashmir from Indian rule. Besides being unjust—the United States had no qualms about supporting terrorists fighting to free Afghanistan from Soviet rule or Nicaragua from Sandinista rule—such a move would undoubtedly strengthen the hand of

Islamic revivalists and redouble Islamabad's determination to keep its atomic bombs and perhaps produce more of them. The irony is that the Reagan administration did exactly the opposite in order to further its own political agenda: it lifted the terrorist status from Iraq—which really *did* bankroll assassinations and other dirty deeds—in order to clear the way for arming it.

And there is another long-term booby trap as well. America's tilting in favor of some nations getting the bomb puts it at risk of being black-mailed into becoming the world's policeman, like it or not. That, too, could have exceedingly dangerous consequences. When South African President F. W. de Klerk announced that his country had built and then dismantled six atomic bombs, the news media correctly seized upon it as a big story. Lost in most of the coverage, however, was an even more important and ominous announcement. De Klerk claimed that had the white regime been seriously threatened by masses of rampaging blacks, it was prepared to take one of its bombs to the Kalahari test site and prepare it for detonation. At that point, in the midst of a crisis in which blacks and whites were slaughtering each other, a "confidential indication of the deterrent capability would be given to one or more of the major powers, for example the United States, in an attempt to persuade them to intervene," he said. Another South African was even more blunt. "The thinking was, if we were attacked from the north, we would have taken one of the devices to the Kalahari and tested it—then turned to the United States and said, 'We need you to send the Marines.'" In fact, that is close to what happened in 1987. De Klerk's predecessor readied the South African nuclear test site in the Kalahari after Cuban and Angolan ad-vances. The United States saw the activity and along with the Soviet Union proposed peace talks.

It would not have been the first time the United States was forced to quickly respond to an imminent threat of nuclear war. During the Yom Kippur War in 1973, after the National Security Agency intercepted Israeli messages ordering Jerichos to be readied and SR-71 spy planes saw the large doors of the missile bunkers being opened, the United States re-sponded by sending more than 20,000 tons of conventional military equip-ment to Israel on an emergency basis and placing U.S. forces around the world on alert to discourage Kremlin intervention. Later, in 1990, the crisis was on the Indian subcontinent, when another signal intercept indicated that the Pakistanis were readying their own atomic bombs for use against India while photographic evidence showed that they seemed to be evacuating the Kahuta nuclear research facility. That was the data that sent Robert M. Gates scurrying to Pakistan and India to dampen the dangerously escalating situation. Seven months later, when Iraqi Scuds slammed into Tel Aviv and Haifa, the United States had to rush Patriots to Israel, agree to divert substantial aircraft in a fruitless search for mobile Scuds and, according to one U.S. general on the scene, allow the Israeli Defense Ministry to "nominate" more than 100 Iraqi targets for destruction, including rail and highway junctions and key links in the electrical power grid.

In each instance, there were two possibilities. One was that the United States heard and saw what it thought it did, forcing it to frantically prevent a catastrophe. The other was that the Israelis and Pakistanis were bluffing with the knowledge that since the Americans had been instrumental in either providing nuclear technology or at least not impeding it, and therefore knew how dangerous the situation really was, they would take the emergency with utmost seriousness and intervene. Either way, encouraging the development of Islamic bombs, Jewish bombs, and Afrikaaner bombs, all instruments of blackmail, has thrust the United States into the unwilling and dangerous role of a mediator that could get caught in the superweapon equivalent of crossfire or, at very least, that has to devote a great deal of energy and resources to the prevention of one close call after another. This calls for change.

Far from being a panacea, Mutual Assured Destruction becomes increasingly likely as the weapons of Armageddon spread, particularly among nations with populations that are obsessed with devout rage and revenge. MAD's absurdity was made clear in May 1988, when Ronald Reagan and Mikhail Gorbachev embraced in Red Square within yards of the White House military officer who carried U.S. nuclear war codes. Using those codes to launch a preemptive attack against the Soviet Union or respond to one would have incinerated the very spot upon which the two men stood. Gorbachev's own codes, of course, were not far away. Both leaders, personally hostage to each other—as were their countries— had come to depend upon a high order of trust. It bore fruit a few years later when each side began reducing its tactical nuclear missiles in Europe without the customary verification procedures. This was finally possible because, like the officers on their nuclearized ships, Reagan and Gorbachev had come to realize that the calamity such weapons could bring made them useless for all but the insane and that they were therefore ridiculously burdensome. They had come to understand that trust would better serve their needs than the constant threat of mutual annihilation.

The argument that MAD works is as flawed as an epidemiological study that uses a dozen subjects. Not only is forty-five years a relatively short trial period, but conditions themselves are changing radically and for the worse. During most of the cold war few nations had nuclear weapons, and none of those that did were obsessed with racial or ethnic hatred. Now, the number has gone up and so has the blood feud factor. That has led to more sudden lurches to the "brink." Going to the brink of nuclear war often enough could make the participants so complacent that they get sloppy handling it, which could lead to gross miscalculations, or it could impel them to up the ante each time in order to maintain credibility and not look foolish. Either possibility courts calamity.

The United States needs to replace its subjective approach to the spread of superweapons with one that is consistently evenhanded and that the Second and Third Worlds will come to see as fair. This means it must not only categorically halt the spread of chemical, biological, missile, and nuclear technology, but supplement that policy by prohibiting the export of sensitive knowledge that can be derived from meetings like the infamous DOE detonation conferences. While respecting academe and the necessity to keep scientific knowledge freely flowing, we think a clear distinction should be made between sharing AIDS research data, for example, and teaching foreign scientists how to implode fission warheads. The argument that such information is freely available anyway only underscores the rationale for ending such meetings. It is appalling that the most insignificant old secrets—the internal structure of the U-2's wing, for instance, which was designed in 1955 and which has been minutely inspected by both the Russians and Chinese who shot the planes down—remains classified while the apparatus that produced the first atomic bomb, the blueprints for two ballistic missiles, and software or diagrams for setting off atomic and hydrogen warheads are freely available. All warheads being equal, so to speak, the effect of being hit by a V-2, a Pershing-2, or a Minuteman-2 is the same.

The entire U.S. export control regime as it relates to dual-use superweapon technology needs to be systematized, as does the ponderous, contentious, and uncommunicative governmental structure that alleges to control it.

What is required in the first instance is a tight and effective interagency communication system, in the opinion of McGeorge Bundy, John Kennedy's national security adviser and a veteran of the Cuban missile crisis. Kennedy's administration was the first to take proliferation seriously. Such a system would be a model upon which a larger international network could be patterned. Bundy expressed optimism about crimping superweapon proliferation on at least three scores. He noted that since the number of nations that want the supers is relatively small, preventing them from acquiring the weapons is easier than it would be trying to stop a stampede. And Bundy noted, too, that nuclear weapons' and long-range missiles' complicated nature and dependence on key parts make their technology easier to stop. The most important of those parts or technology are the ones that weaponize or guide a system, that turn a launch vehicle into a ballistic missile or a short-range fighter into a long-range strike aircraft. Finally, he maintained that computers and instant communication not only can keep track of immense inventories of relevant dual-use technology and who is requesting it, but can be used by federal agencies to share information and enforce uniform standards.

John Ellicott, the Washington lawyer who was on the National Academy of Sciences panel that produced *Finding Common Ground*, the study of U.S. export control problems and solutions, echoed Bundy on the need for common standards and close cooperation between agencies.* The study upon which he worked described an existing control regime so ponderous, inefficient, self-contradictory, and politicized that it amounts to a quagmire that makes doing legitimate business overseas needlessly difficult while perpetuating the leaking of dangerous technology. Chief among the problems it cited are a multiplicity of statutes, many of them uncoordinated and supervised by different congressional committees; competing agencies and control regimes; jurisdictional disputes; licensing complexity; overlapping enforcement; outdated and confusing control lists; and the ineffective resolution of disputes between enforcement agencies that result from unclear guidelines and therefore widely differing interpretations of what constitutes sensitive technology.

If Bundy, Ellicott, the others on the National Academy of Sciences panel, and many experts in and out of government who have studied the subject are correct, and we are persuaded they are, then a fundamental change is necessary in U.S. export policy. A list of sensitive dual-use

---

*National Academy of Sciences, *Finding Common Ground: U.S. Export Controls in a Changed Global Environment*, Washington: National Academy Press, 1991.

technology needs to be developed and circulated at home and abroad. Such a list could help a regime to become a world model and add impetus for toughening the international agreements. At the same time, interagency and international cooperation should be sharply increased, both through institutional restructuring and data sharing.

Placing proliferation at the head of national security concerns would be a radical departure from recent U.S. policy. Proliferation has been encouraged as a way to reward friends, bribe proxies, and support the U.S. business community. Typical was Reagan's decision in 1984 to pressure the U.N. to freeze the IAEA's already paltry $200 million a year overall budget and the $60 million it used for safeguard inspections around the world. By the hypocritical calculus of Reaganomics, a pared-down budget would force the IAEA to work more efficiently. No such standard was applied to the nation's armed forces, however, which received an increase in appropriations so large that it was mainly responsible for catapulting the deficit to $4 trillion.* Nor did Reagan show an interest in coordinating the activities of the agencies responsible for curtailing illegal exports, since that would have violated his implacable belief in a free market that was unfettered by government, no matter how reckless the consequences. "He let them fight it out," Ellicott noted, sourly. The result of such willful neglect was trickle-down superweapons.

That is why the Clinton administration's nonproliferation initiative, as unveiled in a speech before the General Assembly on September 27, 1993, was important. "As weapons of mass destruction fall into more hands, even small conflicts can threaten to take on murderous proportions," Clinton told the delegates and others, adding that "if we do not stem the proliferation of the world's deadliest weapons, no democracy can feel secure." He went on to call for an international agreement banning the production of plutonium and highly enriched uranium for weapons; a comprehensive ban on nuclear weapons testing; a new effort to curb chemical and biological weapons by pushing for ratification of the Chemical Weapons Convention by 1995 (which his own country had not ratified); and thwarting the spread of ballistic missiles by transforming the MTCR from a mere agreement to a set of formal rules "that command universal adherence."

The ban on production of plutonium and enriched uranium implied

---

*Reagan had run on a platform that called for a constitutionally mandated balanced budget, a position that was quietly abandoned after he took office.

a strengthening of the IAEA and even suggested the possibility that IAEA inspectors could monitor the fissile material taken out of dismantled U.S. warheads and the production sites in the United States where bomb-grade material is made. Such visits would mark a sharp departure from previous policy, which held that foreigners intrusively poking around the nation's nuclear weapons production facilities not only compromised security but amounted to an infringement of U.S. sovereignty. (However grandiose Clinton's plan for the IAEA, its effort would be counterproductive unless the agency's budget for safeguard inspections matched its mandate. A malnourished IAEA would only invite its being used to mask diversions, as Jafar Jafar did.)

To be sure, Clinton's suggestions were part of a control regime: a fix. Yet they reflected a sea change that was political, one that, as he put it, "made nonproliferation one of our nation's highest priorities." If U.N. inspectors snooping at uranium and plutonium production sites was a contentious issue, so was the idea of a permanent moratorium on nuclear weapons testing. Many respected scientists maintained that testing the weapons was necessary not only to design new ones more adapted to changed political circumstances—the "minis," for example—but for safety's sake. The new policy reflected the Oval Office's awareness that proliferation had already gone critical. For it to work, the American leadership would have to use every lever it had, working them simultaneously and with unambiguous consistency.

That would be hard enough. But Clinton made a further point of telling the United Nations that world economic prosperity, certainly including that of his own country, was also a linchpin of the world he envisioned. This, he hastened to add, meant that some hardware and technology could in fact be exported without risking further proliferation (a point made by Ellicott and the others in *Finding Common Ground*).

So even as his administration, like Bush's, was forcing the Russians to abandon the Indian rocket deal, it was preparing (for example) to relax its own rocket export standards. The idea, which could have been concocted while tumbling down the rabbit hole, was that opening such exports would induce more nations to join the MTCR because doing so would allow them increased access to U.S. space-launch technology. In fact, it would undoubtedly inspire those who already had similar technology—Brazil, China, India, Israel, North Korea, and South Africa, to name only six—to sell what they had to other seekers of ballistic missiles.

"We have crippled entire industries while the French, the Germans, and everybody else is selling all over the globe," complained Representative Sam Gejdenson, the Connecticut Democrat whose state is the home of United Technologies, Sikorsky, and Electric Boat, which produces submarines. Yet at least five of his colleagues, including Senators Claiborne Pell, a Rhode Island Democrat, and Jesse Helms, a North Carolina Republican, were not persuaded. The new policy would "open a substantial loophole in the MTCR," they warned National Security Adviser Anthony Lake, "since participants would be free to export ballistic missile technology under the guise of 'peaceful' space launch technology."

Presidential leadership remains the key to an effective control regime. "Through the vehicle of the NSD [National Security Directive], the President should provide guidance on the fundamental objectives for all national security export controls . . . and the direction for achieving those aims," the National Academy of Sciences panel concluded. Ellicott put the requirement more bluntly. There is a need, he said, to "knock heads together" at the highest level.

McGeorge Bundy was of the same mind. The impetus for an effective control regime, he said, must come directly from the White House and be overseen by either the Director of Central Intelligence or the National Security Adviser. Which one gets the job is less important than the degree of clout he is given. "Word has to go down the line," Bundy explained. "When somebody challenges it, the DCI or National Security Adviser has to be able to say to him, 'Do you want to tell the President about this?' " Bundy, reaching back to his own days in the White House, savored the exquisitely subtle yet powerful nuance of such moments and smiled. "That is usually effective."

While we agree that the United States should take the lead in forging an effective antiproliferation control regime, and that the President ought to put that challenge at the top of the foreign policy agenda, we are convinced that depending on such a strategy to the exclusion of wider responses would be fruitless. Trying to stop superweapon proliferation with only an export control regime would be like trying to stop drug use by intercepting smugglers when the controlled substances are being produced at home anyway. The only strategy that can hope to work requires a common political resolve that evolves into mutual trust. That, in turn, requires a fresh outlook and radical thinking.

The strategy needs to start with demonstrating to aspiring superweapon states that owning the devices is as economically counterproductive as it is futile and dangerous. Right now, the opposite is happening. Buying uranium and plutonium that is taken from Russian and other former Soviet weapons and the weapons themselves, for example, has been hailed as a positive step toward the strategic arms build-down. And it is. But at the same time it has the pernicious effect of putting a high value on the weapons. That sends the wrong signal to Japan, which is accumulating both elements, and to nations like Argentina and Brazil that have serious economic problems. Seeing that, David Kay has explained, would lead the South Americans to think "My God, if we'd only continued our program we could have sold it off." It is therefore important to be careful about paying ransom for fissile material or real or potential weapons for fear that it will lead to the creation of systems specifically to be bought out. The better way is to convince potential proliferators that building superweapons in any guise inevitably leads to an unacceptable political, economic, and social drain.

More fundamentally, the West has to take the rest of the world seriously, not on a selective basis—as a market, an energy source, or a geopolitical pawn—but in its totality. In other words, it is time for the Third World to be taken seriously for what it is, not for how it affects the West. At least two instances in which India and Pakistan almost started a nuclear conflagration went virtually unreported in the Western news media, for example, because the developments were not thought of as affecting the West.

The political corollary of paying exorbitant sums for plutonium and weapons is paying complete attention to Third World nations only after they acquire, or are close to acquiring, enough superweapons to threaten the West. Every non-Western nation understands that, aside from their supposed use in settling old scores, having atomic bombs is a proven way to get everyone's attention: to be taken seriously. As David Kay has noted, the British have said that the only reason they remain on the U.N. Security Council is because they have nuclear weapons (though it is hard to tell whether they are bragging or complaining).

Giving Germany and Japan permanent membership on the council, he added, would not only reflect their growing importance, but would in effect reward them for not having nuclear weapons. That could have at least two important effects, one subtle, one not. The obvious effect would be to demonstrate that it is not necessary to carry an equalizer to gain political prominence in the world community. Less obviously, it would show any nation tempted to acquire nuclear weapons that those who already have them really do believe that they are potentially harmful to the world's health and therefore ought to be abandoned. Continued American and Russian nuclear disarmament and a permanent test moratorium would reinforce the message.

This represents a radical departure from foreign policy as it has been practiced for more than a millennium. But looked at from the long perspective, foreign policy as usual has not succeeded in either reducing tension or ending war. The persistent undercurrent of feeling in the United States and elsewhere within the Western alliance after the end of the cold war is a vague but real sense of malaise that is occasionally reflected in this question: How come we don't feel good because we won? The easy answers are that helping our old foes back on their feet is costly both emotionally and economically and, besides, the world is in recession and there are plenty of problems to worry about at home.

But that misses the underlying problem. Foreign policy as usual— realpolitik as practiced by statesmen from Julius Caesar to Klemens Metternich to Henry Kissinger—is becoming not only irrelevant but dangerously counterproductive. We don't feel good because on some subliminal level we understand that yet again we haven't really won at all. Blood, deep psychic involvement, and a vast amount of treasure were spent to eliminate one danger only to have it replaced by an even greater one. A single ideological opponent has vanished. But in its place there are multiple atomic snakes that we armed and that are fully prepared to destroy each other, and us in the process, for reasons that are irrational and culturally unfathomable to us.

The Department of Defense's reflexive reaction is to draw a bead on new, multiple targets. The general in charge of the U.S. Strategic Command, for example, takes it upon himself to build and test computer models that would enable the United States to aim nuclear weapons at threatening Third World nations. "Deterrence may not work in the old Soviet-American terms," General Lee Butler said, "but I'm convinced that having nuclear weapons still matters." That sentiment was shared by those of his comrades in arms who wanted to resume nuclear weapons testing, in the process breaking a test moratorium with Moscow and sending a clear message to the proliferators that their goal was legitimate. They wanted to begin testing "mini-nukes" and developing a base of 3,500 new targets, they let it be known, as a way of scaring, not the Russians, but Third World nations. Unlike an attack by their former foe, however, they may never even know where a Third World attack has come from.

Traditional foreign policy and military strategy have become anachronistic because armed alliances, economic zones, and distinct regional imperatives are melting into a common political environment that is becoming as indivisible as the natural one. The United States, Canada, western Europe, and far-flung bastions like Australia and New Zealand are now in it for keeps with China, Japan, India, Pakistan, Iran, Brazil, and even with Armenia, Bosnia, and Azerbaijan. As every dwelling in the "global village" is vulnerable to deadly pandemics like AIDS, so can it be targeted for atomic annihilation. And there is no place to hide. Mutual trust must therefore replace mutual assured destruction everywhere, just as it has between the old cold war antagonists, or a cataclysm must sooner or later follow. This is no longer utopian idealism. It is a matter of life and death.

# APPENDIX 1:

# NUCLEAR FLASHPOINTS

**June 1967:** Israel arms its first two nuclear weapons at Rafael, following an Egyptian reconaissance run over Dimona the day before.

**October 8, 1973:** As Syrian and Egyptian troops approach Israel proper, Israel orders its arsenal of twenty nuclear weapons on alert for possible use against military headquarters in Damascus and Cairo.

**May 1974:** India detonates its first nuclear explosive device.

**October 14–21, 1984:** Pakistan and India threaten each other's nuclear facilities with conventional attacks. Indian nuclear forces on alert.

**January 1987:** Pakistan and India again near war, with Pakistan using this crisis to cold-test its nuclear device to ensure that it will work against India. Indian nuclear forces on alert.

**November 1987:** South Africa, following a defeat at the hands of Angolan-Cuban forces, orders its nuclear test range at Vastrap to be restarted in anticipation of a test of an atomic bomb.

**May 15–20, 1990:** Pakistan and India again near war, with Pakistan assembling its first two nuclear weapons for use against India. Later, it assembles five others. Indian nuclear forces on alert.

**January 17, 1991:** Israel puts its nuclear forces on alert for the third time during a war, this time after Iraq attacks Tel Aviv and Haifa with Scuds.

# APPENDIX 2:
# THIRD WORLD WEAPONS
# DEVELOPMENTS

**THIRD WORLD NATIONS POSSESSING NUCLEAR WEAPONS**

| | | | |
|---|---|---|---|
| Ukraine | China | Belarus | Pakistan |
| Kazakhstan | Israel | India | North Korea |

**THIRD WORLD NATIONS PURSUING NUCLEAR WEAPONS**

| | |
|---|---|
| Iran | Libya |
| Iraq | Algeria |

**THIRD WORLD NATIONS WITH QUIESCENT NUCLEAR PROGRAMS**

| | |
|---|---|
| Argentina | Brazil |
| South Africa | South Korea |

**THIRD WORLD NATIONS WATCHED FOR NUCLEAR WEAPONS DEVELOPMENT**

Egypt
Indonesia

## THIRD WORLD NATIONS WITH CHEMICAL WEAPONS PROGRAMS

| | | |
|---|---|---|
| Iran | Pakistan | South Africa |
| Iraq | India | Vietnam |
| Syria | China | Yugoslavia [Serbia] |
| Israel | Burma | Cuba |
| Egypt | Taiwan | Chile |
| Libya | North Korea | Romania |

## THIRD WORLD NATIONS WITH BIOLOGICAL WEAPONS CAPABILITY

| | | | |
|---|---|---|---|
| China | Syria | Pakistan | Libya |
| Iraq | Egypt | Taiwan | North Korea |
| Iran | India | South Africa | Cuba |
| Israel | | | |

## THIRD WORLD NATIONS WITH BALLISTIC MISSILE CAPABILITY

| | | | |
|---|---|---|---|
| China | Iran | Syria | India |
| South Korea | Argentina | Ukraine | Pakistan |
| Iraq | Egypt | Israel | North Korea |
| Brazil | Libya | Yugoslavia [Serbia] | Kazakhstan |

# NOTES

## 1. Iraq: Lawrence of Arabia Meets Dr. Strangelove

**High-prestige:** Derek Boothby in "The Hunt for Saddam's Secret Weapons," "Nova," WNET, January 12, 1993.

**DIA analysts:** "Intelligence Successes and Failures in Operations Desert Shield/Storm," U.S. House of Representatives, Committee on Armed Services, August 1993, p. 35.

**Kay and plutonium production:** A talk Kay gave to the Program of Non-Proliferation Studies at the Monterey Institute of International Studies, Monterey, California, on February 10, 1993.

**The first attack on Tuwaitha:** "F-117 Pilots, Generals Tell Congress About Stealth's Value in Gulf War," *Aviation Week & Space Technology*, May 6, 1991, p. 66.

**The F-117A raid:** Ibid.

**Pentagon overestimates and the flatbeds:** From a highly knowledgeable source who spoke on condition of anonymity.

**Sharing satellite intelligence:** "Democrats Press C.I.A. Nominee on Giving Iraq Secrets About Iran," *The New York Times*, September 18, 1991.

**Horner:** "Iraqi Nuclear Weapons Capability Still Intact," *Aviation Week & Space Technology*, July 1, 1991, p. 23.

**Gates:** From the transcript of his remarks before the Comstock Club, Sacramento, on December 15, 1992. The address was titled "Weapons Proliferation: The Most Dangerous Challenge for American Intelligence."

**Kay's figure** is from his paper, "The IAEA—How Can It Be Strengthened?" presented at the Woodrow Wilson Center conference December 12, 1992, on "Nuclear Proliferation in the 1990s: Challenges and Opportunities," p. 2.

**Kay's fifteen nukes a year:** From Windrem's interview with him in November 1992.

**Information on the entire enterprise** is from Jay C. Davis and David A. Kay, "Iraq's Secret Nuclear Weapons Program," *Physics Today*, July 1992, p. 21.

**Kay's accolade:** From a Windrem interview, March 5, 1992.

**"Ragheads":** From an interview with a Pentagon official on June 23, 1991.

**All the documents,** including Lawrence's, are reported in "How Iraq Reverse-Engineered the Bomb," *IEEE Spectrum*, April 1992, p. 64.

**The Jafar family background:** From Windrem interviews with David Kay and Hamid Jafar. There were several interviews with Kay. The Hamid interviews were February 29 and March 2, 1992.

**Jafar's time in London:** "Il Dottor Stranamore abita a Bagdad," *Corriere della Serra*, September 30, 1991 (translated by the author, Claudio Gatti).

**Geneva visit:** Ibid.

**Harwell information** is from the first interview with Hamid. Jafar's access to the calutron is noted by a source who requested anonymity.

**"Mechanism"** is from a top-secret report, "Al-Atheer Plant Progress Report for the Period from 1 January 1990 to 31 May 1990," Ministry of Industry and Military Industrialization, Petrochemical Project-3, p. 6. The report was translated into English by the United Nations and constituted the annex of the IAEA's "First Report on the Sixth IAEA On-Site Inspection in Iraq Under Security Resolution 687 (1991), 22–30 September 1991," and was released on October 8, 1991.

**Jafar's life-style and experience at the Imperial College:** "Il Dottor Stranamore abita a Bagdad."

**Recruiting drive:** "Saddam's Nuclear Weapons Dream: A Lingering Nightmare," *The Washington Post*, October 13, 1991.

**Saddam's trip to France:** Steve Weissman and Herbert Krosney, *The Islamic Bomb*, New York: Times Books, 1982, p. 93.

**"first Arab attempt":** Ibid., p. 249.

**Sharistani:** *The Islamic Bomb*, pp. 252–55; "Il Dottor Stranamore abita a Bagdad"; and an internal memorandum from Kroll Associates titled "Jafar Dhia Jafar."

**The reactor attack:** *The Islamic Bomb*, pp. 5–7.

**Sharistani's arrest:** *The Islamic Bomb*, p. 252.

**Sharistani in jail and the offer:** "Il Dottor Stranamore abita a Bagdad."

**The capitulation:** Ibid.

**Partying Kuwaitis:** February 1, 1991, interview with an Egyptian who studied there at the time.

**Sami Arajj:** Windrem interview with David Kay in Washington on May 18, 1993.

**Saclay:** Kenneth Timmerman, *The Death Lobby: How the West Armed Iraq*, Boston: Houghton Mifflin, 1991.

**The fate of defectors:** David Kay, "Iraqi Inspections: Lessons Learned," *Eye on Supply*, No. 8, Winter 1993, p. 93.

**Meshed's recruitment:** Timmerman, *The Death Lobby*.

**Meshed's and the prostitute's murder and the Techint explosions:** *The Death Lobby*, pp. 69–70, and *The Islamic Bomb*, pp. 239–43.

**Saddam's continuing pursuit:** *The Death Lobby*, pp. 103–4.

**Deceiving the IAEA:** "Saddam's Nuclear Weapons Dream: A Lingering Nightmare."

**Saddam's proliferation statement:** The Iraqi Atomic Energy Commission's annual report, 1982–83, unnumbered page in the appendix.

**Jafar's boast:** "Saddam's Nuclear Weapons Dream: A Lingering Nightmare."

**The underground reactor:** Interview with David Kay, May 18, 1993.

**The French role in providing precursor chemicals:** Thomas Whiteside, "The Yellow Rain Complex—II," *The New Yorker*, February 18, 1991, p. 67.

**Camouflaged buildings:** "Iraq's Secret A-Arms Effort: Grim Lessons for the World," *The Washington Post*, August 11, 1991, and "Saddam's Nuclear Weapons Dream: A Lingering Nightmare."

**The Yugoslav connection:** "Saddam's Secret Bomb," *U.S. News & World Report*, November 25, 1991, pp. 38 and 40. The light fence is reported in Glenn Zorpette, "How Iraq Reverse-Engineered the Bomb," *IEEE Spectrum*, April 1992, p. 20.

**Transformers:** "Saddam's Secret Bomb," *U.S. News & World Report*, November 25, 1991, p. 36.

**Bar codes:** Davis and Kay, "Iraq's Secret Nuclear Weapons Program," p. 25.

**Construction equipment:** From an interview with von Wedel and from his unpublished manuscript, *From the Gates of Babylon to the Gates of Hell*. A source on the House Banking Committee confirms von Wedel's account.

**Twenty bombs a year:** Kay's talk at Monterey on February 10, 1993.

**Modem:** Ibid.

**Al Atheer:** Tim Ripley, "Iraq's Nuclear Weapons Programme," *Jane's Intelligence Review*, December 1992, p. 554, and Davis and Kay, "Iraq's Secret Nuclear Weapons Program," pp. 26–27.

**Kay's remarks** are from one of the interviews.

**Internet and the modems:** The Windrem interview with David Kay on May 18, 1993.

**Kolb:** "Germans Arrested on Iraqi Exports," *The New York Times*, August 18, 1990; also Robert Windrem, "Iraq's Most Lethal Weapons," *Popular Science*, February 1991, p. 55.

**Al Multhanna production rates** were deduced by W. Seth Carus based on data made publicly available by William H. Webster to the Senate Committee on Government Affairs on February 9, 1989. (See Carus's monograph, *The Genie Unleashed: Iraq's Chemical and Biological Weapons Production*, Washington: The Washington Institute for Near East Policy, 1989, p. 8.)

**The figure for Iranian chemical weapon casualties** is widely quoted. See, for example, Carus's *The Genie Unleashed: Iraq's Chemical and Biological Weapons Production*, p. 3. Barzani's complaint is from "U.S. Says It Monitored Iraqi Messages on Gas," *The New York Times*, September 15, 1988.

**Horner's gas testimony:** "F-117 Pilots, Generals Tell Congress About Stealth's Value in Gulf War," *Aviation Week & Space Technology*, May 6, 1991, p. 66.

**The U.N. at Al Taqqadum:** "Annex, Report by the Executive Chairman of the Special Commission Established by the Secretary-General Pursuant to Paragraph 9 (b) (i) of Security Council Resolution 687 (1991)," pp. 26–27.

**The German firms** were listed in "Germans Arrested on Iraqi Exports," *The New York Times*, August 18, 1990.

**Hussein's warning to Israel:** "Iraq Chief, Boasting of Poison Gas, Warns of Disaster if Israelis Strike," *The New York Times*, April 3, 1990.

**Care in bombing:** "Iraqi Nuclear Weapons Capability Still Intact," *Aviation Week & Space Technology*, July 1, 1991, p. 23.

**The biological agents** are from the "Report by the Executive Chairman of the Special Commission," p. 30. Their effects were described by Dr. Eileen Choffnes, a staff member of the U.S. Government Affairs Committee in an interview with Windrem on January 22, 1993.

**The two orders** are from a packet of materials that were attached to a letter sent by Human Rights Watch to Rolf Ekeus, Chairman of the U.N. Special Commission on Iraq, on December 29, 1992.

The number of weapons in the Iraqi CW arsenal is from an address by CIA Director Robert M. Gates, "Weapons Proliferation: The Most Dangerous Challenge for American Intelligence," delivered to the Comstock Club, Sacramento, California, December 15, 1992.

**Malkian's response:** " 'I Was Sure It Was Chemical Weapons and That I Was Dead,' " *The New York Times*, January 19, 1991.

**Terrorist activities:** "Arms Control: U.S. and International Efforts to Ban Biological Weapons," U.S. EAO report, EAO/NSIAD-93-113, December 23, 1992, pp. 55–56.

**Application-specific:** A report, "Foreign Supplies to the Iraqi Nuclear Programme," written by the IAEA's Eighth Inspection Team on December 11, 1991.

**Leybold Heraeus through Du Pont:** Ibid.

**The three German and one French firm:** The IAEA Board of Governors, "Report on the Thirteenth IAEA On-Site Inspection in Iraq Under Security Council Resolution 687 (1991), 14–21 July 1992," August 17, 1992.

**Brazil's sales under the table:** Gary Milhollin and Diana Edensword, "Saddam's Nuclear Army," Washington: The Wisconsin Project on Nuclear Arms Control, July 18, 1993, pp. 2–5.

**Piva's influence:** From a highly knowledgeable source who requested anonymity. His remarks are from "An Interview with General Hugo Piva," *Veja* (São Paolo), January 20, 1993.

**Leading off the trail:** "Iraqi Inspections: Lessons Learned," p. 98.

**Defector:** "Iraqi Nuclear Installations," a news report on National Public Radio which aired on June 3, 1991.

**FOIA and "all my life":** "The Hunt for Saddam's Secret Weapons."

**Shot bullets:** "Report by the Executive Chairman of the Special Commission," p. 8.

**The water tower and chase:** Leslie Thorne, "IAEA Nuclear Inspections in Iraq," *IAEA Bulletin*, Vol. 34, No. 1, 1992, p. 20, and "The Hunt for Saddam's Secret Weapons."

**Wood's statement:** "Saddam's Secret Bomb," p. 38.

**Boothby:** "The Hunt for Saddam's Secret Weapons."

**"We've found it" and 20,000:** "The Hunt for Saddam's Secret Weapons."

**Jafar's "historic document" remarks:** An IAEA videotape of the confrontation made on September 23. The personnel plea is also from IAEA tape as it appeared on "The Hunt for Saddam's Secret Weapons."

**The importance of the documents:** "First report on the Sixth IAEA On-Site Inspection in Iraq Under Security Council Resolution 687 (1991), 22–30 September 1991," released on October 8, 1991, and subsequently called "First Report."

**Al Atheer's bomb progress:** Ministry of Industry and Military Industrialization, Petrochemical Project-3, "Al Atheer Plant Progress Report for the Period from 1 January 1990 to 31 May 1990," Number 172S/697, 11 November 1990.

**Obtaining software:** "Nuclear Proliferation" hearings, House Energy and Commerce Committee's Oversight Committee, April 24, 1991.

**Twenty bombs a year:** "The Hunt for Saddam's Secret Weapons."

**Twelve to eighteen months:** Kay, as reported on "The Business of the Bomb," "Adam Smith's Money World," WNET, January 14, 1993.

**In place and on the payroll:** "Iraqi Inspections: Lessons Learned," p. 98.

**Microfilm:** Ibid. Kay maintained that he saw some of it.

**The open question:** "First Report," p. 4.

**"We now have the capability":** "Saddam's Secret Bomb," p. 42.


## 2. PAKISTAN: A HORRIBLE EXAMPLE

**Bhutto's meeting with Rafsanjani, Beg's offer, and the events of June 1990:** From multiple interviews with highly knowledgeable sources and participants who did not wish to be identified.

**Ishaq Khan's role in the execution of her father:** Peter Truell and Larry Gurwin, *False Profits*, Boston: Houghton Mifflin, 1992, p. 82.

**The 1,000-year threat:** "Another India-Pakistan War Is Building," *The Wall Street Journal*, May 24, 1990. The $5 million appropriation: Leonard S. Spector, "India-Pakistan War: It Could Be Nuclear," *The New York Times*, June 6, 1990.

**"I think it's criminal":** Benazir Bhutto interview with Windrem and Fred Francis on September 11, 1992, in Islamabad.

**The suitcase:** "Gorbachev Lost Nuclear Control, Russians Report," *The New York Times*, August 23, 1992.

**Oakley's warning:** From highly knowledgeable sources who did not wish to be identified.

**The $250 million in computers:** U.S. Department of Commerce document, "Approved Applications to Pakistan Closed Out 10/01/86 Through 10/16/90," *Exports and Reexports*, pp. 1 and 2.

**Computers and other equipment:** "Approved Applications," pp. 1 and 2. Congressional investigators: Windrem interview in November 1992 with a congressional investigator who wished to remain anonymous.

**Bhutto's three requests:** Interview with one of her aides on March 23, 1993.

**Bhutto's discourse with Ishaq Khan and Beg:** The interview with her.

**"Nuclear coup":** A highly informed source who did not wish to be identified.

**Poverty statistics** are from the United Nations Human Development Report, 1992, and *The New Book of World Rankings*, 3rd ed., 1991, as provided by Sen. John Glenn in testimony on "U.S./Pakistan Nuclear Issues" before the U.S. Senate Foreign Relations Committee on July 30, 1991, and hereafter referred to as the Glenn testimony.

**"Substantial amount of time":** Jeffrey T. Richelson, *The U.S. Intelligence Community*, 2nd ed., Cambridge: Ballinger, 1989, p. 242.

**The weapons test cooperation:** Declassified DIA "Incoming Message," of June 19, 1991, and titled "Pakistan Use of Chinese Nuclear Weapons Test Facilities," p. 1. This was confirmed by a Russian nuclear weapons scientist who spoke with the understanding that he would not be named.

**The 1993 reactor and centrifuge expansion projects:** "Pakistan to Boost Enrichment Plant," *Financial Times*, July 10, 1993.

**The $300 million:** An interview with Pakistani ambassador to the United States, Mrs. Abida Hussain, in September 1992. The number of missiles: "China Said to Sell Pakistan Dangerous New Missiles," *Los Angeles Times*, December 4, 1992. K-8s: "Karakoram K-8 Trainer Makes Air Show Debut," *Aviation Week & Space Technology*, March 9, 1992, pp. 42–45.

**"Horrible example":** Benazir Bhutto, *Daughter of the East*, London: Mandarin Paperbacks, 1989, p. 86.

**Anemic:** A background interview with a U.S. Department of State official on August 1, 1991.

**Airport installations and the equipment:** A report, "Pakistan—Basic Interpretation," by Christopher Larsson of the Stockholm-based Space Media Network. The accompanying satellite photographs are dated March 8, 1987.

**Accelerated nuclear program:** Glenn testimony.

**Pentagon assessment:** Ibid.

**High-level spy:** *The U.S. Intelligence Community*, p. 242.

**Beyond beyond reasonable doubt:** Interview with a knowledgeable CIA analyst on April 28, 1993.

**Buckley:** Glenn testimony.

**U.S. bomb analysis and the mock-up:** Gary Milhollin and Gerard White, "A New China Syndrome: Beijing's Atomic Bazaar," Outlook, *The Washington Post*, May 12, 1991.

**Casey's plan and the U.S. and Saudi contributions:** Mohammad Yousaf and Mark Adkin, *The Bear Trap: Afghanistan's Untold Story*, London: Leo Cooper, 1992, pp. 81–97, 189–90, and 192–93.

**Increasing concern and Chinese participation:** *Daughter of the East*, p. 258.

**White House reaction:** Windrem's interview with Glenn on October 14, 1992.

**Galbraith and Bhutto:** *Daughter of the East*, p. 258, and a highly knowledgeable source.

**Conciliatory and reference to material disappeared:** Ibid., p. 260.

**Cranston's remarks:** Sreedhar, *Pakistan's Bomb: A Documentary Study*, New Delhi: ABC Publishing House, 1986, p. 258.

**Casey's forays:** *The Bear Trap*, pp. 78–80.

**The number of people visiting the weapons labs:** U.S. Senate Government Affairs Committee report in October 1989. Thin shells: U.S. Department of Energy, Defense Programs, Office of International Security Affairs, "Technology Security," Vol. 1, March 1988.

**Bryen:** Windrem interview on September 1, 1992.

**Krytrons and x-rays:** Glenn testimony.

**NTG:** Cameron Binkley, "Twenty-four Foreign Firms Reported to Have Been Engaged in Illicit Nuclear Weapons-Related Trade," Monterey: Monterey Institute of International Studies, 1992, pp. 7–8.

**"Blind eye":** Interview of October 14, 1992.

**Critical mass and Zia's statement:** Glenn testimony.

**Khan admission:** Seymour M. Hersh, "On the Nuclear Edge," *The New Yorker*, March 29, 1993, p. 59.

**Beg's cold test:** "Pakistani Quoted as Citing Nuclear Test in '87," *The New York Times*, July 25, 1993. His denial was carried in the *Times* the next day ("Pakistani Denies A-Test").

**Attack and response:** *The Bear Trap*, pp. 189–206.

**Scowcroft:** Interview with the Bhutto aide.

**Oakley's advice:** From highly knowledgeable sources who wished to remain anonymous.

**Haft-2:** "Assessment of Pakistan's Missile Capability," *Missile Monitor*, No. 3, Spring 1993, pp. 4–11.

**Fragmentation:** "Afghanistan, Always Riven, Is Breaking into Ethnic Parts," *The New York Times*, January 17, 1993.

**Dispersed facilities:** Larsson's Space Media material; Leonard S. Spector, *Nuclear Ambitions*, Boulder: Westview Press, 1990, pp. 89–117.

**The 70-megawatt reactor:** Foreign Broadcast Information Service, JPRS Report, *Proliferation Issues: Russian Foreign Intelligence Service Report: Proliferation of Weapons of Mass Destruction*, April 28, 1993, p. 65.

**The 5 percent specification:** *Nuclear Ambitions*, p. 93.

**Mock-up:** "On the Nuclear Edge," p. 61.

**The meeting with Webster:** From highly knowledgeable sources who wished to remain anonymous.

**Bhutto's meeting with Bush** was described by a highly knowledgeable source who did not wish to be identified.

**Events in Kashmir:** From a high-ranking U.S. government intelligence official.

**Missiles:** Sarwar Naqvi, Minister and Deputy Chief of Pakistan's Mission to the United States, in an interview in December 1992.

**Indian military strength:** Col. Trevor N. Dupuy, *Future Wars*, New York: Warner Books, 1993, p. 57–58.

**The 100 figure** is from an interview with Gary Milhollin on December 1, 1992. The CIA estimate is from a State Department official interviewed on August 1, 1991.

**The Pakistani estimate** is from a highly knowledgeable source who did not wish to be named, and "Former Military Official on Nuclear Program," FBIS-NES-92-239, December 11, 1992, p. 57.

**Nuclear-capable F-16s and Barlow's dismissal:** "On the Nuclear Edge," pp. 71–72.

**C-130 atomic bombers:** "NBC Nightly News," December 1 and 2, 1992.

**NSA intercept:** "On the Nuclear Edge," p. 65.

**Satellite reconnaissance and the analyst's recollection:** Ibid., p. 65.

**Aim at Tarapur:** Ibid.

**Atomic bomb threat:** "Destroyer of Worlds," *Far Eastern Economic Review*, April 30, 1992, pp. 23–26.

**The Gates–Ishaq Khan–Beg meeting:** Ibid., p. 67.

**The Gates trip and its consequences:** From a highly knowledgeable source who did not wish to be named.

**The effect on Singh:** Shekhar Gupta with W.P.S. Sidhu and Kanwar Sandhu, "A Middle-Aged Military Machine," *India Today*, April 30, 1993, pp. 22–30.

**Most dangerous nuclear situation:** "On the Nuclear Edge," p. 56.

**The seven-bomb story** was broken by NBC News in a two-part series on December 1 and 2, 1992. Two days later, the *Los Angeles Times* broke the news of the M-11 delivery. The bomb and missile stories provoked a debate in the Indian parliament which included calls for war by Hindu nationalists.

**Mrs. Hussain:** Windrem interview in September 1992.

**The two efforts to explain away the bomb:** "Pakistan Tells of Its A-Bomb Capacity," *The New York Times*, February 8, 1992.

**India's position:** From an interview with an Indian diplomat on September 4, 1992. He wished to remain anonymous.

**India's upgraded weapons program:** Windrem interview with a Department of State official on September 4, 1992. He wished to remain anonymous.

**Fighter and aircraft carrier capability:** U.S. intelligence source.

**"They lied to us!":** Windrem interviews with Pressler and Glenn on October 14, 1992.

**Rafsanjani's courting of Ishaq Khan** could be confirmed neither by U.S. intelligence sources nor by the People's Mojahedin.

**Iran and the defense bill:** "The Temptation of Pakistan," *Foreign Report (The Economist)*, March 25, 1993, p. 1.


## 3. A BEWILDERING VARIETY OF POISONOUS SNAKES

**Kalam's "flower" remark:** "Agni: Chariot of Fire," *India Today*, June 15, 1989, p. 12.

**Agni's potential targets:** Ibid., p. 10.

**The dream war:** "India Enters the Missile Age," *Sunday*, March 13–19, 1988, p. 35.

**Soviet tactical nuclear missiles in Cuba:** "Fidel Castro's Theater of Now," *The New York Times* Op-Ed Page, January 20, 1992.

**Cruise missiles:** "Cruise Missiles Becoming Top Proliferation Threat," *Aviation Week & Space Technology*, February 1, 1993, p. 26.

**The indigenous quote** is from "Agni: Chariot of Fire," p. 10.

**The missile expert** was Sidney Graybeal, who made the statement in a discussion with Burrows in Chicago on February 6, 1992. NASA's willingness to sell the launch vehicle is also mentioned in Gary Milhollin, "India's Missiles—with a Little Help from Our Friends," *The Bulletin of the Atomic Scientists*, November 1989, p. 32.

**The sharp reaction to the Agni test and the technology sale episode:** Janne E. Nolan, *Trappings of Power: Ballistic Missiles in the Third World*, Washington: The Brookings Institution, 1991, pp. 1–2.

**The State Department computer and microchip memo:** "State Department Munitions Control Investigation Summary," May 22, 1989. It was written to Assistant Special Agent Scott Tripp from Case Agents Richard Drangstveit and Claude Nebel.

**The French and German contributions:** Milhollin's "India's Missiles—with a Little Help from Our Friends," pp. 32 and 34.

**PSLV:** Raj Chengappa, "Joining the Big Boys," *India Today*, April 15, 1993, pp. 56–58. The article's subtitle is "With PSLV, India is poised to enter the superpower club for space launchers."

**ABR 200 (I):** "Indians Test Air-Breathing Engine," *Space News*, February 22–28, 1993, p. 7.

**Rao's remark:** "ISRO's Rao Shrugs Off U.S. Space Trade Ban," *Space News*, February 22–28, 1993, p. 7. "Big boys" is from "Joining the Big Boys," p. 56.

**Rafsanjani's remark:** "U.S. Nuclear Technology Tactics Vex Iran," *The New York Times*, November 18, 1991.

**Long-range ballistic missiles and their capabilities:** Nolan's *Trappings of Power*, pp. 66 and 68–69. Also see Duncan Lennox, "The Global Proliferation of Ballistic Missiles," *Jane's Defence Weekly*, December 23, 1989, pp. 1384–85; James Bruce, "The Middle

East Missile Race," *Jane's Defence Weekly*, April 1, 1989, p. 553; and Janne E. Nolan and Albert D. Wheelon, "Third World Ballistic Missiles," *Scientific American*, August 1990, pp. 34–40. The H-2 is described in some detail in Craig Covault, "Japan Forging Aggressive Space Development Pace," "Japan's New H-2 Launch Site Rivals Largest U.S., European Facilities," and "Mitsubishi Leads Privatization Effort as First H-2 Boosters Are Fabricated," *Aviation Week & Space Technology*, August 13, 1990, pp. 336–39; 341–44, and 362–64.

**Israel's A-bombs:** Seymour M. Hersh, *The Samson Option*, New York: Random House, 1991, p. 291.

**Western European reconnaissance:** "WEU Study Group Envisions Spy Satellite Program," *Space News*, February 1–7, 1993, p. 3.

**Material on chemical weapons,** submarines, space reconnaissance, and tactical and antiship missiles is from testimony given by Rear Admiral Thomas A. Brooks, Director of Naval Intelligence, to the Seapower, Strategic, and Critical Materials Subcommittee of the House Armed Services Committee on Intelligence, March 7, 1991. The 121-nation figure is from "Cruise Missiles Becoming Top Proliferation Threat."

**The Israeli F-4s:** Hersh, *The Samson Option*, p. 216.

**Conventional arms exports and imports:** Alfred Rosenblatt, "Grappling with the Arms Trade," *IEEE Spectrum*, September 1991, p. 60.

**The cost of Rabta** is from a U.S. intelligence source. The Algerian figure is from a Chinese source that did not wish to be identified. Iraq's expenditures are from the U.N. Special Commission. Indonesia's is from *Energy and Technology Review*, April 1983. Argentina's is from interviews with U.S. officials, Lawrence Livermore National Labs, May 1990. Brazil's is from a paper delivered at a University of Maryland conference by Fernando da Souza, "Non-Proliferation and the Press," May 5, 1991, pp. 4–6.

**Poisonous snakes:** "C.I.A. Nominee Wary of Budget Cuts," *The New York Times*, February 3, 1993.

**The new modes adopted** by arms sellers in the 1980s were outlined by Andrew L. Ross, a professor at the U.S. Naval War College, in a paper, "The Political Economy of the Arms Market," presented on February 6, 1992, at the American Association for the Advancement of Science annual meeting.

**The benefits from arms trade:** Ibid.

**Saddam's haggling** over avionics is well told by Kenneth R. Timmerman in *The Death Lobby: How the West Armed Iraq*, Boston: Houghton Mifflin, 1991, p. 31.

**South African sale:** Ronald Walters, *South Africa and the Bomb*, New York: Lexington Press, 1987, p. 131.

**Pakistani sale:** S. Chandrashekar, "An Assessment of Pakistan's Missile Capability," *Missile Monitor*, Spring 1993, p. 4.

**Aerospatiale's ad** ran in *Aviation Week & Space Technology*, May 27, 1991, pp. 64–65. Thomson CSF's ad also ran in the magazine (February 24, 1992, pp. 8–9, to take only one example).

**Thomson CSF's contribution to Iraq:** Timmerman, *The Death Lobby*, pp. 212–14 and 336–37.

**The list of French military and civilian projects,** and the quote from *Le Monde*, are from Timmerman's *The Death Lobby*, p. 32.

**Kalam's statement:** "An Embargo Cannot Throttle Us," *Frontline*, June 10–23, 1989, p. 10.

**Brazil's overcommitment and subsequent problem:** From a highly knowledgeable source who spoke on condition of anonymity.

**The Brazilian firm Engasa** is described in Timmerman's *The Death Lobby*, pp. 43, 180, and 290.

**Avibras:** U.S. Congress, Office of Technology Assessment, *Global Arms Trade*, OTA-ISC-460, Washington, D.C.: U.S. Government Printing Office, June 1991, p. 149.

**The Iranian Scud purchase:** Timmerman, *The Death Lobby*, p. 288.

**The existence of Scud D:** Testimony given by Central Intelligence Agency Director Robert M. Gates to the Senate Governmental Affairs Committee on January 15, 1992.

**China's attitude** about nonproliferation was articulated by Ralph Cossa of the National Defense University's Institute for National Strategic Studies in a paper, "Great-Power Political Realignment in Northeast Asia," presented on February 9, 1992, at the AAAS annual meeting in Chicago.

**A. Q. Khan's remark about bigotry:** Sreedhar, *Pakistan's Bomb: A Documentary Study,* New Delhi: ABC Publishing House, 1986, pp. 185–86.

**Malkani and deployment:** "Demands Growing for an India That's Truly Hindu," *The New York Times,* January 24, 1993.

**The NPT and the worries of Third World signatories:** *Arms Control and Disarmament Agreements,* Washington: United States Arms Control and Disarmament Agency, August 1980, p. 86.

**The congressional witnesses** were quoted in "Germans Accused of Exporting Arms," *The New York Times,* May 3, 1989.

**Qaddafi's dream,** which he claimed to have abandoned in order to maintain good relations with Greece, is from "Qaddafi Tells of Plan to Attack U.S. Bases," *The New York Times,* May 8, 1990.

**The French missile transfer:** "French Missile Technology May Land in Libya," *The Washington Times,* July 18, 1989.

**Article VI of the NPT:** Ashok Kapur, "Dump the Treaty," *Bulletin of the Atomic Scientists,* July/August 1990, p. 22.

**The forcing of missile buyers** to go to Third World suppliers is mentioned in "Missile Proliferaton Survey of Emerging Missile Forces," No. 88-642F (revised), Washington: Congressional Research Service, February 9, 1989, p. CRS-4.

**The Indian editorial:** "Significance of Agni," *Frontline,* June 10–23, 1989.

**The Russians in Algeria and Libya:** "Nuclear Emigres Work in Libya," *The Washington Times,* February 24, 1992. This was conformed by U.S. intelligence officials. The Russians had worked in the nuclear weapons program for more than three decades. North Korea and China: From a Burrows interview with a highly knowledgeable Russian. The Russian government made some effort to curtail the exodus, but with limited effect. See, for example, "MSR Recommends Secret Carriers Stay at Their Places," *Izvestia,* December 21, 1992. The article reported that thirty-six Russian nuclear scientists headed for North Korea were "detained" at the Moscow Airport on their way to Pyongyang. It said the scientists had been promised the equivalent of $3,000 a month for their work. (The MSR succeeded the KGB.)

**Kay had by then left the IAEA** and was working for the London-based Uranium Institute, an industry organization. ("Arms Experts Fear Nuclear Blackmail," *Aviation Week & Space Technology,* January 4, 1993, pp. 61–62.)

**Dr. Harvey R. Colten** is a leading immunologist and head of Children's Hospital in St. Louis.

**The interview with Segla:** "Farewell to Arms?" "MacNeil/Lehrer News Hour," Public Broadcasting System, October 28, 1991.

**The tighter German laws:** "Germany Acts to Curb Arms Exports," *The New York Times,* January 24, 1992.

**Bush's arms control proposal:** "Bush Unveils Plan for Arms Control in the Middle East," *The New York Times,* May 30, 1991. Also see "Cheney Says U.S. Plans New Arms Sales to the Middle East," *The New York Times,* June 5, 1991.

**The Saudi fighter order:** "NBC Nightly News," February 24, 1992.

**Power to superpower:** "China Builds Its Military Muscle, Making Some Neighbors Nervous," *The New York Times,* January 11, 1993.

**The end of sanctions against China:** "U.S. Lifts Its Sanctions on China Over High-Technology Transfers," *The New York Times,* February 22, 1992.

**The *Times*'s observation:** "Beyond Start II: A New Level of Instability," *The New York Times,* January 10, 1993.

## 4. "Shop Till You Drop"

**The picture scene:** Paul von Wedel, *From the Gates of Babylon to the Gates of Hell*, an unpublished manuscript, p. 79, and hereafter referred to as von Wedel.

**"Aid procurement and to report on":** Secret British Foreign and Commonwealth document, "PQs on Iraqi Procurement," November 9, 1989.

**Funding:** United States District Court for the Northern District of Georgia, Atlanta Division, *United States of America v. Christopher P. Drogoul et al.*, February 28, 1991, p. 33.

**Electrical usage:** Interviews with intelligence and congressional sources in October 1990 for Sa'ad-16 and November 1992 for Ash Sharqat.

**More than 65 percent:** *U.S. v. Christopher P. Drogoul et al.* sentencing memorandum, p. 7.

**BNL data:** Frederick B. Lacey, Banca Nazionale del Lavoro, "Report of the Independent Counsel," Part 1, December 8, 1992, p. 17, and hereafter called the Lacey report.

**Initial permission from Rome:** United States District Court for the Northern District of Georgia, Atlanta Division, *U.S. v. Christopher P. Drogoul et al.*, February 28, 1991, p. 8. That was the day the war for Kuwait ended.

**Medium-term loans:** *U.S. v. Christopher P. Drogoul*, passim.

**The cost of Ash Sharqat:** Jay C. Davis and David A. Kay, "Iraq's Secret Nuclear Weapons Program," *Physics Today*, July 1992, p. 23.

**Badush's cost:** "Iraq—Low-bidder for Dam Construction," *Middle East Economic Digest*, September 28, 1985, p. 13.

**Automobile industry:** "Schools Brief," *The Economist*, January 23–29, 1993, p. 80.

**Costs, including the Olympics:** "Proposed Major Iraqi Projects," *Middle East Executive Reports*, May 1989, p. 17.

**Necklace:** *U.S. v. Christopher P. Drogoul et al.*, p. 53. Von Wedel noted that he had seen New and Drogoul "necking" in the branch's parking lot (von Wedel). New's role is from the Lacey report, pp. 20–21.

**GI Joe watch:** von Wedel, p. 21.

**Babil's articles of incorporation,** updated to January 11, 1991, were translated by the Congressional Research Service. Pierre Drogoul's activities and the interest they aroused by French intelligence are from "Saddam in France," *Mednews*, August 3, 1992, p. 4.

**The financial arrangement between father and son:** United States District Court for the Northern District of Georgia, *U.S. v. Christopher P. Drogoul*, Government's Sentencing Memorandum, No. 1:91-CR-078-01-MHS, September 11, 1992, pp. 45–46.

**German intelligence:** German intelligence document, April 5, 1990, "Iraq Activities in the Area of . . . ," p. 6.

**GM:** von Wedel, p. 80.

**Pushing on the plane:** Kenneth Cline, "Lavoro Bank Scandal: The Inside Story," *Southern Banker*, June 1990, p. 21.

**Hussein Kamel:** von Wedel, p. 82.

**The tour of Nasser:** von Wedel, p. 83.

**Alphajet:** Kenneth R. Timmerman, *The Death Lobby*, Boston: Houghton Mifflin, 1991, p. 333.

**The car scene:** von Wedel, p. 90. Von Wedel also described the scene to Windrem in an October 1990 interview.

**The displays:** "Iraq to Build Own Jets, Says Minister," *The Baghdad Observer*, April 28, 1989.

**Hamid's remarks:** Telephone interview with Windrem on February 29, 1992.

**Terms of the Crescent agreement:** an analysis done by MRC Oil Division of Oxford, England, dated March 9, 1992, and provided to Windrem.

**Hamid's knowing about his brother's work:** Ibid.

**The projected Fina deal:** "Company with Ties to Iraq Military Tried to Buy Fina," *Oil Express*, March 16, 1992, pp. 4–5; "J.C. Penney Business Services Inc. Has Signed

Fina Inc. to a Six-Year Credit Card Processing Contract," *CardFax*, September 16, 1991.

**The gold-plated pistol:** Letter from A. M. D. Willis and J. P. Carver, Clifford Chance Law Firm, to Allan George, dated February 3, 1992.

**The letters of credit:** *U.S. v. Christopher P. Drogoul*, passim, and interviews.

**Thompson CSF:** "Machine Tool Review," an IAEA report on machine tools found in the Iraqi nuclear weapons plants, dated June 15, 1992.

**The 2,500 letters:** "The Arming of Iraq," "Frontline," PBS, Autumn/Winter 1990, and based on an interview with Alan Friedman of the *Financial Times*.

**The bust:** Kenneth Cline, "Scandal in Atlanta: Secret Loans to Iraq," *American Banker*, August 8, 1992, p. 12.

**Von Wedel's home:** Kenneth Cline, "Lavoro Bank Scandal: The Inside Story," *Southern Banker*, June 1990, p. 6.

**The meeting in London:** Lacey report, pp. 38–39.

**The firing and his clearing of New York and Rome:** Ibid., pp. 39 and 77–80, respectively.

**The charges** are from *U.S. v. Christopher P. Drogoul*, passim.

**Machine tool use:** "Machine Tool Review," an IAEA report of June 15, 1992.

**Waldegrave and Young:** "Matrix-Churchill: Export of Lathe Equipment to Iraq," a secret UK "Eyes Only" memorandum from J. R. Young, Middle East Department, Foreign & Commercial Office, London, and a cover letter from N. K. Darroch, personal secretary to William Waldegrave, both dated February 6, 1989.

**SNEC:** "SNEC Cases of Interest," a secret internal memorandum from the Bureau of Oceans and International Environmental and Scientific Affairs, Department of State, November 21, 1989, pp. 1–3.

**Baker, Eagleburger, and the CCC:** "As 'Iraqgate' Unfolds, New Evidence Raises Questions of Cover-Up," *The Wall Street Journal*, October 9, 1992.

**Shoob:** "Disillusioned With Government, Judge Is Thorn in Side of U.S. Prosecutors," *The New York Times*, October 9, 1992.

**Lacey's case:** Lacey report, pp. 77–82.

**A. Q. Khan's reception:** *Nucleonics Week*, August 29, 1991.

**Khan's expressions of gratitude:** Sreedhar, *Pakistan's Bomb: A Documentary Study*, New Delhi: ABC Publishing House, 1986, pp. 195 and 198–99.

**The Saudi-Contra deal:** "The Dirtiest Bank of All," *Time*, July 29, 1991, p. 45.

**"Have anybody killed":** Ibid., p. 45.

**Murder, rape:** Ibid.

**The sheiks' cuts and deals:** Memorandum by Joseph Bodansky, a consultant to the House Republican Task Force on Terrorism, sent to Rep. David McCullum in the summer of 1991.

**Zia's going to the hospital:** U.S. Congress, Committee on Foreign Relations, 102 Cong., 1st Sess., "The BCCI Affair," August 1, 1991, p. 26.

**The investigative report:** "BCCI Aided Nuclear Project," *The Guardian*, July 26, 1991.

**Khan's defense and the Houston three:** Ibid.

**Underwriting computers:** Mark Potts, Nicholas Kochan, and Robert Whittington, *Dirty Money: The Inside Story of BCCI, the World's Sleaziest Bank*, Washington: National Press Books, 1992, p. 173.

**Habib's letter of credit,** dated May 1, 1987, was HEB/1119/87. It in turn drew on BCCI, Leadinhall St., London.

**The secret Tikriti fund:** Kenneth R. Timmerman, *The Death Lobby*, Boston: Houghton Mifflin, 1991, p. 272.

**Brazil's and the other nations' foreign debts:** *World Development Report 1991: The Challenge of Development*, World Bank, New York: Oxford University Press, May 1991, Table 1, p. 244.

**Brazil's submarine program** is sketched in "The Political and Security Concerns That Drive the Nuclear Aspirations of the Near Nuclear States," a paper by Fernando de Souza

Barros, a Brazilian physicist, dated May 5, 1991. The admiral's quote, as repeated by Barros, appeared in the *Brazilian Navy Review*, January 1988.

**The VLS launcher and U.S. concern about it:** "Brazil Chafes at Missile Curbs," *Space News*, October 14–20, 1991.

**The nuclear program:** "Brazil Uncovers Plan by Military to Build Atom Bomb and Stops It," *The New York Times*, October 9, 1990.

**Bomb-grade enriched uranium:** Barros's paper, p. 5, where he states that by 1996 Brazil will easily be able to produce large quantities of the material.


## 5. DOCTORS OF DEATH

**Cardoen's morality remark:** Interview with Windrem in Santiago on March 28, 1990.

**The investigator,** who wished to remain anonymous, made the remark in January 1993 after an exhaustive investigation of Cardoen's and Bull's efforts on behalf of Iraq.

**Piva's role:** "The Bombs Barely Missed Brazilian Heads," *Jornal Do Brasil*, September 3, 1990, p. 34.

**The South Africa-Chile-Israel-Taiwan connection:** Windrem interview with Abdul Minty, Chairman of the Worldwide Campaign Against Apartheid, on June 4, 1990.

**Iraq's G-6 policy:** Ibid.

**The creation of Cardoen's empire:** Interview with Windrem on July 18, 1990.

**Cardoen's credit to Kennedy:** Interview of March 28, 1990.

**The cluster bomb figure:** Interview by Windrem on July 18, 1990.

**The $200 million figure:** News release by the United States Attorney for the Southern District of Florida dated April 3, 1992, which accompanied *United States of America v. Swissco Properties et al.*

**The April 7 factory** is described in detail in "How Minister Helped British Firms to Arm Saddam's Soldiers," *The Sunday Times* (London), December 2, 1990.

**Scrap metal:** "Nightline," ABC, September 13, 1991.

**The LTV steel deal:** Swissco memorandum to Cardoen signed by G. R. Sipp on July 13, 1988.

**Filling the helicopter vacuum:** Cardoen's sales brochure, "Cardoen 206L-III Attack Helicopter."

**Specifications for the 206L-III** are in the Cardoen brochure. Also see "Cardoen's Single-Place Bell 206L," *Rotor & Wing International*, May 1990, p. 6.

**The description of the civilian uses:** Interview of July 18, 1990.

**The agricultural aspect of the helicopter:** August 1990 Windrem interviews with the FAA officials charged with approving its airworthiness, as well as an interview with Cardoen in Santiago on March 28 of that year.

**Details of Moyle's murder:** "Bloodstains Give Lie to Claim That Briton's Death Was Suicide," *The Independent* (U.K.), May 27, 1990; "Missing Documents Add to Doubts on Journalist's Suicide," *The Times* (London), May 30, 1990; "Murder Most Foul?" *The Times* (London), May 30, 1990; "Chile Judges Say British Journalist Was Murdered," *The Sunday Times* (London), June 3, 1990.

**The Cardoen-Iraq-Moyle connection:** "Briton's 'Killing' Linked to Iraqi Arms Sale," *The Independent* (London), May 20, 1990. Also see David S. Harvey, "The Mysterious Case of a Chile-Iraq Arms Connection," *Armed Forces Journal International*, January 1991, pp. 37–38.

**Cluster bombs to Ethiopia:** An Agence France Presse story, "Chile-Ethiopia," October 12, 1990.

**The end of Ethiopian cluster bombs:** "Chile Halts Cluster Bomb Sales to Ethiopia," *The Financial Times*, October 21, 1990.

**The Pentagon report,** dated December 17, 1990, was "Cardoen Issues," prepared by DTSA's Technology Security Operations office for the U.S. Customs Service. See p. 21.

**Cardoen's Florida property** included the Angelica Gardens Development at Lakes of Avalon; the Royal Palm North Development, Lakes Plaza, and Swissco Corporate Center in Miami Lakes; the Victoria Lakes residential development in Pembroke Pines; and 892 acres near the Orlando International Airport, part of which constituted the Orlando Corporate Centre. *(U.S. v. Swissco et al.,* United States District Court, Southern District of Florida, 92-0788, April 3, 1992, pp. 2–4.)

**Giangrandi's and Swissco's roles:** *Nasser Beydoun v. Carlos Cardoen et al.,* Circuit Court of the Eleventh Judicial Circuit, Dade County, Florida, 90-43689, pp. 2 and 3.

**The Grahams** are listed on the warranty deed, along with Augusto Giangrandi, Cardoen's chief lieutenant, as trustee.

**The Cardoen-Graham connection:** "Arms Dealer Was a Big Fundraiser for Graham," *Roll Call,* April 30, 1992, p. 32.

**Ricardson, Theberge, and the CIA:** "Nightline," ABC, September 13, 1991.

**The trigger sting:** NBC News "Expose," January 19, 1991.

**The press release** is R-91-039, "U.S. Customs Agents Seize Attack Helicopter."

**Cardoen's complaint and the text of his letter:** U.S. embassy's report of July 18, 1991.

**The CIA fax and its effect:** Interviews with Customs agents on February 24, 1993.

**"I am not Julio Iglesias":** "Interview With Arms Manufacturer Carlos Cardoen," FBIS-LAT-93-025, February 9, 1993, p. 36.

**Bull's childhood:** William Lowther, *Arms and the Man,* Toronto: Doubleday Canada, Ltd., 1991, pp. 16–20.

**Murphy's observation:** Kevin Toolis, "The Man Behind Iraq's Supergun," *The New York Times Magazine,* August 26, 1990, p. 48.

**The V-3:** "The Man Who Made the Supergun," "Frontline," PBS, February 12, 1991.

**The funding of HARP:** G. V. Bull and C. H. Murphy, *The Paris Guns and Project HARP,* Hereford: Verlag E. S. Mittler & Sohn, 1988, p. 145.

**Activities at Barbados:** D'Arcy Jenish, "The Man With the Golden Gun," *Maclean's,* April 22, 1991, p. 47.

**HARP's legacy:** James Adams, *Bull's Eye,* New York: Times Books, 1992, pp. 104–5.

**The writer** is D'Arcy Jenish, "The Man With the Golden Gun."

**"Morons":** "The Man Behind Iraq's Supergun," p. 50.

**Ranges for the big gun:** Bull and Murphy, *The Paris Guns and Project HARP,* p. 232.

**Polar orbit Martlets:** "The Man With the Golden Gun," p. 49.

**The SRC-PRB arrangement:** William Lowther, *Arms and the Man,* Toronto: Doubleday Canada, Ltd., 1991, p. 103.

**Frost and Clancy:** Adams, *Bull's Eye,* pp. 145–50.

**OMC's letter of permission to Bull, sent by William Robinson, its director:** Adams, *Bull's Eye,* pp. 154–55.

**CIA stonewalling:** "The Man Who Made the Supergun."

**SRC's shipment to South Africa** and events leading up to it were the subject of a House subcommittee investigation, the results of which were released on March 30, 1982. "At the very least, this episode suggests serious negligence on the part of the [Central Intelligence] Agency," the report said. "At most, there is a possibility that elements of the CIA purposely evaded U.S. policy." (Adams, *Bull's Eye,* p. 204.)

**The Chinese connection:** Ibid., pp. 208–10.

**The Chinese plant:** Ibid., p. 213.

**WA 021:** Ibid., p. 212.

**The Yugoslav connection:** Lowther, *Arms and the Man,* p. 164.

**The cranes:** Dale Grant, *Wilderness of Mirrors,* Scarborough: Prentice-Hall Canada, 1991, pp. 171–73.

**The Navy cannon:** Interview Windrem did with Fred Quelle, formerly of ONR, on November 21, 1991.

**The workshop proceedings** are outlined in "Proceedings: Intercontinental Cannon and Orbiter Technology Workshop," 4–5 November 1985, DARPA/STO, 1400 Wilson Blvd.,

Arlington, Va. 22101. Also see Larry B. Stotts, DARPA, "Summary of Information for FOI Inquiry," 91-FOI-1692, September 25, 1991. The workshop was not classified.

**Sarkis Soghanalian:** Adams, *Bull's Eye*, pp. 210–11.

**He claimed:** "The Arming of Iraq," "Frontline," PBS, Autumn/Winter 1990.

**Bastards:** Grant, *Wilderness of Mirrors*, p. 188.

**The two big guns:** Lowther, *Arms and the Man*, pp. 200–201. Also see Timmerman, *The Death Lobby*, p. 300.

**Michel's visit to the OMC:** "Who Killed Gerald Bull," "60 Minutes," CBS-TV, September 17, 1990.

**Babylon's specifications, as well as the 350- and 600-millimeter versions:** Trade and Industry Committee, House of Commons, "Exports to Iraq: Project Babylon and Long Range Guns," Second Report, Session 1991–92, London: Her Majesty's Stationery Office, March 13, 1992, p. xxi. Also see Adams, *Bull's Eye*, p. 229.

**Details for the supergun-satellite launcher:** "Preliminary Proposal for Satellite Launcher Using Sadam [sic] Rockets," prepared by SRC Engineering, Geneva, for the Iraqi Ministry of Industry and Military Industrialization, 1988, pp. 1–10.

**Launcher versus cannon:** "Exports to Iraq: Project Babylon and Long Range Guns," p. xx.

**The satellite launcher combinations:** Ibid.

**The intelligence analysis** is from a knowledgeable source who requested anonymity.

**The military guns' numbers:** "Exports to Iraq: Project Babylon and Long Range Guns," p. xxi.

**Cowley's remarks:** "The Arming of Iraq."

**Third stage:** Interview with a U.S. intelligence official on April 19, 1993.

**Bull's other weapons:** Interview with a U.S. intelligence official in February 1993.

**Threats and Bar-David:** "The Man Who Made the Supergun."

**The SRC connections:** Alan George, "Supergun Company Acted as Middleman for Iraq Deals," *The Middle East*, October 1990. The firms are listed in "Exports to Iraq: Project Babylon and Long Range Guns," pp. xxii and xxiii. Also see "Papers Reveal Extent of Supergun Links," *The Guardian*, March 13, 1992, and "Spanish Link to Iraqi Supergun," *Financial Times*, May 26/27, 1990.

**Seizure of crates:** Adams, *Bull's Eye*, p. 250.

**Aziz's remark:** "Britain Seizes Tube Going to Iraq," *The New York Times*, April 13, 1990.

**The seizures:** "Greece Seizes a Truck Carrying Arms to Iraq," *The New York Times*, April 21, 1990, and "Exports to Iraq: Project Babylon and Long Range Guns," p. xvii.

**The test:** Adams, *Bull's Eye*, pp. 242–43.

**Reports on problems with Big Babylon:** U.N. Special Commission report on the ballistics team's visit to Jabal Hamrayn.

**The model:** "Exports on Iraq: Project Babylon and Long Range Guns," p. xxxii.

**Bull's assassination** has been described many times; see Adams, *Bull's Eye*, p. 14; Lowther, *Arms and the Man*, p. 271; and Grant, *Wilderness of Mirrors*, pp. 1–2. The shooting was reported in "Gerald Bull, 62, Shot in Belgium; Scientist Who Violated Arms Law," *The New York Times*, March 25, 1990.

## 6. LOOTING THE STOREHOUSE OF KNOWLEDGE

**Saddam at Aberdeen:** "The Arming of Iraq," "Frontline," PBS, Autumn/Winter, 1990. The visit was recounted by Neil Livingston, a writer specializing in chemical weapons.

**CIA attitudes on cooperation:** Hearing on "Security Weaknesses and the Nuclear Weapons Laboratories," U.S. Senate Government Affairs Committee, October 11, 1988, p. 14.

**CDC shipments and the statement:** Reported by Windrem on "NBC Nightly News" on April 11, 1990.

**The analyst who talked** about the Iraqis was Peter Zimmerman, a Los Alamos physicist and member of the Strategic Arms Treaty (START) negotiating team.

**The explosion,** erroneously reported to have taken place at Al Hillah, was reported in "Hundreds Reported to Have Died in Iraqi Explosion," *The New York Times*, September 7, 1989.

**RDX was listed as an export control item in** *The Militarily Critical Technologies List*, Washington: Office of the Under Secretary of Defense, Research and Engineering, October 1986, p. 17-7. Also listed were cyclotetramethylenetetranitramine, or HMX (high melting point explosive), which is even better than RDX as an A-bomb detonator, and two others, TATB and PETN.

**Petroleum explosion:** "Petroleum-Depot Explosion Acknowledged by the Iraqis," *The New York Times*, September 8, 1989.

**Bazoft's execution** was reported in "Denying Pleas, Iraq Hangs British-Based Reporter," *The New York Times*, March 16, 1990.

**The GAO investigation:** "Nuclear Nonproliferation: Better Controls Needed Over Weapons-Related Information and Technology," GAO/RCED-89-116, Washington: United States General Accounting Office, June 1989, p. 19.

**Tracking requests:** Ibid., pp. 3–4.

**The GAO study of foreigners at DOE labs:** *Nuclear Nonproliferation: Major Weaknesses in Foreign Visitor Controls at Weapons Laboratories*, GAO/RCED-89-31, October 1988, p. 38.

**The background checking problem and sloppy administration:** Ibid., pp. 3–4.

**The first individual's tour at Oak Ridge** was spelled out in his Request for Approval of Alien Participation in Unclassified Research (RAAPUR), dated May 16, 1979, and by a letter requesting an extension of his research written by J. J. Vogt, Director of Employee Relations, on April 2, 1981. Information on the other is from his RAAPUR.

**Partom's and Ganani's visit to Los Alamos** is described in considerable detail in U.S. Senate, Committee on Governmental Affairs, "Security Weaknesses at the Nuclear Weapons Laboratories," 100th Congress, 2nd Sess., October 11, 1988, pp. 251–358.

**Du Val** was the Acting Deputy Assistant Secretary for Operations of the DOE's Office of Defense Programs. His remark is from the hearing cited above, p. 30.

**The Chinese theft at Livermore:** "Chinese Atom-Arms Spying in U.S. Reported," *The New York Times*, November 22, 1990.

**The archive V-weapon and Jupiter material:** National Public Radio report, "Missile Tech," by Neil Conan, June 20, 1990.

**Hardware exports:** Ibid.

**The nuclear-related high explosives:** *The Militarily Critical Technologies List*, Washington: Office of the Under Secretary of Defense, Research and Engineering, October 1986, p. 17-7.

**Bryen's remarks about the computer:** "NBC Nightly News," June 30, 1989.

**Cutting out intelligence agencies** happens frequently, according to a number of sources familiar with the situation.

**Bryen's two kinds of difficulty:** NBC interview of June 2, 1989.

**Roberts's phone conversation** was with Jeffrey Tripp, as noted by Roberts. The note appears as item 4 in the "Chronology of U.S. Sales to Iraq," an off-the-record account compiled by Consarc.

**The Pentagon official** who cited the Karbala weapons facility did so on condition of anonymity.

**MIMI's disclaimer:** "Chronology of U.S. Sales to Iraq," item 8.

**Bryen's observations and opinions about the furnace deal (and the computers for Sa'ad-16):** "The Arming of Iraq," a "Frontline" series program made for public television, which aired on September 11, 1990.

**The Hewlett-Packard export** to Salah al Din was uncoverd by the Wisconsin Project on Nuclear Arms Control, as reported in "Military Exports to Iraq Come Under Scrutiny," *The New York Times*, June 25, 1991, and on "NBC Nightly News," June 30, 1989.

**The Blazer alteration:** Ibid., p. 4.

**The rocketcase episode:** Gary Milhollin, "Licensing Mass Destruction: U.S. Exports to Iraq: 1985–1990," Washington: Wisconsin Project on Nuclear Arms Control, June 1991, p. 2.

**The Scud attack:** "Scud Missile Hits a U.S. Barracks, Killing 27," *The New York Times*, February 26, 1991.

**Commerce's and State's computer problems:** U.S. Congress, House Government Operations Committee, "Strengthening the Export Licensing System," 102–137, July 2, 1991, p. 13.

**Confusion over MTCR rules:** Ibid., p. 11.

**NRC approval of the uranium to Romania:** Administration and congressional sources.

**FAE's use and current status:** Honeywell Aerospace & Defence, U.K., *A Preliminary Study for Development of a FAE Warhead for Application to a Ballistic Missile: Mid Study Progress Report*, Copy No. 6, November 1984, p. 13.

**Smith** made his presentation in Minneapolis on March 28 and 29, 1984, with Gareth Thornton, the manager of the Operational Analysis Department of Honeywell Control Systems, Ltd. Smith's position at IFAT consisted of placing contracts with industry. He and Thornton had worked together at another firm, and he was therefore using his past affiliation to place the contract. HCSL in turn used Honeywell's Defense Systems Division in Minnetonka as an internal subcontractor. It is notable that Smith played down the missile's potential to Honeywell officials. Details of his presentation are from an internal memorandum from J. D. Beckmann of Honeywell's Mission Analysis Division to Gary M. Lehr, not otherwise identified, dated April 4, 1984, pp. 1–2. It will hereafter be called the Beckmann memorandum.

**The objection** is from the Beckmann memorandum, p. 4.

**FAE effects:** *FAE Warhead Analysis Final Report*, Minnetonka, Minn.: Mission Analysis Group, Honeywell Defense Systems Division, December 1984.

**Van Anraat, Tanaka, Greenberg, and Hinkleman:** Keith F. Girard, "Poison Profits," *Regardie's*, November 1990, pp. 61–64.

**The money transfer and illegal documentaton:** Ibid., p. 66.

**The Iranian angle:** Ibid., pp. 62 and 67–68.

**The sting and its result:** Ibid., pp. 67–70.

**Turnbaugh's observation:** Girard, "Poison Profits," p. 62.

**The meeting in London and Supnick's role:** "Operation Exodus," *The Sunday Times* (London), April 1, 1990.

**The sting** was reported on "NBC Nightly News" on March 28 and 29, 1990. See also "Atom Bomb Parts Seized in Britain En Route to Iraq" and "Artful Hunt for Smuggler Suspects," *The New York Times*, March 29, 1991.

**The report:** Committee on Science, Engineering, and Public Policy, National Academy of Sciences, *Finding Common Ground: U.S. Export Controls in a Changed Global Environment*, Washington: National Academy Press, 1991.

**Commerce:** Ibid., pp. 191–92.

**Ellicott:** Burrows interview on March 20, 1992.

## 7. GERMANY: EXPORTS ÜBER ALLES

**Schlosser's award:** Kenneth R. Timmerman, *The Death Lobby*, Boston: Houghton Mifflin, 1992, p. 70.

**Degussa's involvement with the Jews and with Zyklon B:** Interview with Prof. Peter Hayes of Northwestern University on October 3, 1991; "Iraq Gas in Nazi Probe," the London *Sunday Mirror*, January 27, 1991; a Reuters report on February 15, 1989, citing "How Auschwitz Got Its Zyklon B," *Jerusalem Post*, February 10, 1989; and an extensive article, "German Firm Accused Over Iraqi War Gas," in the London *Daily Telegraph*, February 10, 1991. Referring to his company's wartime connection to Degesch, Hans-

Joachim Nimtz, a Degussa spokesman, was quoted in the Reuters story as saying: "Not one Degussa official was ever convicted of war crimes. The Degesch officials were executed." Also see Richard Breitman, *The Architect of Genocide: Himmler and the Final Solution*, New York: Alfred A. Knopf, 1991, p. 203.

**Degussa's role in the atomic bomb program:** David Irving, *The German Atomic Bomb*, New York: Da Capo Press, 1967, p. 198. Also see Barbara Rogers and Zdenek Cervenka, *The Nuclear Axis: The Secret Collaboration Between West Germany and South Africa*, New York: Times Books, 1978, pp. 35–36.

**Data on the company:** *International Directory of Corporate Affiliations*, Vol. 1, Wilmette, Ill: National Register Publishing Company, 1991; *International Corporate 1000 Yellow Book*, Vol. 4, No. 1, New York: Monitor Publishing Company, 1991; and *Moody's International Manual*, Vol. 1, New York: Moody's Investors Service, 1990.

**The Yongbyon reactor and associated intelligence:** "The Yongbyon Puzzle," *Asiaweek*, March 9, 1990; Leonard S. Spector and Jacqueline R. Smith, "North Korea: The Next Nuclear Nightmare?" *Arms Control Today*, March 1991; "N. Korea—Set to Join the 'Nuclear Club'?" *Jane's Defence Weekly*, September 23, 1989; and "Photos Indicate N. Korean Growth in Nuclear Ability," *Space News*, March 12–18, 1990.

**Degussa's beryllium and zirconium deals:** Undated complaint filed by Benjamin Oberholtzer, Director of Commerce's Office of Export Enforcement, a signed consent agreement between Degussa and Commerce dated March 15 and 27, 1990, respectively, and a Commerce Department news release, BXA 90-10 dated March 28, 1990: Commerce Imposes $800,000 Fine on a West German Firm for Alleged Illegal Re-exports. Also see Cameron Binkley, "Twenty-four Foreign Firms Reported to Have Been Engaged in Illicit Nuclear Weapons-Related Trade," Monterey Institute of International Studies, undated, p. 3. Windrem's Freedom of Information Act request to Commerce for the complete file on the fine levied against Degussa was denied, as was a subsequent appeal.

**The documents' movement to Iraq and possibly elsewhere:** Department of Defense memorandum dated November 15, 1991, and provided to Windrem.

**Werner's involvement with Iraq:** Telex from the GIPRO project office at Sa'ad-16 to Gildemeister Projecta regarding equipment suppliers.

**Burma:** Martin Smith, "The Burmese Way to Rack and Ruin," *Index on Censorship*, October 1991, pp. 43–45.

**The attempted shipment** of the furnace to Libya was reported by *Der Spiegel*, September 9, 1991, and *Frankfurter Rundschau* on September 11, 1991.

**The export** was changed by the BAW (German Ministry of Foreign Trade) on April 26 to coincide with changes in NATO export regulations. (BAW's Runderlassaussenwirtschaft 10/91.)

**The linking of Leybold and Degussa to the centrifuges:** Sources on the IAEA's inspection team and others in the Department of Defense.

**The Leybold-Degussa-Iraq link:** "Foreign Supplies to the Iraqi Nuclear Program," U.N. press release 91/47 of December 11, 1991.

**Information about the "Leybold Suite" and its contents:** Conversation with the technical expert on January 16, 1992.

**The Bonn meeting** was outlined in a memorandum from Meed International to Ali on August 11, 1989. Meed, based in London, was an Iraqi front company, according to the U.S. Treasury Department.

**The Leybold precision instruments story** was broken by *Der Spiegel* on October 7, 1991. The company's points were made in lengthy response by Degussa's Corporate Communications/Public Relation Department on October 2, 1991, to written questions submitted by Windrem.

**Werner Hein:** "NBC Nightly News," February 4, 1992.

**The House complaint** is from U.S. House Committee on Government Operations, "Strengthening the Export Licensing System," No. 102-137, July 2, 1991, pp. 21–22. The report did not identify Leybold by name because of privacy restrictions in the export law. But the authors obtained the complete license application file, which specifically names Leybold as the exporter.

**Bryen expressed his anger** over the Leybold transaction in an inteview with Windrem on December 4, 1991.

**The correspondence** between Balu and Leybold is dated September 4, 1992.

**Berman's letter** is dated September 9, 1992.

**H & H and Huetten's exploits:** JPRS Report, "Proliferation Issues: Germany, Exporters of Death," JPRS-TND-91-007L, July 25, 1991, pp. 39–40 and 42.

**The H & H indictment:** "Two Charged with Helping Iraq Arms Plan," *The Wall Street Journal*, March 25, 1993.

**Lutz's remark:** "Hitler's Slave Labourers Sue for 'Back Pay'," *The Sunday Times* (London), April 15, 1990.

**Siemens wartime recruiting:** "Charges of Crimes Against Humanity Made Against Three Directors of Siemens in Berlin," *The New York Times*, February 9, 1947.

**Farben's killing 30,000 inmates:** Interview with Prof. Peter Hayes, a historian at Northwestern University, on October 3, 1991.

**The efficient ventilation system:** "Charges of Crimes Against Humanity Made Against Three Directors of Siemens in Berlin."

**Blass's remarks:** Interview with Windrem January 9, 1991.

**Gansel's remarks:** Interview with Windrem which aired on "NBC Nightly News" on September 25, 1991.

**Hayes's observation about corporate responsibilities:** Interview of October 3, 1991.

**Leybold's export percentage:** Randy Reydell, "The Supply Side of Nuclear Proliferation: A Look at West Germany," *Energy and Technology Review*, April 1983, pp. 17–25.

**The Siemens data:** Windrem's interview with Volker Schmidt-Wellenburg on January 7, 1991.

**The list of critical exports** from German companies is from a U.S. Senate Foreign Relations Committee addendum to the IAEA inspection team's report, dated January 5, 1993.

**German machine tools:** "Machine Tool Review," an IAEA report on machine tools found in Iraqi nuclear facilities, dated June 15, 1992.

**The raid and quote:** "Weapons Exports," *Der Spiegel*, July 13, 1992.

**Fat substitute:** Richard Breitman, *The Architect of Genocide: Himmler and the Final Solution*, New York: Knopf, 1991, p. 37.

**Japanese participation:** From a highly knowledgeable source.

**The BND's ignored reports** are treated in some detail in Thomas C. Wiegele, *The Clandestine Building of Libya's Chemical Weapons Factory*, Carbondale: Southern Illinois University Press, 1992, pp. 82–91.

**The Hong Kong ruse** and Imhausen's and SIG's involvement with Pharma 150 were detailed by the German news magazine *Stern* on January 26, 1989, as reported by the Foreign Broadcast Information Service in FBIS-WEU-89-018, January 30, 1989, pp. 2–3.

**Imhausen's fee:** "German Confesses on Libyan Plant," *The New York Times*, June 14, 1990.

**The Teleperm M Hong Kong ruse:** FBIS-WEU-89-018, p. 3.

**Teleperm M's true use and that of the field multiplexers:** Ibid.

***The Times* article** was titled "U.S. Thinks Libya May Plan to Make Chemical Weapons."

**Siemens denial that it knew the Teleperm M was going to Libya:** Interview with Volker Schmidt-Wellenburg on January 7, 1991.

**The *Stern* story** on the submarines appeared in the April 19, 1990, issue as excerpted by FBIS-WEU-90-079-A, April 24, 1990.

**Schmidt-Wellenburg's remarks:** Interview with Windrem in Munich on January 7, 1991.

**The remark about Siemens** having been repeatedly "misled" is from a source who wished to be anonymous.

**Genscher's proposal and the State Department's reaction:** "A U.S.-Bonn Split on Libya Is Seen," *The New York Times*, March 8, 1990.

**The withdrawal of records:** Senate Foreign Relations Committee hearings (January 24, 1989; March 1, 1989; May 9, 1989) on the "Chemical and Biological Weapons Threat,"

p. 67. The article was "U.S. Thinks Libya May Plan to Make Chemical Weapons," *The New York Times*, December 24, 1987.

**The charges against Hippenstiel-Imhausen:** "German Is Charged in Libyan Case," *The New York Times*, March 23, 1990.

**Hippenstiel-Imhausen's guilty plea:** "German Confesses on Libyan Plant," *The New York Times*, June 14, 1990.

**His sentencing:** "German Is Jailed in Sale to Libya," *The New York Times*, June 28, 1990.

**Imhausen's retention of the profit from Rabta:** Private investigator's report.

**The first report of the fire** was "Plant Said to Make Poison Gas in Libya Is Reported on Fire," *The New York Times*, March 15, 1990.

**The initial hoax story** was "U.S. Says Fire at Libya Arms Plant May Be a Hoax," *The New York Times*, March 31, 1990.

**For a later hoax story** and mention of the old tires, see "U.S. Says Evidence Points to Hoax in Fire at Libyan Chemical Plant," *The New York Times*, June 19, 1990.

**The use of paint:** "Phony Fire?" Washington Roundup, *Aviation Week & Space Technology*, April 16, 1990, p. 15.

**The cable from Stuttgart,** dated August 10, 1990, and carrying reference number 1244, was titled: "Imhausen: Plans for a Second Poison Gas Plant in Libya?"

**Gates's testimony** about production at Rabta and the development of Sebha was given to the Senate Govenmental Affairs Committee hearing on "Weapons Proliferation in the New World Order" on January 15, 1992.

**The director's answer** is from Burrows interview of Müller on March 19, 1992, in Washington.

**Administrative changes:** Ibid.

**The law:** "Outline on the Act to Amend the Foreign Trade and Payments Act Establishing a Federal Export Office," an undated precis from the Federal Republic of Germany's Embassy in Washington in March 1992.

**Designated jailbird:** Müller interview.

**The furnaces:** "Where Governments Fail: The Case of Leybold AG," *Mednews*, October 12, 1992, pp. 2, and 6.

**Hempel:** "60 Minutes," CBS, April 16, 1989.


## 8. THE YARD SALE AT THE END OF HISTORY

**Data on the SS-18** is from "Aerospace Forecast & Inventory," *Aviation Week & Space Technology*, March 9, 1987, p. 175.

**The fee** is from "A Soviet Company Offers Nuclear Blasts for Sale to Anyone With the Cash," *The New York Times*, November 7, 1991. The $300 fee appeared on the one-page Chetek flier.

**Chetek and Iraq-Kuwait:** Letter sent by Viktor N. Mikhailov and A. D. Kuntzevich in September 1991, a copy of which was obtained by Canadian Centre for Arms Control and Disarmament in Ottawa.

**Workers' salaries:** "60 Minutes," CBS-TV, May 17, 1992.

**"Sole proprietor" and infrastructure:** Mark Hibbs, "Soviet Firm to Offer Nuclear Explosives to Destroy Wastes," *Nucleonics Week*, October 24, 1991, p. 1.

**Chetek's wares are from its fliers:** "Large-Platform Gobal Space System/XXI Century Project," "Re-Processing Aluminum, Copper and Magnesium Alloys [sic] Chips," "Ultra-Dispersed [sic] Diamonds (UDD) . . . ," "Production of Bottlenecked Vessels (Drums) From Aluminum Used in Food Industry," "The Technological Know-How of Electronic Beam Generators," all undated, and all carrying the firm's address and its telephone and fax numbers: 206 57 35 206 56 and (095) 200 32 62 200 20 95, respectively.

**Mikhailov's plans for Chetek:** Windrem interview in Washington on October 22, 1991.

**Early days at the secret facility** are described in Andrei Sakharov, *Memoirs*, New York:

Alfred A. Knopf, 1990. The author obliquely refers to the H-bomb as "The Third Idea" (Chapter 12).

**Tutnev and Andrushin** were identified by a source who did not want to be identified.

**The paper** was Albert Petrovich Vasilyev, Nikolay Korneyevich Prikhodko, and Vadim Aleksandrovich Simonenko, "Underground Nuclear Blasts . . . to Improve the Ecological Situation," *Priroda*, February, 1991, pp. 36–42.

**Dmitriev's remarks** are from his address on the influence of nuclear weapons on the environment and research of radioactive pollution given on April 23, 1991.

**Mikhailov and the audience:** Windrem interview with Tariq Rauf, Senior Research Associate of the Canadian Centre for Arms Control and Disarmament, in Moscow in October 1991.

**Lamb's remark:** "Soviet Concern Has Explosive Solution for Toxic Waste," *The Wall Street Journal*, October 25, 1991.

**The CCACD demand** is mentioned in a letter from Rauf to Windrem of October 24, 1991.

**Wolfson:** "A Soviet Company Offers Nuclear Blasts for Sale to Anyone With the Cash."

**KGB:** From a knowledgeable source who did not wish to be identified.

**Kay's observation** is from David Kay, "The IAEA—How Can It Be Strengthened?" a paper delivered at the Woodrow Wilson Center's Conference on "Nuclear Proliferation in the 1990's: Challenges and Opportunities," December 1–2, 1992.

**Havel's remarks:** "Rio and the New Millennium," *The New York Times*, June 3, 1992.

**Novaya Zemlya:** "A Scramble for Data on Arctic Radioactive Dumping," *Science*, July 31, 1992, p. 608. For a more comprehensive update, including findings from a Russian report, see "Russians Describe Extensive Dumping of Nuclear Waste," *The New York Times*, April 27, 1993.

**Aral Sea:** Murray Feshbach and Alfred Friendly, Jr., *Ecocide in the USSR*, New York: Basic Books, 1992, p. 73. The comment on the first stages is from p. 173.

**The three sites:** Thomas B. Cochran and Robert Standish Norris, *Soviet Nuclear Warhead Production*, Washington: National Resources Defense Council, pp. 8–10.

**Total residents** is from *Yomiuri Shimbun*, November 17, 1991. The 100,000 number is from Mark Hibbs, " 'Vulnerable' Soviet Nuclear Experts Could Aid Clandestine Weapons Aims," *NuclearFuel*, October 28, 1991, p. 4. The 6,000–7,000 figure is from a highly knowledgeable source who wished to remain anonymous. Other sources say it is closer to 3,000–5,000 (interview with Evgeniy Mikirin, director of nuclear fuel cycle programs at MAPI, at ministry headquarters on October 14, 1991).

**"Special contingents":** Aleksandr Solzhenitsyn, *The Gulag Archipelago*, New York: Harper & Row, 1974, p. 407.

**Radiation at Chelyabinsk-40:** *Soviet Nuclear Warhead Production*, p. 17.

**Chelyabinsk-40 and Kyshtym:** Cochran and Norris, *Soviet Nuclear Warhead Production*, pp. 18–25.

**The econuke paper** was "Underground Nuclear Blasts . . . to Improve the Ecological Situation," previously cited.

**Loose Cannon:** Interviews Windrem conducted with Arkin in April, June, and December 1991, the most extensive of which occurred in Washington on December 14. Arkin also arranged for Windrem to have access to several Greenpeace meetings in London and Berlin at which the operation was discussed. Windrem also accompanied Arkin to the abandoned bunker and was in Berlin the morning Arkin met the lieutenant.

**Cheney:** "U.S. Fears Spread of Soviet Nuclear Weapons," *The New York Times*, December 16, 1991.

**The number of nuclear weapons that are man-portable:** December 14, 1991, interview with Arkin.

**45,000 nukes:** "Russian Says Soviet Atom Arsenal Was Larger Than Was Estimated," *The New York Times*, September 26, 1993.

**Gates made the remark** in an address, "Weapons Proliferation: The Most Dangerous Challenge for American Intelligence," at the Comstock Club of Sacramento, California, on December 15, 1992.

**Plutonium and HEU:** Interviews with Russian officials, including Mikirin, in October 1991.

**The storage facility:** "Proliferation Watch," a publication of the U.S. Senate Committee on Government Affairs, Vol. 3, No. 3, May–August 1992, p. 2.

**Purchasing uranium:** "U.S. to Buy Russian Uranium," *The Washington Post*, September 1, 1992, and "U.S. to Buy Uranium Taken From Bombs Scrapped by Russia," *The New York Times*, September 1, 1992.

**Kazakhstan's force:** "Kazakhstan to Sign Treaty, Eliminate Nuclear Arms," *Aviation Week & Space Technology*, May 25, 1992, p. 23.

**The warhead count:** "U.S., Russia, Bargain for Enriched Uranium," *Aviation Week & Space Technology*, January 11, 1993, p. 29 (from a report by the Harvard Project on Cooperative Denuclearization).

**The return of the Belarusian warheads:** "Belarus Shows the Way on Arms" (editorial), *The New York Times*, February 8, 1993.

**Dismantling SS-19s:** "U.S. Says Ukraine Has Begun Dismantling Nuclear Missiles," *The New York Times*, July 28, 1993.

**Possible problems in Russia:** Interview with a U.S. analyst on February 1, 1993.

**Gravity bomb codes:** Interview with a government analyst on December 3, 1992.

**670 cruise missiles:** Testimony by Bruce G. Blair of the Brookings Institution to the European Subcommittee of the Senate Foreign Relations Committee, June 24, 1993.

**The Ukrainian nuclear situation:** William C. Potter, "Who Controls Nuclear Missiles in Ukraine?" October 26, 1992, Monterey Institute for International Studies, paper, pp. 2–3.

**Yukhnovsky:** "Official: Ukraine Will Sell Its Nuclear Weapons," AP, November 5, 1992.

**Idiots:** "Ukraine Could Seize Control Over Nuclear Arms," *The Washington Post*, June 3, 1993.

**"We have a treasure":** "Ukraine Asks Aid for Its Arms Curb," *The New York Times*, November 13, 1992.

**Perkovich's observations are from his Trip Report:** "Moscow Nuclear Arms Reduction Workshop," July 2, 1992, pp. 2–3.

**Beryllium:** "The Arming of Iran," "Frontline," PBS, 1993.

**SS-18s and sausage machines:** "From Missile Maker to Sausage Stuffer," *The Washington Post*, January 30, 1992.

**Dual-use exports from the four countries:** William C. Potter, "The True Story About Nuclear Exports From the FSU," October 30, 1992, pp. 1–4.

**Cesium and the mafia:** "Theft of Radioactive Materials in Russia Reaches Alarming Proportions," *Izvestia*, November 19, 1992.

**The Monterey study** is William C. Potter and Eve E. Cohen, "Nuclear Assets of the Former Soviet Union," CIS Nonproliferation Project, Center for Russian and Eurasian Studies, Monterey Institute of International Studies, October 1992, p. II. In addition, Windrem interviewed Potter in October 1992.

**Iranian reactors:** "Iran and Russia Sign Pact to Build Nuclear Plants," PRNewswire, November 2, 1992.

**The Kazakhstan nuclear connection:** Interview with U.S. State Department official who requested anonymity.

**Training the North Koreans and refusal of the blueprint sale:** Windrem interview with a high-ranking official of the Kurchatov Institute in Moscow on October 12, 1991. The institute played a key role in the transfer of technology.

**Reactor sales:** Interview with Mikirin.

**The heavy water shipment:** Soviet bills of lading dated October 1983. Shishkin's remarks are from an interview with Windrem in Minatom headquarters in Moscow.

**The BN-800 denial** is from the interview of October 14, 1991.

**The BN-800 brochure,** six pages long, was in Russian and English and gave specifications for the reactor.

**Brown's idea:** "First Aid for Russian Science," *Science*, February 14, 1992, p. 793.

**Babayan:** "Russian Computer Scientists Hired by American Company," *The New York Times*, March 3, 1992.

**Closing the gap with Japan:** "Use Ex-Soviet Scientists to Top Japan," *The Philadelphia Inquirer*, February 26, 1992.

**Fusion:** "U.S. Plans to Hire Russian Scientists in Fusion Research," *The New York Times*, March 6, 1992.

**The academy recommendations** are from a report, "Reorientation of the Research Capability of the Former Soviet Union," Washington: National Academy Press, 1992.

**The International Science and Technology Centers** are described briefly in "Technology Centers for Russian Scientists," *The Bulletin of the Atomic Scientists*, October 1992, p. 46.

**Nunn-Lugar:** Dunbar Lockwood, "Dribbling Aid to Russia," *The Bulletin of the Atomic Scientists*, July/August 1993, pp. 39–41.

**Gallucci:** Eve Cohen, "Nonproliferation in the Former Soviet Union: The Role of International Science and Technology Centers," *Eye On Supply*, Summer 1992, p. 66.

**The number of Russian scientists:** Windrem interview with Mikirin on October 14, 1991, and Burrows and Windrem interview with a U.S. government analyst on March 17, 1992.

**One million scientists:** News media briefing by top Defense Intelligence Agency analysts on February 27, 1992.

**Biopreparat:** "Planning a Plague," *Newsweek*, February 1, 1993, pp. 40–42.

**The five favorites** from a knowledgeable source who required anonymity.

**Mironov and Kurchatov:** "Fears Grow of Soviet Nuclear Brain Drain," *Financial Times*, January 13, 1992.

**Libyan and Algerian Russian specialists** is from a highly knowledgeable source who requested anonymity.

**China and North Korea:** From a knowledgeable source who required anonymity.

**Weapons reductions:** "Post-Soviet Arms Industry Is Collapsing," *The New York Times*, June 9, 1992.

**Lobachev's remark:** "NBC Nightly News," October 23, 1991.

**Bor:** Brochure "Bor Complex" put out by Aviaexport in Moscow.

**AS-16:** Norman Friedman, "It's Dangerous Out There . . . ," *Proceedings*, October 1992, p. 122.

**Energia:** "Russia Seeks U.S. Buyer for World's Biggest Rocket," *The New York Times*, July 9, 1991.

**Rocket material** is from a series of brochures called "Liquid Rocket Engines," put out by NPO Energomash in Moscow.

**The Indian release** was "Indian Import of Rocket Engine from Russia: Background & Facts," Washington: Embassy of India, May 6, 1992.

**Yeltsin and the rockets:** "Despite U.S., Yeltsin Backs Rocket Deal with India," *The New York Times*, Janaury 30, 1993.

**Carrot and stick:** "U.S. Warns Russia on Missile Fuel Sales," *The New York Times*, June 23, 1993; "U.S. Sets Penalty for Russian Firms," *The New York Times*, June 25, 1993; "Russia Backs Away from India Deal," *Space News*, July 19–25, 1993; "India Asserts It Will Develop Rocket Engines," *The New York Times*, July 18, 1993.

**Seitz's observation** is from "U.S. Is Shopping as Soviets Offer to Sell Once-Secret Technology," *The New York Times*, November 4, 1991.

**"Nasties" and Litavrin:** "Moscow Insists It Must Sell the Instruments of War to Pay the Costs of Peace," *The New York Times*, February 3, 1993.

**Scientists, S-300s, and Nankou:** "China's Buying Spree," *Far Eastern Economic Review*, July 8, 1993, pp. 24 and 26.

**Backfires, centrifuges, and labs:** Windrem interview with a highly knowledgeable congressional investigator.

**Reactors, planes, and subs:** "NBC Nightly News," December 22, 1992.

**The Ukraine MIGs:** "Ukrainian MIG-29s Tour Canada, U.S. After Receiving Navaids," *Aviation Week & Space Technology*, June 1, 1992, p. 51.

**The source of the KH-11 imagery** was Samuel Loring Morison. The pictures were in "Satellite Pictures Show Soviet CVN Towering Above Nikolaiev Shipyard," *Jane's Defence Weekly*, August 11, 1984, pp. 171–73.

**Sale of the *Varyag*:** "Chinese Buy Russian Carrier," *Proceedings of the Naval Institute*, September 1992, p. 123.

**Shevardnadze:** "Shevardnadze Tries to Arrange Economic and Military Cooperation with Iran," *Izvestia*, January 20, 1993.

**Tarasiuk:** "Russian Plans Review Panel to Halt Illegal Arms Exports by High Officials," *Aviation Week & Space Technology*, March 2, 1992, p. 22.

**Shlekov:** "60 Minutes," CBS-TV, May 17, 1992.

**Semtex's reappearance:** "Farewell to Arms?" "MacNeil/Lehrer News Hour," PBS, October 28, 1991.

**Washington appeal:** "U.S. Asks Prague Not to Sell Weapons to Syria and Iran," *The New York Times*, May 8, 1991.

**The arms bunker** was reported on-site by Windrem.


## 9. ISRAEL: ATOMIC SOVEREIGNTY

**Lawrence's quote** is from T. E. Lawrence, *Seven Pillars of Wisdom*, New York: Dell Publishing Co., 1963, pp. 246 and 253. "Sun's Anvil" is from the film *Lawrence of Arabia*.

**Operation details of the mission** such as altitude, speed, maneuvering, and communication are from gun camera film released by the Israeli Air Force.

**KH-11 imagery:** Seymour M. Hersh, *The Samson Option*, New York: Random House, 1991, pp. 3–17.

**The visit to the NRC:** "Israelis Queried NRC About Effect of Bombs," Associated Press, June 19, 1981.

**The best account of the attack on Osirak** is Dan McKinnon's *Bullseye Iraq* (also published as *Bullseye One Reactor* and *Bullseye One*), New York: Berkley Books, 1987.

**"Resounding halt":** Shlomo Nakdimon, *First Strike*, New York: Summit Books, 1987, p. 20. This account is not footnoted and blatantly pro-Israeli. It also suffers from some dubious reporting. The author, for example, describes King Hussein of Jordan looking up at the Israeli planes as they passed over his yacht and making "a shrewd estimate of their flight path" while his brow was "furrowed" (p. 212).

**Raz made the remarks** at a news conference in Israel on May 16, 1991, in the aftermath of coalition attacks against other Iraqi nuclear facilities.

**The Israeli alert:** *The Samson Option*, pp. 225 and 236–37.

**The number of chemical weapons:** Iraqi CBW orders captured by the Kurds (see Chapter 1).

**Iraqi tests:** Windrem interview with a high-ranking Israeli military intelligence official on January 16, 1991.

**Peres's remark:** Shimon Peres, *David's Sling*, London: Weidenfeld and Nicolson, 1970, p. 31.

**Ben-Gurion and Bergmann:** *The Samson Option*, pp. 22 and 23.

**"You empty head":** Knesset debate on September 23, 1993.

**1967 alert:** Interview with Israeli scientist quoting the Hebrew-language memoirs of General Israel Lior, the military aide to Prime Minister Levi Eshkol, and Munya Maridor, first director of Rafael.

**Six hours:** Windrem interviews in June 1992 with a former American weapons lab scientist who had been briefed by a top Israeli nuclear expert.

**The existence of the chemical weapons facility** at Dimona was first revealed by Mordechai Vanunu in his interviews with the London *Sunday Times* in 1986 and updated in "Israeli

May Give Up Nuclear Edge," *The Los Angeles Times*, February 2, 1993. The existence of the biological weapons facility is from various sources, including a Windrem interview in February 1991 with an American scientist who visited the Israel Institute for Biological Research, and "Israel Germ Warfare Expert," UPI, September 8, 1985.

**"Non-NATO allies":** "Discrimination and Nonproliferation," *Proliferation Watch*, July–August 1991, p. 1.

**Schiebel's ties** are from interviews with staff members on the committees.

**"They've studied them all":** A highly knowledgeable strategic analyst who spoke on condition of anonymity.

**Reagan-Begin cooperation:** Ilan Peleg, *Begin's Foreign Policy, 1977–1983: Israel's Move to the Right*, New York: Greenwood Press, 1987, pp. 198–99.

**Strategic corridor:** Analysis of SPOT and Soyuzcarta satellite imagery. Missile ranges are from a highly knowledgeable source.

**The spokesman** was Gennady Gerasimov, as quoted in "Moscow Concern at 'Israel Ballistic Missile Launch,' " *Financial Times*, September 16–17, 1989.

**Ne'eman's career** is from his curriculum vitae and from Amir Oren, "Sea, Territory, Energy, Nucleus," *Davar* Friday Supplement, July 20, 1990, p. 1.

**Israel's targets:** Interview with Yuval Ne'eman, "Sea, Territory, Energy, Nucleus," *Davar* (Jerusalem), July 20, 1990.

**The Committee of Thirty:** *The Samson Option*, pp. 66–67.

**Loans-grants:** "A Close Look at U.S. Aid to Israel Reveals Deals That Push Cost Above Publicly Quoted Figures," *The Wall Street Journal*, September 19, 1991.

**The oil:** "Israeli Nuclear-Capable Missiles: 1995," Wisconsin Project on Nuclear Arms Control, October 5, 1989, p. 4. Deal on 155-mm gun: "Minutes from Meeting Held in Tel Aviv Between H. E. General M. Dayan, Foreign Minister of Israel and H. E. General H. Toufanian, Vice Minister of War, Imperial Government of Iran," July 18, 1977, pp. 3–4. The record of the meeting, stamped "Top Secret," was found by Iranian students.

**"Several billion dollars":** Communication from CIA Director R. James Woolsey to Senator John Glenn, August 27, 1993.

**The Patriot saga** is from "Defense Dept. Confirms Patriot Technology Diverted," *Aviation Week & Space Technology*, February 1, 1993, pp. 26–27, and "Gates: China Has U.S. Missile Secrets," *The Washington Times*, January 5, 1993.

**Arens and Milhollin:** Interviews with Tom Brokaw on "NBC Nightly News," March 12, 1992. Also see "Arms Export Report Further Strains U.S.-Israeli Ties," *The New York Times*, March 15, 1992, and "Cheney Presses Israeli on Chinese Missile Aid Issue," *The New York Times*, March 17, 1992.

**GAO and Arrow:** "A Missile Under Fire," *U.S. News & World Report*, June 28, 1993, pp. 40–41.

**The Indian connection:** "Our Priorities Are Common," *India Today* (Q and A with Peres), June 15, 1993, pp. 22–23.

**Bourges-Maunoury's remark:** *David's Sling*, p. 57.

**Steps leading to Dimona:** *The Samson Option*, pp. 36–43.

**"Screwed":** Ibid., p. 42.

**"Atoms for Peace":** Louis Toscano, *Triple Cross*, New York: Birch Lane Press, 1990, p. 97.

**Saclay:** *The Samson Option*, p. 28.

**Ben-Gurion's remarks:** David Ben-Gurion, *Israel: A Personal History*, New York: Funk & Wagnalls, 1971, p. 660.

**Photointerpretation:** *The Samson Option*, pp. 47–55.

**Dale's report** was in airgram A-742, "Current Status of the Dimona Reactor," April 9, 1965.

**The suitcase bomb:** *The Samson Option*, p. 220.

**Soreq** is described in Peter Pry, *Israel's Nuclear Arsenal*, Boulder: Westview Press, 1984, pp. 7–9.

**The disappearances:** *Israel's Nuclear Arsenal*, pp. 28–29, and Yossi Melman and Dan Raviv, *Every Spy a Prince*, Boston: Houghton Mifflin, 1990, pp. 107–8.

**Dimona and its reprocessing facility** are described in *Triple Cross*, pp. 21–23, and by Frank Barnaby, *The Invisible Bomb*, London: I. B. Tauris, 1989.

**Dimona's production level:** "Israel and Nuclear Weapons," CRS Issue Brief IB87079, Washington: Congressional Research Service, updated April 16, 1990, p. 3.

**The role of computers:** "The Need for Supercomputers in Nuclear Weapons Design," U.S. Department of Energy, January 1986.

**LAKAM and the U.S.:** *Every Spy a Prince*, pp. 104–5.

**The articles by W. H. Goldstein,** J. Oreg, and A. Bar-Shalom were in *Physical Review A*, August 1988 and May 1989.

**The Israeli scientists:** Department of Energy, Office of International Affairs, Requests for Foreign National Unclassified Visit or Assignment to Los Alamos, 1986–1990.

**Partom's research interest** was described in her Request for Foreign National Unclassified Visit or Assignment of June 27, 1988. Her host and coworker was Kay H. Birdsell of Los Alamos's Earth and Space Sciences Division.

**Partom's published paper** was "Equivalent One-Dimensional Coefficient for Hydrodynamic Dispersion in a Circular Tube," Los Alamos National Laboratory, September 1986.

**Vrooman** wrote the letter of assurance to David B. Waller, Assistant Secretary, International Affairs and Energy Emergencies, on July 14, 1988.

**Computer access:** "U.S. Has Given Nuclear-Weapons Data to Several Nations, Senate Panel Finds," *The Wall Street Journal*, August 7, 1989.

**The letter to Segal** was dated February 26, 1987, and transmitted by fax (011-972-4-794509).

**Partom's letter to Hoffman** was dated May 19, 1990.

**The asking price** is from the affidavit of Special Agent Steven J. Bosseler made in June 1990, p. 37.

**Boasting:** "Engineer Held in Illegal 'Star Wars' Sales," *The Los Angeles Times*, June 16, 1990.

**The IDA study** was "Critical Technology Assessment in Israel and NATO Nations," IDA Memorandum Report M-317, Alexandria: Institute for Defense Analysis, April 1987, pp. 1–2.

**Berated:** "Arens Says Israel Expects to Launch Spy Satellite," Reuters, March 6, 1991.

**Ne'eman's statement on trust:** Steve Weissman and Herbert Krosney, *The Islamic Bomb*, New York: Times Books, 1981, p. 18.

**Ne'eman's remark:** "Israel Puts a Satellite in Orbit a Day After Threat by Iraqis," *The New York Times*, April 4, 1990.

**Offeq resolution:** "Israeli Satellite Advances," *Signal*, December 1989, p. 10.

**Sahvit's real range:** Steven E. Gray, "Israeli Missile Capabilities: A Few Numbers to Think About," Lawrence Livermore National Laboratory, October 7, 1988, p. 4.

**Amos:** "IAI Gives Details of Amos Satellite," Foreign Broadcast Information Service-NES-92-073, April 15, 1992, p. 45; "Launch of Amos Satellite Set for December," FBIS-NES-92-071, April 13, 1992, p. 26; and "Israeli Satellite Advances," *Signal*, December 1989, p. 10.

**Dolphins:** "The Mideast Goes MAD," *The Washington Post*, July 15, 1990; "Final Debate Begins on Submarine Purchase," *The Jerusalem Post*, August 19, 1990; "Bonn to Build Two Subs for Israel," *The Independent*, November 27, 1989; and "Israel Will Get Cruise Missile Submarines," *The Jerusalem Post*, May 28, 1990.

**Arrow's cost and percentage division:** Marvin Feuerwerger, "The Arrow Next Time? Israel's Missile Defense Program for the 1990s," The Washington Institute Policy Papers, No. 28, Washington: The Washington Institute for Near East Policy, 1991, pp. 28 and 31.

**"Chutzpah":** Ibid., p. 30, in reference to Yeshayahu Ben-Porat, "Chutzpah by the Name of Arrow," *Yediot Aharonot*, March 22, 1991, p. 7.

**The poll:** "Poll Shows Support for Nuclear Arms Transfer," FBIS-NES-91-157, August 14, 1991, p. 22.

## 10. THE CRESCENT OF CRISIS: PLOWSHARES INTO SWORDS

**For the *"pied noir"* feeling about Algeria,** see "Still Aching for Algeria, 30 Years After the Rage," *The New York Times*, July 20, 1992.

**The French test:** Lewis A. Dunn, "Military Politics, Nuclear Proliferation, and the 'Nuclear Coup d'Etat,' " *The Journal of Strategic Studies*, May 1978, p. 38.

**Early Chinese nuclear history:** Richard W. Fieldhouse, *Nuclear Weapons Databook*, NWD-91-1, "Chinese Nuclear Weapons: A Current and Historical Overview," Washington: Natural Resources Defense Council, March 1991, pp. 12–13.

**Wang Enmao's adventure** is briefly told in Donald H. McMillen, "The Urumqi Military Region: Defence and Security in China's West," Working Paper No. 50, Canberra: The Strategic and Defence Studies Center, Australian National University, March 1982, p. 6. Also see "Mao Calls Truce with Rebel General in Bomb Province," *The Sunday Times* (London), July 2, 1967, and "Military Politics, Nuclear Proliferation, and the 'Nuclear Coup d'Etat,' " p. 39.

**The Malaysian imam:** "Everything the Other Is Not," *The Economist*, August 1, 1992.

**The diplomat** was quoted in "Sudan Presses Its Campaign to Impose Islamic Law on Non-Muslims," *The New York Times*, June 1, 1992.

**Tunisia's revivalist numbers:** "Tunisia Puts Nearly 300 Muslim Militants on Trial," *The New York Times*, August 3, 1992.

**The Islamic roundup:** "Islam Resumes Its March," *The Economist*, April 4, 1992, p. 47.

**Arafat:** "Arafat Warning Fundamentalists on Violence in Occupied Lands," *The New York Times*, November 10, 1992.

**A traveler:** Robert D. Kaplan, "Shatter Zone," *The Atlantic*, April 1992, p. 24.

**Demirel's statements:** "Turkish Premier Voices Worries Over Pull of Ethnic Conflict in Caucasus," *The Washington Post*, March 19, 1992.

**The Russian reaction to the nuclear start-up:** Windrem's interviews with the officials in Moscow in October 1991.

**The Iran-Saudi moves:** "To Counter Iran, Saudis Seek Ties With Ex-Soviet Islamic Republics," *The New York Times*, February 22, 1992.

**Weapons inventories:** Statement of Rear Admiral Thomas A. Brooks, Director of Naval Intelligence, before the Seapower, Strategic, and Critical Materials Subcommittee of the House Armed Services Committee on Intelligence Issues, March 7, 1991. Also see "Middle East Arms Control and Related Issues," CRS Report to Congress, 91-384F, Washington, D.C.: Congressional Research Service, May 1, 1991, pp. CRS-73–87.

**Indigenous production and Turkish subs:** Admiral Brooks's testimony.

**The Mauritanian connection:** "Photos Show Iraq Missile Launchers in Mauritania," *The Washington Times*, March 30, 1990, and "U.S. Fears Iraq Is Seeking Long-Range Missile Site," *The New York Times*, April 24, 1990.

**The Algerian statement:** "Algeria Acknowledges China Helping It Build Nuclear Reactor," Agence France Presse, April 30, 1991.

**Cross's mission:** "China Helps Algeria Build First Arab Atom Bomb," *The Sunday Times* (London), April 28, 1991.

**The analyst's observation** is from "China Helps Algeria Develop Nuclear Weapons," *The Washington Times*, April 11, 1991.

**Advice on adapting the weapons:** Ibid.

**Algerian radio:** "UK Claims of Plans to Build Bomb Denied," Foreign Broadcast Information Service-NES-91-082, April 29, 1991, p. 5.

**Inspectors:** "Algeria Opens Nuclear Reactor to Inspection," Reuters, February 27, 1992.

**The airport explosion:** "Blast at Algiers Airport Kills 9 and Wounds 100," *The New York Times*, August 27, 1992.

**Tolba:** "Crackdown Seems to Lead Algeria into Chaos," *The New York Times*, August 20, 1992.

**Antiterrorism:** "Algeria Descends into More Chaos," *The New York Times*, July 29, 1992.

**The Libyan-Indian connection:** "Indian Official Says Qaddafi Sought Atom-Arms Technology in 70's," *The New York Times,* October 10, 1991.

**The Iran connection:** "U.S. Thinks Libya May Plan to Make Chemical Weapons," *The New York Times,* December 24, 1987.

**Qaddafi's remarks,** delivered to students at the Higher Institute of Applied Social Studies at Al Fatah University in Tripoli on April 18, 1990, were carried in Arabic by the Tripoli Television Service.

**Lutz Kayser's remark:** "Otrag Missile Firm to Hold Tests in Libyan Desert," FBIS-WEU-80-187, September 19, 1980.

**The agents and reconnaissance:** From a highly knowledgeable source.

**Sebha:** "Libya Said to Be Readying New Chemical Weapons Plant," Agence France Press, May 5, 1990. The report quoted an article in *Der Spiegel* that named "Western intelligence" as its source and made reference to a similar article in *Bunte,* another news magazine. Three years later, work on the facility was still in progress, according to U.S. intelligence. See "U.S. Says Libya Is Building a 2d Poison-Gas Plant," *The New York Times,* February 18, 1993.

**Tarhuna:** "Thais' Work in Libya Brings a U.S. Warning," *The New York Times,* October 26, 1993.

**The transfer to Iran:** Janne Nolan, *Trappings of Power,* Washington, D.C.: Brookings Institution, 1991, p. 24.

**Saddam's complaint** is from "Libya Wants CSS-2," *Flight International,* May 14, 1988.

**The attempt to buy CSS-2s:** Ibid.

**The money:** "Look What I Found in My Backyard," *The Economist,* May 27, 1989, p. 44.

**Tauwiwa:** "Qadhafi's Secret Missile Oasis: German Technician's Revelations," *Stern,* May 21, 1987, pp. 20–26.

**Intelligence:** "Libya's Ballistic Missile," "ABC News This Morning," April 28, 1987. Also see "Libya Is Developing SSM," *Flight International,* May 23, 1987.

**SU-24s:** "Soviet Sale of SU-24 Deepens Concern About Mideast Weapons Proliferation," *Aviation Week & Space Technology,* April 10, 1989, p. 19.

**The IL-76:** "Soviets Sold Libya Advanced Bomber, U.S. Officials Say," *The New York Times,* April 5, 1989.

**C-130 and Mirage F-1:** "Libya Takes Key Step to Extend Range of Bombers," *The New York Times,* March 29, 1990.

**Nuclear-weapons-related activity:** Foreign Broadcast Information Service, JPRS Report, *Proliferation Issues: Russian Foreign Intelligence Service Report: Proliferation of Weapons of Mass Destruction,* April 4, 1993, pp. 47–48.

**Chemical weapons:** Admiral Brooks's congressional testimony on March 7, 1991. Egypt, along with thirteen other countries, was listed as "probably" possessing the weapons in order to protect the accuracy of the assessment, and therefore of the sources and methods used to make it. The Russian Foreign Intelligence Service expressed no doubt on the matter, according to an undated report issued by the Foreign Broadcast Information Service early in 1993.

**TU-16s and subs:** "Middle East Arms Control and Related Issues," CRS, May 1, 1991, pp. CRS 75–77.

**The end of Condor:** "Egypt Drops Out of Missile Project," *The Washington Post,* September 20, 1989. Helmy was reported in "U.S. Rocket Expert Pleads Guilty in Egyptian Smuggling Case," *The New York Times,* June 11, 1989, and was the subject of a long article, "How the U.S. Caught an Alleged Smuggler of Arms Parts to Egypt," *The Wall Street Journal,* April 4, 1989.

**The tourists and al-Mahgoub:** "Patterns of Global Terrorism: 1990," Washington, D.C.: U.S. Department of State, April 1991, p. 26.

**Al-Turabi:** Profile of al-Turabi, *The Los Angeles Times,* April 6, 1992.

**The Pentagon analyst** did not wish to be identified.

**Iran backing revivalists:** "Arabs Raise a Nervous Cry Over Iranian Militancy," *The New York Times,* December 21, 1992.

**Ankara, Bangkok, and the pilgrimage:** "Patterns of Global Terrorism: 1990," pp. 29 and 31.

**CSS-2:** "Middle East Arms Control and Related Issues," p. CRS-90, and Timothy V. McCarthy, "A Chronology of PRC Missile Trade and Developments," Monterey: Monterey Institute of International Studies, February 12, 1992, p. 13, by way of Aaron Karp, "Ballistic Missile Proliferation," *SIPRI Yearbook: World Armaments and Disarmament: 1991*, Stockholm International Peace Research Institute, p. 325. Estimates of the number of missiles delivered varies enormously, and in one case was put at 120, which is unlikely. Thirty-six is probably the most accurate number. ("A Saudi Surprise?" *Foreign Report*, The Economist Newspaper, Ltd., January 10, 1991, p. 1.)

**For speculation about nukes,** see, for example, "State, Pentagon Worry About Saudi Missiles," *The Washington Times*, May 12, 1988, and "U.S. Caught Napping by Sino-Saudi Missile Deal," *The Los Angeles Times*, May 4, 1988.

**The advanced Saudi base:** "The Arming of Saudi Arabia," "Frontline," the Documentary Consortium, WNET, February 16, 1993.

**Riyadh-Teheran:** "In Victory, Afghanistan Can't Find Peace," *The New York Times*, July 27, 1992.

**The Syrian payment:** Internal Senate Foreign Relations Committee memorandum of November 21, 1990.

**$26 billion:** Embassy of Saudi Arabia newsletter, "Pakistan Moves to Settle Nuclear Plant Purchase," January 1991, p. 1.

**Pakistan:** Kyodo News Service, January 31, 1990.

**Gates's estimates** are from his "Weapons Proliferation: The Most Dangerous Challenge for American Intelligence," speech to Comstock Club, Sacramento, Calif., December 15, 1992.

**The estimates for restarting the Iraqi weapons programs** are from a highly knowledgeable source who requested anonymity.

**Bleeding and revivalists:** "Iraq's Gamble: Sharp Words, Dull Claws," *The New York Times*, January 18, 1993.

**Conventional weapons:** "Middle East Arms Control and Related Issues," pp. CRS 91–92.

**The M-9 sale:** "Potent Office Weaves Web in China Arms," *The New York Times*, August 21, 1991.

**Baker:** Kenneth R. Timmerman, "Weapons of Mass Destruction: The Cases of Iran, Syria, and Libya," Los Angeles: Simon Wiesenthal Center, 1992, pp. 70–71.

**The M-9s and Scud Cs:** A source that requested anonymity. And see "China-Syria Missile Deal Concluded, Officials Say," *The Los Angeles Times*, July 14, 1988, and "China to Supply 'Undefined Number' of Missiles," FBIS-NES-89-145, July 31, 1989, p. 38.

**Scud C shipment:** "U.S. Tracks a Korean Ship Taking Missile to Syria," *The New York Times*, February 21, 1992, and "Search Gone Awry," *Aviation Week & Space Technology*, March 16, 1992.

**The tests:** "Israel Says Syria Is Testing Advanced Scud Missile," *The New York Times*, August 15, 1992.

**The Scud-small arms deal and the missile plants:** "Iran-Syria Deal Revealed as Scuds Near Gulf Ports," *The Washington Times*, March 10, 1992.

**Syrian chemical weapons and the French official:** "Weapons of Mass Destruction," pp. 59–63.

**Chemical sites and inventories:** Ibid., p. 60.

**Hama:** The internal Senate Foreign Relations Committee memorandum.

**Nuclear weapons:** "Bush's Misguided Israel-Bashing," *The Washington Post*, October 3, 1991 (Lally Weymouth column). Also see "Syria-Iran Defence Links Arouse Western Suspicion," *Financial Times*, March 9, 1992.

**The new embassy and mission upgrade:** "Iran Opens Embassy in Tajikistan," Reuters, January 10, 1992.

**Jakarta:** "A Movement in Search of Itself," *Newsweek*, September 14, 1992, p. 43.

**The Kilos and McCoy:** "Iran's New Submarine, Built by Russia, Stirs Concern in U.S. Navy," *The Wall Street Journal*, November 16, 1992.

**The $7 billion buildup:** "Iran Said to Commit $7 Billion to Secret Arms Plan," *The New York Times*, August 8, 1992.

**Conventional arms:** "Middle East Arms Control and Related Issues," pp. CRS-78-79.

**The weapons bill:** "Counting Iran's New Arms Is the Easy Part," *The New York Times*, April 26, 1992.

**The $6 billion:** "Iran Steps Up Military Buildup, Raises New Fears," AP, February 11, 1992.

**Rafsanjani's remark:** "U.S. Nuclear Technology Tactics Vex Iran," *The New York Times*, November 18, 1991.

**Chemicals against Iranians and their effectiveness:** Matthew Meselson, "Chemical Weapons, Anti-Chemical Protection, and the Ascendancy of the Defense," a paper presented at the AAAS annual meeting on February 18, 1990.

**Possession of chemical weapons:** Admiral Brooks's testimony of March 7, 1991, p. 58. Also see Elisa D. Harris, "Stemming the Spread of Chemical Weapons," *The Brookings Review*, Winter 1989/90, p. 41. Iran also tried to buy poison-producing strains of fungus from Canada and the Netherlands, but the effort was blocked. ("Iran Is Said to Try to Obtain Toxins," *The New York Times*, August 14, 1989.)

**Locations other than Qazun and the Scud warheads:** "Weapons of Mass Destruction," pp. 33–34.

**The Scud C test:** "U.S.: Iran Fired Ballistic Missile," *The Washington Times*, May 24, 1991.

**Missile sales:** Discussions with various analysts.

**Nuclear history:** "Tehran Steps Up Nuclear Drive," AP, July 17, 1991.

**Bushehr and the European refusals:** Ibid.

**Brazil:** "Iran Seeking Nuclear Technology from Brazil," Agence France Presse, December 2, 1991.

**Argentina:** "Government Holds Up Shipment of Nuclear Material to Iran," AP, February 5, 1992.

**India:** "India Won't Sell Nuclear Reactor to Iran, Official Says," AP, November 20, 1991.

**The ten-year agreement:** "A Chronology of Iran's Nuclear Program," *Eye on Supply*, No. 7, Fall 1992, p. 11.

**The reactor purchase:** "China to Provide Atomic Reactor," London *KEYHAN*, JPRS-TND-90-016, September 20, 1990, p. 33.

**The Russian reactors:** "Iran and Russia Sign Pact to Build Nuclear Plants," PRNewswire, November 2, 1992.

**Pakistani training:** "Iran's Lethal Secret," *The Washington Post*, October 18, 1992.

**The PMI material** was released by Mohammed Mohadessin at the group's Washington office on June 4, 1991.

**U.S Intelligence assessments and Mohajerani's remarks:** "Officials Say Iran Is Seeking Nuclear Weapons Capability," *The Washington Post*, October 30, 1991. Also see "Iran's Nuclear Plans Worry U.S. Officials," *The Los Angeles Times*, January 27, 1991, and "Report Says Iran Seeks Atomic Arms," *The New York Times*, October 31, 1991.

**Sharistani:** "Iranian Sources Reveal: Iraqi Nuclear Scientist Sharistani Alive, Residing in Tehran," *Sawt al-Kuwait*, May 16, 1992, FBIS-NES-92-100, May 22, 1992.

**The duping of Jannekens:** David Kay, "The IAEA—How Can It Be Strengthened?" a paper prepared for delivery at the Woodrow Wilson Center on "Nuclear Proliferation in the 1990s: Challenges and Opportunities," December 1–2, 1992.

**Turksat:** "Turkey Extends a Helping Hand," *World Press Review*, July 1992, p. 13. (From *Neue Zurcher Zeitung*.)

**TRT:** "Turkey Is to Broadcast to 6 Ex-Soviet Lands," *The New York Times*, April 12, 1992.

**The remarks about conflict:** "Turkey Is Looking for Advantages in Region's New Ex-Soviet Nations," *The New York Times*, June 27, 1992.

**Afghanistan Scud firings:** U.S. Congress, House Committee on Ways and Means, "Administration and Enforcement of U.S. Export Control Programs," 102–72, 102nd Cong., 1st sess., 18 April and 1 May 1991, p. 113.

**Per capita income:** "The Next Islamic Revolution," *The Economist*, September 21, 1991, p. 58.

**Language proficiency:** "Russian Sahibs Go Home," *The Economist*, August 8, 1992, pp. 29–30.

**The Slavic retreat:** Sophie Quinn-Judge, "Retreat from Empire," *Far Eastern Economic Review*, October 25, 1990, pp. 23–24.

**"Children":** "Russian Sahibs Go Home."

**Tyuratam "for us":** "Baykonyr Space Station Important Asset for Kazakhstan," Agence France Presse, August 30, 1991.

**The Tyuratam riot:** "Soldiers Riot at Baikonur," *Aviation Week & Space Technology*, March 2, 1992, p. 15, and "Riots Bring Reduction of Troops at Baikonur," *Space News*, August 10–16, 1992, p. 21.

**"One big family":** "Suspected Moslem Separatists Blow Up China Bus," Reuters, February 21, 1992.

**Common knowledge of atomic bombs:** "Soviet Disarmament Ambassador Warns That Republics Know How to Build Nukes," Agence France Presse, October 4, 1991. The remark was made by Sergei Batsanov, the CIS representative to a U.N. disarmament conference in Geneva.

**European missile defense:** "European ABM Defense Plans Anticipate Middle East Threat," *Aviation Week & Space Technology*, August 10, 1992, p. 22.

## 11. INDIA AND PAKISTAN: OUR GOD CAN LICK YOUR GOD

**The power and research reactors:** Leonard Spector, *Nuclear Ambitions*, Boulder: Westview Press, 1990, pp. 83–87.

**The Kahuta episode** was related to Windrem by Gary Milhollin, who said he heard it from a Pakistani participant. Also see "Ex-President Discusses Nuclear Program, Politics," *The Muslim* (Islamabad), July 23, 1993.

**The series of crises:** *Nuclear Ambitions*, pp. 66–68.

**The continuing crises:** Ibid., pp. 66–78; "Pakistan's Threat Perception of India," *The Muslim* (Islamabad), September 9, 1992; and "NBC Nightly News," December 1 and 2, 1992.

**The Bible series threat:** "Tales from the Bible on TV Survive Islam Threat in India," *The New York Times*, April 12, 1993.

**"Dirty fish":** "Hindu Rage Against Muslims Transforming Indian Politics," *The New York Times*, September 17, 1993.

**Hussain's remark:** Windrem interview at the Embassy on September 4, 1992.

**The start of Pakistan's centrifuge:** Interview with A. Q. Khan published by the Rawalpindi *Nawai Waqi*, February 10, 1984, and reprinted in Sreedhar, *Pakistan's Bomb: A Documentary Study*, New Delhi: ABC Publishing House, 1986, pp. 184–85.

**India's standard image:** Steve Weissman and Herbert Krosney, *The Islamic Bomb*, New York: Times Books, 1981, p. 130.

**No foreign components:** Ibid., p. 129.

**India's relationship with China** is nicely summarized in Brahma Chellaney, "South Asia's Passage to Nuclear Power," *International Security*, Summer 1991, pp. 48–51.

**Canadian, French, and American help:** Ibid., pp. 130–31.

**The two scientists:** Ibid.

**The $2.3 billion estimate** was made by Thomas W. Graham at University of Maryland seminar on Nuclear Proliferation and the Press, May 14, 1991.

**U.S. involvement in the West-East Pakistan situation:** Seymour M. Hersh, *The Price of Power*, New York: Summit Books, 1983, pp. 444–64. See p. 464 in particular.

**The strategist** was Humayun Akhtar, quoted in *The Muslim*, September 9, 1992.

**Five biological warfare facilities:** Foreign Broadcast Information Service JPRS Report, *Proliferation Issues: Russian Foreign Intelligence Service Report: Proliferation of Weapons of Mass Destruction*, April 4, 1993, p. 54.

**Best microchip designers:** Geoffrey Kemp and Selig Harrison, "India and America," Washington, D.C.: Carnegie Endowment for International Peace, 1993.

**Smuggled water:** *Nuclear Ambitions*, p. 73.

**Details of Hazira** are from a fax of January 11, 1991, from Enzio von Kuehlmann-Stumm, Siemens AG Corporate Press Department, to Windrem.

**Milhollin on possible violation of the NPT:** From his fax to Windrem dated January 4, 1991.

**The Trudeau and Gandhi vignettes:** *The Islamic Bomb*, p. 133.

**Eating grass or leaves:** Ibid., p. 161.

**Bhutto's remark to Kissinger:** Ibid., p. 163.

**Zia ul-Haq** made the statement in an interview with a Bahraini newspaperman. He is quoted in "Pakistan, Iraq, and the Islamic Bomb?" *Proliferation Watch*, Senate Committee on Governmental Affairs, November–December 1990, p. 2.

**The NPT's provisions:** *Arms Control and Disarmament Agreements*, Washington, D.C.: U.S. Arms Control and Disarmament Agency, 1980, pp. 88–89.

**The scene under the tent:** *Pakistan's Bomb*, pp. 114–17.

**Khan's background:** Ibid., pp. 195–200.

**The A. Q. Khan episode:** *The Islamic Bomb*, pp. 175–80.

**Butt** is from *The Islamic Bomb*.

**Ul-Haq:** Government sentencing memorandum in the case of *United States of America v. ul-Haq*, Eastern District of Pennsylvania, 87–283, September 22, 1992, and other court documents.

**Horrible example:** Benazir Bhutto, *Daughter of the East*, London: Mandarin Press, 1988, p. 86.

**Poincet's remark:** Ibid., p. 171.

**The chronology of events from 1976 to 1984** is from the *Congressional Record*, "Pakistan's Dispossessed Bomb," passim.

**Khan's letters to his network** were seized by the Royal Canadian Mounted Police on August 29, 1980, and were used in the prosecution of three Pakistanis who illegally exported centrifuge components home (*Pakistan's Bomb*, pp. 23–58).

**The possible Iraq-Pakistan connection:** *Proliferation Watch*, Vol. 1, No. 5, July 1990.

**Events in 1980** are from the *Congressional Record*, Senate, S 15880, "Pakistan's Dispossessed Bomb," Vol. 135, No. 161, November 16, 1989.

**Inam ul-Haq's remarks:** "NBC Nightly News," December 2, 1992.

**A. Q. Khan's remarks to the librarians:** Foreign Broadcast Information Service-NES-90-215, November 6, 1990, p. 71.

**The "asset" remark:** FBIS-NES-90-176, September 11, 1990, p. 73.

**Khan's nationalistic outpouring** is from an interview that appeared in *Rawalpindi Nawai Waqt*, February 10, 1984.

**The Chinese-Pakistani bomb plans:** Gary Milhollin and Gerard White, "Bombs from Beijing: A Report on China's Nuclear and Missile Exports," Washington, D.C.: Wisconsin Project on Nuclear Arms Control, May 1991, p. 2.

**Agni's launch and benefits:** Dilip Bobb and Amarnath K. Menon, "Chariot of Fire," *India Today*, June 15, 1989, p. 10.

**Kalam's remarks:** Ibid., p. 12.

**The creation of the National Committee for Space Research:** Janne Nolan, *The Trappings of Power*, Washington, D.C.: Brookings Institution, 1991, p. 41.

**The acquisition of Scout technology:** Gary Milhollin, "India's Missiles—With a Little Help from Our Friends," *The Bulletin of the Atomic Scientists*, November 1989, pp. 31–32.

**The Soviets' contribution to the space program:** *Trappings of Power*, p. 42.

**DFVLR help:** Gary Milhollin, "West German Aid to India's Rocket Program," a research report, Washington, D.C.: Wisconsin Project on Nuclear Arms Control, April 11, 1989, pp. 10–11.

**The French/German efforts:** Milhollin, "India's Missiles—With a Little Help from Our Friends," pp. 32–34.

**Details of the IGMDP** are from W. Seth Carus, "India's Ballistic Missile Program" (draft), Newport, RI: Naval War College Foundation, December 1, 1989, p. 7.

**The Indian correspondent** was Pushpindar Singh, "India's Agni Success Poses New Problems," *Jane's Defence Weekly*, June 3, 1989, p. 1052.

**The Prithvi test:** "After Testing Missile, India Holds Talks with Pakistan," *The New York Times*, August 19, 1992.

**The hydrogen bomb and beryllium material:** "Signs Found India Building an H-Bomb," *The Washington Post*, May 19, 1989.

**India's reaction to Webster's remarks** is from a State Department transmission of May 22, 1989, p. 52.

**The ICBM material:** "India Proposes Building of ICBM," *Defense & Foreign Affairs Weekly*, June 5–11, 1989, p. 1.

**The use of Pakistan in backchanneling to China:** *The Price of Power*, pp. 356, 359, and 365–66.

**The aid package:** Smith and Cobban, "A Blind Eye to Nuclear Proliferation," *Foreign Affairs*, Summer 1989, p. 58.

**Reagan's letters to Wright** were written on December 17, 1989, and on November 10, 1988.

**Pakistan's seven nuclear weapons:** "NBC Nightly News," December 1 and 2, 1992, as well as "News Forum," November 25, 1990. Senator Daniel Patrick Moynihan, a member of the Senate Foreign Relations Committee, said in response to a question that "Last July, the Pakistanis machined six nuclear warheads, and they still got them. Now, that's the first Islamic country with delivery systems—F-16s—and the warheads." Moynihan and other members of the committee had been briefed by the CIA earlier in the fall.

**Subrahmanyan's remarks** are from the introduction to *Pakistan's Bomb* by Sreedhar, p. xv.

## 12. THE REAL CHINA SYNDROME

**The May 21, 1992, test:** "Powerful Underground Nuclear Explosion in China," AP, May 21, 1992.

**Largest-ever:** "Missile Diplomacy," *The Economist*, June 6, 1992. Also see "Chinese Set Off Their Biggest Nuclear Explosion," *The New York Times*, May 22, 1992.

**ASLV, the gamma-ray satellite, polar satellite launch vehicle, and the remote sensing satellite:** "India Succeeds with Third ASLV Launch Attempt" and "India's IRS-1C Satellite to Offer Sharper Images," *Space News*, May 25, 1992, pp. 6 and 11, respectively. Also see "Critical India Rocket Launch Set for End of May," *Space News*, May 18–24, 1992, p. 14.

**"Goodwill":** "Missile Diplomacy."

**Agni:** "India Successfully Tests a Medium-Range Missile," *The New York Times*, May 31, 1992.

**The exercise:** Ibid.

**Biological weapons:** Interviews with congressional staff members on April 27, 1993.

**The three new types of weapons:** "Chinese Coveting Offensive Triad," *Aviation Week & Space Technology*, September 21, 1992, p. 20. Also see "China Builds Its Military Muscle, Making Some Neighbors Nervous," *The New York Times*, January 11, 1993.

**The document** is from "As China Looks at World Order, It Detects New Struggles Emerging," *The New York Times*, April 21, 1992.

**Old territories:** "China Builds Its Military Muscle, Making Some Neighbors Nervous."

**The pledges of nonproliferation:** Gary Milhollin and Gerard White, "Bombs from Beijing: A Report on China's Nuclear and Missile Exports," Washington, D.C.: Wisconsin Project on Nuclear Arms Control, May 1991, p. 15.

**Li's NPT announcement:** "China Backs Pact on Nuclear Arms," *The New York Times*, August 11, 1991.

**The Algerian reactor:** "Bombs from Beijing," p. 16.

**Possible military aid:** "China May Be Giving A-Arms Aid to Algeria," *The Los Angeles Times*, April 12, 1991.

**Nuclear customers** are in "Bombs from Beijing," pp. 16–19. Missile sales are listed chronologically in Timothy V. McCarthy, "A Chronology of PRC Missile Trade and Developments," Monterey: Monterey Institute of International Studies, February 12, 1992. In addition, see U.S. Senate Committee on Governmental Affairs, *Proliferation Watch*, March-April 1991, pp. 1–4.

**COSTIND's leaders:** William C. Triplett II, "China's Weapons Mafia," *The Washington Post*, October 27, 1991.

**Military structure:** John W. Lewis, Hua Di, and Xue Litai, "Beijing's Defense Establishment: Solving the Arms Export Enigma," *International Security*, Spring 1991, pp. 88–92.

**Individual corporate responsibilities** are in "China's Defense Industrial Trading Companies," VP-1920-271-90, Washington, D.C.: Defense Intelligence Agency, September 1990, and in "China's Weapons Mafia."

**Arms sales to Myanmar:** "Burmese Warning on Arms Buildup," *The New York Times*, November 19, 1991.

**J-6s and J-7s:** Richard A. Bitzinger, "Arms to Go," *International Security*, Fall 1992, p. 88.

**Fifty percent:** From a highly knowledgeable source who requested anonymity.

**Number three position:** Richard F. Grimmet, "Trends in Conventional Arms Transfers to the Third World by Major Supplier, 1982–1989," 90-298F, Washington, D.C.: Congressional Research Service, June 19, 1990, pp. CRS 4–5.

**Deng's reaction to the CSS-2 sale:** "Beijing's Defense Establishment: Solving the Arms Export Enigma," p. 96.

**M-11 data** can be found in "China's M11 Revealed," *Jane's Defence Weekly*, April 9, 1988, p. 655. Also see "China Has Sold 'A Small Number' of Missiles to Pakistan: Official," Agence France Presse, June 20, 1991, and "Pakistan Seeks Chinese Missile, U.S. Believes," *The Wall Street Journal*, April 5, 1991.

**Unveiling the M-9 and sales negotiations:** "A Chronology of PRC Missile Trade and Developments," pp. 5 and 7.

**M-9 data:** *SIPRI Yearbook 1988: World Armaments and Disarmament*, New York: Oxford University Press, 1988, p. 53, and "New Chinese Mobile SRBM," *News Review on East Asia*, February 1987, p. 135. Also see "Pakistan Seeks Chinese Missile, U.S. Believes."

**Zhu's statement** is from the transcript, "Statements by PRC Ambassador Zhu Qizhen on Proliferation Issues," Federal Information Systems Corp., June 27, 1991.

**The M-9 and M-11 chronology:** "A Chronology of PRC Missile Trade and Developments," pp. 9–22.

**Poison gas and Biden's remarks:** "Chinese Reported to Weigh Sale of Poison Gas Chemicals to Libya," *The New York Times*, June 7, 1990.

**The second factory:** "Chinese Move Seen as Aiding Libya in Making Poison Gas," *The Washington Times*, July 12, 1990.

**The political situation vs. the former Soviet Union:** Ellis Jaffe, "China After the Gulf War: The Lessons Learned," a paper prepared for the Center for National Security Studies, Los Alamos National Laboratory, November 1991, pp. 9–10.

**Silkworms:** "Merchants of Death," *Newsweek*, November 18, 1991, p. 38.

**The new dimension:** Paper by Liu Jinglian, "Reflection on the Gulf War and Lessons Drawn from It," given at the Los Alamos National Laboratory on February 2, 1990, p. 2.

**Budgets:** "China to Reward Army with 13% Increase in Military Budget," *The New York Times*, March 22, 1992.

**The "Third Line":** "Nuclear Tibet: Nuclear Waste and Nuclear Weapons on the Tibetan Plateau," a report by the International Campaign for Tibet, Washington, D.C., 1993, p. ix.

**The "863" plan:** U.S. Department of State telex no. 089557, from the Secretary of State to various recipients, March 25, 1993.

**MIG-31s:** "China Seeks to Build MIG-31," *Aviation Week & Space Technology*, October 5, 1992, pp. 27–28.

**The deal with Iran:** "Chinese Coveting Offensive Triad," *Aviation Week & Space Technology*, September 21, 1992, pp. 20–21.

**Use of nuclear test facilities:** From a declassified Department of Defense document of June 1991.

**Observations:** September 1992 interview with a highly knowledgeable source who did not wish to be identified.

**Lances and F-15Es:** "A Chronology of PRC Missile Trade and Developments," p. 7, and "Saudi Purchase of Chinese Missiles Changes Middle East Military Balance," *Aviation Week & Space Technology*, March 28, 1988, p. 30.

**"Stability":** "China Seeks Leverage—Finds Criticism—for Arms Sale to Saudis," *Christian Science Monitor*, April 8, 1988.

**Al Joffer and Al Sulaiyl:** "A Chronology of PRC Missile Trade and Developments," p. 13.

**The finding of the CSS-2 and the crisis:** Interview with an Arab source who requested anonymity.

**Wu's reply to Shultz:** "U.S. Caught Napping by Sino-Saudi Missile Deal," *The Los Angeles Times*, May 4, 1988.

**"Responsible way":** "A Chronology of PRC Missile Trade and Developments," pp. 9, 11, and 12.

**Bush's remarks and the computers:** "Bush Renewing Trade Privileges for China, But Adds Missile Curbs," *The New York Times*, May 28, 1991.

**The Department of State official** spoke on condition of anonymity.

**"You can't make it useful":** "State, Pentagon Worry About Saudi Missiles," *The Washington Times*, May 12, 1988.

**The chemical-nuclear possibility:** Ibid.

**The visit to Argentina and Brazil:** "A Chronology of PRC Missile Trade and Developments," p. 4.

**The two tests:** "Soviet and People's Republic of China Nuclear Weapons Employment Policy and Strategy," TCS-654 775-72, Copy 3, Washington, D.C.: Defense Intelligence Agency, March 1972, pp. II–21 and Table 1: Chinese Communist Nuclear Tests.

**Soviet help:** Ibid., p. II–6.

**"Everything you've got":** Michael R. Beschloss, *The Crisis Years*, New York: Edward Burlingame, 1991, p. 43.

**Chinese tests, arsenal, and retargeting:** Richard Fieldhouse, "China's Mixed Signals on Nuclear Weapons," *The Bulletin of the Atomic Scientists*, May 1991, p. 40.

**The power plant:** "China Sells Nuclear Power Plant to Pakistan," AP, December 31, 1991. Also see "China's First Nuclear Power Plant Put into Operation," AP, December 18, 1991.

**Daya Bay:** "China Makes Nuclear Pledge," Agence France Presse, April 2, 1991.

**Indian heavy water:** "Bombs from Beijing," p. 4.

**"Sheer fabrication":** "China Denies Helping Iraq Build Nuclear Power Plant," AP, July 3, 1991.

**Sales to Iraq:** "Bombs from Beijing," p. 17.

**The separator, reactor, and statement:** "China Acknowledges Nuclear Sales to Iran," Agence France Presse, November 4, 1991.

**The calutrons:** Ibid.

**Finishing the German-French reactor and increased trade:** "Report Says PRC to Supply Nuclear Technology," FBIS-NES-91-138, July 18, 1991, p. 38.

**"Sheer fabrication":** "China Denies Plans to Sell Iran Nuclear Weapon Technology," Reuters, June 27, 1991.

**The Syrian reactor:** "Israel Concerned About Chinese Nuclear Reactor Sale to Syria," Agence France Presse, November 29, 1991.

**Algeria and the NPT:** "Algeria Offers Atom Arms Vow," *The New York Times*, January 8, 1992.

**Iraqi scientists and uranium:** Ibid.

**Congressional testimony and the leak:** "China May Be Giving A-Arms Aid to Algeria."

**The CIA and Kennedy:** "Algerian Reactor Came from China," *The New York Times*, November 15, 1991.

**Special economic zones:** "A Great Leap Forward," *The Economist*, October 5, 1991, pp. 19–22.

**Retrenchment:** "Foreign Trade Barriers," 1991 National Trade Estimate Report, Office of the United States Trade Representative, p. 43.

**U.S.-China import-export figures:** Ibid.

**The administration position** was often articulated. See, for example, "U.S. Lifts Its Sanctions on China Over High Technology Transfers," *The New York Times*, February 22, 1992.

**Rizvi:** "Has China Sold Out the Third World?" *World Press Review*, December 1991, pp. 12 and 14. (From the independent weekly *Dialogue* of Dacca.)


## 13. EAST ASIA: THE OTHER RING OF FIRE

**Warrant and punishment:** "Ministry Takes Measures in Chang Defection Case," FBIS-CHI-88-064, April 4, 1988, p. 80.

**"Ungentlemanlike":** "Atom [sic] for Peace," *China Post* (Taiwan), April 3, 1988.

**Washington's clampdowns:** Steve Weissman and Herbert Krosney, *The Islamic Bomb*, New York, Times Books, 1981, pp. 152–53.

**Ten weapons:** Leonard S. Spector and Jacqueline White, *Nuclear Ambitions*, New York: Basic Books, 1990, p. 60.

**Shaping bomb cores:** A highly knowledgeable source who requested anonymity.

**The reactor's closing:** "Taiwan to Close Nuclear Reactor," *The Washington Post*, March 24, 1988.

**The reprocessing plant:** "Taipei Halts Work on Secret Plant to Make Nuclear Bomb Ingredient," *The New York Times*, March 23, 1988.

**Pei-fen's letter:** "Papers Link Missing Scientist to Alleged Plan to Make Nuclear Weapons," AP, March 13, 1988.

**Ships, submarines, and planes:** "Military Presence: U.S. Personnel in the Pacific Theater," GAO/NSLAD-91-192, Washington, D.C.: General Accounting Office, August 1991, p. 112. The cost in fiscal 1989, the last year available, was $16.8 billion (p. 26). The Japanese and South Korean contributions are from pp. 10 and 11.

**Japanese and Korean cuts:** Ibid., pp. 10 and 11.

**Congress acted through the National Defense Authorization Act for Fiscal Years 1990 and 1991:** Ibid., p. 20.

**Singapore:** "Singapore and the Problems of Success," *The Economist*, August 22, 1992, p. 25.

**Toshiba:** "Chinese Missiles Tied to Japanese," *The New York Times*, September 16, 1992.

**The East German ships to Indonesia:** "Combat Fleets," *Proceedings*, October 1992, p. 125.

**An Indian-Japanese alliance** is treated at some length in George Friedman and Meredith Lebard, *The Coming War with Japan*, New York: St. Martin's Press, 1991, p. 389.

**Singapore's F-16s:** U.S. Congress, Office of Technology Assessment, *Global Arms Trade*,

OTA-ISC-460, Washington, D.C.: U.S. Government Printing Office, June 1991, p. 125.

**The quoted analyst:** "Taiwan Getting New U.S. Arms to Offset China," *Los Angeles Times*, December 22, 1990.

**The SU-27s:** Tai Ming Cheung, "Loaded Weapons," *Far Eastern Economic Review*, September 3, 1992, p. 21.

**Bih:** "Taiwan Launches Aggressive Arms-Buying Program," AP, August 29, 1991.

**Cobras:** "Taiwan Getting New U.S. Arms to Offset China."

**Patriot components:** "U.S. Clears Way for Made-in-Taiwan Missiles," *Los Angeles Times*, January 12, 1992.

**The naval vessels:** "Taiwan to Buy Six More Submarines from the Netherlands: Report," Agence France Presse, October 2, 1991.

**F-16s:** "Bush Approves, Defends F-16 Sale to Taiwan," Reuters, September 2, 1992.

**Mirage:** "Sale of Mirage 2000-5s to China Wins Approval," *Aviation Week & Space Technology*, November 23, 1992, p. 32.

**Sky Horse:** "Propping Up a Fading Friendship," *Far Eastern Economic Review*, October 27, 1978, p. 18.

**MIT:** "Taiwanese Program at MIT Ended," *The Washington Post*, July 16, 1976. One MIT official was quoted in the article as saying that the engineers were returning to a top-secret military research institute. It was Chungshan.

**Green Bee:** "Taiwan's Space and Missile Programs," *International Defense Review*, 8/1989, p. 1077.

**Sky Horse:** James Katz, ed., *Arms Production in Developing Countries*, Lexington, MA: Lexington Books, 1984, p. 311, and an article in *Lien Ho Pao* (Taipei), November 11, 1982.

**Article IX:** Richard Halloran, "Chrysanthemum and Sword Revisited: Is Japanese Militarism Resurgent?" Honolulu: The East-West Center, 1992, pp. 9–10.

**MacArthur and the court:** Ibid., p. 10.

**Plutonium background:** "Dangerous Cargo," *The Economist*, April 18, 1992, pp. 32–33.

**The departure:** "Plutonium Shipment Leaves France for Japan," *The New York Times*, November 8, 1992.

**Fabrication problems:** "Japan Says Technical Problems Will Force Storage of Plutonium," *The New York Times*, November 28, 1992.

**The sea change and weapons conversion:** "Japan Thinks Again About Its Plan to Build a Plutonium Stockpile," *The New York Times*, August 3, 1992.

**Gridlock:** "First Batch of Plutonium Fuel Transported," *Nuke Info Tokyo*, July/August 1992, p. 7.

**Naval escort:** "Japan to Ship Plutonium Amid Rising Concerns," *The Washington Post*, April 5, 1992.

**"N minus six months":** "Chrysanthemum and Sword Revisited," pp. 17–18.

**The Moon and Halley:** William E. Burrows, *Exploring Space: Voyages in the Solar System and Beyond*, New York: Random House, 1991, p. 429.

**Akiyama:** "Soviets Send First Japanese, a Journalist, into Space," *The New York Times*, December 3, 1990, and "Japanese Journalist Reaches Soviets' Space Station Aboard Commercial Flight," *Aviation Week & Space Technology*, December 10, 1990, pp. 23–24.

**The three astronauts:** "First Japanese Shuttle Astronaut Set for 1991 Spacelab J. Flight," *Aviation Week & Space Technology*, August 27, 1990, pp. 72–75.

**Mamoru Mohri:** "Sketches of the 7 Astronauts Aboard Shuttle Endeavor," *The New York Times*, September 14, 1992.

**The agreement with Russia:** "Japanese, Russians to Sign Space Accord in September," *Space News*, August 31–September 6, 1992, p. 39.

**The space shuttle:** "Japanese Refining Unmanned HOPE Orbiter for Planned 1996 Launch," *Aviation Week & Space Technology*, April 3, 1989, pp. 57–58.

**Spaceport:** "Japan Preparing New Spaceport Facilities for H-1, H-2 Rockets," *Aviation Week & Space Technology,* July 14, 1986, pp. 51–56.

**Lunar base:** "Japan Readies First Moon Mission Launch as Companies Seek Lunar Base Role," *Aviation Week & Space Technology,* January 8, 1990, p. 20.

**H-1 and H-2:** "Japan Forging Aggressive Space Development Pace," *Aviation Week & Space Technology,* August 13, 1990, passim. Also see "Japanese Select Launcher with Heavy-Lift Capacity," *Aviation Week & Space Technology,* August 13, 1984, pp. 162–63.

**J-1:** "Japan to Offer J-1 Solid Rocket for Launch of Small Payloads," *Aviation Week & Space Technology,* August 10, 1992, pp. 47–49.

**The satellites:** "Japan Plans Ambitious Satellite Expansion," *Space News,* July 8–14, 1991, pp. 8 and 10; Hughes Fact Sheets SCG 86301B/2M/4-78 and SCG 856329A/3500/3-85; "Japan to Get More Use from JERS-1 Satellite," *Space News,* June 8–14, 1992, pp. 6 and 13; "Japan Plans New Generation of Remote Sensing Satellites," *Aviation Week & Space Technology,* July 13, 1992, pp. 66–67; and "Japan Set to Launch Satellite for Ocean Remote Sensing," *Aviation Week & Space Technology,* February 16, 1987.

**The FSX project** is described in "Joint FS-X Team at Work; Detailed Design Phase to Start Next Year," *Aviation Week & Space Technology,* July 29, 1991, p. 44.

**Protectionist and racist:** *Global Arms Trade,* p. 112.

**Hagi:** "Tokyo, Unsure of U.S., Talks of Developing Its Own Arms," *The New York Times,* June 28, 1989.

**AAM-3:** "Japanese Missiles," *Aviation Week & Space Technology,* December 3, 1990, p. 13.

**Ryozo Tsutsui:** "Tokyo, Unsure of U.S., Talks of Developing Its Own Arms."

**Mach-5 engine:** "Japan Leads Team Effort to Test Mach 5 Powerplant," *Aviation Week & Space Technology,* August 17, 1992, pp. 48–49.

**Yamato:** "Unpropelled to Stardom," *The Economist,* April 27, 1991, p. 90, and "Ship Sails on High-Tech, 'Silent' Drive," *The Washington Post,* June 17, 1992.

**Hoffman's indictment** was in the United States District Court for the Central District of California, February 1990. Also see News Release: "Los Angeles Man Indicted for Illegal Export of Space Craft and Missile Technology," U.S. Attorney's Office, Los Angeles, California, November 15, 1990, and "Engineer Held in Illegal 'Star Wars' Sales," *Los Angeles Times,* June 16, 1990.

**The navigation and missile parts:** "Japanese Defence Group Fined Over Illegal Arms Sale," *Financial Times,* March 13, 1992, and "Arms Sale to Iran Charged in Japan," *The New York Times,* July 6, 1991. The company was Japan Aviation Electronics Industry, which was affiliated with NEC. Toshiba was the firm that transferred the propeller technology to the U.S.S.R.

**Internal pressure:** From a highly knowledgeable source who did not wish to be identified.

**Troops abroad:** "Japan's Parliament Votes to End Ban on Sending Troops Abroad," *The New York Times,* June 26, 1992.

**The official's quote:** Ibid.

**Boutros-Ghali and Mozambique:** "U.N. Chief Presses Japan for Peacekeeping Troops," *The New York Times,* February 19, 1993.

**Watanabe:** "Japanese Discuss Expanded Role in Peacekeeping for the Military," *The New York Times,* January 10, 1993.

**G-1:** "A Chronology of North Korean Nuclear Developments," Monterey: Emerging Nuclear Suppliers Project, May 13, 1991, p. 5.

**The expert** was Gary Milhollin in "North Korea's Bomb," *The New York Times,* June 4, 1992.

**Antiaircraft guns:** "Jittery Asia Has Visions of a Nuclear North Korea," *The New York Times,* April 7, 1991.

**Yongbyon** is described in detail in the excellent article by Joseph S. Bermudez, Jr., "North Korea's Nuclear Program," *Jane's Intelligence Review,* September 1991, pp. 404–11.

**Hee Young Chae:** Search warrant filed on October 18, 1991, in U.S. District Court for the Central District of California for 16436 Tulsa Street, Granada Hills.

**Ko:** "Defector Says North Korea Close to Making Nuclear Weapons," AP, September 13, 1991.

**Gates:** "U.S. Agencies Split Over North Korea," *The New York Times*, March 10, 1992.

**Sixty-two pounds:** "North Korea Building Plant Capable of Making Nuclear Weapons," AP, April 24, 1991.

**Six to eight:** Gary Milhollin, "Pursuing the Bomb in North Korea," Washington: Wisconsin Project on Nuclear Arms Control, June 3, 1992.

**Woolsey and Eagleburger:** Gates testimony before the Senate Government Affairs Committee, February 24, 1993.

**Commando raid:** "Defense Minister's Reported Comment on Possible Raid Creates Flap," AP, April 12, 1991.

**$1 billion investment:** Windrem interview with a congressional source in Washington on June 19, 1993. Also see "Israel Seeks to Keep North Korea from Aiding Iran," *The New York Times*, June 20, 1993.

**No Patriots:** "Jittery Asia Has Visions of a Nuclear North Korea."

**Patriots:** "Government Reportedly Buying Patriot Missiles to Counter Scud Threat," AP, October 8, 1991.

**The U.S. withdrawal and Roh's declaration:** "South Korea to Keep Out All Atom Arms," *The New York Times*, November 9, 1991.

**Inspection:** "Seoul to Permit Nuclear Inspections," *The New York Times*, December 12, 1991.

**The pledge:** "Seoul Says It Now Has No Nuclear Arms," *The New York Times*, December 19, 1991.

**Japanese demands:** Mark Hibbs, "Bilateralism, Supply Controls Emerge as New Nonproliferation Paths," *Nucleonics Week*, January 16, 1992, p. 18.

**SPOT:** "The Yongbyon Puzzle," *Asiaweek*, March 9, 1990, p. 17. That issue's cover posed the question "Does North Korea Have the Bomb?" in front of a mushroom cloud.

**The denial:** "North Korea Defends Atom Plant," *The New York Times*, June 1, 1991.

**The North–South accord:** "Look, No Bomb," *The Economist*, January 4, 1992, p. 30.

**Safeguards:** "North Korea Signs Accord on Atom-Plant Inspections," *The New York Times*, January 31, 1992.

**The document:** "North Korea Reveals More About Its Nuclear Sites," *The New York Times*, May 7, 1992.

**Plutonium:** "North Korea Confirms It Has Produced Plutonium at Experimental Facility," AP, May 15, 1992.

**Blix:** "N. Korean Plutonium Plant Cited," *The Washington Post*, May 17, 1992.

**Deception:** "C.I.A. Chief Says North Koreans Are Hiding Arms Projects."

**Trucks and underground:** "Bomb Bluffers?" *The Economist*, May 16, 1992.

**Sharing satellite imagery and chemical data:** "West Knew of North Korea Nuclear Development," *The New York Times*, March 13, 1993.

**North Korea's change of heart:** "North Korea Rebuffs Nuclear Inspectors, Reviving U.S. Nervousness," *The New York Times*, February 1, 1993.

**Blix's reaction:** "Atom Agency Said to Issue Demand to North Korea," *The New York Times*, February 11, 1993.

**Kim Il Sung's remarks:** "North Korea Spurns Nuclear Agency Demand," *The New York Times*, February 14, 1993.

**Only a matter of time:** "West Knew of North Korea Nuclear Development."

**The official** did not wish to be identified.

**Biological and chemical weapons and the long-range missile:** Foreign Broadcast Information Service JPRS Report, *Proliferation Issues: Russian Foreign Intelligence Service Report: Proliferation of Weapons of Mass Destruction* (undated), pp. 61–62.

**Re-embracing the NPT:** "North Korea Says It Won't Pull Out of Arms Pact Now," *The New York Times*, June 12, 1993.

**Intelligence estimates:** Highly knowledgeable sources who requested anonymity.

**Clinton's warning and the response:** "Clinton, in Seoul, Tells North Korea to Drop Arms

Plan," *The New York Times*, July 11, 1993, and "Clinton's Warning Irks North Korea," *The New York Times*, July 13, 1993.

**Generals in Cuba:** Interview with José Oro, a defector from the Cuban nuclear program, on May 1, 1991.

**Nodong-1 test:** "Korean Missile Threat," *Aviation Week & Space Technology*, July 5, 1993, p. 17; "Missile Is Tested by North Koreans," *The New York Times*, June 13, 1993.

**Japan's reaction:** "Japan Shifts Its Stand on Ruling Out A-Bomb," *The Washington Post*, July 9, 1993.

**Kim Jung Il:** An intelligence source who wished to remain anonymous. The information about his life-style comes from two North Korean movie stars who defected. His position is described in "North Korean Chief's Son Gains Military Post," *The New York Times*, April 10, 1993.

**Korean collaboration and strategy:** *Global Arms Trade*, pp. 132–35.

**Honest John and Nike-Hercules:** *Ground Defence International*, November 1979, p. 36.

**The longer-range missile:** "South Korea," *Asian Survey*, January 1979, p. 43, and James Katz, *Arms Production in Developing Countries*, Lexington, MA: Lexington Books, 1984, p. 228.

**Answering the Scud threat:** Janne E. Nolan, *Trappings of Power*, Washington, D.C.: The Brookings Institution, 1991, pp. 91–95.

**The IRBM:** Gerald M. Steinberg, "Two Missiles in Every Garage," *Bulletin of the Atomic Scientists*, October 1983, p. 43.

**The satellite:** "Korea to Launch Nation's 1st Research Satellite by 1996," *The Korea Times*, May 21, 1987.

**The hard-liners and Han Sung Joo:** "Wary of North Korea, Seoul Debates Building Atomic Bomb," *The New York Times*, March 19, 1993.

**Reprocessing plant:** From a highly knowledgeable source who requested anonymity.


## 14. THE WORLD MISSILE: TWO CASE HISTORIES

**Helmy's background:** U.S. Congress, House Subcommittee on Oversight, *Administration and Enforcement of U.S. Export Control Programs* (102–72), 102nd Cong., First Session, April 18 and May 1, 1991, pp. 142–43.

**The $1 billion** is from figures supplied by Warner Bros., Touchstone (Disney), 20th Century Fox, and Columbia. His other films include *Black Joy, Absence of Malice, The King of Comedy, Brazil, Stripper, Family Business, Q & A, Guilty by Suspicion*, and *The Power of One*. Since Milchan's primary role was that of a financier, he did not always appear in a film's credits, so he may have been involved in more than twenty-four pictures.

**Abbott and McKeown:** Andrew Yule, *Losing the Light: Terry Gilliam and the Munchausen Saga*, New York: Applause Books, 1991, pp. 1 and 3.

**The Kosmos caper:** A highly knowledgeable source who spoke on condition of anonymity.

**Dichmont** was interviewed by Windrem.

**Striking resemblance:** "U.S. Says Data Suggest Israel Aids South Africa on Missile," *The New York Times*, October 27, 1989. DSP satellites were designed primarily to warn of a missile attack against the United States by pinpointing the positions and tracks of an enemy missile launch. They have also been routinely used to collect intelligence data on Soviet, Chinese, and other missile tests.

The 1962 start-up date is from the top-secret transcript of a meeting between General E. Weizman, Israel's Minister of Defense, and General H. Toufanian, Iran's Vice Minister of War, in Tel Aviv on July 18, 1977, to discuss military cooperation. Weizman correctly noted that Jericho was initially developed with help from France.

**The DIA reported** "a probably SRBM" fired "in an easterly direction from South Africa's Arniston Missile Test Range." The assessment noted that Armscor called the missile a booster rocket and further noted that the Arniston facility was "particularly appropriate for the development of ballistic missiles." Defense Intelligence Agency, Directorate for Current Intelligence, "Special Assessment: South Africa: Missile Activity (U)," July 5, 1989, p. 9.

**Think tank:** NBC News report on October 26, 1989. Also see Richard MacWilliams, *Armscor, South Africa's Arms Merchant*, McLean, VA.: Brasseys, 1989.

**Rhoodie's lament:** Eschel Rhoodie, *The Real Information Scandal*, Pretoria: Orbis SA (PTY) Ltd, 1983, pp. 110–11.

**Rhoodie and Milchan:** Jonathan Bloch and Andrew Weir, "The Adventures of the Brothers Kimche," *The Middle East*, April 1982, p. 26. Milchan gave contradictory accounts of his role, alternately saying that he loathed South Africa because of apartheid and admitting his role but adding that he "couldn't sleep at night" because of it. ("The Mogul with Muscle and Money," *The Jerusalem Post*, March 17, 1992, and "A Mogul's Bankroll and Past," *Los Angeles Times*, February 28, 1992. Also see Mervyn Rees's and Chris Day's 1980 book, *Muldergate* [Johannesburg: Macmillan of South Africa], which described Milchan as one of Rhoodie's "front men.")

**Peres's letter to Rhoodie** was dated November 22, 1974.

**Arming Jericho:** Richard Sale and Geoffrey Aronson, "Exporting Nuclear Triggers: The Strange Case of Richard Smyth," *Middle East Report*, May-June, 1987, p. 40. Dayan's condition: Stephen Green, *Living by the Sword: America and Israel in the Middle East 1968–87*, Brattleboro: Amana Books, 1988, pp. 89–91.

**The Israeli-South African uranium-tritium connection:** "Nuke Bombshell: Govt to Get Rhoodie Awakening," *The City Press* (Johannesburg), April 18, 1993, p. 1; Eschel Rhoodie, *The Real Information Scandal*, Durban: Orbis SA (PTY) Ltd, 1983, pp. 522–24; Seymour M. Hersh, *The Samson Option*, New York: Random House, 1991, p. 156; and an interview with a former high-ranking South African official on May 3, 1993.

**The Israeli-Iranian missile connection:** "Documents Detail Israeli Missile Deal With the Shah," *The New York Times*, April 1, 1986. Much of the deal was recorded in top-secret minutes of relevant meetings: "Minutes From Meeting Held in Tel Aviv Between H. E. General M. Dayan, Foreign Minister of Israel, and H. E. H. Toufanian, Vice Minister of War, Imperial Government of Iran," July 18, 1977, and a second one between Weizman and Tufanian the same day.

**Gabriel to Skorpion:** DIA report, "South Africa-Israel Military Cooperation and Technology Transfer Continues (U)," December 1986, p. 3.

**The sales angle** is from the DIA subreport, "The Israeli Security Assistance Connection: A Key to Diplomatic Relations with Sub-Saharan Africa (U)," undated, p. 2.

**The Indian Ocean test** is from various sources. See, for example, Desmond Ball, "The U.S. VELA Nuclear Detection Satellite (NDS) System: The Australian Connection," Reference Paper No. 70, The Australian National University, Canberra, October 1981, pp. 7–8. A highly informed former Soviet analyst, like his U.S. counterparts, put the blast in the three-kiloton range.

**"Full-blown":** From a highly knowledgeable source who requested anonymity.

**Participation in certain activities:** Director of Central Intelligence, "The 22 September 1979 Event," Interagency Intelligence Memorandum, December 1979, p. 10.

**The defense strategy report** was prepared for the Director of Central Intelligence, dated January 1980, and released on July 10, 1990.

**South Africa's "peaceful" program:** "Space Research Myth Cloaks Nuclear Missile Development," *SouthScan*, September 18, 1992, p. 268.

**"Rebuffed":** "U.S. Knew of 2 Nations' Missile Work," *The Washington Post*, October 27, 1989.

**"Taboo" and the response:** "Rabin Tells Cabinet: No U.S. Technology Transfers to South Africa," AP, October 29, 1989.

**"On its own":** "State Dept. Sees No Israel-South Africa Transfer," *The Washington Post*, October 28, 1989.

**Kissinger-Meir:** *The Samson Option*, p. 230*n*.

**Tenth-generation:** Interview by Windrem on June 8, 1992.

**Milchan's early years:** "Mystery Milchan," *The Jerusalem Post Magazine*, February 21, 1986.

**Peres and Milchan:** Interviews with two former South African officials, February 18 and March 22, 1993.

**Rhoodie, Milchan, and joint propaganda:** Interview with a former South African official on February 18, 1993, and from *The Real Information Scandal*, p. 796.

**Condo:** Mervyn Rees and Chris Day, *Muldergate*, Johannesburg: Macmillan of South Africa, 1980.

**Penetration:** The February 18 interview.

**Smyth, Milchan, and Milco's start-up:** "Computer Expert Used Firm to Feed Israel Technology," *The Washington Post*, October 31, 1986.

**The Milco-Heli connection:** *United States of America v. Richard Kelly Smyth*, United States District Court, Central District of California, CR 85-493-PAR, August 15, 1985, p. 6.

**Another 70:** Milco International five-year business report, 1983, and an interview with former Assistant U.S. Attorney William Fahey on March 21, 1993.

**Domestic use and pentodes:** Interview with William F. Fahey, Assistant U.S. Attorney, on June 2, 1992.

**Nuclear and missile items** are listed in Milco records and were mentioned by two of its directors who served from 1980 to 1982.

**Special oscilloscopes and fuel:** An analysis of Milco International reports by a U.S. intelligence analyst on June 18, 1992.

**Milhollin:** Interview on August 10, 1992.

**The analyst** spoke on condition of anonymity.

**Benny:** Interview with an FBI agent, who requested anonymity, on June 24, 1992.

**Beihl's experience** is from an extensive interview on June 4, 1992.

**Mainhardt's role:** Interview with Windrem on February 3, 1993. Also see "Computer Expert Used Firm to Feed Israel Technology," *The Washington Post*, October 31, 1986.

**Circumstances of the discovery** are from an interview with a Customs Service case agent who requested anonymity, on Terminal Island, California, on June 2, 1992.

**Milchan's disclaimer:** NBC News interview on May 16, 1985.

**The first call:** Interview with Milchan on June 8, 1992.

**Federal investigators:** *United States of American v. Richard Kelly Smyth*, pp. 6–7, and Customs agent interviews, June 1992.

**Carter's story** is from a Windrem telephone interview on July 2, 1992.

**The request to Israel:** United States District Court, Central District of California, "Application of the United States to Request the Assistance of the Judiciary of Jerusalem, Israel," *United States of America v. Richard Kelly Smyth*, August 9, 1985. The Customs Service subpoena is from the same case and carries the same date.

**Krytrons to South Africa:** "Richard K. Smyth," undated U.S. Customs Service document.

**The end of the nukes and the Israeli connection:** "South Africa's 16-year Secret: The Nuclear Bomb," *The Washington Post*, May 12, 1993, and "South Africa's Secret Nuclear Program: From PNE to a Deterrent," *Nucleonics Week*, May 10, 1993, p. 3.

**Julia:** Joseph S. Bermudez, Jr., "Ballistic Missile Development in Egypt," Monterey: Monterey Institute of International Studies, February 26, 1992, p. 49.

**IFAT and the Egyptian contract:** *United States of America v. Abdelkader Helmy, et al.*, United States District Court for the Eastern District of California, S-89-201-RAR, November 7, 1989, p. 2.

**Consen-IFAT:** Ibid.

**Consen SA's activity and products:** Dun & Bradstreet report 48-164-8178, dated October 14, 1988.

**Hammer:** Simon Henderson, *Instant Empire*, San Francisco: Mercury House, 1991, pp. 157–58.

**Condor-1 background and Bratschi:** "Secret Project Condor," *Stern*, August 25, 1988, p. 190.

**Condor-1 at Paris and MBB's design divisions:** Ibid.

**The Saudi's $1 billion** was reported by Keith Smith, an IFAT employee. (J. D. Beckmann Honeywell memorandum to Gary M. Lehr of April 4, 1984, p. 2.)

**The MBB connection and 400 times the price:** "Secret Project Condor."

**KOLAS** was briefly reported by *Aviation Week & Space Technology*, in two articles: "New Missile," Industry Observer, November 7, 1988, and "West German," Industry Observer, February 13, 1989. Other material is from answers to questions submitted to Martin Marietta.

**The secret decrees (604 of April 9, 1985, and 1315 of August 13, 1987):** "Cavallo Gives Details of 'Secret' Deal with Iraq," FBIS-LAT-91-018, p. 26.

**The "nonconventional"** is from part of an untitled and undated Israeli intelligence report.

**Description of the tunnel** is based on Windrem's reporting at the scene.

**Khairat's Salzburg office:** "Ballistic Missile Development in Egypt," p. 51.

**Iraq's grievances:** "Secret Egypt-Iraq Accord Collapses," *Financial Times*, June 12, 1989.

**Consultations from 1984:** *Administration and Enforcement of U.S. Export Control Programs*, p. 144.

**The wish list** is from accounting statements, invoices, discarded notes, and other exhibits used in *United States of America v. Abdelkadar* (sic) *Helmy*, United States District Court for the Eastern District of California, S-89-201-RAR, November 7, 1989. The dollar amount is from Exhibit 11, which also listed $35,787 for services, bringing the total to $649,915.

**Huffman's connection** is described in *Administration and Enforcement of U.S. Export Control Programs*, p. 118 passim, in *United States of America v. Abdelkader Helmy*, and through invoices for material he purchased (e.g., $1,820 to Vega Precision Laboratories in Vienna, Virginia, for two model 826U-1 swept back pointer antennas, dated May 23, 1988).

**Surveillance:** *Administration and Enforcement of U.S. Export Control Programs*, pp. 116–20, and an affidavit by David E. Burns, Customs Investigator, U.S. Customs Service.

**The reference to Schrotz** by Khairat is from p. 5 of the phone tap. The car bombing and related events: Kenneth R. Timmerman, *The Death Lobby*, Boston: Houghton Mifflin, 1991, pp. 296–97.

**C-130:** News release by David F. Levi, U.S. Attorney for the Eastern District of California, dated April 21, 1989.

**Egypt's abandonment of Condor:** "Condor Project 'in Disarray,' " *Jane's Defence Weekly*, February 17, 1990, p. 295, and "Egypt Drops Out of Missile Project," *The Washington Post*, September 20, 1989.

**"Stonewalling":** "Argentina's President Battles His Own Air Force on Missile," *The New York Times*, May 13, 1991.

**First stages and guidance systems:** "Argentina Lagging on Missile Pledge," *The New York Times*, August 19, 1992. The missing plans: "U.S. Concern Over Argentine Missile Link to Baghdad," *Financial Times*, March 9, 1992.

**Gonzalez:** "Argentina, Acceding to U.S., Ends Missile Program," *The New York Times*, May 30, 1991.

**Explosions:** "Argentina Lagging on Missile Pledge."

**Capricornio, the military missile:** "Spain Unveils Rocket Program," *Defense News*, May 18–24, p. 1992.

**Menem's declaration:** "Menem on Space Activities for Peaceful Purposes," FBIS-LAT-91-208, October 28, 1991, p. 24.

**Bush's concern:** "Iraq's Involvement in Condor II Project Viewed," *Somos* (Buenos Aires), January 28, 1991.

## 15. THE TERRIFYING ALTERNATIVE

**The Pentagon expert** spoke on condition of anonymity.

**Maraging steel and parallel computing:** *India Today*, April 15, 1993, p. 58.

**Stubborn generals:** Robert A. Divine, *The Sputnik Challenge*, New York: Oxford University Press, 1993, p. 25.

**Chinese M-11s:** "China Breaking Missile Pledge, U.S. Aides Say," *The New York Times*, May 6, 1993.

**Ballistic missile threat:** Horner's remarks at the Thirtieth Space Congress, Cocoa Beach, Florida, on April 28, 1993.

**Accelerated aid:** "U.S. to Speed Money to Bolster Yeltsin," *The New York Times*, September 23, 1993.

**Export ban:** "U.S. to Curb Exports of High-Tech Goods to China," *The New York Times*, August 26, 1993.

**Satellite sales:** "President Clinton Slaps China With Satellite Export Restrictions," *Satellite News*, August 30, 1993.

**Atomic test:** "Clinton Asks China to Halt Atom Test," *The New York Times*, September 18, 1993.

**Air safety:** "Eye on Olympics, China Pursues Air Safety," *The New York Times*, September 16, 1993.

**Terrorist status:** "Pakistan Is Facing Terrorist Listing," *The New York Times*, April 25, 1993.

**De Klerk:** "South Africa Says It Built 6 Atom Bombs," *The New York Times*, March 25, 1993.

**Nominating targets:** Windrem interview with an Air Force general who participated in Desert Storm. General Charles A. Horner, who led the coalition air forces, denied that the Israelis nominated any targets in an interview with Burrows on April 28, 1993.

**Pakistani bluff:** From a highly knowledgeable source who did not wish to be identified.

**Bundy's opinions** are from a Burrows interview on November 30, 1992.

**List of problems:** National Academy of Sciences, *Finding Common Ground: U.S. Export Controls in a Changed Global Environment*, Washington: National Academy Press, 1991, pp. 86–105.

**The IAEA budget freeze:** "The U.N.'s Nuclear Detectives," *Defense Monitor*, March 20, 1993.

**Clinton's initiative:** Speech before the United Nations on September 27, 1993.

**New rocket policy:** "Administration to Relax Rocket Export Rules," *Space News*, August 16–22, 1993.

**Gejdenson, et al.:** "White House Plans Export of Rocketry," *Portland* (Maine) *Press Herald*, August 10, 1993 (from *The Los Angeles Times*).

**The Panel's conclusion:** *Finding Common Ground*, p. 188.

**Knocking heads:** The Burrows interview.

**Selling off the program:** David Kay, "Iraqi Inspections: Lessons Learned," *Eye on Supply*, Winter 1993, p. 94.

**Britain, Germany, Japan, and the U.N.:** Ibid.

**Butler:** "Head of Nuclear Forces Plans for a New World," *The New York Times*, February 25, 1993.

**Resumed testing:** News brief in *Time*, May 17, 1993, p. 13.

# Index

# Photo Credits